Accounting and Regulation

Roberto Di Pietra · Stuart McLeay
Joshua Ronen
Editors

Accounting and Regulation

New Insights on Governance, Markets and Institutions

Springer

Editors
Roberto Di Pietra
Department of Business and Law
University of Siena
Siena
Italy

Joshua Ronen
Stern School of Business
New York University
New York
USA

Stuart McLeay
The University of Sydney
Sydney, NSW
Australia

ISBN 978-1-4614-8096-9 ISBN 978-1-4614-8097-6 (eBook)
DOI 10.1007/978-1-4614-8097-6
Springer New York Heidelberg Dordrecht London

Library of Congress Control Number: 2013940763

Printed on acid-free paper

Springer is part of Springer Science+Business Media (www.springer.com)

Contents

Contributors

Walter Aerts is full Professor at the Department of Accounting and Finance (Faculty of Applied Economics) at the University of Antwerp (Belgium). He also teaches at the Antwerp Management School. He holds a Ph.D. in Applied Economics and a Master in Commercial Engineering from the University of Antwerp. Before entering academia he has been working as a financial executive in the utility sector for nearly two decades. He teaches financial reporting and analysis, internal control and risk management, and international financial reporting standards. He is a member of the IFRS committee of the Belgian Accounting Standards Board ('CBN'). He is Associate Editor of the British Accounting Review. His research interests are narrative impression management, internal control and corporate governance, institutional perspectives on accounting, and comparative disclosure research. He has co-authored several books and publications in various academic journals, such as Accounting, Organizations and Society, Abacus, Journal of Accounting and Public Policy, Accounting and Business Research, Corporate Governance: An International Review, Journal of Business Finance and Accounting and European Accounting Review.

Miguel Arce is Associate Professor in Accounting and Finance at the University of Valencia (Spain). He holds a Degree in Economics and Business Studies and Ph.D. in Business by the University of Valencia. He is the Director of the Master of Science in Accounting and Auditing by the University of Valencia. He has occupied visiting positions in Lancaster University and Southampton University. His research interests are in the areas of financial reporting and financial analysis, mainly economic consequences of accounting and accounting policy choice related to financial institutions. He has published several books and articles in Spanish and international journals. He has been a member of several research projects funded by the Spanish Government, the Instituto de Contabilidad y Auditoría de Cuentas (ICAC) and Asociación Española de Contabilidad y Administración de Empresas (AECA).

Daniela Argento received her Ph.D. in "Public Management and Regulated Sectors" at the Department of Business and Social Studies, University of Siena, Italy. She is currently Senior Lecturer in "Business Administration and Accounting" at the Center for Business Studies of Kristianstad University College (Sweden). Her research interests include corporate disclosure, organizational change and governance, and accounting issues in local utilities.

Michael Bromwich is the CIMA Professor of Accounting and Financial Management emeritus at the London School of Economics since September 2006. After qualifying as an accountant with the Ford Motor Company he took a B.Sc. (Econ) Degree in Economics at the LSE. In 1970, he was appointed the first Professor of Accounting at the University of Cardiff. He has published some 100 articles including articles in The Accounting Review, AOS, Abacus, and Management Accounting Research. He is a Past President of CIMA (1987/1988). With Bob Scapens, he is a founding editor of the international journal Management Accounting Research in 1989. He has written a number of books, including *The Economics of Capital Budgeting* (1976). His book with Al Bhimani, *Management Accounting: Evolution not Revolution* was important in determining the importance of activity-based costing and management to the profession. His most recent book with Al Bhimani is *Management Accounting: Retrospect and Prospects.*

Frank Clarke is Emeritus Professor of Accounting at the University of Newcastle, and Honorary Professor of Accounting at The University of Sydney; has held appointments at the Universities of Newcastle, Sydney, Glasgow, Canterbury (New Zealand), and Lancaster. He is a past editor and currently a consulting editor of Abacus, the fourth oldest and one of the leading Anglo-American accounting academic journals. He is the author or joint author of 9 books, numerous articles in refereed and business journals, and is a frequent presenter at international conferences and contributor to the secular financial press (with Dean).

Christina Dargenidou is a Senior Lecturer in Finance in the Xfi Centre for Finance and Investment at the University of Exeter, England. She completed her Ph.D. thesis at Bangor University while holding a doctoral research fellowship funded by the European Commission (HARMONIA network). Before her appointment at Xfi, she was a financial analyst at the National Bank of Greece. Christina Dargenidou has published accounting and finance research studies in Journal of Business, Finance and Accounting, European Accounting Review and Abacus.

Judy Day has recently retired from her post at Manchester Business School, UK, where she was Professorial Fellow in Accounting from 2007 to 2012. Prior to that, she was Professor of Accounting at the Open University and Senior Lecturer in Accounting at the London School of Economics and Political Science. Her research interests are in debt contracting and the role of financial reporting in emerging economies. She is a member of the Institute of Chartered Accountants in England and Wales.

Graeme Dean is Emeritus Professor of Accounting and formerly Head of Discipline of Accounting at The University of Sydney, has held visiting appointments at several overseas universities, Glasgow, Graz, Canterbury, Cardiff, Munich, and Frankfurt. He was the sole editor (1994–2009) of Abacus, the fourth oldest and one of the leading Anglo-American accounting academic journals. Dean has published several books and books of readings and nearly 50 refereed journal articles. With Frank Clarke, Dean has traced ideas about the development of accounting for inflation, their transportation from European to Anglo-American countries. Also they have examined asset valuation and auditing issues through the lens of company failures, leading to (with co-author Kyle Oliver) *Corporate Collapse: Accounting, Regulatory and Ethical Failure* being published by Cambridge University Press in 1997, and a second (substantially) revised edition appearing in 2003; with an edition in Chinese in 2006.

Roberto Di Pietra is a full Professor in Accounting and Business Administration at the Department of Business and law, University of Siena. He received a Ph.D. in Accounting and Business Administration from the University of Pisa in 1997; he has also received a specialization in Banking in 1993. Di Pietra's main research interests are in International Accounting (IFRS and Financial statements, IFRS and Corporate Governance, Accounting regulation, IAS and organizational learning), in Auditing and in Accounting History. He is also EB member of Accounting in Europe, Financial Reporting, Revista Espanola de Contabilidad y Financiaccion de Empresa, and Financial Reporting. Since 2007, he is the Editor-in-Chief of the Journal of Management and Governance.

Begoña Giner is Professor in Accounting and Finance at the University of Valencia (Spain). She holds a Degree in Business Studies and Ph.D. in Business by the University of Valencia, and a Master of Science in Accounting and Finance by the London School of Economics. She has been a Member of the European Financial Reporting Advisory Group (EFRAG). Currently, she is the President of the European Accounting Association (EAA) and is a member of the IFRS Advisory Council. Her research interests are in the areas of financial reporting and financial analysis, mainly economic consequences of accounting and accounting policy choice. She has published several books and numerous articles in Spanish and international journals (e.g., Abacus, Accounting and Business Research, European Accounting Review, Journal of Business, Finance and Accounting, Journal of Management and Governance, Revista Española de Financiación y Contabilidad-Spanish Journal of Finance and Accounting). She has been a member of two European projects funded by the EU: INTACCT and HARMONIA.

Christopher Humphrey is a Professor of Accounting at Manchester Business School (MBS), England. The Manchester Accounting and Finance Group (MAFG) at MBS is one of the leading European research units in its field. Christopher's involvement with auditing research stretches back to the mid-1980s and he has published a wide body of work on auditing and related issues, including audit expectations, audit quality, audit planning, developments in auditing methodologies, audit regulation, and audit liability. He has specialized in recent years in the field of international audit regulation and the historical development of the International Federation of Accountants (IFAC). Christopher is on the editorial board member of a wide range of international accounting and auditing journals. He was head of the Accounting and Finance group at Manchester for 5 years (2001–2006) and is now Chair of the UK's Conference of Professors of Accounting and Finance (CPAF). He has been a co-opted academic member of the governing Council of the Institute of Chartered Accountants in England and Wales (ICAEW), and currently sits on the ICAEW's Technical Strategy Board, and is a Director of the Chartered Accountants' Trustees Ltd.

Aziz Jaafar is a Lecturer in Accounting at Bangor University Business School, Wales. He has also taught at MARA University of Technology, Malaysia, Henan University of Technology, China, and Aberystwyth University, Wales. Aziz Jaafar has prior audit and management consultancy experience with an international accounting firm, and his main research interests are in the quality of international financial reporting, particularly in the measurement of harmonization and standardization. Aziz Jaafar has published research studies in Abacus, British Accounting Review and Accounting in Emerging Economies.

Ann Jorissen is full Professor of Accounting at the University of Antwerp, Belgium. Her primary research areas include international accounting, corporate governance and management control. She has published in Accounting, Organizations and Society, Accounting and Business Research, the European Accounting Review, Accounting in Europe, Journal of Accounting and Public Policy, Corporate Governance: An International Review, Family Business Review, Entrepreneurship: Theory and Practice and Review of Business and Economics. She is active in the EAA, she has served as member or chair on a number of EAA committees and is current the President-Elect of the EAA.

Jonathan Karpoff is the Washington Mutual Endowed Chair in Innovation and Professor of Finance at the University of Washington's Foster School of Business. Jon's research seeks to understand how Adam Smith's Invisible Hand works, or does not work, to coordinate economic activities ranging from fisheries management to arctic exploration to corporate governance. His articles have received the Griliches Prize, Sharpe Award, and several other best paper awards. Jon teaches Executive, MBA, and Ph.D. finance students, and seeks to inspire an appreciation for the insights of economic analysis in everyday life. He also serves as Associate Editor for The Journal of Finance, Journal of Financial Economics, Journal of Financial and Quantitative Analysis, and Management Science, and is a member of the Board of Trustees for The Financial Management Association International.

Roland Königsgruber has obtained a Master's degree in International Relations from Yale University and a Ph.D. and Habilitation qualification in Accounting from Karl-Franzens-University Graz, Austria. He started his career as a consultant for Ernst and Young Consulting (now part of Cap Gemini) and joined academe as a research assistant and later post-doctoral researcher at the University of Graz where he also served as Chairman of the Curriculum Commission for Bachelors' and Masters' Degrees in Business Studies. He was closely involved in the set-up of the Center for Accounting Research and the establishment of the doctoral program in accounting, reporting, and taxation. After a visiting professorship at the University of Constance in Germany, he currently works as an Assistant Professor in Financial Accounting at Vrije Universiteit Amsterdam in The Netherlands. His main research interests lie in the interaction between public policy making, accounting regulation, and financial reporting. His research encompasses a broad methodological range from analytical modeling and archival empirical research to experimental economics. Recent papers have been published in the European Accounting Review, Accounting in Europe and the Journal of Management and Governance, among others.

Scott Lee is the Lincy Professor of Finance at the University of Nevada at Las Vegas. He earned his Ph.D. at the University of Oregon and has taught at Texas A&M University, the University of Utah, and the Santa Chiara Study Center in Castiglion Fiorentino, Italy. Scott teaches corporate finance and valuation analysis. His research focus is on the economic and managerial labor market repercussions of accounting misrepresentation, fraud, and bribery. Other areas of interest include financial distress and the unintended consequences of regulation. His work appears in the Journal of Financial Economics, Journal of Finance, Journal of Political Economy, Journal of Financial and Quantitative Analysis, Journal of Law & Economics, and Strategic Management Journal. Scott grew up as a printer in his family's weekly newspaper in Southeastern Wyoming. He has owned and operated a commercial salmon fishing business in a remote part of Kodiak Island, Alaska since 1976.

Nadine Lybaert is Professor of Accounting at the Faculty of Business Economics at Hasselt University, Belgium, and Guest Professor at the University of Antwerp. She is associated with the Research Center for Entrepreneurship and Innovation (KIZOK) at Hasselt University. Her research interests include a wide array of financial accounting topics. She has published in Accounting and Business Research, the European Accounting Review, International Journal of Accounting, Journal of Accounting and Public Policy, Family Business Review, Management Decision, Small Business Economics, Entrepreneurship and Regional Development.

Jerry Martin is an Associate Professor of Finance at the Kogod School of Business, American University in Washington, DC. He teaches courses in corporate finance and quantitative analysis. Jerry's research focuses on securities regulation and enforcement activities, capital structure, corporate payout policy, financial distress, and Warren Buffett. His articles have appeared in Journal of Financial Economics and Journal of Financial and Quantitative Analysis and he is co-editor of Capital Structure and Corporate Financing Decisions a Wiley publication. He currently serves on the advisory board of a hedge and exchange traded fund, economic fellow and chair of the FCPA Task Force at George Mason University School of Law, Law & Economics Center, Searle Civil Justice Institute and an expert witness in corporate malfeasance and bankruptcy cases. His research has directly affected the way in which damage estimates are calculated in financial misrepresentation lawsuits in state and federal district courts. As one of a few academics that study Warren Buffett, he is often quoted in Bloomberg News and other press and his research has been featured in Wall Street Journal, Business Week, Forbes, the New York Times and other publications throughout the world and has made numerous personal appearances on CNBC, Bloomberg Television, and National Public Radio. Prior to embarking on his academic career, Dr. Martin spent 17 years in the private sector as President and CEO of TMI Aircraft Finance, LLC and TMI Leasing, LLC and in both finance and marketing for two subsidiaries of Textron Inc.; Textron Financial Corporation and Bell Helicopter Textron and was responsible for financing over $1 billion in aviation equipment worldwide. Jerry received his Ph.D. and M.S. degrees in Finance and M.B.A and B.B.A. in Marketing, from Texas A&M University.

Stuart McLeay is Professor of Accounting at the University of Sydney, Australia, and he is also Emeritus Professor of Accounting and Finance at the University of Sussex, England. He completed his Ph.D. at the International Center for Research in Accounting at Lancaster University, England. A qualified chartered accountant, Stuart Mcleay has more than 10 years prior experience with the European Investment Bank, Price Waterhouse, and other international audit firms, and in the university sector as a pension fund chair and audit committee member.

Raf Orens is Assistant Professor of Financial Accounting at Lessius, Department of Business Studies, and Associate Researcher with the Department of Accountancy, Finance & Insurance, Faculty of Business Economics at KU Leuven. In 2007, he obtained his doctoral degree in Applied Economics at Hasselt University. His main research interests are: international accounting standard setting, earnings quality, non-financial reporting, and analysts' behavior. He published in Accounting and Business Research, the European Accounting Review, Accounting in Europe, the International Journal of Accounting, and Journal of Accounting and Public Policy.

Joshua Ronen is Professor of Accounting at the Stern School of Business, New York University. He earned a BA and a CPA Degree in Economics from the Hebrew University and a Doctorate (1969) in Business Administration from Stanford University. Prior to joining the Stern School of Business at New York University, he served as a member of the faculty of the University of Chicago's Graduate School of Business. He has been a visiting professor and lectured at leading academic institutions in many countries. He served as associate director of research for the AICPA Accounting Objective Study Group. He also served as President of the Price Institute of Entrepreneurial Studies, and as Director of the Vincent C. Ross Institute of Accounting Research at the Stern School of Business, New York University.

Anna Samsonova is a Lecturer in Accounting in the Manchester Business School, University of Manchester. Anna's research covers a range of topics, including audit reforms in the context of a transitional economy, various aspects of accounting and audit regulation, transnational policy processes and networks, and others. Anna is a member of the European Auditing Research Network.

Ann Tarca Ph.D., MAcc, BCom, FCA is a Winthrop Professor in the Business School at the University of Western Australia (UWA). She has over 20 years teaching experience, with the last 15 years being spent at UWA working with both undergraduate and postgraduate students. She has a keen interest in improving teaching and learning practices and in preparing students for the challenges of professional practice. She is a lead author on the textbook *Accounting Theory* (7th Edition, Wiley, Australia) and has served on the Education Committee of the American Accounting Association. As a chartered accountant, Ann has strong links with the accounting profession. Her research focuses on financial reporting standards, regulation and practice, with a particular emphasis on international issues. She has published in well recognised international journals including Abacus, Accounting and Business Research, Accounting and Finance, British Accounting Review, European Accounting Review, and the International Journal of Accounting and serves as a reviewer and on journal boards for the Journal of International Accounting Research, Accounting and Finance, and the Australian Accounting Review. Ann is an active member of the International Association for Accounting Education and Research (IAAER) and the International Group of the American Accounting Association, serving on doctorial consortia and various committees. During 2011–2012, she was Academic Fellow for the IFRS Foundation Education Initiative in London.

Peter Taylor is currently Professor of Accounting at Manchester Business School and also Emeritus Professor of Accounting in the University of Liverpool. He has held academic posts at the University of Sheffield and in the University of Wales. His research interests include debt contracting and debt covenants, with particular respect to the role of financial reporting, and financial reporting systems change in transition and emerging economies.

Stuart Turley is professor of Accounting at the University of Manchester, England. Since 2001 he has been an academic member of the Auditing Practices Board, which sets practice and ethical standards for auditors in the UK and Ireland. He is also a member of the Scientific Committee of the European Auditing Research Network and the Research Committee of the Institute of Chartered Accountants in Scotland, and serves on the editorial boards of several journals. Stuart Turley is a past editor of the British Accounting Review and the International Journal of Auditing.

Leo van der Tas is full professor at Tilburg University, The Netherlands and is technical partner at Ernst & Young Accountants LLP in The Netherlands. Heearned a Ph.D. at Erasmus University Rotterdam, The Netherlands. He is a member of the advisory bodies of the International Accounting Standards Board, the European Securities and Markets Authority's (ESMA), Sanding Committee on Corporate Reporting and the Authority for Financial Markets (AFM). His main research area is international financial reporting in which he published articles inThe European Accounting Review, Accounting and Business Research, Journal ofAccounting and Public Policy, and Abacus.

Geoffrey Whittington is Emeritus Professor of Financial Accounting at the University of Cambridge and a Senior Associate of the Judge Business School, attached to the Center for Financial Analysis and Policy. He is a Chartered Accountant and has a Doctorate in Economics from Cambridge University. From 2001 to 2006, he was a full-time member of the International Accounting Standards Board. He has held Chairs of Accounting at the Universities of Edinburgh, Bristol, and Cambridge and served as a part-time member of the UK Monopolies and Mergers Commission, the Accounting Standards Board for the UK and Ireland (ASB), and many other public and professional committees. Academic and professional honors include the ACCA/BAA Distinguished Academic of the year Award, an honorary doctorate from the University of Edinburgh, and the Founding Societies' Centenary Award of the Institute of Chartered Accountants in England and Wales.

Mahbub Zaman is Associate Professor of Accounting at the University of Manchester, England, and is currently the Accounting & Finance Ph.D. Program Director. His main research interests are in auditing and corporate governance, and he has published widely on the effect of audit committees on financial reporting, internal controls and risk management and external audit; auditor independence, nonaudit services and ethical standards; the demand for audit and assurance services in different institutional and regulatory settings. Mahbub Zaman is a member of the European Auditing Research Network, and has served on British Accounting Association Auditing and Corporate Governance special interest groups. His research has been published in Accounting, Auditing & Accountability Journal, Accounting Forum, British Accounting Review, Corporate Governance: An International Review, Critical Perspectives in Accounting, and the Journal of Management & Governance.

Acronyms

AAA	American accounting association
AAER	Accounting and auditing enforcement release
AC	Audit committee
ACCA	Association of chartered certified accountants
AICPA	American institute of certified public accountants
APB	Accounting principles board
ARC	Accounting regulatory committee
ASAF	Accounting standards advisory forum
ASB	Accounting standards board
BOD	Board of directors
CBCA	Canada business corporations act
CEO	Chief executive officer
CFO	Chief financial officer
CNC	French national council of accounting (*Conseil National de la Comptabilité*)
CNDCEC	Italian national board of professional and chartered accountants (*Consiglio Nazionale dei Dottori Commercialisti ed Esperti Contabili*)
CPA	Certified (or chartered) public accountant
CSR	Corporate social responsibility
DOJ	Department of justice
DP	Discussion paper
DPA	Deferred prosecution agreement
EAA	European accounting association
EBIT	Earnings before income, tax
EBITDA	Earnings before income, tax, depreciation, and amortization
EC	European commission
ED	Exposure draft
EFRAG	European financial reporting advisory group
EIASM	European institute for advanced studies in management
EPS	Earnings per share
EU	European union
EVA	Economic value added

FAS	Financial accounting standards
FASB	Financial accounting standards board
FCPA	Foreign corrupt practices act
FRRP	Financial reporting review panel
FSI	Financial statement insurance
FV	Fair value
GAAP	Generally accepted accounting principles
GAO	US general accounting office
GDP	Gross domestic product
GFC	Global financial crisis
HC	Historical cost
IAASB	International auditing and assurance standards board
IAS	International accounting standards
IASB	International accounting standards board
IASC	International accounting standards committee
IASCF	IASC foundation
ICAC	Spanish institute of accounting and auditing (*Instituto de Contabilidad y Auditoria de Cuentas*)
ICAEW	Institute of certified accountants of England and Wales
IFRIC	International financial reporting interpretations committee
IFRS	International financial reporting standards
IOSCO	International organization of securities commissions
MC	Management commentary
MD&A	Managements discussion and analysis
MEP	Members of the European parliament
NPA	Non-prosecution agreement
NPV	Net present value
NSS	National standard-setters
OFR	Operating and financial review
OFT	Office of fair trading
OIC	Italian accounting standards setter (*Organismo Italiano di Contabilità*)
PAT	Positive accounting theory
PCAOB	Public company accounting oversight board
PHC	Perfect historical cost
PIIGS	Portugal, Ireland, Italy, Greece, Spain
PV	Present value
RI	Residual income
RICO	Racketeer influenced and corupt organizations act
ROE	Return on equity
ROI	Retutn on investments
ROS	Return on sales
SAC	Standards advisory council
SARG	Standards advice review group
SEC	Securities and exchange commission

SFAS	Statement of financial accounting standard
SIC	Standing interpretations committee
SOX	Sarbanes-oxley act
SPE	Special purpose entities
TEG	Technical expert group
US	United States

Chapter 1
Introduction

Roberto Di Pietra, Stuart McLeay and Joshua Ronen

Accounting research offers two complementary approaches to the understanding of regulation. Under the first of these, regulation is seen as affecting management behavior, not only at the operational level of the firm, but also at the strategic level. Managerial behavior, in this context, is also conditioned to a great extent by different modes of corporate governance, and of critical importance are the conflicts of interest that may exist between managers and owners, the impact these conflicts can have on the process of preparing financial statements, and the consequences for both internal and external parties, including regulators.
The second approach models the determinants of accounting regulation, and also considers the nature and quality of the accounting information that is produced and disseminated within different regulatory frameworks. Under this approach, the study of accounting regulation seeks to improve the efficacy and efficiency of regulation, at both the national and international levels. Such research spans the following areas of investigation, amongst others: theories of the evolution of accounting rules;[1] regulatory instruments that enable the enforcement of accounting rules, and the role of the institutions that represent interests gained

[1] Theories of the evolution of accounting rules are addressed by, amongst others, Watts and Zimmerman (1978), Bromwich (1985) and Horngren (1985).

R. Di Pietra (✉)
Department of Business and Law, University of Siena, Piazza San Francesco 7, 53100 Siena, Italy
e-mail: dipietra@unisi.it

S. McLeay
The Business School, The University of Sydney, Room 314, Building H69, NSW 2006, Australia
e-mail: stuart.mcleay@sydney.edu.au

J. Ronen
Stern School of Business, New York University, 44 West 4th Street, 10-71, New York, NY 10012, USA
e-mail: jronen@stern.nyu.edu

R. Di Pietra et al. (eds.), *Accounting and Regulation*,
DOI: 10.1007/978-1-4614-8097-6_1,

through regulatory privileges;[2] and the application of political pressure on bodies issuing accounting rules, through lobbying and related forms of influence.[3]

In this context, regulatory policies are seen as guiding and influencing a series of decisions, initiatives, and processes that lead to the issuance of new accounting rules. The study of these processes has become particularly significant in the case of the International Financial Reporting Standards issued by the IASB, due to the increasingly important and global role taken on by this institution and the political significance that its work has acquired over the last decade.

Indeed, the study of accounting regulation exhibits a strong awareness of the political, economic, and social nature of accounting rules and their application. Accounting is far more than a highly technical discipline: it interacts profoundly with the forces of economics and politics, guiding strategic decisions made in both national and, increasingly, international contexts. To fully understand the technically complex solutions adopted for the collection and representation of information within financial statements, an appreciation is required of the forces that have shaped and defined the accounting rules in use. In this sense, contemporary research draws on knowledge and competences from a range of different but related fields of thought, including information economics, regulatory economics, sociology, and political science.

The need to provide capital markets with accounting information that is credible, reliable, and complete is increasingly evident, as dramatically confirmed by recent corporate scandals.[4] In this sense, the need for robust analysis of the impact of economic forces on accounting regulation is ever more pressing. At the same time, aspects such as the prominent role of the IASB, the ongoing convergence with the FASB, and the process of accounting modernization launched by the European Commission, all constitute clear evidence of the interaction between politics and accounting.

An earlier treatment of the linkages and interactions between accounting and political and economic forces is the volume edited by Christian Leuz, Dieter Pfaff and Anthony Hopwood, entitled The Economics and Politics of Accounting, International Perspectives on Research Trends, Policy, and Practice (Oxford Press 2004). In this book, the contributing authors examined how accounting is entwined with politics in many different respects, not only with regard to geopolitics, such as those surrounding the transition from European Directives on financial statement preparation to the use of international accounting standards, but also with respect to institutional engagement in the process of accounting law making and accounting standard setting, the broader relationship with corporate governance models, and, last but not least, the political economy underlying changes in

[2] See for example Benston (1980), Jönsson (1991), Mitchell and Sikka (1993), Robson (1993), Cooper and Robson (2006).

[3] See for example Walker and Robinson (1993, 1994) and Klumpes (1994).

[4] For examples of corporate scandals linked to creative accounting, and the regulatory failure involved, see Clarke et al. (2003), Clarke and Dean (2007), Jones (2011).

accounting method, such as the adoption of the fair value model and the valuation of goodwill. These initial efforts serve to highlight how much is to be understood, and further examined, in the area of applied research that we present here as 'Accounting and Regulation'.

1.1 The Siena Workshops on Accounting and Regulation

Between 1998 and 2010, five Workshops on Accounting and Regulation were held in Siena (one every 3 years). The first Workshop was planned by Angelo Riccaboni (current Rector of the Università degli Studi di Siena) and Stuart McLeay.[5] Beginning with the second Workshop, this three yearly meetings have been jointly organized with the European Institute for Advanced Studies in Management (EIASM). Since the first event, which was held in the impressive setting of the Certosa di Pontignano (a retreat in the Tuscan hills outside Siena), a significant number of researchers interested in Accounting and Regulation have attended the Siena Workshops. As can be seen from Table 1.1, over the five Workshops, close to two hundred research papers have been presented, including guest presentations at opening plenary sessions and at regular symposia dedicated to the conceptual framework of accounting.

A total of 194 papers presented and discussed in the Workshops to date have been authored or co-authored by scholars from 25 countries. This community of researchers is international, drawing on participants from a number of different countries (12 countries were represented in the first Workshop and 16 in the last) (Table 1.2).

With regard to the international focus of the research studies involved, we can discern three types of paper presented during the course of the five workshops on Accounting and Regulation. In some, the authors approached their subject with reference to the particular characteristics of a specific accounting jurisdiction, or country; in others, they carried out a (more or less extensive) cross-national comparison among different jurisdictions, in relation to a single issue; in yet others, lastly, the papers address a topic that, by nature, is not specific to a particular national context but reflects rather an essentially global viewpoint (see Table 1.3).

The above classification highlights the increase in research examining Accounting and Regulation within a specific national context; typically these papers investigate the effects of adopting IFRS within the jurisdiction of a particular country. Even greater increase can be seen in the number of papers dedicated to general issues that are not restricted to a specific context or geographical

---

[5] See McLeay and Riccaboni (2000) for a preliminary volume of research papers on Accounting and Regulation. For an insight into related work disseminated in Italy, see Di Pietra et al. (2001) and Riccaboni and Di Pietra (2003).

Table 1.1 The Siena workshops on accounting and regulation

	1998	2001	2004	2007	2010	Total
Papers submitted	52	68	44	86	93	343
Papers included in the workshop program	29	27	28	46	64	194
Workshop participants	56	78	53	83	91	361
Parallel sessions	10	12	12	18	23	75
Plenaries and symposia	1	1	2	3	2	9

Table 1.2 Papers presented at the Siena workshops (by country)

		1998	2001	2004	2007	2010	Total
1	Australia	4	2	1	4	3	14
2	Austria	1		1	2	1	5
3	Belgium			1	5	3	9
4	Brazil		1				1
5	Canada		1		1		2
6	Cyprus				1		1
7	Czech Republic					1	1
8	Denmark				1		1
9	Finland			1	2		3
10	France	1	1	3	1	2	8
11	Germany		2	3	1	6	12
12	Greece	1		1			2
13	Ireland	2	1	1			4
14	Italy	2	5	3	10	17	37
15	Japan	1					1
16	Netherlands	1		1	2	3	7
17	New Zealand					2	2
18	Poland				1		1
19	Portugal		1	1	2	2	6
20	Slovenia				1	1	2
21	Spain	1	1	1	3	3	9
22	Sweden	1		2	1	3	7
23	Turkey					2	2
24	UK	12	9	6	5	13	45
25	USA	2	3	2	3	2	12
		29	27	28	46	64	194

Table 1.3 Styles of international accounting research

(Number of research papers)	1998	2001	2004	2007	2010	Total
Papers related to a specific jurisdiction	15	9	10	18	31	83
Papers that compare cross-nationally	5	4	5	14	9	37
Papers with a global perspective	9	14	13	14	24	74
	29	27	28	46	64	194

area (e.g., papers dedicated to the processes of IFRS issuance of standards or to those related to the IASB Framework). The number of papers presenting the results of comparative investigations involving two or more countries, or even a broad sample of countries, appears to have increased more moderately. Focusing on the 83 papers that make specific reference to a certain country, Table 1.4 reveals that they refer to a total of 24 countries.

Finally, with regard to the specific research issues investigated in the 194 papers presented in the five workshops held in Siena over the last 12 years, we have classified the contributions using the keywords provided in each paper, as presented below.

Table 1.5 reveals a certain consistency, in that the issues most frequently dealt with have substantially remained the same. The table shows that the Siena Workshops on Accounting and Regulation have regularly debated aspects of governance (23), disclosure (20), and auditing (19), as well as theories of regulation (19), specific instances of accounting in regulated industries (17), and the regulatory consequences of practices such as earnings management (15). Furthermore, this research community has been instrumental in bringing forward new evidence, and in developing new thinking, concerning the regulatory implications

Table 1.4 Studies of accounting regulation in specific jurisdictions

(Number of research papers)	1998	2001	2004	2007	2010	Total
Australia	4	1			2	7
Austria		1				1
Belgium				1	1	2
China			1			1
Cyprus				1		1
France	1	1	1		1	4
Germany		1	1	1	4	7
Greece	2		1			3
Ireland	1					1
Italy	2	2	1	8	10	23
Japan	1					1
Korea					1	1
Netherlands	1					1
Poland				1		1
Portugal		1	1		1	3
Russia			2			2
Spain		1		1	2	4
Slovenia				1	1	2
South Africa				1		1
Sweden			1	1	3	5
Turkey					1	1
UK	3	1	1	1	3	9
USA				1	1	2
	15	9	10	18	31	83

Table 1.5 Key words

(Number of research papers)	1998	2001	2004	2007	2010	Total
Governance	3	4	6	3	7	23
Disclosure	3	3	0	6	8	20
Auditing	1	1	2	9	6	19
Theories of regulation	6	2	0	6	5	19
Accounting in regulated industries	3	3	2	3	6	17
Earnings quality/management	0	0	3	4	8	15
Financial reporting	1	3	1	1	6	12
Standard setting	0	2	5	2	3	12
Compliance and enforcement	3	2	4	2	0	11
Regulatory systems	4	2	0	3	0	9
SMEs	1	0	0	3	3	7
The management report	0	0	0	1	5	6
Risk reporting	0	2	1	0	3	6
Accounting standardization	1	3	1	0	0	5
Financial instruments	0	3	1	0	1	5
Lobbying	0	1	1	2	1	5

of financial reporting (12), the processes and institutions of standard setting (12), and the degree of compliance and enforcement (11).

The tables above identify the salient issues: the importance of economic-financial information and its use; the role of standard setters, including the IASB;[6] and the institutional frameworks of oversight and enforcement.[7] Table 1.5 also clearly illustrates the importance of financial reporting problems, including the scope of disclosure and the quality of accounting, and emerging issues such as those surrounding the management report.[8] These observations motivate and explain the structure of this volume dedicated to Accounting and Regulation.

The volume is divided into five sections:

1. Introduction.
2. Audit.
3. Financial Consequences.
4. Fair Value.
5. Reporting Behavior.

In each section, we include some of the outstanding papers that have been presented and discussed at the Workshops on Accounting and Regulation in Siena since 1998 where research issues have been reconsidered over the years that have

---

6 On the history and political economy of international standard setting, see Camfferman and Zeff (2007) and Botzem (2012). See also Allen and Ramanna (2013).

7 For an insightful discussion of the social and political dimensions of audit oversight, see Power (1999, 2000, 2003) and Sikka (2009).

8 A useful exposition of the implications of regulation theory for corporate disclosure can be found in Bertomeu and Magee (2011), Wagenhofer (2011).

passed since they were presented in Siena, or since their original publication, or where it has proved useful to take account now of changes that have taken place, especially on the international scene, the original papers have been adapted accordingly. In some cases, the authors have included an insightful postscript in this regard.

As editors of this volume and co-organizers of the Siena Workshops on Accounting and Regulation 1998–2010, we are particularly pleased and honored that many authoritative researchers have accepted our invitation to participate in the compilation of this volume. Sincere thanks for their support for the project go to Walter Aerts, Miguel Arce, Daniela Argento, Michael Bromwich, Frank Clarke, Christina Dargenidou, Judy Day, Graeme Dean, Begoña Giner, Christopher Humphrey, Aziz Jaafar, Ann Jorissen, Jonathan Karpoff, Roland Königsgruber, Scott Lee, Gerald Martin, Anna Samsonova, Ann Tarca, Peter Taylor, Stuart Turley, Geoffrey Whittington and Mahbub Zaman.

References

Allen, A., & Ramanna, K. (2013). Towards an understanding of the role of standard setters in standard setting. *Journal of Accounting and Economics, 55*(1).

Benston, G. J. (1980). The establishment and enforcement of accounting standards: Methods, benefits and costs. *Accounting and Business Research, 11*(41).

Bertomeu, J., & Magee, R. (2011). From low-quality reporting to financial crises: Politics of disclosure regulation along the economic cycle. *Journal of Accounting and Economics, 52*(2/3).

Botzem, S. (2012). *The politics of accounting regulation: Organizing transnational standard setting in financial reporting*. USA: Edward Elgar Publishing.

Bromwich, M. (1985). *The economics of accounting standard setting*. Prentice–Hall: Hemel Hempstead.

Camfferman, K., & Zeff, S. (2007). *Financial reporting and global capital markets : A history of the international accounting standards committee, 1973–2000*. Oxford: Oxford University Press.

Clarke, F., & Dean, G. (2007). *Indecent disclosure: Gilding the corporate lily*. Cambridge: Cambridge University Press.

Clarke, F., Dean, G., & Oliver, K. (2003). *Corporate collapse: Accounting regulatory and ethical failure*. Cambridge: Cambridge University Press.

Cooper, D., & Robson, K. (2006). Accounting, professions and regulation: Locating the sites of professionalization. *Accounting, Organizations and Society, 31*(4/5).

Di Pietra, R., McLeay, S., & Riccaboni, A. (2001). La regolazione del Bilancio di esercizio: Modelli teorici ed esperienza italiana. *Rivista dei Dottori Commercialisti, 6*.

Horngren, C. (1985). Institutional alternatives for regulating financial reporting. *Journal of Comparative Business and Capital Market Law, 7*.

Jones, M. (2011). *Creative accounting, fraud and international accounting scandals*. NewYork: Wiley.

Jönsson, S. (1991). Role making for accounting while the state is watching. *Accounting, Organizations and Society, 16*(5/6).

Klumpes, P. (1994). The politics of rule development: A case study of Australian pension fund accounting rule–making. *Abacus, 30*(2).

Leuz, C., Pfaff, D., & Hopwood, A. (2004). *The economics and politics of accounting, international perspectives on research trends, policy, and practice*. Oxford: Oxford Press.

McLeay, S., & Riccaboni, A. (2000). *Contemporary issues in accounting regulation*. Berlin: Kluwer Academic Publishers.
Mitchell, A., & Sikka, P. (1993). Accounting for change: Institutions of accountancy. *Critical Perspectives on Accounting*, *4*, March.
Power, M. (1999). *The audit society: Rituals of verification* (Trans.). Oxford: Oxford University Press. La società dei controlli, Rituali di verifica, Edizioni di Comunità, Turin (2002).
Power, M. (2000). The audit society—second thoughts. *International Journal of Auditing*, *4*(1).
Power, M. (2003). Auditing and the production of legitimacy. *Accounting, Organizations and Society*, *28*(4).
Riccaboni, A., & Di Pietra, R. (2003). *Il caso italiano di regolazione contabile: Caratteri e recente evoluzione*. Atti del Convegno internazionale di Rimini, aprile 2002, RIREA, Roma, 2003 (pp. 59–104).
Robson, K. (1993). Accounting policy making and "interest": Accounting for research and development. *Critical Perspectives on Accounting*, *4*(1).
Sikka, P. (2009). Financial crisis and the silence of the auditors. *Accounting, Organizations and Society*, *34*(6/7).
Wagenhofer, A. (2011). Towards a theory of accounting regulation: A discussion of the politics of disclosure regulation along the economic cycle. *Journal of Accounting and Economics*, *52*(2/3).
Walker, R., & Robinson, P. (1993). A critical assessment of the literature on political activity and accounting regulation. *Research in Accounting Regulation*, *7*, jai Press.
Walker, R., & Robinson, P. (1994). Competing regulatory agencies with conflicting agendas: Setting standards for cash flow reporting in Australia. *Abacus*, *30*(2).
Watts, R., & Zimmerman, J. (1978). Towards a positive theory of the determination of accounting standards. *Accounting Review*, *54*(2).

Chapter 2
Corporate Collapse: Regulatory, Accounting and Ethical Failure

Frank Clarke and Graeme Dean

Abstract Outlined below are some underlying ideas pursued in our *Corporate Collapse: Accounting, regulatory and ethical failure*, which first appeared in 1997, revised in 2003, followed by a Chinese translation in 2006. Primarily case-based, it examined material over many decades in several countries, but mainly concentrated on Australian *causes célèbres*. Also detailed is our later book *Indecent Disclosure: Gilding the corporate lily*, published in 2007—it is theme based, reviewing similar material, but post-2000. Very little had changed during the 10 years interregnum, despite regulators' and governments' promises of rigorous corporate reforms. Both books were set against a background of repeated official inquiries into discrepancies between what corporations had disclosed about their trading affairs and their actual financial outcomes. The matters in focus have been concerns over many decades. They continue to be, as regulatory reforms have been piecemeal and ill-directed. The recent global financial crisis (GFC) revealed behavior suggesting that it is more likely the 'truth' that under the present regulatory regimes many corporations habitually 'gild the lily'.

This Chapter includes some material first published under the title "Corporate Collapse: Regulatory, Accounting and Ethical Failure" (Cambridge University Press) in 1997 and 2003, which is augmented by the author's comments by way of a post-script on further developments on the *Corporate Collapse*. The chapter is based on the original paper presented at the First International Workshop on Accounting and Regulation in 1998.

F. Clarke · G. Dean (✉)
The Business School, The University of Sydney, Room 314, Building H69, Sydney, NSW 2006, Australia
e-mail: graeme.dean@sydney.edu.au

F. Clarke
e-mail: frank.clarke@sydney.edu.au

R. Di Pietra et al. (eds.), *Accounting and Regulation*,
DOI: 10.1007/978-1-4614-8097-6_2,

2.1 Backdrop: Consider Some of Those Inquiries and Regulatory Responses

As the dust settled in the US in the mid-2000s Enron emerged as a watershed in corporate affairs. The *Crooked E* was the catalyst for the Bush administration's sudden interest in corporate America not living up to its financial reporting responsibilities, particularly its dismal performance in meeting even its quarterly earnings disclosures. Against a backdrop of other US failures at Sunbeam, Cendant, Waste Management, Tyco, Adelphia, Qwest, and (say) Vivendi, plus the frequency of early 2000s restatements downward from quarterly earnings predictions (Clarke and Dean 2007), Enron was possibly the straw that broke the *corporate* camel's back. Enron was too big and too well connected with Capitol Hill to ignore. And all the more so when WorldCom collapsed soon afterwards. However, as a commentator noted, this period and events had all been seen before –'with their Gilded Age predecessors, combining financial legerdemain and political influence peddling'.[1]

As in the 1930s, the regulatory response was swift. Somewhat attempting to mimick Roosevelt's 1930s New Deal 'truth in securities' mantra, 'corporate governance reform' dominated the first decade of the twenty-first century. New *rules of corporate engagement* in the US were promulgated through the 2002 *Sarbanes- Oxley Act* (SOX). Supposedly the 'problem was fixed'!

Australia in the early 2000s also had its equivalent Enron-like dramas. They were in the form of the collapses and subsequent revelations of financial distress at (for example) insurer HIH and the telecommunications company One.Tel (*Corporate Collapse*, 2003, Chaps. 15 and 16). Australian regulatory response was likewise swift, though, as in the US, underpinned by questionable wisdom. For arguably, with the subsequent failures in Australia of Westpoint, Opes Prime, ABC Learning, Centro, Allco, Babcock and Brown and the like, matters worsened. Once again corporate governance matters have been up front in the regulatory rhetoric—this time the plea primarily has been to ensure auditor independence and to rein in unreasonable executive remuneration. By mid-2001 the federal government had postured with its commissioning of an inquiry which produced the Ramsay (2001) Report, *Independence of Australian Company Auditors: Review of current Australian requirements and proposals for reform.* There, auditor independence was the main focus. It was submitted for ministerial approval in October of that year. Concerns about executive remuneration practices would await inquiry until the end of the decade when Australia's Productivity Commission released its final report into *Executive Remuneration in Australia* (2010).

The follow-up legislative initiatives took longer than in the US. There was greater resistance to endorsing government-imposed black-letter law prescriptions. In Australia the proposed independence and other audit-related reforms promoted

---

[1] S. Jacoby, review of Skeel (2004), in *Business History Review* (2005, No. 3).

by the Ramsay Report were eventually included in deliberations by the federal government as part of its ongoing corporate and economic law reform program (CLERP). After a lengthy submission and review process legislative reforms would eventually be proposed in the September 2002 *CLERP* 9 Discussion paper, *Corporate Disclosure—Strengthening the Financial Reporting Framework*. The enactment of the *Corporate Law Economic Reform Program (Audit Reform and Corporate Disclosure) Act* on 30 June 2004 included a number of reforms to the *Corporations Act 2001* (Cth).

Drawing on such developments, the contestable claim being made by some at that time was that corporate governance was no longer a *fad*, that the altered system now had teeth. But attempts to water-down the regulations were just over the horizon.

Concurrently with the Enron fallout, European courts and regulators were busy untangling the Parmalat failure in Italy. There, the somewhat different corporate ownership structure of 'closely held' shareholding patterns (in contrast with the diffused US, capital-ownership pattern), revealed that misleading disclosure was a critical factor in befuddling regulators, financiers and the investing public at large. Members of the well-placed Tanzi family were claimed to be the corporate malefactors. Their alleged deeds rivalled those in Italy a quarter of a century earlier by 'God's bankers', Michele Sindona and Roberto Calvi in the Banco Ambrosiano affair,[2] and in the US three-quarters of a century earlier of the likes of the household names, Carlo Ponzi, Ivar Kreuger and Samuel Insull. Particularly significant is that neither the different legal framework underpinning (say) Parmalat's incorporation nor different board structures, prevented a stark similarity between the alleged deceptive acts by Parmalat and those by its contemporary US corporates. Nor did the rules relating to auditor appointments of the kind subsequently injected into the Sarbanes–Oxley regime.

Meanwhile in Australia ASIC was riding high, having achieved minor convictions of HIH's Ray Williams and Rodney Adler though on charges not directly related to the causes of HIH's collapse in 2001. So it was not surprising that

---

[2] See AAP item, '64 face charges as Parmalat case starts', *Australian Financial Review*, 7 June 2006, p. 66. Coincidentally, the circumstances of Calvi's supposed suicide (he was found dead hanging from scaffolding under London's Blackfriars Bridge, with rocks attached to his legs, and with his pockets stuffed with thousands of pounds in cash) were re-examined in a trial of five persons charged with having murdered him—see *BBC News* as reported BBC News, 18 May 2004; on the web at:<http://news.bbc.co.uk/go/pr/fr//1/hi/world/europe/3732485.stm>(downloaded 25 August 2006); and 'Calvi murder trial opens in Rome', *BBC News* as reported BBC News, 06 October, 2005; on the web at:<http://news.bbc.co.uk/2/hi/europe/4313960.stm >(downloaded 20 September 2006). An original inquest of Calvi's death had returned a suicide verdict. See also Raw (1992). For an update on the trial outcome see Wikipedia which reports that 'On 7 May 2010, the Court of Appeal confirmed the acquittal of Calò, Carboni and Diotallevi. The public prosecutor Luca Tescaroli commented after the verdict that for the family "Calvi has been murdered for the second time." On November 18, 2011, the court of last resort, the Court of Cassation confirmed the acquittal.' (http://en.wikipedia.org/wiki/Roberto_Calvi accessed 12/11/2012).

Australia's corporate regulator ASIC pursued recovery of $90 million from One.Tel's Jodee Rich and Mark Silbermann for overseeing trading by an alleged insolvent One.Tel—ASIC was only partially successful. In 2009 Rich was found not guilty by Justice Robert Austin (see *Australian Securities and Investment Commission v Rich* (2009) NSWSC 1229). Earlier, other One.Tel directors and executive members had been convicted on various charges. Of particular interest in the One. Tel deliberations were the insights into the workings of non-executive directors in the revelations by Lachlan Murdoch and James Packer that they are able to recall very little about their involvements with One.Tel, other than that they were 'profoundly misled' by the disclosures to them of the company's financial performance and position. A *performance* and *position* so poor as to cost their companies in the order of $900 million! Amongst other things, their performances raised a cloud over the corporate governance movement's claim of the invaluable monitoring role of independent, non-executive directors.

Throughout 2006 other matters involving corporate groups and difficult to unravel transactions were being examined. Evidence was taken at the federal government's Cole Commission of Enquiry into alleged bribes associated with the Australian Wheat Board Ltd's contracts for the sale of wheat to Iraq under the United Nations' 'Oil-for-food' program. Under scrutiny were allegations that monies were reported as 'trucking fees' under the AWB program so as to not disclose alleged kick-backs to Saddam Hussein's Iraqi government in contravention of UN rules. At issue was who knew what, and when it was known. Disclosure was again the issue. On the final days of the Cole Enquiry directors and other witnesses revealed contrary disclosures to those previously in the public domain for years.[3]

On the other side of the country at that time, the Western Australian Supreme Court was considering two major corporate group imbroglios. Those deliberations would continue for years. In the first, ASIC claimed that the directors of the Westpoint property group had misled investors about the use of funds raised by its 'mezzanine' finance companies through an apparent use of a loophole in the corporate reporting regime. Westpoint allegedly used investment schemes to seek funds from investors via $2 companies rather than licensed responsible entities. In this context, questions emerged in respect of the corporate regulator's supposed inaction, evoking questions such as 'Did ASIC fail over Westpoint?'. Legitimate grounds were raised here for asking whether the national regulator's role should be that of an (essentially) *ex post* corporate policeman, apprehending and prosecuting, or of a more proactive agent bringing pressure to create an orderly commercial

---

[3] Lee (2006) and 'AWB's $US8 m to be sanitised, deductible', *Australian Financial Review*, 28 September 2006, p. 5. The Cole Report was released in late November 2006, recommending that actions be taken *inter alia* in respect of tax offences, money laundering, terrorist financing, and breaches of the Corporations Law. The allegations of the trucking fees being bribes were not supported. These previously undisclosed matters epitomise the difficulties that persist in Australia's so-called *continuous*, but what still amounts to *indecent* disclosure system. Corporate governance issues were clearly to the fore in the AWB affair.

environment. Westpoint's particulars recalled Australia's notorious 1990s Estate Mortgage Trusts real estate property saga, with its convoluted shuffling of funds between trusts investing in several property projects that already had obtained supposedly secured finance. Such similarities would emerge in late 2010 with matters revealed relating to the collapse in 2009 of Trio Capital (see *Parliamentary Joint Committee on Corporations and Financial Services inquiry into the collapse of Trio Capital*, www.gov.au). Commonalities include complex corporate structures and equally complex financing arrangements, factors that eventually cost unaware investors dearly, many of whom were pensioners.[4]

A second 2006 case before the WA Supreme Court, *The Bell Group Limited (In Liquidation) and Ors v Westpac Banking Corporation and Ors*[5] had begun over decade earlier with interlocutory hearings. The Bell Group liquidator, with the financial backing from the WA Insurance Commission, had sought legal action to the tune of up to $1.5 billion (including interest on the amount being sought over more than 15 years). This action concerned the allegation 'that when the [twenty major—Australian and overseas] banks took security for [the $250 million] loans in 1990 they knew the companies were close to insolvency'.[6] The main case finished in October 2006. By then, it was the longest running court case in Australia's history with over 400 days of evidence in 3 years, estimated legal costs of $300 million, 63,000 items of evidence and more than 36,000 pages of transcript, not to mention the many trees that had been felled in response to the legal discovery process. Eventually Justice Neville Owen held in favour of the litigants in 2009. It would not be long before the banks appealed the decision—as this monograph goes to press, a three-judge panel of the Court of Appeal of Western Australia by a 2-1 decision upheld the $AUD1.56 billion awarded by Supreme Court of Western Australia Justice Owen in 2009 and added additional interest, damages and costs of litigation to the judgment.

Briefly, the *Bell* action involved financing arrangements entered into as the Bell Group (comprising around 80 companies) sought loan refinancing from six major Australian and overseas banks, in response to what some have described as a financial meltdown in 1989 and 1990. The liquidator argued that the banks agreed to extend (restructure) loans to the Bell group of companies, provided they obtained senior security over other unsecured creditors. It needs to be understood that, previously, nearly all debt had been arranged primarily on a negative pledge basis.[7] At issue is how to assess solvency or insolvency from internal and reported financial information within a group setting.

---

4 Unexpected collapses of entities in 2012 in Australia's property trust non-banking sector reveal that little has changed. This, notwithstanding ASIC's 2007 disclosure guidance for that sector following the Westpoint particulars.

5 *The Bell Group Limited (In Liquidation) and Ors v Westpac Banking Corporation and Ors.* Supreme Court of Western Australia Action No. CIV 1464 of 2000.

6 Jacobs 2006.

7 See Dean et al. (1995).

2.2 A Primary Theme

The general theme coursing through our 1990s analyses, such as those in *Corporate Collapse …* (1997) is that *creative*, misleading, accounting is more the consequence of compliance with the Accounting Standards of the day than deviations from them. The significant point is that auditors face an uphill task when the financial statements are inherently misleading. Little did we anticipate that a decade later accounting would play a vital role when mark-to-market accounting became a critical issue in respect of banks' disclosures during the GFC.

Corporate failures provide unique insight into how accounting misleads. In this respect we draw an analogy with how autopsies inform. For, more can be learned about the way things work from enquiry into anomalies—in this case why companies have stopped operating efficiently, than from the myriad *Do it Yourself* explanations of how they succeed. It would seem that so many of the companies that collapsed reported healthy states almost up to immediately before they collapsed. Post failure investigations revealed what had actually been their positions year by year. In this way the company became the 'control' in the analysis.

Further, the GFC experience introduced a novel twist. Novel, insofar as the banks' defense against mark-to- market prescriptions was to argue that openly, disclosing their financial problems, was worse for the public than hiding them. Yet, only by analyzing the *reported* against the *actual* (from investigations) has it been possible to show how the drift in their actual financial states was not revealed in the accounts. Why? Primarily because accounting data prepared (mainly) in accord with the Accounting Standards then, as now, do not disclose a company's *wealth* and *progress.*

2.3 Secondary Themes

2.3.1 Very Little Changes

The 2000s failures in Australia and elsewhere were no different—for whereas most of the failures examined over many decades entailed some deviant behaviour, for the most part their accounting complied generally with the Standards. Compliance with the standards mostly produced grossly misleading data. At the margin there is always likely to be deviation. In some instances the deviations from the approved practices made more sense and possibly produced data that were more informative than would have compliance with the current Standards.

Over time, such occurrences are not all that unusual—Samuel Insull's depreciation accounting in the 1920s often made more sense than the conventions of the time, namely, his alternative replacement reserve accounting to 'depreciation' being regarded merely an *allocation of cost* (McDonald 1962). Regarding consolidation accounting consider more recently Australian corporate mariner

Adsteam's tactics to avoid the use of misleading consolidation techniques Clarke et al. 2003, Chap. 11). There, misleading consolidation data were avoided, though arguably for the wrong motives.

As we demonstrate in *Indecent Disclosure* (2007, Chap. 9) analysis of consolidated data in accord with the Standards is shown to be grossly misleading, based upon false premises, employing senseless procedures, and invoking analyses contradicting both company law and financial fact.

This continues. Consider again the Enron case—most of its supposed manipulation of SPEs was in accord with SEC approved practices. Of course some of Enron's practices were not. But even those that were compliant produced misleading data. Enron's *mark-to-model* method of recording periodic gains on energy contracts *up-front* had been approved by the SEC in the early 1990s—so for 10 years it was basically a compliant practice. Consider the general rules for bringing into account periodic gains on construction contracts—in principle, how different from what Enron did are they?

Consider how perverse the allegations that WorldCom improperly *capitalized expenses*. No doubt WorldCom over-stepped the bounds of common sense. But conventional accounting practice is essentially an expense capitalization system. The boundary is a grey line.

Think about the reasoning underpinning accrual accounting. WorldCom's manipulations could just as easily have occurred without any intention to deceive, mislead, or improperly massage the outcomes. And similarly, consider Waste Management and their depreciation policies on their vehicle fleet.

2.3.2 Feral and Creative Data: Auditors on a Hiding to Nothing

Most companies do not collapse. And most that do, have had only a small engagement in accounting practices designed to deceive. In contrast most companies comply with the prescribed Accounting Standards. Contemplate the consequence of that—if misleading data are more the consequence of compliance with the Standards than deviation from them—the misleading data arising from the intention to deceive is a relatively minor problem, and those arising from compliance are by far, the major problem. Yet *creative* accounting is generally presented to be the result of the intention to deceive. Arguably that is back-to-front—it makes more sense to label 'misleading' the data that arise from the intent to deceive —*feral* accounting, and the misleading data arising from compliance with the Standards with the best of intentions—*creative* accounting.

Contrary to the recent attacks on auditors, a reasonable take is that auditors are poorly served by those setting the accounting standards. Regulation 'by sanction' is the common regulatory mode in the western world. ASIC, Australia's corporate regulator, almost annually threatens local auditors with a 'get tough' monitoring of their clients' compliance with the accounting standards currently in vogue. Arguably, the post-2005 IFRSs are little better than the national Standards that preceded them in respect of making an auditor' task possible.

Our proposition is that the auditors cannot win, that they are between a rock and a hard place when they report that the financials 'comply with the standards' and yet 'show a *true and fair view*. They are almost certain to be stating the impossible. Sometime, somewhere, somehow, someone amongst their number will be found *wanting* when quizzed on how compliance with (now the IFRSs).

Standards could likely show a 'true and fair view' of a financial performance and financial position of a legal entity. For that rests upon the perfectly reasonable proposition that *true and fair* means something sensible in a functional sense. Eventually, sometime down the track, accountants are going to be quizzed in Court about the serviceability of the data prepared in accord with the Standards—whether for example, they show the wealth and progress of a business entity, whether they can be used to determine a business's likely solvency, calculate for it a meaningful: rate of return, earnings per share, the financial relationship between debt and equity, asset backing, and the like.

The answers to such a quiz would have to be *generally no*, once financially meaningful explanations were settled as to what each of those financial indicators are indicative. In this regard consider the deliberations of Justice Middleton in the 2010 Centro case [*Australian Securities and Investments Commission v Healey* (2011) FCA 717 (27 June 2011)] and related civil class actions.

They may prove to be a watershed. Issues to the fore there include what is meant by financial position and solvency and whether standards compliance versus true and fair view should have dominance.[8]

2.3.3 Serviceability: The Consumerism Criterion

Against that background it is reasonable to argue that the same general criterion that applies to consumer protection (in respect of virtually everything other than accounting data) ought to apply to accounting data—that accounting data ought to be serviceable in the uses ordinarily made of them. And we can readily observe how published financial statement data are used to make those financial evaluations, and to calculate or otherwise derive those financial indicators. Furthermore, there is little dispute regarding as to what those derivatives are indicative. We don't have to know whether, or if so how, those financial indicators are used in decision making. It is unequivocal that general purpose financial statement data are used in that way, at least. As a minimum they ought to be fit in those uses. We label that *serviceability*—a simple quality criterion that one might expect everyone to understand and, indeed, expect to govern quality in their world of goods and

[8] Bowers (2012), Lenaghan (2012).

services. It is curious that nothing like that is said about accounting in the current cacophony on corporate governance—the primary quality criterion elsewhere protecting the public interests doesn't get a mention!

2.3.4 Consolidation and Misrepresentation

Most of the commentaries regarding companies' financial performance and financial position draw upon the data in consolidated financial statements, yet they are the most misleading aggregations of financial data. They rest upon a number of propositions that contradict both financial commonsense and the law. They lift the corporate veil and thereby offend the capital boundary rule; the notion of a *group* is an accounting fiction; the notions of 'group' assets, liabilities, revenues and expenses, do not accord with the legal financial outcomes of the transaction. For consolidation techniques inject data that frequently do not appear in the financials of the separate related companies, require a 'not-at-arms-length' assumption irrespective of the transactions' commercial reality, and require the application of the standards to the consolidated data that can produce opposite outcomes to those reflected in the accounts of the constituent companies.

Interestingly, at the time this publication is being finalised Australian legislative reforms have relieved Australian parent companies of disclosing their financials to their shareholders [Corporations Amendment (Corporate Reporting Reform) Act 2010, *Improving Australia's Corporate Reporting Framework*]. Only consolidated data, supplemented with aggregative parent data, need to be published. Curiously, most company analyses appearing in the business press entail the analysis of consolidated data only. Yet nobody (human or artificial) owns a share in a 'corporate group' *per se*. Shareholders of Australian listed companies are thus to be denied under such a reform (in most instances) the financial statements of the companies in which they *do* hold shares. A very peculiar practice, indeed!

Consolidated data are thus extremely creative. Nonetheless, virtually every financial assessment and evaluation made of listed companies continues to be on the basis of them. Most of those assessments and evaluations are nonsensical, counterfactual! The James Hardie affair in Australia illustrated the extent of the general confusion regarding the group notion and consolidated financial data—and the related issues of directors' obligations. Many, including politicians and financial journalists, have paraded their misunderstandings of financial reality and legal status.

James Hardie has justified all of our complaints regarding the group notion and the accounting for the group. It is no surprise that corporate groups have played a significant role in corporate failures. The general public, company officers, and (it seems) legislators and regulators are conditioned into accepting misinformation that fuels corporate distress. This point is reinforced in our 2005 article, Clarke and Dean (2005b).

2.3.5 *True and Fair: A Functional Corporate Governance Test*

In Chapters 17 and 18 of *Corporate Collapse* … (2003) we argued that the accounting profession by failing to impose prescriptions through which the data would be serviceable is abandoning its historical ethos. By placing the primary focus on complying with the Standards—comparability of methods has replaced comparability of outcome. Most of the 'conceptual framework' drafts specify *relevance*, *reliability*, *comparability* and *understandability* as the essential qualitative characteristics of general purpose financial statements. But none of the Standards, collectively or individually (including more recently the IFRSs) has explained how those characteristics emerge from compliance with them. Accountants' professionalism is at stake (West 2003). Though the *true and fair* criterion is a quality heritage that accountants uniquely enjoy, it is treated rather shabbily by them. Yet, *serviceability* is the qualitative characteristic that makes financial statement data true and fair.

Note, were it that the data in general purpose financial statements were serviceable, they would have to be 'relevant, reliable, comparable, and understandable'. Whatever the financial outcomes they would be exposed in the wash-up of it all. Whatever Boards of Directors had done, no matter in whose interests they acted; whatever use was made of the intangibles at their disposal; whatever the acumen applied to running their company; irrespective of the supposed inducements to act in their own or ethical ways; independently or otherwise; whether the auditors were independent or not, been rotated or are long-serving, had or had not provided non-audit services, all would be reflected in the financial outcomes. The corporate governance rules, like most of the talk of corporate sustainability, Triple Bottom Line reporting and the like, are promoted arguably because the financial statements do not inform of the financial outcomes from how companies are managed, including the economic outcomes of whatever use is made of the financially measurable and the non-financial non-measurable resources at their disposal. Recall, all the governance rules and the *avant garde* accounting movements are directed toward adding value—and if we take a stakeholder point of view, perhaps adding value to meet a kind of Pareto optimum.

Corporate failure is a natural enough event. As Schumpeter and others have noted—failures are necessary. They are the product of the capitalist winds of *creative destruction*. It is reasonable in a world of scarce resources to argue that companies unable to add value by their operations ought to be liquidated. But an orderly commercial environment is a necessary condition for mature economies. Those acting in markets need to be adequately and equally informed. Only then can proper risk/return assessments be made. But a pervading feature of failures has been their unexpected nature; *unexpected* by virtue of the means of advising companies' financial wealth and progress being neither true nor fair.

2.3.6 Indecent Disclosure: A Dubious Legacy

Central to those discussions are questions regarding the reliability, accuracy and overall probity of corporate financial disclosures. Contestable phrases or words, often touted by regulators and standards setters, imply a desire either to achieve *quality in accounting information* or *transparency*. Such issues are supposed to be at the forefront of those seeking to produce an international conceptual framework, viz the IASB and FASB who jointly continue to undertake such an exercise. While not questioning the motives, elsewhere the current authors have provided an assessment of the less than fruitful outcomes accompanying earlier national exercises that were underpinned by similar desires.[9]

The above illustrations are important for the light they throw on the role of financial disclosure in creating the orderly commercial environment, essential to the proper functioning of market economies. Importantly, the defaults and anomalies might be taken to be indicative of the new corporate governance mechanisms biting into and exposing corporate wrongdoing. However, on closer analysis they frequently emerge to be repeat performances of the *indecent disclosure* by companies over the past nearly 170 years. Matching the current corporate governance regimes against those of the past offers little comfort, for they indicate that, for the most part, the current regimes contain 'more of the same'. Little that is new has been introduced. It would seem unlikely that the judicial reviews of failures already examined or those under current review would have been prevented had the latest IFRSs been in place in their current formats.

In fact, the current talk of corporate governance and the various codifications, schema and recommendations might be doing more harm than good. For if, as we argue here, the regimes specified are impotent, passing them off as panaceas for corporate ills is likely to lure investors into a sense of false security. There is a burgeoning literature reporting research associating compliance with the various governance regimes and 'superior corporate performance'. In contrast, there is little addressing the problems of the modern corporation in this age of globalisation. 'Legacy thinking' draws upon experiences in the different corporate environments of the past, seducing would-be reformers into massaging the past ways of dealing with corporate problems, without much explicit recognition of differences between the past and the present. A critical issue is whether the conventional corporate form with which most are familiar (and in respect to which the current governance regimes are directed) can indeed be governed adequately, if by 'governing' we are referring to its original notion of controlling or *steering*.[10]

---

[9] A special issue of *Abacus*, Vol. 39, No. 3, October 2003 contains several articles that discuss the positive and negative aspects of those national conceptual framework exercises. The current authors were among several expressing their views.

[10] In an earlier unpublished work, IIR Corporate Governance seminar, October (2002) Clarke and Dean noted that the word 'governance' is taken arguably from the Greek *cybernetics* (or Latin *gubenatore*) which refers to the ability of the navigator effectively to steer a vessel—a skill

The relatively easy access to international capital markets and the ease with which companies might move between alternative jurisdictions, possibly eased the way for the doubtful practices underpinning the GFC. Globalisation certainly made it easier to exploit perceived advantageous trading, labour, stock exchange listing, and financial disclosure rules. Such corporate antics militated against exercising control over conventional corporate structures with updated versions of past regulatory mechanisms. For these had already failed to override arrangements less sophisticated and less complex than those to which they were then being applied. There is little ground to expect that they ever will be any more successful in the future than they were in the past.

As briefly noted earlier the (now Ireland-based; previously Netherlands and before that Australian-based) James Hardie group's contemporary, worldwide ongoing battle with governments, unions and the victims of asbestos related diseases, is a salient example of the problems with the conventional corporate structure. That the form of the corporation as it is generally understood and accepted, has a legitimate *place* in modern society is contestable. Doubt that the grouping of subsidiaries under the umbrella of 'limited liability within limited liability'—can provide a net benefit for a modern commercial society is evoked by the conflict between commercial and legal realities inherent in the notion of a sacrosanct *corporate veil*. That situation is exacerbated by the seeming inconsistency between the traditional notion of the corporate objective to maximise shareholder wealth. Especially so in view of the now popular notions of: corporate social responsibility, the limiting of financial statements to only those 'Standards compliant' to show present financial position and past financial performance, the potential conflict between legal obligations and alleged ethical responsibilities and the frequent misunderstanding of public perceptions regarding the nature of the corporate vehicle and the reality of it. Possibly, the Hardie asbestos affair has better served to highlight those matters than various other failures.

The series of transactions in 1997/98 involving the Lang Corporation (loosely described as the Patricks/MUA Waterfront affair) perhaps comes a close second.[11] The legislative likes of the US's *Sarbanes–Oxley*, Australia's *CLERP 9* and the ASX Corporate Governance Council's *Corporate Governance Guidelines* (and their equivalents elsewhere) have poured out rules in particular for the internal management of corporations. In contrast, the Hardie affair has drawn an outpouring of proposed rules regarding companies' interactions with the public at large. Of particular interest is the manner in which the debate regarding Hardie's

---

(Footnote 10 continued)
that required information about the vessel's current position, the speed it is travelling, sea currents, other vessels' positions, land etc. Information needed was spatial and required continual updating. This was again discussed in Clarke and Dean (2005a). Walker and Walker (2000), similarly note that governance has its roots in Greek, where the relevant word can mean 'manage', 'oversee', 'direct' or lead'.

[11] For details of the way the use of the corporate veil in the *Waterfront* affair affected employees' entitlements see Dean et al. (1999); see also Clarke and Dean (2007).

alleged misdeeds has renewed the personification of corporate ethics. But whereas the artificial persona of the corporation has been translated (as we noted above) into an almost human equivalent, in a twist its true fictional character has been reinforced by the NSW state government's threats to 'lift the corporate veil'. This sanction would be imposed were Hardie to not meet its perceived financial obligations to those suffering from or having died as a consequence of its asbestos products.

In mid 2006 a partial proposal was put forward by the NSW Attorney-General. It sought to have a federal inquiry examine ways to prevent the type of episode at James Hardie. There, aptly illustrated was the problem of a wealthy (solvent) parent company avoiding responsibility for the personal injury and death compensation obligations of insolvent subsidiary companies'.[12] This reform did not occur. But the significance of the issue had been stressed.

In a curious way, the plight of those victims of asbestos-related diseases has made it clear, possibly the clearest in around 170 years, that the corporate structure (especially where groups are prevalent) is not sacred. At the end of the day, if it is no longer serving commerce in the way the UK Gladstone Committee and those 1840s politicians intended when pressing the British Parliament to enact the *Companies Act of* 1844 (with its general registration provisions), the present company structure can and ought to be changed.

That possibility doesn't seem to have been contemplated by those reacting to the successive waves of corporate collapses and crises over the past century. Particularly over the past several decades when shareholders', finance and trade creditors' and (more recently) employees' financial woes have been to the fore. It is no surprise then, that the solutions are being presented in the form of corporate governance rules framed with an underlying assumption that accepts without question the current form of the corporate vehicle. The modern corporation with its 'limited liability within limited liability' facility, shareholder sovereignty and corporate veil framework, is assumed to be untouchable.

A peculiar feature of the current debate over corporate shenanigans is the similarity they bear to those revealed following the 1929 crash and ensuing Depression. The financial statements of many companies then were grossly misleading. Grossly misleading, not only by virtue of deliberate acts of deceit, but also as a consequence of following the prescribed accounting conventions (rules) of the day, possibly with the best of intentions. Now, as then, few seem to appreciate the prospect that the reported financials of the companies that have not failed, those deemed the current high-fliers and 'travelling swimmingly', are equally misleading as were those that crashed or were noted to be in trouble. In the early 1930s the general lead taken in the US was to specify accounting 'rules' (incorrectly labelled then, and now, as 'principles') for the processing of financial aspects of business transactions, and disclosure rules for reporting the financial outcomes of them.

---

[12] Sexton (2006). See also *ASIC Media Release 07–35* 'ASIC commences [civil] proceedings relating to James Hardie', 14 February 2007.

That push for rules (enabling the 'tick-a-box' mentality) to govern accounting practices that has been pursued for the best part of 80 years, underpinned by the idea that comparability would be achieved were each company's financials prepared to accord with the same rules. The mistaken proposition is that uniformity of essentially *input* and processing rules would produce uniform *output* in the form of comparable financial statements. Yet the falsity in the reasoning of that proposition was clearly demonstrable, and clearly evidenced by the variances in the outputs in the financial statements of companies following the same rules.

Few seem to recall that, just as in the 1920s when the UK Royal Mail's drawing upon past profits to pay current dividends accorded with the generally accepted accounting disclosure *rules* of the day,[13] Enron's (and more recently in the GFC, the shadow banking sector's) use of special purpose entities to hide debt was facilitated by a professionally prescribed [and ad-hoc, not theoretically driven] ownership *rule*. Nor do they recall that the mark-to-model valuations to bring prospective profits to account had regulatory approval, as did the 1970s Australian financier-cum-property company, Cambridge Credit's 'front-end-loading' mechanism to calculate current profits while in the new millennium WorldCom's expense capitalisation was arguably the product of the conventional accrual system that differed little from Australia's Reid Murray's capitalisation of development expenses in the 1960s. Little has been recalled in the context of WorldCom's woes of the UK's Rolls-Royce's 1970s fall following its capitalisation of the costs of developing its innovative RB-211 engine (see Gray 1971). Waste Management's alleged depreciation charge scam is as much a product of accountants' contestable idea that depreciation is an easily manipulable 'allocation of cost', rather than a 'decrease in price'. Again, that the same problem had arisen with US airline companies in the 1950s passes without mention. Perversely, following the rules has emerged a legitimate, often as much well-intentioned as intentionally deceitful, means of misleading accounting, a simulacrum of a quality mechanism.

Significantly, the practices causing the shaking of heads in outrage in the March 2000 dotcom crash and then also in the 2007–2008 GFC have, in one form or another, all happened previously. In other disciplines the habitual recurrence of undesirable events would provoke thoughts that perhaps there was something awry with the system within which they were being repeated. And certainly, failed means of preventing the repetition of unwanted outcomes would be abandoned. Curiously, in business matters the response of legislators and professional

---

[13] Green and Moss (1982), support this claim, noting that the defence 'case made much of the auditor's use of the phrase "after adjustment of taxations reserves" to describe the falsification of the 1926 and 1927 accounts. They were also able to plead that, rightly or wrongly, the secret transfer of inner reserves was a fact of life in large conglomerate companies, particularly in the shipping industry where transfers were an accepted method of ironing out the effects of the business cycle. In this the evidence of Lord Plender was especially persuasive. As a result Kylsant and Morland were cleared of the balance sheet charges'. Notably the complexity of the structure is captured by Green and Moss's reference to the Royal Mail being a conglomerate.

standards setters has been precisely the opposite. The vacillation surrounding the mark-to-market of (in particular banks') securities during the GFC bears witness to companies' penchant for 'not telling it how it is'. The failed remedies of the past have not only been repeated, in most instances they have been multiplied—more rules of the kind known to have failed in the past have been replicated with a vengeance, even though their deterrent effect and their clout when imposing penalties on individuals for wrongdoing have dismal histories.

Throughout all this the ways and means of lessening culpability have been encouraged by regulators. Plea-bargaining which has become the norm in the US and seems to be growing in Australia is apt. Regulators have traded off their responsibility to apprehend and penalise wrongdoers with the prospect of the potentially easier convictions of others. At times, achieving 'heads on poles' has dominated. This has been at the expense of the presumably critical regulatory quest of achieving an orderly financial market. Plea-bargainers trade their guilt to become primary witnesses for prosecuting regulators. Andrew Fastow, for instance, was a primary witness against Kenneth Lay and Jeffrey Skilling in the Enron case. The evidence shows that the case against those officers rests more upon what their previous collaborators disclose, than what the regulatory machinery has uncovered from examining public data. In the Australian cases against HIH offenders, an HIH executive Bill Howard turned 'Crown witness', in return for indemnity against conviction. It may not be unkind to suggest that the sentiment underlying Roosevelt's (perhaps apocryphal) quip that 'you have to set a thief to catch a thief' still prevails. Legend has it that Roosevelt was responding to criticism that he had appointed Joseph Kennedy (then considered by many to be a modern-day robber baron) to be the first head of the newly formed SEC in 1934.[14]

Lack of transparency, misleading disclosure—*indecent disclosure*—characterised traumatic failures of the Enron, HIH variety. In particular, annual statements of financial performance and financial position have not presented accurate, reasonably reliable, portrayals of companies' dated wealth and periodic financial progress. In today's and yesterday's jargon they have not ensured 'transparent', 'truthful' financial reporting. Were they to have done so, for the most part the financial outcomes disclosed would have facilitated informed evaluations, signalled the appropriate questions to ask of managers and executives, alerted those with an eye for wrongdoing. It would have been irrelevant how company directors had acted—with propriety or with deception, in their own best interests or in the interests of the shareholders or a wider stakeholder cohort, with or without regard for social and environmental wellbeing, with or without business acumen. Fair dealing is a hallmark of a civilised society. It is grossly *indecent* that the commercial environment lacks the *order*, the *framework*, necessary for fair dealing. There is a real lack of trust by participants based on a perception that the regulated market system is actually a 'fair game'. The mark-to-market episode during the

[14] See Chatov's (1975); and more recently, David Radler's SEC plea bargain in return for being a witness against Conrad Black (*Australian Financial Review*, 19 March 2007, p. 11).

GFC has more than justified that perception. It is consistent with many participants' view that the market fails to operate *as if*, as Oscar Wilde's Sir Robert Chiltern quipped in *An Ideal Husband*, it has a 'commercial conscience'. Recall the earlier James Hardie observations.

So, it is probably not surprising that during the GFC those who opposed the move to have banks and other financial institutions mark-to-market their financial assets, jumped on the bandwagon. Quickly, there were cries of 'told you so' from those who opposed the introduction of the relevant accounting standards FAS 157 in the US and international financial reporting standard (IFRS) 39 in Europe. Academics soon followed suit (see Katz 2008; Ryan 2008; Whalen 2008; Magnan 2009). US politicians such as past Speaker in the US House, Newt Gingrich, enthusiastically mouthed such a litany with the apparent approbation of 2008 Republican Presidential candidate John McCain. The refrain was that having to write-down assets to their market prices had 'caused' the financial collapses of Bear Sterns, Lehman Brothers, AIG, and Northern Rock, and the near collapse of numerous others. That causation chain is said therefore to have necessitated the $US700b *cash for trash* bailout in the US. It was also suggested that Iceland's near bankruptcy was another 'fair value' (mark-to-market) casualty. Such sentiments soon resurfaced in the discourse surrounding Ireland's bankruptcy and the sovereign debt problems of Europe's so-called 'PIIGS', namely Portugal, Ireland, Italy, Greece and Spain.

Thus, having to report market prices were, for some, the cause of the GFC crisis, or at the very least that they unnecessarily exacerbated it. This was by no means the first time that the use of market values had been the subject of controversy in the US and elsewhere (Dean and Clarke 2010). In 2005 numerous countries adopted the International Accounting Standards (IAS), including IAS 39 which specified that certain financial instruments (which featured particularly in bank balance sheets) be accounted for at 'fair value through profit and loss'—that is, that they be *marked-to-market*. In 2007 a renewed US push for the application of a current value accounting system came with the FASB's promulgation of FAS 157. And, whereas FAS 157 was voluntary with respect to many assets, other FASs permitted current values to be used. Where assets were 'held for sale' or for 'trading' it meant that, like their European counterparts, US banks and other financial institutions (securities firms, mutual funds, hedge funds and the kind) had to mark-to-market many of their financial instruments.

Consider Greece's sovereign debt crisis. It aptly illustrates the impact of false or misleading messages. There, Lynn (2011) alleges that (what amounts to) deliberately false communication by the Greek Government to the European Union countries, understating the level of Greek debt, paved the way for Greece's entry into the EU and the Eurozone. Moving away from Continental Europe, O'Toole (2009) claims that Ireland's politicians were bathing in a false impression of their country's financial position, fully knowing that its building bubble was about to implode. Again, alleged communication of false financial information had disastrous effects when the truth was revealed.

Mark-to-market matters came to a head after Lehman Brothers' collapse in October 2008, when Congress rose to the cause. Accusations we heard above suggested the mark-to-market rule of FAS 157 'caused the financial crisis'[15]. This illustrated a misunderstanding of accounting's communicative role of informing financial decisions, by 'telling it how it is'.

As well as the management intent issue about whether financial assets are held-for-sale, another major bone of contention was the noted necessity under FAS 157 to write down financial assets, given an *inactive market*. Market inactivity was presumed by many to be 'temporary'. The continuing inactivity for several years highlights the lacuna in such an argument. The proposition put was that marking-to-market failed to take into account the future prospects of the assets, that (in particular for the banks') capital was being eroded erroneously and that doing so exacerbated the credit crisis. Accounting's mark-to-market prescriptions were said by some to be exacerbating the financial system's *procyclicality*. In their *Alchemists of Loss*, Dowd and Hutchison (2010: 310) opine that 'In the event, FAS 157's timing was terrible' for Goldman Sachs and Bear Stearns.

The FASB attempted to meet the inactive markets problem by injecting FAS 157 with a *fair value hierarchy* of assets for valuation purposes—those that it labelled, respectively: *level 1*—for which a market and its prices were available; *level 2*—where a market for like assets allowed some discretion by owners regarding which prices they chose and; *level 3*—where the markets are inactive, and owners could mark-to-model or 'mark-to-myth' as Buffett (quoted in Davies 2010: 114) called it. The recent IASB's IFRS 13 (2011) has adopted the same 3-level hierarchy in its measurement standard equivalent to FAS 157.[16] But the hierarchy did little for some. It merely exposed their perilous state—Goldman Sachs was, for example, shown to have level 3 assets amounting to '3 times its capital', and Bear Stearns $28 billion in level 3s with 'a net equity position of only 11.1 billion' (Dowd and Hutchison 2010: 311).

Complaints from compliant institutions being forced to make considerable write-downs as a result of mark-to-market accounting (FAS 157 in particular in the US) were common, as evident in this comment by Zandi (2009: 237): 'The [mark-to-market] rules put pressure on institutions to quickly adjust the book value of their assets to market prices … markdowns were so large and cut so deeply into their capital that it threatened their survival … To keep this from happening in the future mark-to-market accounting rules could be tweaked so that changing assets [read also liabilities] values could be phased in over time … Banks would still have to lower their holding as prices fell, but not as rapidly'.

The introduction of the mark-to-market accounting rules has been perceived a serious problem. Munchau (2011: 211), for example, noted that 'If accounting

---

[15] Magnan and Makarian (2011: 216) note the following as examples of this group: Katz (2008), Whalen (2008), Gingrich (2009) and Zion et al. (2009).

[16] The hierarchy is arbitrary—others have been proposed, entailing up to five levels.

rules had not been temporarily relaxed many banks and insurance companies would have had to file for bankruptcy'.

2.4 The Anguish of the Sad Experiences over the Last 15 Years

The hullabaloo from 1997 to the present has not been without its benefits. Misleading reporting of financial outcomes has been at the centre of the numerous inquiries into and prosecutions for corporate wrongdoing. Inappropriate disclosures have been noted. Earnings management practices were alleged to have facilitated companies like Enron, WorldCom, Tyco, Vivendi, Waste Management, Sunbeam, Disney and the like in the US to meet analysts' quarterly earnings predictions. Allegedly they underpinned many of the analysts' questionable 'buy' recommendations uncovered by Attorney-General Eliot Spitzer, and to have assisted the alleged tactics of some, like the US analyst guru, Jack Grubman, to push up WorldCom's share price.[17]

A spotlight on financial disclosure has evoked the questioning not only of the rules directing how companies account and report, but also whether the system should remain *rules-based* or become a more *principles-based* system.[18] A primary claim by many regulators has been that the rules are followed frequently, but the intention underpinning them is not. But there has been little compelling argument to support the proposition that the principles said to underpin the post-2005 IFRSs (of whatever persuasion) differ from the earlier described rules (sometimes labelled principles) prescribed by national accounting bodies. That convoluted debate has witnessed those promoting the IFRS to argue that they, in contrast with the practices in accord with the rules promulgated by (for example) the US Financial Accounting Standards Board, are principles-based. But the debate is bereft of any undergirding, primary principle identified, suggested or specified. The discussions related to the joint IASB/FASB Conceptual Framework exercise which began in mid-2006 continue to fail to accept that any accounting conceptual framework needs to be grounded in the realities (principles even) of commerce, linking accounting with the ethical, legal, financial, economic, metrical and other foundations of business (Chambers 1991).

Achieving this on an international basis is a huge challenge. Consider one such principle, the legal (based on ethical) *true and fair view* principle. One might presume that the British (and European generally) true and fair criterion governing the quality of financial disclosures, has the historical and potential technical credentials to fit that role. From our analyses, outlined above, we find it curious that it

[17] Anon (2002).

[18] See, inter alia, AAA Financial Accounting Standards Committee (AAAFASC), 'Evaluating concept-based vs rules-based approaches to standard setting' (2003); Schipper (2003).

is not universally accepted by practitioners nor standards setters as a basis for overriding a required compliance with the rules, viz the accounting standards specified.

Our analyses suggest that, repeating history, rules will prevail. This is a situation which, in the present climate, conveniently satisfies auditors' responsibility to form and report an opinion as to whether a company's financials are truly and fairly indicative of, or fairly present, its wealth and progress. For whereas auditors' performances have been criticised in the fallout from company failures, given the faulty foundations of accounting, their verification task is all but an 'impossibility'.[19] It is suggested *in Corporate Collapse* and pursued further in *Indecent Disclosure* that it is problematic whether extant accounting standards (including IFRSs) facilitate or hinder the making of such professional judgments about whether accounts show a true and fair view.

Unexpected corporate failures, warped ideas regarding the function of accounting, the production of financial data that are not serviceable for the uses habitually made of them and dodgy accounting that doesn't *tell it how it is*, demonstrate, that in the corporate world all that glitters certainly is not gold.

References

Anon (2002). Is Jack Grubman the worst analyst ever?, *CNN Money*.

Bowers, S. (2012). Share price ruling this year. *The Australian Financial Review*, 48.

Chambers, R. J. (1991). Accounting and corporate morality—the ethical cringe. *Australian Journal of Corporate Law*, *1*(1), 9–21.

Chanos, J. (2009). We need honest accounting: Relax regulatory capital rules if need be, but don't let banks hide the truth. *Wall Street Journal, 23*.

Chatov, R. (1975). *Corporate financial reporting*. NY: Free Press.

Clarke, F., & Dean, G. (2005a). Corporate governance: A case of misplaced concreteness?. *Advances in public interest accounting,* 11, *Corporate Governance: Does any size fit*? (Elsevier: JAI, 2005a), pp. 15–39.

Clarke, F., & Dean, G. (2005b). Corporate officers' views on cross-guarantees and other proposals to "lift the corporate veil". *Company and Securities Journal*, 23, 299–320.

Clarke, F., & Dean, G. (2007). *Indecent disclosure*. Cambridge: Cambridge University Press, pp. 41–44.

Clarke, F. L., Dean, G. W., & Oliver, K. G. (1997). *Corporate collapse: Regulatory, accounting and ethical failure*. Cambridge: Cambridge University Press.

Clarke, F., Dean, G., & Houghton, E. (2002). Revitalising group accounting: Improving accountability. *Australian Accounting Review, 12*, pp 58–72.

Clarke, F., Dean, G., & Oliver, K. (2003). *Corporate collapse: Accounting, regulatory and ethical failure, rev* (2nd ed.). Cambridge: Cambridge University Press.

[19] This point was demonstrated throughout, using case particulars, in Clarke et al. (1997, 2002) and then again in Clarke and Dean's 2007).

Clarke, F., Dean, G., & Margret, J. (2008). Solvency solecisms: corporate officers' problematic perceptions'. *Australian Accounting Review*, 71–80

Dean, G. W., & Clarke, F. L. (2010). 'Unresolved methodological questions at the cross-section of accounting and finance. In T. Wise & V. Wise (Eds.), *A Festschrift for Bob Clift, special issue of International Review of Business Research Papers*, (Vol. 6(5), pp. 20–32).

Dean, G., Clarke, F., & Houghton, E. (1995). Cross guarantees and negative pledges: A preliminary analysis. *Australian Accounting Review*, *5*, 48–63.

Dean, G., Clarke, F., & Houghton, E. (1999). Corporate restructuring, creditors' rights, cross guarantees and group behaviour. *Company and Securities Law Journal*, *17*, 73–102.

Davies, H. (2010) *Financial Crisis: Who is to Blame*?, Malden, MA: Polity Press.

Dowd, K., & Hutchinson, M. (2010). *Alchemists of loss: How modern finance and government intervention crashed the financial system*. New York: John Wiley.

Gray, R. (1971). *Rolls on the Rocks: The history of Rolls Royce*, Tisbury, Salisibury

Green, E., & Moss, M. (1982). *A business of national importance: The royal mail shipping group, 1902–1937*. London and New York: Methuen.

Gingrich, N. (2008) 'Suspend mark-to-market now!', Forbes, 29 September. Online Available http://www.forbes.com/2008/09/29/mark-to-market-opedcx_ng_0929gingrich.html (accessed 21 September 2011).

Jacobs, M. (2006). Bell fight goes down to the wire as case winds up. *Australian Financial Review*, 9.

Katz, I. (2008). *SEC recommends keeping fair-value rule with changes*. Bloomberg.

Lee, T. (2006). Clarity comes too late for Cole's liking. *Australian Financial Review*, 4.

Lenaghan, N. (2012). Centro chiefs had the jitters. *The Australian Financial Review*, 48.

Lynn, M. (2011) *Bust: Greece, the Euro, and the Sovereign Debt Crisis*, Hoboken, NJ: John Wiley

Magnan, M. (2009). Fair value accounting and the financial crisis: messenger or contributor?, Working paper, CIRANO—Scientific Publications Paper No. 27.

Magnan, M., & Markarian, G. (2011). Accounting, governance, and the crisis: Is risk the missing link? *European Accounting Review*, *20*(2), 215–231.

McDonald, F. (1962). *Insull*. Chicago: Chicago University Press.

Munchau, W. (2011). *The meltdown years: The unfolding of the global economic crisis*. New York: McGraw Hill.

O'Toole, F. (2009) *Ship of Fools: How Corruption and Stupidity Sank the Celtic Tiger*, London: Faber & Faber.

Productivity Commission Report. (2010). *Executive Remuneration in Australia, Australian Government printer;* http://www.pc.gov.au/projects/inquiry/executive-remuneration, Australian Government Printer, accessed on 6 March 2012.

Ramsay, I. (Chairman) (2001). *Independence of Australian company auditors: Review of current Australian requirements and proposals for reform, Australian Government Printer.*

Raw, C. (1992). *The money changers: How the Vatican Bank enabled Roberto Calvi to steal $250 million for the heads of the P2 Masonic Lodge*. London: Harvill.

Ryan, S. (2008) '*Accounting in and for the sub-prime crisis*', The Accounting Review, 83: 1605–1639.

Schipper, K. (2003). Principles-based accounting standards. *Accounting Horizons*, 17(1), 61–72.

Sexton, E. (2006). Nothing to stop another Hardie. *Sydney Morning Herald*, 17–18.

Skeel, D. (2004). *Icarus in the boardroom: The fundamental flaws in corporate America and where they came from*. Oxford: Oxford University Press.

Walker, R. G., & Walker, B. C. (2000). *Privatisation—sell off or sell out?:The Australian experience*. Sydney: ABC Books.

West, B. P. (2003). *Professionalism and accounting rules*. London: Routledge.

Whalen, R. C. (2008). The subprime crisis: cause, effect and consequences, Networks Financial Institute Policy Brief No. 2008-PB-04. Online. Available http://ssrn.com/abstarct=1113888. Accessed 12 Sept 2011.

Zandi, M. (2009). *Financial shock*. Upper Saddle River, NJ: FT Press.

Zion, D., Varshney, A., & Cornett, C. (2009). *Focusing on fair value*. Credit Suisse Equity Research Report, June 27.

Chapter 3
Post-Enron Reform: Financial Statement Insurance, and GAAP Re-Visited

Joshua Ronen

Abstract The fact that auditors are paid by the companies they audit creates an inherent conflict of interest that is endemic to the relation between the firm (the principal) and the auditor (the agent). I analyze a financial statement insurance mechanism that eliminates the conflict of interest auditors face and properly aligns their incentives with those of shareholders thus mitigating market inefficiencies arising from uncertainty regarding the quality of financial statements. Instead of appointing and paying auditors, companies would purchase financial statement insurance that provides coverage to investors against losses suffered as a result of misrepresentation in financial reports. The insurance coverage that the companies are able to obtain is publicized, as are the premiums paid for that coverage. The insurance carriers would then appoint and pay the auditors who attest to the accuracy of the financial statements of the prospective insurance clients. Firms announcing higher limits of coverage and smaller premiums would distinguish themselves in the eyes of the investors as companies with higher quality financial statements. In contrast, those with smaller or no coverage or higher premiums will reveal themselves as those with lower quality financial statements. Every company will be eager to get higher coverage and pay smaller premiums lest it be identified as the latter. A sort of Gresham's law in reverse would be set in operation, resulting in a flight to quality.

3.1 Introduction

On October 16, 2001, Enron Corp. announced that it was reducing its after-tax net income by $544 million and its stockholders' equity by $1.2 billion. Because of accounting errors, Enron announced on November 8 that it was restating its

J. Ronen (✉)
Stern School of Business, New York University, New York, USA
e-mail: jronen@stern.nyu.edu

R. Di Pietra et al. (eds.), *Accounting and Regulation*,
DOI: 10.1007/978-1-4614-8097-6_3,

previously reported net income for the years 1997–2000. The result of this restatement was a reduction in stockholders' equity of $508 million. Within a month equity was lower by $1.7 billion (18 % of the 9.6 billion previously reported on September 30, 2001). On December 2, 2001, Enron filed for bankruptcy under Chap. 11 of the United States Bankruptcy Code. As catastrophic as this event may have been, it proved to be only the beginning of a series of stunning revelations of accounting irregularities by major corporations that were the darlings of Wall Street: WorldCom, AOL, Metromedia Fiber Networks, Qwest Communications; the list goes on and on. The number of restatements keeps rising, from fifty-a- year in the early 1990s to well over two-hundred-a-year now. What happened?[1]

Can the roots of the calamities be traced back to Federal Reserve Chairman Alan Greenspan's famous 1996 warning of investors' "irrational exuberance"?[2] Are they a manifestation of the "infectious greed [that] seemed to grip much of our business community,"[3] which, on July 16, 2002, Greenspan impugned as responsible for the stock market's woes? Is it the foolishness of investors, coupled with the bursting of the stock market's bubble; or the depleted morality of the Chief Executive Officers (CEOs)? Is it the tendency to "cook" the books? Perhaps the collapse could be ascribed to the failure of the "gatekeepers": the auditing profession, or rather the industry it has become, boards of directors, audit committees, and the regulators. If the watchdogs misbehaved, is it because of moral turpitude or perverse incentives? And are the bright line financial reporting standards perchance the other culprits, encouraging designs to circumvent them and making it easier for auditors to acquiesce in some accounting and disclosure playfulness?

Sifting through all these causes can be a nightmare to any diagnostician. It may be tempting to suggest that all have contributed to the situation in varying degrees, but such a sweeping conclusion offers no constructive policy remedies. Effective crisis resolution requires sharp distinctions: which of the implicated circumstances are truly harmful, and which are benign, possibly even salubrious when considered in isolation? Among the potentially baneful conditions, which can be cured by reform and which are resistant to legislative or regulatory intervention? Finally,

---

[1] This Chapter includes a reprinted article first published under the title "Post-Enron Reform: Financial Statement Insurance, and GAAP Re-visited" in the Stanford Journal of Law, Business and Finance in 2002, which is followed by the author's comments by way of a post script on further developments on the Financial statement insurance based on the original paper presented at the Third International Workshop on Accounting and Regulation in 2004.

[2] Greenspan (1996), The Challenge of Central Banking in a Democratic Society, Address at the Annual Dinner and Francis Boyer Lecture of The American Enterprise Institute for Public Policy Research (Dec. 5, 1996).

[3] Federal Reserve Board's Semiannual Monetary Policy Report to the Congress Before the US S. Comm. on Banking, Housing., and Urban Affairs, 107th Cong. (2002) (statement of Alan Greenspan, Chairman, Federal Reserve), available at http://www.federalreserve.gov/boarddocs/hh/2002/july/testimony.htm.

considering those ills that are susceptible to effective treatment, who would be the savior, government or the free market?

Not all remedies are equally effective. For example, although we all may be enraged that certain individuals and companies violated our trust, prosecution, and ultimate punishment may not adequately deter wrongdoing: intentional misrepresentation is difficult to discover or prove. Overhauling the regulatory structure and adding layers of supervision and monitoring by the government would be at best inefficient and socially wasteful. After all, the SEC already had vast authority to monitor and punish.[4] It is indisputable that optimistic investors and a depleted reservoir of ethics contributed to disaster.

But little can be done in the short run to fill the ethics reservoir, nor is it necessarily desirable to curb investors' enthusiasm. Rather, the solution lies in a market mechanism that realigns the incentives of the players of this economically vital financial game: let honesty be pursued in the self-interest of CEOs, Chief Financial Officers (CFOs), boards of directors, and the auditors; and eliminate the perverse incentives that are pervasive under the current social arrangement. Below I focus on financial statement insurance as such a market mechanism. I contend that it holds the promise of improved alignment of incentives, and hence better quality audits, more transparent and truthful financial statements, fewer shareholders' losses, more accurate pricing of securities, and, finally, more efficient resource allocation. This solution can be complemented and reinforced by a General Accepted Accounting Principles (GAAP) reform that redefines what components in the financial statements should be subjected to audit. Specifically, financial statement elements that inherently are not verifiable should not be audited; they are simply not auditable. They should be presented separately from the verifiable–the audited. Although these two remedies are mutually reinforcing, they can be implemented independently: each contributes.

Before I address financial statement insurance and the proposed GAAP changes, I present arguments that suggest that the critical—albeit not the sole—cause of the recent debacles was misaligned incentives of the auditors. In particular, a coincidence of circumstances, not all harmful by themselves, created an environment within which the misaligned incentives of the auditors brought about a failure in the gate-keeping function. Thus, the main conclusions I draw are the following:

- "Irrational exuberance" or the stock market bubble was not the source of the problem; rather, it magnified the payoffs for unethical conduct;
- Greed is harmless unless it is manifested in unethical actions;

[4] The SEC has the authority to establish generally accepted accounting and auditing standards, to review the financial statements registered with the SEC by most publicly traded corporations, to discipline CPAs who sign such statements (by rejecting statements they sign or by suspending or barring the CPAs from SEC practice), and to conduct investigations and recommend possible criminal inquiries to the Department of Justice.

- Society is better off when its members are more ethical, but ethical profiles are difficult to change in the short term;
- Ethical conduct is responsive to incentives: rewards and punishments;
- Market incentives, if feasible, are more effective and less socially costly than those that are created by legislation or governmental regulation. At the very least, they complement the latter;
- Financial statement insurance constitutes one such market-mediated set of incentives;
- Separation between verifiable (to be audited) and unverifiable (not to be audited) elements of financial statements sharpens investors' awareness of risks and so improves resource allocation.

3.2 The Role of "Irrational Exuberance," "Infectious Greed," and the Stock Market Bubble

Three themes have dominated the media recently: "cooking" the books by corporate America, the "irrational exuberance" in the 1990s, and the "infectious greed" plaguing our society. The themes are closely related; exuberant investors, rushing to buy stock when earnings exceed expectations by as little as a penny, tempt greedy executives to "cook" the books. Was the exuberance "irrational"? Is the greed infectious and hence baneful? Were the books "cooked"?

Exuberance—the enthusiasm evinced in the bidding up of the prices of securities, especially those of high technology firms—is embedded in beliefs about the firms' prospects. Even if optimism about the new technologies of the 1990s permeated the markets, there is nothing "irrational" about beliefs that, even with initial losses, entrepreneurial firms will do well in the future. Besides, early investors in successful new technologies earn a greater than normal return on their investment. Beyond that is the increase in the "winner's" social standing for having been a seer; throughout history people have venerated prophets. An examination of this proposition historically will disclose that it was true in many situations: from railroads to automobiles, airplanes, electronics, computer hardware, and software. It is also true that there are many examples where highly touted new technologies did not pay off. Consider, for example, cold fusion and wind and solar energy. Yet the ultimate failure of a venture does not imply that the prior beliefs that led investors to embark on it were "irrational," just as "rational" beliefs do not guarantee ultimate success. As to the state of optimism, no judgment can be rendered on its rationality: it reflects a subjective model of where the economy is headed, formed by each individual's scanning of the surrounding environment. It could be seen just as rational in the 1990s as pessimism is today.

What about greed? The American Heritage Dictionary of the English Language, defines it as "an excessive desire to acquire or possess more than what one needs or deserves, especially with respect to material wealth."[5]

Under our capitalist system, need is not the criterion for allocating material wealth. Instead, the claim for the allotment of wealth is the marginal contribution to the economy, i.e., what one deserves. But our highly competitive economic system will not allow the misappropriation of wealth by the undeserving, unless the undeserving has misrepresented—"cooked" the books. Before we turn to this "cooking" theme, however, note that if deserving, the "desire to acquire or possess" is no longer "excessive," nor are the desirous "greedy." They would be the ambitious entrepreneurs who fuel our economic engine. The more infectious their ambition, the faster the engine will accelerate.

Did corporate America "cook" the books? Some—the less ethically endowed—probably did. Most others, using their discretion under GAAP to choose from a range of resulting earnings numbers, must have signaled their genuine optimism regarding the future; hence the rosy numbers that now seem unsustainable. Indeed, many of the accounting numbers reported in financial statements reflect largely nonverifiable expectations. Giving credence to them requires the same degree of optimism on the part of investors. Thus, the so-called "bubble" of the 1990s may well have resulted from a sanguine vision of the future—shared by both executives and investors.

The bubble and its bursting are a reflection of the cycle of optimism giving way to pessimism. Neither can be asserted to be irrational. The more pointed question—whether we are better off without booms and busts—has no easy answers. It is likely the bubbles are the agent of technological "creative destruction" that promises the forward leaps beyond. An economy without optimism is a stagnant economy. On balance, therefore, I conclude that exuberance, greed, and bubbles are not necessarily the axis of evil that Federal Reserve Chairman Alan Greenspan makes them appear to be. What transforms ambition into the infectious greed that Greenspan deplores are the incentives to "cook" the books, which are made all the more potent by the allure of profits that the stock market bubble and investors' exuberance make possible. Because auditors have been tempted to wink at, or even encourage, accounting gimmicks such as the creation of Special Purpose Entities (SPEs), allowing Enron to hide debt and losses, or the possibly improper recording of swap transactions among telecommunication companies, the Enron affair became possible, and the Tyco and WorldCom scandals that followed. But what made the auditors wink? And what made CEOs and CFOs so desirous of that wink? Clearly the paucity of ethical standards and values contributes, but so do the

[5] American Heritage Dictionary of the English Language (4th ed. 2002), *available at* http://education.yahoo.com/reference/dictionary/index.html.

perverse incentives driving the actions of these players. I turn next to a discussion of the roles played by ethics and incentives. This discussion will convince the reader, I hope, first, that at least in the short term, incentives are required to elicit ethical conduct, and, second, that market incentives are necessary beyond legislative and/or regulatory reform.

3.3 The Importance of Ethics for the Accounting Profession

Ethical behavior is vitally important to businesses, but it plays a far more critical role in the attestation of auditors to financial statements. Ethical behavior is a necessary condition for investors to benefit from the auditors' product—the credibility of the auditors' attestation to financial statements. Society can consume the output of goods provided by businesses (such as automobiles, tobacco, perfumes, etc.,) managed by unethical individuals, although this may not be true to the same extent in the case of "modern economy" businesses that supply knowledge products. Yet society cannot rely on the financial reports of these businesses if it perceives a possibility of misrepresentation. Thus, society would not be able to use auditors' attestation services without perceiving the auditors to be ethical. Hence, in addition to the skill and competence required to detect misrepresentations or omissions in financial statements, for auditors it is of equal or even greater importance to possess the ethical trait of rendering an honest opinion.

Indeed, the importance of ethical conduct to accountants cannot be overstated. It has always been recognized that accounting was a special profession as far as public interest was concerned. Nowhere has this point been made as sharply as by former "Chief Justice Warren Burger", making the distinction between lawyers and accountants.

By certifying the public reports that collectively depict a corporation's financial status, the independent auditor assumes a public responsibility transcending any employment relationship with the client. The independent public accountant performing this special function owes ultimate allegiance to the corporation's creditors and stockholders, as well as to the investing public. This "public watchdog" function demands that the accountant maintain total independence from the client at all times and requires complete fidelity to the public trust.[6]

In the following sections, I elaborate on how the demand for ethical auditors is derived from the demand for truthful financial statements.

---

[6] United States v. Arthur Young & Co., 465 U.S. 805, 817–18 (1984).

3.3.1 Ethics as an Economic Good

From an economic standpoint, I define unethical behavior as purely self-interested behavior that inflicts harm on others. It characterizes a self- interested individual who prefers a course of action associated with some benefit while the damage caused to others is large.[7] The standard economic model for the rational agent is that of a purely self-interested individual. Within a business, the objective of stockholders is to maximize value. Accounting can be viewed as part of the necessary self-controls instituted by representatives of stockholders (boards of directors, BODs)—assuming BODs' interests are aligned with shareholders' interests—to bound the feasible actions that managers and employees can take. The cost-benefit trade-off involves balancing the increased cost of more elaborate accounting and internal controls against the benefits of more efficiently directed self-interested behavior.

First, suppose ideally that investors directly observe the degree to which managers (agents) engage in ethical behavior, and, furthermore, that all relevant parties' interests are perfectly aligned. What quantum of ethics can we expect to be exhibited in such a utopian world? Agents likely exhibit varying degrees of ethical behavior. The more unethical would covet consumption at the expense of others to a larger degree than the relatively more ethical. Under the preferable social arrangement, wherein incentives are perfectly aligned, it should be in the self-interest of corporations to elevate ethical standards governing the behavior of their officers and employees. Thus, suppose the BOD believes management and other employees rank low on the ethical scale. It would then direct the investment of some corporate resources in improving the internal control and audit systems to avert the higher potential costs of fraud, chicanery, embezzlement, and other detrimental (to itself) self-interested behavior on the part of its officers and employees. High ethical standards would result in net savings to the corporation, which would require less internal control and audit services. If more managers of corporations are known to be ethical, auditors would need to invest less effort, reducing audit fees and the total social cost of ensuring such credibility of financial statements as would allow proper functioning of the capital markets. Were the market to realize that a given corporation has become more ethical, such as by ridding itself of the unethical and hiring the ethical, the value of the corporation would increase by the amount of anticipated savings in the consumption of control and audit services. In this sense, accounting controls and ethical conduct can be viewed as economic substitutes.

---

[7] *See* Koford and Penno (1992), *Accounting, Principal-Agent Theory, and Self-Interested Behavior, in* Ethics and Agency Theory 127 (N. E. Bowie et al. eds., 1992). This is the definition of unethical behavior generally articulated or implied in the economic literature.

3.3.2 External Audits as Substitutes for Unobserved Ethical Endowments

Unfortunately, investors cannot directly observe the degree to which managers' actions are ethical. Managers with high ethical standards wish to advertise their "righteousness" to enhance the value of their shares. Yet nothing prevents managers with low ethical standards from engaging in false advertising. To guarantee to potential purchasers the truth of their advertisement, high-quality managers will hire auditors to attest to the veracity of the disclosures: the auditors will opine that there are no material misrepresentations in the client's financial statements (the advertisements). Just as substitution between ethics and accounting and auditing controls occurs within the organization, a similar substitution will be manifested externally: organizations with a higher concentration of unethical agents will require a greater investment of external audit resources.

For their attestation to be credible, the auditors must be perceived as "objective" and "neutral" qualified outsiders. They need to exert effort in detecting potential misrepresentation and to convince investors that they have done so. Potential penalties must face auditors who do not conduct their job appropriately. Without such penalties, auditors' pursuit of their own self- interest may induce them to collaborate with the "poor quality" managers, diminishing the credibility of the financial reports. Presumably, in attempting to minimize such penalties, the auditors will have an incentive to apply such audit procedures as will enable them to detect biases in management's representations. SEC enforcement actions and suits, and civil suits brought by stockholders, have constituted these penalties. The Sarbanes–Oxley Act of 2002 (the Act), imposes harsher penalties on directors and officers and restrictions on auditors' services.[8]

So far, however, the existing deterrents have proved to be ineffective in curbing abuses. One needs only to scan the headlines announcing one accounting irregularity after another to entertain no doubts about the failure of the current system. Furthermore, there is no reason to hope the increased potential fines and imprisonment terms introduced by the Act will make any more than a marginal dent in the tendency to "cook the books" over the long haul. Why?

[8] Sarbanes–Oxley Act, Pub. L. No. 107-204, 116 Stat. 745 (2002). The Act prohibits auditors from providing most of the traditional nonaudit services, such as bookkeeping, financial information systems design, appraisal services, fairness opinions, actuarial services, internal audit services, management functions, investment banking, legal and other expert services unrelated to the audit, and any other services deemed by the Public Company Accounting Oversight Board to be impermissible. *Id.* (§ 201). The Act also requires that all services (with some minor exceptions) be preapproved by the audit committee and that such pre- approvals be disclosed in public reports. *Id.* (§ 201–202).

3.3.3 The Perverse Incentives of Auditors

The problem is that the incentives driving auditors' behavior are not properly fine-tuned to elicit unbiased reports. In the current social arrangement, auditors operate under perverse incentives: they are paid by the companies they audit and hence they are beholden to the CEOs and CFOs who ultimately decide on the hiring of their services. While, theoretically, auditors are supposed to be the agents of the shareholders, in practice it is management that engages the auditor. Shareholders admittedly vote on management's recommendation of which auditor's services to hire, but the decision is effectively handed over to management: widely dispersed share ownership and the mechanism of proxy voting result in many shareholders giving their proxy votes to management, and others refrain from voting altogether.

This arrangement creates an inherent conflict of interest that is endemic to the relation between the client (the principal) and the auditor (the agent). The client-principal (management) who engages the auditor ultimately pays for the services and hence de facto structures the compensation of the auditor- agent to elicit such actions (opinions) of the auditor as would best serve his own interests. The fear of losing an indefinite stream of future audit fees—even without the added allure of nonaudit services now mostly barred by the Act—effectively guarantees that the auditor complies with management's wishes.

The threat of legal liability is not sufficiently fine-tuned to balance the incentive of doing management's bidding.

Moreover, the expected cost of litigation and other penalties is recouped on the average from the auditees, albeit in an economically distorted fashion: the auditor does not recoup his expected litigation costs from each client in proportion to the latter's contribution to the risk of the auditor being litigated against or fined and to the consequent damages the auditor suffers. In other words, the recoupment from any client is not commensurate with the damages the particular client causes. This results in an inefficient allocation of risk and resources.

Furthermore, the recoupment is made out of the client-corporation's resources, thus diminishing the wealth of shareholders who purchased the shares at prices potentially inflated as a result of misrepresentations. Consider the irony: instead of the shareholders being protected, they end up partially shouldering the cost and burden of perpetuating the cozy cohabitation of auditor and management. Some, perhaps plaintiffs' attorneys, may argue that the liability exposure of the auditors is not high enough and that it should be increased sufficiently to deter malpractice. Yet in addition to failing to address the misallocation of risk and resources, increasing exposure to liability and instituting draconian penalties may drive auditors out of the business of auditing—certainly not a welcome prospect.

I conclude that no exogenous force—legislation, regulation, enforcement, or litigation—can satisfactorily resolve the intractable conflict of interest. I would argue that only severing the agency relation between the client-management and the auditor can remove the inherent conflict of interest. We need to create instead an agency relationship between the auditor and an appropriate principal–one whose economic interests are aligned with those of investors, who are the ultimate intended beneficiaries of the auditor's attestation. Such a realignment of interests would restore the "complete fidelity to the public's trust" that Chief Justice Burger insisted on in his opinion cited above.[9]

Who, in the context of a free market mechanism, can serve the role of such a principal? I maintain that the insurance carriers are an eminently reasonable candidate. The scheme I am proposing is Financial Statement Insurance. To this I turn next.

3.4 Financial Statement Insurance

Financial Statement Insurance (FSI) would make for a significant change in the principal-agent relationship. Instead of appointing and paying auditors, companies would purchase financial statement insurance that provides coverage to investors against losses suffered as result of misrepresentation in financial reports. The insurance coverage that the companies are able to obtain is publicized, along with the premiums paid for the coverage. The insurance carriers then appoint—and pay—the auditors who attest to the accuracy of the financial statements of the prospective insurance clients.

Those announcing higher limits of coverage and smaller premiums will distinguish themselves in the eyes of the investors as the companies with higher quality financial statements. In contrast, those with smaller or no coverage or higher premiums will reveal themselves as those with lower quality financial statements. Every company will be eager to get higher coverage and pay smaller premiums lest it be identified as the latter. A sort of Gresham's law in reverse would be set in operation, resulting in a flight to quality.[10] Below I sketch the major elements of the FSI mechanism.[11]

---

[9] *See supra* note 5 and accompanying text.

[10] Sir Thomas Gresham was a financier born in London, England in 1519. Knighted in 1559, he was for a time the English ambassador at Brussels. "Gresham's Law" is an economic observation attributed to him: if there are two coins of equal legal exchange value, and one is suspected to be of lower intrinsic value, the "bad" coin will tend to drive the other out of circulation, as people will hoard the "good" coin. *See* Webster's World Encyclopedia: The Cambridge Biographical Encyclopedia (Webster's Millennium 2002 CD-ROM, 2002).

[11] For further background information on the FSI mechanism, see Ronen and Cherny (2002) *Is Insurance a Solution to the Auditing Dilemma?*, Nat'l Underwriter, Life and Health/Fin. Services Edition, Aug. 12, 2002, at 26.

3.4.1 The FSI Procedure

The FSI underwriting procedure starts with a review of the potential insured. The review is performed, on behalf of the FSI carrier, by an expert risk assessor, who investigates the nature of conditions such as the following:

- The nature, stability, degree of competition, and general economic health of the industries in which the potential insured operates;
- The reputation, integrity, operating philosophy, financial state, and prior operating results of the potential insured's management;
- The nature, age, size, and operating structure of the potential insured;
- The potential insured's control environment and significant management and accounting policies, practices, and methods;
- The FSI process might proceed as follows (see Fig. 3.1):

Step 1: The potential insured requests an insurance proposal from the FSI carrier. The proposal contains, at a minimum, the maximum amount of insurance being offered and the related premium. Typically, it also specifies a schedule of amounts of coverage below the maximum along with associated premiums. The proposal request is made prior to the preparation of the potential insured's shareholders' proxy on the basis of the underwriting review described above. The reviewer can be the same auditor who will eventually audit the financial statements.

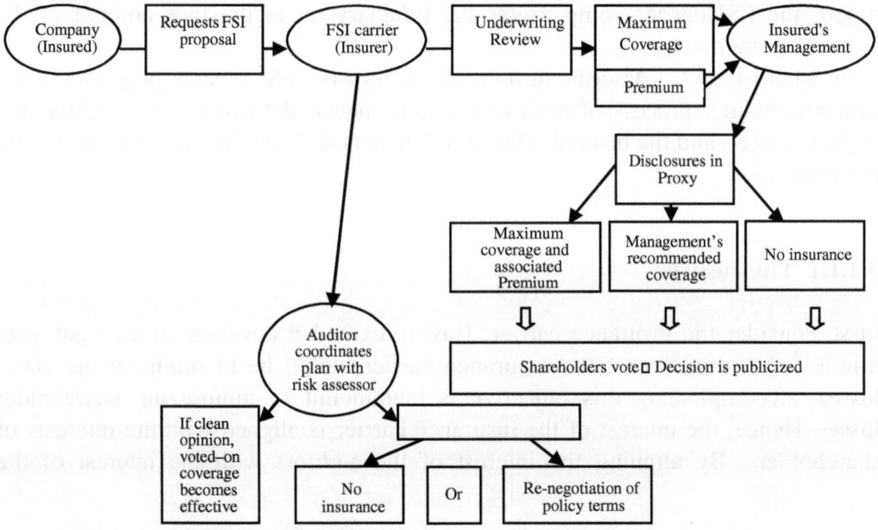

Fig. 3.1 The FSI process

Step 2: The proxy offers the following alternatives. The maximum amount of insurance and related premium as offered in the insurance proposal. The amount of insurance and related premium recommended by management. No insurance.

Step 3: If either of the insurance options set forth in Step 2 is approved, then the reviewer and the auditor cooperatively plan the scope and depth of the audit to be conducted.

Step 4: If, after the audit, the auditor is in the position of rendering a clean opinion, the policy is issued. That is, the originally proposed coverage and premium will be binding on the insurance carrier if the auditor's opinion turns out to be clean. If the auditor's opinion is qualified the insurer will not provide any coverage unless the company can then renegotiate different terms with the insurer, which would depend on the auditor's findings and reasons for qualification. To the extent the policy terms are renegotiated, the new agreed-upon terms would be publicized.

Step 5: The auditor's opinion will contain a paragraph disclosing the amount of insurance that covers the accompanying financial statements and the associated premium. The FSI concept also contemplates an expeditious claims settlement process. The FSI carrier and the potential insured cooperatively select a fiduciary organization whose responsibility is to represent the financial statement users when a claim is made. Part of the fiduciary's responsibility is the assessment of claims before notifying the FSI carrier.

After the fiduciary notifies the FSI carrier of a claim, the FSI carrier and fiduciary mutually select an independent expert to render a report as to whether there was an omission or misrepresentation and whether it did give rise to the amount of losses that resulted. Within a short time after receiving the expert's report, the FSI carrier compensates the fiduciary up to the face amount of the policy for the damages.

In what follows, I describe in more detail how the FSI scheme plays out in the decision-making process of each of its participants: the insurer, the auditor, the capital market, and the insured. Figure 3.2 depicts stylistically the relations among the parties.

3.4.1.1 The Insurer

First, consider the insurance carrier. Having extended coverage at a certain premium,[12] the objective of the insurance carrier would be to minimize its claim losses. Accomplishing this objective is tantamount to minimizing shareholder losses. Hence, the interest of the insurance carrier is aligned with the interests of shareholders. By aligning the interest of the auditors with the interest of the

[12] How the premium is determined is discussed in the proceeding paragraph.

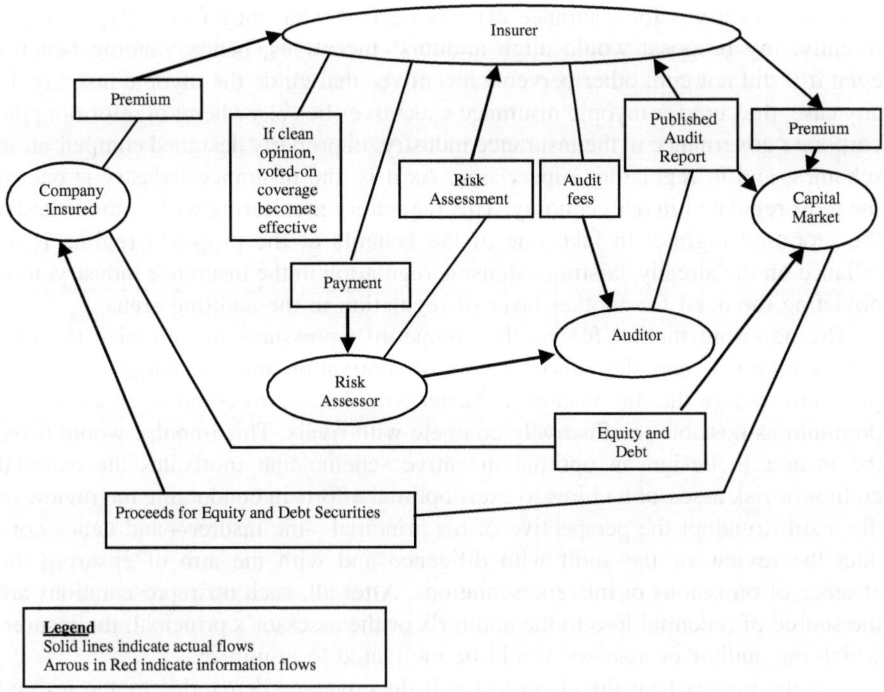

Fig. 3.2 Relationships among the parties

insurance carrier who hires the auditor's services, we are able to align the interest of the auditors, by extension, with the interests of shareholders.

Now I turn to the process by which the magnitude of the premium is determined. The insurer is subject to the checks and balances of the market. This market tension ensures that the premium is determined in as accurate a fashion as possible. The first market force is one that pressures the insurer to assess as low a premium as possible. This is the force of competition. Because the insurance industry is competitive, to ensure maintaining or expanding market share any insurer would wish to minimize the premium for a given amount of coverage he extends to the insured. On the other hand, the opposing market force induces the insurance carrier to charge a premium that is sufficient to cover the expected claim costs and other expenses, including the industry-wide profit designed to compensate for the entrepreneurial and managerial services the insurers provide. If the premium is not high enough, the insurer would not be able to survive.

Some may argue that short-horizon insurers may low ball—charge too low a premium relative to the risk undertaken by extending the coverage to gain market share—and skim the market. Yet if that is likely to happen under my proposed regime, it is equally likely to happen under the existing regime, in which the insurers provide directors and officers insurance that includes coverage for the corporations as well. In other words, the proposed regime would not introduce perverse incentives for insurance carriers beyond what they face today. Put differently, my proposal would align auditors' incentives, hence yielding benefits even if it did not cure other perverse incentives that guide the myopic insurers. In any case, the cure for myopic insurance executives lies elsewhere: in reforming the corporate governance in the insurance industry, in properly designed compensation schemes, and in regulatory supervision. As it is, the insurance industry is one of the most regulated in our economy. This regulatory monitoring will continue under the proposed regime. In fact, one of the benefits of the proposed regime is its reliance on the already existing extensive regulation in the insurance industry, thus obviating the need for another layer of regulation in the auditing arena.

The opposing market forces, the competitive pressures to minimize the premiums charged, and the survival-induced motivation not to charge too low a premium, ensure that the insurance carrier would strive to compute as accurate a premium as possible to effectively compete with rivals. This impulse would drive the insurer to design an optimal incentive scheme that motivates the external auditor or risk assessor he hires to exert optimal efforts in conducting the review or the audit: to adopt the perspective of his principal—the insurer—and hence conduct the review or the audit with diligence and with the aim of ensuring the absence of omissions or misrepresentations. After all, such misrepresentations are the source of potential loss to the auditor's or the assessor's principal, the insurer, which the auditor or assessor would be motivated to minimize.

Can the insurer bear the claim losses if the coverage demanded by the insured and supplied by the insurer is very large? There are two answers to this question. First, suppose we fix coverage under the proposed regime at the same level investors recover under the current regime. This means that, in equilibrium, the premiums paid under the proposed regime would at most equal the total cost to corporations of directors' and officers' insurance, audit fees, and the additional litigation settlement costs they incur as a result of class-action suits filed against them.[13] Under this condition, the coverage would be affordable—it is the same as under the current regime. The auditors' incentives, however, would be better aligned with those of shareholders, thus eliminating the conflict of interest and improving audit quality. That is, other things being equal, the proposed regime would be superior at least from the standpoint of improved audits.

Now suppose we relax this hypothetical ceteris paribus condition and allow for the possibility that the coverage extended under the proposed regime would exceed the insurance coverage under the current regime. Will the insurance industry have the capacity to pay? The answer to this question is yes because, unlike property and casualty insurance for example, the losses insured against—decreases in the valuation of companies resulting from omissions or misrepresentations in the financial statements—can be hedged in the capital markets with properly

[13] Below I shall argue that for the same coverage the equilibrium magnitude of the premiums paid under my proposed regime would be less than under the existing regime because of the improved audit quality, improved financial statement quality, and hence smaller shareholder losses.

constructed derivatives, the exercise of which can be made contingent on the same triggering events that cause loss to shareholders, i.e., the financial statement and audit failures that are manifested in omissions or misrepresentations. Specifically, the insurer can buy a special put option with a duration that corresponds to the period covered under the policy.[14] The put would be exercisable upon a stock price decline of the insured that was determined to have resulted from misrepresentations or omissions in the insured's financial statements. Investment funds (pension funds, mutual funds, and the like) would be willing to sell these puts for less than the price of general puts (that are not conditional on misrepresentations) and would thus enable the insurer to reinsure whichever portion of the coverage he wishes not to retain at an affordable cost. The put sellers can minimize their exposure on these written puts by constructing portfolios that are well diversified with respect to the risk of misrepresentations and omissions. The assessment of such risks can be provided by independent rating organizations akin to bond rating agencies, such as Standard & Poor's Corp.

The incentive to assess accurate premiums creates the insurers' demand for review and risk assessment services. These can be, but need not be, conducted by the same auditor who ultimately opines on the financial statements. At the same time, having determined the premium, the incentive not to extend the contemplated coverage upon the discovery of large risks creates a demand for the familiar external audit. This audit, which would be of higher quality than under the current regime, will ultimately determine whether the insurer agrees to extend the coverage. If the opinion is clean, the coverage becomes effective. If the opinion is qualified for a variety of reasons, either the coverage is withdrawn, or the insurer renegotiates a different coverage and premium, the magnitudes of which would depend on the reasons for the qualification. Thus, two layers of monitoring protect the insurer: the initial risk review and assessment that helps determine the tentative coverage to be extended and the associated premium, and the external audit that finally determines whether the tentative agreement (policy) would become effective. The sequence of activities is necessitated by (1) the need to contract at the beginning of the fiscal year (or the end of the prior fiscal year) on coverage and the premium so that these can be publicized and made available for the capital markets to assess the quality of the financial statements and to accurately price the securities (as a result of making portfolio decisions) and (2) the subsequent need to conduct the external audit, geared toward assuring the absence of material loss-causing misrepresentations. The plan for the external audit would be prepared in consultation with the insurer—the principal—and the risk assessor who conducted the initial review so that the details of the plan would be tailored to the findings of the initial risk review. Such a coordinated audit plan would de-emphasize the mechanical sample testing of journal postings and emphasize the more costly but more meaningful verification of assets and revenues.

---

[14] A put option is a contract giving its owner the right to sell a fixed number of shares of a specified common stock at a fixed price at any time on or before a given date.

3.4.1.2 The Auditor

In the current social arrangement, the auditor's perspective is not aligned with that of shareholders, but rather mirrors the perspective of his clients—effectively management. The auditor finds it difficult to deviate from the client's perspective because of the inherent non-verifiability of many elements of the financial statements. Management generates the data and prepares the financial statements, which it then presents to the auditor. The auditor tests for accuracy and evaluates the statements for compliance with GAAP. In most of the recent revelations regarding accounting irregularities, it seems that the issue was not the accuracy of the underlying data, but the way the data were classified and presented in the financial statements; as examples, consider liabilities that are recorded as revenues or expenses that are recorded as assets. In many cases, while the data available are accurate, projections based on these data cannot be verified by the auditor. Consequently, he would have insufficient grounds to dispute the subjective valuations made by the client.

Indeed, even though the financial statements are allegedly based primarily on historical transactions, most of these past events play themselves out in the future. The cash flow expected to be generated must be predicted. In many of these instances, such as the valuation of residual interests in securitized financial assets, the estimation of these future cash flows is largely subjective, resulting in wide ranges of numbers that can be quantified as assets on the balance sheet. The evaluation of such forward-looking events requires the examination of assumptions that are based either on past experience or on models that forecast the probability of given outcomes. In stable environments, these models can yield relatively objective numbers. In volatile environments, however, they can result in misleading numbers. In the latter case, the ability of the auditor to verify the numbers is significantly impeded. In the current regime, managers would argue the validity of the assumptions until proven wrong. The auditor's incentives, influenced by the fear of loss of an indefinite stream of future audit fee revenues from the client he audits, would almost assuredly cause the auditor to give the client the benefit of the doubt.

By contrast, under the proposed regime, because of the incentive structure that realigns the auditor's interest with the insurer's, the auditor would be predisposed to insist on a greater degree of verifiability before acquiescing in management's valuations. The auditor would be identifying with the persons or entities that would suffer a loss in the event of a misrepresentation or omission in the financial statements. Although this greater insistence on verifiability may cause management to be less willing to undertake ventures that perforce require the evaluation of forward-looking consequences of transactions and hence to exhibit greater risk aversion, this may not be a bad outcome from a societal point of view. The system should overall result in a better balance between risk-taking and the needs of financial statement users. Companies would attempt to balance their quest for higher returns against the avoidance of being penalized by the capital markets for unreliable numbers in the financial statements presented.

Under the proposed regime, the auditor would choose the audit quality so as to maximize his expected compensation.[15] Because the compensation scheme is designed by the insurance carrier, the auditor would decide on the quality that is optimal from the standpoint of the insurer, and hence the shareholders. Specifically, the auditor would attempt to maximize the difference between the audit fee revenue he expects from the insurer and the expected costs of misrepresentations and omissions. This attempted maximization would induce him to choose the optimal audit quality. The insurer has at its disposal potent penalties to deter the auditor from deviating from the desired quality. Unlike the current regime, in which a bad audit may cause a loss of the client's engagement and some expected litigation costs, under the proposed regime the auditor faces two kinds of penalties that an audit failure can trigger. The first is his tort liability pursuant to the contractual relationship between him and the insurance carrier. The second is the threat of losing the possibly very many clients the insurer has assigned him to audit. Note the change in the market structure: under the current regime the auditor–client relationship is one-to-one; under the proposed regime the relationship is one to many: the auditor and many auditees assigned by the insurer. The threat of losing many auditees' engagements upon an audit failure that is related to only one of these auditees is a very potent penalty.

3.4.1.3 The Market

For the purpose of this discussion, I assume that the stock market is semi-strong efficient; publicly available information is unbiasedly and quickly impounded in the market prices of stocks.[16] Hence, the publicized coverage that the shareholders of the insured approved and the premium paid to obtain that coverage would provide a credible signal to the marketplace regarding the underlying quality of the financial statements, i.e., the degree to which they may include omissions or misrepresentations. The FSI mechanism would satisfy the conditions required for a signaling equilibrium.[17] The larger the coverage the insured purchases, the larger the premium the company must pay; but for any given coverage, the better the quality of the financial statements, the smaller the premium the insurer will assess. The more effective the internal accounting and auditing controls and the corporate governance system in place, the more likely the risk assessor hired by the insurer will assess lower risk, in turn resulting in the insurer's assessing a lower premium. The better the quality of the review and risk assessment process, the more accurate

---

[15] What I mean by quality in this context is the combination of effort that the auditor exerts on the job and the level of his objectivity and freedom from bias.

[16] Consider, however, the so-called "anomalies," such as the post-announcement drift, that can be explained within a rational market, as shown by in A. Dontoh et al., *On the Rationality of Post-announcement Drift*, 8 J. Acct.. Stud. 69–104, 2003.

[17] *See generally* Riley (1979), *Informational Equilibrium*, 47 Econometrica 331, 333–36 (1979) (discussing the relevant conditions).

the premium assessment. Thus, the better the quality of the financial statements, the lower the cost borne by the insured for a given coverage. Equivalently, for a fixed premium, insureds with better quality financial statements will be able to purchase more coverage. This means that the conditions for a signaling equilibrium would be satisfied under the financial statement insurance mechanism (some additional technical conditions would be easy to satisfy as well), so the publicized pair of signals, the coverage and the premium (along with disclosures of significant terms of the insurance policy), would be a credible signal to the markets regarding the underlying quality of the insured's financial statements. The market would be able to compare different companies and reckon which presents more reliable financial reports. Given the semi-strong efficiency of the market, these different qualities would be priced into the securities offered by the insureds to the public or traded in the secondary markets.

But this is not the whole story. Consider the policy coverage. Since the FSI procedure requires that the coverage be approved by the shareholders, and since the coverage is common knowledge, in that it is publicized both in the proxy and in all financial reports issued by the insured, the market is made aware of the coverage, and having priced it into securities, an implicit contractual agreement would have been formed. The market would come to understand the limit to which it is to be indemnified in the case of loss. Although a plaintiff class may still be able to sue for damages beyond the limits of the policy, it seems less likely that it would prevail: the investors were put on notice regarding the limit of the policy coverage and will have paid less for the security with the lower coverage and thus protected themselves in advance against the risk of misrepresentations. This would have the effect of practically limiting the exposure to the policy coverage and hence decreasing the dead weight loss to society caused by lengthy litigation.

The implication of the pricing of the financial statements' quality is that the traded securities would be more complex instruments than the ones we have under the current regime. The securities would reflect two additional dimensions: the coverage shareholders can claim upon the triggering event of misrepresentation or omission, and the underlying reliability of the financial statements, as reflected in the premium for the given coverage. This more accurate pricing of the securities would provide more precise signals to institutional and individual investors to help them better channel their savings and capital to worthy projects. Companies undertaking more promising ventures would be able more reliably and credibly to transmit information about the potential of these ventures to the markets, and hence to obtain funds to finance them more cheaply and easily. Resources would be allocated more efficiently; social investment would yield a higher return.

3.4.1.4 The Company—the Insured

Now we come full circle back to the company purchasing the insurance. Under the proposed regime, a company with better quality financial statements would have an incentive to signal its superiority to the marketplace by demonstrating that it can obtain higher coverage at a lower premium relative to other companies in its industry. It would do so because it reckons that the coverage it obtains and the premium it pays would be made public, and, furthermore, would be viewed by the market as credible signals of the true quality of its financial statements. As a result, the company knows that its securities would be priced at a higher level, thus decreasing its cost of capital and increasing its ability to finance worthy projects. Companies with poorer quality financial statements would be forced to reveal the truly lower quality and reliability of the financial reports because they would not be able to obtain the same coverage as the better companies (companies with better quality financial statements) except by paying a higher premium; recall that the risk assessment conducted by the insurer's agent would have resulted in a higher premium, commensurate with the poorer quality the assessor would have discovered. Thus, the company with poorer quality financial statements would have no choice but to reveal the true state of its financial reports: either it is forced to pay the higher premium or it would decide not to purchase any insurance. Both occurrences will reveal the truth.

For the company with poorer quality financial statements, this is not a happy state of affairs. It cannot pretend that it is one of the better companies: the insurer would impose the necessary discipline by having the company's management and internal controls reviewed as a condition for extending the coverage and determining the premium. Moreover, the coverage would not be extended if the external auditor does not issue a clean opinion. Reckoning that if the coverage is not extended, a significant drop in the stock price would ensue, the company would refrain, ex ante, from attempting to emulate the better companies by purchasing high coverage that would likely not be extended were the external auditor to decline to issue a clean opinion. Of course, in addition, the potential emulator would have had to pay a higher premium at the outset because of the unfavorable findings by the risk assessor. What is such a company to do? It now would reckon that it is in its best interest to improve its internal accounting and auditing controls so as to qualify for the higher coverage and the lower premium. That is, it would now compete with the better companies by actually improving its systems so that the risk assessor would induce the insurer to assess a low premium, correctly signaling to the marketplace the improved quality of the insured. Formally, the company would choose the quality of its financial statements to maximize the difference between the proceeds of shares it issues and the premium it has to pay for the insurance, recognizing at the same time, that the premium would be set by the insurer so as to minimize its claim losses and that it would assess the premium conditional on the findings of the risk assessor it hires for the purpose and would extend the coverage conditional on the external auditor issuing a clean opinion.

3.4.2 Recapitulation

The FSI scheme effectively eliminates the conflict of interest so evident in the aftermath of Enron and its sequels. But as I have shown, financial statement insurance has other important benefits: the credible signaling of financial statement quality and the consequent improvement of such quality, the decrease in shareholder losses, and the better channeling of savings to worthy projects.

Are there additional remedies for what ails financial reporting today? In my introductory remarks to this essay, I alluded to the bright line financial reporting standards that some blame for the malaise. Below I argue that FSI, if implemented, would facilitate an accounting approach based on underlying principles rather than detailed rules. On the other hand, without the incentive alignment proffered by FSI, having underlying principles without detailed rules govern accounting practice can be hazardous to investors' financial health.

3.5 Principles and Rules

I now turn to the recent debate regarding rules and principles. It has been argued that the US model of specifying rules that must be applied has allowed or encouraged firms such as Andersen to accept procedures that, while conforming to the letter of the rules, violated the basic objectives of GAAP accounting. For example, while SPEs in Enron usually appeared to have the minimum required three percent of independent equity, Enron in fact bore most of the risk. The contention is that general principles such as UK GAAP that require auditors to report a "true and fair view" of an enterprise are preferable to the over-specified US model, and that the US model encourages corporate officers to view accounting rules as analogous to the Tax Code.[18] Indeed, the contrast drawn with UK GAAP has also caught the attention of the popular press. Consider, for example, the following quotation from a recent Wall Street Journal article: Sir David Tweedie, the retiring chairman of the International Accounting Standards Board, testifying before Congress on Feb. 14, explained, "Companies want detailed guidance because these details eliminate uncertainties about how transactions should be structured. Auditors want specificity because these specific requirements limit the number of difficult disputes with clients and may provide a defense in litigation. Securities regulators want detailed guidance because these details are thought to be easier to enforce."

While this rationale makes sense on one level, it fails on another. It engenders a mindset among accountants, auditors and managers to ask the wrong question: "Is it legal?" instead of "Is it right?" High-priced lawyers and skilled merchant bankers can often find a way through the thicket of regulations because human ingenuity is such that it is impossible to cover every possibility... The alternative to this rule-based approach is one pursued by IASB. In the words of Sir David: "Put simply, adding the detailed guidelines may obscure, rather than highlight, the

[18] *See* Benston and Hartgraves (2002), *Enron: What Happened and What We Can Learn From It*, 21 J. Acct. and Pub. Pol'y 105, 126 (2002).

underlying principle. The emphasis tends to be on compliance with the letter of the rule rather than on the spirit of the accounting standard."

"Our approach," Sir David explains, by contrast, "requires both companies and their auditors to exercise professional judgment in the public interest. Our approach requires a strong commitment from preparers to financial statements that provide a faithful representation of all transactions and a strong commitment from auditors to resist client pressure. It will not work without those commitments."

Sir David's bottom line: "There will be more individual transactions and structures that are not explicitly addressed. We hope that a clear statement of the underlying principles will allow companies and auditors to deal with those situations without resorting to detailed rules."[19]

I served as associate director of research at the AICPA-appointed "Trueblood Objectives Group," which issued a report on the objectives of financial statements.[20] This report, along with a companion volume of selected papers,[21] was the precursor for the Conceptual Framework that guides the Financial Accounting Standards Board (FASB)'s setting of detailed standards. At the time, some of the committee's members viewed the objectives that later became the "Conceptual Framework" as a sort of a constitution to guide the promulgation of standards, just as the United States Constitution governs the legislation of statutes and the case law. I interpret the recent clamor for principles and against rules as an appeal to make do with the Conceptual Framework without the detailed standards issued by the FASB. In other words, let the Conceptual Framework alone govern practice—the guidelines it offers should suffice for the accountants to report a "true and fair view." Yet, without FSI, auditors' incentives are not aligned with shareholders, and although the Conceptual Framework formulates desirable objectives of financial reporting, it leaves ample room for corporate managers to misrepresent unless potent incentives are in place that motivate telling the truth.

It may be useful at this point to dwell on the rationales for and against uniformity—the finely specified and detailed rules, and flexibility—the application of general guiding principles that accord entities the freedom to choose among different accounting treatments to best reflect a "true and fair view." Traditionally, uniformity of standards and detailed rules have been championed because they allegedly enhance credibility. Uniform application decreases the ambiguity of results and variation in reported numbers. Hence, it enhances comparability and possibly decreases audit costs (by minimizing disputes with clients about accounting choices). Yet increasing uniformity also decreases the flexibility of management in making accounting choices, and hence limits its ability to signal expectations about the prospects of the company that are not shared by the public. In other words, compulsory uniformity of standards or detailed rules constrains managers' ability to "best" convey their superior knowledge about the past,

---

19 Wriston (2002), *The Solution to Scandals? Simpler Rules*, Wall St. J., Aug. 5, 2002, at A10.

20 1 AICPA, Objective of Financial Statements (1973).

21 2 AICPA, Objective of Financial Statements (1974).

present, and future. If discretion is accorded the manager over which accounting methods to apply in the particular circumstances, he will, if he has incentives to report or signal honestly what he knows, employ the combination of methods that best reflects the "economic reality" of the company. Restricting his choice to a single method or even to a specific menu of such methods limits his ability to convey truthful information if he has incentives to do so. Along with the flexibility, therefore, incentives should be aligned to elicit truthful information from management.

Thus, unless existing deterrents of false reporting are insufficient, the solution is not to limit the information flow by legislating rules of reporting that must be universally followed. Rather, the solution is to increase incentives for truthful reporting and give managers a choice of reporting rules to apply once they have the incentive to report truthfully. Suppose, for example, the manager knows which of four states—A, B, C, or D—occurred. (Say it is state C). If he wishes to report truthfully and he has the freedom to choose a reporting mechanism, he would be able to correctly signal that state C has indeed occurred. If he is provided with a limited menu of mechanisms whereby he could only report coarser partitions, he may be able to report only that either state C or state D has occurred; hence, a loss of information would ensue.

Generally, the role of the Conceptual Framework is to specify the characteristics of the set of information disclosures that would result in efficient resource allocation. Even if not translated into detailed rules, such principles or framework would be useful as benchmarks against which to evaluate the adequacy of accounting practices once properly aligned incentives are in place. As indicated, however, without FSI incentives are not properly aligned with those of shareholders. Therefore, in the current regime, the use of the Conceptual Framework, or for that matter any set of general principles, including those prevalent in the UK, as a sole guide for practice is a hazardous proposition, strewn with pitfalls. The historical proliferation of detailed standards that Wriston deplores in his Wall Street Journal column[22] did not come about in a vacuum. The creation of the FASB as a full-time board, and the formulation of objectives of financial statements, both came on the heels of major accounting abuses and the "pooling mania" of the 1960s. Indeed, left on its own under the "guidance" of the general principles—far less detailed than the FASB's standard—promulgated by the FASB's predecessor, the Accounting Principles Board (APB), the profession did not curb the abuses. The accounting profession created the full-member board (the FASB) with the promise to issue detailed standards to avert the governmental takeover of the standard-setting function. Standards were issued mostly to plug exploitable loopholes. The problem was then, and still is now, the perverse incentives causing the abuses, not the detailed standards. Both the abuses and the

[22] *See supra* note 20 and accompanying text.

detailed standards they triggered were symptoms of the bad incentives. It is simply wrong to think that the rules caused the abuses.[23]

However, implicating incentives alone does not do justice to a very complex problem. A careful analysis of the underlying dynamics of financial reporting reveals two fundamental problems: (1) perverse incentives afflicting both corporate management and auditors; and (2) the non-verifiability of many quantifications currently included in the financial statements, which makes financial statements in their present format under existing GAAP essentially non-auditable.

This second fundamental problem requires some elaboration. Today's financial statements are a blend of largely verifiable, but uninformative, depictions of past transactions and largely unverifiable, but possibly informative, projections of future outcomes. Under existing GAAP, many of those projections of the future are assigned respectable seats in the balance sheets of companies as assets, and a good portion of these end up being reflected as revenues. As an example, consider the Interest Only Strip, shown as an asset in the balance sheets of specialty finance companies under Financial Accounting Standard (FAS) 140.[24] This asset is simply the present value of a future stream of unrealized income, recorded as current income. Its valuation is highly subjective, acutely sensitive to even very miniscule changes in assumptions. It is extremely difficult, even for a well-intentioned auditor, to effectively dispute and reject the projection of a manager wishing to prettify his financial statements. Or consider Rebecca Smith's report on Enron's Braveheart venture (incorporated on December 28, 2000): "Enron assigned the partnership a value of $124.8 million based on its projections of the revenue and earnings potential of the Blockbuster Venture, according to company documents."[25] It is this sort of largely unverifiable intangible that makes financial statements in this era of technological innovation so difficult to audit and make it so hard to opine as to whether they present a "true and fair view."[26]

One cannot overestimate the insidious effects of such intangibles. These projections, perforce, are made by management, which, as an insider, is in a better position to forecast the outcome of its own decisions and plans. Yet these forecasts constitute "private information" of the management. Typically such private information cannot be perfectly verified ex post. Without the ability to peer into

---

23 In any case, an overriding GAAP rule is the principle of "substance over form," by which adherence to the literal rules may violate GAAP. *See* Qualitative Characteristics of Accounting Information, FASB Concept Statement No. 2 160 (Financial Accounting Standards Bd. 1991).

24 Accounting for Transfers and Servicing of Financial Assets and Extinguishments of Liabilities Research and Dev. Arrangements, Statement of Financial Accounting Standards No. 140 (Financial Accounting Standards Bd. 2000).

25 R. Smith, *Show Business: A Blockbuster Deal Shows How Enron Overplayed Its Hand, Company Booked Big Profit From Pilot Video Project That Soon Fizzled Out, "I Just Couldn't Believe It,"* Wall St. J., Jan. 17, 2002, at A1.

26 We do encounter sweeping admonitions in the press to the effect that accountants should make sure that "GAAP fairly portrays the underlying economics." *See* S. Liesman, *SEC Accounting Cop's Warning: Playing By Rules May Not Ward Off Fraud Issues*, Wall St. J., Feb. 12, 2002, at C1 (quoting Michael Young, a defense attorney who specializes in securities fraud).

the manager's mind, we can only observe, in hindsight, whether his forecasts were accurate. We cannot assert that he did not truly believe that the forecasts he made were truthful. Under these circumstances, in equilibrium, and on the average, managements' presentations will not be truthful.[27] Even the detailed standards did not prevent the unverifiable intangibles from creeping into the financial statements. Imagine what would happen if we rely only on "underlying principles!" Thus, I conclude that under the existing regime, detailed rules, improved so as to rule out fair valuations that are based on projections by the privately informed insiders, are a necessary evil.

With some GAAP reform,[28] however, the introduction of FSI may make it possible to minimize the rules and emphasize reliance on the Conceptual Framework in the day-to-day business of making accounting decisions. Under FSI, the auditor who adopts the perspective of the insurer, and hence the perspective of investors, would insist on such accounting choices that conform with the Conceptual Framework as would approximate as closely as possible the "true and fair view" of the enterprise that he, the auditor, perceives after having completed his audit. The potential for misleading the investors would be minimized.

3.6 Potential GAAP Improvements

There is room for improvements in the Conceptual Framework and in the specification of which reported numbers should be subjected to audit. Under the prevalent accrual basis of accounting, projections, typically reflecting future events that management can predict better than the auditor, are endemic to financial reporting. Projection enters into the quantification of accounts receivable, inventory, liability for warranty, and so on. Assets may be reflected at the amount paid to acquire them (verifiable but largely uninformative), at the amount of their expected benefits (possibly informative but mostly unverifiable), or at a blend of both. While investors need to assess the future of the companies they buy and sell, only the past can be verified. The dilemma is pervasive, perhaps existential—not unique to accounting—recalling Kierkegaard's lament: "Life can only be understood backwards; but it must be lived forwards." It is deplorable that the accounting regulators have allowed the intangibles—the soft, unverifiable projections—to contaminate potentially verifiable financial statements. Blended with the verifiable, they are mostly hidden from vision: witness the obfuscation in Enron's financials. The projections, perforce emanating from companies' management, are plagued by future uncertainty, undue optimism and exuberance, or worse, prevarication; not even the most skilled auditors can verify them.

---

[27] Ronen and Yaari (2002), *Incentives for Voluntary Disclosure*, 5 J. Fin. Mkts. 349, 362, 372-73 (2002).

[28] *See infra* Part VI.

The statement of the problem points to the solution: unbundle the verifiable past from the unverifiable future while providing both in the financials. Present systematically the projections (the unverifiable), and along with these but separately from them an account, over time, of how the projected future unfolded as evident in what now has become the past—the realizations (the verifiable).[29] By displaying the expectations and the realizations explicitly, side-by-side, investors will reap two benefits.

First, over time they will be able to evaluate how managements' projections pan out and thereby jointly judge their ability to anticipate the future or their proclivity to be optimistic or deceitful. Admittedly, this will not cure the occasional ambitious executive's unsavory proclivities if he reckons his rosy projections will inflate the value of his stock or options, which he can then sell at great profit and jump ship before the storm (Enron comes to mind again).

But investors would not be fooled; herein lies the second benefit of this suggested solution. Having decoupled the realizations—the verifiable—from the expectations—the unverifiable, auditors will attest only to the former; this is what they do best. The projections—chancy and unreliable—cannot be verified, so they cannot be audited. Instead, perhaps just like cigarette packages, they should explicitly carry the label: "These projections may be hazardous to your financial health." Knowing that the projections are unverifiable and potentially hazardous, investors will beware. To the skeptic who may protest that this could discourage investments and risk-taking, my answer would be that investors are better off being aware of the risks they are taking rather than taking risks unaware. A more efficient economy will emerge.

This suggested GAAP reform thus entails three distinct, albeit potentially complementary elements:

1. Separation of unverifiable projections from verifiable realizations;
2. Having the auditor attest only to the latter;
3. Assuming FSI is implemented, the auditors can rely on the Conceptual Framework without the detailed rules, with more impunity: auditors' incentives are sufficiently aligned to minimize abuses.

FSI is an essential remedy. Even if GAAP is reformed as suggested and the auditors attest only to the verifiable, incentives must be properly aligned. The verifiable realizations themselves vary in the degree of their verifiability: they include more than just cash. Although they exclude long-term projections such as the predictions of earnings from intangibles or contracts that may extend over many years into the future, they do include projections that span relatively shorter periods. In other words, the verifiable will include short- term accruals. For example, sales revenue will still be recorded upon realization—when the earnings generating process is essentially completed and collectibility is reasonably

[29] *See generally* Ronen and Sorter (1972), *Relevant Accounting,* 45 Bus. 258, 258-282 (1972) (providing a detailed description of how such a financial reporting system can be implemented).

assured. This sales transaction would be defined as a realization—verifiable and subjected to audit. Yet many of the recently publicized abuses, Worldcom, Enron, and others, resulted from the misrecognition of revenue. Thus, even with this GAAP reform, auditors will need to be sufficiently motivated to apply the necessary degree of skepticism.

Items (1) and (2) above can be beneficially implemented independently of FSI. They can also complement FSI in synergistically magnifying the benefits. In particular, in conjunction with FSI, these reforms will make it more feasible to do away with the bright line rules that greatly offend a growing number of critics.

3.7 A Future Role for the FASB

What would be the role of the FASB or any other "standard-setting" body in an FSI regime where a modified Conceptual Framework, as suggested above, would govern, and where there is no demand for the promulgation of detailed standards? I envisage a vital role—akin to that of the courts—of laying down the "case law" of financial reporting.

Disputes will inevitably arise between the auditor working for the insurer and the management of the company being audited with respect to how best to apply the Conceptual Framework to a particular transaction or situation. It is in this context that the FASB can play a role akin to that of a court. Presumably possessing accounting expertise and rich practical experience, the accounting board members can offer guidance that helps resolve disputes that arise in the process of auditing. The FASB can develop a compendium of specific applications of the Conceptual Framework to transactions in the process of providing guidance to the disputing partners. Such a compendium could serve successfully as the "case law" of financial reporting, just as the case law in the judicial domain successfully serves the nation's judges.

3.8 Conclusion

In the introduction of this essay, I enumerated several causes implicated in the media and in academe in precipitating the "accounting" meltdown: irrational exuberance, infectious greed, the stock market bubble, moral turpitude of executives, unethical accountants, non-audit services, and related "ills."

I have argued that the conflict of interest that inheres in the auditor– client relationship probably is the major culprit, reinforced and fed by some other factors. Bubbles and exuberance merely magnify the payoffs so that executives are more tempted to "cook the books" and the auditors' conflict of interest is aggravated.

The reform measures adopted so far, including the Act, are inadequate. A market-based solution that properly realigns auditors' incentives is a necessary complement. I suggest a particular market mechanism, Financial Statement Insurance, for implementation. The insurance yields multiple benefits, only one of which is the vitally important elimination of the auditors' inherent conflict of interest. The publicization of the insurance coverage and the premium under the particular mechanism I am suggesting will credibly signal the quality of the insured's financial statements. These signals will be priced into the equity and debt securities and thereby make the prices of these financial instruments better guides for investments. As a result of this better channeling of savings into the reliably worthier projects, social dividends will be earned. At the same time, companies will have incentives to improve the quality of their financial statements and do so. This, along with the consequent improvement in audit quality, will result in fewer misrepresentations and accordingly in fewer suits and stakeholder losses; the deadweight social cost of litigation will significantly diminish.

Financial statement insurance is a free market mechanism, so it should not require new legislation. Nonetheless, the market institutions that would be responsible for implementing it, the insurers, the insured, and the risk assessors, will need to gear up for the necessary contractual arrangements. This may be time consuming. It therefore may be advisable to jumpstart the remedial process through an interim regulatory initiative, one that is temporary and that would "self-destruct" once the market institutions have been able to set up the required infrastructure. For example, the SEC could mandate financial statement insurance at some minimum coverage, where the minimum could be determined as, for example, a properly computed multiple of the largest negative earnings surprise experienced by the insured over the last three or five years. A federal insurer could be incorporated for this purpose; that would be financed mostly by the premiums collected from the insureds. This organization's accumulated experience will inform and guide the market as to the appropriate risk pricing. With time, the market institutions will replace the government, bringing an end to the temporary engagement.

Furthermore, independently of this mechanism but potentially complementing it, I also suggest GAAP reforms: separation of the unverifiable from the verifiable in financial reports, and presentation of management's projections in the financial statements along with the consequent realization. This will allow investors to judge managers' skill in forecasting. Also, to improve the reliability of the audit, the auditor should attest only to the verifiable. In this way, investors would become more aware of the risks surrounding their investments. Together with FSI, or even with FSI alone, a financial reporting practice that relies solely on general principles, a Conceptual Framework, will become possible; the need for detailed rules would be obviated.

References

Benston, G. J., & Hartgraves, A. L. (2002). Enron: What happened and what we can learn from it. Journal of Accounting and Public Policy, *105*, 126.

Greenspan, A. (1996). The challenge of central banking in a democratic society, address at the annual dinner and Francis boyer lecture of the American enterprise institute for public policy research. 5 Dec 1996.

Koford, K., & Penno, M. (1992). Accounting, principal-agent theory, and self-interested behavior. In N. E. Bowie et al. (Eds.), Ethics and agency theory 127.

Riley, J. G. (1979). Informational equilibrium. Econometrica, *331*, 333–336.

Ronen, J., & Cherny, J. (2002. Is insurance a solution to the auditing dilemma? Nat'l Underwriter, Life and Health/Fin. Services Edition. 12 Aug 2002 at 26.

Ronen, J., & Sorter, G. H. (1972). Relevant accounting. Bus *45*, 258–282.

Ronen, J., & Yaari, V. (2002). Incentives for voluntary disclosure. Journal of Financial Markets, *5*(3), 349–373.

Wriston, W. (2002). The solution to scandals? Simpler rules. Wall Street Journal. 5 Aug 5 2002, at A10.

Chapter 4
Accounting Standard Setting in Two Political Contexts

Roland Königsgruber

Abstract In addition to private-sector standard setters, a number of public actors are involved in accounting standard setting. So the question arises toward which actor lobbying will be directed by firms or individuals wishing to influence the outcome of the standard setting process. This chapter presents a simple game-theoretic analysis of the standard setting process to identify the pivotal actor who will be the target of influencing activities. Analysis of the model suggests that "political" lobbying is more likely to happen in the EU than in the US. Furthermore it is suggested that if the relevant standard setters wish to achieve harmonization of accounting standards between the EU and the US, European companies have more lobbying leverage than their American counterparts because there are more European veto players than American ones. It is argued that in the future these structural forces will become more important as the historic intellectual dominance of the FASB over the IASB recedes.

This Chapter includes a reprinted article first published under the title "A Political Economy of Accounting Standard Setting" in the Journal of Management and Governance in 2010, which is followed by the author's comments by way of a post script on further developments on the Accounting standard setting processes based on the original paper presented at the Fourth International Workshop on Accounting and Regulation in 2007. The author wishes to thank in particular Kees Camfferman and Stephen Zeff whose insightful comments (Journal of Management and Governance, 15: 297–304) contributed to the present revision.

R. Königsgruber (✉)
Center for Accounting Research, University of Graz, Universitätsstraße 15 8010 Graz, Austria
e-mail: roland.koenigsgruber@uni-graz.at

R. Di Pietra et al. (eds.), *Accounting and Regulation*,
DOI: 10.1007/978-1-4614-8097-6_4,

4.1 Introduction

Accounting standard setters have often been criticized for giving undue influence to individual, mostly corporate, actors and being subject to regulatory capture. A recent addition to the criticisms voiced is the fear of too much political interference preventing "objective" accounting standards. This chapter identifies public and/or political organizations which have veto power over accounting standards. It then presents a simple model of the political process to determine how this veto power influences the standard setting process and to identify situations where companies and managers have incentives to engage in "political" lobbying of the accounting standard setter, i.e., to try to influence accounting standards by approaching political actors instead of participating in the due process of accounting standard setting. The model is applied to the different institutional frameworks in which accounting standard setting takes place in the United States and in Europe.

Managers or corporations may wish to retain the ability to conceal unpleasant financial information or the ability to manage earnings to present constant growth or positive financial results (e.g., Burgstahler and Dichev, 1997; Burgstahler and Eames 2003, 2006). In order to do so they have incentives to exert influence on financial reporting standards. Major international accounting standard setters follow a due process approach giving companies the ability to express their views and have them taken into account. However, managers pursuing one of the objectives mentioned above generally do not wish to express their preferences in full view of the investing public. Instead, they may use good personal contact to political decision-makers in order to gain leverage over the standard setter. Former FASB Chairman Dennis Beresford (2001) states that Congressional intervention in the standard setting process is taken very seriously by the Board. A point can be made that such activities have a detrimental effect on the objectivity and unbiasedness of financial information reported according to standards thus politically influenced (Zeff 1993, 2002).[1]

Traditionally, research in lobbying has used empirical methodology and has taken comment letters sent to the standard setter as the basis of their analysis[2] (e.g., Watts and Zimmerman 1978; Deakin 1989; Dechow et al. 1996 for lobbying in the United States; MacArthur 1988; Georgiou 2002 for lobbying in the United Kingdom; Larson 1997; Jorissen et al. 2006 and 2012 for lobbying of the International Accounting Standards Committee/International Accounting Standards Board). Georgiou (2004) finds that the use of comment letters is correlated with the use of other means of lobbying. This gives some justification to the use of comment letters as a proxy for a company's overall lobbying posture. However, more lobbying may go on "behind the scenes" and recent work has begun to use

[1] Some researchers have suggested that admitting limited competition among accounting standard setters instead of granting them a monopoly would reduce political interference in the accounting standard setting process (Benston et al. 2003; Dye and Sunder, 2001; Sunder 2002a, b).

[2] More recently, interpretations have become a subject of research in addition to standards. E.g., Larson (2007) and Bradbury (2007).

monetary contributions to politicians as a proxy for political lobbying. Ramanna (2008) finds that firms that have incentives to lobby against the elimination of pooling as an acceptable accounting method for business combinations can be linked via political contributions to Congress persons who became involved against the Financial Accounting Standards Board (FASB) proposal on this issue. Johnston and Jones (2006) identify three significant accounting issues under consideration by the FASB from 1999 to 2000 and find that firms' political lobbying expenditures are associated with their interest on those issues. Both studies present evidence of political influence on accounting standards under a private sector standard setting regime.

The American Institute of Certified Public Accountants (AICPA) is quite open about its efforts to influence public policy making in Washington. In its journal it prides itself of having influence on policy outcomes by understanding the policy-making process and by being able to deliver timely information (Lee and Rudd 1988; Lee 1988). Unsurprisingly, an empirical study of political action committee contributions found that members of the accounting profession gave significantly greater contributions to legislators who were members of committees having jurisdiction over accounting affairs (Thornburg and Roberts 2008). The study's findings are consistent with the access hypothesis which predicts that special interest groups donate in order to get in a position where they can provide information to a relevant policy-maker. Despite the subject's empirical relevance, so far little published economic theory work on lobbying in accounting standard setting exists.[3] This chapter is an attempt to fill this void and presents a game-theoretic analysis of financial reporting standard setting in a political context.

The remainder of the chapter is organized as follows: Section 4.2 discusses different systems of accounting regulation and the possibilities they respectively offer for participation in the regulatory process. Section 4.3 introduces and analyzes a model of accounting standard setting in a political context. Section 4.4 builds on these results to analyze corporate lobbying. Section 4.5 discusses the findings and concludes.

4.2 Systems of Accounting Regulation

"Political" lobbying in order to influence financial reporting standards has been observed in many jurisdictions. Zeff (2006) cites instances from the United States, Canada, the UK, Sweden and international lobbying on IASB standards. However,

---

[3] The rare exceptions include Sutton (1984) who models lobbying in a Downsian framework of political action; Lindahl (1987) who extends that framework to coalition building; Amershi et al. (1982) who study strategic aspects of lobbying arising in a multi-period, multi-issue setting; and Chung (1999) who studies private information involuntarily released by the act of lobbying. These theoretical studies attempt to inform traditional, comment letter-based lobbying research. They do not address behind-the-scenes political lobbying.

possibilities for exerting political influence vary according to country. This chapter analyzes the institutional setup in the United States and in the European Union. Traditionally, studies in comparative international accounting have distinguished between an Anglo-Saxon or American and a Continental model of accounting regulation. Whereas the US has a long tradition of standard setting by an organism belonging to the private sector[4] Continental European countries are characterized by a larger role given to legislation in accounting regulation.[5] In Germany, the government sets broad principles in accounting via the commercial code while referring to the *Grundsätze ordnungsmässiger Buchführung (GoB)*, literally the principles of orderly book-keeping, for situations not covered by the law (Flower and Ebbers 2002). GoB are determined in a *market for interpretations* by the decisions of judges in court, the expertise of practitioners and publications by academic accountants (Merkl-Davies 2004). This gives companies and managers the opportunity to influence accounting practice on either the legislative or the interpretative level. A further notable difference is in the participation of academic accountants in the development of accounting rules. Whereas there is traditionally high involvement by accounting academics in Germany (McLeay et al. 2000), few academics participate in the standard setting process in the US by submitting comment letters (Tandy and Wilburn 1996). In France, state involvement in accounting goes back to Colbert's Edict of 1673. In the twentieth Century, The Vichy Government sponsored development of a general accounting code which was absorbed into later regulation (Colasse and Standish 1998, 2004).

A 2002 act by the European Union, known as the IAS regulation, radically altered this situation for listed companies (Véron 2007). The regulation which went into effect in 2005 mandates consolidated group reporting by companies with securities traded on a stock exchange to adhere to International Accounting Standards/International Financial Reporting Standards (IAS/IFRS) as issued by the International Accounting Standards Board (IASB) and endorsed by the European Union.[6] Listed companies in the EU henceforth have to apply accounting standards which are developed by a private organization operating in a very similar manner to the US standard setter. However, the political system in which this standard setter is embedded differs strongly between the two jurisdictions. It will be argued here that despite the similarities of the immediate process of developing accounting standards the differences on the political level influence companies' lobbying incentives and are likely to lead to different standard setting outcomes. This is consistent with the view that the European Union's implicit objective in

[4] See Zeff (2005a, b) for a history of the evolution of accounting standard setting in the US.

[5] An overview over international differences in accounting regulation and practice can be found in Nobes and Parker (2006) or Flower and Ebbers (2002).

[6] Annual accounts, which in Europe are often linked to tax accounting, still have to be prepared in accordance with national law in most countries. However, the IAS regulation gives member states of the EU the option to permit or require IAS/IFRS also for annual accounts and reporting by non-listed companies.

mandating IFRS was to counter US hegemony in accounting standard setting (Dewing and Russell 2008).[7]

In the United States, the legislator has endowed the Securities and Exchange Commission (SEC) with the power to promulgate and enforce financial reporting standards in the Securities Acts of 1933 and 1934. The SEC in turn has delegated the rule-making power to organizations of the private sector, since 1973 to the Financial Accounting Standards Board. Since the right to regulate can be removed by the body that granted it accounting regulation can be seen as a two-level principal-agent relationship between the Congress and the SEC and between the SEC and the FASB.[8] Both the legislator and the SEC thus have veto power over standards promulgated by the FASB (Beresford 1995). Horngren (1985) illustrates this hierarchical relationship as depicted in Fig. 4.1:

The institutional setup for standard setting in the European Union is less straightforward. The IAS regulation stipulates that before IAS/IFRS become applicable in the European Union the Commission has to decide that they are conducive to the European public good and meet certain qualitative criteria. In this task the Commission follows a so-called comitology procedure (e.g., Bergstrom 2005) and is supported by three newly created bodies. The European Financial Reporting Advisory Group (EFRAG) represents private-sector interests and is financed by federations representing business, accountants and auditors, banks, and similar organizations. Its work is reviewed on behalf of the European Commission by the Standards Advice Review Group (SARG), which is composed of independent accounting experts appointed by the Commission. The Accounting Regulatory Committee (ARC) represents member states' governments and is staffed by civil servants from national ministries. After a new standard or interpretation is promulgated by the IASB, EFRAG's Technical Expert Group (TEG) reviews it and issues an advice on its adoption to the Commission. SARG reviews this advice within 3 weeks in order to assess whether it is well balanced and objective. Taking into account EFRAG's advice, the Commission prepares draft regulation to adopt the new standard or interpretation and sends it to the ARC which either agrees or recommends rejecting it. If the ARC recommends rejection, the Commission can either return the matter to EFRAG for further review or send it to the Council of Ministers for a final decision (Brackney and Witmer 2005). A recent change in the European Union's comitology procedures has made the so-called *regulatory procedure with scrutiny* applicable to the endorsement

[7] Porter (2005) notes a surprising willingness of US government officials to bring US rules more in line with international ones. Perry and Nölke (2006, 2007), on the other hand, argue that harmonization between IFRS and US GAAP favours the Anglo-Saxon over the Rhenish economic model. Similarly, Martinez-Diaz (2005) and Botzem and Quack (2006) see the reason for the international accounting standard setter's success in the strong alignment of its core values with the interests of the Securities and Exchange Commission.

[8] Mattli and Büthe (2005) argue that the desire to benefit of existing expertise and to shift blame for failures constitute two prime reasons for delegating authority to a private actor in accounting standard setting.

Fig. 4.1 Accounting standard setting hierarchy in the United States

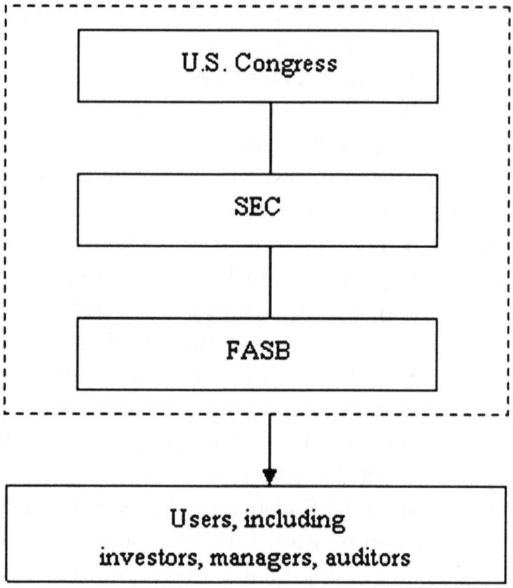

process. This means that both the European Parliament and the Council can overturn an implementing measure of the Commission within three months' time on the grounds that the Commission has exceeded its implementing powers or that the draft is not compatible with the aim or the content of the basic instrument (i.e., the IAS regulation). The process is illustrated in Fig. 4.2:

Assuming that the member states' governments' interests are represented on a civil servant level by the Accounting Regulatory Committee and that therefore the Council will not veto a standard deemed acceptable by the ARC this process gives veto power to three institutions. First, the European Commission which takes into account EFRAG's advice but is not bound to it under applicable comitology procedures. Second, the ARC representing national governments. And third, the European Parliament whose members are elected by the population of the European Union. Arguably, these actors are constrained by the terms of the IAS regulation in their veto decisions. However, the phrasing employed in the regulation which requires a new standard to be "conducive to the European public good" to be endorsed seems to give *carte blanche* to the actors involved. Figure 4.3 illustrates this veto relationship between the IASB and public European actors. Note that there are two substantial differences to the hierarchical relationship in the US depicted in Fig. 4.1: First, there is no hierarchy between the individual veto players, i.e., no actor can undo another player's veto. And second, the hierarchy suggested in Fig. 4.3 only extends to individual standards which can be vetoed by the European veto players. In contrast to this situation the two veto players in the US, the SEC and Congress, can threaten the standard setter's very existence.

The description of the respective political processes in accounting regulation in the European Union and the United States suggests that despite a similar structure

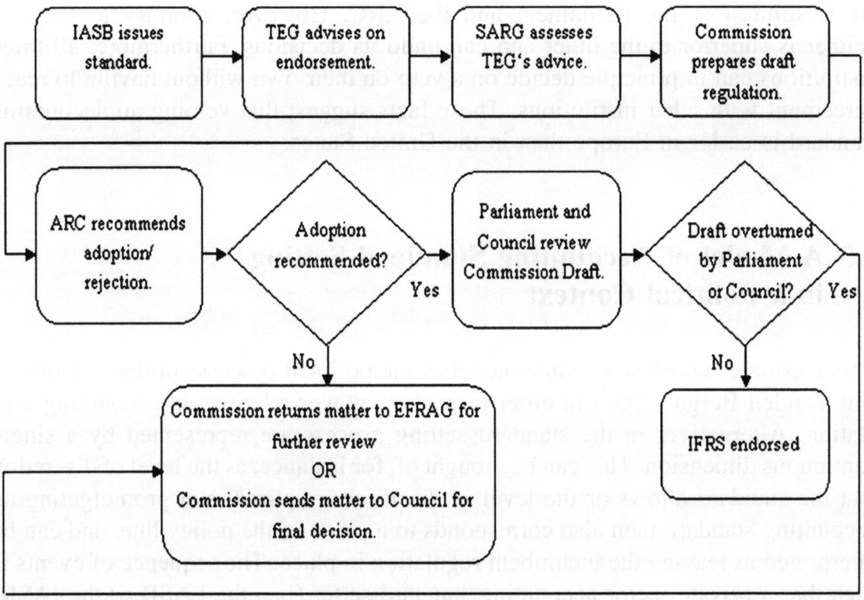

Fig. 4.2 Endorsement process for accounting standards in the EU

Fig. 4.3 Veto players in accounting standard setting in the European Union

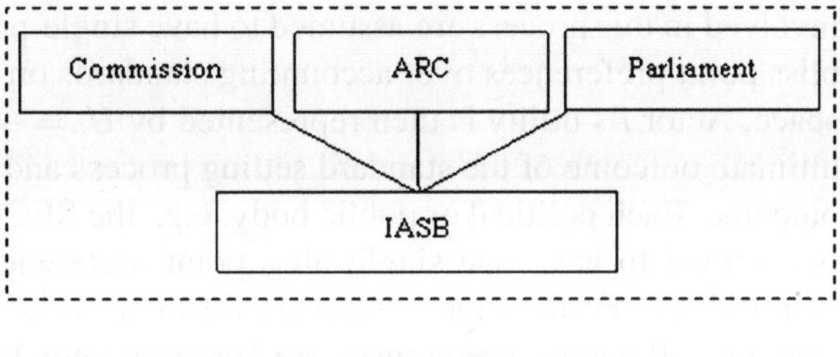

of the immediate process of accounting standard setting—the IASB and the FASB follow an almost identical due process approach to standard setting—the possibilities for influencing standards are fairly different in the two regions due to differences in the political environment. In the US, a new standard has to overcome the potential rejection by two veto players: the Securities and Exchange Commission and the legislator. The SEC can veto any standard or simply refuse to enforce it. However, the SEC is subject to oversight by Congress and Congress can therefore undo an SEC veto by legislatively mandating the enforcement of the standard. On the other hand, Congress also has the ultimate veto power over the standard. There is, at the same time, a countervailing force working against political mingling in the standard setting process: since a legislative act requires the consent of both Chambers of Congress and the President a legislative veto over an accounting standard will only occur if all three agree on it. In the European Union there are three actors with de facto veto power over accounting standards, the Commission, the Parliament and the ARC. However, contrary to the US, neither is superior to the other and can undo its decisions. Furthermore, all three institutions can in principle decide on a veto on their own without having to reach agreement with other institutions. These facts suggest that vetoing an accounting standard is easier in Europe than in the United States.

4.3 A Model of Accounting Standard Setting in a Political Context

This section establishes a simple model of the political process similar to Holburn and Vanden Bergh (2004) in order to analyze power relations in accounting regulation. Alternatives in the standard setting process are represented by a single continuous dimension. This can be thought of, for instance, as the level of discretion that the standard allows or the level of disclosure required. Not promulgating an accounting standard then also corresponds to a point on the policy line, and can be interpreted as leaving the incumbent regulation in place. The sequence of events is such that a private sector accounting standard setter (i.e., the FASB or the IASB) promulgates a new standard or a new interpretation subsequent to which public or political actors with veto power decide whether to accept that standard or to veto it and thereby reinstate the status quo before issuance of the new standard. All actors involved in this process are assumed to have single-peaked, linear, and symmetrical bliss point preferences over accounting standards on the single-dimensional policy space. Actor i's utility is then represented by $U_i = -|\hat{s} - s_i|$ where $\hat{s}$ represents the ultimate outcome of the standard setting process and s_i represents actor i's optimal outcome. Each political or public body, e.g., the SEC or the European Commission, is assumed to have one single bliss point preference, independent of its internal composition. Furthermore, complete information is assumed throughout the analysis, i.e., all actors' preferences are common knowledge.

4.3.1 Accounting Standard Setting in the United States

In the United States, accounting standards are promulgated by the Financial Accounting Standards Board. However, the right to develop mandatory standards has been delegated to the FASB by the Securities and Exchange Commission (SEC) and the SEC retains veto power over individual standards and can refuse to apply them. Furthermore, any accounting standard can be voided of its content by law, which then has higher authority than a SEC decision as well. Alternatively, the law could also theoretically order the SEC to take back a veto and acknowledge a given standard. The legislative process is such that passing a bill requires the consent of the Senate, the House, and the President. To keep the model simple

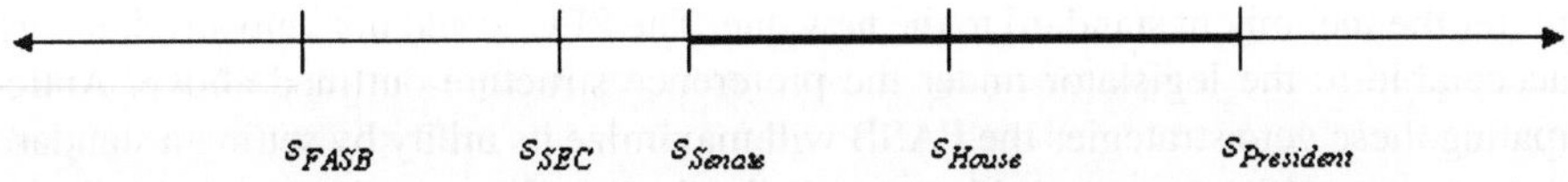

Fig. 4.4 A possible distribution of preferences over accounting standards in the US

and tractable we abstract from the possibility of Congress to overcome a presidential veto. Then the game is played as follows: FASB develops and promulgates an accounting standard, the SEC decides whether to veto it, and the legislator decides whether to override any regulation with a law. Such a dynamic game is solved by the usual technique of backward induction: the institutions involved in the legislative process, i.e., the House, the Senate and the President, decide whether to intervene in the standard setting process by vetoing either the new standard or by undoing a veto by the SEC. Anticipating this, the SEC will only veto a new accounting standard if it prefers the incumbent standard to the new one and foresees that its veto will not be overruled by a legislative act. Under complete information the FASB will in turn anticipate both the SEC's and the legislator's reaction and choose its preferred standard among the set of standards that will not be vetoed.

For illustrative purposes, Fig. 4.4 shows a possible distribution of preferences over accounting standards.[9] The subscripts denote the respective organizations potentially involved in the standard setting process. The range between the extreme preferences on either side of the three actors involved in the legislative process, i.e., the Senate, the House and the President, is called the Political Core and highlighted in Fig. 4.4 by a bold line. Points farther to the left on the single-dimensional policy line correspond to smaller numerical values in the following analysis. The eventual outcome in this situation depends on where on the policy line the incumbent standard lies as this is the fallback that will prevail if a potential new standard gets vetoed. If, for instance, the incumbent standard lies to the right of the President's preferred point $s_{\text{President}}$, the FASB can fully impose its own preferences, $\hat{s} = s_{\text{FASB}}$. The SEC will not veto this standard because $-|s_{\text{FASB}} - s_{\text{SEC}}| > -|SQ - s_{\text{SEC}}|$ where SQ denotes the status quo, i.e., the incumbent standard. Similarly, the legislator will not veto the standard because $-|s_{\text{FASB}} - s_{\text{Senate}}| > -|SQ - s_{\text{Senate}}|$ implying that at least the Senate will not agree to a legislative solution vetoing the new standard and reinstating the status quo. If, on the other hand, the incumbent standard falls sufficiently to the left of the President's preferences, the legislators will veto any new standard s if $-|s_{\text{Senate}} - s| < -|SQ - s_{\text{Senate}}|$ as in that case all three legislative institutions will

[9] A possible intuition for this particular distribution of preferences might be as follows: the accounting standard setter considers a standard with very little discretion (left-most point on the policy line) optimal. The SEC is sympathetic to the FASB's point of view but somewhat more willing to compromise. The three political actors, possibly under the influence of corporate lobbying, prefer a higher degree of flexibility in accounting (points farther to the right on the policy line).

prefer the incumbent standard to the new one. The SEC would not veto any standard acceptable to the legislator under the preference structure outlined above. Anticipating these veto strategies the FASB will maximize its utility by setting a standard $\hat{s} = s_{\text{Senate}} - (SQ - s_{\text{Senate}})$. More generally, these findings can be stated as follows:

Under the US accounting regulatory system, the FASB can fully impose its preferred standard if and only if either both the SEC and at least one of the three legislative institutions prefer this standard to the incumbent one or if all three legislative institutions prefer this standard to the incumbent one.

The logic is straightforward: if the SEC prefers the new standard to the incumbent one it will not veto it and if at least one of the legislative institutions prefers it, no law will be passed vetoing the standard. Similarly, if all three legislative institutions prefer the new standard to the incumbent one they will overrule a potential SEC veto by law. If, on the other hand, all three legislative institutions prefer the incumbent standard to the new one, they will veto it independently of the SEC's preferences. Analogously, if the SEC and at least one legislative institution prefer the incumbent standard to the new one, the SEC will veto it and the legislator will not agree on overturning this veto. Anticipating a veto, the FASB will, of course, adopt a standard that is as close to its preferred one as possible without being vetoed. This analysis implies that if the FASB is not fully satisfied with the incumbent standard, having the right of initiative of setting a new standard, it will only promulgate a new standard under the following conditions which ensure that there exists some new standard which the FASB prefers to the incumbent one and which will not be vetoed.

If $s_{\text{FASB}} \neq SQ$, then the FASB will promulgate a new standard if and only if *neither* of the following two conditions apply: (a) SQ lies outside of the Political Core and s_{FASB} is even farther outside on the same side of the Political Core than SQ; (b) SQ lies on one side of s_{SEC} and at least one legislative institution's preferred point and s_{FASB} lies even farther on the same side.

If conditions (a) or (b) apply, the logic delineated above implies that *any* standard s which the FASB prefers to the status quo, i.e., which is closer to its preferred point on the single-dimensional policy line, will ultimately be vetoed. In case (a) the political institutions agree on issuing a law vetoing the standard. In case (b) the SEC vetoes the standard and the political institutions will not agree on overriding that veto. Anticipating this, the FASB will not attempt to promulgate a new standard. On the other hand, if neither of these two conditions applies, there is at least *some* standard s that is closer to the FASB's optimal standard which will not be vetoed though not necessarily its optimal standard $s_{\text{FAS}B}$ itself.

4.3.2 Accounting Standard Setting in the European Union

The European Union follows a different approach to developing accounting standards. It uses standards promulgated by the international accounting standard setter IASB after a specific endorsement procedure designed to ensure that a new standard is conducive to European interests. The European Commission is advised in this process by EFRAG and has to obtain the assent of the ARC. The European Parliament and the Council subsequently assess whether the Commission has not exceeded its implementing powers by suggesting endorsement of a given standard and has adhered to the terms set out in the IAS regulation. Arguably, as discussed in Sect. 4.2, this gives veto power to three institutions acting independently from one another: the Commission, the ARC and the European Parliament. In a first step it is assumed that the IASB wants any new standard to be endorsed by the European Union even if this implies compromising on its contents. The implications of relaxing this assumption will be discussed below. To begin the discussion, Fig. 4.5 shows a possible distribution of preferences over accounting standards.

The subscripts denote the respective organizations potentially involved in standard setting. Points farther to the left on the policy line again correspond to smaller numerical values in the analysis. A major difference to the graphical depiction of the US system illustrated above lies in the absence of a Political Core. This is because under the European system any veto player can act on its own whereas a legislative veto in the United States requires the consent of three actors. Since in the EU no veto player is superior to any other in the sense that it can override a veto from another actor the veto players' sequence of actions is inconsequential for solving the game by backward induction. The IASB moves first by promulgating a new standard, anticipating the veto players' actions. After the promulgation of the standard the Commission, the ARC and the European Parliament will decide independently whether to veto the new standard, or, more correctly, to refuse its endorsement. Again, the outcome of the game depends on the fallback option, that is to say the incumbent standard SQ. In the situation depicted in Fig. 4.5, if $s_{\mathrm{ARC}} \leq SQ \leq s_{\mathrm{Parliament}}$, i.e., if the incumbent standard falls somewhere between the extreme preferences of the veto actors, no change of the incumbent standard is possible. This is because any change would leave at least one veto player worse off and would therefore be vetoed. If either $SQ < s_{\mathrm{ARC}}$ or $SQ > s_{\mathrm{Parliament}}$ the IASB can impose some new standard closer to its own preferences. For $SQ \leq s_{\mathrm{ARC}} - (s_{\mathrm{IASB}} - s_{\mathrm{ARC}})$ or $SQ \geq s_{\mathrm{Parliament}} + (s_{\mathrm{Parliament}} - s_{\mathrm{IASB}})$ the IASB can fully impose its own preferences, $\hat{s} = s_{\mathrm{IASB}}$, since all veto players will then prefer this new standard to the status quo. For less extreme values of SQ, the IASB has to compromise and will issue a new standard that leaves the ARC (for $SQ < s_{\mathrm{ARC}}$) or the European Parliament (for $SQ > s_{\mathrm{Parliament}}$) indifferent between the new standard and the incumbent one. These findings can be generalized as follows:

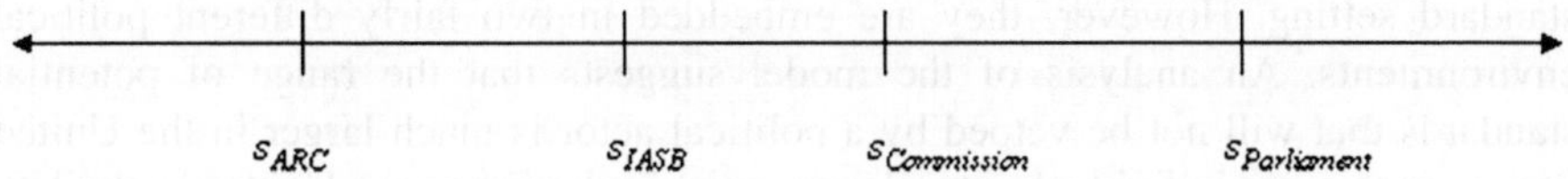

Fig. 4.5 A possible distribution of preferences over accounting standards in the EU

Under the EU accounting regulatory system, the IASB can fully impose its preferred standard if and only if one of the following cases applies: (a) $SQ \leq \min\{s_{ARC}, s_{Commission}, s_{Parliament}\} - |s_{IASB} - \min\{s_{ARC}, s_{Commission}, s_{Parliament}\}|$ or (b) $SQ \geq \max\{s_{ARC}, s_{Commission}, s_{Parliament}\} + |\max\{s_{ARC}, s_{Commission}, s_{Parliament}\} - s_{IASB}|$.

Conditions (a) and (b) ensure that the IASB's preferences relative to the incumbent standard and to the three veto players' preferences are such that the IASB can promulgate a standard that it finds fully satisfying without having to compromise in order to prevent a veto. This necessitates that all three veto players prefer this standard to the incumbent one. Intuitively, this will be the case if either the incumbent standard and the IASB's preferred standard are both on the same side of all veto players' preferences but the IASB's preferences are less extreme than the status quo or if the status quo is so extreme compared to all veto players' preferences that the IASB's favorite standard is preferred to the incumbent one by all even though it may "go too far" from at least some veto players' point of view.

If at least one veto player prefers the incumbent standard to the proposed new one it will be vetoed. As in the American case, the IASB would anticipate a veto and refrain from issuing such a standard. However, the fact that the IASB cannot promulgate a standard fully compatible with its preferences does not necessarily mean that it cannot pass some new standard that it prefers to the incumbent one. A standard exists which is both preferred to the incumbent one by the IASB and by all veto players in the following cases:

If $s_{IASB} \neq SQ$, then the IASB will promulgate a new standard if and only if either (a) $SQ < \min\{s_{ARC}, s_{Commission}, s_{Parliament}\}$ and $s_{IASB} > SQ$ or (b) $SQ > \max\{s_{ARC}, s_{Commission}, s_{Parliament}\}$ and $s_{IASB} < SQ$. Intuitively, this means that for a new standard to be feasible the incumbent standard has to fall outside of the range between preferences of all three veto players. If this is not the case, any new standard will leave at least one veto player worse off and therefore get vetoed. A second necessary condition for the IASB to be able to obtain a standard preferred to the status quo is that its own preferences are at the same side relative to the status quo as all the veto players' preferences are. If its own preferences relative to the veto players' are even more extreme than the incumbent standard, it is not in a position to ensure a move toward its own preferred point.

4.3.3 Implications for Accounting Harmonization

The relevant accounting standard setters for the United States and the European Union, the FASB and the IASB, respectively, follow a very similar approach to standard setting. However, they are embedded in two fairly different political environments. An analysis of the model suggests that the range of potential standards that will not be vetoed by a political actor is much larger in the United States since more individual veto players exist in the European Union. In the US, all three political actors have to prefer a common position to a proposed standard in order to override it. In the EU, to the contrary, three actors have individual veto-power over a standard. This suggests a higher propensity of EU political actors to veto an IASB standard than of US political actors to veto a FASB standard.

Interestingly, this institutional structure also suggests an important difference in incentives for political interference in accounting standard setting. In the United States, the final outcome of the standard setting process is more likely to differ from the standard setter's initial preference if the political actors' preferences are similar. This is because the three legislative institutions have to agree in order to overturn a FASB standard. Conversely, in the European Union, the final outcome of the standard setting process is more likely to differ from the standard setter's initial preference if the political actors' preferences are dissimilar. In the EU, political actors have individual veto powers and do not have to agree in order to overturn a standard. Therefore the more dissimilar their individual preferences are the more likely it is that at least one political actor will have incentives to veto any given standard proposed by the IASB.

The FASB and the IASB are engaged in an effort towards international convergence of accounting standards (e.g., Schipper 2005). This has both been welcomed as leading to more international comparability in financial reporting numbers (Tarca 2004) and criticized as too restrictive to take into account regional differences (Stecher and Suijs 2012). Given the similarity in the structure of the two standard setting bodies, it is reasonable to treat them as belonging to the same epistemic community (Haas 1992) and assume that their preferences over accounting standards are fairly similar. However, their effort to achieve convergence is subject to veto from the relevant political authorities. Any common standard that the two standard setters wish to promulgate therefore needs to fulfill the requirement of not being subject to a veto by either the US or the EU political actors who have veto power over it. The analysis above suggests that if there are continental differences in preferences over an accounting standard and if the two standard setters nevertheless wish to achieve convergence in the area of that standard the final outcome is likely to be closer to European preferences than to American ones. This is the case because any common standard has to "pass" more veto threats on the part of European actors than American ones. This result stands in contrast to claims that the European Union gives too much ground to American hegemony in financial reporting regulation (Dewing and Russell 2004).

4.3.4 Recent Experiences with Political Interference in the European Union

There have been several instances in which European institutions have mingled with accounting standard setting by the IASB in recent years. Two cases will be briefly presented to illustrate the logic outlined above. In 2004, IFRIC 3 Emission Rights was issued. In its recommendation to the European Commission EFRAG concluded that this Interpretation did not meet the requirements of the 'true and fair view' principle and that it did not meet the criteria of understandability, relevance, reliability and comparability. EFRAG therefore suggested not endorsing it. Anticipating a rejection by the EU, the IASB decided to withdraw the Interpretation and has not yet announced an estimated completion date for its subsequent Emissions Trading Schemes project.[10] Despite considering the IFRIC a correct Interpretation of existing standards, the Board thus withdrew it when foreseeing that it would not be endorsed, highlighting the power of the European Commission and its advisory body, EFRAG.

A second instance where a European Union institution initially opposed endorsement of a standard was IFRS 8 Operating Segments. In this case the European Parliament expressed concerns about the impact of the standard and requested an impact assessment from the Commission. Contrary to IFRIC 3, this initial opposition only delayed endorsement which was ultimately granted. It is interesting to compare these two cases, one of which ended with the endorsement of the standard as originally promulgated by the IASB while the other one led to the withdrawal of the Interpretation by the standard setter. Arguably, the different outcomes were caused by some major differences between the two cases. First, while the European Parliament expressed reservations about the IFRS 8 both EFRAG and the ARC supported it. Preventing its endorsement would therefore probably have imposed political costs on individual Members of the European Parliament (MEPs). Second, while IFRIC 3 was in principal universally applicable, it was to a degree tailored toward the European new cap-and-trade emissions trading scheme whereas IFRS 8 brought international segment reporting in line with the respective US standard SFAS 131. Rejecting IFRS 8 would therefore have impacted more on the harmonization effort between international and US standards than rejecting IFRIC 3, again leading to potential political costs for MEPs. Arguably, then, Parliament did not expect to ultimately prevent endorsement of the standard but rather wanted to make its voice heard in order to manifest its clout and gain leverage over future standards by demonstrating its veto power.

4.4 Corporate Lobbying in Accounting Standard Setting in the US and EU Context

The analysis presented in Sect. 4.3 has implications for firms' lobbying decisions. No specific assumptions are made about the origin of the lobbyists' preferences but according to empirical results (e.g., Beresford 1993) she is more likely to belong to the preparer sector (e.g., corporate management or auditors) than to be a user of financial statements (e.g., banks or financial analysts). Assuming that lobbying is costly and marginally shifts the preferences of the actor toward whom it is

---

[10] See IAS Plus (2008) and IASB (2008) for more details.

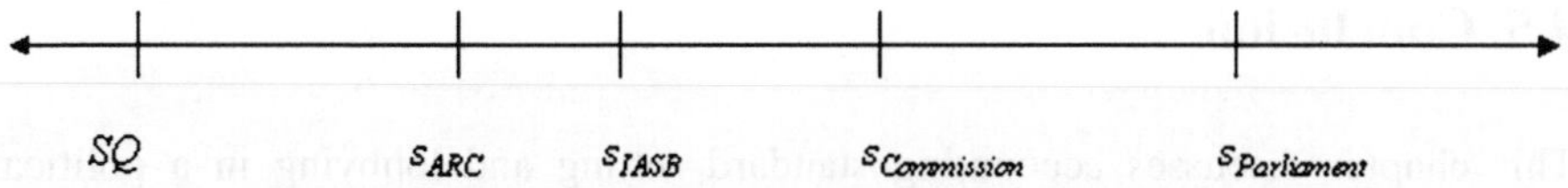

Fig. 4.6 A possible distribution of preferences over accounting standards in the EU

directed, firms have to decide whom to lobby in order to have an impact on the final outcome of the standard setting process. They will not expend resources to influence an actor's preferences if ultimately the standard passed is not affected. We will call the actor whose preferences are decisive the pivotal actor (Holburn and Vanden Bergh 2004) and resort to a graphical depiction of the situation in the European Union in order to present the argument. Assume the preferences are as presented in Fig. 4.6:

In this case the IASB can fully impose its preferred standard since all veto players prefer s_{IASB} to the incumbent standard SQ. In this case a lobbyist wishing to change the outcome of the standard setting process will direct his lobbying toward the standard setter as shifting the IASB's preferences will directly impact the ultimate standard. If, on the other hand, the status quo lay somewhat to the right of its current position such that $s_{\mathrm{ARC}} - SQ < s_{\mathrm{IASB}} - s_{\mathrm{ARC}}$ the IASB would no longer be in a position to impose its will. If it promulgated a standard corresponding to its own preferences the ARC would prefer the status quo and veto the proposed new standard. In this case directing lobbying toward the IASB and marginally shifting its preferences would be a waste of money since the ultimate outcome of the standard setting process would not be altered. In that case the pivotal actor is the ARC and rational lobbyists will direct their efforts towards it. Note that if one actor's preferences are pushed far enough by means of lobbying another actor may become pivotal. In Fig. 4.6, once the IASB's preferences have shifted beyond the point characterized by $2{\cdot}s_{\mathrm{ARC}} - SQ$, the ARC will become pivotal.

Generalizing this argument we observe that the pivotal actor, towards whom lobbying will be directed in the first place, will be the accounting standard setter in exactly those cases where the standard setter can fully impose its preferred standard. It will be a political actor in all other cases. Since we have argued in Sect. 4.3 that the private sector standard setter enjoys more flexibility in the US than in the EU in the sense that it can impose its preferred standard more often it follows that lobbying will be political rather than directed towards the accounting standard setter more frequently in the European Union than in the United States.

It can be seen from the discussion in Sect. 4.3 that if the standard setter cannot fully impose its preferred standard the pivotal actor in general will be the political actor whose preferences are closest to the FASB in the US and the political player whose preferences are farthest from the IASB in the EU. The reason for this is that due to the way the legislative system works in the United States, it is sufficient to convince one political actor in order for a new standard not to be vetoed. In the European Union, on the other hand, all three political players need to be convinced since they have veto power individually.

4.5 Conclusion

This chapter discusses accounting standard setting and lobbying in a political context. It establishes and analyzes a simple model of the political process and derives predictions about the outcome of accounting standard setting under the threat of a political veto. The base model is applied to a US and an EU context. The relevant accounting standard setters, the FASB in the United States and the IASB for the EU show great similarities and follow an almost identical due process when developing new accounting standards. They are, however, embedded in an entirely different political context and as a result the outcome of the standard setting process will often differ even when both standard setters have identical preferences over an ideal accounting standard.

An analysis of the respective systems of financial reporting regulation in the European Union and the United States finds that a higher number of individual players are endowed with veto power over accounting standards in the EU than in the US. Anticipating potential vetoes, the relevant standard setter will promulgate only standards that all players who individually have the power of veto prefer to the status quo. Holding everything else constant the analysis gives rise to three main predictions:

(a) Political and public sector actors in the European Union have a bigger say in financial reporting regulation than their counterparts in the United States;
(b) Harmonization between standards applicable in the European Union (i.e., IFRS) and standards applicable in the US should be biased toward the European position;
(c) The presence of more veto players implies greater weight of political actors in Europe. Therefore, lobbying is more likely to be addressed toward a political actor in the EU than in the US.

Ironically, the relative power advantages of the European Union stemming from the existence of numerous veto players in the endorsement process has been somewhat offset by a recent decision by the SEC which has been pushed for by the European Union. In 2007, the SEC decided to accept from foreign private issuers in their filings with the Commission financial statements prepared in accordance with IFRS (SEC 2008; Jamal et al. 2008). However, only those financial statements prepared in accordance with IFRS *as issued by the IASB* are deemed acceptable. This in turn punishes any deviation of IFRS *as endorsed by the European Union* from the complete set of IFRS since that imposes costs of reconciliation of financial statements to US GAAP on European firms listed in the US. It is, however, not clear that the implicit power shift toward the US position motivated the SEC's decision.

While direct lobbying of the accounting standard setter via comment letters is a much researched subject, studies on the political aspects are rare despite their acknowledged importance. Both conceptual and empirical work on the politics of accounting standard setting represent a fruitful area for research. The propositions presented above can be operationalized and tested empirically. Measuring political lobbying is easier in the United States than in Europe due to the availability of data on political contributions. However, public statements of politicians on accounting matters, such as the famous letter French President Jacques Chirac sent to Commission President Romano Prodi, can be taken as proxies for political positions.

At first glance, existing evidence seems to contradict some of the main predictions outlined above. There are more documented instances of political lobbying in the US than in the EU and the direction of convergence between the International Financial Reporting Standards and US GAAP appears to be mostly in the direction of the FASB-issued American standards (Camfferman and Zeff 2011). Arguably, however, both effects are driven by temporary causes which are likely to recede in importance, as time goes by. First, the FASB as the heir to a decades-long tradition of private-sector standard setting enjoys considerable reputation world-wide. The IASB and its predecessor organization, the IASC, on the other hand for the most part of their existence lacked any powers, its promulgated standards being mandatory nowhere. With the adoption of the IAS regulation by the European Union and the subsequent rapid increase in the number of countries requiring financial statements to be prepared according to IAS/IFRS, the IASB's prestige also drastically increased, neutering the previous advantage of the American standard setter. At the same time, incentives for lobbying political actors involved in the endorsement process only existed since the passage of the IAS regulation. Second, the IASB may cater to US interests in an effort to obtain the SEC's approval also for US firms. However, either the US also commits to use IFRS in which case the IASB's incentives to please its potential clients diminish. Or it does not, which should ultimately convince the IASB of the futility of its effort. Either way, this does not seem to be a lasting influence on IASB decision making. The forces identified in this chapter, on the other hand, are structural and should come to predominate once more temporary forces recede to the background.

References

Amershi, A., Demski, J., & Wolfson, M. (1982). Strategic behavior and regulation research in accounting. *Journal of Accounting and Public Policy, 1*(1), 19–32.

Benston, G., Bromwich, M., Litan, R., & Wagenhofer, A. (2003). *Following the Money*. AEI-Brookings Joint Center for Regulatory Studies: The Enron Failure and the State of Corporate Disclosure.

Beresford, D. (1993). Frustrations of a standard setter. *Accounting Horizons, 7*(4), 70–76.

Beresford, D. (1995). How should the FASB be judged? *Accounting Horizons, 9*(2), 56–61.

Beresford, D. (2001). Congress looks at accounting for business combinations. *Accounting Horizons, 15*(1), 73–86.

Bergstrom, C. (2005). *Comitology: Delegation of Powers in the European Union and the Committee System*. Oxford: Oxford University Press.

Botzem, S., & Quack, S. (2006). Contested rules and shifting boundaries: International standard setting in accounting. In M.-L. Djelic & K. Sahlin-Andersson (Eds.), *Transnational*

Governance: Institutional Dynamics of Regulation (pp. 266–286). Cambridge: Cambridge University Press.

Brackney, K., & Witmer, P. (2005). The European Union's role in international standards setting. *CPA Journal, 75*(11), 18–27.

Bradbury, M. (2007). An anatomy of an IFRIC interpretation. *Accounting in Europe, 4*(2), 109–122.

Burgstahler, D., & Dichev, I. (1997). Earnings management to avoid earnings decreases and losses. *Journal of Accounting and Economics, 24*(1), 99–126.

Burgstahler, D., & Eames, M. (2003). Earnings management to avoid losses and earnings decreases: Are analysts fooled? *Contemporary Accounting Research, 20*(2), 253–294.

Burgstahler, D., & Eames, M. (2006). Management of earnings and analysts' forecasts to achieve zero and small positive earnings surprises. *Journal of Business, Finance and Accounting, 33*(5/6), 633–652.

Camfferman, K., & Zeff, S. (2011). Comment on 'a political economy of accounting standard setting'. *Journal of Management and Governance, 15*(2), 297–304.

Chung, D. (1999). The informational effect of corporate lobbying against proposed accounting standards. *Review of Quantitative Finance and Accounting, 12*(3), 243–269.

Colasse, B., & Standish, P. (1998). State versus market: Contending interests in the struggle to control french accounting standardisation. *Journal of Management and Governance, 2*(2), 107–147.

Colasse, B., & Standish, P. (2004). The development and decline of law in french accounting regulation. *Journal of Management and Governance, 8*(4), 407–429.

Deakin, E. (1989). Rational economic behavior and lobbying on accounting issues: Evidence from the oil and gas industry. *Accounting Review, 64*(1), 137–151.

Dechow, P., Hutton, A., & Sloan, R. (1996). Economic consequences of accounting for stock-based compensation. *Journal of Accounting Research, 34*(Supplement), 1–20.

Dewing, I., & Russell, P. (2004). Accounting, auditing and corporate governance of European listed countries: EU policy developments before and after enron. *Journal of Common Market Studies, 42*(2), 289–319.

Dewing, I., & Russell, P. (2008). Financial integration in the EU: The first phase of EU endorsement of international accounting standards. *Journal of Common Market Studies, 46*(2), 243–264.

Dye, R., & Sunder, S. (2001). Why not allow FASB and IASB standards to compete in the U.S.? *Accounting Horizons, 15*(3), 257–271.

Flower, J., & Ebbers, G. (2002). *Global Financial Reporting*. Basingstoke: Palgrave.

Georgiou, G. (2002). Corporate non-participation in the ASB standard-setting process. *European Accounting Review, 11*(4), 699–722.

Georgiou, G. (2004). Corporate lobbying on accounting standards: Methods, timing and perceived effectiveness *Abacus, 40*(2), 219–237.

Haas, P. (1992). Introduction: Epistemic communities and international policy coordination. *International Organization, 46*(1), 1–35.

Holburn, G., & Vanden Bergh, R. (2004). Influencing agencies through pivotal political institutions. *Journal of Law, Economics and Organization, 20*(2), 458–483.

Horngren, C. (1985). Institutional alternatives for regulating financial reporting. *Journal of Comparative Business and Capital Market Law, 7*, 267–289.

IAS Plus. (2008). *IFRIC 3 emission rights*, http://www.iasplus.com/interps/ifric003.htm. Accessed 31 July 2008.

IASB. (2008). *Emissions tradings schemes*, http://www.iasb.org/Current+Projects/IASB+Projects/Emission+Trading+Schemes/Emission+Trading+Schemes.htm. Accessed 31 July 2008.

Jamal, K., Benston, G., Carmichael, D., Christensen, T., Colson, R., Moehrle, S., et al. (2008). A perspective on the SEC's proposal to accept financial statements prepared in accordance with international reporting standards (IFRS) without reconciliation to U.S. GAAP. *Accounting Horizons, 22*(2), 241–248.

Johnston, D., & Jones, D. (2006). How does accounting fit into a firm's political strategy? *Journal of Accounting and Public Policy, 25*(2), 195–228.

Jorissen, A., Lybaert, N., Orens, R., & Van der Tas, L. (2012). Formal participation in the IASB's due process of standard setting: A multi-issue/multi-period analysis. *European Accounting Review, 24*, 693.

Jorissen, A., Lybaert, N. & Van de Poel, K. (2006). Lobbying towards a global standard setter—Do National characteristics matter? An analysis of the comment letters written to the IASB. In G.N. Gregiou, M. Gaber (Eds.). *International accounting. Standards, regulations, and financial reporting*. London: Elsevier.

Larson, R. (1997). Corporate lobbying of the International Accounting Standards Committee. *Journal of International Financial Management and Accounting, 8*(3), 175–203.

Larson, R. (2007). Constituent participation and the IASB's International Financial Reporting Interpretations Committee. *Accounting in Europe, 4*(2), 207–254.

Lee, B., & Rudd, R. (1988). Beltway wisdom: Rules of the game. *Journal of Accountancy, 166*(3), 76–77.

Lee, B. (1988). Because members deliver. *Journal of Accountancy, 166*(3), 82–92.

Levitt, A. (2002). *Take on the Street*. New York: Pantheon Books.

Lindahl, F. (1987). Accounting standards and Olson's theory of collective action. *Journal of Accounting and Public Policy, 6*(1), 59–72.

MacArthur, J. (1988). Some implications of auditor and client lobbying activities: A comparative analysis. *Accounting and Business Research, 19*(73), 56–64.

Martinez-Diaz, L. (2005). Strategic experts and improvising regulators: explaining the IASC's Rise to global influence, 1973–2001. *Business and Politics*, *7*(3), Article 3.

Mattli, W., & Büthe, T. (2005). Global private governance: Lessons from a National model of setting standards in accounting. *Law and Contemporary Problems, 68*(3–4), 225–262.

McLeay, S., Ordelheide, D., & Young, S. (2000). Constituent lobbying and its impact on the development of financial reporting regulations: Evidence from Germany. *Accounting, Organizations and Society, 25*(1), 79–98.

Merkl-Davies, D. (2004). Regulation and enforcement of financial reporting in Austria. *Journal of Management and Governance, 8*(2), 199–225.

Nobes, C., & Parker, R. (Eds.). (2006). *Comparative International Accounting* 9th Ed.). Upper Saddle River: Prentice-Hall.

Perry, J., & Nölke, A. (2006). The political economy of International Accounting Standards. *Review of International Political Economy, 13*(4), 559–586.

Perry, J. & Nölke, A. (2007). The power of transnational private governance: Financialization and the IASB. *Business and Politics*, *9*(3), Article 4.

Porter, T. (2005). Private authority, technical authority, and the globalization of accounting standards. *Business and Politics*, *7*(3), Article 2.

Ramanna, K. (2008). The implications of unverifiable fair-value accounting: Evidence from the political economy of goodwill accounting. *Journal of Accounting and Economics, 45*(2–3), 253–281.

Schipper, K. (2005). The introduction of international accounting standards in Europe: Implications for international convergence. *European Accounting Review, 14*(2), 101–126.

SEC. (2008). Acceptance from foreign private issuers of financial statements prepared in accordance with international financial reporting standards without reconciliation to US GAAP http://www.sec.gov/rules/final/2007/33-8879.pdf. Accessed 31 July 2008.

Stecher, J. & Suijs, J. (2012). Hail, Procrustes. Harmonized accounting standards as a Procrustean bed. *Journal of Accounting and Public Policy, 31*(4), 341–355

Sunder, S. (2002a). Regulatory competition for low cost-of-capital accounting rules. *Journal of Accounting and Public Policy, 21*(2), 147–149.

Sunder, S. (2002b). Regulatory competition among accounting standards within and across international boundaries. *Journal of Accounting and Public Policy, 21*(3), 219–234.

Sutton, T. (1984). Lobbying of Accounting standard-setting bodies in the U.K. and the U.S.A.: A Downsian analysis. *Accounting, Organziations and Society*, *9*(1), 81–95.

Tandy, P., & Wilburn, N. (1996). The academic community's participation in standard setting: Submission of comment letters on SFAS Nos 1–117. *Accounting Horizons, 10*(3), 92–111.
Tarca, A. (2004). International convergence of accounting practices: Choosing between IAS and US GAAP. *Journal of International Financial Management and Accounting, 15*(1), 60–91.
Thornburg, S., & Roberts, R. (2008). Money, politics, and the regulation of public accounting services: Evidence from the Sarbanes–Oxley Act of 2002. *Accounting, Organizations and Society, 33*(2–3), 229–248.
Véron, N. (2007). *The Global Accounting Experiment*. Brussels: Bruegel Blueprint Series.
Watts, R., & Zimmerman, J. (1978). Towards a positive theory of the determination of accounting standards. *Accounting Review, 53*(1), 112–134.
Zeff, S. (1993). The politics of accounting standards. *Economia Aziendale, 12*(2), 123–142.
Zeff, S. (2002). "Political" lobbying on proposed standards: A challenge to the IASB. *Accounting Horizons, 16*(1), 43–54.
Zeff, S. (2005a). The Evolution of U.S. GAAP. The political forces behind professional standards, part I. *CPA Journal, 75*(1), 19–27.
Zeff, S. (2005b). The evolution of U.S. GAAP. The political forces behind professional standards, part II. *CPA Journal, 75*(2), 19–29.
Zeff, S. (2006). Political lobbying on accounting standards—National and international experience. In C. Nobes & R. Parker (Eds.), *Comparative international accounting* (9th ed., pp. 189–218). Upper Saddle River: Prentice-Hall.

Chapter 5
Constituents' Participation in the IASC/IASB's due Process of International Accounting Standard Setting: A Longitudinal Analysis

Ann Jorissen, Nadine Lybaert, Raf Orens and Leo van der Tas

Abstract In order to increase its legitimacy as worldwide accounting standard setter, the International Accounting Standards Committee (IASC) reformed in 2001 its due process of standard setting with the purpose of instigating a more widespread constituents' participation in terms of stakeholder diversity and geographical diversity. Using a multi-period/multi-issue research design, this study sets out to analyze whether constituents' participation changed after the reform in comparison to the period before the reform. An analysis of 7,442 comment letters sent to the standard setter over the periods 1995–2007 reveal that conclusions are different according to the topic on the agenda of the standard setter. Constituents' participation with regard to financial-instruments-related issues did not change after the reform. These topics always generated widespread interest from all corners of the world and from all types of constituents. Participation in response to non-financial instruments-related proposals, increased after the reform, especially due to a much more active participation of constituents from G4+1 countries.

This chapter includes the paper originally titled "Lobbying toward the IASB: A multi-issues analysis of participation in the due process of standard setting" and discussed at the Third International Workshop on Accounting and Regulation in 2007.

A. Jorissen (✉)
University of Antwerp, S. B. 331, Prinsstraat 13, 2000 Antwerpen, Belgium
e-mail: ann.jorissen@ua.ac.be

N. Lybaert
Hasselt Universiteit (University of Limburg), Antwerpen, Belgium
e-mail: nadine.lybaert@uhasselt.be

R. Orens
Lessius—Business Studies, Korte Nieuwstraat 33, 2000 Antwerpen, Belgium
e-mail: Raf.Orens@kuleuven.be

L. van der Tas
Tilburg University, Tilburg, The Netherlands
e-mail: leo.van.der.tas@nl.cy.com

R. Di Pietra et al. (eds.), *Accounting and Regulation*,
DOI: 10.1007/978-1-4614-8097-6_5,

5.1 Introduction

For the International Accounting Standards Board (IASB), being a private organization, gaining legitimacy is a key issue for its acceptance as a global standard setter (Johnson and Solomons 1984; Wallace 1990; Larson 2007). In order to gain this legitimacy, a standard setter needs sufficient authority, a substantive due process, and a procedural due process (Johnson and Solomons 1984; Wallace 1990). A procedural due process relates to the fact that the standard setter must provide an adequate and impartial opportunity for interested parties to provide input to the standard setting process (Wallace 1990). However, simply affording the opportunity to provide input is not a sufficient condition to gain legitimacy. A common view in the literature with regard to the legitimacy of a standard setter is that widespread participation of all constituents in the process of standard setting is of utmost importance (Johnson and Solomons 1984; Dyckman 1988; Wallace 1990; Tandy and Wilburn 1992; Larson 2007; Richardson and Eberlein 2011). This participation in the process of standard setting is considered important because it generates information which can help the standard setter gauge the potential reaction of interest groups to its standards (Dyckman 1988; Tandy and Wilburn 1992).

It became evident in the 1990s that the International Accounting Standards Committee (IASC) board could not claim the necessary legitimacy for global leadership in international accounting standard setting. In order to take up this leading role in developing global high-quality standards, the IASC board restructured itself in order to reinforce its credentials as a legitimate worldwide accounting standard setter (Camfferman and Zeff 2007). In 2001, the IASC reformed its structure and due process of standard setting in order to allow more widespread participation and to stimulate involvement of constituents in the due process of international accounting standard setting. With this reform the standard setting process changed into two major ways. First, the standard setting body, i.e., the IASB, is set up as an independent technical body. Its predecessor, the IASC, was a more representative body, where board members represented the view of a particular group of constituents (often the accounting profession). Second, the due process now resembles more to the FASB's due process of standard setting. This change was a result of the pressure exerted by the G4+1[1] (Street 2005, 2006; Bhimani 2008). During the financial crisis in 2008, the due process of standard setting of the IASB together with the outreach to constituents was again criticized.

[1] The G4+1 are the standard setters of Australia plus New Zealand, Canada, the UK and the US, and the IASC as observer.

A major drive for this critique was "supposed" lack of input constituents had in the promulgation of financial-instruments-related standards.

Given the criticisms expressed in 2008 with regard to constituents' participation, this study sets out to analyse whether or not constituents' participation in the due process of international accounting standard setting changed after the reform of the standard setter in 2001. Considering the criticisms with regard to stakeholder participation expressed in the wake of the financial crisis, we analyse whether constituents' participation differs according to the topic of a proposal on the agenda of the standard setter (i.e., being financial instruments-related or not). In order to answer these questions, we examine whether constituents' formal participation after the reform of the standard setter is different in terms of stakeholder diversity and in terms of geographic diversity from constituents' representation in the due process before the reform of the standard setter in 2001. By collecting formal participation data over a period of 12 years (1995–2007) we are able to detect long-term patterns in the evolution of constituents' participation and find out whether or not this participation became more widespread and diverse over time and whether or not this diversity was associated with the topic of the proposed standard. Stakeholder diversity as well as geographic diversity in constituents' participation contributes to the legitimacy of the global standard setter (Larson 2007; FCAG 2009).

To study the long-term evolution in constituents' participation in the due process of international accounting standard setting over time, we choose as unit of analysis the formal participation of constituents in the international accounting standard setting process. Formal participation consists of writing comment letters when the standard setter solicits responses from its constituents by publishing discussion papers and exposure drafts for comments.[2] This choice with respect to the unit of analysis is taken for a number of reasons. First, formal participation of constituents gained in importance after reform of the standard setter in 2001, as a technical, independent expert model replaced the representative board model. Second, as information on informal participation methods is not publicly available, it is almost impossible in a multi-period/multi-issue study to collect data on all participation methods (formal as well as informal) used by constituents for all issues on the agenda of the standard setter for a lengthy period of time. Third, empirical evidence is available that the use of formal participation methods by constituents is linked to their use of informal participation methods (Georgiou 2004), so that evidence obtained on formal participation can be extended to participation in general.

In this study, we analyse constituents' formal participation in international accounting standard setting over a period of 12 years (1995–2007). The year 1995

[2] We consider only comment letters written in response to discussion papers and exposure drafts preceding the issue of IFRS. We do not consider comment letters written in the process of issuing draft SIC Interpretations (Standard Interpretation Committee) and draft IFRIC Interpretations which both relate to the Interpretation of the standards. With discussion papers, we refer to both discussion papers (IASB) and to draft statements of principles (IASC).

was chosen as the start of the period of analysis since, at that time, the prominent role of the IASC in international accounting standard setting became assured through decisions of the International Organization of Securities Commissions (IOSCO) to use International Accounting Standards (IAS) for listing purposes and the European Commission (EC) New Accounting Strategy to consider IAS for the preparation of consolidated accounts for listed firms. Subsequently, since 6 years elapsed between 1995 and reform of the standard setter, an equal period of 6 years was chosen following the reform of the standard setter. The end of this 12 year period coincides with the start of the financial crisis. Over this 12 year period, we analyse 7,442 comment letters sent to the standard setter.

The results of this longitudinal analysis reveal that the evolution of the diversity in formal constituent participation is significantly associated with the topic on the agenda of the international accounting standard setter. If we focus on the comment letters sent to documents (discussion papers and exposure drafts) dealing with elements of measurement, recognition and disclosure of financial instruments, we do not observe a significant increase in participation of the different stakeholder groups after the reform of the standard setter except for the associations of financial preparers, the national standard setters and the consultants. If we focus on the geographic distribution of constituent participation related to financial instruments issues, we observe that when these issues are on the agenda of the standard setter constituents from Western code law countries as well as from Western common law countries are almost equally represented, especially in the group of preparers. When recognition, measurement, and disclosure issues not related to financial instruments issues are on the agenda of the standard setter, constituents' participation increased significantly after the reform for most types of stakeholder groups. If we consider the geographic diversity of constituents when measurement, recognition and disclosure issues not related to financial instruments are on the agenda of the standard setter, we observe that many comment letters are written by constituents of the G4+1 countries, being the constituents of the UK, the US, and Australia. If we split up participants according to the characteristics of the capital market of their country or the gross domestic product (GDP) per capita of their country, we observe that constituents from countries with medium or lower GDP per capital and from countries with emerging or developing capital markets are still under represented in the due process of international accounting standard setting. The following three stakeholder groups did not change their participation behavior over time regardless of the topic of the standard: The accounting profession, the academics, and the actuaries. These findings reveal that the abolishment of the representative board model did not trigger a higher formal participation of the accounting profession. The participation of the users of financial information in the due process of standard setting even decreased significantly over time.

In the light of the criticisms on stakeholder representation in the due process of international accounting standard setting, we find a more widespread geographic diversity in constituents' participation when financial instruments-related issues are on the agenda of the standard setter in comparison to participation with regard to other topics on the agenda of the standard setter. Constituents from Western common law countries as well as Western code law countries are actively involved when financial instruments-related proposals are discussed. When measurement/ recognition and disclosure issues, not related to financial instruments, are on the agenda of the standard setter, constituents from former G4+1 countries send the majority of the comment letters after the reform of the standard setter. The results of this longitudinal analysis indicate that the IASB needs to use other mechanisms to pursue inputs from its stakeholders in the following instances: Input from the user group on all topics discussed by the IASB, input from countries with lower and medium GDP per capita and from countries with emerging or less developed capital markets.

This chapter proceeds as follows. In the next section we describe the context of the study and the reform of the due process of standard setting. In the third part we pay attention to the literature and discuss the method of analysis. In the fourth part, we present the results and the fifth part concludes this chapter.

5.2 From International Accounting Harmonization Toward Global Accounting Standard Setting

In this section, we briefly discuss the changing role of the international accounting standard setter over time. Thereafter, we focus on the changes in the due process of international accounting standard setting in the period of our study.

5.2.1 The Changing Role of the International Accounting Standard Setter

In 1973, when the IASC was established, its main objective was to promote the global harmonization of accounting standards on the basis of the IASs it issued. The parties in charge for this promotion were the accounting member bodies. During the first two decades of its existence, the IASC was an international accounting standard setter among a number of other players in this field, such as the European Union (EU), the United Nations (UN), and the Organization for Economic Cooperation and Development (OECD) (Wallace 1990). In that period, the IASC had to compete for its authority and the accounting member bodies had to see that the IASC's mission of international accounting harmonization would succeed. In the mid-nineties, the IASC was the only organization to claim prime responsibility for promoting international accounting harmonization or standardization on a world-wide basis (Emenyony and Gray 1996). This was the result of decisions of two important players. First, in 1995, the IASC reached an agreement with IOSCO that envisaged that, by March 1998, IOSCO would recommend to its members (i.e., major securities regulators throughout the world) that accounts drawn up in accordance with IAS should be accepted for foreign listings.[3] Second, the EC announced an important change in its policy on accounting harmonization, in its communication 'Accounting Harmonization: A new strategy vis-à-vis international harmonization'. The EC, in developing its new accounting strategy, decided to envisage the possibility of accepting IAS for listed companies instead of setting up a European accounting standards setting body [EC, COM 95(508)]. In May 2000, IOSCO formally accepted the IAS's 'core standards' as a basis for cross-border securities listings worldwide, although some countries (notably the US) still required reconciliations of items such as earnings or stockholder equity to US Generally Accepted Accounting Principles (GAAP). In the same year, the EC [COM2000 (359)] proposed that all EU listed firms should use one set of accounting standards for financial reporting purposes. These decisions boosted the IASC's ambition to become the global accounting standard setter.

In the requirements to become a global standard setter, the structure and board composition of the IASC were sources of criticism, because board members merely represented accounting bodies, which also provided a large part of the funding. It became evident in the 1990s that the IASC board could not claim the necessary legitimacy for global leadership in international accounting standard setting. In order to take up this leading role in developing global high-quality standards, the IASC board restructured itself in line with FASB in order to reinforce its credentials as a legitimate worldwide accounting standard setter (Camfferman and Zeff 2007). In this reform process, the IASC showed extensive willingness to alter its structure and operating mechanisms to appeal to US preferences (Bhimani 2008). The International Accounting Standards Committee Foundation (IASCF) and the IASB were created, whereby the IASCF became responsible for the funding of the organization and the IASB became the standard setting body as successor to the IASC. The IASB is conceived as an independent technical body, whereas the IASC was more a representative body. The restructuring meant that the representative model was abandoned and replaced by a technical expert model in which members are independent and by definition required to be neutral judges seeking the truth (Colson et al. 2009). Board members no longer represent the view of a particular group of constituents, like they did under the IASC regime. Together with the restructuring of the standard setter, its due process of standard setting was altered as well. Up until 2008, it seemed that the restructuring of 2001 had been able to overcome the criticisms of the late nineties. However, when the financial crisis hit the world in 2008, the international accounting standard setter became again highly criticized and as a result a system of public monitoring (installation of the Monitoring Board) was added to the system of international accounting standard setting.

[3] IOSCO took this step after the IASC had completed its 'Comparability Project'. With the Comparability Project, which began in 1989 with the issuance of ED 32, the IASC had started a major movement to address criticisms about the allowance of so many alternatives in its accounting standards. The Comparability Project resulted in the revision and reissuance of 10 IASs, which took effect on January 1, 1995.

5.2.2 The Process of Standard Setting of the IASC and the IASB

Accounting standards were developed by the IASC/IASB according to a due process of standard setting, which changed over the years. We discuss these changes in the due processes of standard setting below.

5.2.2.1 The IASC's due Process of Standard Setting

Initially, the IASC did not invest a lot of effort in seeking the views of users of its standards, and relied principally on the pledge of its members (i.e., the accounting member bodies) to use their best endeavors to ensure that IASs were adopted in their respective countries (Wallace 1990). This might have been the most appropriate strategy to start with, but it did not seem to work, and the legitimacy of the IASC to set corporate financial reporting standards at the global level was regularly questioned (Wallace 1990).

Up until 1989, the IASC developed its standards with a selected group of interested parties who were invited by the IASC to comment on their projects. The public never got access to the information and comments requested by the IASC from these selected parties. These fairly confidential procedures changed in 1989, when ED 32 on the comparability of financial statements was issued. ED 32 was the first document issued to the public for comment. As a result, the due process of standard setting became more open from 1989 onwards (Larson 1997) since constituent parties were able to participate in the due process of standard setting by means of the production of comment letters. The IASC started at the end of the eighties with the public release of exposure drafts and comment letters written in response to these ED. Further public hearings were also organized (Wyatt 1992). While many IASC deliberations and their votings were still done privately, there was much greater openness compared to the seventies and the early eighties (Guenther and Hussein 1995).

The due process of standard setting of the IASC started with the addition of a project to the IASC Board's agenda (Knorr and Ebbers 2001). Afterward, the Board of the IASC set up a Steering Committee to develop a statement of principles, an exposure draft and ultimately an International Accounting Standard. Each Steering Committee was chaired by a Board representative and usually included representatives of accountancy bodies from at least three other countries. Such a Committee may also include representatives of organizations which were represented on the Board of the IASC, representatives of the Consultative Group or experts on a particular topic. The IASC was anxious to obtain input from a wide range of users and preparers of financial statements at the early stages of the development of IASs. Therefore, the IASC formed a Consultative Group including representatives of users' and preparers' organizations (Cairns 1997).

The Board of the IASC reviewed in detail all the recommendations of the Steering Committees. The procedure for the development of an IAS was as follows:

- The Steering Committee developed a draft statement of principles which was issued for comment;
- The Steering Committee reviewed the comments on the draft of principles and normally agreed with a final statement of principles, which was submitted to the Board for approval as the basis for an exposure draft of a proposed IAS;
- After revision and with approval of at least two-thirds of the Board, the exposure draft of a proposed IAS was published for comment;
- The Steering Committee reviewed the comments on the exposure draft and prepared a draft IAS for consideration by the Board;
- The Board reviewed the draft IAS. After revision and with the approval of at least three-quarters of the Board the standard were approved.

When in 2001 the IASB was installed as a result of the reform of the IASC, an open process of standard setting was established that is similar to the standard setting process adopted by the US standard setter (FASB) and the UK standard setter (ASB). This similarity is a result of the fact that the G4+1 played an important role in reform of the standard setter (Street 2005, 2006; Camfferman and Zeff 2007).

5.2.2.2 The IASB's due Process of Standard Setting

From 2001 onwards, the standard setting process became the responsibility of the IASB, whereby initially a number of individual board members got the task to liaise with important national standard setters (namely the US, the UK, Canada, France, Germany, Japan, Australia, and New Zealand). This liaison task was abolished half way the first decade of the twenty first century. The due process of standard setting of the IASB consists of six stages: Stage I: Setting the agenda [this is done in cooperation with the Standards Advisory Council (SAC)]; stage II: Project planning; stage III: Development and publication of a discussion paper; stage IV: Development and publication of an exposure draft;—stage V: Development and publication of an International Financial Reporting Standards (IFRS) and stage VI: Procedures after an IFRS is issued.

The methods constituent parties can use in order to influence the standard setting process differ according to the stage of the standard setting process. The mechanisms range from formal to informal meetings, questions in public hearings and the submission of comment letters. In the due process of the IASB, the following opportunities for input can be distinguished: (a) Participation in the development of views as a member of the SAC; (b) participation in advisory groups; (c) submission of an issue to International Financial Reporting Interpretations Committee (IFRIC); (d) submission of a comment letter in response to a discussion document; (e) submission of a comment letter in response to an exposure draft; (f) participation in public round-table discussions; and (g) participation in field visits and field tests. In addition, there are informal ways like private sessions with individual staff and board members.

In the IASC's due process of standard setting comment letters were written in response to draft statements of principles (discussion papers) and exposure drafts of IAS. With regard to the IASB's due process of standard setting, comment letters can be used to influence the outcome of stage III (discussion papers) and stage IV (exposure drafts) of the standard setting process. The production of these comment letters is the unit of analysis of the empirical part of the paper.

5.3 Literature and Research Design

5.3.1 The Participation Literature

Most publications on the international accounting standard setter relate to its structure, its influence, the financing system, and the functioning of the standard setter (e.g., Wallace 1990; Flower 1997; Kirsch 2006; Camfferman and Zeff 2007; Fulbier et al. 2009; Botzem and Quack 2009; Burlaud and Colasse 2011; Bengston 2011; Königsgruber 2010; Zeff 2012). Fewer articles study in an empirical way constituents' participation in the international accounting standard setting process.

Participation studies in the extant literature have primarily used a single-issue approach in single country studies as well as in multi-country studies (e.g., Kenny and Larson 1993; Guenther and Hussein 1995; MacArthur 1996, 1999; Larson and Brown 2001; Jorissen et al. 2006). Through a single-issue approach, constituents' participation and their drivers to participate in the due process of standard setting are studied by focusing on attempts in response to just one standard at a time. Although the examination of participation in response to a single-issue standard offers some distinct advantages, for example, ease in measuring variables of interest, such as the lobbying position, it also has some important disadvantages (Georgiou 2005). Most importantly, single-issue studies cannot reveal any patterns in a lobbying strategy since a sole lobbying decision is likely to be 'a single move in a multimove political regulatory game' (Amershi et al. 1982, p 20). Amershi et al. (1982) observe that lobbying is likely to be a multi-issue, multi-period process, especially for professional lobby organizations such as industry associations or unions. Limiting the investigation to a single-issue may present methodological problems because the behavior of certain lobbying agents can only be understood by taking a long-term view and considering multiple issues. According to Elbannan and McKinley (2006), single-issue studies further neglect the impact of the attributes of standards on constituent participation in the due process. Attributes do vary from standard to standard and that might explain why constituents participate in relation to some standards but not others. Further single-issue studies often suffer from small sample size (Georgiou 2005). So the limitations of single-issue studies can be overcome by using a multi-issue/multi-period approach which involves studying participation behavior on more than one issue and over a period of time (Larson 1997; Georgiou 2005; Elbannan and McKinley 2006).

Less empirical research exists that employ a multi-period/multi-issue approach (e.g., Larson 1997, 2007; Jorissen et al. 2012). The limited number of multi-period/multi-issue studies examining participation toward the international accounting standard setter so far, only analyse participation within one time frame (1st time frame—participation only under the IASC, e.g., Larson 1997; 2nd time frame-participation only under the IASB, e.g., Larson 2007; Jorissen et al. 2012). These studies focus on stakeholder diversity within constituent participation and examine mainly the differences between preparers' participation versus user participation, based on Sutton's theory (1984) as well as the drivers of mainly preparers' participation based on the insights of the positive accounting theory of Watts and Zimmerman (1978, 1986). Using a multi-issue/multi-period approach, we examine constituents' participation over a longer period of time than prior studies and compare these participation figures over time using a consistent data-collection and data-classification method for a 12 year period. Our research design also allows us to study the impact of the topic of the proposed standard on long-term constituents' participation.

5.3.2 *Research Design*

In this section, we present the data collection and the data classification methods used to analyse the changes in constituents' participation. Next, we introduce the methods of analysis employed together with the measurement of the research variables.

5.3.2.1 Data Collection Method and Data Classification Method

Our longitudinal analysis begins in 1995, when it became clear that the IASC would become a major player in the development of IAS with a view toward worldwide acceptance. In 2001, the international accounting standard setter was reformed to enhance its mission as global standard setter (see Sect. 5.2). For our period of analysis, we have chosen an equal time frame before and after the reform of the standard setter. Since a period of 6 years elapsed between 1995 and the reform, we also include a period of 6 years after the reform. The end of this period also coincides with the start of the financial crisis when the legitimacy of the IASB as global accounting standard setter was criticized. Over this period of 12 years, 90 documents were issued for comment by the standard setter: 45 documents were issued for comment over the period 1995–2001 by the IASC and 45 documents were issued over the time frame 2001–2007 by the IASB.

We study constituents' formal participation through collecting data on the comment letters written by constituents in response to these documents. With regard to the comment letters sent in response to the documents issued for comment during the period 1995–2001 by the IASC, we collect the data from the archives of the IASB. We obtain the information on comment letters sent in response to the proposals issued for comment by the IASB (2001–2007) from analysing the comment letters posted on the IASB website. For the whole period of study, our dataset consists of 7,442 comment letters: 2,910 comment letters sent to the IASC in the period 1995–2001, and 4,532 comment letters sent to the IASB in the period 2001–2007. An overview of the number of comment letters sent in response to each document issued for comment by the IASC/IASB is listed in appendix.

After collection of the comment letters, each comment letter is classified according to the character of the originating party and subsequently according to its geographic origin. First, we assign each of the 7,442 comment letters into one of the classes of constituent parties as mentioned in par. 19 of the preface to the IASB (2005): Preparers, the accounting profession, users, national standard setters, stock exchanges, governments, individuals, academics, or other interested parties. We subdivide the group of preparers into the following four subcategories: (1) individual commercial, industrial and service companies, corporate preparers; (2) associations of these corporate preparers; (3) individual financial institutions (including insurance companies and mutual funds), financial preparers; and (4) associations of these financial preparers. The accounting profession is classified into two subgroups: Audit firms and associations of accountants and auditors. For the group of other interested parties, we opt to use two subgroups: Actuaries and consultants. We classify investors, financial analysts, consumer organizations, or other parties relying on financial statement information for decision making purposes as users.

Before classifying each comment letter into one of these categories, we make the following choices. First, similar to Larson (1997), we group individuals with ties to specific organizations with those organizations. Only when the author of the comment letter stated explicitly that s/he was writing in her/his own name, we do not assign the comment letter to an organization, but classify the letter under individuals. Next, when a joint response is classified, the category to which the first mentioned author belongs is chosen. In almost all cases, the second and following authors belong to the same category of constituents. A third major choice is that we classify responses of subsidiaries of multinational corporations under the multinational corporation itself. Finally, within the category of stock exchanges, we also include supervisory authorities of financial markets.

With regard to geographic classification, we classify a letter to the country of origin of the sender (being an individual or an organization). So, we assign individual preparers to a single individual country according to the official's legal location of the headquarters of the group. In those cases where the sender in an organization having members from various countries, or that is active in more than one country, the comment letter is classified as 'international' and not assigned to an individual country. For consultants and users alike, the country of origin of the comment letter is taken into account. For individuals, the address of the sender on the letter is used for country classification purposes.

Following this system, two investigators classified each sender of a comment letter independently to the main constituent and to a geographic location. When classification is not obvious from the content of the comment letter, a search on Internet is conducted to obtain more information about the sender. After these procedures, a few cases remain where the letter can be classified to more than one constituent party.[4] So the reader should be aware that in a very limited number of cases, an arbitrary assignment cannot be avoided; however, as these cases are less than 1 % of the total number of comment letters analzed, this does not affect constituent distribution in the different steps in the IASB process.

5.3.2.2 Measurement of Variables and Method of Analysis

To examine the evolution in stakeholder diversity we test whether the lobby intensity of the various stakeholder groups is significantly different before and after the reform of the standard setter. For the analysis of constituents' geographic distribution, we use those comment letters that we could assign to a single country. So our population for the geographic analysis include all countries from which at least one constituent party has sent a comment letter to the IASC/IASB over the time period 1995–2007. This population include 89 countries. We group the participating countries based on their legal origin, cultural region, capital market development, and per capita GDP. These groups are similar to classifications used in Leuz (2010), with the exception that we limit the classification according to the legal origin in the classification between the code law and the common law system. The assignment of countries to cultural regions is based on Schwartz (2004) and Licht et al. (2007). Both studies identify following cultural regions which we also employ in our study: African, English speaking, Far East, Latin American, Mediterranean, Western Europe, and Eastern Europe. All former G4+1 countries are included in the English speaking countries together with a.o. Kenya, India, Ireland, South Africa, and Zimbabwe. The Mediterranean countries consist of the Arab countries around the Mediterranean Sea and Turkey.

A country's capital market development is based on MSCI (2012). This organization classifies countries either belonging to developed, emerging, and frontier

---

[4] There are a few examples where a straightforward assignment is not evident, like an academic working for the Big Four, but writing in his own name (was assigned to academics); an organization having corporations, financial institutions and academics as members (was assigned to associations of corporate preparers); a corporation involved in the financing and development of real estate projects (was assigned to individual corporate preparers) or a governmental organization providing consulting on reporting standards (was assigned to governments).

capital markets following criteria based on economic development, liquidity requirements, and market accessibility criteria (MSCI 2012). Countries that are not classified in one of these three groups are "standalone" countries having equity markets with a limited number of listed firms. Since both frontier countries and standalone countries only submit a few number of comment letters, we opt to combine these country groups and label these countries as developing capital markets. This procedure leads to the classification of the lobbying countries into three groups: Developed, emerging, and developing capital markets. Finally, we group countries based on their per capita GDP, provided by the World Bank (2006). We split the countries into three clusters: Low income, middle income, and high income. The low income cluster in our study encompasses the countries that the Word Bank identifies as a low income country (GDP per capita of $875 or less) or as lower middle income country ($876–3,465). The middle and high income clusters include, respectively, countries belonging to the upper middle income group ($3,466–10,725) and the high income group ($10,726 or more).

In order to isolate whether constituent behavior differs according to the topic of the proposal on the agenda of the standard setter, we classified the group of documents issued for comment by the standard setter into three subcategories depending on the topic of the proposal. We created the following three subpopulations: Proposals dealing with financial instruments-related issues, proposals dealing with recognition, measurement, and disclosure issues not related to financial instruments and proposals relating to the convergence project of the IASB and the FASB. The proposals related to financial reporting by private enterprises (Small and Medium Sized Enterprises) and to the structure and the governance of the standard setter were not included in any of these subgroups. We compare the stakeholder participation on financial instruments proposals with the other proposals having an impact of the recognition, measurement, and disclosure of financial statement information. In a subsequent step, we exclude in this latter group the convergence projects (all these proposals include significant recognition, measurement, and disclosure issues) since the lobby intensity of US constituents on these projects might bias the participation figures toward the IASB.

5.4 Results

This section discusses first the findings on the evolution of stakeholder diversity in constituents' participation in the process of international accounting standard setting over time. Subsequently, it addresses the evolution of the geographic diversity in constituents' formal participation in this process.

5.4.1 Stakeholder Diversity in Constituents' Participation in International Accounting Standard Setting

We start with a general overview of constituents' participation over time. The findings set forth in Table 5.1 present the absolute number of comment letters written to the IASC and the IASB for all proposals, together with the proportion of comment letters written by the different stakeholder groups to the standard setter.

Table 5.1 shows that preparers write almost half of all comment letters received by the IASC and the IASB. This proportion with respect to the total number of comment letters received by the standard setter is almost identical in the two time frames. The accounting profession was the second largest producer of comment letters both before and after reform of the standard setter. After the reform of the IASC into the IASB, national accounting standard setters are the third most important group of constituents, writing about 15 % of all comment letters to the IASB. The increased participation of national standard setters is in fact no surprise, since many of them saw their authority erode after the decision of the EU and the

Table 5.1 Stakeholder distribution of the lobby intensity to IASC and IASB

Constituent party	Absolute number of comment letters		Proportion of comment letters		Number of comment letters allocated to a country	
	IASC	IASB	IASC (%)	IASB (%)	IASC	IASB
Preparers	**1,295**	**1,962**	**44.5**	**43.3**	**1,208**	**1,789**
Individual corporate preparers	622	588	21.4	13.0	622	585
Association of corporate preparers	226	432	7.8	9.5	175	356
Individual financial preparers	245	465	8.4	10.3	245	465
Associations of financial preparers	202	477	6.9	10.5	166	383
Non-preparers	**1,615**	**2,570**	**55.5**	**56.7**	**1,223**	**2,012**
Accounting profession	975	1157	33.5	25.5	722	822
Audit firms	*248*	*288*	*8.5*	*6.4*	*12*	*15*
Associations of accountants and auditors	*727*	*869*	*25.0*	*19.2*	*710*	*807*
Users	90	66	3.1	1.5	83	64
National standard setters	191	683	6.6	15.1	128	627
Stock exchanges	86	112	3.0	2.5	53	47
Governments	28	90	1.0	2.0	26	78
Individuals	90	168	3.1	3.7	80	124
Academics	69	107	2.4	2.4	68	101
Other interested parties	86	187	3.0	4.1	63	149
Consultants	*24*	*98*	*0.8*	*2.2*	*24*	*97*
Actuaries	*62*	*89*	*2.1*	*2.0*	*39*	*52*
Total	**2,910**	**4,532**	**100**	**100**	**2,431**	**3,801**

Notes This table reports the total number of comment letters written by each constituent party to the IASC and IASB as well as the proportion of comment letters written by each constituent party to the IASC and IASB

Australian FRC, among others, to require mandatory IFRS application for listed companies. Since then, national standard setters have had to relinquish their standard setting authority for listed companies to the IASB. This participation rate indicates that national standard setters still wish to play a role in standard setting for listed companies. Users hardly participate formally in the standard setting process. These findings confirm earlier empirical results on constituent participation in the international accounting standard setting process based on Sutton's hypothesis (1984) that users participate significantly less than preparers (Larson 1997; Jorissen et al. 2012). The figures in Table 5.1 show that within international accounting standard setting, the unbalance between preparers and users got even worse over time, since users write significantly fewer comment letters per document issued by the standard setter after the reform than before. So an element of critique with regard to stakeholder representation in the due process of international accounting standard setting is the absence of the users of financial information in the formal participation stage.

Next we focus on the changes in stakeholder participation over time in relation to the topic of the proposal on the agenda of the standard setter (i.e., financial instruments-related, other recognition/measurement and, disclosure issues with and without convergence projects). In order to study in greater depth these changes in the behavior of the individual stakeholder groups, we analyse the average number of comment letters per request for comment, sent by the different categories of constituents in response to the discussion papers and exposure drafts issued by the IASC/IASB. Additionally, the proportion of comment letters is considered as well and computed as the number of comment letters written by that party for each proposal issued by the IASC or the IASB divided by all comment letters written in response to that proposal. The tables, discussed below, all present the average figures and proportions, together with the results of the significance tests (based on the Mann–Whitney U test). These tests give an indication as to whether the level of participation of each constituent has changed significantly between time frames. Table 5.2 presents the evolution in constituent participation over time in terms of stakeholder diversity whereby participation is presented in function of the topic of the proposed standard.

In panel A of Table 5.2, which presents the data with regard to participation when financial instruments-related proposals are on the agenda of the standard setter, we observe that only three different stakeholder groups increased their participation significantly after the reform in comparison to before the reform based on the average number of comment letters written per proposal. These constituents are the association of financial preparers, the national standard setters, and the governments. The data in panel B reveal that the participation behavior with regard to non financial instrument related proposals increased for many more stakeholder groups significantly between the period before the reform and after the reform of the standard setter. The association of corporate preparers, individual financial preparers and associations of financial preparers, national standard setters, stock exchanges, governments and consultants participate significantly more after the reform of the standard setter. The individual corporate preparers, the

Table 5.2 Stakeholder distribution of the lobby intensity to IASC and IASB categorized by attribute of the standard

Constituent party	Mean IASC	Mean IASB	Z-value	Proportion IASC	Proportion IASB	Z-value
Panel A: Financial instruments						
Number of proposals	**10**	**9**		**10**	**9**	
Preparers	30.800	53.222	−1.675*	0.380	0.495	−1.307
Individual corporate preparers	9.800	9.667	−0.452	0.130	0.091	−1.308
Associations of corporate preparers	4.900	7.667	−1.319	0.068	0.074	−0.327
Individual financial preparers	8.400	14.778	−1.603	0.101	0.131	−0.817
Associations of financial preparers	7.700	21.111	−2.375**	0.081	0.198	−2.578***
Non-preparers	27.400	43.000	−1.881*	0.620	0.505	−1.307
Accounting profession	17.000	21.000	−1.558	0.458	0.259	−2.124**
Audit firms	5.100	5.333	−0.515	0.154	0.067	−2.205**
Associations	11.900	15.667	−1.637	0.304	0.192	−1.796*
Users	0.900	0.556	−0.182	0.008	0.005	−0.044
National standard setters	2.400	14.000	−3.700***	0.042	0.176	−3.594***
Stock exchanges	2.800	3.000	−0.083	0.068	0.026	−2.206**
Governments	0.700	1.778	−1.826*	0.007	0.018	−1.899*
Individuals	1.700	0.778	0.000	0.016	0.006	−0.221
Academics	1.100	0.889	−0.313	0.016	0.007	−0.927
Other interested parties	0.800	1.000	−0.684	0.006	0.008	−0.682
Consultants	0.200	0.222	−0.115	0.001	0.002	−0.114
Actuaries	0.600	0.778	−0.475	0.004	0.006	−0.566
Total	58.200	96.222	−1.757*			
Panel B: Measurement, recognition, and disclosure proposals						
Number of proposals	**34**	**30**		**34**	**30**	
Preparers	28.206	45.567	−2.294**	0.388	0.396	−0.108
Individual corporate preparers	15.176	16.300	−0.249	0.212	0.144	−2.684***
Associations of corporate preparers	4.971	10.000	−3.204***	0.077	0.093	−0.962
Individual financial preparers	4.588	10.800	−3.598***	0.054	0.089	−3.414***
Associations of financial preparers	3.471	8.467	−2.944***	0.046	0.070	−2.239**
Non-preparers	37.765	57.567	−3.304***	0.612	0.604	−0.108
Accounting profession	22.824	24.267	−0.451	0.386	0.283	−3.552***
Audit firms	5.647	6.267	−1.355	0.092	0.077	−1.910*
Associations	17.176	18.000	−0.458	0.294	0.205	−3.464***
Users	2.324	1.867	−1.914*	0.033	0.014	−3.307***
National standard setters	4.559	15.033	−6.459***	0.079	0.173	−5.651***
Stock exchanges	1.559	2.567	−1.797*	0.020	0.023	−1.107
Governments	0.588	1.767	−3.037***	0.009	0.016	−2.324**
Individuals	2.029	4.267	−1.714*	0.028	0.032	−0.574
Academics	1.647	2.633	−0.264	0.026	0.019	−0.875

(continued)

Table 5.2 (continued)

Constituent party	Mean IASC	Mean IASB	Z-value	Proportion IASC	Proportion IASB	Z-value
Other interested parties	2.235	5.167	−2.511**	0.031	0.045	−1.762*
Consultants	0.647	2.633	−2.808***	0.009	0.020	−2.549**
Actuaries	1.588	2.533	−1.278	0.022	0.024	−0.579
Total	65.971	103.133	−3.034***			
Panel C: Measurement, recognition, and disclosure proposals excluding convergence projects						
Number of proposals	**34**	**19**		**34**	**19**	
Preparers	28.206	39.368	−0.677	0.388	0.366	−0.742
Individual corporate preparers	15.176	15.526	−0.836	0.212	0.139	−2.439**
Associations of corporate preparers	4.971	8.421	−1.764*	0.077	0.090	−0.603
Individual financial preparers	4.588	8.579	−2.050**	0.054	0.075	−2.053**
Associations of financial preparers	3.471	6.842	−1.414	0.046	0.062	-1.192
Non-preparers	37.765	50.789	−1.642*	0.612	0.634	−0.742
Accounting profession	22.824	21.947	−0.539	0.386	0.310	−2.012**
Audit firms	5.647	5.947	−0.685	0.092	0.089	−0.427
Associations	17.176	16.000	−0.780	0.294	0.221	−2.087**
Users	2.324	1.579	−2.436**	0.033	0.011	−3.122***
National standard setters	4.559	13.684	−5.434***	0.079	0.190	−4.841***
Stock exchanges	1.559	2.211	−0.822	0.020	0.023	−0.677
Governments	0.588	1.105	−1.491	0.009	0.012	−1.176
Individuals	2.029	3.158	−0.019	0.028	0.025	−0.607
Academics	1.647	1.632	−1.045	0.026	0.013	−1.723*
Other interested parties	2.235	5.474	−2.135**	0.031	0.051	−1.889*
Consultants	0.647	2.737	−1.935*	0.009	0.021	−2.107**
Actuaries	1.588	2.737	−1.256	0.022	0.030	−0.863
Total	65.971	90.158	−1.391			

Notes This table reports the average number of comment letters sent to the IASC and IASB by constituent party and categorized by attribute of the standard. The z-value indicates the Mann–Whitney U test to identify the significance in the evolution in the number of comment letters sent by each constituent party to the IASC and IASB. ***, **, * denote significance at the 1, 5, and 10 % levels, respectively

academics, and the actuaries are the only three groups of which the formal participation behavior did not change significantly between the two time frames with regard to non financial instruments-related proposals. With regard to the users of financial information, the average number of comment letters written in response to requests for comment of the international accounting standard setter even decreased significantly. Comparing panel A with panel B show that after the reform of the standard setter, financial preparers' interests in non financial instruments-related proposals increased, although financial preparers write on average more comment letters to financial instruments-related issues compared to other issues for which responses were solicited. Both panels (A and B) show that especially preparers' participation through associations became more common after the reform. Most of the non-preparers group write fewer comment letters in response to financial instruments-related proposals than in response to non financial instruments-related proposals.

If we exclude convergence issues from the population of non financial instruments-related proposals, we observe that only individual financial preparers, associations of corporate preparers, national standard setters and consultants increased their participation significantly after the reform of the standard setter (panel C, Table 5.2). These data show that the increase in the participation with regard to non financial instruments-related proposals are to a large extent driven by the proposals in the frame of the convergence project on the agenda of the standard setter.

So with regard to the question, whether or not stakeholder diversity increased after the reform of the standard setter in comparison to before the reform, our answer differs according to the topic on the agenda of the standard setter. The number of comment letters received by the standard setter in relation to measurement, recognition and disclosure issues not related to financial-instruments proposals increased significantly after the reform and we also notice an increase in diversity of stakeholder representation with regard to these issues. When measurement, recognition, and disclosure topics not related to financial instruments are under discussion, 60 % of the comment letters stem from non-preparers. Half of these letters come from the accounting profession and about 30 % of them are written by national standard setters. Although the accounting profession is no longer technically represented on the standard setting board due to the change from the representative model to the technical independent model, the accounting profession did not increase significantly their formal participation efforts to counterbalance this loss of direct influence over the standard setting process. We have to note that convergence proposals are to a large extent the driver of this increase in constituents' participation with regard to non financial instruments-related issues. If we focus on participation in response to financial instruments-related issues, we notice a decrease in diversity as after the reform 50 % of the comment letters sent to the standard setter now originate from preparers, in contrast to 40 % before the reform of the standard setter. In the category of the non-preparers again the accounting profession and the national standard setters write the bulk of the comment letters.

5.4.2 Geographic Diversity in Constituents' Participation in International Accounting Standard Setting

For the analysis of the geographic distribution of constituents with regard to formal participation in international accounting standard setting we divide the respondents into international organizations (including large international audit firms), respondents from code law countries and respondents from common law countries. We use the variable *legal origin* as a starting point in the geographic analysis; later in this chapter, we focus on other geographical characteristics. For both periods, we assigned about 84 % of all comment letters to a single country. We further observe a strong increase from the earlier to the later period in the number of countries from which the international standard setter receives at least one comment letter. The IASC received in the first period (1995–2001) comment letters from 58 individual countries, while the IASB received in the second period (2001–2007) submissions from 81 individual countries. The increase in the number of countries participating post-reform, compared to before the reform, is mainly due to the participation of countries in Central America and South America, the former USSR and a limited number of African and Asian countries with a code law background. African and Asian countries participating before as well as after the reform of the standard setter all have a common law background (they are all commonwealth countries).

If we consider constituents' participation from a geographic perspective, panel A of Table 5.3 highlights that common law countries increase their lobbying intensity significantly for financial instruments. Within this group, especially preparers and non-preparers from the EU and Oceania devote more efforts in writing comment letters to the IASB. Probably this was the most expected result of the approval of the EU Regulation that required EU listed groups on EU stock exchanges to comply with IFRS, than of the reform of the standard setter. Further, we notice that preparers from code law countries do not participate more after the reform of the IASB, except countries from Eastern Europe that do not belong to the EU. In contrast, non-preparers from code law country groups lobby more.

With regard to financial instruments-related topics, we conclude that the geographic diversity of the participants taking into account whether they originate from a code law versus a common law background is more balanced, than in the case of non financial instruments-related issues. We further find a significant increase in participation to non financial instruments-related proposals after the reform of the standard setter from constituents from different parts of the world (Table 5.3, panel B and C). However, Table 5.3 highlights that most comment letters on these proposals originate from constituents with common law background, especially in the group of non-preparers. We hence conclude that in terms of a country's legal origin, the geographic distribution of participants is more balanced when financial instruments-related proposals are on the agenda of the standard setter compared to non financial instruments-related proposals.

If we split the population of respondents according to the different cultural regions from which they originate, we notice that the English speaking countries, on an average double their participation effort in terms of average number of comment letters sent per proposal (see Table 5.4). Specifically, almost all comment letters from English speaking countries stem from G4+1 countries. In addition, many constituents from Western European countries take part in the due process of standard setting. Potential explanations for the dominance of English speaking countries in the process of standard setting are the constituents'

Table 5.3 Geographic distribution of the lobby intensity to IASC and IASB based on legal origin and categorized by attribute of the standard

Legal origin	Preparers			Non-preparers		
	Mean IASC	Mean IASB	Z-value	Mean IASC	Mean IASB	Z-value
Panel A: Financial instruments						
Number of proposals	**10**	**9**		**10**	**9**	
Code law	17.600	25.444	−1.354	8.100	13.333	−2.344**
Africa	0.000	0.111	−1.054	0.000	0.778	−3.008***
Asia	1.100	1.778	−0.912	1.800	2.444	−1.807*
EU + EFTA	16.400	23.000	−1.394	6.300	9.000	−1.859*
Other Europe	0.000	0.556	−2.297**	0.000	0.444	−1.930*
Central America	0.000	0.000	0.000	0.000	0.222	−1.534
South America	0.000	0.000	0.000	0.000	0.333	−1.936*
Oceania	0.100	0.000	−0.949	0.000	0.111	−1.054
Common law	10.900	21.222	−1.843*	11.200	19.111	−1.964*
Africa	0.200	0.778	−2.063**	1.300	0.556	−1.980*
Asia	1.000	0.111	−1.145	1.100	3.778	−3.028***
EU	4.000	12.444	−2.179**	2.900	7.111	−2.892***
North America	3.900	3.111	−0.373	3.800	2.556	−0.501
Oceania	1.800	4.778	−2.171**	2.100	5.111	−2.199**
Panel B: Measurement, recognition, and disclosure proposals						
Number of proposals	**34**	**30**		**34**	**30**	
Code law	15.088	18.000	−1.198	11.118	16.967	−3.833***
Africa	0.000	0.067	−1.065	0.176	0.267	−0.357
Asia	0.353	1.367	−3.376***	2.088	3.500	−3.541***
EU + EFTA	14.735	15.667	−0.761	8.206	11.933	−3.315**
Other Europe	0.000	0.133	−2.182**	0.088	0.633	−4.326***
Central America	0.000	0.033	−1.065	0.206	0.300	−0.861
South America	0.000	0.733	−1.517	0.294	0.267	−0.268
Oceania	0.000	0.000	0.000	0.059	0.067	−0.128
Common law	11.353	24.600	−3.414***	18.088	28.500	−2.748***
Africa	0.882	1.300	−1.047	1.912	1.967	−0.097
Asia	0.176	0.233	−2.087**	2.853	4.233	−2.888***
EU	5.206	13.000	−3.998***	4.294	10.600	−5.068***
North America	2.794	6.833	−0.163	5.794	5.933	−1.801*
Oceania	2.294	3.233	−0.475	3.235	5.767	−3.363***
Panel C: Measurement, recognition, and disclosure proposals excluding convergence projects						
Number of proposals	**34**	**19**		**34**	**19**	
Code law	15.088	14.737	−0.019	11.118	14.895	−2.054**
Africa	0.000	0.000		0.176	0.368	−0.894
Asia	0.353	1.632	−3.161***	2.088	2.947	−2.140**
EU + EFTA	14.735	12.789	−0.399	8.206	10.684	−1.455
Other Europe	0.000	0.158	−2.363**	0.088	0.421	−2.838***
Central America	0.000	0.000		0.206	0.263	−0.473
South America	0.000	0.158	−1.338	0.294	0.158	−0.919

(continued)

Table 5.3 (continued)

Legal origin	Preparers			Non-preparers		
	Mean IASC	Mean IASB	Z-value	Mean IASC	Mean IASB	Z-value
Oceania	0.000	0.000		0.059	0.053	−0.093
Common law	11.353	22.316	−1.691*	18.088	24.316	−1.022
Africa	0.882	0.789	−0.655	1.912	1.632	−1.029
Asia	0.176	0.158	−1.088	2.853	3.474	−1.544
EU	5.206	11.105	−2.346**	4.294	9.211	−3.846***
North America	2.794	7.211	−1.137	5.794	5.000	−2.165**
Oceania	2.294	3.053	−0.219	3.235	5.000	−2.023**

Notes This table reports the average number of comment letters sent to the IASC and IASB by legal origin and categorized by attribute of the standard. The z-value indicates the Mann–Whitney U test to identify the significance in the evolution in the number of comment letters sent by each legal origin to the IASC and the IASB. ***, **, * denote significance at the 1, 5, and 10 % levels, respectively

familiarity with private accounting standard setting (most of the constituents are from G4+1 countries) and the familiarity with the language employed (Standish 2003).

If we focus on those geographical differences and classify the writers of the comment letters according to the per capita GDP in their country or the development status of their domestic stock market, we observe that most comment letters originate from countries with a high GDP per capita and more developed stock markets. Although more constituents from emerging or developing countries are involved in the formal participation in accounting standard setting after the reform of the standard setter, the number of comment letters written by these countries is still limited. This implies that the IASB needs to consider other mechanisms to receive input from constituents of those economies with regard to the economic consequences of their proposals in these countries. Up until the last revision of the objectives of the IASB on 26th of January 2010, it was clearly stated that the IASB in developing standards should take into account the special needs of emerging economies. However, in the last revision of the objectives of the standard setter, the word "emerging economies" was removed from the objectives and replaced by the words "types of entities in diverse economic settings". One could wonder whether this change in the wording of the objectives implies less attention for the needs of the emerging economies.

In order to refine this geographic analysis to an individual country-level, we zoom in on those countries which can be classified as frequent lobbyers. We classify a country as frequent lobbyer, when preparers as well as non-preparers from a country have responded to at least half of the proposals issued by the standard setter. Following these criteria, we consider eight countries as frequent lobbyers, namely Australia, France, Germany, South Africa, Switzerland, the Netherlands, the UK and the USA. Table 5.5 reveals that within this group of

Table 5.4 Geographic distribution of the lobby intensity to IASC and IASB based on cultural region, capital market development and GDP, and categorized by attribute of the standard

Country characteristic	Preparers			Non-preparers		
	Mean IASC	Mean IASB	Z-value	Means IASC	Mean IASB	Z-value
Panel A: Financial instruments						
Number of proposals	**10**	**9**		**10**	**9**	
Cultural region						
African	0.200	0.778	−2.063**	1.300	1.333	−0.050
English speaking	9.700	20.333	−1.967**	9.000	16.000	−2.008**
Far East	2.200	1.889	−0.563	2.600	5.111	−2.573**
Latin America	0.000	0.000	0.000	0.000	0.556	−2.673***
Mediterranean	0.000	0.222	−1.534	0.100	0.000	−0.949
Western Europe	16.400	22.667	−1.310	6.300	8.556	−1.783*
Eastern Europe	0.000	0.778	−3.008***	0.000	0.889	−2.291**
Capital market development						
Developing markets	0.000	0.667	−1.928*	0.600	2.778	−2.997***
Emerging markets	0.400	1.778	−2.594***	1.400	3.778	−2.371**
Developed markets	28.100	44.222	−1.512	17.300	25.889	−1.722*
Per capita GDP						
Low	0.200	0.111	−0.516	0.700	2.444	−2.464**
Medium	0.200	1.444	−2.679***	1.200	2.667	−2.214**
High	28.100	45.111	−1.594	17.400	27.333	−1.886*
Panel B: Measurement, recognition, and disclosure proposals						
Number of proposals	**34**	**30**		**34**	**30**	
Cultural region						
African	0.882	1.367	−1.096	2.059	2.233	−0.172
English speaking	10.294	23.067	−3.442***	13.824	22.800	−2.870***
Far East	0.500	1.567	−3.857***	3.971	7.000	−4.025***
Latin America	0.000	0.767	−1.517	0.588	0.667	−0.522
Mediterranean	0.029	0.000	−0.939	0.471	0.200	−1.724*
Western Europe	14.735	15.600	−0.741	7.706	11.467	−3.473***
Eastern Europe	0.000	0.233	−2.961***	0.588	1.100	−2.174**
Capital market development						
Developing markets	0.059	0.700	−2.344**	2.971	2.300	−1.272
Emerging markets	0.882	2.400	−2.166**	2.676	5.733	−4.333***
Developed markets	25.500	39.500	−2.106**	23.559	37.433	−3.238***
Per capita GDP						
Low	0.029	0.267	−1.547	2.176	2.333	−0.528
Medium	0.882	2.533	−2.100**	2.824	3.733	−1.773*
High	25.529	39.800	−2.127**	24.206	39.400	−3.528***

(continued)

Table 5.4 (continued)

Country characteristic	Preparers			Non-preparers		
	Mean IASC	Mean IASB	Z-value	Means IASC	Mean IASB	Z-value
Panel C: Measurement, recognition, and disclosure proposals excluding convergence projects						
Number of proposals	**34**	**19**		**34**	**19**	
Cultural region						
African	0.882	0.789	−0.655	2.059	2.000	−0.485
English speaking	10.294	21.368	−1.738*	13.824	19.632	−1.468
Far East	0.500	1.737	−3.167***	3.971	5.842	−2.488**
Latin America	0.000	0.158	−1.338	0.588	0.474	−0.326
Mediterranean	0.029	0.000	−0.748	0.471	0.158	−1.874*
Western Europe	14.735	12.737	−0.418	7.706	10.211	−1.700*
Eastern Europe	0.000	0.263	−3.113***	0.588	0.895	−0.638
Capital market development						
Developing markets	0.059	0.211	−0.648	2.971	2.000	−0.983
Emerging markets	0.882	1.579	−0.773	2.676	4.474	−2.731***
Developed markets	25.500	35.263	−0.529	23.559	32.737	−1.420
Per capita GDP						
Low	0.029	0.105	−1.135	2.176	1.947	−0.294
Medium	0.882	1.684	−0.703	2.824	2.947	−0.481
High	25.529	35.263	−0.529	24.206	34.316	−1.764

Notes This table reports the average number of comment letters sent to the IASC and IASB by cultural region, capital market development and GDP. The z-value indicates the Mann–Whitney U test to identify the significance in the evolution in the number of comment letters sent by group of countries based on culture, capital market development and GDP to the IASC and the IASB. ***, **, * denote significance at the 1, 5, and 10 % levels, respectively

frequent lobbyers constituents in the UK increased their participation effort most substantially. As mentioned before, this increase is probably more driven by the fact that the status of IFRS changed in the UK from voluntary to mandatory. We observe that after the UK, German constituents write the most comment letters with regard to financial instruments-related issues, followed by Switzerland and France. With regard to measurement, recognition, and disclosure issues not related to financial instruments, the UK and the US constituents write on average the most comment letters if we consider the preparers followed by preparers from Switzerland, Germany, and France. If we focus on the non-preparers, the three former G4+1 countries namely the UK, the USA, and Australia write most of the comment letters.

So again we notice differences according to the topic on the agenda of the standard setter. Non financial instruments-related issues generate most comments from G4+1 members, whereas in case of financial instruments, France, Germany, and Switzerland are as active as the constituents from G4+1 countries, at least in the preparers group.

Table 5.5 Lobby intensity of the main countries involved in comment letter writing to IASC and IASB categorized by the attribute of the standard

Country	Preparers			Non-preparers		
	Mean IASC	Mean IASB	Z-value	Mean IASC	Mean IASB	Z-value
Panel A: Financial instruments						
Number of proposals	**10**	**9**		**10**	**9**	
Australia	1.800	3.667	−1.708*	1.500	2.778	−1.921*
France	4.300	4.333	−1.487	1.000	1.000	0.000
Germany	2.300	7.222	−1.816*	1.600	2.444	−2.112**
South Africa	0.200	0.778	−2.063*	0.900	0.333	−2.489**
Switzerland	4.700	4.111	−0.536	0.300	0.222	−0.374
The Netherlands	3.200	1.000	−0.566	1.200	1.000	−1.668
UK	3.700	11.556	−2.229**	2.600	6.111	−2.600**
USA	3.600	3.111	−0.373	2.400	1.333	−0.673
Panel B: Measurement, recognition, and disclosure proposals						
Number of proposals	**34**	**30**		**34**	**30**	
Australia	2.265	2.933	−0.055	2.412	4.167	−3.106***
France	2.118	3.400	−2.368**	1.088	1.233	−0.811
Germany	2.471	3.600	−1.236	1.500	2.800	−3.917***
South Africa	0.853	1.300	−1.135	0.882	1.067	−0.636
Switzerland	5.294	4.867	−0.664	0.882	0.633	−1.476
The Netherlands	2.588	1.033	−1.411	0.912	1.067	−1.672*
UK	4.912	12.367	−4.086***	4.088	9.467	−4.669***
USA	2.324	6.000	−0.041	4.059	3.967	−2.422**
Panel C: Measurement, recognition, and disclosure proposals excluding convergence projects						
Number of proposals	**34**	**19**		**34**	**19**	
Australia	2.265	2.947	−0.381	2.412	3.737	−2.220**
France	2.118	2.632	−0.946	1.088	0.947	−0.622
Germany	2.471	3.053	−0.285	1.500	2.737	−3.090***
South Africa	0.853	0.789	−0.586	0.882	0.895	−0.022
Switzerland	5.294	4.158	−1.158	0.882	0.526	−1.860*
The Netherlands	2.588	0.947	−1.733*	0.912	1.105	−1.769*
UK	4.912	10.526	−2.429**	4.088	8.263	−3.553***
USA	2.324	6.842	−0.822	4.059	3.263	−2.646***

Notes This table reports the average number of comment letters sent to the IASC and IASB from the countries that lobby frequently. The z-value indicates the Mann–Whitney U test to identify the significance in the evolution in the number of comment letters sent by each country to the IASC and the IASB. ***, **, * denote significance at the 1, 5, and 10 % levels, respectively

5.5 Conclusion

As a private organization, legitimacy is a key issue for the IASB's acceptance as global standard setter. In this respect, participation of a diversity of constituents in a process of standard setting is of critical importance. Based on an analysis of 7,442 comment letters sent to the international accounting standard setter over the period 1995–2007, we observe an increase in the number of constituents that participate formally in the international accounting standard setting process.

Overall, the data indicate that preparers write the majority of comment letters to the IASB and indirect participation of preparers through their associations increased after the reform of the standard setter. A stakeholder group which decreased its formal participation are the users, whereas the participation of the accounting profession, the academics, and the actuaries did not change over time. A stakeholder group which became very active in formal participation after the reform are the national accounting standard setters. This does not come as a surprise since the national standard setters handed-over the standard setting authority for listed companies to the IASB.

Our conclusions with regard to the evolution of constituent participation over time differ according to the topic on the agenda of the standard setter and according to the type of constituent, being a preparer or non-preparer. We notice that constituents' participation over time increased most significantly for measurement, recognition, and disclosure issues that do not contain financial instruments-related issues. However, the geographic diversity is more biased for these proposals compared to financial instruments, since most of the comment letters stem from members of the former G4+1 and in particular from Australia, the UK and the US. Especially the UK increased its formal participation activities drastically after the reform of the IASC into the IASB. So we notice a biased geographic diversity with regard to non financial instruments-related issues.

If we consider financial instruments-related topics, the data reveal that especially in case of the preparers next to the UK, the Swiss, the Germans, and the French preparers wrote a lot of comment letters. Constituents from countries with developed markets and high GDP per capita are still the overwhelming majority of the participants. In relation to the critics expressed with regard to constituents' participation in the international accounting standard setting process at the time of the financial crisis, we notice that especially with regard to financial instruments-related issues, the geographic representation of constituents, especially of preparers, is the most diverse of all actions undertaken by constituents in response to the proposals of the standard setter. The critics, with regard to stakeholder representation are more applicable to non financial instruments-related proposals, were the responses which are dominated by the former G4+1 countries.

Around the time of the reform of the standard setter many elements were altered (change in due process, change from representative body to an independent standard setting body) or decisions were taken (change from voluntary IAS compliance to mandatory IAS compliance in a number of countries). As a result it is difficult to exactly pinpoint the trigger for the observed change in constituents' participation behavior since these observed changes can be a result of a number of elements at work at the same time. The fact that from 2005 onward the UK companies have to comply on a mandatory basis, is probably the largest trigger for this increase. This increase has as a result that the views of the G4+1 constituents are well represented among responses in reply to recognition, measurement, and disclosure issues not related to financial instruments.

Appendix: Documents issued for comment by the IASC and the IASB

No	Topic	FI	MR	CVG	Date	Number of comment letters
Documents issued for comments by the IASB						
1	ED: Group cash-settled share-based payment transactions (proposed amendments to IFRS 2 share-based payment and IFRIC 11 IFRS 2—group and treasury share transactions)		X		Dec. 2007	44
2	ED: Amendments to IFRS 1 first-time adoption of international financial reporting standards and IAS 27 consolidated and separate financial statements		X		Dec. 2007	64
3	ED of proposed amendments to IAS 39 financial instruments: Recognition and measurement (exposures qualifying for hedge accounting)	X			Sep. 2007	75
4	ED 9: Joint arrangements		X	X	Sep. 2007	115
5	Discussion paper: Preliminary views on insurance contracts		X	X	May 2007	162
6	ED of a proposed IFRS for small- and medium-sized entities				Feb. 2007	162
7	ED state-controlled entities and the definition of a related party: Proposed amendments to IAS 24		X		Feb. 2007	72
8	ED: Amendments to IFRS's first-time adoption of international financial reporting standards cost of an investment in a subsidiary		X		Jan. 2007	49
9	Discussion paper: Fair value measurement		X	X	Nov. 2006	136
10	Discussion paper: Preliminary views on an improved conceptual framework for financial reporting		X	X	July 2006	179
11	Exposure draft of proposed amendments to IAS 32 financial instruments: Presentation and IAS 1 presentation of financial statements: Financial instruments puttable at fair value and obligations arising on litigation	X			June 2006	88
12	Proposed amendments to IAS 23 borrowing costs		X	X	August 2006	87
13	Proposed amendments to IAS 1 presentation of financial statements		X	X	July 2006	129

(continued)

(continued)

No	Topic	FI	MR	CVG	Date	Number of comment letters
14	Proposed amendments to IFRS 2—vesting conditions and cancellations		X		May 2006	56
15	Discussion paper: Measurement bases for financial reporting—measurement on initial recognition		X		March 2006	86
16	Discussion paper: Management commentary		X		Feb. 2006	112
17	ED 8 operating segments		X	X	Feb. 2006	105
18	Proposed amendments to IAS 27 Consolidated and separate financial statements		X	X	Nov. 2005	94
19	Proposed amendments to IFRS 3 business combinations		X	X	Oct. 2005	164
20	Draft Technical Correction (DTC) 1 Proposed amendments to IAS 21 the effects of changes in foreign exchange rates—net investment in a foreign operation		X		Oct. 2005	33
21	Proposed amendments to IAS 37 provisions contingent liabilities and contingent assets and IAS 19 employee benefits		X		Oct. 2005	123
22	Draft memorandum of understanding on the role of accounting standard-setters and their relationships with the IASB				August 2005	66
23	IFRS 6 exploration for and evaluation of mineral resources and, as a consequence, an amendment to IFRS's first-time adoption of international financial reporting standards		X		June 2005	24
24	Staff questionnaire on possible modifications of the recognition and measurement principles in international financial reporting standards (IFRSs) for use in IASB standards for small and medium-sized entities (SMEs)				June 2005	98
25	ED 7 financial instruments: Disclosures	X			Oct. 2004	104
26	Proposed amendments to IAS 39 transition and initial recognition of financial assets and financial liabilities	X			Oct. 2004	37
27	Proposed amendments to IAS 39 cash flow hedge accounting of forecast intragroup transactions	X			Oct. 2004	57
28	Proposed amendments to IAS 39 financial guarantee contracts and credit insurance	X			Oct. 2004	61
29	Discussion paper: Preliminary views on accounting standards for small- and medium-sized entities				Oct. 2004	120

(continued)

(continued)

No	Topic	FI	MR	CVG	Date	Number of comment letters
30	Proposed amendments to IFRS 3 business combinations–combinations by contract alone or involving mutual entities		X		August 2004	77
31	Proposed amendments to IAS 19 employee benefits-actuarial gains and losses, group plans and disclosures		X		August 2004	92
32	Proposed amendments to IAS 39 financial instruments: Recognition and measurement: The fair value option		X		July 2004	116
33	IASB deliberative process				June 2004	50
34	ED 6 exploration for and evaluation of mineral resources		X		May 2004	72
35	ED fair value hedge accounting for a portfolio hedge of interest rate risk	X			Dec. 2003	122
36	ED 4 disposal of non-current assets and presentation of discontinued operations		X	X	Dec. 2003	85
37	ED 5 insurance contracts		X		Dec. 2003	134
38	ED 3 business combinations		X	X	Nov. 2003	128
39	Amendments to IAS 32 financial instruments: Disclosure and presentation and IAS 39 financial instruments: Recognition and measurement	X			Sep. 2003	207
40	ED 2 share-based payment		X		Sep. 2003	242
41	Improvements to IAS		X		April 2003	159
42	ED 1 first-time application of international financial reporting standards		X		Feb. 2003	83
43	IAS 19 employee benefits—the asset ceiling		X		April 2002	34
44	Preface to international financial reporting standards				April 2002	77
45	Discussion paper: Accounting for share-based payment (second invitation)		X		Dec. 2001	164
	Total					**4,532**
46	Proposed IAS 39 implementation guidance questions and answers (batch 6)	X			Nov. 2001	23
47	Issue papers—extractive industries		X		June 2001	52
48	Draft standard and basis for conclusions—financial instruments and similar items	X			June 2001	122
49	Proposed IAS 39 implementation guidance questions and answers (batch 5)	X			April 2001	19
50	Proposed IAS 39 implementation guidance questions and answers (batch 4)	X			Nov. 2000	20
51	Discussion paper: Accounting for share-based payment		X		Oct. 2000	29
52	ED 68 income tax consequences of dividends (limited revisions of IAS 12)		X		Sep. 2000	33

(continued)

(continued)

No	Topic	FI	MR	CVG	Date	Number of comment letters
53	Proposed IAS 39—implementation guidance questions and answers (batch 3)	X			Sep. 2000	14
54	ED 67 employee benefits (limited revision of IAS 19)		X		Sep. 2000	39
55	ED 66 financial instruments: Recognition and measurement and other related standards (limited revision of IAS 39)	X			Sep. 2000	42
56	Discussion paper: Leases: Implementation of a new approach		X		July 2000	29
57	G4+1 special report: Reporting interests in joint ventures and similar arrangements		X		July 2000	9
58	Proposed IAS 39 implementation guidance questions and answers (batch 2)	X			July 2000	19
59	Proposed IAS 39 implementation guidance questions and answers (batch 1)	X			July 2000	31
60	Issues paper: Insurance		X		May 2000	138
61	Discussion paper: Accounting for non-reciprocal transfers, excluding contributions by owners		X		May 2000	5
62	ED 65 agriculture		X		Jan. 2000	63
63	Discussion paper: Reporting financial performance		X		Dec. 1999	54
64	Discussion paper: Shaping the IASC for the future				Dec. 1999	85
65	ED 64 investment property		X		Oct. 1999	122
66	Discussion paper: Recommendations for achieving convergence on the methods of accounting for business combinations		X		March 1999	35
67	ED 63 events after balance sheet date		X		Feb. 1999	54
68	ED 62 financial instruments: Recognition and measurement	X			Sep. 1998	119
69	ED 61 business combinations		X		Nov. 1997	24
70	ED 60 intangible assets		X		Nov. 1997	99
71	ED 59 provisions, contingent liabilities and contingent assets		X		Nov. 1997	100
72	ED 58 discontinuing operations		X		Nov. 1997	78
73	ED 57 interim reporting		X		Oct. 1997	82
74	ED 55 impairment of assets		X		August 1997	92
75	ED 56 leases		X		July 1997	105
76	DSOP discontinuing operations		X		July 1997	58
77	Discussion paper: Accounting for financial assets and financial liabilities	X			July 1997	173
78	DSOP agriculture		X		April 1997	43
79	ED 54 employee benefits		X		Jan. 1997	141
80	DSOP provisions and contingencies		X		Jan. 1997	80
81	DSOP interim reporting		X		Nov. 1996	62

(continued)

(continued)

No	Topic	FI	MR	CVG	Date	Number of comment letters
82	ED 53 presentation of financial statements		X		Oct. 1996	88
83	ED 52 earnings per share		X		June 1996	77
84	ED 51 reporting financial information by segment		X		June 1996	79
85	Issues paper: Retirement benefits—other employee benefits		X		June 1996	57
86	Issues paper: Interim financial reporting		X		June 1996	40
87	ED 33 income taxes		X		March 1996	45
88	ED 50 intangible assets (goodwill and R&D)		X		Nov. 1995	88
89	DSOP presentation of financial statements		X		June 1995	62
90	ED 49 income taxes (revision of ED 33)		X		May 1995	81
	Total					**2,910**

Notes This table presents the accounting proposals issued by the IASC (1995–2001) and the IASB (2001–2007). The table indicates for each proposal whether the proposal is considered as a financial instrument proposal (FI), a recognition and measurement proposal (MR), or a convergence proposal (CVG)

References

Amershi, A., Demski, J., & Wolfson, M. (1982). Strategic behaviour and regulation research in accounting. *Journal of Accounting and Public Policy, 1*(1), 19–32.

Bengsston, E. (2011). Repoliticalization of accounting standard setting-the FASB, the EU and the global financial crisis. *Critical Perspectives on Accounting, 22*(6), 567–580.

Bhimani, A. (2008). The role of a crisis in reshaping the role of accounting. *Journal of Accounting and Public Policy, 27*, 444–454.

Botzem, S., & Quack, S. (2009). (No) limits to Anglo-American accounting? reconstructing the history of the international accounting standards committee: A review article. *Accounting, Organizations and Society, 34*, 988–998.

Burlaud, A., & Colasse, B. (2011). International accounting standardisation: Is politics back? *Accounting in Europe, 8*(1), 23–47.

Cairns, D. (1997). The future shape of harmonization: a reply, *The European Accounting Review, 6*(2), 305–348.

Camfferman, K., & Zeff, S. (2007). *Financial reporting and global capital markets: A history of the international Accounting Standards Committee 1973–2000*. Oxford: Oxford University Press.

Colson, R., Benston, G., Carmichael, D., Christensen, T., Jamal, K., Moehrle, S., et al. (2009). Response to FAF exposure draft, 'proposed changes to oversight, structure, and operations of the FAF, FASB, and GASB'. *Journal of Accounting and Public Policy, 28*(1), 51–57.

Dyckman, T. (1988). Credibility and the formulation of accounting standards under the financial accounting standards board. *Journal of Accounting Literature, 7*, 1–30.

Elbannen, M., & McKinley, W. (2006). A theory of the corporate decision to resist FASB standards. *Accounting, Organizations and Society, 37*(7), 601–622.

Emenyony, E., & Gray, S. (1996). International accounting harmonization and the major developed stock market countries: An empirical study. *The International Journal of Accounting, 31*(3), 269–279.

Financial Crisis Advisory Group (FCAG). (2009). *Report of the financial crisis advisory group*, consulted at 26 June 2012 at http://www.ifrs.org/nr/rdonlyres/2d2862cc-befc-4a1e-8ddc-f159b78c2aa6/0/fcagreportjuly2009.pdf.

Financial Stability Forum. (2009). *Report of the financial stability forum on addressing procyclicality of the financial system*. http://www.fsforum.org/publications/r_0904a.pdf. Accessed June 2010.

Flower, J. (1997). The future shape of harmonization: The EU versus the IASC versus the SEC. *The European Accounting Review, 6*(2), 281–304.

Fulbier, R., Hitz, J., & Sellhorn, T. (2009). Relevance of academic research and researcher's role in the IASB's financial reporting standard setting. *Abacus, 45*(5), 455–492.

G20. (2009). *Declaration on strengthening the financial system.* London 2 April 2009. http://www.g20.org/Documents/Fin_Deps_Fin_Reg_Annex020409-1615final.pdf. Accessed Dec 2010.

Georgiou, G. (2002). Corporate non-participation in the ASB standard-setting process. *European Accounting Review, 11*(4), 699–722.

Georgiou, G. (2004). Corporate lobbying on accounting standards methods, timing and perceived effectiveness. *Abacus, 40*(2), 219–237.

Georgiou, G. (2005). Investigating corporate management lobbying in the UK accounting standard-setting process: A multi-issue/multi-period approach. *Abacus, 41*(3), 323–347.

Guenther, D., & Hussein, A. (1995). Accounting standards and national tax laws: The IASC and the ban on LIFO. *Journal of Accounting and Public Policy, 14*, 115–141.

High-Level Group of Financial Supervision in the EU. (2009). Report http://ec.europa.eu/internal_market/finances/docs/de_larosiere_report_en.pdf. Accessed June 2010.

Johnson, S., & Solomons, D. (1984). Institutional legitimacy and the FASB. *Journal of Accounting and Public Policy, 3*(3), 167–183.

Johnston, D., & Jones, D. (2006). How does accounting fit into a firm's political strategy? *Journal of Accounting and Public Policy, 25*, 195–228.

Jorissen, A., Lybaert, N., & van de Poel, K. (2006). Lobbying towards a global standard setter—do national characteristics matter? An analysis of the comment letters written to the IASB. In G. N. Gregiou & M. Gaber (Eds.), *International accounting standards, regulations and financial reporting*. Amsterdam: Elsevier.

Jorissen, A., Lybaert, N., Orens, R., & van der Tas, L. (2012). Formal participation in the IASB's due process of standard setting: A multi-period analysis. *The European Accounting Review*,. doi:10.1080/09638180.2010.522775.

Kenny, S., & Larson, R. K. (1993). Lobbying behavior and the development of international accounting standards: The case of IASC's joint venture project. *The European Accounting Review, 2*(3), 531–554.

Kenny, S. Y., & Larson, R. K. (1995). The development of international accounting standards: An analysis of constituent participation in standard-setting. *The International Journal of Accounting, 30*(4), 283–301.

Kirsch, R. (2006). *The international accounting standards committee: A political history*. London: IASC.

Knorr, L., & Ebbers, G. (2001). IASC. In D Ordelheide, & KPMG (Eds.), *Transnational Accounting* (2nd ed.). Palgrave, New York.

Königsgruber, R. (2010). A political economy of accounting standard setting. *Journal of Management and Governance*,. doi:10.1007/s10997-009-9101-1.

Larson, R. K. (1997). Corporate lobbying of the international accounting standards committee. *Journal of International Financial Management and Accounting, 8*(3), 175–203.

Larson, R. K. (2007). Constituent participation and the IASB's international financial reporting interpretations committee. *Accounting in Europe, 4*(1–2), 207–254.

Larson, R. K., & Brown, K. L. (2001). Lobbying of the international accounting standards committee: The case of construction contracts. *Advances in International Accounting, 14*, 47–73.

Leuz, C. (2010). Different approaches to corporate reporting regulation: How jurisdictions differ and why? *Accounting and Business Research, 40*(3), 229–256.

Licht, A., Goldschmidt, C., & Schwartz, S. (2007). Culture rules: The foundation of the rule of law and other norms of governance. *Journal of Comparative Economics, 35*(4), 659–688.

MacArthur, J. B. (1996). An investigation into the influence of cultural factors in the international lobbying of the international accounting standards committee: The case of E32, comparability of financial statements. *The International Journal of Accounting, 31*(2), 213–237.

MacArthur, J. B. (1999). The impact of cultural factors on the lobbying of the international accounting standards committee on E32: Comparability of financial statements: An extension of MacArthur to accounting member bodies. *Journal of International Accounting, Auditing and Taxation, 8*(2), 315–335.

MSCI (2012) *Index Definitions*. Available at http://www.msci.com/products/indices/tools/. Consulted on 10 May 2012.

Richardson, A., & Eberlein, B. (2011). Legitimating transnational standard-setting: The case of the international accounting standards board. *Journal of Business Ethics, 98*, 217–245.

Schwartz, S. (2004). Mapping and interpreting cultural differences around the world. In H. Vinken, J. Soeters, & P. Ester (Eds.), *Comparing cultures* (pp. 43–73). Leiden: Brill Academic Publishers.

Standish, P. (2003). Evaluating national capacity for direct participation in international accounting harmonization: France as a test case. *Abacus, 39*(2), 186–210.

Street, D. (2005). *Inside G4+1: The working group's role in the evolution of the international standard setting process*. London: Centre for Business Performance, ICAEW.

Street, D. (2006). The G4's role in the evolution of the international accounting standard setting process and partnership with the IASB. *Journal of international Accounting, Auditing and Taxation, 15*, 109–126.

Sutton, T. G. (1984). Lobbying of accounting standards-setting bodies in the UK and the USA: A Downsian analysis. *Accounting, Organizations and Society, 9*(1), 81–95.

Tandy, P., & Wilburn, N. (1992). Constitution participation in standard-setting: The FASB's first 100 statements. *Accounting Horizons, 6*(2), 47–58.

Wallace, O. (1990). Survival strategies of a global organization: The case of the IASC. *Accounting Horizons, 4*(2), 1–22.

Watts, R. L., & Zimmerman, J. L. (1978). Towards a positive theory of the determination of accounting standards. *The Accounting Review, 53*(1), 112–134.

Watts, R. L., & Zimmerman, J. L. (1986). *Positive accounting theory*. Englewood Cliffs: Prentice-Hall.

World Bank. (2006). *World development report 2007: Development and the next generation*. Washington, DC: The World Bank.

Wyatt, A. (1992). An era of harmonization. *Journal of International Management and Accounting, 4*(1), 63–80.

Zeff, S. (2012). The evolution of the IASC into the IASB and the challenges it faces. *The Accounting Review, 87*(3), 807–837.

Chapter 6
A Crisis of Identity? Juxtaposing Auditor Liability and the Value of Audit

Christopher Humphrey and Anna Samsonova

Abstract Despite attempts to find appropriate regulatory solutions, the issue of the civil liability of statutory auditors and the perceived need for some form of liability limitation continues to evoke divergent views and reactions. The analysis in this chapter indicates that such divergence is characteristic not just of the positions taken by various stakeholder groups but also of the differences in the nature and scope of auditor liability regimes adopted in individual countries. This chapter uses such analysis to suggest that the auditor liability debate and the continuing search for a regulatory solution has potentially hindered more focused consideration of the professional identity of auditors, their capacity to meet public expectations and the extent to which such capacity (and achievements) varies across countries and the differing cultural contexts in which auditors work.

6.1 Introduction

"The problem confronting the profession today is to see to it that the liability is 'clearly defined', and that the extent of damages bears some reasonable relationship to the gravity of the accountant's offense" (Carey 1965, p. 415). "If audit is to

---

This Chapter includes the paper originally titled "Re-Thinking Auditor Liability: the case of the European Union's Regulatory Reform" and discussed at the Fifth International Workshop on Accounting and Regulation in 2010.

C. Humphrey · A. Samsonova (✉)
Accounting and Finance Group, Manchester Business School, University of Manchester, Manchester, UK
e-mail: Anna.Samsonova@mbs.ac.uk

C. Humphrey
e-mail: Chris.Humphrey@mbs.ac.uk

R. Di Pietra et al. (eds.), *Accounting and Regulation*,
DOI: 10.1007/978-1-4614-8097-6_6,

be reformed to help to prevent another global financial crisis, there needs to be a real debate on the issue of auditor liability" (Davies, ACCA's Technical Head 2012).[1]

The above statements made nearly half a century apart lead to the intriguing observation that, despite many years of debate and a number of regulatory attempts to develop public policy solutions, the issue of the civil liability of statutory auditors still continues to be one of the most concerning for the accountancy profession. The profession has for many years pointed to the rise in litigation against auditors by both their clients and third parties that rely on the audit opinion for decision making (Talley 2006). Critics of the profession often represent such activity as a signal of the public's distrust in the ability of auditors to perform their duties properly, a perception that was significantly reinforced by notable corporate collapses such as Enron in 2001 and Lehmans in 2008 (Sikka 2008; Quick et al. 2008). The profession, however, routinely emphasises the inequitable, punitive and untenable nature of such a legal position, pointing to 'an epidemic of litigation' (Arthur Andersen & Co. et al. 1992, p. 1), an 'outrageous level of current claims' (ICAA 1995, p.11), and the possibility that 'many audit firms face the risk of Armageddon' (Ward 1999, p. 388).

Some record claims brought against auditors in recent years, such as the £2bn negligence claim made by the British insurer Equitable Life against Ernst and Young and the $1 bn lawsuit against KPMG for their audit of the failed US sub-prime lender New Century Financial[2] have been used by the profession to lend further momentum to the above arguments, with the Big 4 audit firms regularly stressing that the consequences of any such litigation threatened the audit profession's survival. Or as Martyn Jones, the UK's national audit technical partner for Deloitte, concluded 'Armageddon still exists', pointing, in the process, to the

[1] See *'A shared shield'*, ACCA website (www.accaglobal.com/en/member/cpd/auditing-assurance/planning/sharper-shield.html).

[2] In the first case, Ernst and Young and its former client services partner, Kevin McNamara, were initially held responsible in 2008 for more than 20 instances of a lack of professional competence during an audit of Equitable Life and fined £4.2 m. However, after the appeal, the initial ruling was overturned and the fine reduced to £500,000. In the second case, the creditors of the New Century, America's second largest subprime lender which collapsed in April 2007, claimed that KPMG's audits were 'recklessly and grossly negligent'. Such an assessment was also echoed in the 2008 report prepared by the US Department of Justice appointed examiner Michael Missal. This argued that KPMG contributed to the New Century's failings 'in critical ways', for example, by suggesting alternative methods for calculating the company's reserves needed to cover defaulting loans. In July 2010, it was reported, however, that the lawsuit was resolved in a settlement where KPMG LLP was required to pay $44.75 m. Such appeals and associated settlements, though, have not tended to quell the level of debate, with critics of the profession in the press expressing a sense of bafflement at how auditors could not have a certain degree of responsibility for failing to spot scandals of the magnitude of, for example, the Equitable Life case (e.g. see Ruth Sutherland in her article in the Observer (6/10/10) entitled "Equitable case shows it's time for regulators to bring auditors to book" (see http://www.guardian.co.uk/business/2010/jun/06/equitable-life-ernst-and-young).

damaging effects of actual and potential litigation 'on partners, potential partners and people thinking of joining the firm, when the firm is not freely able to contract' [3].

Such comments or responses on the part of the profession have been underpinned by its desire to see (or promote the case for) reform of auditors' 'joint-and-several' liability[4], replacing it with alternative, more constrained liability arrangements, such as capped or proportionate liability[5]. The profession, and particularly its leading firms, have committed to active processes of political engagement in the pursuit of reform, both at national and international levels (e.g. see Roberts et al. 2003; Humphrey and Samsonova 2012). The success of such efforts, however, is open to question. In the UK, for instance, long-running campaigns on the part of the profession for auditor liability limitation have for many years emphasised the catastrophic consequences of non-action both for the country's auditing community and the public at large (see Accountancy Age 1993, 1994a, 1994b; Accountant 2003; Sunday Times 2004). Revisions to the Companies Act were secured in 2006, but they did not specify any limitation of liability in tort law and instead stipulated that the appropriateness and terms of any such limitation should be the subject of a contractual agreement between the auditor and the company's shareholders. In the US, the Big 4 firms' responses in 2008 to the draft report by the US Treasury's Advisory Committee on the Auditing provided another illustration of their desire to convince the government of the case for auditor liability limitation (see Centre for Audit Quality 2008a; Ernst and Young 2008; Grant Thornton 2008; Centre for Audit Quality 2008b). However, the final draft of the Treasury's Advisory Committee's report failed to list auditor liability as an area recommended for reform.

It is evident that there are countries that have chosen to adopt some form of statutory auditor liability limitation (e.g. Australia, Austria, Belgium, Germany, Greece and Slovenia) and that some of these choices can be seen to be as a consequence of lobbying campaigns by the profession as well as a combination of associated contextual factors. In Australia, for example, a series of reforms of auditor liability led to the introduction in 2004 of proportionate liability, replacing the previous principle of joint and several liabilities. Furthermore, some individual states in the country (such as New South Wales) have since introduced a liability cap in addition to the proportionate liability regime required by law and in combination with compulsory indemnity insurance. Apart from a considerable support for limited liability expressed by Australian auditors, the above changes were also said to be driven by the fact that the insurance market for professional services was

---

[3] See 'Hands off the auditors' 'deep pockets', *Financial Times*, 12 October 2005. http://www.ft.com/cms/s/0/102da602-3b85-11da-b7bc-00000e2511c8.html

[4] Such a regime means that any audit partner accused of wrongdoing can be required to pay the entire amount of damages irrespective of whether the damages were caused by the unprofessional audits or by the wrongdoing of other parties, such as the company's management.

[5] Proportionate liability is a regime where an auditor can be asked to compensate for the damages caused but only in proportion to the degree of his/her culpability.

considered deeply dysfunctional and, therefore, a liability reform was thought to be necessary as a way to bring the level of available insurance in line with the level of audit supply[6].

Furthermore, individual country examples continue to be used as grounds for action in other countries. In its recent report 'Audit reform: aligning risk with responsibility', for example, the UK's association of chartered certified accountants (ACCA) pointed to the experiences of Australia and other countries that introduced limited liability arrangements in tort law as a way to make a point that 'the argument for reforming the liability rules has been widely accepted' (ACCA 2011, p. 8). Nevertheless, the profession's efforts to secure liability reform at the international level have certainly not delivered the desired harmonised, 'one-size-fits-all' auditor liability regime. For instance, the much anticipated Recommendation issued in the European Union (European commission 2008), while encouraging the European Member States to introduce a form of limited liability for auditors, did not impose on them any definitive obligation to do so. Further, the European Commission's more recent Green Paper on auditing did not even make any mention of the subject as a live topic of regulatory reform (for more discussion, see Humphrey and Samsonova 2012).

In this chapter, we consider the underlying causes of what is an uneasy status quo, with audit liability limitation being a subject that has, at different times, attracted considerable momentum, engagement and frustration on the part of the profession, regulators and stakeholders. Such analysis strongly suggests that a broad-based, long-standing international consensus on auditor liability limitation reform is, for varying reasons, unlikely to materialise. Further, we argue that allowing auditor liability debate to be dominated by the search for such a regulatory solution is serving to detract from more serious consideration of the auditor's professional identity and his/her capacity to meet public expectations, particular to the differing countries in which they work.

The remainder of the chapter is structured as follows. The following section will problematise the issue of auditor liability, reviewing the competing set of arguments for and against reform. Section 6.3 and 6.4 of the chapter demonstrate the challenges that liability reformers face, first, by presenting evidence of residing differences in national regimes of auditors' civil liability and, second, by reviewing recent attempts at harmonising the rules for auditor liability across EU Member States. The closing section reflects on such regime differences and attempts to secure auditor liability reform, both within and across countries, arguing that underpinning debates and reform agendas is a more fundamental problem of professional identity and a pressing need to know more about the world of auditing.

6 See an evidence statement by Lee White, a Chief Executive Officer at the Australian Institute of Chartered Accountants, made as part of the enquiry led by the Select Committee on Economic Affairs of the British House of Lords into audit market concentration in the UK in November 2010 (House of Lords 2010, p. 151).

6.2 Competing Perspectives on Auditor Liability Limitation

The subject of auditor liability and the need for its limitation has been associated with a diversity of, often conflicting, attitudes and views expressed by the regulatory community, users of audit reports and the audit profession. Over the years, it has evolved into one of the most controversial aspects of auditing, dividing stakeholder opinions into those that see the 'joint and several' (i.e. unlimited) liability regimes adopted in many countries as necessary and appropriate to the important role that auditors play in a society and those that claim such regimes are too onerous and require some form of limitation.

Arguments in favour of limiting liability have been based on the premise that as businesses (their stakeholders and their accounting systems) have become numerous, larger and more complex, the risk and economic consequences of audit failure have risen significantly, and left auditors 'unduly exposed' to litigation, with a growing number and scale of legal claims against them. O'Malley (1993, p. 7) saw a clear cause and effect relationship in the sense that 'any effort on the profession's part to meet these (rising) public expectations always seems to generate newer and even more unrealistic expectations that will almost certainly produce increased litigation'. The rise of litigation against the profession from the 1960 s onwards in countries such as the US, appears to have due to a mix of factors, including legislative changes, numerous corporate collapses in the economic downturn of the late 1960s and early 1970s and the growing commercial success of the profession (which was suspected as helping to portray them as attractive litigation targets)—coupled with a concern that such commercialisation (especially in terms of the pursuit of revenue growth through a rise in consulting activities) was undermining the profession's commitment to auditor independence and the quality of audit work. A more active and interventionist regulatory stance by the SEC was also seen as playing a key factor, with the 1966 criminal action brought against Lybrand, Ross Brothers and Montgomery for its audits of Continental Vending Machines[7], a New York City-based maker of vending equipment, according to Brewster (2003), not only being a 'shock to Lybrand, and to the rest of the profession, for that matter' (p. 118), on a scale comparable to that of the Enron debacle, but a case that 'opened the litigation floodgates' (p. 146). Brewster goes on to note, for example, that, before 1969, Price Waterhouse had seen only three cases of audit-related litigation in its history, whereas by the early 1970s, the number of such cases had jumped to 40–50. By 1990, the US government had filed over a dozen lawsuits with claims in access of $2 bn. At another level, one could

[7] The case became the first in the US history where criminal charges were brought against auditors who were found guilty of conspiracy even though they did not personally benefit from providing unprofessional audits. Specifically, the jury accused the auditors of having made a false and misleading statement by having inappropriately issued an unqualified opinion on fraudulent financial reports prepared by the Vending Machines.

witness some significant developments in law establishing auditors' duties in relation to third parties that, particularly in the 1970s widened the range of parties that could claim damages against auditors) (Lys 2005; Baker and Prentice 2007, 2008), together with a continuing series of corporate scandals around the world (which included, in the late 1980s and early 1990s, cases such as Barings, BCCI, Maxwell/Mirror Group, Polly Peck, Praise the Lord (PTL) Industries and the multiple Savings and Loan collapse in the US) that significantly undermined public trust in auditors' ability to do their job properly. By the late 1990s, it was being reported that total damages claimed against auditors each year in the UK alone were well in excess of £1 billion (Ward 1999), while others asserted that litigation had become the most significant contributor to the growing cost of an audit and represented perhaps the biggest threat to the audit profession (Siliciano 1997).

Furthermore, there has been emerging empirical evidence suggesting that a growing number of legal cases against auditors have had a significant effect on the auditors' ability to perform their duties properly, and particularly, on the quality of audit judgement (Koch and Schunk 2009). Specifically, some senior audit professionals claimed that auditors increasingly adopt a more apprehensive approach to taking a 'professional stands' as a consequence of an increased litigation risk; and that this situation can impair the overall quality of financial reporting (O'Malley 1993). Accordingly, limiting auditor liability has been presented as a way to tackle the problem of defensive behaviours that auditors develop as a way to shield themselves from the possibility of litigation. Also, it has been argued that strict liability regimes can force experienced auditors to abandon the profession or make newly qualified professionals reluctant to enter, which has a longer term, detrimental effect on overall standards of audit quality (Hill Metzger and Wermert 1994).

Some, albeit again within the profession, have gone so far as to suggest that unlimited liability may negatively influence the economy as a whole. The roots of this argument rest in the multifaceted nature of the role served by the auditor and the capacity of a liability regime to upset the delicate balance associated with such a function. To some extent, the risk of litigation is linked to the very nature of auditing where auditors' owe a duty of care to the company's owners (and by association, to third parties reasonably expected to rely on the audit report in their decision making); however, it is the management that auditors are in contact with during an audit. In essence, auditing involves balancing off often conflicting interests and objectives of different economic agents, with an understanding that any one failure to do so may lead to a legal claim. Furthermore, investors of a troubled company often turn to its auditor for compensation, regardless of the nature or degree of the auditor's involvement, as the company itself is often insolvent. This phenomenon, referred to as the "deep pockets" syndrome (Palmrose 1997) has been said to be further exacerbated by the fact that auditors have been required to hold professional indemnity insurance, which *de-facto*, reinforces a perception of auditors as underwriters possessing sufficient funds to compensate for losses incurred. In conditions of unlimited liability, auditors' capacity to mitigate litigation risk, especially to third parties, has been held to centre on their power to choose their audit clients—and, in consequence, to exhibit a greater reluctance to take on any clients that they perceive as overly risky. A company which cannot attract the services of an audit firm with the highest reputation may find, subsequently, that its financial accounts are not regarded to have the same, or a satisfactory, level of credibility and trustworthiness, making it more difficult for them to secure external funding (in the form of equity investment or bank lending), with, ultimately, adverse consequences for the country's general economic development (Ward 1999).

Despite this range of argument and rationalisation in favour of limiting auditors' civil liability, there has been strong opposition to any such moves. Among other things, the opponents of limiting liability have argued that any form of limitation would damage innocent plaintiffs by significantly reducing the likelihood of them recovering the damages suffered and effectively shielding auditors who failed to meet their professional duties. As such, it is argued that a system of 'joint and several' liability encourages fair treatment of vulnerable third parties while maintaining social justice (O'Malley 1993). It has been also regularly pointed out that audit firms have failed to provide real evidence of the true impact economic impact of litigation against auditors (as most cases are settled outside court)—and that the amount of compensation awarded by the courts is not as overwhelming as auditors have claimed (Gwilliam 2006) and that final settlements are often significantly lower than the initial damages claimed (Cousins et al. 1999). In this regard, the argument put forward by the proponents of unlimited liability has been that the problem of 'catastrophic litigation' has been created by a profession that has increasingly put commercial priorities above social obligation. From this perspective, the calls for liability limitation are seen as camouflaging or not giving due respect to the commercial success of the largest accounting firms and diverting the public's attention from fundamental issues, such as ruling standards of audit quality and effectively leaving society to deal with the consequences of audit failure (Sikka 2008). It has also been argued that the obligation on a profession claiming to serve the public interest requires it to be vigilant in exercising its professional judgement, and not seeking legalistic solutions more compatible with the role of and societal expectations held out for technicians (see Merino and Kenny 1994).

The profession's response has been that cases like Enron have provided categorical proof of the cataclysmic consequences of audit failure and the demonstrably inequitable nature of an unlimited liability regime that can bring a whole audit firm down on the basis of one audit failure[8]. Such arguments are, in turn, countered by critics who have argued that the problems at Arthur Andersen, Enron's auditor, were more systemic in nature (e.g. see Levitt 2003) and that the fate of Andersen was sealed, not by the peculiarities of the liability regime, but by

[8] A series of major law suits is widely cited as having led to the Chap. 11 bankruptcy filing by Levanthol Horwath in November 1990, which prior to its collapse had been the seventh largest audit firm in the US.

the damage that the Enron case had done to its reputation, integrity and capacity to provide high quality audits.

A further line of argument has been to use the deterrent effect that auditors utilise themselves as an indication of the inherently intangible benefits of the audit. Just as auditors emphasise that the true benefit of the audit depends not just on what auditors detect through their work but also what their presence deters and prevents, advocates of a strict liability regime have emphasised its importance in ensuring that auditors deliver in terms of their public accountability, especially their duty of care to third parties that rely on their opinion. Here, it is argued that any limitation of liability would adversely affect auditors' incentives to perform their duties properly, and as a result, further undermine public confidence in the reliability of financial reporting (Gietzmann et al. 1997). From this perspective, the risk or 'threat' of litigation has been seen as a vital means for guiding auditors' behaviours, or, rather, providing a deterrent effect, constraining auditors' freedom of action in a context where the quality of audit work is inherently difficult to observe. In this sense, a distinction has been made between the self-interest of the audit profession in promoting limited liability and the public's desire for auditors to commit fully to the fulfilment of their social duties (Cousins et al. 1999).The counter-argument put forward by the auditing profession has continued to be that a punitive liability regime encourages defensive as against creative and insightful auditing, with auditors spending more time protecting their own position, obeying the rule but not the spirit of accounting and auditing regulations and ultimately performing audits which less serve the public interest. The aforementioned 2011 report by the ACCA illustrates that this argument has not lost favour in the profession, when stating that litigation 'leads to so-called defensive auditing, accusations of 'boiler plate' opinions and a reputation for the profession as being excessively cautious and conservative' (ACCA 2011, p. 6).

6.3 A Diversity of National Regimes of Auditor Liability

The degree and intensity of competing perspectives on auditor liability limitation is bolstered, if not fuelled, by the level of diversity in national auditor liability regimes. The examples provided in this section are illustrative of the diversity of national legislative approaches to the civil liability of statutory auditors. One source of variation relates to the scope of auditors' liability exposure and the principle of *joint and several liability*, which means that any audit partner accused of wrongdoing can be required to pay the entire amount of damages irrespective of whether the damages were caused by an unprofessional audit or by the wrongdoing of other parties, such as the company's management. Common ways of limiting liability exposure include setting a cap on the amount of damages claimed against auditors or applying the principle of proportionality where the damages are awarded in proportion to the auditor's degree of wrongdoing. As far as auditor liability to third parties is concerned, despite the significant expansion of global capital markets and the scale and diversification of corporate activity, together with the importance of financial reports as a source of information about corporate performance, there is generally quite an adherence to restricting auditor liability primarily to claims by contractual parties.

The United States of America is a country where the issue of auditor liability has long been recognised as an area of concern. Amendments to Rule 23 of the Federal Rules of Civil Procedure adopted in 1966 triggered a subsequent growth in the number of securities class actions (Mahoney 2009) and a sharp rise in litigation against auditors that was duly characterised as a 'litigation explosion' (Minow 1984). A further increase in the number of lawsuits filed against auditors in the wake of the 'Savings & Loan crisis' (involving a collapse of nearly a quarter of all American savings and loan associations during the late 1980s and early 1990s (Knapp 2011) stimulated a full-scale lobbying campaign, led by the then Big 6 largest audit firms and the American Institute of Certified Public Accountants (AIPCA), to reform US securities laws. These efforts resulted in the passing of the Private Securities Litigation Reform Act (PSLRA) in 1995, making the US the first country to introduce a principle of proportionality—such that auditors' liability had to be determined in proportion to their actual degree of culpability (see Roberts et al. (2003) for a detailed analysis). This contrasted to the previous position, which advocated the principle of *joint and several* liability—although the latter continues to be applied in cases where auditors have intentionally breached securities' laws or for certain claims by small investors (e.g., where the investor's net worth is at least $200,000 and the claim made against the auditor represents 10 % or more of this net worth). However, those criticising the 1995 Act pointed out that it made the audit firms exempt from being sued in a private, class action, which effectively meant that the US Securities and Exchange Commission (SEC) became the only body that could instigate litigation against the firms (p. 186), although its capacity for action also appeared to have been limited by the 1994 Supreme Court decision *in Central Bank of Denver N.A. versus First Interstate Banks of Denver*. This eliminated the 'aiding and abetting a securities law violation' that had been a prime weapon that plaintiffs had used in arguing their case against the audit firms, which arguably made it more difficult for the SEC to sanction the auditors subsequently (Brewster 2003).

Interestingly, while the US auditor liability regime reflects the specific nature of the country's accountancy culture, some similarities have been drawn to the French system, which also emphasises the role of an auditor in safeguarding the economic interests of a society as a whole, as opposed to just company owners. In this regard, the French Companies Act of 1966 ('Loisur les Societes Commercials no. 66–537') states that auditors owe a duty of care to the client company, individual shareholders and various third parties, providing that the plaintiff can prove the causal link between the fault of the auditors and the damages claimed. The same law also outlines the principle of proportionality which, like in the US, governs the treatment of the auditors' liability exposure (Chung et al. 2010). Giudici (2010) reports a perception that a US auditor is 'serving multiple principles: the company, the investors, the general public' because the country's securities laws do not specifically require that an auditor be appointed by the client company's shareholders and hence auditors' duty of care is not restricted to the shareholders only[9].

The treatment of auditors' responsibility towards third parties has been significantly influenced by, or reflected in, case law development. In 1931, the highest court of New York in the seminal *Ultramares Corp. versus Touche* case considered whether an auditor was liable also to unknown third parties falling outside the auditor-client contract. The court ruling in this case, which was widely applied subsequently, effectively introduced a near-privity standard (although it did reject the specific claim made by the 'third party' against the auditor in the case). In subsequent years, the scope of third-party liability extended with the introduction of the 'restatement rule' which was first applied in 1968 in the *Rusch Factors versus Levin* case and was later embodied in Sect. 552 of the Restatement (Second) of Torts (1976) imposing third-party liability on professionals who supply inaccurate information to their client which is also relied on by non-clients, such as creditors, investors, and others stakeholder groups (Scherl 1994; Al-Shawaf 2012). The main difference between the near-privity and restatement principles is that the latter 'does not require that the identity of specific third parties be known to the auditor, only that they be members of a limited group known to the auditor' (Chung et al. 2010, p. 67). Also, some jurisdictions began to apply a 'reasonable foreseeability' rule, first established in the ruling of the New Jersey Supreme Court in *Rosenblum vs. Adler* (1983). This rule stipulated that an auditor is liable to all parties that he or she can reasonably foresee as potential users of an audit report. It is also worth noting in this regard the Sarbanes–Oxley Act (SOX) 2002 subsequently introduced a definition of a third party that included not just users of financial statements but also users of any non-financial reports that help to decide whether or not one can rely on the audit of such statements, including those produced by the audit firms themselves (e.g. firms' registration documents) or regulators (e.g. PCAOB inspection reports).

Claims of the significant negative effects of litigation have been behind the recent attempts by the auditing profession in the US to push for amendments to statutory law in order to cap auditor liability exposure. For example, the Centre for Audit Quality, an organisation set up by the AICPA with membership of over

---

[9] In the US, apart from the PSLRA, examples of other key pieces of legislation covering the issue of auditor liability include relevant sections of the Securities Act of 1933, the Securities Exchange Act of 1934, and the Racketeer Influenced and Corrupt Organizations Act (RICO) enacted in 1970. Section 10(b) of the 1934 Securities Exchange Act, for example, which is used most frequently as a basis upon which the damaged parties bring federal suits against auditors, deems it unlawful to use 'any manipulative or deceptive device in contrivance of ··· (the securities) rules and regulation as the (Securities and Exchange) Commission may prescribe as necessary or appropriate in the public interest or for the protection of investors'. In addition, section 11 of the 1933 Securities Act gives the parties affected as a result of unprofessional audits a right to take action against an auditor of a company that files a registration statement that contains 'an untrue statement of a material fact or omitted to state a material fact'. Both sections place the burden of proving the materiality of misstatements and the causality between such misstatements and the losses incurred on the plaintiffs themselves.

800 audit firms, heavily criticised the proposals by the US Treasury's Advisory Committee on the Auditing Profession for reforming the US audit market because the proposals failed to respond to the Centre's previous urging to address the 'catastrophic litigation' that the Centre felt was in danger of 'destroying the profession' (see Center for Audit Quality 2008a, 2008b). To substantiate their claims, auditors submitted key statistics showing that claims against the six largest US audit firms amounted to 'an astounding $140 billion(Oberly 2008, p. 6). Despite significant support for such arguments from some of the country's regulatory institutions (including the Committee on Capital Markets Regulation and the United States Chamber of Commerce), the final version of the Treasury's report did not mention liability as an area recommended for reform.

In the UK, the decision by the British House of Lords in the *Caparo* case of 1990 substantially reshaped the treatment of auditor liability by British courts by promoting a more narrowly specified set of conditions under which auditors were considered to owe a duty of care (Napier 1998). According to the Caparo judgement, in the absence of extraordinary circumstances, auditors owed a duty of care to the client company only, and specifically, the company's owners as a collective body. Hence, any third-party claims against auditors could be satisfied only if specific criteria were met (De Poorter 2008)—although subsequent years did see some expansion of privity by the British courts, fuelled by the increasing public pressure for the liability regime to account for the needs of a variety of financial statement users, such as individual shareholders, directors and various third parties (Gwilliam 2004; Pacini et al. 2000).

Like their counterparts in the US, British audit firms have taken an active role in their engagement with the country's accounting professional and regulatory circles in their advocacy of limited liability. Sikka (2008), for example, shows how intense lobbying activities carefully orchestrated by the UK's largest audit firms led to the passage of theLimited Liability Partnerships Act of 2000. This allowed UK audit firms to do what their North American counterparts had done for some time which is to form Limited Liability Partnerships (LLPs), in addition to the existing right (established in the 1989 Companies Act) to incorporate as companies. Unlike ordinary partnerships, LLPs have a separate legal personality and so, in the event of litigation, the claimed amount of damages is first recovered from the audit firm's assets and a partner is only liable for his own wrongdoing and not for the wrongdoing of his/her co-partners. In 2001, Ernst and Young was the first Big audit firm to register as a LLP with the intent that it would offer a greater protection to its individual partners and their personal assets. However, neither incorporation nor LLPs offer total liability protection and the so-called 'catastrophic' claim which may result in the failure of an individual audit firm is still a risk for any such incorporated firm or LLP.

A significant recent development was the revised Companies Act 2006 which allowed auditors to stipulate a contractual liability limitation in their engagement letter for any negligence, breach of duty, or breach of trust on the part of the auditor in relation to the audit (see Turley 2008). Any such limitation, however, has to be on an annual basis and be approved by a shareholder resolution.

The liability limitation agreement (LLA) also had to be 'fair and reasonable', allowing the courts to override/amend any such agreement if it considered the agreement not to be so. Interestingly, the 2006 Companies Act also introduced additional arrangements to strengthen the emphasis on auditors' accountability to users, which were widely seen as counterbalancing provisions for liability limitation. Among such arrangements was a new criminal offence, punishable by an unlimited fine, for auditors who 'knowingly or recklessly' provide a false audit opinion.

Since LLA were first permitted, their use has been impeded by a number of factors. Roach (2010), in this regard, points to the vague nature of LLAs which makes their application problematic. He further notes that the guidance issued by the UK's Financial Reporting Council (FRC 2008), while providing some important clarifications, still left some questions unanswered, such as the subsequent responsibility of a company director whose recommendation of the adoption of an LLAs is followed by an action in which the company's auditor is found to be negligent? Roach reported a generally unfavourable reaction to LLAs by the users of audit reports, such as institutional investors and that the whole viability of LLAs was significantly threatened by the SEC's rejection of such a contractual liability limitation on the grounds that they represented a major breach of auditor's independence (a move which saw the SEC seek to prevent UK audit firms with US-listed clients from entering into any LLA)[10]. Such a stance by the SEC is not only suggestive of substantial differences in views of the most appropriate liability arrangements and the required scope of the auditor's duty of care adopted in the two countries, but demonstrates that the issue of auditor liability limitation should not be viewed in (national) isolation. The SEC's reaction also presents a significant hindrance to the operations of the audit firms themselves as a large number of FTSE 100 companies (which form the firms' primary client base) also have their stock traded in New York and, therefore, find themselves having to follow the SEC requirements.

Such national variation in liability regimes, when coupled with the global nature of audit firms' operations, means that the firms' liability exposure is not constant and always subject to alteration and modification as a result of different jurisdictional action. Interestingly, the audit profession's success in securing liability limitation is quite varied, with significant concessions being granted in countries that had already established quite strict liability arrangements. For instance, in Canada, auditors are required to compensate for damages incurred by the plaintiff if the latter is able to prove that the harm suffered can be directly attributed to the actions of the auditors. The 1997 Hercules versus Ernst & Young case reinforced this position by concluding that company investors have no right to sue the auditor in cases where financial statements are found to contain misstatements on the ground that auditors owe a duty of care primarily to the contractual party (Puri and Ben-Ishai 2003; Chung et al. 2010). Canadian auditors, like their British and

[10] See, for example, 'Auditor liability deals blocked', *Financial Times*, 11th March 2009.

American colleagues, can also form LLPs, while amendments to the Canada Business Corporations Act (CBCA) in 2001 saw *joint and several* liability being replaced with capped proportionate liability arrangements—with the audit profession being noted as the major driving force behind the reform (Puri and Ben-Ishai 2003). Under such arrangements, the scope of damages that the auditor can be held liable for is to be in proportion to the degree of his/her wrongdoing, although the auditor can still be required to cover up to a maximum of 50 % of the amount of damages awarded by the court against another defendant (such as company management) when the latter is insolvent. Such provisions only apply to cases of violation of the CBCA and not, for example, to violations of securities law.

The cap on auditor liability claims introduced in Germany has, over the years, been increased, a move, ironically, advocated by German auditors themselves in the hope of warding off any possible government measures seeking to increase the rights of third parties (Gietzmann and Quick 1998). The current legal provisions in Germany limit auditors' contractual liability to €1 mn per audit and €4 mn for the audit of listed companies. Such a monetary cap, however, refers only to claims by the client, unlike countries like Belgium, Austria and Greece where the cap also covers liability to third parties (Gietzmann and Quick 1998; Kohler et al. 2008).

In environments with a relatively high level of litigious activities against auditors, laws stipulating auditor liability, while varied, can be expected to be relatively well developed and detailed in terms of both stipulating the scope of auditors' liability exposure as well as the range of parties that can claim damages against auditors. In contrast, auditor liability rules in less litigious environments are often characterised by laws and regulation which are more general in their provisions. In Belgium, for example, where despite a few high-profile cases, litigation against auditors is comparatively low, national law has not introduced any specific requirements for auditor's liability to third parties. Effectively this means that, since the 1970s when the national legislator mandated the publication of company financial reports, auditors have been considered liable to any party that relies on such reports as a source of information. And so, Belgian auditors are believed to owe a duty of care not just to the company shareholders but a wide range of other stakeholders, such as company employees, creditors and other groups, which underscores the significant emphasis that the country places on auditors' social roles (De Poorter 2008). Belgium did recently introduce an absolute cap on liability, but as Roach (2010) notes, such a cap 'was not based upon realisation that the principle of joint and several liability coupled with the deep pockets syndrome is inherently unfair', as in the UK, but was 'to improve the level of domestic insurance cover' available to auditors' (Roach 2010, p. 11).

There are also national environments where the issue of auditor liability limitation has clearly been assigned less social importance and significance. One example is Russia where 'Western'-style auditing was introduced more than two decades ago but, at the time of writing, there are still no laws or regulations of a business or audit-specific nature that explicitly define auditors' civil liability. Instead, such liability is determined with reference to the provisions of the Civil Code, article 15 of which states that 'a person whose rights have been violated can demand full compensation for the damages incurred, unless laws and regulations exist that impose restrictions on the amount of compensation'. Furthermore, the focus in the Code is on the economic consequences of a contractual relationship where 'individuals and companies are free to determine their respective rights and responsibilities as part of an agreement between them as long as such an agreement is not in contradiction with the existing legislation' (article 1). This means that the Russian statutes contain no legislative provisions that stipulate an auditor's liability to third parties. Samsonova (2012), for example, notes in this regard that 'identifying the causality between the damages suffered by the plaintiff and the auditors' actions is problematic' and that 'unlike the existing litigation practices in mature audit environments, audit standards are rarely used as a reference in Russian courts' (p. 31). This assessment was reinforced by a series of court cases filed in 2001–2002 by a number of minority shareholders of a Russia's energy giant Gazprom against the company's auditor PricewaterhouseCoopers (PwC). The shareholders accused PwC of approving several deals that allegedly resulted in asset losses worth billions of US dollars and of having issued a misleading audit opinion. The Moscow Arbitration Court, however, did not consider the quality of the audit work and whether it was up to 'standard', but rejected the claims on the basis that it was not the company's shareholders but its management that entered into the agreement with the auditor (for a discussion, see Korchagina 2002).

6.4 The Uneasy Task of Harmonising Auditor Liability Rules

In many areas of financial reporting and audit regulation, a common approach to dealing with national diversity has been to contemplate attempts at reducing it through processes of standardisation and harmonisation. Indeed, the promotion of international standards and the harmonisation of practice across nations has very much become the norm in today's globalised world, with cross-country variation increasingly represented as an obstacle to economic integration and growth and certainly not an aid to the promotion of corporate transparency and accountability. Clear evidence of such a trend lies in the global standards and codes advocated by bodies such as the Financial Stability Board (FSB) and the World Bank/IMF. In the field of accounting and auditing, the growing international recognition of the work of the International Accounting Standards Board (IASB) and the International Auditing and Assurance Standards Board (IAASB) reflect the significance global commitment to the harmonisation of accounting and auditing practices. Similar cooperative commitments in relation to the issue of auditor liability issue can be seen to be particularly relevant given that the nature of liability risks faced by the audit profession, and specifically the large international audit networks, extend across national boundaries and is no longer unique to any one specific national environment. However, the success in signing countries up to the global adoption of international accounting and auditing standards stands in some contrast to the level of success that has been achieved in terms of harmonising national regimes of auditor liability. An illustration of the problems that have been encountered in this area is now provided by reviewing the attempt to harmonise national auditor liability regimes within the context of the European Union (EU).

In 2007, a public consultation was launched (Directorate General for Internal Market and Services 2007a) to collect stakeholder views on the need for and appropriate methods of limiting auditor liability. The documents resulting from the consultation process, such as the response letters and the EU reports interpreting these responses, are striking in that they demonstrate significant differences of opinion across key stakeholder groups. The audit profession was virtually the only group of respondents that expressed a unanimous support for some form of auditor liability limitation. Other interest groups, however, demonstrated far less unity on the subject of auditor liability limitation. Importantly, as Fig. 6.1 shows, the variation in views on the need for limited liability and various mechanisms for delivering such limitation attributable to their different national origin and the nature of auditor liability regimes adopted in their respective countries.

Specifically, the investment community argued that the case for reform at the EU level had not been made as there was no convincing evidence to suggest that the existing levels of litigation could bring down an audit network. Furthermore, there was a clear split in opinions submitted by members of the banking sector, with French representatives strongly rejecting a need for any form of liability limitation while representatives of other Member States expressed a view that such limitation was beneficial in terms of improving audit choice. For the French banking community, limiting liability was anticipated as having a detrimental

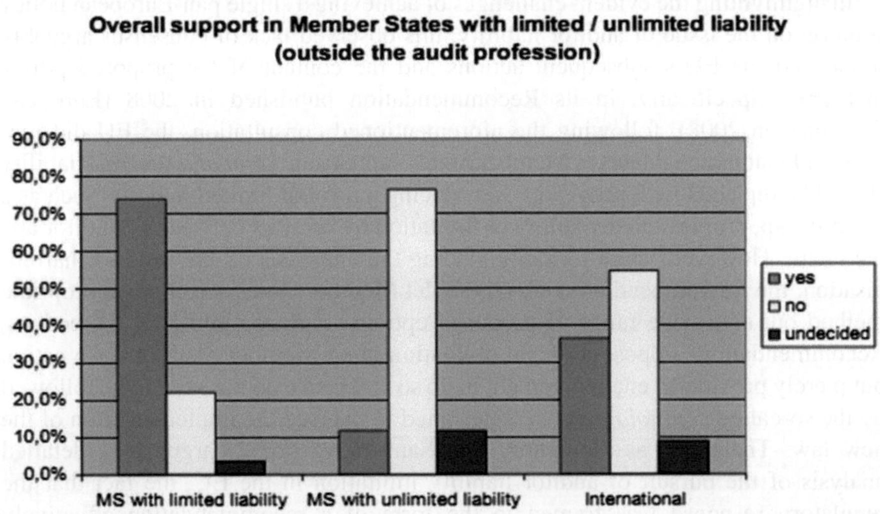

Fig. 6.1 Stakeholder views based on the country of origin. *Source* Directorate general for internal market and services 2007b, p. 7

effect on audit quality and was not an appropriate way of dealing with current levels of audit market concentration. The response of European corporate also lacked uniformity with members of the French corporate sector opposing the reforms, while companies from the countries where liability cap had been introduced (such as Germany) expressing views in support of limited liability.

Significantly, the opinions of individual Member States' governments and regulatory agencies failed to demonstrate a united front as to whether or not auditor liability should be limited and, if so, what was the most suitable limitation method. In their response letter, the Swedish Supervisory Board of Public Accountants, for example, refrained from explicitly commenting on the proposed nature or appropriateness of the liability reform proposed by the EU and simply stated its belief that any regulatory action should be based on some general principles rather than on detailed provisions (Directorate General for Internal Market and Services 2007b). Also, the Swedish Ministry of Justice stressed that the European Commission should introduce new regulatory measures only if they impose no restrictions on individual Member States' decisions as to the most appropriate mechanism for implementation, noting that the Swedish government had previously undertaken its own study looking into how best to limit auditor liability. Furthermore, the Finnish government's Ministry of Trade and Industry made reference to a similar type of a country-wide study published in 2006 and suggested that, in the context of the EU as a whole, the ability of the Member States to change the existing liability regimes was not sufficiently well understood and hence, there was a need for further investigation and analysis before any decision was made at the EU level. And finally, representatives of French regulators demonstrated strong opposition to regulatory reform that would lead to any form of limited liability.

In highlighting the evident challenges of achieving a single pan-European policy solution on the issue of auditor liability, this observed lack of consensus arguably influenced the EU's subsequent actions and the content of the proposed policy measures. Specifically, in its Recommendation published in 2008 (European Commission 2008), following the aforementioned consultation, the EU did recommend that national laws in Member States supporting '*joint and several*' liability should be replaced with provisions introducing a form of limited liability, such as a liability cap, proportionate liability or limitation by contract between an auditor and the client. However, while formally placing the emphasis on the need for harmonisation, the Recommendation effectively let Member States select the appropriate method out of a wide range of proposed options. Further, unlike EU Directives, Recommendations impose no legal obligation upon Member States to take action but merely provide an encouragement to do so and hence do not need to be followed by the so-called *comitology* process designed to oversee the implementation of the new law. Therefore, as Humphrey and Samsonova (2012) argue in a detailed analysis of the pursuit of auditor liability limitation in the EU, the fact that the regulatory response was framed in the form of a recommendation effectively suggests that the EU had refrained from fully addressing the problem of national diversity of liability regimes in Europe.

6.5 A Struggle over Liability or Identity?

The above discussion has vividly illustrated the problematic nature of the issue of auditor liability in terms of both the sheer degree of variation in the national approaches to such an issue and difficulties of achieving a policy solution which would be deemed satisfactory for different stakeholders and in relation to different environments. In many respects, a struggle to find such a solution is akin to a struggle to reconcile the diverse opinions and standpoints as to the nature of the auditor's identity and the social value of audit. Humphrey and Samsonova (2012) have argued that auditor liability should be viewed as not merely a mechanism for restraining auditor behaviours but, in a broader sense, as an instrument of social control whose functionality is determined with reference to some more fundamental values and norms adopted in the institutional environment where such an instrument is employed—such as the general role that auditing plays in a society, context-specific understandings of social justice and accountability, the influence of the state on shaping the notions of audit professionalism, and others. Variation in liability rules across countries may therefore be seen as an indication of the extent to which national actors have different views as to the identity and roles that should be attributed to an auditor in terms of maintaining important functional and social values and norms. In other words, the emphasis and punitive strength of auditor liability arrangement may be less in less litigious settings not simply because of a lower risk of litigation, but also because of the relatively lower level of importance that such a society places on auditing in comparison to, for example, government oversight. In this respect, Humphrey and Samsonova (2012) view auditor liability as part of 'a broader system of accountability' and argue that 'strict and punitive systems of public oversight over auditors (regulatory accountability), the strong collegial effects of peer pressure on auditors' daily routines (peer accountability) or the extent and effectiveness of criminal liability for intentional negligent conduct by auditors can greatly diminish the significance of civil liability as a key mechanism to guide and discipline auditor behaviour' (p. 49).

If appreciation of differences in contextualised understandings of audit objectives can help better understand the roots of the persistent variation in the countries' auditor liability regimes and, as the case of the EU shows, the challenges of harmonising such regimes, the question has to be asked as to what are the most appropriate policy responses going forward? The chapter has illustrated the wide spectrum of opinions on the appropriate scope of liability exposure and perceived need for liability limitation among various stakeholder groups. In many ways, such a state of affairs may be seen as a reflection of an equally long-standing debate regarding the existence of an audit expectations gap. Just as we may debate whether auditors are delivering audits of the quality expected and desired by users of audit services and whether they should be providing additional functions and services, we can discuss whether auditors should be responsible to a narrower or broader range of stakeholders, whether litigation claims against auditors are 'fair' or 'punitive', and whether audit firms are commercially powerful and successful or highly vulnerable to the vagaries and catastrophes of legal action.

It may be appropriate to see the EU's Recommendation as a staging post from which the profession globally can build a stronger case for (further) liability limitation. Alternatively, it may be that the relative silence at EU levels on this issue, post the Recommendation, suggests that any sense of advancement by the profession towards its desired goals, is overstated. It could even be argued that the debate is no closer to a conclusion and that seeking a set of liability arrangements that would be deemed appropriate to all parties involved, including auditors and users of their services, remains a monumental and, probably, an impossible task. Over the years, we have seen auditor liability discussed from various perspectives reflecting different sets of priorities and interests. The range of arguments developed in the course of such discussions has varied, from those advanced by an audit profession that sees liability limitation as the key for tackling the problems of poor audit judgement and defensive audit behaviour (effectively trading limited liability for promised improvements in audit quality) to those emphasising limitation as a way to reduce entry barriers for smaller audit firms and hence address the problem of audit market concentration. While the basic logic behind such arguments has been substantially questioned by critics suggesting that the profession has overstated the scale and seriousness of its liability exposure (in the form of realised court decisions against auditors) (e.g. see Gwilliam 2004, 2006), may be the key message to take from such discussion is to shift the policy focus from trying to come up with 'the best' or the 'least bad' solution for the liability problem and to give more attention to fundamental questions about auditing and the achievements of audit practice. Rather than being a subject in which energy and attention is devoted to the identification of an all-embracing solution, auditor liability limitation should be seen as opportunity for gaining greater understanding of the achievements, lived experiences and expectations of (and those held for) auditors.

Arguably, one of the reasons as to why the liability debate is still alive is because there continues to be a lack of clarity in the minds of the public as to what it is that auditors do and the particular social identity and functioning of audit. Instead of debating whether or not limiting auditor liability is an effective means of tackling issues of audit quality, audit market concentration or something else, one should reverse such a debate to consider how addressing such issues may in turn help tackle the liability dilemma. In other words, there is a chance that continued efforts to improve audit standards, standards' compliance as well as the visibility of the audit process may lead to the long-running liability saga solving itself. This is not an easy policy route or one guaranteed to deliver concrete results. But it has one distinct advantage—in that we arguably know much less about differences in the social significance and achievements of audit practice than we do about differences in auditor liability regimes.

It has been suggested on numerous occasions that the best form of liability limitation is quality auditing work—after all, no court is going to find auditors liable for having done a good audit! The conundrum highlighted by the profession is that demanding regulatory and punitive liability regimes are said to engender a form of audit that is more rigid and less embracing/trusting of the very professional judgement that makes for a quality audit. Accordingly, it is claimed that the best, preventive, forms of liability limitation cannot come without first securing legislative liability limitation. But, such legislative reform is not going to come (and has not come) when the complainants are seen to be massively commercially successful organisations or when their case is seen as being based on cross-country liability regime comparisons in which the role of, and respect for, audit varies significantly. In this respect, the underlying crisis that auditors face is not one of liability per se, but as mentioned earlier, one of professional identity and achievement. It is one thing for the audit profession to claim a commitment to serving the 'public' interest, but to secure desired liability reform, this commitment is going to have to be suitably recognised and appreciated not only by the 'public' but also the profession itself. This is not to say that there will ever be one blanket-styled reform of auditor liability that is suitable in all national jurisdictions and contexts. Indeed, it may well be that the issue of auditor liability is a moving feast, a polemic that shifts in focus and emphasis as social demands, expectations and social contexts change. However, it is always likely to be the case that the more that is known of the world of auditing, the achievements and lived experiences of auditors and those to whom auditors are accountable, the more chance there is that liability regimes will be socially 'fit for purpose'.

References

ACCA (2011) Audit reform: aligning risk with responsibility. *Report*. May. London: ACCA.

Accountancy Age (1993). Big firms lead push to cap audit liability, 1.

Accountancy Age (1994a). Audit liability campaign shifts to public interest, 10.

Accountancy Age (1994b). Audit liability—we are not crying wolf this time, 10.

Accountant (2003) Urgent need for liability reform. 25th April, 2.

Al-Shawaf, H. T. (2012). Bargaining for salvation: how alternative auditor liability regimes can save the capital markets. *University of Illinois Law Review, 2012*, 501–536.

Andersen A & Co., (1992) Coopers and Lybrand, Deloitte and Touche, Ernst and Young, KPMG Peat Marwick, price waterhouse, the liability crisis in the United States: impact on the accounting profession. *Journal of Accountancy*, 174(5): 19–23.

Baker, C. R., & Prentice, D. (2007). The evolution of auditor liability under common law. *Journal of Forensic Accounting, 8*, 183–200.

Baker, C. R., & Prentice, D. (2008). The origins of auditor liability to third parties under United States common law. *Accounting History, 13*, 163–182.

Brewster, M. (2003). *Accountable: how the accounting profession forfeited a public trust*. New Jersey: Wiley.

Carey, J. L. (1965). *The CPA plans for the future*. New York: American Institute of Certified Public Accountants.

Center for Audit Quality (2008a). *Report of the major public company audit firms to the department of the treasury advisory committee on the auditing profession*. http://www.thecaq.org/publicpolicy/data/TRData2008-01-23-FullReport.pdf.

Center for Audit Quality (2008b). *Comment letter by Cynthia M. Fornelli, executive director, regarding draft report addendum 17–19*. http://comments.treas.gov/_files/CAQComment letter62708FINAL.pdf.

Chung, J., Farrar, J., Puri, P., & Thorne, L. (2010). Auditor liability to third parties after Sarbanes-Oxley: an international comparison of regulatory and legal reforms. *Journal of International Accounting, Auditing and Taxation, 19*, 66–78.

Cousins, J., Mitchell, A., & Sikka, P. (1999). Auditor liability: the other side of the debate. *Critical Perspectives of Accounting, 10*, 283–312.

De Poorter, I. (2008). Auditor's liability towards third parties within the EU: a comparative study between the United Kingdom, the Netherland, Germany and Belgium. *Journal of International Commercial Law and Technology, 3*(1), 68–75.

Directorate General for Internal Market and Services (2007a). *Commission staff working paper: consultation on auditors' liability and its impact on the European capital markets*. Brussels: European Commission.

Directorate General for Internal Market and Services (2007b). *Consultation on auditors' liability: summary report*. Brussels: European Commission.

Ernst & Young (2008).*Comment letter regarding draft report and draft report addendum* 25–26.

Financial Reporting Council (2008), Guidance on Auditor Liability Limitation Agreements, London: FRC, June 2008. See http://www.frc.org.uk/about/auditorliability.cfm

Gietzmann, M. B., & Quick, R. (1998). Capping auditor liability: the German experience. *Accounting, Organizations and Society, 23*(1), 81–103.

Gietzmann, M. B., Ncube, M., & Shelby, M. J. (1997). Auditor performance, implicit guarantees, and the valuation of legal liability. *International Journal of Auditing, 1*(1), 13–30.

Giudici, P. (2010). Auditors' roles and their multi-layered liability regime. Working paper. Italy: Free University of Bozem-Bolzano.

Gwilliam, D. R. (2004). Auditor liability: law and myth. *Professional Negligence, 20*(3), 172–181.

Gwilliam, D. R. (2006). Audit quality and audit liability—a musical vignette. *Professional Negligence, 22*(1), 37–52.

Hill, J., Metzger, M., & Wermert, J. (1994). The spectre of disproportionate auditor liability in the savings and loan crisis. *Critical Perspective on Accounting, 5*(2), 133–177.

House of Lords (2010). *Auditors: market concentration and their role. Volume II: Evidence*. London: House of Lords.

Humphrey, C., & Samsonova, A. (2012). Transnational governance in action: the pursuit of auditor liability reform in the EU. Working paper. Manchester Business School, UK: University of Manchester.

ICAA (1995). *Opportunity, equity and fairness*. Edmonton: Institute of Chartered Accountants of Alberta.

Knapp, M. (2011). *Contemporary auditing; real issues and cases*. South-Western, USA: Mason.

Koch, C. W. & Schunk, D. (2009). Limiting auditors' liability? - experimental evidence on behavior under risk and ambiguity. Working paper. http://papers.ssrn.com/sol3/papers.cfm?abstract_id=982027.

Kohler, A.G., Marten, K-U., & Quick, R. (2008). Audit regulation in Germany: improvements driven by internationalization. In R. Quick, S. Turley, & M. Wilekens. (Eds.) 'Auditing, trust and governance: developing regulation in Europe'. Routledge: London: 111–143.

Korchagina, V. (2002). Big five discuss auditing problems. *The Moscow Times*.

Lys, T. (2005). Discussion: the evolution of lawsuits against auditors—determinants, consequences, and solutions. *Journal of Economics and Management Strategy, 2*(3), 427–433.

Mahoney, P. G. (2009). The development of securities law in the United States. *Journal of Accounting Research, 47*(2), 325–347.

Merino, B. D., & Kenny, S. Y. (1994). Auditor liability and culpability in the Savings and Loan industry. *Critical Perspectives on Accounting, 5*(2), 179–193.

Minow, N.N. (1984). Accountants' liability and the litigation explosion. *Journal of Accountancy* 70.

Napier, C. (1998). Intersections of law and accountancy: unlimited auditor liability in the United Kingdom. *Accounting, Organizations and Society, 23*(1), 105–128.

O' Malley, S. F. (1993). Legal liability is having a chilling effect on the auditor's role. *Accounting Horizons, 7*(2), 82–87.

Oberly, K. (2008). *Written testimony of Kathryn, A. Oberly (Americas Vice Chair and General Counsel, Ernst & Young LLP) before the Federal Advisory Committee on the Auditing Profession to U.S. Department of the Treasury*. http://www.ustreas.gov/offices/domestic-finance/acap/submissions/06032008/Oberly060308.pdf.

Pacini, C., Hillison, W., & Sinason, D. (2000). Auditor liability to third parties: an international focus. *Managerial Auditing Journal, 15*(8), 394–406.

Palmrose, Z. (1997). Audit litigation research: do merits matter? an assessment and directions for future research. *Journal of Accounting and Public Policy, 16*, 355–378.

Puri, P., & Ben-Ishai, S. (2003). Proportionate liability under the CBCA in the context of recent corporate governance reform: Canadian auditors in the wrong place at the wrong time? *Canadian Business Law Review, 39*, 36–50.

Quick, R., Turley, S., & Wilekens, M. (2008). *Auditing, trust and governance: developing regulation in Europe* (pp. 205–222). London: Routledge.

Roach, L. (2010). *Auditor liability: liability limitation agreements, working paper*. UK: University of Portsmouth.

Roberts, R. W., Dwyer, P. D., & Sweeney, J. T. (2003). Political strategies used by the US public accounting profession during auditor liability reform: the case of the private securities litigation reform act of 1995. *Journal of Accounting and Public Policy, 22*, 433–457.

Samsonova, A. (2012). *Local sources of a differential impact of global standards: the case of international standards of auditing in Russia, working paper*. UK: Manchester Business School, University of Manchester.

Scherl, J. (1994). Evolution of auditor liability to noncontractual third parties: balancing the equities and weighing the consequences. *The American University Law Review, 44*, 255–289.

Sikka, P. (2008). Globalization and its discontents: accounting firms but limited liability partnership legislation in Jersey. *Accounting, Auditing and Accountability Journal, 21*(3), 398–426.

Siliciano, J. A. (1997). Trends in independent auditor liability: the emergence of a sane consensus? *Journal of Accounting and Public Policy, 16*(4), 339–353.

Sunday Times (2004). Big four battle liability laws. 2nd May; 8.

Talley, E. L. (2006). Cataclysmic liability risk among big 4 auditors. *Columbia Law Review, 106*(7), 1641–1697.

Thornton G. (2008). *Comment letter regarding draft report and draft report addendum* 4. http://comments.treas.gov/_files/GTCommentlettertoACAPJune2008_FINAL.p.

Turley, S. (2008). Developments in the framework of auditing regulation in the United Kingdom. In Quick, R., Turley, S. and Wilekens, M. (Eds.) Auditing, *Trust and Governance: Developing Regulation in Europe*. London: Routledge; 205–222.

Ward, G. (1999). Auditors' liability in the UK: the case for reform. *Critical Perspectives on Accounting, 10*(3), 387–394.

European Commission (2008). *Commission recommendation of 5/VI/2008 concerning the limitation of the civil liability of statutory auditors and audit firms, 2008/473/EC*. Brussels: European Commission.

Chapter 7
The Corporate Governance Effects of Audit Committee

Stuart Turley and Mahbub Zaman

Abstract This chapter provides a synthesis and evaluation of empirical research on the governance effects associated with audit committees. Given recent policy recommendations in several countries aimed at strengthening these committees, it is important to establish what research evidence demonstrates about their existing governance contribution. A framework for analyzing the impact of audit committees is described, identifying potential perceived effects which may have led to their adoption and documented effects on aspects of the audit function, on financial reporting quality and on corporate performance. It is also shown that most of the existing research has focused on factors associated with audit committee existence, characteristics, and measures of activity and there is very little evidence on the processes associated with the operation of audit committees and the manner in which they influence organizational behavior. It is clear that there is no automatic relationship between the adoption of audit committee structures or characteristics and the achievement of particular governance effects, and caution may be needed over expectations that greater codification around factors such as audit committee members' independence and expertise as the means of "correcting" past weaknesses in the arrangements for audit committees. The most fundamental question concerning what difference audit committees make in practice continues to be an important area for research development. For future research we suggest: (1) greater consideration of the organizational and institutional contexts in which audit committees operate; (2) explicit theorization of the processes associated with

This Chapter includes the paper published the Journal of Management and Governance, Vol. 8, no. 3, 2004, pp. 305–332.

S. Turley · M. Zaman (✉)
University of Manchester, Manchester M13 9PL, UK
e-mail: mahbub.zaman@mbs.ac.uk

S. Turley
e-mail: stuart.turley@mbs.ac.uk

R. Di Pietra et al. (eds.), *Accounting and Regulation*,
DOI: 10.1007/978-1-4614-8097-6_7,

audit committee operation; (3) complementing extant research methods with field studies; and (4) investigation of unintended as well as expected consequences of audit committees.

7.1 Introduction

During the past two decades audit committees (henceforth ACs) have become a common mechanism of corporate governance internationally. Originally non-mandatory structures used by a minority of corporations, more recently numerous official professional and regulatory committees in many countries have recommended their more universal adoption and have advocated expanded roles for ACs. The Sarbanes–Oxley Act of 2002 in the US, the report of the Australian Treasury (2002) and the recommendations of the Smith Committee (2003) and the Higgs (2003) review in the UK (Turley and Zaman 2003) are recent examples. The objective of this chapter is to evaluate the extent to which research evidence demonstrates corporate governance effects associated with the operation of ACs in private sector corporations.[1] This evaluation incorporates consideration of perceived effects that may have led to AC adoption and demonstrated effects on the audit function, financial reporting quality, and corporate performance.

While no a priori position on the efficacy of ACs for alleviating weaknesses in corporate governance is adopted in this chapter, it can be noted that regulators, governmental bodies, and researchers in many countries have raised questions about ACs' effectiveness and their contribution to governance (Sommer 1991; Wolnizer 1995; Lee 2001; Turner 2001). The incidence of high profile corporate failures, notably in the period since 2000, involving fraud, poor accounting, and failure of internal control have provided at least anecdotal evidence to support concerns about the adequacy of the monitoring provided by ACs. Such events have accentuated concerns that have been expressed over a somewhat longer period. For example, researchers and commentators have argued that many AC members lack critical attributes such as independence, expertise and experience in oversight (Vicknair et al. 1993; DeZoort 1997; Cohen et al. 2002; Guy and Zeff 2002), that the level of interaction between the AC and auditors is variable, undermining the AC's value as an effective vehicle for pursuing shareholders' interests (Hatherly 1999), and that whether ACs are actually discharging their important responsibilities is not sufficiently understood (Kalbers and Fogarty 1993). Some have also

[1] There are significant differences between the private sector and public sector contexts within which ACs have been established. These differences are particularly marked with respect to the institutional and governance arrangements the AC is intended to contribute to and the current governance climate in which the role of ACs is being developed. For this reason this chapter focuses on private sector organizations alone.

argued that the adoption of ACs may be primarily symbolic (Kalbers and Fogarty 1998) and that the benefits associated with them are more rhetorical than substantive (DeZoort 1997).

Recent years have seen attempts to enhance the role of ACs to address governance issues [for example, Cadbury (1992) in the UK; AARF (1997) in Australia; and the Blue Ribbon Committee (1999) in the US], followed by significant corporate failures such as Enron in which the adequacy of the AC has been questioned (Powers 2002; Benston and Hartgraves 2002), followed in turn by further attention to ACs' responsibilities and the qualities necessary for AC effectiveness [see for example, SEC (2002) in the US; Australian Treasury (2002); and Smith Committee (2003) in the UK]. Given, on the one hand, the continued reliance on and development of rules for ACs in the governance policy arena and, on the other hand, the concerns expressed about the realization of the intended benefits from having ACs as part of the governance structure for corporations, the question of what is the impact of ACs on specific aspects of governance in practice is of considerable importance. It is this question that this chapter seeks to address by evaluating available empirical evidence about the impact of ACs on a number of governance factors. While the governance environment continues to change in the aftermath of Enron and similar cases, evaluation of existing demonstrated effects associated with ACs is relevant in forming expectations about the likely results of current regulatory change, in establishing benchmarks against which the future impact of such change can be evaluated and in guiding the emphasis of future research.

The remainder of the chapter is structured as follows. The next section sets out a framework of potential areas of impact within which the evidence on the corporate governance effects of ACs can be evaluated. Section 6.3 establishes the evidence of AC impact—perceived incentives associated with their adoption, effects on the audit function, effects on financial reporting quality, and effects on corporate performance. Section 6.4 provides a summary of the evaluation of evidence, concluding remarks, and suggestions for future research.

7.2 A Framework for Reviewing Audit Committee Effects

The concept of ACs is not new [see, for example, Tricker (1978); Collier (1996); DeZoort (1997); and Lee and Stone (1997), for evidence on their development]. What is notable, however, is the extent of their promotion and subsequent adoption by listed companies in several countries during the past quarter century (Morse and Keegan 1999). There have been major changes over time in the context in which ACs operate and cultural and structural differences internationally will influence their operation, but overall there has been an increasing degree of codification and harmonization of "best practice". The growing global acceptance of the AC as a relevant governance structure, including recent efforts toward increasing legislation, in a wide variety of environments can be linked to claims made in professional and governmental reports about AC benefits on a number of aspects of corporate

Table 7.1 A framework of expected AC effects

Area of impact	Examples of effects
Structural incentives	Factors associated with AC adoption and potential reduction in agency costs
	Links with other governance arrangements, e.g., large audit firms
	Reduction in directors' legal liability
Audit function	Selection and remuneration
	Independence of external auditors
	Impact on the audit process and on auditor communication
	Monitoring of internal control and audit
Financial reporting quality	Impact on errors and irregularities
	Adoption of accounting standards and accounting policy choice Legal/regulatory action for defective reporting
	Audit qualifications
Corporate performance	Impact of AC adoption on share prices and wealth creation

governance (see Appendix 1 for examples of such statements). These potential areas of expected benefit can be used to establish a broad framework for evaluating the evidence on effects associated with the existence and operation of ACs. This framework of impact issues is set out in Table 7.1.

7.2.1 Structural Incentives

Arguments associated with the promotion of ACs emphasize their potential contribution to, for example, the relationships between directors, investors, and auditors, the discharge of accountability and directors' execution of their responsibilities. They suggest ACs influence the balance of power in accountability and audit relationships. Whether or not this interpretation is valid, not least in terms of perceived or implied benefits, may be revealed by the circumstances that are associated with adoption (and non-adoption) of AC structures or particular AC characteristics such as level of expertise and independence. Although such factors do not in themselves provide evidence of actual effects in practice, it can indicate something about the motivations associated with ACs in governance structures and the organizational circumstances in which accountability benefits are most strongly perceived. Studies of the factors associated with formation in non-mandatory settings can thus provide evidence on the expected effects of ACs and the justification for AC requirements.

7.2.2 *Effects on the Audit Function*

A second aspect of the case for ACs is their impact on external audit and internal control and audit. It has often been as a consequence of reviews of alleged weakness in audit effectiveness that recommendations for AC requirements have been made and actual outcomes in this area are therefore an important subject for evaluation. The potential for ACs to influence a number of factors concerning external and internal audit is asserted in professional literature and in policy documents. It is therefore appropriate to consider what evidence is available regarding the effects of ACs on the audit function in practice. ACs could be expected to have an impact on the appointment, removal and remuneration of auditors, the content and extent of audit work, auditor independence, and the resolution of disputes between auditors and executive management. The evidence of the effects of ACs on the internal audit function and on internal controls and risk management also needs to be considered (Zaman 2001). The AC can strengthen the internal audit function (COSO 1994; Turnbull 1999) and internal audit can in turn be an important resource to the AC in fulfilling its responsibilities. It is also argued that ACs should be responsible for overseeing management's assessment of business risk and that they can strengthen management's ability to identify and assess both internal and external risks and hence potential opportunities and challenges facing the entity in achieving its operating, financial, and compliance goals.

7.2.3 *Effects on Financial Reporting*

ACs comment upon and approve choice of accounting policies, and they can be expected to influence a company's approach to financial reporting, levels of disclosure and adherence to standard practice. Over many years, various claims have been made about the potential contribution of ACs to improving financial reporting (Marsh and Powell 1989; APB 1994; ICAEW 1997). ACs are expected to monitor the reliability of the company's accounting processes and compliance with corporate legal and ethical standards including the maintenance of preventive fraud controls. An interesting aspect of research on the financial reporting effects of ACs is the manner in which proxies for reporting quality are created, relying on both analysis of actual reported numbers and more negative signals of poor quality, such as regulatory action against companies.

7.2.4 *Effects on Corporate Performance*

A fourth and final area of potential impact concerns whether the existence of an AC as a governance mechanism results in better corporate performance or wealth effects for investors. It may seem tenuous to draw a direct link between the AC and company performance, but recommended management and governance structures are intended to lead to improved control and better management practices, and this in turn could be associated with positive improvements in performance on behalf of investors.

The connection between particular governance structures and characteristics and corporate performance has become a notable theme in some recent research following corporate failures and it is therefore appropriate to examine whether this line of approach offers any insights and evidence on the value of ACs in companies.

7.3 Effects on Corporate Audit Committee

This section of the chapter evaluates the extent to which empirical research provides evidence of ACs' governance impact in each of the four principal areas introduced above, i.e., (1) structural incentives for the adoption of ACs; (2) effects on the audit function; (3) effects on financial reporting quality; and (4) impact on corporate performance.

7.3.1 Structural Incentives

Several studies have conceptualized AC formation in an agency framework (Jensen and Meckling 1976; Fama and Jensen 1983), and have examined the link between proxies for agency costs and AC presence in organizations where ACs have been introduced voluntarily. Essentially, this strand of research looks for evidence that ACs are perceived as effective mechanisms for reducing agency costs. Several factors associated with agency costs have been tested, including company size, leverage, inter-corporate stockholding, national stock market listing, and extent of managerial ownership, but examination of the incentives for AC formation using these variables has produced mixed results, as illustrated in Table 7.2.

7.3.1.1 Company Size

Tests of an association between company size and the formation of ACs have reported inconsistent findings and do not provide unequivocal support for the suggestion that reduction of agency cost is the primary factor in voluntary adoption of ACs. While some studies (Pincus et al. 1989; Adams 1997) have found a significant positive relationship between company size and AC formation, others using similar definitions of size have not found any significant relationship (Bradbury 1990; Collier 1993; Menon and Williams 1994). Size has been found to

Table 7.2 Illustrative studies AC adoption and activity in an agency framework

Variable	Study						
	Pincus et al. (1989)	Bradbury (1990)	Collier (1993)	Menon and Williams (1994)	Adams (1997)	Turpin and DeZoort (1998)	Collier and Gregory (1999)
Company size	+SR	NSR	NSR	NSR	+SR	+SR	NSR
Leverage	NSR	NSR	+SR	NSR	+SR	NSR	NSR
Top tier Audit firm	+SR	NSR	NSR	NSR			+SR
Management Ownership	−SR	NSR	−SR	NSR		NSR	
Assets in place		NSR	NSR		NSR		
Inter corporate Holdings		+SR					
Dominant CEO			NSR				−SR
No of Shareholders			NSR				
Stock market listing	+SR					NSR	

Note ± SR: positive/negative significant relationship; NSR: no significant relationship be significant in explaining firms' decisions to include a separate AC report in the annual report to shareholders but interestingly other agency variables were not found to be associated with such voluntary reporting (Turpin and DeZoort 1998).

7.3.1.2 Leverage

Jensen and Meckling (1976) suggest that, because of the conflicting interests of managers and debtholders, higher leverage increases debtholders' need to monitor managers. Managers have incentives to control the agency cost of debt and can do so by providing increased monitoring through ACs. Again, as shown in Table 7.2, the research evidence on the influence of leverage on the formation of ACs is inconclusive. For example, Pincus et al. (1989) found only mixed evidence that AC formation is associated with higher leverage and concluded that there is no strong support for an association between the agency cost of debt and voluntary AC formation. In a contrasting result, Collier (1993) asserted that his UK study is 'unique in highlighting gearing as a significant factor' (p. 429). Although Adams (1997) provides some support for Collier's (1993) findings, other studies provide contrary evidence, failing to find a significant positive relationship between leverage and AC formation (Eichenseher and Shields 1985; Bradbury 1990; Menon and Williams 1994). There is also evidence that leverage is not a significant factor associated with the level of AC activity, as measured by the number and duration of meetings (Collier and Gregory 1999) or with the likelihood of a firm including a separate AC report in its annual report (Turpin and DeZoort 1998).

7.3.1.3 Other Agency Factors

Within an agency framework a number of other variables have also been tested for their association with voluntary formation of ACs, but overall with no more conclusive results. For example, while some studies have found a negative relationship between the level of management ownership and AC formation (Pincus et al. 1989; Collier 1993), others have not found any significant relationship (Bradbury 1990; Menon and Williams 1994; Turpin and DeZoort 1998). Tests have also shown no significant association between the voluntary formation of ACs and assets in place (Bradbury 1990; Collier 1993; Adams 1997), the number of shareholders (Collier 1993), and the existence of a dominant chief executive officer (CEO) (Collier 1993). Evidence has, however, been reported of a significant negative relationship between the presence of a dominant CEO and AC activity, as indicated by frequency and duration of meetings (Collier and Gregory 1999). Although a positive relationship between national stock market listing and AC formation has been found (Pincus et al. 1989), suggesting that ACs may reflect the greater information and monitoring demands of the stock market investors, this influence does not hold when extended to voluntary disclosure of an AC report (Turpin and DeZoort 1998). The existence of a large inter-corporate stockholding increases the probability that a firm will have outside directors, thereby increasing the probability that a firm maintains an AC (Bradbury 1990).

Existence does not constitute effectiveness, and the mere formation of an AC does not mean that boards of directors actually rely on ACs to enhance their monitoring ability (Menon and Williams 1994). Other attributes have also been tested as potential indicators of AC impact in practice. AC activity, measured by the frequency of meetings, has been found to increase with firm size and with increases in the proportion of outsiders on the board (Menon and Williams 1994). Collier and Gregory (1999) found the number and duration of AC meetings to be negatively related to the presence of a dominant CEO and positively related to top tier[2] audit firms. There is some evidence that companies with strong CEOs have a higher probability of placing insiders and interested directors on ACs than those with relatively weaker CEOs (Klein 1998a) and also that the ACs of strong CEO companies tend to meet less frequently than their counterparts (Klein 1998a; Collier and Gregory 1999). However, the number and duration of AC meetings are very crude measures of AC activity which may depend not only on the size and nature of a company's business, but also on the scope of the AC's activities and more fundamentally on the extent and nature of communication outside AC meetings.

A further potential indicator of effectiveness that has been used to test the link between agency cost proxies and the quality of AC monitoring is the inclusion of members in the AC with relevant experience. Lee and Stone (1997) found that the composition of ACs is not related to agency costs but is significantly related to the background of the CEO and AC chair, and concluded that their evidence was inconsistent with the agency paradigm that has guided much research on monitoring and control.

Overall, the empirical evidence on the formation of, and/or reliance on, ACs provides very limited support for viewing their effects solely in terms of managing the costs associated with agency related factors. Given this conclusion, a number of suggestions, including the adoption of alternative approaches, for AC research are made in the final section of this chapter.

7.3.1.4 Association with Large Auditing Firms

Auditing firms may have incentives to encourage the formation of ACs. It is argued that an AC enhances the independence of the auditor from management, which in turn can be important in protecting the auditor from allegations of inadequate auditing associated with business failure or fraud (Mautz and Neumann 1970). Large audit firms should have more incentive to promote ACs among their clients than smaller firms, and the rate of voluntary formation for different categories of auditor could indicate a link with auditor incentives.

[2] The term ''top-tier'' refers generically to the leading group of firms that currently comprise the Big-4, and previously over time the Big-5, Big-6 or Big-8 audit firms.

There is some evidence of an association between the use of top-tier audit firms and the formation of ACs. For example, evidence has been reported for the US showing a positive relationship between a company being audited by a top-tier audit firm and the existence of an AC (Pincus et al. 1989). Similarly, in circumstances where an incumbent auditor is replaced by a smaller audit firm, an AC is not likely to be formed (Eichenseher and Shields 1985; Bradbury 1990; Menon and Williams 1994). Although this association is consistent with many observations on the competitive nature of the market for audit services (Pong and Turley 1997), it need not imply causality as both the engagement of a top-tier auditor and the adoption of an AC could simply reflect other company variables. Despite finding some evidence that companies with auditors outside the top-tier were less likely to have formed ACs, Collier (1993) confirmed that having a top-tier auditor was not a significant factor influencing AC formation, although a significant positive relationship has been found between top-tier auditors and AC activity (Collier and Gregory 1999).

7.3.1.5 Legal Protection

ACs can provide evidence that the board of directors has exercised due care in performing its prescribed duties which in turn would be expected to reduce the board's legal exposure and there is some early evidence of a perception among auditors and directors, both executive and non-executive, that an AC provides some legal protection to the directors as evidence of due diligence in the fulfillment of their responsibilities (Mautz and Neumann 1970). It has also been suggested that the increase in adoption of ACs in the US during the late 1970s was a monitoring response to increasing director liability, primarily stemming from the Foreign Corrupt Practices Act (FCPA) of 1977, and by implication that a perceived effect of ACs is lower liability costs (Eichenseher and Shields 1985). However, the legal protection explanation of the benefits and effects of ACs is likely to be influenced by the particular legal context in different national environments and so is not compelling as a universal explanation for the development of ACs internationally.

7.3.2 *Effects on the Audit Function*

A second theme relevant in evaluating the governance contribution of ACs is their impact on the external and internal audit function. There are several research questions of interest in this area. Does the AC affect the selection, retention, and removal of the auditor or influence the level of audit fees? Has auditor independence improved as a result of having ACs? What is the likelihood that the AC will support either the auditors or management in a dispute? How do ACs impact on the internal control and risk management processes in companies? Many of the claimed benefits of ACs are linked to these questions. This section discusses evidence dealing with such issues.

7.3.2.1 Auditor Selection

A potential effect of ACs relating to external auditor appointments is that they may exhibit a bias in favor of large auditors, for example due to past connections or reputation and associated perceptions of audit quality. Evidence from early studies examining auditor selection in the US in the 1980s did not support the existence of an AC bias leading to the selection of large, better-known auditing firms over smaller, less well-known firms (Kunitake 1981, 1983; Eichenseher and Shields 1985; Cottell and Rankin 1988). While there was evidence of a tendency for companies with an AC to select a top-tier audit firm at the time of a change in auditor, this behavior was also exhibited in companies without an AC and the evidence did not suggest any statistically significant AC effect on this tendency (Eichenseher and Shields 1985; Cottell and Rankin 1988).

More recent research has reported that ACs which do not include employees and that meet at least twice per year are more likely to select auditors specializing in the company's industry (Abbott and Parker 2000). Archambeault and DeZoort (2001) reported results which suggested that neither the existence of an AC nor its level of activity (proxied by the number of AC meetings) had a negative and significant relationship with auditor switches identified as suspicious. However, there was a negative and significant relationship between suspicious auditor switches and the proportion of independent directors, the proportion of AC members with experience in accounting, auditing and finance, and the size of the AC.

7.3.2.2 Auditor Remuneration

A related question to that of auditor selection is the effect of ACs on auditor remuneration. Despite the considerable volume of research on audit fees, evidence of AC effects on fees is rather limited. One difficulty is that different rationales suggest that ACs could result in increased fees or decreased fees. If an AC seeks to enhance audit quality, the impact could be to increase the audit fee. Conversely, if existence of an AC is associated with increased internal control strength, a reduced fee would be expected. Collier and Gregory (1996) examined these propositions and found a significant positive relationship for the first but no significant relationship for the second. The authors conclude that 'there is no conclusive evidence to suggest that (ACs are) effective in engendering a stronger internal control environment that is reflected in reduced audit fees' (p. 195).

Evidence that the proportion of non-executive directors has a positive and significant impact on audit fees, which is consistent with increased nonexecutive representation encouraging more extensive auditing, is provided by O'Sullivan (2000) based on an examination of the 1992 fees of 402 UK companies. Intriguingly, however, this research did not test whether the presence of an AC affects audit fees, but a study by the same author (O'Sullivan 1999) using the 1995 audit fees for a sample of 146 UK companies found no evidence that board and AC characteristics influence audit pricing.

The potential for research on AC's involvement and influence in audit fee determination is much broader than the limited examination it has so far received. In this context it is interesting to note that DeZoort (1997) found that AC members ranked external auditor selection and fee approval as relatively unimportant compared to other oversight duties. The AC's perceptions of auditor quality will inevitably influence its approach to auditor selection and remuneration and those perceptions are influenced by AC members' prior exposure to different size audit firms (Knapp 1991). Survey results indicate that audit team factors, such as the level of partner/manager attention given to the audit, are perceived by AC chairs to have a greater effect on audit quality than factors such as the relative significance of total fees paid to the audit firm. There is also evidence that AC members perceive that large audit firms are more likely to disclose material errors that they discover than are local firms and that a learning curve effect in the early years of an audit appointment results in a gradual improvement in auditor quality (Schroeder et al. 1986).

7.3.2.3 Auditor Independence

A longstanding element in the rationale for ACs is their potential effect on the relationship between the external auditor and management and consequent benefit for auditor independence (Cohen Commission 1978). Some evidence on this issue is provided by studies that have examined the effect of AC existence on users' perception of independence. The presence of ACs has been found to create a perception of enhanced auditor independence and more reliable financial reporting among financial statements users (Gwilliam and Kilcommins 1998). Similarly, a small sample study of 20 bankers considering loan applications has identified greater reliance on financial statements given information on the presence of ACs than given information on their absence (Tsui et al. 1994). It is, however, difficult to draw general conclusions from these exploratory and survey studies. The observed effects could be due to the fact that the subjects' attention was drawn specifically to the existence of an AC or otherwise, and may not represent normal decision processes in practice.

A second source of evidence on the contribution of ACs to auditor independence is their behavior in situations where there is a dispute between the external auditor and executive management. Confidentiality limits the research potential in this area, but a limited amount of questionnaire and experimental test results are available. In an early experimental survey, Knapp (1987) examined factors affecting AC support for auditors, rather than management, in audit disputes. The results suggested that AC members, on average, tended to support the auditors, rather than management, in the conflict scenarios where the dispute involved objective technical standards and the auditee was in a weak financial position.

Similar more recent work identified greater independent director experience and greater audit knowledge as associated with higher AC support for an auditor who advocated a 'substance over form' approach in a dispute with client management (DeZoort and Salterio 2000). Given the evidence of significant disagreements between executive management, external auditors, and AC chairs concerning the appropriate level of financial statement disclosure (Haka and Chalos 1990), the effects of ACs on auditor independence may be much more complex than can easily be captured in survey studies (Spira 1999).

7.3.2.4 Auditor Process and Reporting

Given the adoption of new audit methodologies (Bell et al. 1997; KPMG 1999; Lemon et al. 2000) and concerns about the external reporting of audit findings (Hatherly et al. 1998; Manson and Zaman 2001), the impact of ACs on the external audit process and on auditor communication is an important issue. Although there is some evidence that auditors gather information on corporate governance primarily at the preplanning and the planning stages (Cohen and Hanno, 2000), there is limited research evidence of AC impact on the audit process. Practicing auditors have characterized their meetings with the AC as normally entailing the auditor reporting on significant issues, rather than an active two-way exchange or a proactive process on the part of the AC (Cohen et al. 2002). Interestingly the auditors believed that ACs are not effective and not powerful enough to resolve contentious matters with management.

Some indication of the effects of ACs on the outcome of the audit may be gleaned from Beattie et al.'s (2000) investigation of interactions between finance directors and audit engagement partners in the UK. The authors found that the existence of an AC was not associated with the extent of changes to financial statements. ACs were, however, found to reduce the confrontational intensity of interactions between auditors and management by increasing the level of discussion and reducing the level of negotiation. While in interviews, practicing auditors state that their discussions with ACs or boards never affect the type of audit report issued (Cohen et al. 2002), investigation of a link between AC independence and audit reporting has found that the greater the percentage of grey directors on the AC, the lower the probability that the auditor will issue a going-concern audit qualification (Carcello and Neal 2000, 2003).

7.3.2.5 Internal Controls and Risk Management

Although numerous articles in the professional literature discuss the control and risk management roles of ACs, the academic literature on the impact of ACs in these areas is rather limited. Evidence based on experience in an individual company is provided by Allison (1994) who illustrates a case where the AC has become an integral element in the internal control system of an enterprise. Analysis of 11 AC reports, for the US fiscal year 1990, found that all the companies reported that their ACs review and monitor internal controls (Rezaee and Farmer 1994, p. 18). An interesting consideration in this context is the suggestion that internal auditors and managers believe that where the internal audit function is outsourced it might be difficult for ACs and boards to come to an overall opinion on the effectiveness of internal control (Assiri and Sherer 2000).

A related question is the role of ACs in the hiring and firing of the chief internal auditor. In the US, for example, the NCFFR (1987) advocated that ACs should review the appointment and dismissal of the chief internal auditor. The limited empirical evidence on this issue, from a survey of US chief internal auditors, suggests that ACs are involved in appointment and dismissal decisions in 33 and 38 % of companies, respectively (McHugh and Raghunandan 1994). Only in 14 % of such cases did the chief internal auditor have unrestricted access to the AC, and, concerning the question of independence, the authors found that a strong majority of internal auditors, particularly those in smaller companies, perceived that vesting the AC with authority over appointment and dismissal would enhance internal auditor independence, improve oversight by the AC, and improve the ability of the internal auditor to get action on audit findings.

Some evidence is available that the more independent the AC is from executive management the more active is its approach to internal audit. This higher degree of activity on internal audit matters did not however extend to involvement in decisions to dismiss the chief internal auditor (Scarbrough et al. 1998). Survey evidence from auditors and directors in Singapore, where ACs are mandatory, reported that, although the existence of a strong AC is perceived to enhance the effectiveness of an external audit and to help the company prevent and detect errors in the financial statements, there was doubt among respondents about whether a strong AC would help the company to prevent and detect control weaknesses and fraud (Goodwin and Seow 2002).

It has been reported that AC members rank internal control evaluation as the most important AC oversight responsibility after financial statement review (DeZoort 1997). However, a difficulty with researching this area is identifying generalized signals of internal control impact. In an examination of whether experience affects AC members' oversight judgments, it was found that AC members with financial experience made internal control judgments more like auditors than did members without experience, suggesting that relevant expertise can make a difference in AC member oversight of internal controls and risk management (DeZoort 1998).

7.3.3 Financial Reporting Effects

A further area of significant interest is the effect of ACs on financial reporting quality. The basic question is whether financial reporting is different in the presence of ACs compared to their absence. Identifying signals of financial reporting quality may be difficult but can be attempted either through analysis of actual reported financial numbers, for example to consider whether, ACs improve companies' earnings quality, or through negative signals of problems in financial reporting, for example instances of apparent or alleged errors, fraud, and irregularities (see Table 7.3). The growing volume of research in this area generally falls into two categories: studies which have examined the effect of AC presence (absence) on various measures of financial reporting quality (for example, DeFond and Jiambalvo 1991; Beasley 1996; Dechow et al. 1996; McMullen 1996; Peasnell et al. 1999); and those more concerned with testing particular AC characteristics, such as meetings, independence and members' backgrounds (for example, Abbott et al. 2000; Beasley et al. 2000; Parker 2000; and Windram and Song 2000).

Evidence of a positive link between AC existence and the quality of financial reporting has been provided by analysis indicating that earnings overstatements, as indicated by prior period adjustments to correct errors in previous reports, are less likely among companies that have ACs (DeFond and Jiambalvo 1991) and that companies manipulating earnings are less likely to have an AC (Dechow et al. 1996). Evidence has also been documented that ACs are associated with a reduced incidence of errors and irregularities in financial statements, as identified by a number of indicators of financial reporting quality (McMullen 1996).[3] In the UK, action against companies by the Financial Reporting Review Panel (FRRP) for defective financial statements has been used as an equivalent signal to SEC Enforcement Actions in the US. While, for a sample of 47 UK firms subject to FRRP action, Peasnell et al. (1999) did not report a significant relationship between FRRP action and presence of ACs, Windram and Song (2000) found a significant negative relationship between FRRP action and the AC's financial literacy, the frequency of AC meetings and the number of outside directorships held by AC members.

What is not resolved by these studies on reporting quality is whether the improvements in financial reporting are specifically due to the existence of ACs or whether certain AC characteristics and reporting outcomes are both the product of other corporate variables. A particularly interesting finding relating to this is that the presence of ACs does not significantly affect the likelihood of fraud (Beasley 1996), although the proportion of outside members on the board of directors was found to be lower for firms experiencing financial statement fraud than for no-fraud firms and a significant negative relationship was also found between the likelihood of fraud and both the percentage of gray directors on the board and the percentage of independent directors. Although based on a small sample of only 26 companies, the results suggest board composition, rather than the presence of ACs, may be significantly more likely to reduce the likelihood of financial statement fraud.

In the UK context, the association between board composition and earnings management activity in both the pre- and post-Cadbury periods has been examined (Peasnell et al. 2000). Results for the post-Cadbury period indicate less

---

[3] These are shareholder litigation alleging fraudulent financial reporting; correction of reported quarterly earnings; SEC enforcement actions; illegal acts; and auditor turnover involving a client-auditor accounting disagreement.

Table 7.3 Illustrative Studies of ACs and Financial Reporting Quality

Signal of reporting quality	Studies	AC-related variables						
		Exist-ence	Size	Meetings	Independence	Expertise	AC outside director-ships	Outside directors on board (%)
Fraud (SEC action)	Beasley (1996)	NSR						−SR
	Dechow et al. (1996)	−SR						-SR
	Beasley et al. (2000)	−SR						
	McMullen (1996)	−SR		−SR	−SR			
	Abbott et al. (2000)			−SR	−SR			NSR
FRRP action	Peasnell et al. (1999)	NSR						
	Windram and Song (2000)			−SR		−SR	−SR	−SR
Earnings management	Abbott et al. (2000)		NSR	−SR	−SR	NSR		NSR
	Parker (2000)			−SR	−SR			−SR
	Peasnell et al. (2000)	NSR						−SR
	DeFond and Jiambalvo (1991)	−SR						
Audit qualification	Carcello and Neal (2000)				−SR			
	Carcello and Neal (2003)							

Note ±*SR* positive/negative significant relationship; *NSR* no significant relationship income-increasing accrual management to avoid earnings losses or earnings declines when the proportion of nonexecutive directors is high. However, no evidence was found of an association between the degree of accrual management and the proportion of nonexecutive directors in the pre-Cadbury period. Consistent with Beasley's (1996) finding, it appears the proportion of nonexecutive directors is significant in explaining reduced earnings management rather than the increasing use of ACs in the post-Cadbury period (Peasnell et al. 2000).

Neither of the above studies examined the effect of AC characteristics, but evidence is now being reported that these are important in explaining, inter alia, cross-sectional differences in financial reporting quality (Wright 1996; Klein 2002; Abbott et al. 2000; Parker 2000). Analyst ratings of financial reporting quality are higher for companies with lower percentages of directors, particularly AC members, who are either relatives of officers, or have some business relationships with the firm, i.e., gray directors; and firms violating SEC reporting standards have a significantly higher percentage of insiders and grey directors on their AC (Wright 1996). AC independence has also been found to be positively related to the informativeness of financial accounting information for equity valuation and negatively related to the degree of bargaining power that the CEO commands over the board (Klein 2002).

Recent studies have reported that independent and active ACs are associated with a decreased likelihood of both fraud and nonfraudulent earnings misstatements (Abbott et al. 2000), but also that AC size and AC expertise are not significantly related to reduced earnings misstatements Abbott et al. (2000). Similarly, income-increasing accounting has been found to be constrained by independent ACs and by public disclosure of ACs responsibility for monitoring financial reports (Parker 2000). Among companies subject to SEC AAERs, Beasley et al. (2000) found that fraud firms have fewer ACs, less independent ACs, fewer AC meetings and less internal audit support than non-fraud firms.

While some of the variables representing AC characteristics have been associated with mixed findings, it is noticeable that both AC meetings (a measure of AC activity) and the independence of AC members have consistently been found to be associated with a lower likelihood of problems in financial reporting quality (see Table 7.3). The fact that corporate failures and irregularities occur in companies with ACs complying with, or even exceeding, recommended best practice illustrates the importance of understanding the process associated with AC operations. For example, Enron provides an example which counters the proposition that financial literacy among AC members will lead to effectiveness (Benston and Hartgraves 2002). While ACs may be enhanced by certain characteristics (such as independence and expertise), these attributes alone are unlikely to deliver an improvement in financial reporting quality. This conclusion indicates that the character and operations of ACs may be fruitful areas for research into the conditions under which the anticipated benefits of ACs can be realized.

7.3.4 Corporate Performance Effects

A final area of potential AC impact is corporate performance. As noted earlier, it is important to be clear whether particular benefits or effects are due to the existence of ACs as such or if they are a result of other features of corporate governance. A growing body of literature has examined the relationship between board characteristics and corporate performance. Positive findings on this issue could imply that ACs, being a subcommittee of the board with a majority of outside directors, might lead to similar performance effects.

Taking as a starting point the idea that good corporate governance is equated with good corporate performance, some researchers have examined whether the inclusion of outside directors on the board enhances corporate performance and the returns to shareholders (Klein 1998b). Examples of the available evidence relevant to this issue include the finding that the stock market reaction to announcements of poison pills is positive when the board has a majority of outside directors and negative when it does not (Brickley et al. 1994), and that characteristics of the board of directors' and ownership structure are significant determinants of the likelihood that a firm is a target of hostile take-over attempts (Shivdasani 1993). Results of this nature are consistent with the proposition that outside directors do perform an important role in corporate governance and serve the interests of shareholders.

A relevant avenue of research concerning possible AC impact on performance, though not one yet fully exploited, is the investigation of the links between board membership characteristics and shareholder wealth effects. As an example, in a study of the returns to shareholders of bidding firms in tender offers, Byrd and Hickman (1992) reported that the average announcement date abnormal return is significantly less negative for bidding firms on whose boards at least half the seats are held by independent outside directors. Examination of the wealth effects associated with appointments of an outside director by management indicates that the appointment is accompanied, on average, by significantly positive excess returns, although most boards are numerically dominated by outsiders before the appointment. This suggests that outside directors are viewed as likely to act in the interests of shareholders (Rosentein and Wyatt 1990).

Future research on the relationship between ACs and corporate performance should also recognize the conclusions from other general reviews addressing the relationship between board composition, board leadership structure, and corporate performance. Dalton et al. (1998) found little consistency in results and concluded that, in general, neither board composition nor board leadership structure has been consistently linked to corporate financial performance. This view is supported by Weisbach and Hermalin's (2000) conclusion, based on a survey of the economic literature on boards of directors, that board composition is not related to corporate performance, although board size is negatively related to corporate performance.

Some evidence on the wealth effects specifically related to ACs is provided by Wild (1994, 1996) in his test of the proposition that the formation of the AC enhances earnings quality. It was hypothesized that if the AC enhances the quality of reported earnings, then release of earnings reports after AC formation would be accompanied by greater revisions in users' expectations of future company performance than before the formation of the AC. The findings indicate a significant increase in stock returns variability, specifically 20 % greater than for earnings reports prior to AC formation, leading to a conclusion that the "evidence is characteristic of effective audit committees that substantially enhance the quality of reported earnings" (p. 274).

7.4 Summary and Conclusions

In an environment where, following a number of major corporate scandals, AC effectiveness has been criticized and changes are being introduced to strengthen the AC's governance contribution, understanding the existing body of evidence concerning the effects of ACs is important—for formulating expectations regarding the likely impact of policy changes and for establishing the benchmark for testing the impact of those changes. Taken together, the evidence discussed in the previous Section suggests a number of general observations concerning the development of future research priorities of relevance to these questions that can help inform the continuing debate on regulatory policy and its implementation in practice.

7.4.1 Research Focus

Attempts to infer perceived benefits by examining the structural incentives associated with choices over AC adoption and characteristics do not suggest a clear accepted model of the role of ACs in corporate governance in practice. In part this may be due to the weakness of proxy measures used to represent and test different governance scenarios, but it also indicates the need to dig deeper to develop a more complete understanding of the ACs in practice.

The predominant emphasis in extant research is on testing incentives for the use of ACs within an agency framework, where the underlying proposition is that an effect of the AC will be to reduce agency costs. Overall, however, the empirical evidence that the use of ACs is intended to achieve a reduction in agency costs is very limited. It is unsurprising that certain company characteristics, used as proxies for agency costs, are correlated strongly with the adoption of ACs, and the existence of such a relationship does not point unambiguously to motives for the use of ACs. Important research issues include the interaction between ACs and other aspects of governance arrangements, particularly attributes of board composition in general and why, even if ACs do indeed reduce agency costs, preference is given to ACs over other means of achieving the same goal. It could be important to establish whether the effects on external audit, financial reporting, and corporate performance are simply due to the mix of insiders and outsiders on the board or whether particular governance structures such as ACs really make a difference.

There is considerable scope for further study of AC effects on all aspects of the audit and financial reporting process. The evidence on the link between AC presence, and more recently AC characteristics, and financial reporting quality raises some important questions. It also remains the case that there are a number of areas of potential impact on which as yet only limited evidence is available. Such areas include the effect of ACs on aspects of internal control, internal audit and risk management. Similarly, although the research on board composition suggests that ACs, as a subcommittee of the board, may fulfill a useful role, it does not provide direct evidence of AC impact on corporate performance.

Even where evidence has been found of association between ACs and governance outcomes, there remains very little understanding of the methods of operation whereby these effects are brought about. Policy on ACs has tended to emphasize characteristics of the committee and its members, but the processes through which the AC's activities are conducted and the impact on other organizational processes and the behavior of other participants are of at least equal importance. Extant research provides very little understanding of these processes. While there is some evidence of a correlation between financial reporting characteristics and governance arrangements, further research is needed to establish issues relating to the processes and impact unique to ACs.

A limiting feature of much of what has been researched on ACs is that it has resulted from studies in which the primary subject has not been ACs but rather topics such as auditor independence, auditor tenure and financial reporting quality. In such studies, researchers tend merely to add an AC variable to their model of, for example, audit fees or financial reporting quality. The fact that AC issues are often a secondary concern in the research design inevitably limits the contribution of such studies to the understanding of AC operations and effects. ACs should be the primary subject of future research, rather than simply another variable included in a model.

7.4.2 Research Framework: Need to Reconceptualize Acs

The evaluation of the evidence of AC effects suggests that there is a case for focusing attention on the institutional and organizational features, particularly the dynamics relating to the AC process that lead to certain effects. Clearly there are variations in the degree of effectiveness between ACs and the context and nature of AC activities that appear to be associated with particular effects need to be investigated more fully. This issue might require rather different types of research than those that have so far been prominent. It could be said that much of the research to date has been developed around theories of the existence of ACs but that for the future there is a need to give greater attention to possible theories of operation.

The fact that extant research has primarily adopted an agency perspective may have to some extent constrained insights about the operation of ACs and how the manner in which AC activity is conducted is linked to impact in corporate enterprises. ACs do not operate in a vacuum and their operation and effects cannot be adequately examined without regard to the institutional and organizational context in which they function and the power relationships which are intrinsic to that context.

The ways in which ACs affect behavior within organizations is an open and potentially interesting area for future research. AC effects need to be examined in the context in which they operate so that due account can be taken of the relational dynamics in and around the AC, and the interaction of the AC with other internal structures of the entity. It should also be recognized that the personality of AC members, particularly that of the AC chair, and the underlying corporate culture are potentially important factors affecting the operation and effects of ACs. Within the individual organization, these factors may be particularly important in determining AC impact and their link to AC effects warrants investigation.

7.4.3 A Case for Qualitative Methods

Much of the existing body of AC research has been based on large samples, utilizing publicly available and/or questionnaire data which rarely reflect the practical reality of ACs' operation and their effects. The impact of ACs cannot be adequately investigated using solely questionnaire surveys and analysis of databases. Qualitative research methods incorporating case studies and interviews provide significant potential for researching ACs' activities in the organizational and institutional context in which they operate. In particular, cases may allow identification of specific independence and audit process effects and recognition of the complex environment of the AC and the interaction of the AC with other parties such as executive management and auditors. There are a number of reasons for believing this area of effect could be of particular significance.

First, in the context of the debate on corporate governance, the interaction between the AC and auditors is potentially an important means of enhancing overall governance. The issues surrounding auditor independence and the appointment and retention of auditors, including the negotiation of fees and the provision of nonaudit services, need to be examined in more detail. Second, communication between the AC and auditors clearly has the potential to influence auditors' work programmes, both through direct suggestion and through the onus it places on auditors to be able to justify their intended approach. Potentially the audit process is made more visible than previously. Third, as the methodologies employed by the audit firms continue to evolve, and particularly in recent years as a tension has arisen between the

'attest' and 'consultancy' attributes of the audit (Jeppesen 1998), the degree to which the methodologies meet the expectations of ACs will be of interest. Finally, in exercising influence over both internal control and external audit there are different potential strategies available to ACs, with varying implications for external audit. How ACs make relevant choices and the circumstances in which, for instance, external audit costs are increased or decreased should be investigated.

7.4.4 Concluding Remarks

It is clear that there is no automatic relationship between the adoption of AC structures or characteristics and the achievement of particular governance effects. The mixed results associated with, for example, tests for association between ACs and aspects of the audit function and the quality of financial reporting suggest that particular rules on ACs cannot be relied upon to deliver a consistent impact. This observation is of relevance in the policy arena at a time when greater reliance is being placed on codification around such factors as AC members' independence and expertise as the means of ''correcting'' past weaknesses in the arrangements for ACs. That is not to say that such characteristics are not valuable and worthy of promotion but caution may be needed over expectations that greater standardization will deliver guaranteed standard governance contributions.

This chapter has sought to illustrate and evaluate the nature and extent of available empirical evidence of the governance impact of ACs, through the benefits apparent in the structural incentives for the adoption of ACs and their effects on the audit function, on financial reporting quality and on corporate performance. Evaluation of this evidence offers a mixed picture—while some evidence of beneficial effects has been established, on many areas of expected benefits the findings thus far are either inconclusive or very limited, leaving plenty of scope for further investigation. Future research should incorporate (1) greater consideration of the organizational and institutional contexts in which ACs operate; (2) explicit theorization of the processes associated with AC operation; (3) complementing extant research methods with field studies; and (4) investigation of unintended (behavioural) as well as expected consequences of ACs.

Appendix

> Increasingly, companies will be expected to demonstrate good governance in order to access the world's capital markets. The fact that a company has an audit committee may boost investor confidence in its governance practice (Price Waterhouse 1997).

> There is no doubt that audit committees can play a major role in bringing about greater accountability by companies and in restoring confidence in financial reporting (Lindsell 1992).

(Audit committees can) help directors meet their statutory and fiduciary responsibilities, especially as regards accounting records, annual accounts and the audit (Collier 1992).

An audit committee is unique in that it provides a forum where directors, management, and auditors can deal together with issues relating to the management of risk and with financial reporting obligations (AARF 1997).

The independent nature of the audit committee should result in the internal audit department assuming a greater responsibility in the financial reporting process. This role should, in turn, promote improvements in the internal control structure, resulting in heightened integrity in the financial reporting process (Apostolou 1990).

(Audit committees) provide a framework within which the external auditor can assert his independence in the event of a dispute with management (and) strengthen the position of the internal audit function, by providing a greater degree of independence from management (Cadbury 1992).

Audit committees have an important role to play in enhancing the perceived independence of internal and external audit (Price Waterhouse 1997).

The audit committee of a company's board of directors can play a crucial role in preventing and detecting fraudulent reporting (NCFFR 1987).

(Audit committees have the potential to) improve the quality of financial reporting, by reviewing the financial statements on behalf of the board (and to) create a climate of discipline and control which will reduce the opportunity for fraud (Cadbury 1992).

References

AARF. (1997). Audit Committees: Best Practice Guide, Australia: Australian Accounting Research Foundation, Australian Institute of Company Directors and Institute of internal Auditors.

Abbott, L. J., & Parker S. (2000). Auditor selection and audit committee characteristics. *Auditing: A Journal of Practice and Theory*, 19(2), 47–66.

Abbott, L. J., Park, Y., & Parker, S. (2000). The effects of audit committee activity and independence on corporate fraud. *Managerial Finance, 26*(11), 55–67.

Adams, M. (1997). Determinants of audit committee formation in the life insurance industry: New Zealand evidence. *Journal of Business Research, 38*(2), 123–129.

Allison, D. L. (1994). Internal auditors and audit committees. Internal Auditor, February, pp. 50–55.

APB. (1994). *The audit agenda*. London: Auditing Practices Board.

Apostolou, B. (1990). The role of internal auditor communication with the audit committee. *Internal Auditing Fall, 6*(2), 35–42.

Archambeault, D., & DeZoort, T. (2001). Auditor opinion shopping and the audit committee: an analysis of suspicious auditor switches. *International Journal of Auditing, 5*, 33–52.

Assiri, S. M., & Sherer M. (2000). *Outsourcing the internal audit function: an empirical evaluation of benefits and pitfalls*. Paper presented at the 6th Annual Midyear AAA Auditing Section Conference, California.

Australian Treasury. (2002). Corporate disclosure: strengthening the financial reporting framework. CLERP9, Department of Treasury, Commonwealth of Australia. http://www.treasury.gov.au.

Beasley, M. S. (1996). Board of director composition and financial statement fraud. *Accounting Review, 71*(4), 443–465.

Beasley, M. S., Carcello, J. V., Hermanson, D. R., & Lapides, P. D. (2000). Fraudulent financial reporting: consideration of industry traits and corporate governance mechanisms. *Accounting Horizons, 14*(4), 441–454.

Beattie, V., Fearnley, S., & Brandt, R. (2000). Behind the audit report: a descriptive study of discussions and negotiations between auditors and directors. *International Journal of Auditing, 4*, 177–202.

Bell, T., Morris, F., Solomon, I., & Thomas, H. (1997). *Auditing organizations through a strategic-systems lens*. Montvale, NJ: KPMG Peat Marwick LLP.

Benston, G. J., & Hartgraves, A. L. (2002). Enron: what happened and what we can learn from it. *Journal of Accounting and Public Policy, 21*, 105–127.

Blue Ribbon Committee. (1999). *Report and recommendations of the blue ribbon committee on improving the effectiveness of corporate audit committees*. NY: NYSE and NASD.

Bradbury, M. E. (1990). The incentives for voluntary audit committee formation. *Journal of Accounting and Public Policy, 9*, 19–36.

Brickley, J. A., Coles, J. L., & Terry, R. L. (1994). Outside directors and the adoption of poison pills. *Journal of Financial Economics, 35*, 371–390.

Byrd, J. W., & Hickman, K. A. (1992). Do outside directors monitor managers? Evidence from tender offer bids. *Journal of Financial Economics, 32*(2), 195–221.

Cadbury Committee. (1992). *Financial aspects of corporate governance*. London: Gee Publishing Ltd.

Carcello, J. V., & Neal, T. L. (2000). Audit committee composition and auditor reporting. *Accounting Review, 75*(4), 453–467.

Carcello, J. V., & Neal, T. L. (2003). Audit committee characteristics and auditor dismissals following 'new' going-concern reports. *Accounting Review, 78*(1), 95–118.

Cohen, J., & Hanno D. (2000). Auditors consideration of corporate governance and management philosophy in preplanning and planning judgments. *Auditing: A Journal of Practice and Theory, 19*(2), 133–146.

Cohen Commission. (1978). Report of the commission on auditors' responsibilities, AICPA.

Cohen, J., Krishnamoorthy, G., & Wright, A. M. (2002). Corporate governance and the audit process. *Contemporary Accounting Research, 19*(4), 573–594.

Collier, P. (1992). *Audit committees in large UK companies*. London: ICAEW Research Board.

Collier, P. (1993). Factors affecting the formation of audit committees in major UK listed companies. *Accounting and Business Research, 23*(91A), 421–430.

Collier, P. (1996). The rise of the audit committee in UK quoted companies: a curious phenomenon? *Accounting, Business and Financial History, 6*(2), 121–140.

Collier, P., & Gregory, A. (1996). Audit committee effectiveness and the audit fee. *European Accounting Review, 5*(2), 177–198.

Collier, P., & Gregory, A. (1999). Audit committee activity and agency costs. *Journal of Accounting and Public Policy, 18*, 311–332.

COSO. (1994). Internal control: Integrated framework. New York: Coopers and Lybrand/Committee of Sponsoring Organizations of the Treadway Commission.

Cottell, P. G., & Rankin, L. J. (1988). Do audit committees bias auditor selection? *Akron Business and Economic Review, 19*(4), 87–103. Winter.

Dalton, D. R., Daily, C. M., Ellstrand, A. E., & Johnson, L. J. (1998). Meta-analytic review of board composition, leadership structure and financial performance. *Strategic Management Journal, 19*, 269–290.

Dechow, P. M., Sloan, R. G., & Sweeney, A. P. (1996). Causes and consequences of earnings manipulation: An analysis of firms subject to enforcement action by the SEC. *Contemporary Accounting Research, 13*(1), 1–36. Spring.

DeFond, M. L., & Jiambalvo, J. (1991). Incidence and circumstances of accounting errors. *Accounting Review*, July *66*(3), 643–655.

DeZoort, F. T. (1997). An investigation of audit committees' oversight responsibilities. *Abacus, 33*(2), 208–227.

DeZoort, F. T. (1998). An analysis of experience effects on audit committee members' oversight judgments. *Accounting Organizations and Society, 23*(1), 1–21.

DeZoort, F. T., & Salterio, S. (2000). The effects of corporate governance experience and financial reporting and audit knowledge on audit committee members' judgments. Working Paper, University of South Carolina.

Eichenseher, J. W., & Shields, D. (1985). Corporate director liability and monitoring preferences. *Journal of Accounting and Public Policy, 4*, 13–31.

Fama, E., & Jensen, M. (1983). Separation of ownership and control. *Journal of Law and Economics, 26*, 301–325.

Goodwin, J., & Seow, J. L. (2002). The influence of corporate governance mechanisms on the prevention and detection of control weaknesses, fraud and error: The perceptions of auditors and directors. *Accounting and Finance, 42*, 195–233.

Guy, D. M., & Zeff, S.A. (2002). Independence and objectivity: Retired partners on audit committee. *CPA Journal* July, pp. 31–34.

Gwilliam, D., & Kilcommins, M. (1998). The impact of audit firm size and audit committee on perceptions of auditor independence and financial statement reliability in Ireland. *Irish Accounting Review, 5*(1), 23–56.

Haka, S., & Chalos, P. (1990). Evidence of agency conflict among management, auditors, and the audit committee chair. *Journal of Accounting and Public Policy, 9*, 271–292.

Hatherly, D. (1999). The future of auditing: The debate in the UK. *European Accounting Review, 8*(1), 51–65.

Hatherly, D., Innes, J., & Brown, T. (1998). Free-form reporting and perceptions of the audit. *British Accounting Review, 30*(1), 23–38.

Higgs, D. (2003). *Review of the role and effectiveness of non-executive directors*. London: Department of Trade and Industry.

ICAEW. (1997). *Audit committees: A framework for assessment*. London: ICAEW Audit Faculty.

Jensen, M. C., & Meckling, W. H. (1976). Theory of the firm: managerial behavior, agency costs and ownership structure. *Journal of Financial Economics, 3*(4), 305–360.

Jeppesen, K. K. (1998). Reinventing auditing, defining consulting and independence. *European Accounting Review, 7*(3), 517–541.

Kalbers, L. P., & Fogarty, T.J. (1993). Audit committee effectiveness: an empirical investigation of the contribution of power. *Auditing: A Journal of Practice and Theory*, *12*(1), 24–49.

Kalbers, L. P., & Fogarty, T. J. (1998). Organizational and economic explanations of audit committee oversight. *Journal of Managerial Issues, 10*(2), 129–151.

Klein, A. (1998a). Economic determinants of audit committee composition and activity. Stern School of Business Working Paper, New York University.

Klein, A. (1998b). Firm performance and board committee structure. *Journal of Law and Economics, 41*, 275–303.

Klein, A. (2002). Audit committee, board of directors characteristics and earnings management. *Journal of Accounting and Economics, 33*, 375–401.

Knapp, M. C. (1987). An empirical study of audit committee support for auditors involved in technical disputes with client management. *Accounting Review, 62*(3), 578–588.

Knapp, M. C. (1991). Factors that audit committee members use as surrogates for audit quality. *Auditing: A Journal of Practice and Theory*, *10*(1), 35–52.

KPMG. (1999). *The financial statement audit: Why a new age requires an evolving methodology.* Montvale, NJ: KPMG LLP.

Kunitake, W. (1981). Do audit committees favor the large CPA firms. *Journal of Accountancy*, August, pp. 43–45.

Kunitake, W. (1983). Auditor changes by audit committees and outside directors. Akron Business and Economic Review, Fall, pp. 48–52.

Lee, T. (2001). A crisis of confidence: US auditing in the 21st century. *International Journal of Auditing, 5*(1), 1–2.
Lee, T., & Stone, M. (1997). Economic agency and audit committees: Responsibilities and membership composition. *International Journal of Auditing, 1*(2), 97–116.
Lemon, W. M., Tatum, K. M., & Turley, W. S. (2000). *Developments in the audit methodologies of large accounting firms*. London: Auditing Practices Board.
Lindsell, D. (1992). Blueprint for an effective audit committee. *Accountancy*, December, p. 104.
Manson, S., & Zaman, M. (2001). Auditor communication in an evolving environment: Going beyond SAS 600 auditors' reports on financial statements. *British Accounting Review, 33*, 113–136.
Marsh, H. L., & Powell T. E. (1989). The audit committee charter: Rx for fraud prevention. *Journal of Accountancy*, February, pp. 5–57.
Mautz, R. K., & Neumann, F. L. (1970). *Corporate audit committees*. Illinois: Bureau of Economic and Business Research, University of Illinois.
McHugh, J., & Raghunandan, K. (1994). Hiring and firing the chief internal auditor. *Internal Auditor*, August, pp. 34–39.
McMullen, D. A. (1996). Audit committee performance: An investigation of the consequences associated with audit committees. *Auditing: Journal of Practice and Theory*, *15*(1), 87–103.
Menon, K., & Williams, J. D. (1994). The use of audit committees for monitoring. *Journal of Accounting and Public Policy, 13*, 121–139.
Morse, A., & Keegan, M. (1999). *Audit committees: Good practices for meeting market expectations*. London: PricewaterhouseCoopers.
NCFFR. (1987). *Report of the national commission on fraudulent financial reporting* (Treadway Commission), New York: AICPA.
O'Sullivan, N. (1999). Board characteristics and audit pricing post-cadbury: A research note. *European Accounting Review, 8*(2), 253–263.
O'Sullivan, N. (2000). The impact of board composition and ownership on audit quality: Evidence from large UK companies. *British Accounting Review, 32*, 397–414.
Parker, S. (2000). *The association between audit committee characteristics and the conservatism of* financial *reporting*. Paper presented at the American Accounting Association 2000 Annual Conference.
Peasnell, K.V., Pope P., & Young S. (1999). *Characteristics of firms subject to adverse financial reporting review panel rulings*. Paper presented at the Financial Accounting and Auditing Research Conference, 12–13 July, SOAS, University of London.
Peasnell, K. V., Pope, P., & Young, S. (2000). Accrual management to meet earnings targets: UK evidence pre- and post- Cadbury. *British Accounting Review, 32*, 415–445.
Pincus, K., Rusbarsky, M., & Wong, J. (1989). Voluntary formation of corporate audit committees among NASDAQ firms. *Journal of Accounting and Public Policy, 8*, 239–265.
Pong, C., & Turley, S. (1997). Audit firms and the market. In M. Sherer & S. Turley (Eds.), *Current issues in auditing*. London: Paul Chapman.
Powers Report. (2002). Report of Investigation by the Special Investigative Committee of the Board of Directors of Enron Corporation, February.
Price Waterhouse. (1997). *Audit committees: A study in European corporate governance*. London: Price Waterhouse.
Rezaee, Z., & Farmer L. E. (1994). The changing role of the audit committee. Internal Auditor, Spring, pp. 10–20.
Rosentein, S., & Wyatt, J. G. (1990). Outside Directors, Board independence, and Shareholder Wealth. *Journal of Financial Economics, 26*, 175–191.
Scarbrough, D. P., Rama, D. V., & Raghunandan, K. (1998). Audit committee composition and interaction with internal auditing: Canadian evidence. *Accounting Horizons, 12*(1), 51–62.
Schroeder, M. S., Solomon, I., & Vickrey D. (1986). Audit quality: The perceptions of audit committee chairpersons and audit partners. *Auditing: A Journal of Practice and Theory*, *5*(2), 86–94.

SEC. (2002). Disclosure required by section 404, 406 and 407 of the Sarbanes-Oxley Act of 2002, securities and exchange commission release no. 33-8138. http://www.sec.gov/rules/proposed/33-8138.htm.

Shivdasani, A. (1993). Board composition, ownership structure, and hostile take-overs. *Journal of Accounting and Economics, 16*, 167–198.

Smith Committee. (2003). Audit committees: Combined code guidance, Financial Reporting Council.

Sommer, A. A. (1991). Auditing audit committees: An educational opportunity for auditors. *Accounting Horizons, 5*(2), 91–93.

Spira, L. (1999). Independence in corporate governance: The audit committee role. *Business Ethics: A European Review, 8*(4), 262–273.

Tricker, R. I. (1978). *The independent director: A study of the non-executive director and of the audit committee*. Croydon: Tolley.

Tsui, J., Subramaniam, N., & Hoy J. S. (1994). The effects of audit committees on bankers' perceptions of auditor independence. *Corporate Governance: An International Review*, April, *2*(2), 101–107.

Turley, S., & Zaman, M. (2003). Public policy on corporate audit committees: Case study evidence of current practice. Occasional Research Paper No. 35, Association of Chartered Certified Accountants, London.

Turnbull. (1999). Internal control: Guidance for directors of listed companies incorporated in the UK. London: ICAEW.

Turner, L. E. (2001). Audit committees: A Call for Action. Speech delivered at the Conference on Accounting Irregularities II: What's an Audit Committee To Do? 21 February 2001, Atlanta, Georgia.

Turpin, R. A., & DeZoort, F. T. (1998). Characteristics of firms that include an audit committee report in their annual report. *International Journal of Auditing, 2*, 35–48.

Vicknair, D., Hickman, K., & Carnes, K. C. (1993). A note on audit committee independence: Evidence from the NYSE on ''grey'' area directors. *Accounting Horizons*, Mar, *7*(1), 53.

Weisbach, M. S., & Hermalin, B. J. (2000). *Board of directors as an endogenously determined institution: A survey of the economic literature*. Working Paper: University of Illinois.

Wild, J. (1994). Managerial accountability to shareholders: Audit committees and the explanatory power of earnings for returns. *British Accounting Review, 26*, 353–374.

Wild, J. (1996). The audit committee and earnings quality. *Journal of Accounting, Auditing and Finance, 11*(2), 247–276.

Windram, B., & Song, J. (2000). *The effectiveness of audit committees: Evidence from UK companies in the Post-Cadbury period*. Paper presented at the British Accounting Association Annual Conference, University of Exeter.

Wolnizer, P. W. (1995). Are audit committees red herrings? *Abacus, 31*(1), 45–66.

Wright, D. W. (1996). Evidence on the relation between corporate governance characteristics and the quality of financial reporting. Working Paper, University of Michigan.

Zaman, M. (2001). Turnbull: generating undue expectations of the corporate governance role of audit committees. *Managerial Auditing Journal, 16*(1), 5–9.

Chapter 8
The Role of Debt Contracts and Debt Covenants in Corporate Governance: Reflections on Evolution and Innovation

Judy Day and Peter Taylor

Abstract This chapter discusses aspects of the role of debt contracts and covenants in corporate governance. It reviews evidence on types and incidence of debt covenants in both public and private debt and discusses evidence on contemporary developments in debt contracting practice and newly emerging debt covenants, placing debt covenant practice in historical context, and stressing the evolutionary nature of covenants. We observe patterns in empirical evidence on covenant types and usage, noting that covenants lose and gain popularity or relevance, with some new covenants appearing. Traditional explanations of choice in debt contracting associated with agency costs and contracting costs provide only partial explanations of change and we explain covenant evolution using the literature on financial innovation. Influences on covenant evolution include changing law and regulation, new opportunities to manage risk, exogenous shocks and crises, the influence of cyclical and structural economic factors, and advances in theory. We conclude that it is important to extend existing research on innovation in debt contracting and covenants to include studies of the development of specific covenants, agents of change and costs and benefits of innovation. Such research will help ensure modelling of debt covenants in empirical research in accounting and finance is sensitive to institutional realities.

This chapter includes the paper originally titled "Debt Contracting costs, corporate governance and accounting choice: reflections on the Positive Accounting Theory model" and discussed at the First International Workshop on Accounting and Regulation in 1998.

J. Day · P. Taylor (✉)
Manchester Business School, The University of Manchester, Manchester, UK
e-mail: peter.taylor@mbs.ac.uk

J. Day
e-mail: j.day@lse.ac.uk

R. Di Pietra et al. (eds.), *Accounting and Regulation*,
DOI: 10.1007/978-1-4614-8097-6_8,

8.1 Introduction

In an earlier paper (Day and Taylor 1998), we examined the role of debt contracting and debt covenants in corporate governance. That paper discussed the form and content of debt contracts; it reviewed evidence on types of covenants which at that time had been observed in debt contracts; and presented evidence on perceptions of the role served by covenants in solving the creditor problems recognised by agency theory and their role in controlling creditor-firm relationships. In addition, we examined issues raised by the nature of debt contracts and the contracting process, focusing in particular upon standardisation versus customisation in debt contracts. Many aspects of debt contracting have remained broadly as outlined in our earlier paper but in the intervening period significant areas have changed and developed. In this chapter, we concentrate on those changes and developments. Our discussion will focus on the evolution of restrictive covenants found in corporate debt contracts, considering *inter alia*: the factors which have determined that evolution, the nature of the evolution, focusing in particular on changes in forms and uses of restrictive debt covenants and the accounting implications of the changes in debt covenant practices which we document. Our particular emphasis, as in the earlier companion paper, is upon accounting-based covenants and other broadly comparable non-quantitatively expressed restrictive covenants with a financial or accounting focus.

Covenants[1] have a long legal history as part of contractual arrangements, especially in relation to real property (see Rowley 1953, on restrictive covenants in English Law). Covenants also have a long history as control restrictions applied within business relationships within firms, as indicated for example in Hejeebu's (2005) work on covenants in employment contracts issued by the English East India Company in the seventeenth century. In relation to corporate debt, covenants and other restrictions on management of indebted companies emerged during the railway reorganisations in the US in the 1890s (see Rodgers 1965; Tufano 1997). Restrictive covenants and accounting-based covenants in particular have for many years been included in debt contracts written under arrangements typical of US (Smith and Warner 1979) and UK (Day and Taylor 1995) institutional conditions. However, relatively little has been published on the origins of accounting-based debt covenants nor on the process by which new covenants emerge. Some evidence suggests that accounting-based restrictive debt covenants first became common in US bank lending in the 1950s and that they subsequently became established in the UK in the following decade through lending associated with North Sea oil and gas project financing (Donaldson and Donaldson 1982). Thereafter, accounting-based and other restrictive covenants have become an integral feature of bilateral and syndicated lending by financial institutions in the

[1] Covenants are agreements between two or more legal personalities, entered into in writing and under seal, whereby either party stipulates the truth of certain facts, or promises to perform or give something to the other, or to abstain from the performance of certain things.

US and UK. Restrictive covenants have also been a common feature of publicly issued corporate debt but different contracting practices from private debt contracts have been both hypothesised and observed. International institutional connections have facilitated the transfer of covenants into corporate loan documents in countries in the US/UK sphere of finance and legal influence such as Australia, Canada, South Africa, and Singapore (Ormrod and Taylor 2004). Latterly, debt covenants have come to be used beyond this and covenants now appear to be increasingly common in lending involving corporate borrowers and lenders from developed country legal jurisdictions and financial systems where they were not formerly encountered. Evidence is also emerging that debt covenants are used in corporate lending in some developing countries. This international spread of debt covenants confirms the existence of forces which have operated to transfer a corporate governance mechanism via debt markets.

It has been long accepted that practice in covenant use has differed consistently and markedly between private and public debt markets in that covenants have been significantly more common in private debt than public debt (Smith and Warner 1979) due to differences in contracting costs in the two settings. Both empirical evidence and costly contracting theory have suggested that covenants appear to be more actively monitored and acted upon by lenders of private debt than by holders of public debt. Notwithstanding these accepted patterns, observation of market practices in contracting for publicly issued corporate debt indicates the extensive use of covenants when debt is high yield. Evidence from academic research and observation of market practice also indicates that the nature of the covenants used in private corporate debt contracts appears to have changed significantly through time. This chapter reviews evidence on the types and forms of accounting-based covenants which have been observed by researchers and we note that evolution in covenant types has taken place. We observe that new forms of accounting-based covenants have emerged (e.g. covenants using direct measures of cash flow or indirect cash flow indictors such as earnings before interest, tax, depreciation and amortisation (EBITDA)) and have become widely used, whilst well established and previously widely used covenants such as gearing have declined in use. Evidence is also presented that some hitherto neglected covenants (e.g. current ratio covenants) are in fact widely used in certain corporate lending contracts. Alternative approaches to the management of the private debt agency relationship using covenants have also evolved in the form of "covenant-lite" contracting whereby maintenance covenants and other contracting devices common in high-yield bonds have been transferred to other market segments. Hence, a broad spectrum of covenant-based contracting can now be observed in markets, encompassing traditional "covenant-heavy" bank lending contracts, through looser covenanted contracts, to "covenant-lite". These developments can be associated with, *inter alia*, changes in debt market structure but also with wider economic considerations. Also observable is a tendency through time for change in the types and forms of covenants used in debt contracts, both private and public. This suggests that it is important to document those changes in covenant practices themselves but also that it is valuable to examine the processes by which these changes take place and to seek to identify the drivers of these changes. Thus, the form and content of debt contracts cannot be considered as static and debt covenants must be viewed as evolving, changing by both innovation and obsolescence, and we consider the nature and implications of such changes in this chapter.[2]

We consider the issues discussed in this chapter to be significant for a number of reasons. Debt covenants remain important in the functioning of debt markets as devices to control agency costs and hence continue to be key elements of market-based corporate governance. The widening international use of covenants in private debt markets means that debt covenant-based corporate governance is assuming greater international importance. For these reasons, it is important to understand the changes which have occurred in debt contracting practice in relation to covenants. Covenants have been widely used by researchers in accounting and finance as, *inter alia*, sources of managerial incentives and proxies for agency costs in relation to those incentives, in studies of accounting choice. However, even in this respect change may be observed. Positive Accounting Theory (PAT) as developed from the work of Watts and Zimmerman (1978) and others may be characterised as taking the form of covenants as given and then seeking to predict what accounting choices managers might make given these covenants. More recent empirical accounting literature has tended to focus on the extent to which debt markets have shaped financial reporting practices by considering what kind of accounting rules debt holders demand (see for example Ball et al. 2008; Kim et al. 2011). Thus, we argue that it is important for researchers to appreciate the evolutionary development of debt covenant practices in order to fully understand the functioning of corporate debt markets to ensure *inter alia* that methodology and models incorporating debt covenants appropriately reflect actual practice.

The chapter is organised as follows: in the following section, we consider theoretical perspectives and empirical evidence on the use of debt covenants, focusing in particular on accounting-based debt covenants in both public debt and private debt, and review some contemporary developments in debt market practice on covenants; section three discusses the literature on financial innovation; section four seeks to apply research on financial innovation to innovation in debt covenants; and section five contains our conclusions.

[2] In this chapter although we focus on the evolution of one aspect of debt contracting practice, namely changes in types and incidence of accounting-based covenants, this is not to say that other aspects of debt contracting relevant to corporate governance do not also evolve. Analysis of the nature and implications of inter-temporal change in lenders' and borrowers' responses to covenant violation, lenders' monitoring practices, measurement practices and other aspects of debt contracting must await further research.

8.2 Debt Covenants: Theoretical Perspectives and Empirical Evidence

Despite the long legal and commercial history of covenants more generally, the form, content and purposes of debt contracts and associated debt covenants were established as a central element in the accounting and finance literature by pioneering research on theoretical aspects of corporate governance only in the last quarter of the twentieth century (as in Jensen and Meckling 1976; Kalay 1982) and manuals of US institutional arrangements for debt contracting as analysed by Smith and Warner (1979). In essence, this works posits that debt contracts and the covenants therein seek to mitigate the agency costs of lenders arising from the ability of firm owners and managers to transfer wealth from lenders by diluting their claims on the firm, through excessive dividend payments, excessive borrowing, asset substitution and underinvestment. Efficiently constructed debt contracts will reflect not only the reduction of agency costs but the costs of bonding and monitoring the terms of those contracts (see Day and Taylor 1998, Sect. 3.3).

The analysis by Smith and Warner (1979) of the debt contracting practices and "boilerplates"[3] reported in the American Bar Foundation's *Commentaries on Indentures* (American Bar Foundation 1971), formed the basis for much subsequent research. Other sources on US practice at that time [for example *Moody's Industrial Manual* (Moody, various years), Simmons (1972), and Castle (1980)] added to Smith and Warner's findings. No UK authority comparable to the American Bar Foundation *Commentaries* was subjected to academic analysis at that time but examination of later UK sources confirm broadly equivalent patterns in debt contracting practice for the UK (see Encyclopaedia of Forms and Precedents 2010, Lingard 1995, and Association of Corporate Treasurers 1991).[4] Empirical research testing hypotheses on accounting choice based on the work of Smith and Warner (1979) followed quite quickly, (as in Bowen et al. 1981; Daley; Vigeland 1983; Holthausen and Leftwich 1983), and such work was based on assumptions that Smith and Warner's findings were representative of actual practice rather than merely professional recommendations.

This distinction is important due to the use in empirical research of proxies for covenants based on institutional and theoretical research rather than direct data on covenants themselves. Confidentiality constraints on the direct observability of the terms of private debt contracts, as well as limitations imposed by financial reporting, have been a continuing problem for empirical research, as have the problems of collecting data from public issues of debt. The debt to equity ratio for example has frequently proxied for closeness to violation of debt covenants and hence for the presence of debt contracting cost incentives. The effectiveness of this proxy is predicated on either the presence of maximum gearing restrictions in debt

---

[3] In its legal sense "boilerplate" refers to standard and often predetermined contract provisions.

[4] The outline structure of standard form debt contracts is discussed in Day and Taylor (1998) pp 174–175.

contracts; or, where gearing covenants are not present, balance sheet gearing proxying for related non-gearing covenants (such as minimum interest cover or direct borrowing restrictions); gearing proxying for other covenants (such as minimum net worth, dividend restrictions, or restrictions on working capital); or there being an underlying economic or statistical link between levels of gearing and likelihood of covenant violation. Research into the robustness of proxies has produced mixed results. Duke and Hunt (1990) found a significant positive association between gearing and the presence of covenants restricting dividends, working capital, and net assets, but not the presence of gearing covenants themselves. Other research noted that such proxies contained measurement error (e.g. Mohrman 1993) or were subject to interpretational difficulties (Ball and Foster 1982; Leftwich 1990). Dichev and Skinner (2002) provide direct evidence on the validity of the leverage variable frequently used in the literature as a proxy for closeness to debt covenants. While they found that leverage was negatively related to covenant slack, the correlation was modest in economic terms, implying that leverage is a fairly noisy proxy for managers' incentives under debt covenants. This suggests that gearing might be a weak proxy for closeness to debt covenant violation. Thus, research investigating the contents of actual debt contracts, both public and private, has been important in establishing the validity of assumptions of empirical research. Such research has found broad correspondence between debt market practice and the findings of theoretical research but has also uncovered some important differences and irregularities. It has also indicated change and development in the types and uses of covenants and hence this research remains importance as covenants evolve. We shall now review the main literature on types and incidence of accounting-based covenants, looking first at publicly issued debt and then at private debt, and then consider contemporary developments in debt market practice on covenants.

8.2.1 Evidence on Covenants in Public Debt

Early research was directed at evidence on the form and content of covenants in public issues of debt. Kalay (1982) examined *Moody's Industrial Manual* over the period 1956–1975 and concluded that dividend covenants were very common in US public debt, with 85 % of firm debt reported on by *Moody's* containing a net income-based dividend restriction. Smith and Warner (1979) had reported a smaller proportionate use of dividend restrictions (23 %) but a very large incidence of accounting-based restrictions on borrowing (90 %) expressed through gearing. Whittred and Zimmer (1986) reported four main types of financial covenant found in contracts for debentures, unsecured notes and convertible notes publicly listed in Australia, namely gearing (liabilities to total tangible assets), secured liabilities to total tangible assets, prior charges to total tangible assets and interest cover. Stokes and Tay (1988) provided further Australian evidence from the market for convertible notes, confirming some of Whittred and Zimmer's findings but observing no covenants on interest cover or prior charges, but finding very common restrictions on asset disposal (in 80 % of their sample) and borrowings (in 97 % of their sample). Francis (1989) studied covenants in a random sample of 45 publicly issued debentures in the US, finding six covenants to be regularly present, relating to payment of principal and interest, requirements to make sinking fund provisions, restrictions on sale and leaseback transactions, restrictions on mergers and constraints on dividends. She found no covenant restrictions on working capital, net worth, or current ratios. Francis reported her findings to be consistent with *Moody's Industrial Manual*. Duke and Hunt (1990) examined a sample of mainly public debt contracts based on *Moody's Industrial Manual*, and found approximately 50 % of firms subject to a dividend restriction (based mainly on retained earnings), approximately one-third of firms facing working capital or current ratio covenants, and 28 % facing gearing restrictions. In a study of contracts governing 108 issues of public debt in the UK, Citron (1995) found that 35 % contained accounting-based covenants, the majority of which related to gearing.

Begley and Freedman (2004) analysed the content of samples of public debt in the US for three time periods, 1975–1979, 1989–1993 and 1999–2000. They noted a sharp decline in the use of accounting-based covenants in public lending agreements in the 25 years covered by their study. In particular, they observed that the incidence of accounting-based restrictions on dividends and additional borrowing fell from being present in nearly half of their sample in the period 1975–1979, to 25 % in the 1989–1993 sample, and to only 10 % in the 1999–2000 sample. They noted also that while restriction of additional borrowing tended to be signalled in the earliest period by the gearing ratio, in the two later periods interest cover was the typical covenant form for the borrowing restriction and, moreover, interest cover tended to reflect profit adjusted for non-cash items such as depreciation, amortisation and gains and losses on disposal of assets.

Mather and Peirson (2006) analysed a sample of 36 recently issued Australian public debt contracts and compared their finding to those of Whittred and Zimmer (1986). They reported substantial changes between the two studies in the types of accounting-based covenants used. Mather and Peirson found that covenants were less restrictive and that the types of covenants used were more heterogeneous than observed by Whittred and Zimmer. They concluded that in the Australian market there had been a significant reduction in the use of gearing covenants (measured as total liabilities to total tangible assets or as secured liabilities to total tangible assets) with only 28 % of their sample including such covenants. The greater variety of covenants was reflected in 47 % of their sample having other restrictions on liabilities (including two contracts with a restriction on the maximum contingent liabilities to net tangible assets), 17 % of contracts having covenants restricting minimum interest cover as well as covenants stipulating a minimum dividend cover restriction and 12 % having net worth and current ratio covenants.

8.2.2 Evidence on Covenants in Private Debt

Access to private debt contracts is problematic, making research into their contents difficult to conduct. However, evidence is available for several countries. Press and Wientrop (1990) analysed a sample of mainly private debt contracts for the US and observed approximately 60 % of sample firms being subject to dividend restrictions, and approximately 50 % of the sample facing gearing, minimum net worth and working capital covenants. Covenants based on interest cover or cash flows were rare. Citron (1992a, b) analysed a sample of UK bank loan contracts and found the three most common financial ratio covenants to relate to minimum tangible net worth, interest cover and gearing (measured as borrowings over net worth), 50 % of his sample of contracts containing all three. Day and Taylor (1997) confirmed the conclusions of Citron for the UK, finding that the three financial covenants which were in most regular use related to interest cover, balance sheet gearing and minimum tangible net worth. Cotter (1998) in a study of Australian private debt contracts found the covenants most likely to be included were restrictions on leverage (as the ratio of total liabilities to total tangible assets), interest cover (as EBIT/to gross interest expense), current ratio and prior charges ratio (as the ratio of prior charges to total tangible assets). She noted, as also did Whittred and Zimmer (1986), that restrictions on dividends were not applied to large companies. The absence of dividend restrictions in conventional private debt contracts was also observed for the UK by Day and Taylor (1995) and Leuz et al. (1997) for Germany. In contrast, Healy and Palepu (1990) noted that dividend restrictions were the most commonly encountered covenants in US debt contracts. Day and Taylor (1997) also reported the rarity in UK debt contracts governing conventional corporate borrowing of covenants involving cash flows (for example ratios of operating cash flows to interest payments or operating cash flows to dividends). Only one company from a sample of 44 companies studied by Day and Taylor reported the presence of cash flow covenants *per se* in its debt contracts, with one other indicating that such covenants had been present in the past.[5] The comparative rarity of cash flow covenants at that time may be explained in several ways: the information content of cash flows may have been captured in other covenants; definitional difficulties for cash flow covenants despite cash flow disclosures being mandated by regulators; accrual accounting information having superior information content in certain contracting situations (e.g. for borrowers with structurally irregular cash flows); or cash flow covenants being perceived by lenders as potentially distorting managerial incentives in businesses where incentive systems are strongly profit-related (as argued by Leuz et al. 1997).

[5] Two further companies, whilst not having actual cash flow covenants, had covenants in contracts applicable to US loans which were similar to cash flow covenants. In addition, two companies had contracts which required the provision of cash flow forecasts and two others had contracts which identified cash flow shortfalls as events of default.

Ramsay and Sidhu (1998) obtained access from large Australian law firms to a sample of 16 anonymised private contracts for corporate debt, including 2 boiler-plate contacts and 14 actual contracts. They found a wider range of covenants than reported for Australian public debt by Whittred and Zimmer (1986) and Stokes and Tay (1988). Accounting-based covenants were not observed in the two boiler-plate contracts but were present in all the actual contracts. The most common accounting-based covenant was a gearing restriction (present in 11 cases and subject to various definitions of balance sheet numbers), followed by interest cover (10 cases, of which 6 were profits-based and 4 were based on profits adjusted for non-cash items such as depreciation, effectively EBITDA), restriction on secured debt (6 cases, of which four were as a gearing ratio), and current ratio (two cases). A range of other accounting-based covenants was used to tailor specific contracts including six cases of minimum net worth restriction, two cases of accounting-based restriction of dividends (restricted to a maximum proportion of net profit after tax), and one case of minimum operating cash flows to total finance charges. Mather (1999) undertook interview research involving 48 loan officers from 19 Australian and foreign banks operating in Australia to identify accounting-based covenants in Australian private debt contracts. Mather asked interviewees to use a Likert scale to assess frequency of use of covenants and seven main accounting covenants were identified as arising. The most common were interest cover and maximum debt or gearing ratio (each of which arose almost always), whilst minimum dividend cover, cash flow-based financial covenants and maximum level of secured debt were the least likely to be used (arising sometimes), with minimum working capital and minimum net tangible worth arising usually. A later study by Mather and Peirson (2006) analysed a sample of 41 recent Australian private debt contracts. In accordance with theory, they found that the sample of private debt contracts contained a greater number, variety and collectively more restrictive set of accounting-based covenants than the public debt contracts reported in the same study (see above). Interest cover covenants were commonly used in the contracts studied, with 78 % of the contracts including such a covenant. Most contracts had some restriction on liabilities with ratios setting maximum total liabilities to total tangible assets or secured liabilities to total tangible assets being the most common (42 and 22 % of contracts, respectively). The private debt contracts also commonly included covenants requiring minimum current ratios (46 %) as well as a minimum net worth (49 %). In addition, there were numerous other types of covenants present such as maximum turnover ratios, minimum net profit and restrictions on contingent liabilities, operating lease rentals and capital expenditure. Consistent with Cotter (1998) and Ramsay and Sidhu (1998) for Australia, and with other researchers elsewhere, Mather and Peirson reported the absence of covenants based on cash flow information. Mather and Peirson also noted differences in accounting rules associated with financial covenants used in the private debt contracts when compared to public debt.

Dichev and Skinner (2002) analysed data from *Dealscan*, a database of details from private lending agreements for a sample of US private lending agreements, to test proxies for closeness to debt covenants. Two types of accounting-based covenants were used for their test of proxies, namely the current ratio and net worth covenants, chosen because they lead to frequent violations, are widely used and are relatively well-defined. They also restricted the data for their proxy tests to large syndicated commercial loans issued by US banks between 1989 and 1999. However, as a side benefit to their main theme Dichev and Skinner provided some evidence on the incidence of other covenants (this for the period 1993–1999). They reported 12 covenants as occurring. The most common ratios were those most frequently represented in other research, namely: gearing (variously expressed as debt to tangible net worth, leverage, and debt to equity); interest cover, fixed charge cover and debt service cover (the first two of which were of almost equal importance); minimum tangible net worth; and current ratio restrictions. Interestingly, they also reported several cash flow-based covenants, of which debt to cash flow was the most common covenant of all 12 covenants reported, appearing in most loan contracts. Two other covenants involving cash flow were much less common and were senior debt to cash flow and cash flow interest cover. Thus, for the period covered, traditional covenants were still dominant but cash flow-based covenants were beginning to become significant, at least for large US firms. However, as Dichev and Skinner note, "cash flow" was subject to varying definitions (e.g. operating cash flow and EBITDA) which was indicative of tailoring of contracts.

UK data for a similar period was analysed by Moir and Sudarsanam (2007). They studied covenants in private debt using a questionnaire survey of UK corporate treasurers at the 200 largest non-financial quoted UK companies with the survey reporting on practice *circa* 1999. Of the 72 responding firms, 17 conceded no financial covenants and of those reporting accounting-based covenants the most frequently occurring covenants related to gearing (28 of 72 using a ratio of debt to total net worth and 7 of 72 a limit on secured borrowing), interest cover (34 of 72) and minimum tangible net worth (19 of 72). Most interesting was the reporting of three covenants with novel elements: a restriction of debt to a multiple of EBITDA (13 of 72); a variant on interest cover measured as the ratio of interest cost to EBITDA (7 of 72) and a gearing restriction measured as debt to market capitalisation (one instance). Moir and Sudarsanam observe that all the instances of the covenant restricting debt to a multiple of EBITDA arose in debt contracts signed between 1997 and 1999 and refer to the comment of one corporate treasurer who was negotiating new debt during 1999 who cited this covenant as one that many lenders were seeking at that time.

8.2.3 Some Contemporary Developments in Debt Market Practice on Covenants

The review of evidence set out in the previous two sections suggests a broad tendency for traditional accounting-based covenants, whilst persisting in debt markets, to have declined in relative importance compared with comparatively new covenants based on cash flows and cash flow related measures based on EBITDA. There is evidence from data on market practices and some limited academic research of other tendencies in the development of covenants such as the use of intangibles measures, performance pricing of covenants, the linkage of covenants to credit rating, the phenomenon of "covenant-lite" or event-based covenants and auditor-specific covenants. We shall consider contemporary developments in this section.

We have already noted evidence on the gradual emergence of cash flow-based covenants from academic studies of covenant incidence. Cash flow covenants appear to rely on indirect measures of cash flow such as EBITDA which are used to create cash flow variants of traditional covenants based on leverage (e.g. financial indebtedness to EBITDA) and interest cover (EBITDA to either net or gross interest payments or adjusted EBITDA to total funding costs). Other academic research confirms this tendency but identifies other developments. Huang (2009) noted the presence of excess cash flow sweep covenants in 17 % of borrowers represented in a sample of US loan contracts covering 1995–2006. Such cash flow sweep covenants are designed to "sweep up" free cash flow mandatorily, thereby forcing borrowers to repay debt ahead of schedule. Huang found the presence of such covenants to be motivated by creditor-shareholder conflicts and hence to have clear associations with corporate governance characteristics. Huang reported the presence of such covenants to be positively associated with higher leverage (i.e. where risk shifting by equity holders is more likely), the presence of equity holders in strong firm control positions (e.g. presence of institutional block holders, or firm incorporation in jurisdictions with laws more favourable to hostile takeovers) or when equity holders place higher valuation on excess cash holdings. Maxwell and Shenkman (2010) observe that excess cash flow in such covenants is typically defined as EBITDA minus interest payments, changes in working capital, taxes, capital expenditures and principal payments. Further, the mandated percentage of excess cash flows to pay down debt is based normally both based on leverage and is performance related, declining as leverage declines.

A well established, if cyclical, recent tendency in certain debt markets has been the issuing of debt contracts which are "covenant-lite" in character (Markland 2007). The dominant form of debt covenants as discussed thus far in this chapter are maintenance covenants, that is, contractual obligations which need to be met by the borrower throughout the loan period. Covenant-lite loans replace some or all maintenance covenants with incurrence covenants, that is, covenants which become effective through specific actions of the borrower such as an acquisition or an increase in gearing. Such covenant structures are associated with high yield, highly geared lending, often involving private equity. Covenant-lite lending is a relatively recent phenomenon. The Bank of England (2007), using Standard and Poor's Leveraged Commentary and Data as a source, reported that the average number of maintenance covenants in US leveraged loans declined gradually from 2000 (approximately 4.5 per loan) to 2007 (less than 3 per loan) with incurrence covenants replacing them. Incurrence covenant usage growth was concentrated in 2006–2007 (approximately 4.5 per loan by 2007). Fewer covenant-lite loans were noted in Europe over the period although other sources expected significant growth in such lending (see House of Commons 2007, and May and Verde 2005).

A further contemporary development has been the emergence of loans containing performance-based covenants. Under conventional contracting arrangements, a lender might increase the interest rate on a loan during its lifetime as a response to covenant violation. Alternatively, they might permit, *ex ante* or *ex post* to agreeing the terms of a debt contract, prepayment by a borrower in the event of unanticipated improvements in the borrower's circumstances. With performance pricing a debt contract specifies *ex ante* terms under which a change in the credit quality of a borrower as indicated by measures of credit quality triggers an automatic change in interest rate. Thus, interest charged on a bank loan becomes a function of a borrower's current credit rating or of specified accounting numbers such as debt to EBITDA, gearing, or interest coverage. Asquith et al. (2005) note that while there is evidence of performance pricing being used from the 1970s it only became common in the US in the late 1990s and, in the US at least, was confined to bank lending. They interrogated the Loan Pricing Corporation database from 1994 and generated a sample for analysis of which 41 % contained performance pricing covenants and observed both interest-increasing and interest-decreasing performance pricing in their sample. Performance pricing modifies normal contract options in both cases. Thus, interest-increasing performance pricing allows lenders to increase the interest rate prior to default as borrower creditworthiness declines and interest-decreasing performance pricing modifies normal prepayment options for borrowers by substituting an automatic lowering of interest rate for renegotiation of improved payment terms following unanticipated improvement in borrower performance. Asquith et al. conclude that both forms of performance pricing modify agency costs, namely adverse selection arising from asymmetric information between lender and borrower which has caused a misclassification of credit risk, and adverse selection and moral hazard problems associated with threatening *ex post* settling up. They identified the debt to EBITDA ratio as the most commonly used trigger for both types of performance pricing, being used in 58 % of interest-decreasing performance pricing contracts and 45 % of contracts with interest-increasing performance pricing. Debt ratings were found to be the next most frequently used measure, with fixed charge ratios the least used measure in both types of performance pricing. Asquith et al. concluded *inter alia* that performance pricing had measurable economic effects with lenders offering borrowers an initial interest rate averaging 26 basis points lower when interest-increasing performance pricing provisions were included in a debt contract. Chatterjee (2006), in unpublished research, found evidence of UK companies' debt contracts incorporating performance pricing with the most common trigger for revision of interest rate being the debt to EBITDA ratio, followed by interest cover, fixed charge cover, and minimum tangible net worth. His sample suggested an association of performance pricing with relatively large loans at above average pricing.

Related to performance pricing are covenants linked to credit rating of borrowers' debt, with the aim of such covenants being to control for likelihood of financial distress. Typically, such covenants require the borrower to maintain a minimum credit rating or maintain original credit rating, with technical default arising from down-grade in the credit rating or in the event of credit up-grade, permission to issue additional debt (Norton and Pettengill 1998).

Developments in covenant practice are not confined to innovations in accounting-based measures. Evidence has recently emerged of auditor specific covenants being included in debt contracts by lenders to apply controls over external monitoring of accounting information. Such covenants restrict the appointment of auditors of borrowers' accounts to particular audit firms, typically "Big Four" audit firms.[6] No systematic evidence of the extent of this practice is available and its frequency has been challenged for the UK by the British Bankers Association (see Accountancy Age 2010, 2011). However, its anti-competitive implications suggest that more detailed evidence is likely to emerge in due course. Following the UK Office of Fair Trading's (OFT) provisional decision to make a market investigation reference to the Competition Commission on the supply of statutory audit services to large companies in the UK, the OFT identified in its consultation document of July 2011 a number of market characteristics which might restrict competition including the possibility that banks may impose conditions requiring the use of a Big Four auditor in their dealings with companies of a certain size. In justifying this it stated that:

> Various key participants in the market and witnesses have referred to the existence of such conditions or covenants. For example, the Association of Chartered Certified Accountants told the House of Lords inquiry that banks invariably include requirements in lending agreements for listed companies to use one of the Big Four. Likewise, the FRC [Financial Reporting Council] concluded that there was sufficient anecdotal evidence of banking covenants to require a further investigation of this issue. However, we understand that in at least some cases, such requirements may be softer than contractual agreements. (OFT, 2011 pp. 34–5)

The foregoing discussion of empirical evidence on covenant type and incidence of covenants in both private and public debt is broadly supportive of theoretical conclusions and predictions, but it also shows variety and change in covenant use through time and place, demonstrating the dynamic character of debt contracting practices. However, it begs several important and inter-related questions, namely: why do differences arise through time and place in the types and forms of covenants which are used; why do some covenant forms disappear or become less important; and how and why do new forms of covenant emerge? These questions require us to consider the issue of evolution and innovation of covenants. To seek a theoretical framework to examine this issue, we shall look first at the research literature which has been developed to analyse financial innovation and then consider its applicability to innovation and change in debt covenant practices. The latter discussion will include consideration of research which has looked at debt covenants specifically.

---

[6] As reported in Accountancy Age (2010), a US corporation included the following in a debt contract: "Audited consolidated balance sheets of the group members … [must be] reported on by and accompanied by an unqualified report from a Big Four accounting firm".

8.3 Financial Innovation and Debt Covenants

The explanation that debt covenant usage arises as a result of the interplay of agency costs and contracting costs is well established and can serve as an explanation of innovation in debt contracting since changes in both agency costs and contracting costs, absolutely and relatively, are likely to be associated with changes in debt contracting. However, we might note that such interplay, at least in its most narrow economic sense, is likely to provide only a partial explanation. Tufano (1997) has observed that in addition to the economic explanation for changes in practice in finance there are other perspectives to consider, in particular the legal perspective capturing the legislative context and decisions of courts which frame practice, and a business history perspective which examines the behaviour of particular business actors at particular times. Bringing these various perspectives together suggests that it is necessary to consider innovation in finance as a process which is broader than the economic and the same argument may be applied to debt covenants as a sub-set of finance practice. We might also add that whilst researchers in accounting and finance are often quick to observe the outcome of financial innovation, including the emergence of new forms of debt covenant, research less frequently seeks to examine the origin of such innovations or to investigate the process by which innovation takes place, or indeed to identify the principal actors in the innovation process.

If we consider the innovation process more generally, we may identify two broad aspects: the first is the process of development of a new technique, product or service, and the second is the spread of an innovation from originator outwards to other providers. Research has addressed both aspects of innovation in finance, with contributions to both the theory of financial innovation and empirical studies of it. Such work has focused on finance broadly but some contributions have been made to the study of innovation in debt covenants. We shall first consider research which has sought to explain both the determinants of financial innovation and the process of innovation, and then how research on financial innovations broadly defined has relevance for understanding developments in debt covenants.

8.3.1 Financial Innovation: Determinants and Process

Silber (1975) and Ben-Horim and Silber (1977) are two early studies of financial innovation examining the development of new financial instruments or practices. These are seen as stimulated by the presence of costly and sustained financial constraints faced by firms, innovation becoming economically viable when the value of such constraints is sufficient to cover the costs of innovation. They see the likelihood of innovation being dependent upon the costs of innovation. A narrow view of the source of financial constraints may be that they arise from regulation which leads to the view that most financial innovations seek to circumvent regulatory constraints, some support for which is provided by Kane (1981) who recognises the regulatory dialectic as a cyclical process in which the opposing forces of regulation and regulatee avoidance adapt continually to one another with innovation a key element in the process. In a later chapter, Silber (1983) elaborates his theory by analysing the factors stimulating a range of new financial products and practices between 1970 and 1982 and associating them with specific exogenous economic causes including inflation, interest volatility, developments in information processing and data transmission technology, legislative initiatives and internationalisation (in his case a narrower view than globalisation). He cites the work of Sylla (1982) on innovation of new monetary systems in US economic history as consistent with the stimulating effect of rising costs of adhering to financial constraints, and notes the role of crises in inducing interest groups to innovate products jointly.[7]

Van Horne (1985) sees financial innovation as a response to either market inefficiency or incompleteness. He argues that for a new financial instrument or process to be truly innovative, it must increase market efficiency or make markets complete and hence if financial markets were perfect and complete there would be no opportunities for nontrivial financial innovation. He associates the achievement of greater efficiency with reductions in transaction costs or of differential taxes and other deadweight losses, and identifies increasing completion of markets as arising from the design of new instruments which cannot be replicated by any combination of existing instruments.

Miller (1986), in an important study, notes the widely accepted view that financial innovation arises from attempts to reduce the cost of regulatory constraints on businesses and emphasises the perspective that unanticipated changes in regulations and tax rules have been the prime motivators of financial innovation during the 25 years reviewed in his chapter. He also characterises financial innovations as unforecastable improvements and makes the helpful distinction between transitory, permanent, successful and significant innovations. In this context, he observes that many financial innovations exist in one form or another often for many years before they become prominent, with the catalyst for their recognition being some change in the environment.[8] Miller also observes the existence of an innovation spiral by which new customised financial products are supplied initially by initiating financial institutions at low volumes in customised form, perhaps protected by information asymmetries. When such new financial products become successful and "seasoned" (i.e. tested, robust and shown to have utility) they will tend to migrate from being supplied only by their instigators to

[7] See also Wojnilower (1980) on the role of credit crunches in financial history which emphasises that new financial products are designed to sustain financing flexibility for the firm.

[8] Miller (1986) also provides an interesting and rare example of a case study of the origin and development of a financial innovation, in this case financial futures. His history includes identification of the inventor and main actors in the innovation and the stimulus to it, floating exchange rates, which he describes as the "sand in the oyster".

being supplied by others in more generic forms, to, at the limit, being supplied by markets in standardised form.

Merton (1995) developed a conceptual framework for understanding the dynamics of institutional change in financial intermediation based upon a functional perspective, i.e. by taking the economic functions performed by financial intermediaries as given and seeking the best institutional structure to perform those functions. Although concerned with innovation at the structural level, Merton's work provides insights into innovation at the practical and technical level and using it we may identify a number of factors which drive financial product innovation, namely: theoretical developments in finance[9]; advances in computer and telecommunications technology (which reduce transactions costs); changes in financial infrastructure, including changes in regulation, which support or make necessary product innovation; and market mechanisms which customise then standardise new financial products. Merton identifies financial engineering as the mechanism for implementing financial innovation and identifies its components as: diagnosis (identifying new problems); analysis (finding best solutions given current regulation, technology, and theory); production (of an innovation); and pricing (determining the cost of production and profit margin) and customisation (tailoring the new innovation to the specific needs of customers). Similarly to Miller's innovation spiral, Merton stresses the dynamic interaction that takes place between institutions and/or influential individuals who create and test new financial products and services, and the markets in which they are traded. Markets are created by new products and innovations add to trading volume in existing markets and in turn markets help innovators to create customised or standardised products by lowering the cost of production. In a statistical study at firm level, Heffernan et al. (2008) examined a sample of 1,100 UK financial firms to identify determinants of financial innovation. They found the likelihood of financial innovation increased with firm size, employee education, expenditure on R&D, availability of finance and the extent to which firms cooperate. R&D, cooperation and appropriability were identified as main variables driving success of financial innovation, measured by the percentage share of innovations sold.[10]

Tufano (1995) provides an historical review of securities' innovations and characterises financial innovation as a process of learning and experimentation. This chimes with the views of other researchers, for example Miller's notion of an innovation spiral and his distinction between transitory, permanent, successful, significant, and seasoned innovations, and Merton's emphasis on dynamic interaction between institutions and individuals in the creation and testing of

[9] Merton cites Bernstein (1992) for a detailed description of the interaction between theory and practice in generating major innovations. Many areas of knowledge have periods of vibrant theoretical development but theoretical advances do not necessarily convert to practice as effectively and swiftly as in finance, leaving the question of how innovation takes place open. Perhaps vibrant theory is best viewed as a necessary but not sufficient condition for innovation.

[10] Heffernan et al. also observed regional and sectoral variations; stock broking, fund management and related activities being most innovative.

innovations, new financial products and services and the customising or standardising of new products. Tufano adds an interesting perspective by noting a distinctive characteristic of financial innovations which potentially increases the probability of failure, namely the contractual basis of financial arrangements. Financial arrangements, however innovative, will be based upon contracts and innovative contracts by their nature will be incomplete in that they cannot fully define all rights or how rights might be interpreted in law in what are new arrangements. This will be particularly problematic in the early, proving stage of innovations before they become seasoned and perhaps standardised. A further distinguishing feature of financial innovation has been the relative difficulty, in comparison with non-financial innovation, of securing legal protection for innovations as proprietary knowledge. Trade secret law, trademarks, copyright and patents all provide varying degrees of legal protection and as a result give incentives to innovate by protecting the returns from incurring the costs and risks of innovation. Thus, lack of legal protection for intellectual property rights may restrict financial innovation but it should also be noted that the presence of restrictions may slow or prevent the spread of innovations if monopoly profits are pursued, and that law will not protect against independent development of an innovation or reverse engineering. Petruzzi et al. (1988) provide illustration and examples that, even at the time of their writing, broader interpretations of legal protections were emerging and being extended into the finance sphere but this remains an important issue for financial innovation.[11]

Thus, a narrow but quite rich literature has addressed the processes and determinants of financial innovation. If we seek a summary of determinants, Finnerty (1988) collates the factors identified as motivators for financial innovation in the work of Miller, Silber and Van Horne, a list which also effectively encompasses Merton's subsequent work. Finnerty identifies 11 determining factors for innovation as follows: taxation benefits, transaction costs, agency costs, opportunities to reduce or reallocate risk, opportunities to increase liquidity, regulatory or legislative change, volatility of interest rates, level and volatility of prices, advances in finance theory, accounting changes and technological advances.[12]

---

[11] A well-known case of the legal protection of financial proprietary knowledge is Stern Stewart. The intellectual property section of its website lists five proprietary measures and one other: Economic Value Added (EVA)®, Current Operations Value®, Future Growth Value®, Wealth Added Index™, and Relative Wealth Added™, and Market Value Added (see http://www.sternstewart.com/?content=intellectualprop). EVA® has been subjected to significant academic use and some academic analysis (see Mouritsen 1998; O'Hanlon and Peasnell 1988).

[12] Finnerty (1988) also provides an extensive listing of financial innovations to the date of his paper, together with an analysis of the influence of the factors driving each innovation; see also Finnerty (1992). Other analytical studies of drivers of particular financial innovations are Tufano (1995), which documents financial innovations in the nineteenth and early twentieth centuries and Mason et al. (1995). For case studies of particular innovations see Brown and Smith (1988), Briys and Crouhy (1988), and McConnell and Schwartz (1992), who provide a case study of the origin of the liquid yield option note.

Tufano (1995) provides an alternative and more abbreviated summary of the drivers of financial innovation under two broad headings as, first, the mitigation of increases in costs of supplying financial instruments under changing taxes, law and regulation; and second, exogenous shocks and financial crises, and the influence of life-cycle factors in the economy. This classification echoes closely with those of other researchers considered above. This review provides us with a basis to consider innovation in debt covenants and debt contracting.

8.4 Innovation in Debt Covenants

Tufano's (1995) first category of innovation drivers broadly relates to the mitigation of costs of supply arising from changes in taxation, law and regulation. If this is broadened to encompass international differences, we can observe its relevance as an explanation of differences in debt contracting practice. For example, we noted above the difference in incidence of dividend restriction covenants between Australia, Germany, and the UK, and the US. Leuz et al. (1997) have explained the relative infrequency of dividend covenants in UK and German bank debt contracts relative to their US counterparts as arising from particular aspects of contracting costs, namely the presence of legally mandated rules on dividend distributions in the UK and Germany which were efficient substitutes for private rules which are more costly to negotiate.[13] Thus, the absence of effective mandated rules in the US make privately negotiated rules on dividend restriction relatively efficient in that country, while the presence of publicly provided subsidy in the form of legal rules on dividend restriction in Germany and the UK, and potential litigation costs in the UK, make privately negotiated covenants inefficient. Hence, we may conclude that differences in comparative contracting costs arising from differences in law and regulation can affect the usage of particular covenants internationally. Yaxuan and Wald (2008) came to a similar conclusion on the influence of differences in law in their study of the impact of US state laws on the use of debt covenants. They analysed a sample of US public bond issues from 1987 to 2004 and considered variation in state laws with respect to the use of a minimum asset-to-debt ratio necessary for a dividend payout and found that firms incorporated in states with stricter restrictions on distributions were less likely to include debt covenants that constrain dividend payouts, limit additional debt, or restrict the sale of assets, concluding that US state payout restrictions appeared to be a substitute for the use of certain debt covenants. Similar confirmatory evidence

[13] Other institutional factors explain international differences in the incidence of dividend covenants, for example the risk of lenders who restrict borrowers' dividend policy being deemed in UK law "shadow directors" under Section 251 of the 2006 Companies Act and insolvency legislation; see Day and Taylor (1998) for a further discussion. In considering the two cases of dividend covenants identified in their sample Ramsay and Sidhu (1998) note the similarity of the private definitions and the legal restrictions of dividend payments under then Australian law.

for the influence of regulation on debt contracting comes from Mather and Peirson (2006). We noted above that their analysis of Australian public debt contracts found that the covenant packages had become less restrictive and covenants more heterogenous than found by Whittred and Zimmer (1986) 20 years earlier. In particular, they noted a significant reduction in the use of covenants restricting ratios of total liabilities to total tangible assets and secured liabilities to total tangible assets. Mather and Peirson associated the change in practice with regulatory change in the form of ASX listing rules. Specifically, prior to 1st July 1996, ASX listing rules covering trust deeds for loan securities, unsecured notes and convertible notes required the inclusion of limits to both total liabilities and secured liabilities in trust deeds governing the issue of loan securities executed after 1st July 1979, hence the high incidence of relevant covenants found by Whittred and Zimmer (1986). Deletion and simplification of these rules after July 1996 gave contracting parties greater discretion on including covenants in public debt contracts, thus helping explain the innovations in covenant practice observed.

However, other evidence shows that the influence of law and regulation is mitigated by other determinants of debt contracting practice. For example, evidence from Citron et al. (1997, 1999) found that dividend restriction covenants were almost universal in management buy-out and management buy-in lending agreements in the UK, despite their absence in other types of UK debt contracts.[14] This suggests that relative agency costs can mitigate the regulatory effect since the usage of dividend restriction covenants in MBOs and MBIs is consistent with relatively large agency costs facing lenders in such transactions. Yaxuan and Wald (2008) also note the moderating effect of agency costs. They considered the influence of differences in state antitakeover statutes as well as dividend restrictions and, in contrast to their result on dividend restriction covenants, they found that firms incorporated in states with stronger anti-takeover statutes were more likely to use debt covenants. They concluded that firms with legal anti-takeover protection were more likely to suffer from agency problems and, thus, were more likely to use debt covenants to minimise agency costs.

Tufano (1995) summarised a second broad group of financial innovation drivers as exogenous shocks and financial crises, and the influence of life-cycle factors in the economy. The influence of these innovation determinants is well illustrated in several research studies. Tufano (1997) reports the impact of widespread financial distress in US railway companies, a financial crisis given the importance of that economic sector at that time, on debt contracting. He cites a range of sources who noted that these railway reorganisations led to the emergence of new covenants in securities contracts (see Dewing 1911; Draper 1930; Rodgers 1965; Stetson 1917). These changes in contracting practices arose from inter-related private innovatory

[14] Dichev and Skinner (2002) identify a range of cash flow covenants, including debt to cash flow, as the most common in the specialist area of management buy-outs and buy-ins in the US.

action by banks which changed the design of security contracts, and legal change instigated by courts, an illustration of an innovation spiral (see Miller 1986).[15] Financial distress in US railway companies and associated judicial responses appears to have dramatically affected agency costs, incentivising debt holders to seek greater direct involvement in corporate governance. Tufano notes the emergence in that period of several new contracting responses including contingent charge corporate securities and voting trust terms.[16] Contingent charge securities permitted debt servicing to be deferred without causing default or court intervention. Hence, servicing of contingent charge securities was not fixed but contingent on future economic outcomes. These instruments took two forms: income bonds and preferred stock. With income bonds, the contingency was accounting-based, which meant the requirement to pay interest was based directly on the earnings of the firm.[17]

Voting trust contract terms gave monitoring and other corporate governance powers over indebted company management to, *inter alia*, debt holders and preferred stock holders. Monitoring would be carried out by groups of three to five professional trustees empowered typically for 5 years or until a firm resumed regular dividend payments following reorganisation with trusts empowered to approve new issues of preferred stocks or mortgages and the creation of new senior claims. Whilst these new contracting devices were responses to crisis and enhanced agency costs, they also appear to have been reactions to legal changes which weakened *ex post* the position of secured creditors. Tufano (1997) records a succession of legal judgements in the US where the rights of secured creditors were superseded by the redefinition of existing securities contracts.[18] Thus, new contracting practices responded to legal change by introducing enhanced monitoring to avoid *ex post* judicial intervention.

More recent crises may have contributed to the development of contemporary debt contracting practices noted in section two above. Some recent innovations in monitoring covenants may have associations with crises of confidence in external monitoring by auditors and credit rating agencies and resulting regulatory responses. The use of covenants relating to credit ratings of borrowers (which may

---

[15] We may add to these two influences the role of influential individuals as the focus of innovation. Although not directly concerned with financial innovation Ramirez (1995) and others discuss the influential individual in finance.

[16] Other innovations included preferred stocks and deferred coupon debt instruments.

[17] Tufano reports evidence of earnings manipulation by management to avoid the terms of such covenants through opportunistic redefinition of "capital improvements" as "maintenance expenses" [Tufano's italics], the latter allowing a reduction in earnings and hence interest expense. He also quotes Stetson (1917), a contemporary legal authority on corporate finance on the difficulties of earnings definition and hence legal enforcement of covenant terms in income contingent debt securities by borrowers.

[18] Examples are court permission for issue of receivers' certificates (short-term debt notes issued to provide liquidity to distressed firms which were secured against the firm's assets irrespective of pre-existing collateralisations) and the reversal of established rules giving secured creditors priority over unsecured creditors.

capture increase in default risk more effectively than auditors' judgements) may have been put under strain following high-profile business failures. Kornaggia (2011) notes the pressure from regulators on ratings organisations in the aftermath of the WorldCom and Enron failures and identifies possible negative implications for the continued use of credit rating-based covenants but cites prohibitive costs of rewriting covenants and contracts as a reason for their possible continued use. Likewise, the use of auditor specified covenants may have become more prevalent after Enron and WorldCom with lenders becoming more concerned regarding auditor selection, a tendency enhanced by the provisions of Sarbanes-Oxley.[19]

In an earlier section, we noted the gradual emergence of cash flow-based covenants documented by academic studies of covenant incidence and the predominance of indirect measures of cash flow rather than direct GAAP-mandated cash flow measures in such covenants, a pattern which persisted in the period following the mandating of published cash flow statements by accounting regulators from the late 1980s.[20] Our discussion of financial innovation provides a basis from which to interpret this pattern. Thus, Mather and Peirson's (2006) findings in relation to accounting rules in private debt contracts did not directly support the influence of regulation on covenant practice. Following Ramsay and Sidhu (1998) and Cotter (1998), they noted the continuing absence of covenants based on cash flow information despite cash flow statements being mandatory for Australian companies in reporting periods ending on or after 30 June 1992, a regulatory change which would have reduced the contracting costs of using cash flow covenants. As cash flow-based covenants have emerged they have been based chiefly on EBITDA, an approximation to operating cash flow calculated from accrual numbers, rather than data from GAAP cash flow statements. This suggests that contracting parties see less value in mandated cash flow disclosures than in equivalent privately constructed covenant definitions despite the contracting cost savings associated with publicly mandated accounting numbers. Moir and Sudarsanam (2007) observe that EBITDA is an established proxy for cash flow which provides capacity for debt repayment before fresh capital expenditure but does not represent free cash flow from an economic point of view. It is a privately constructed accounting measure with properties which contracting parties may consider more useful than either EBIT, free cash flow, or GAAP-mandated measures of cash flow. Stumpp (2000) provides an historical perspective on the use of EBITDA as an indicator of a company's ability to service its debt. She contends that EBITDA was initially used in the early 1980s as a means of compensating for goodwill amortisation in companies that had made acquisitions at a substantial premium. EBITDA then began "being used to evaluate cash flow in the extreme for companies in a 'near bankruptcy' state. With time, the concept was

---

[19] According to Jones (2011) both the Enron and WorldCom failures were clearly associated with failures of external audit (see p. 476).

[20] The FASB issued SFAS95, *Statement of Cash Flows*, in the US in November 1987, followed by the ASB's FRS1, *Cash Flow Statements*, in the UK in September 1991, and the IASC's revision of IAS7 in 1992.

increasingly applied to companies with long-lived assets". Stumpp concludes that EBITDA is a relevant measure of cash flow in such cases, but suggests that it is less appropriate for higher-rated and investment grade lending. Thus it is likely that the growing of use EBITDA in covenants illustrates perceived deficiencies in GAAP measures of cash flow in addressing agency costs and the widespread use of EBITDA indicates the presence of both information and network benefits which reduce contracting costs (as discussed by Kahan and Klausner 1997, see below).

Tufano (1995) considered the influence of life-cycle factors in the economy as a potential driver of financial innovation. In this context, Kahan and Klausner (1993) provide evidence on the cyclical nature of covenant usage associated with the volume of take-over activity, suggesting covenant usage and innovation was economically determined and driven by market utility. They analyse developments in the use of anti-takeover covenant provisions (i.e. "event risk covenants" or "poison puts") in bonds in the US. Such covenants in essence provide that if specified takeover-related events occur, bondholders have rights to put their bonds back to the issuing company or have bond interest rates increased to reflect additional takeover-related risk, Thus, beginning in the 1980s, as the volume of leveraged acquisitions and recapitalisations in the US transformed tranches of investment grade bonds into speculative-grade junk bonds, many corporations voluntarily began to extend to bondholders protection from takeover-related losses through covenants in advance of any additional extra-contractual (legal) protections. When takeover activity declined in the US in 1991, the use of change of control covenants declined dramatically. However, Kahan and Klausner find the picture to be more complex than this deterministic, market-driven pattern suggests. They note that the longevity of many corporate bonds, together with the cyclicality of takeover activity, suggests a continuing potential attractiveness to bondholders of anti-takeover covenants and hence a demand-side pressure for them as a long-term contract feature rather than a short-term protection. The variability of their use suggests other determining factors. Kahan and Klausner observe that anti-takeover covenants have tended to reflect managerial interests rather than bondholder interests, but that the balance of such interests moves in favour of bondholders in active takeover periods, suggesting that management is prepared to cede ground to bondholders under market pressure.[21]

Tufano's (1995) view on the influence of life-cycle factors in the economy as potential determinants of financial innovation finds expression in the suggestion of Gompers and Lerner (1996) that changes in bond covenants depend on demand and supply conditions in financial markets and on associated potential agency problems. These explanations may be associated with the innovation of covenant-lite as discussed above. Whitehead (2009) saw cyclical patterns in market conditions as associated with tightening and weakening of covenants and with the growth and decline of covenant-lite, greater liquidity resulting in new sets of

---

[21] Anti-takeover provisions bring into sharp focus the corporate governance role of covenants in mediating relations between bondholders, managers, and shareholders (see Day and Sigfrid 2001).

agency costs reflected in a decline in covenant use and monitoring across dispersed creditors. Frankel and Litov (2007) suggest new debt covenants such as covenant-lite are associated with excess liquidity in financial markets. The Bank of England reported the view that covenant weakening associated with covenant-lite lending appeared partly to reflect intense competition among lenders, allowing borrowers to transfer risk to lenders but was uncertain on whether this tendency was cyclical or structural (Bank of England 2007). The Bank of England noted possible implications of such covenant weakening as being reductions in lenders' monitoring activity to influence management and potentially lower recovery rates in the event of default. Market participants attributed some of the reduction in use of covenants in this period to the increased ability to hedge risk in the credit market and the weakening incentives of banks to screen and monitor borrowers (see Acharya et al. 2007). With such implications, the influence of market-wide factors may result in market participants not always making optimal choices when selecting covenants unless the costs associated with sub-optimal solutions are taken into account in the evaluation of new covenants such as covenant-lite before adoption (Kealhofer 2003).

The foregoing seeks to apply determinants of financial innovation to developments in debt covenants. To understand how innovations spread once a change in debt contracting practices has been instigated in the market, we need to consider the process of innovation rather than its more macro-level determinants. Kahan and Klausner (1997) examined process in a pioneering study of the standardisation, customisation and innovation process for debt contract terms. They focus on the costs and benefits of adopting standardised covenants in place of customisation, and the incentives to incur the switching costs associated with deviation from existing contracting forms. Although individually customised contract terms provide obvious benefits in being directed at ameliorating specific agency costs, two main benefits from adopting standardised contracts or debt covenants are identified: learning benefits and network benefits. Learning benefits are associated with adoption of a contract form that has been used previously and such benefits are not affected by the adoption of a similar contract form by others in future. Where a covenant has a demonstrated utility from past use and has become common, learning benefits arise when a contracting party drafts a contract more efficiently by reducing contracting costs such as errors of drafting or ambiguity or looseness leading to loss of control and attendant agency costs. Other benefits follow from reduced uncertainty due to the validity and robustness of new or standard covenants being established through judicial rulings, giving rise to reduced litigation costs and a common understanding of contract terms by contracting parties. Moreover, as the use of a contract term increases, it becomes more valuable and its use becomes self-perpetuating. We have seen that new covenants may be initially created to enhance the functionality of debt markets, or to introduce an essential improvement in existing contracts, or to respond to a changed contracting environment. This suggests that there may be significant benefits for contracting parties to adopt a new covenant developed elsewhere in the market once learning has occurred and the benefits have been factored into improving the contract term ("seasoning" in Merton's terminology). Kahan and Klausner note that network benefits are associated with the adoption of new covenants. Research also suggests that standardisation may not necessarily lead to the use of optimal contract terms and that the spread of innovation is not always frictionless. Kahan and Klausner (1996) argue that instances of apparent sub-optimality in the use of contracting terms are readily observable, that some standard terms do not work effectively, and that uniformity in contract terms persist where diversity and customisation might be expected. They suggest that agency problems between the principal to a contract and drafting lawyers may lead to undue standardisation and that herd behaviour and cognitive biases may lead to excessive standardisation of terms. Consistently with this Kahan and Klausner (1997) provide evidence that bond underwriters significantly influence the choices of contracting parties. Day and Taylor (1997) confirm the important intermediary role of lawyers in expressing lenders' objectives in debt contracts.

Empirical research has added confirmatory evidence on the potential for sub-optimality in contracting, and the role of influential parties in innovation. Choi and Gulat (2006) use a dataset of sovereign bond offerings from 1995 to 2004 to test the importance of standardisation for modifying provisions relating to payment terms. They provide evidence that standardisation may lead contracting parties to adopt provisions not necessarily out of preference but that standards, nonetheless, may change. They concluded that processes of change were not necessarily rapid or straightforward and that change could occur by way of an "interpretive shock", that is an unexpected change in how an established contract term was interpreted by certain contracting parties.[22] After the shock, bond issuers and investors did not react immediately with a significant shift in contract terms but during an initial lull post-shock, investors and bond issuers gained experience on the effects of the shock on previous practice and then modified terms according. Choi and Gulat reported that borrowers' lawyers who dealt with a high volume of bond offerings were the driving factor behind both the adaptive delay and the resulting significant shift in contract terms.

Thus, consideration of the work examined in this section of the chapter suggests that aspects of the theory developed to explain financial innovation more generally have applicability in explaining evolution in debt contracts and debt covenants. We have observed that a relatively narrow focus on agency costs and contracting costs as explanations of the contents of debt contracts can be usefully broadened both by the introduction of new perspectives such as the identification of key drivers of change, the identification of influential parties in change and a richer texture to the

[22] Their research shows that sovereign bond contracts with modification provisions requiring unanimous consent by bondholders became vulnerable to change with less than unanimous approval through the unexpected use of existing exit consents. After this shock, borrowers and investors did not initially react with a significant shift in contract terms. In time the value of allowing modification of payment terms with less than unanimous consent was accepted and substantial changes in contract terms followed, moving bond contracts even further away from unanimous action clauses toward collective action clauses.

pattern of costs involved in contracting, such as learning and network costs and switching costs. Nonetheless, while we cannot conclude that debt contracting is necessarily always optimal, we can conclude that it is innovative and evolutionary.

8.5 Conclusions

Debt contracts and, in particular, the covenants which they contain continue to play a significant role in corporate governance and in accounting and finance, which is important to researchers. While modern understanding and analysis of debt covenants and debt contracts, at least in academic research and especially in empirical research in accounting, dates from the 1970s and 1980s, we have noted the long history of covenants as devices of legal contractual control and have sought to illustrate the development of debt covenants within an historical context. We have focused on changes in debt contracting practices and changes in covenants through time and, to a lesser degree, on differences in practices in different countries, the latter having come through implicitly in our review of research findings on the incidence of covenants in different jurisdictions. We observe some regular patterns in empirical evidence on covenant types and usage but we also observe that some covenants lose popularity or relevance and others grow in importance or appear for the first time. Understanding of the patterns and drivers of change in debt contracting and covenants has been a relatively neglected area or research but is important. New covenants and new patterns of usage indicate innovation in contracting practices as well as adjustments to market conditions. We examined the literature on financial innovation to seek explanations of why covenants change, what the causes of change might be, and how change takes place. This examination suggests that while the traditional explanation of choice in debt contracting and covenants as arising from the interplay of agency costs and contracting costs can help explain change and innovation, it cannot provide a full explanation. Other influences are at work both in creating the conditions in which new covenants and contracting practices become necessary and in which others are superseded, and in changing agency costs and contracting costs to provide new economic incentive structures. These additional influences include changing law and regulation, including accounting changes, new opportunities to reduce or reallocate risk, exogenous shocks and financial and business crises, the influence of cyclical and structural economic factors and advances in theory. These influences help create the institutional environment which in turn establishes the contracting environment, the structure of contracting costs, and the structure of agency costs. Since debt contracting practices and covenants evolve to reflect their institutional setting under the pressure of innovation, it is necessary to continue research into recording the outcomes of that innovation and evolution so that modelling of debt contracting and covenants costs in empirical research in accounting and finance can be sensitive to the realities of the institutional setting. It is also important to extend the limited research which has been undertaken to date on processes of innovation in debt contracting and covenants, including studies of the development of specific covenants, particular agents of change, and costs and benefits of innovation. Without such research our understanding of the role of debt contracting in corporate governance will be deficient.

References

Accountancy Age. (2010). Restrictive bank covenants keep the Big Four on top, M. Christodoulou, 17th June; Big-Four-only clauses are rare: BBA, M. Christodoulou 18th June 2010.

Accountancy Age. (2011). Auditors respond to Big Four clause investigation, R. Orlik, 24th Mar 2011.

Acharya, V. V., Franks, J., & Servaes, H. (2007). Private equity: Boom and bust? *Journal of Applied Corporate Finance, 19*(4), 44–53.

American Bar Foundation. (1971). *Commentaries on indentures*. Chicago: American Bar Foundation.

Asquith, P., Beatty, A., & Weber, J. (2005). Performance pricing in bank debt contracts. *Journal of Accounting and Economics, 40*, 101–128.

Association of Corporate Treasurers. (1991). *The treasurer's handbook 1991*. London: Hemmington Scott.

Ball, R., & Foster, G. (1982). Corporate financial reporting: A methodological review of empirical research. *Journal of Accounting Research, 20*, 161–234.

Ball, R., Bushman, R., & Vasvari, F. (2008). The debt-contracting value of accounting information and loan syndicate structure. *Journal of Accounting Research, 46*, 247–288.

Bank of England. (2007). Markets and Operations, *Quarterly Bulletin; Second Quarter*, London.

Begley, J., & Freedman, R. (2004). The changing role of accounting numbers in public lending agreements. *Accounting Horizons, 18*, 81–96.

Ben-Horim, M., & Silber, W. (1977). Financial innovation: a linear programming approach. *Journal of Banking & Finance, 1*, 277–296.

Bernstein, P. L. (1992). *Capital Ideas: The improbable origins of modern wall street*. New York: Free Press.

Bowen, R. M., Noreen, E. W., & Lacey, J. M. (1981). Determinants of the corporate decision to capitalize interest. *Journal of Accounting and Economics, 3*(2), 151–179.

Brown, K. C., & Smith, D. J. (1988). Recent innovations in interest rate risk management and the re-intermediation of commercial banking. *Financial Management, 17*(4), 45–58.

Briys, E., & Crouhy, M. (1988). Creating and pricing hybrid foreign currency options. *Financial Management, 17*(4), 59–65.

Castle, G. R. (1980). Term lending: A guide to negotiating term loan covenants and other financial restrictions. *Journal of Commercial Bank Lending, 63*, 26–39.

Chatterjee, A. (2006). *Performance pricing covenants in debt contracts in the UK*. Cambridge: Judge Business School.

Choi, S. J., & Gulat, G. M. (2006). Innovation in boilerplate contracts: an empirical examination of sovereign bonds. *Emory Law Journal, 53*, 929–996.

Citron, D. (1992a). Accounting measurement rules in UK bank loan contracts and accounting policy choice. *Accounting and Business Research, 23*(Winter), 21–30.

Citron, D. B. (1992b). Financial covenants in UK bank loan contracts and accounting policy choice. *Accounting and Business Research, 23*(88), 322–335.

Citron, D. B. (1995). The incidence of accounting-based covenants in UK public debt contracts: an empirical analysis. *Accounting and Business Research, 25*(99), 139–150.

Citron, D. B., Robbie, K., & Wright, M. (1997). Loan covenants and relationship banking in MBOs. *Accounting and Business Research, 27*(4), 277–297.

Citron, D., Wright, M., Robbie, K., Bruining, H., & Herst, A. (1999). Loan covenants, relationship banking and MBOs in default—a comparative study of the UK and Holland. In M. Wright & K. Robbie (Eds.), *MBOs and venture capital—into the next millennium.* Cheltenham: Edward Elgar.

Cotter, J. (1998). Utilisation and restrictiveness of covenants in Australian private debt contracts. *Accounting and Finance, 38,* 181–196.

Daley, L. A., & Vigeland, R. L. (1983). The effects of debt covenants and political costs on the choice of accounting methods: The case of accounting for R&D costs. *Journal of Accounting and Economics, 3*(2), 195–211.

Day, J. F. S., & Taylor, P. J. (1995). Evidence on the practices of UK bankers in contracting for medium-term debt. *Journal of International Banking Law, 11*(5), 394–401.

Day, J. F. S., & Taylor, P. J. (1997). Loan documentation in the UK market for corporate debt: Current practice and future prospects. *Journal of International Banking Law, 7,* 7–14.

Day, J., & Taylor, P. (1998). The role of debt contracts in U.K. corporate governance. *Journal of Management and Governance, 2*(2), 171–190.

Day, J., & Sigfrid, P. (2001). Who needs merger covenants? An analysis of the effects of takeover covenants within a corporate governance perspective. *Journal of International Banking Law, 16*(1), 12–19.

Dewing, A. S. (1911). The position of income bonds, as illustrated by those of the central and georgia railway. *Quarterly Journal of Economics, 25,* 397.

Dichev, I., & Skinner, D. J. (2002). Large-sample evidence on the debt covenant hypothesis. *Journal of Accounting Research, 40*(4), 1091.

Donaldson, J. A., & Donaldson, T. H. (1982). *The medium term loan market.* London: Macmillan.

Draper, C. M. (1930). A historical introduction to the corporate mortgage. *Rocky Mountain Law Review, 2,* 71–98.

Duke, J. C., & Hunt, H. G. (1990). An empirical analysis of debt covenant restrictions and accounting-related debt proxies. *Journal of Accounting and Economics, 12,* 45–63.

Encyclopaedia of Forms and Precedents. (2010). 5th edn. (London: Butterworths).

Finnerty, J. D. (1988). Financial engineering in corporate finance: An overview. *Financial Management* (Winter), *17*(4), 14–33.

Finnerty, J. D. (1992). An overview of corporate securities innovation. *Journal of Applied Corporate Finance* (Winter), *4*(4), 23–39.

Francis, J. (1989). Covenants in US public debt agreements. *Accounting and Finance Research, 28*(2), 326–347.

Frankel, R., & Litov, L. (2007). *Financial accounting characteristics and debt covenants.* Unpublished working paper, Washington University, Saint Louis.

Gompers, P., & Lerner, J. (1996). The use of covenants: An empirical analysis of venture partnership agreements. *Journal of Law and Economics, 39*(2), 463–498.

Healy, P., & Palepu, K. (1990). Effectiveness of accounting-based dividend covenants. *Journal of Accounting and Economics, 12,* 97–123.

Heffernan, S., Xiaoqing, M. F., & Xiaolan, F. (2008). *Financial innovation in the UK.* Unpublished working paper (No 4, July), City University, London.

Hejeebu, S. (2005). Contract enforcement in the English East India company. *The Journal of Economic History, 65*(2), 496–523.

Holthausen, R. W., & Leftwich, R. W. (1983). The economic consequences of accounting choice implications of costly contracting and monitoring. *Journal of Accounting and Economics, 3*(2), 77–177.

House of Commons. (2007). Private equity: Tenth report of session 2006–2007, Vol. 1, HC 567–I, House of Commons Treasury Committee, (London, The Stationery Office).

Huang, R. (2009). *Creditor control of free cash flow.* Philadelphia: Federal Reserve Bank of Philadelphia.

Jensen, M., & Meckling, J. (1976). Theory of the firm, managerial incentives, agency costs and ownership structures. *Journal of Financial Economics, 3*, 305–360.

Jones, M. J. (2011). *Creative accounting, fraud and international accounting scandals*. Chichester: Wiley.

Kahan, M., & Klausner, M. (1993). Anti-takeover provisions in bonds: Bondholder protection or management entrenchment? *UCLA Law Review, 40*, 931–982.

Kahan, M., & Klausner, M. (1996). Path dependence in corporate contracting: Increasing returns, herd behavior and cognitive biases. *Washington University Law Quarterly, 74*, 347–366.

Kahan, M., & Klausner, M. (1997). Standardisation and innovation in corporate contracting. *Virginia Law Review, 83*(4), 713–770.

Kalay, A. (1982). Stockholder-bondholder conflict and dividend restraint. *Journal of Financial Economics, 4*, 211–233.

Kane, E. J. (1981). Accelerating inflation, technological innovation, and the decreasing effectiveness of banking regulation. *Journal of Finance, 36*(2), 355–367.

Kealhofer, S. (2003). Quantifying credit risk II: Debt valuation. *Financial Analysts Journal, 59*(3), 78–92.

Kim, J.-B., Tsui, J. S. L., & Yi, C. H. (2011). The voluntary adoption of international accounting standards and loan contracting around the world. *Review of Accounting Studies, 16*(4), 779–811.

Kornagia, K. J. (2011). Financial distress and bankruptcy. In H. K. Baker, & G. S. Martin (Eds.), Capital structure and corporate financing decisions: *Theory evidence and practice*. London: Wiley, Kolb Series in Finance.

Leftwich, R. (1990). Aggregation of test statistics: Statistics versus economics. *Journal of Accounting and Economics, 12*, 37–44.

Leuz, C., Deller, D., & Stubenrath, M. (1997). An international comparison of accounting-based pay-out restrictions in the United States, United Kingdom and Germany. *Accounting and Business Research, 28*(2), 111–129.

Lingard, J. R. (1995). *Bank security documents* (2nd ed.). London: Butterworths.

Markland, J. (2007). Cov-lite: The new cutting edge in acquisition finance. *Journal of International Banking and Financial Law, 20*, 379–381.

Mason, S., Merton, R. C., Perold, A. F., & Tufano, P. (1995). *Case book in financial engineering, applied studies of financial innovation*. Englewood Cliffs: Prentice-Hall.

Mather, P. (1999). Financial covenants in Australian bank-loan contracts: Incidence, measurement rules and monitoring. *Australian Accounting Review, 9*(17), 2–72.

Mather, P., & Peirson, G. (2006). Financial covenants in the markets for public and private debt. *Accounting and Finance, 46*(2), 285–307.

Maxwell, W., & Shenkman, M. (2010). *Leveraged financial markets: A comprehensive guide to loans, bonds and other instruments*. New York: McGraw-Hill.

May, W., & Verde, M. (2006). Loan volumes surge, covenants shrink in 2005. *Fitch Ratings Credit Market Research, Special Report*. http://www.fitchratings.com/creditdesk/reports/report_frame.cfm?rpt_id=271124 accessed 9 September 2013

McConnell, J. J., & Schwartz, E. S. (1992). The origin of LYONS: A case study in financial innovation. *Journal of Applied Corporate Finance, 5*(1), 40–47.

Merton, R. C. (1995). A functional perspective of financial intermediation. *Financial Management, 24*(2), 23–24.

Miller, M. (1986). Financial innovation: The last twenty years and the next. *Journal of Financial and Quantitative Analysis, 21*, 459–471.

Moir, L., & Sudarsanam, S. (2007). Determinants of financial covenants and pricing of debt in private debt contracts: The UK evidence. *Accounting and Business Research, 37*(2), 151–166.

Moody, (various years). *Moody's Industrial Manual*.

Mohrman, M. (1993). Debt contracts and FAS No. 19: A test of the debt covenant hypothesis. *The Accounting Review, 68*, 273–288.

Mouritsen, J. (1998). Driving growth: Economic value added versus intellectual capital. *Management Accounting Research, 9*(4), 461–482.

Norton, E., & Pettengill, G. (1998). Event risk covenant rating announcements and stock returns. *Journal of Finance and Strategic Decisions, 11*(2), 1–10.

O'Hanlon, J., & Peasnell, K. (1998). Wall Street's contribution to management accounting: the Stern Stewart EVA® financial management system. *Management Accounting Research, 9*(4), 421–444.

Office of Fair Trading. (2011). Statutory audit: Consultation on the OFT's provisional decision to make a market investigation reference to the Competition Commission of the supply of statutory audit services to large companies in the UK, OFT1357, July, London (available at www.oft.gov.uk).

Ormrod, P., & Taylor, P. J. (2004). The impact of the change to international accounting standards on debt covenants: A UK perspective. *Accounting in Europe, 1*, 71–94.

Petruzzi, C., Del Valle, M., & Judlowe, S. (1988). Protection for innovations in Finance. *Financial Management, 17*(4), 66–71.

Press, E. G., & Weintrop, J. G. (1990). Accounting-based constraints in public and private debt agreements: Their association with leverage and importance in accounting choice. *Journal of Accounting and Economics, 12*, 65–96.

Ramirez, C. (1995). Did J. P. Morgan's men add liquidity? Corporate investment, cash flow, and financial structure at the turn of the twentieth century. *Journal of Finance, 50*(2), 661–678.

Ramsay, I., & Sidhu, B. (1998). Accounting and non-accounting-based information in the market for debt: Evidence from Australian private debt contracts. *Accounting and Finance, 38*, 197–221.

Rodgers, C. (1965). The corporate trust indenture project. *The Business Lawyer, 20*, 551–559.

Rowley, R.G. (1953). The benefits of restrictive covenants a survey. *Modern Law Review, 16*(4), 428–434.

Silber, W. (1975). Towards a theory of financial innovation. In W. Silber (Ed.), *Financial innovation*. Lexington: D. C. Heath & Co.

Silber, W. L. (1983). The process of financial innovation. *American Economic Review, 73*(2), 89–95.

Simmons, R. S. (1972). Drafting of commercial bank loan agreements. *The Business Lawyer* (November), *29*(1), 179–201.

Smith, C. W., & Warner, J. B. (1979). On financial contracting: An analysis of bond covenants. *Journal of Financial Economics, 7*, 117–161.

Stetson, F. L. (1917). *Some legal phases of corporate financing reorganization and regulation*. New York: Macmillan.

Sylla, R. (1982). Monetary innovations and crises in American economic history. In P. Wachtel (Ed.), *Crises in the economic and financial structure*. Lexington: D. C. Heath & Co.

Stokes, D., & Tay, K. L. (1988). Restrictive covenants and accounting information in the market for convertible notes: further evidence. *Accounting and Finance, 28*(1), 57–73.

Stumpp, P. (2000). *Putting EBITDA in perspective. Ten critical failings of EBITDA as the principal determinant of cash flow*. Moody's Investors Service. Global Credit Research. Special Comment.

Tufano, P. (1995). Securities innovations: A historical and functional perspective. *Journal of Applied Corporate Finance, 7*(4), 90–103.

Tufano, P. (1997). Business failure, judicial intervention, and financial innovation: Restructuring U.S. railroads in the nineteenth century. *Business History Review, 71*(1), 1–40.

Van Horne, J. C. (1985). Of financial innovations and excesses. *Journal of Finance, 40*(3), 621–631.

Watts, R. L., & Zimmerman, J. L. (1978). Towards a positive theory of the determination of accounting standards. *The Accounting Review, 53*(1), 112–130.

Whitehead, C. K. (2009). The evolution of debt: Covenants, the credit market, and corporate governance. *The Journal of Corporation Law, 34*(3), 641–677.

Whittred, G., & Zimmer, I. (1986). Accounting information in the market for debt. *Accounting and Finance, 26*(2), 19–33. (Australia).

Wojnilower, A. (1980). The central role of credit crunches in recent financial history. *Brookings Papers on Economic Activity, 2*(1980), 277–326.

Yaxuan, Q., & Wald, J. (2008). State laws and debt covenants. *Journal of Law and Economics, 51*(1), 179–207.

Chapter 9
Regulation, Bonding and the Quality of Financial Statements

Christina Dargenidou, Aziz Jaafar and Stuart McLeay

Abstract In this study, we show that the exposure of European firms across European capital markets is associated with significant constraints in financial reporting discretion. By exploiting the variation in the regulatory environment in this setting, we are able to demonstrate that incentives for reducing financial reporting discretion stem from a form of legal bonding within Europe, in the sense of the exposure to at least one capital market with better regulation than the firm's origin. Furthermore, we provide evidence for the presence of reputational bonding in cases where the firm is exposed to capital markets with weaker regulation than the regulation in its home jurisdiction. We corroborate the evidence on reputational bonding by extending this investigation to circumstances that are likely to trigger managers' engagement with more transparency even in the absence of strong legal regulations, such as stock exchange consolidation and geographical proximity.

9.1 Introduction

This chapter discusses how legal and reputational bonding mechanisms in markets can induce a commitment to lower levels of financial reporting discretion by firms that trade their equity internationally. While the concept of legal bonding was

C. Dargenidou (✉)
University of Exeter Business School, University of Exeter, Exeter, UK
e-mail: C.Dargenidou@exeter.ac.uk

A. Jaafar
Bangor Business School, Bangor University, Bangor, UK
e-mail: a.jaafar@bangor.ac.uk

S. McLeay
School of Business, University of Sydney, Sydney, Australia
e-mail: s.j.mcleay@sydney.edu.au

R. Di Pietra et al. (eds.), *Accounting and Regulation*,
DOI: 10.1007/978-1-4614-8097-6_9,

developed initially to account for cross-listings by overseas companies in the regulated US market (e.g., Doidge et al. 2004; Lang et al. 2003a; Huijgen and Lubberink 2005), such bonding to a more demanding regulatory regime has been assumed to have little or no impact elsewhere, particularly in European capital markets (Roosenboom and Van Dijk 2009; Abdallah and Goergen 2008; Cabán-Garcia 2009). This chapter shows how a better understanding of the dynamics across capital markets can lead to the identification of both legal and reputational bonding effects on financial reporting discretion for firms whose equity is traded beyond their domestic borders.

In contrast to prior studies in the area of financial reporting and cross-listing, which focus mainly on the existence of formal quotations on additional stock exchanges, the notion of capital market exposure is based here also on evidence that a firm actually trades its shares in a particular foreign destination, which allows the investigation of a broader and more varied set of multiple exposures.[1] Based on this approach, it is possible to test not only for 'legal bonding', in the sense that the firm is exposed to a capital market which is better regulated than the home jurisdiction, but also to exploit the variation in regulation across Europe to test for the presence of 'reputational bonding', where the firm with better regulation at home is also exposed to capital markets with weaker regulation, in the spirit of Licht et al. (2013).

We also investigate other factors that are likely to trigger greater reporting transparency, even in the absence of strong legal regulation, such as geographical proximity, stock exchange consolidation, and the use of internationally accepted accounting standards.

The findings of the present study suggest that exposure to European capital markets is associated with the firms' adherence to less financial reporting discretion, with this effect mainly driven by reputational bonding and to some extent by legal bonding, mainly in better disclosure regimes.

Reputational bonding effects on financial reporting are also shown to be reinforced by circumstances that enable the monitoring of the firm across jurisdictions. Indeed, despite this exercise being conducted in the pre-IFRS era, the findings here have implications for research on the consequences of mandatory IFRS implementation.

Prior work (Soderstrom and Sun 2007) has already pointed to the variation in legal institutions as a determinant of the financial reporting outcomes of IFRS implementation, and the impact of stock exchange consolidation and proximity suggests an information segmentation factor that improves our understanding of the bonding motivations of firms exposed to European capital markets.

[1] In this regard, exposure may capture formal cross-listings as well as cases where the trading has been initiated without the involvement of the issuer. Although the latter case might work against our hypothesis of legal or reputational bonding, we are able nevertheless to report findings here that are consistent with bonding. Future research could investigate further the implications of the differences between those two kinds of exposure.

9.2 Financial Reporting Quality in Internationally Exposed Firms

High-quality accounting information is expected to attract foreign investors, as it should enable better monitoring of their investment (see Aggarwal et al. 2005). However, foreign investors are at an informational disadvantage relative to local investors in assessing opaque financial reporting, especially in those weaker regulatory environments where earnings management is more likely to be employed to obfuscate disclosures (see Leuz et al. 2003).[2]

This differential demand for accounting information stems from the variation in monitoring costs between local investors and their foreign counterparts. That is to say, investors are probably better equipped to unravel governance problems within the jurisdiction to which they are accustomed and thus incur lower monitoring costs with respect to local firms (Leuz et al. 2010).[3]

It follows then, given that monitoring costs with respect to foreign firms are expected to be greater, that investors may require such firms to exhibit a high level of reporting quality before they buy their shares or in order to continue holding them. Consistent with this view, Bradshaw et al. (2004) show that some corporate managers have tried to address this 'home bias' by making financial reporting choices that will facilitate adequate monitoring by foreign investors.[4]

Further to this evidence, which demonstrates the bias by foreign firms toward financial reporting choices that are compatible with US GAAP, Covrig et al. (2007)[5] reveal that foreign holdings by US mutual funds in stocks originating in poorer information environments and with lower visibility were significantly higher among voluntary IAS adopters. These results imply that managers may

---

[2] The research question addressed in this study draws parallels with prior research on the differential demand for accounting information between public and private firms (Ball and Shivakumar 2005). On one hand, exposure in public equity markets entails the presence of outsider ownership, which relies heavily on financial reporting for evaluating and monitoring the firm. The presence of outsider investors imposes a threshold of financial reporting information quality which public firms need to exceed in order to convince outsiders to buy or continue to hold their shares. In this spirit, the discussion in Burgstahler et al. (2006) implies that outsider investors may be reluctant to supply capital to firms exhibiting poor information quality, where this does not enable the assessment of economic performance. On the other hand, financial reporting information quality is less of a concern among private firms whereby, for typically concentrated ownership structures, information necessary for evaluating and monitoring the firm may be more accessible through private channels.

[3] The idea that local investors have an information advantage is also consistent with Malloy's (2005) finding that geographically proximate analysts are more accurate than other analysts.

[4] The term 'home bias' is used to describe the tendency of investors to overweight portfolios with firms domiciled in their home countries and underweight portfolios with firms located outside of their home countries.

[5] Similar results concerning the impact of the mandatory adoption of IFRS are also reported by Florou and Pope (2012).

address the 'home bias' of foreign investors by adopting high-quality accounting standards, i.e., either IAS/IFRS or US GAAP.

Following Leuz et al. (2010), the study discussed in this chapter employs an accrual-based earnings management indicator to proxy for the quality of financial reporting. The underlying idea here, building on the above, is that managers of firms wishing to attract and retain foreign investors will make financial reporting choices that mitigate investors' monitoring costs by avoiding apparent earnings misrepresentation.

According to a survey of managers' perceptions of earnings quality by Dichev et al. (2013), common indicators of earnings misrepresentation include persistent deviations between earnings and the underlying cash flows, deviations from industry benchmarks, and other peer performance measures, and accrual changes and levels that are large and unexplained. The idea of avoiding earnings misrepresentation as a means of attracting and retaining foreign investors is supported by both Lang et al. (2003a) and Leuz (2006).

Using accrual measures, they show that foreign firms cross-listing in the US exhibit greater accounting transparency than the local firms in their respective home markets. However, evidence from cross-listing in the US may not be sufficient to lend support to the more general hypothesis that international capital market exposure deters managers from earnings misrepresentation, as the impact of a US cross-listing on accounting quality is determined by the strength of the regulatory institutional framework and the richness of the financial reporting information environment in any specific market. The European setting of the analysis reported later in this chapter allows us to revisit this question by taking advantage of the observable diversity in the strength of regulatory environments.

9.3 The Impact of Regulation and Reputation

As mentioned, the relationship between international capital market exposure and financial reporting discretion depends in part on whether firms are exposed to stronger or weaker foreign institutional environments. Legal bonding is the term that we use to describe the effect of exposure to stronger institutional environments abroad. The fact that the firm submits itself to greater scrutiny through cross-listing in a better regulated environment is expected to signal a relative increase in financial reporting quality, and hence a narrowing of accounting choice. Conversely, reputational bonding arises when there is exposure to a weaker institutional environment than is found in the home market.

Potentially, both legal and reputational bonding could be intensified by the often-ignored fact that firms are often exposed to multiple capital markets. The present study attempts to address this complexity by ranking the relative strengths of the institutional environments to which the firm is exposed, i.e., relative to the home market. Then, two discrete cases arise, the first where the firm is exposed to at least one market characterized by a stronger institutional environment, and the second where even the best ranked market where the firm is exposed is weaker than the home market. Therefore, we expect that firms exposed to stronger regulation elsewhere in Europe will exhibit more restraint in financial reporting discretion as a result of legal bonding, as mostly observed so far with respect to cross-listing in US markets.

However, the concept of legal bonding introduced here is not necessarily synonymous to the legal bonding effect typically defined in the context of cross-listing in a US market, where becoming subject to strict private and public enforcement mechanisms increases the defendant's perceived risk of liability (Coffee 2002).[6] Since we examine exposure, and not just the formality of cross-listing, we do not put forward strong arguments on the *de facto* or *de jure* influence of host market regulation on the financial reporting of firms exposed to those markets.[7]

A legal bonding effect might as well result from the firm's efforts to attract and retain foreign investors in a jurisdiction characterized by stronger regulations, by attaining the level of transparency required by the stronger regulations in force there.

As indicated, we also expect a form of reputational bonding to be in place, when firms are exposed to institutional environments that are weaker than in the home market. In order to corroborate the concept of reputational bonding as identified here, we consider circumstances that are likely to bring about greater transparency even in the absence of strong legal regulations.

Evidence from US cross-listings implies that the benefits of reputational bonding are linked to market forces and, more specifically, to increased monitoring by investors (e.g., Lang et al. 2003b; Frésard and Salva 2010), and we consider too that reputational bonding is more likely to arise under circumstances that enable such monitoring. Given the European setting, we identify factors that are likely to promote investors' awareness and monitoring of internationally exposed firms, namely stock exchange consolidation, the use of internationally recognized accounting standards (before the IFRS mandatory adoption), and geographic proximity.

Exchange consolidation can promote greater investor awareness of the firm by facilitating the trading of the firm's equity through a unified marketplace. An opportunity to examine this factor appeared with the formation in 2000 and 2002 of the Euronext stock market from the merger of the Amsterdam, Brussels, Paris, and Lisbon stock exchanges. A less well-known development in the same direction, again involving jurisdictions in our European sample, is the joint trading platform for Nordic and Baltic countries, Norex, established in 1998 by the Swedish and Danish stock exchanges and expanded later to include Norway in 2000 and Finland in 2003 (Nielsson 2007).

---

[6] Subsequent research admits that this concept of legal bonding in the US might not be entirely realistic. For instance, Siegel (2005) argues that the recovery of damages awarded to shareholders by US courts is contingent upon the size of the assets held by the firm in the US.

[7] It is also an open question to which extent European stock exchanges enforce their own jurisdiction's requirements on foreign firms who formally cross-list in their stock markets.

Consistent with market forces prevailing over the disparity among jurisdiction-specific institutional environments, Pownall et al. (2012) establishes an increase in accounting quality for those firms that chose to become listed on the named segments of Euronext relative to non-segment firms.[8]

However, in the period that is examined here, Euronext had limited options for the enforcement of common regulations, and much of the relevant regulation remained jurisdiction specific. Furthermore, the compliance of the participants with the segment requirements appears to be rather limited Pownall et al. (2012). Based on the above, it can be suggested that the impact of Euronext on the financial reporting of firms is likely to be motivated by reputational rather than legal bonding. In a similar vein, here it is argued that increased investor awareness through the channel of exchange consolidation may trigger a form of reputational bonding for firms that are exposed to institutional environments weaker than the home market and also trade within the Euronext or Norex participating jurisdictions.[9]

Motivated by prior research[10] that examines the impact on earnings quality of adopting an internationally recognizable set of accounting standards, where the use of such standards can be seen as a means of addressing the home bias of foreign investors, this factor is also considered as enabling investors' monitoring of firms that are traded in international capital markets.[11]

Nevertheless, as Daske et al. (2013) point out, the voluntary adoption of international standards does not guarantee a commitment to high-quality reporting, which ultimately appears to be determined by managers' incentives. Indeed, in the specific context of firms that are exposed internationally, it could be argued that such incentives may arise from the need to address the adverse consequences of home bias amongst foreign investors. Hence, it is expected that a commitment to less financial reporting discretion by firms reporting under accounting standards that are applied internationally (e.g., IAS/IFRS or US GAAP) is more likely for a

---

[8] Euronext established two voluntary sections of the integrated stock market on which firms could choose to list by pre-committing themselves to enhanced financial reporting quality and corporate governance i.e., quarterly financial reports beginning in 2004; international accounting standards, or a reconciliation of existing information with those standards, beginning in 2004; financial documents in English beginning in 2002; scheduling of at least two meetings annually for analysts; description of corporate governance policy in the annual report; announcement of a schedule for publications and meetings beginning in 2002; publication of key financial information on their websites beginning in 2002 Pownall et al. (2012).

[9] The statistics reported in Pownall et al. (2012), Table 9 do not suggest that internationally exposed firms dominate the Euronext segments. Therefore, we argue that we capture a relationship that is not fully addressed in their study.

[10] See Soderstrom and Sun (2007) for a comprehensive review of related evidence. Also, Karamanou and Nishiotis (2009) argue that the voluntary adoption of IAS is primarily a form of reputation bonding due to the commitment to expanded disclosure and transparency.

[11] An alternative approach is to examine indices of similarity between accounting standards (see Bae et al. 2008). However, the case of internationally accepted accounting standards captures a similar concept here, as their use is assumed to enhance the comparability of financial reporting information.

firm that is exposed across additional European capital markets, consisting of a form of reputational bonding.

Finally, prior research suggests that both information asymmetries and agency costs tend to decrease when capital providers reside closer to the firm (see Wang and Pirinsky (2010) for a review of the relevant literature). To the extent that proximity reduces information asymmetries and agency costs, and thus enables better monitoring of the firm, it is expected that the closer the home and host jurisdictions are, the greater the facility to monitor, and the more managers will exhibit self-restraint against financial reporting discretion.

The intuition behind this hypothesis can be seen in Ayers et al. (2011) who also argue that financial reporting discretion is positively associated with the distance between the firm and its monitoring institutions, conditional upon the costs of financial reporting discretion to outside investors. Based on the extensive evidence on foreign investor home bias, it could be assumed that the costs of financial reporting discretion to outside shareholders are relatively high in a cross-border trading setting.[12] Hence, a conjecture that builds upon the Ayers et al. (2011) argument is that managers may be more under pressure to exercise less discretion when they are aware that foreign investors who have the means to monitor the firm are closer to hand.

Summarizing the discussion above, firms that trade their equity internationally have to address the investor bias toward their home countries. We maintain that managers attempt to counter this bias by becoming subject to stronger regulations or, in the absence of those, by building a reputational asset whose influence is conditional upon circumstances that promote investors' awareness of the firm and facilitate their assessment of its financial situation. It is argued here that either or both avenues induce a commitment to less financial reporting discretion.

9.4 Assessing the Impact of International Capital Market Exposure on Financial Reporting Discretion

Discretion in financial reporting is represented here by the absolute value of the unexpected increase or decrease in working capital, that is, the net change in short-term accruals and short-term deferrals that is not consistent with the firm's operations.[13]

---

[12] Ayers et al. (2011) also note that their findings in the domestic US market should have similar implications for cross-border investment. The present study contributes by testing this conjecture explicitly.

[13] Peasnell, Pope and Young (2005) justify modeling the working capital accrual instead of the total accrual by pointing out that changes in depreciation policy cannot be made very frequently without attracting adverse attention and that modeling other long-term accruals such as environmental liabilities and pension obligations is far too complex. Note that, in the European setting examined here, depreciation policy is anyway often not left to managers to determine and is, instead, guided by tax rules.

We refer to this metric as 'the discretionary net current accrual', or, more briefly, as 'the discretionary accrual'. The discretionary accrual is of particular interest since it is easily derived from reported amounts in financial statements, is known to revert in the short term, and its use in income manipulation in response to a variety of incentives is well understood by the analyst community. Prior research has shown that the measurement of working capital is prone to managerial manipulation with a view to achieving certain performance objectives, chiefly in order to increase earnings through a *positive* discretionary accrual (Burgstahler and Dichev 1997).

More recently, and in the same vein, Ettredge et al. (2010) also provide evidence of the overstatement of working capital accounts as a means of inflating earnings. Yet, while the emphasis in prior research has been attributed largely to the exercise of accounting discretion in a way that is income inflating, there are also reports of the *negative* net accrual being used as a means of building up 'cookie jar' reserves for the future (DeFond and Park 1997; Chaney and Lewis 1998), especially for use in poor performing years.

Hence this study investigates financial reporting discretion in terms of the magnitude of the discretion that is exercised, and more specifically the magnitude of the discretionary net current accrual.[14]

The estimation of the discretionary component of the working capital change requires the modeling of its predicted value, taking into account the underlying business activity. To this end, we follow convention in accounting research and assume that the net current accrual is a function of the change in cash revenues, and that this relation varies across sectors and years.

More specifically, the process of estimating the discretionary accrual applies a performance adjusted version of the modified-Jones model (Dechow et al. 1995) on a cross-sectional basis, rather than a firm-specific time-series approach, due to survivorship bias and sample size concerns. The performance adjustment is proposed by Kothari et al. (2005) and further supported by Cheng et al. (2012) in order to reduce measurement error in the estimation of the discretionary accrual; that is, further to associating the expected level of accruals and deferrals with growth, captured here by the change in cash revenues, a performance adjustment implies that higher levels of performance need to be supported by an increased

[14] Here, the focus is on the type of earnings management that would be obvious to an investor for whom a reduction in discretion would signal a commitment to greater reporting integrity. In fact, evidence suggests that the manipulation of accruals is perceived by the managers themselves as the most common indicator of earnings misrepresentation Dichev et al. (2013). Unlike Cohen et al. (2008) and others, we do not attempt to investigate 'real earnings management', which has a less than obvious effect on current and future financial statements. In the pre-IFRS European context of this study, taking such an approach would present significant problems associated with identifying real earnings management (Roychowdhury 2006). First, given that the availability of cash flow statements was more limited across Europe at that time (LaFond 2005), there are major data reliability and completeness issues, and second there is considerable variation with respect to certain critical accounting rules, such as expensing and capitalizing intangibles including R&D: see Stolowy and Jeny-Cazavan (2001) for a discussion on this topic.

level of investment in working capital, and hence this component of current accruals and deferrals will also be considered as normal, instead of discretionary.

The estimation of discretion in the context of the present study presents further challenges, given the accounting diversity that permeated European jurisdictions in the pre-IFRS era that is examined here (and possibly also in the post-IFRS implementation period). For instance, LaFond (2005) reports significant cross-jurisdictional variation in the methods followed for the recognition of working capital items such as inventories and accounts receivable.

More to the point, a statistical assessment of country and sector effects in financial reporting has established not only significant country variation in terms of accounting for inventories in Europe, but also sector specific variation (Jaafar and McLeay 2007). Such findings may lend some support to the idea that accounting diversity is canceled out to some extent within portfolios of firms sorted by industry, yielding an estimate of the expected net accrual that represents the *typical European firm* within its sector, and also for each year involved.

Considering that our research question is about the financial reporting discretion of firms that originate from a variety of European jurisdictions, whose shares are traded in a number of additional European destinations, this approach is consistent with comparing each company to its direct competitors within a geographic region, a practice that is widespread across analysts and investors. Moreover, it also captures the idea of the deviation from the peer group norm as one of the earnings management 'red flags' suggested by CEOs in Dichev et al. (2013).

Following Kothari et al. (2005), as well as Cheng et al. (2012),[15] who recommend the use of an industry-specific performance adjusted 'modified Jones' model in order to estimate the discretionary component of accruals and deferrals when investigating earnings management, the expectations model we employ here is:

$$\frac{\text{CACC}_{\text{it}}}{\text{TAsset}_{\text{it}-1}} = a_0 + a_1 \frac{1}{\text{TAsset}_{\text{it}-1}} + a_2 \frac{\Delta\text{REV}_{\text{it}} - \Delta\text{REC}_{it}}{\text{TAsset}_{\text{it}-1}} + a_3 \frac{\text{EARN}_{\text{it}}}{\text{TAsset}_{\text{it}-1}} + \omega_{\text{it}} \tag{9.1}$$

where the observable current net accrual (CACC) for firm *i* and year *t* is calculated as $\text{CACC}_{\text{it}} = (\Delta\text{CA}_{\text{it}} - \Delta\text{CASH}_{\text{it}}) - (\Delta\text{CL}_{\text{it}} - \Delta\text{STDEBT}_{\text{it}})$, that is as firm *i*'s change in current assets in year *t* ($\Delta\text{CA}_{\text{it}}$) excluding the change in cash and cash equivalents ($\Delta\text{CASH}_{\text{it}}$) *less* the change in current liabilities ($\Delta\text{CL}_{\text{it}}$) excluding the change in short-term borrowings together with the current portion of long-term debt ($\Delta\text{STDEBT}_{\text{it}}$). As discussed, the determinants of the expected net accrual are the change in cash revenues (i.e., change in revenues $\Delta\text{REV}_{\text{it}}$ minus change in accounts receivable $\Delta\text{REC}_{\text{it}}$) and the return on assets, defined as earnings before extraordinary items and preferred dividends (EARN_{it}) scaled, as are all variables, by total assets at the beginning of the year ($\text{TAsset}_{\text{it}-1}$).

---

[15] Following other authors, the model employed here includes a constant as an additional control for heteroskedasticity not alleviated by using assets as the deflator, and to mitigate problems stemming from an omitted size (scale) variable.

The discretionary net current accrual ($DACC_{it}$), or the proxy for financial reporting manipulation used in the study described in this chapter, is estimated as the residual arising from running regression (9.1) across portfolios of firms sorted by sector and year.

The main research question that is addressed here is whether international capital market exposure is associated with less financial reporting discretion. International capital market exposure here is investigated in terms of exposure to additional European capital markets beyond the firm's home market (EXPOSURE), whose coefficient is expected to be negative. When focusing in particular on the issue of exposure to European capital markets, it is understandable that a firm's shares may be traded on more than one additional exchange.

This aspect of European exposure is captured here by using a variable that measures the number of European jurisdictions in which a firm's shares are found to be traded in addition to its domicile (NUMEX). Including this feature of exposure to additional European markets captures the intuition in Sarkissian and Schill (2009), who argue that there might be different motivations for multiple cross-listings that, in our case, may affect the influence of market exposure over financial reporting discretion. For instance, Sarkissian and Schill (2009) argue that, while the first listing may be motivated by funding needs, sequential listings may not always be motivated by such needs and could be obtained for other reasons, such as currency sourcing.

While here we do not address explicitly the sequence of listing destinations, by controlling only for the number of additional European jurisdictions where a firm's shares are found to be traded, we allow for the related motivations that may dilute the incentives of managers to exercise financial reporting discretion. On the other hand, NUMEX accounts for the enlargement of the investor base, which may in itself be a potential motivation for less financial reporting discretion. Thus, we do not have a prediction for the direction of the sign of this variable.

Model (9.2) sets the base model for testing the impact of international capital market exposure on financial reporting as follows:

$$\mathrm{DACC}_{\mathrm{it}} = b_0 + b_1\mathrm{EXPOSURE}_{\mathrm{it}} + b_2\mathrm{NUMEX}_{\mathrm{it}} + \mathrm{Controls} + u_{\mathrm{it}} \qquad (9.2)$$

A number of control variables that prior research has established to be associated with proxies for earnings management are added to model (9.2). These controls, which alleviate concerns related to omitted variable problems, include firm-level characteristics and jurisdiction level indicators shown in prior research to be associated with earnings management, as well as controls for further exposure to international markets beyond Europe (i.e., regulated US markets NYSE, NASDAQ, and AMEX, plus OTC unregulated US markets, and other international markets beyond Europe and the US).

Firm-level characteristics include analyst following, measured as the average number of analysts following the firm during the year; ownership structure, measured by the percentage of closely held shares; leverage, measured by the ratio of short and long-term debt to equity; audit quality, indicated by a dummy variable taking the value of 1 if the firm is audited by an auditing firm of international standing such as Deloitte, Ernst & Young, KPMG, PriceWaterhouseCoopers, or Coopers & Lybrand; size, measured by the natural logarithm of market capitalization in US$; lagged net operating assets scaled by total assets, capturing the notion that earnings management is constrained by the level of net assets overstatement (Barton and Simko 2002); export orientation, measured by the percentage of foreign sales to total sales; weak performance, indicated by a dummy variable that takes the value of one if the firm reports negative earnings and zero otherwise; growth opportunities, measured by Tobin's Q, the ratio of total assets minus the book value of equity plus the market value of equity to total assets; and debt market considerations proxied by the percentage changes in the book values of equity and total debt.

It is expected that financial reporting discretion is negatively associated with analyst following (Yu 2008) and size (Watts and Zimmerman 1986) since increased monitoring by analysts and shareholders or other regulatory and enforcement bodies arising from the visibility of larger firms might deter managers from making accrual or deferral estimates that might appear opportunistic.

Moreover, while prior research documents a negative association between the presence of established accounting firms and earnings management (Becker et al. 1998), more recent international evidence reports that this influence is conditional upon the institutional environment where the firm operates (Francis and Wang 2008), a factor that we also control for in this study.

On the other hand, the demand for transparent reporting might be compromised among closely held firms initiating a positive association between discretion and more closely held ownership structures (Leuz et al. 2003; Leuz 2006). Similarly, based on a review of the earnings quality literature, Dechow et al. (2010) conclude that weak performance provides incentives to engage in earnings management.

A positive association between financial reporting discretion and growth opportunities may be also expected when the net accrual is employed for signaling purposes. We also predict a positive association between discretion and funding investment opportunities by appealing to shareholders and debt holders. Finally, at the firm level, the percentage of foreign sales controls for the influence of foreign stakeholders on financial reporting discretion.

Other control variables in this study account for the international, and more particularly, the European context that is examined here. We control for the adoption before IFRS of an internationally accepted set of accounting standards across Europe (i.e., IAS, and to a lesser extent, US GAAP) and the impact of a major stock exchange consolidation in the case of Euronext (and, again to a lesser extent, Norex).

Those mechanisms, the most likely to affect firms trading across European capital markets, are also investigated for their potential in enhancing reputational bonding. However, they are included as controls here since it is expected that they also exert an overall effect on financial reporting quality (Barth et al. 2008; Pownall et al. 2012; Daske et al. 2013).

Furthermore, we consider the diversity of tax regimes across jurisdictions, whereby it is predicted that higher tax rates may be associated with more accounting discretion (the tax avoidance hypothesis). Finally, we include industry, year and country effects, so that, in a detailed analysis of the impact of legal and reputational bonding, we may investigate country effects further by taking into account the jurisdiction-specific strength of various aspects of the institutional environment.[16]

9.5 Endogeneity of Financial Reporting Discretion and International Capital Market Exposure

Research on the wider area of cross-listing suggests that the variables that we discuss here as determinants of financial reporting discretion may also be associated with the exposure of the firm to international capital markets.

The decision to cross-list is shown to be driven by the need to fund growth opportunities, to enhance investor recognition of the firm, and to widen the ownership structure for liquidity reasons or as part of the controlling shareholder exit strategy (Pagano et al. 2002; Bancel and Mittoo 2001, 2009). Furthermore, internationally exposed firms tend to be larger (Pagano et al. 2002), grow faster and have more foreign sales (Claessens and Schmukler 2007). They are more visible across the investment community (Baker et al. 2002; Lang et al. 2003b; Abdallah 2008), originate from larger and more open economies, with higher income and better macroeconomic environments (Claessens and Schmukler 2007), and tend to cross-list in familiar markets (Sarkissian and Schill 2004).

An instrumental variables solution to the present endogeneity problems is not feasible, given the difficulty of finding instrumental variables that are correlated with the endogenous regressor but uncorrelated with the error in the structural equation (i.e., satisfying the exclusion restriction).[17]

Hail and Leuz (2009) face a similar dilemma in their study of cross-listing, where they propose employing firm effects and a differences-in-differences research design. According to Hail and Leuz (2009), by using a panel data

---

[16] Wysocki (2004) employs the correlation between earnings management indicators and similar jurisdiction-specific institutional environment factors (disclosure and private–public enforcement indicators).

[17] Applying a Heckman procedure is also inappropriate, considering that the classification of a particular firm as internationally exposed in a given year is not independent from the classification of the same firm in prior years. Indeed, unless there is an explicit delisting, it is very difficult to ascertain when the international exposure ceases to exist. Given the nature of our data, which encompass the strict concept of cross-listing, once we classify a firm as internationally exposed, this classification remains for the period examined here. This sampling assumption should work against our predictions; in other words, if we look for the impact of international exposure where it has ceased to exist, the association should be nonsignificant.

methodology that accommodates firm fixed effects,[18] regressions should mitigate concerns about correlated omitted variables and selection bias based on unobservable, time–invariant firm characteristics (though the authors are still concerned about time-variant selection that is not already captured by time-variant control variables).

Similar selection bias concerns are also addressed by means of a research design that focuses on the change of the status of the firm from 'non-exposed' to 'exposed' across European capital markets. However, given that firms may prepare themselves for international capital market exposure for a few years before the actual event, it is possible that this approach might not be able to capture the impact of the exposure on financial reporting discretion and lead to erroneously weak evidence.[19]

Finally, selection bias can be addressed also by matching firms based on a propensity score estimated from the determinants of the international exposure of the firm. The caveat regarding this methodology is that it mitigates the selection bias based on observables but it does not address selection bias based on unobservables.

In order to corroborate our evidence, each of these alternative approaches[20] is employed throughout the empirical applications of the models proposed here, i.e., the general model in Eq. (9.2) and the models which follow below assessing the impact of legal and reputational bonding on financial reporting discretion.

9.6 Assessing the Impact of Legal and Reputational Bonding on Financial Reporting Discretion

While most prior research has sought evidence of legal bonding in terms of listing in the highly regulated US markets, some research has attempted to uncover

---

[18] While Hail and Leuz (2009) advocate the used of fixed firm effects, we employ random firm effects in order to accommodate the influence of institutional environment of the home market of the firm.

[19] For instance, anticipation and planning of internationalisation may encourage a firm to refrain from financial reporting discretion for a few years before the event in order to present a satisfactory record to prospective foreign investors. More recent research reveals that firms may be found to be involuntarily traded in a foreign jurisdiction (Brüggemann et al. 2012; Brüggemann et al. 2012), and the extent to which less financial reporting discretion has attracted this type of trading without the issuer's involvement is an open question.

[20] More specifically, a propensity score is estimated by matching firms in terms of analyst following, ownership structure, leverage, auditor, size, net operating assets, foreign sales, reporting losses, Tobin's Q, change in equity, change in leverage, country and industry affiliations, and time. The matching addresses only firms that are traded across Europe and firms that are strictly locally traded during the period covered by the study. The logistic regression which underlies the estimation of the propensity score yields an R^2 of 42 %.

similar evidence among non-US markets (e.g., Cabán-Garcia 2009; Roosenboom and Van Dijk 2009; Abdallah and Goergen 2008), with very weak results so far.[21]

We argue that a potential reason underlying the weak or nonsignificant findings of prior research is the lack of consideration of the complexity of the firm's exposure to international capital markets.

As discussed, we address this complexity by ranking the strengths of the institutional characteristics of the markets where the firm is exposed relative to the home market. Then, two discrete cases arise, the first where the firm is exposed to at least one market characterized by a stronger institutional environment, and the second where even the best ranked market to which the firm is exposed is characterized by weaker institutions than the home market.

Therefore, we expect that firms that are exposed to stronger regulation elsewhere will exhibit more restraint in exercising financial reporting discretion as a result of a form of legal bonding. This idea is captured in the construction of the LEGAL BONDING variable that expands the model presented in (9.2) as follows:

$$\begin{aligned} \mathrm{DACC}_{\mathrm{it}} = {} & c_0 + c_1\mathrm{EXPOSURE}_{\mathrm{it}} + c_2\mathrm{NUMEX}_{\mathrm{it}} + c_3\mathrm{LEGAL\,BONDING}_{\mathrm{it}} \\ & + c_4\mathrm{HOME\,REGULATION} + \mathrm{Controls} + v_{\mathrm{it}} \end{aligned} \tag{9.3}$$

where DACC is the discretionary accrual, estimated as the residual arising from running regression (9.1) across portfolios of firms sorted by sector and year; EXPOSURE is a dummy variable taking the value of 1 if the firm's shares are traded in European capital markets additional to the firm's local market and 0 otherwise; NUMEX is the number of additional European jurisdictions where a firm's shares are traded; LEGAL BONDING is a dummy variable that takes the value of one when the firm is exposed to at least one market characterized by a stronger institutional environment than in the home market and zero otherwise; and HOME REGULATION is an indicator of the institutional environment in the firm's home market, based on La Porta et al. (2006) securities regulation indices with respect to disclosure, public and private enforcement.

The important feature of the LEGAL BONDING variable is that it is based on the ranking of all of the destinations of the firm across Europe,[22] using a measure that is relative to the home market score in terms of characteristics of the regulatory environment that are likely to affect financial reporting discretion.

Furthermore, the introduction of this variable affects the interpretation of the variable EXPOSURE. Given that LEGAL BONDING captures exposure to a

---

[21] Roosenboom and Van Dijk (2009) examine the economic benefits of cross-listing in the eight major stock exchanges in the US, the UK, continental Europe, and Japan; Abdallah and Goergen (2008) examine the determinants of cross-listing choice drawing upon 19 markets. More to the point, Cabán-Garcia (2009) examines a sample of 13 European jurisdictions and finds that the foreign regulatory requirements have little or no effect on the reported earnings of European firms cross-listed in European exchanges.

[22] The impact of US and other overseas exposure is addressed separately with discrete dummy variables that are included with the other control variables.

subset of destinations characterized by relatively strong regulatory environments, the c_1 coefficient on EXPOSURE now captures what is likely to be a reputational bonding effect (i.e., the influence of international exposure that is not attributed to legal bonding).[23]

Such an interpretation is also consistent with the Licht et al. (2013) argument that a major difference between legal and reputational bonding is that the former depends on the host country's enforcement whereas the latter may incentivize insiders to follow weakly enforced rules for reputational reasons. Hence, evidence for the presence of legal bonding should be established by a negative and significant coefficient c_3, while evidence for reputational bonding in the context of model (9.3) should be provided by means of a negative and significant coefficient c_1.

Moreover, having controlled for legal bonding, the breadth of exposure NUMEX should now capture the combined effect of relatively weak regulatory environments. A possible prediction with respect to the c_2 coefficient on NUMEX is that the breadth of such exposure could adversely affect the incentives of managers to exercise less financial reporting discretion, i.e., an 'adverse' legal bonding effect denoted by a positive and significant coefficient.

Further to the exposure of the firm to additional regulatory environments captured in model (9.3), the present study also investigates various aspects of these environments that may matter as determinants of financial reporting discretion. In this regard, we follow prior research on cross-listing (Cabán-Garcia 2009) covering the private–public enforcement debate and other disclosure-related aspects of securities regulation.

Cabán-Garcia (2009) adds the disclosure regulation dimension[24] to the enforcement parameters based on a similar argument, i.e., that the choice of a foreign market with high disclosure and governance requirements enables managers to provide a more credible signal about the quality of their firm and of their commitment to higher disclosure and governance standards.

Furthermore, the interaction between disclosure and accrual discretion (our dependent variable) has been shown elsewhere to provide relevant information to investors (Christensen and Demski 2003; Dargenidou et al. 2011). The securities regulation indices employed by Cabán-Garcia (2009), and used here, are based on the La Porta et al. (2006) indices on the disclosure requirements, liability standard, and public enforcement of securities laws.[25]

---

[23] Alternatively, the coefficient on LEGAL BONDING could be considered as the incremental effect of being exposed to at least one market whose regulatory environment is stronger than the home market's.

[24] It is important to note that the disclosure variable that we discuss here refers to disclosure regulation and not voluntary disclosure scores (e.g., CIFAR scores, S&P Transparency, and Disclosure scores, etc).

[25] The disclosure requirements index averages the scores of six areas of disclosure: delivering the prospectus, insiders' compensation, ownership structure, inside ownership, irregular contracts, and related-parties transactions. The liability standard index captures the existence of liability rules thus enabling investors to recover from losses caused by wrong or omitted

An auxiliary empirical question that arises in the context of the present study is the extent to which the influence of legal bonding is significant over and above the influence of the local regulation in the jurisdiction of origin. In the context of cross-listings in the US, both Lang et al. (2006) and Leuz (2006) point out that local regulation has a pervasive effect on cross-listed firms.

In the European context, where the regulation process in the pre-IFRS period was oriented toward harmonization and mutual recognition (Enriques 2006), compared for example to the centralized enforcement mechanisms of the SEC in the US, it may be expected that local institutional characteristics play an even more important role.

The investigation undertaken here is related to Raonic et al. (2004), which also examines the joint effect of market and regulatory forces on the properties of earnings, by modeling relative effects of regulation both in the jurisdiction of origin and in the host jurisdiction level.

In the present study, further to the relative effects of regulation, we also introduce various aspects of regulation in the home market as a determinant of financial reporting discretion. While Raonic et al. (2004) establishes a positive association between regulatory enforcement and conditional conservatism in reported earnings, more detailed evidence in Bushman and Piotroski (2006), which employs the same regulation variables as the ones we use here, confirms the Raonic et al. (2004) findings in terms of the public enforcement aspect of securities regulation, although they find no evidence of the private enforcement aspect. Finally, Wysocki (2004) shows that both the public and private enforcement indicators are negatively correlated with measures of earnings management. Therefore, in the context of model (9.3), we expect that the HOME REGULATION coefficient c_4 will be negative, suggesting not only that local regulation is an important determinant of financial reporting discretion but also, following Wysocki (2004), confirming the validity of our measure of discretion.

Further to legal bonding, here it is argued that international exposure of firms is also driven by reputational bonding. Model (9.3) accommodates this influence by means of the coefficient c_1 on EXPOSURE. In order to corroborate our inference about reputational bonding, we examine various circumstances that are likely to enhance foreign market participants' awareness of the firm.

More specifically, we examine the influence of exchange consolidation, the adoption of internationally recognized accounting standards, and geographical proximity. To this end, we extend the model in (9.3) by incorporating these factors and allowing them to interact with the regulation variables. The interaction allows

(Footnote 25 continued)
information. It combines the scores of liability standards for the issuers and directors, distributors, and accountants. The private enforcement index combines the sub-indices of disclosure requirements and liability standard. The public enforcement index comprises sub-indices on the characteristics and investigative powers of the market supervisor as well as on the existence of criminal and noncriminal sanctions for securities laws violations (Gaban-Garcia 2009).

us to observe the influence of those circumstances both in the presence or absence of legal bonding.

Each reputational bonding mechanism examined here has particularities that are accommodated and discussed in the following models (9.4a–c), which extend model (9.3). More specifically, the models examined are:

$$\begin{aligned}\text{DACC}_{\text{it}} = {} & d_0 + d_1\text{EXPOSURE}_{\text{it}} + d_2\text{NUMEX}_{\text{it}} + d_3\text{LEGAL BONDING}_{\text{it}} \\ & + d_4\text{HOME REGULATION} + d_5\text{EURONEXT}_{\text{it}} + d_6\text{NOREX}_{\text{it}} \\ & + d_7\text{EXPOSURE}_{\text{it}} * \text{EURONEXT}_{\text{it}} + d_8\text{EXPOSURE}_{\text{it}} * \text{NOREX}_{\text{it}} \\ & + d_9\text{LEGAL BONDING}_{\text{it}} * \text{EURONEXT}_{\text{it}} \\ & + d_{10}\text{LEGAL BONDING}_{\text{it}} * \text{NOREX}_{\text{it}} + \text{Controls} + v_{\text{it}} \qquad (9.4\text{a})\end{aligned}$$

The model in (9.4a) accommodates the influence of exchange consolidation, namely the cases of Euronext and Norex. EURONEXT is a dummy variable that takes the value of 1 if the corresponding observation is either a firm that originates in France, Netherlands or Belgium, or whose shares are traded on the exchanges in these three countries after 2001, and similarly for Portugal after 2003. NOREX is a dummy variable that takes the value of 1 if the corresponding observation is a firm that originates in Sweden or Denmark, or whose shares are traded on the exchanges in these two countries after 1998, and similarly for Norway from 2000 and Finland from 2003.

The effect of consolidation on local firms is represented by the coefficients d_5 and d_6 while a reputational bonding effect arising from exchange consolidation is captured by d_7 and d_8. As long as exchange consolidation triggers a reputational bonding effect, we would expect d_7 and d_8 to be negative and significant. Furthermore, the interactions of the exchange consolidation variables with LEGAL BONDING should inform us about the extent to which there is a substitution effect or complementarity.

If exchange consolidation and legal bonding are substitutes, then it would be expected that the effect of the consolidation on financial reporting discretion would be more pronounced in the absence rather than in the presence of a legal bonding background. If the two are complements rather than substitutes, then legal bonding might reinforce the impact of reputational bonding on financial reporting discretion.

Similarly to the effect of exchange consolidation, the impact of adopting internationally understood high-quality accounting standards can be observed for both local and internationally exposed firms. In the model presented in (9.4b), the impact of either IAS or US GAAP on local firms is represented by the coefficients d_5 and d_6, while a reputational bonding effect can be established by means of the coefficients d_7 and d_8.[26]

In the spirit of (9.4a), we also test for interaction effects between legal bonding and accounting standards by means of the coefficients d_9 and d_{10}.

[26] The IAS and US GAAP variables take the value of 1 if the firm is said to report under the respective standards according to Worldscope. The criterion is also used for classifying firms as reporting under IAS in Daske et al. (2013). The latter argue that relevant information on the Worldscope database may be subject to errors; if this is so, then this could work against confirming the hypothesis here.

$$\begin{aligned}\mathrm{DACC_{it}} = {} & d_0 + d_1\mathrm{EXPOSURE} + d_2\mathrm{NUMEX} + d_3\mathrm{LEGAL\ BONDING} \\ & + d_4\mathrm{HOME\ REGULATION} + d_5\mathrm{IAS} + d_6\mathrm{US\ GAAP} \\ & + d_7\mathrm{EXPOSURE} * \mathrm{IAS} + d_8\mathrm{EXPOSURE} * \mathrm{US\ GAAP} \\ & + d_9\mathrm{LEGAL\ BONDING} * \mathrm{IAS} + d_{10}\mathrm{LEGAL\ BONDING} * \mathrm{US\ GAAP} \\ & + \mathrm{Controls} + v_{\mathrm{it}} \end{aligned} \tag{9.4b}$$

Finally, geographical proximity is a variable that pertains only to internationally exposed firms. More specifically, the corresponding variable DISTANCE is estimated by taking the logarithm of (1 + distance in kilometers) where this is measured as the distance in Km between the capital cities of the jurisdictions where a firm is trading its shares.[27]

In the model presented in (9.4c) below, the coefficient of interest is d_1, which, in this context, represents a reputational bonding effect that arises when home and host destination markets are close enough, again in the absence of legal bonding.

$$\begin{aligned}\mathrm{DACC_{it}} = {} & d_0 + d_1\mathrm{EXPOSURE} + d_2\mathrm{NUMEX} + d_3\mathrm{LEGAL\ BONDING} \\ & + d_4\mathrm{HOME\ REGULATION} + d_5\mathrm{DISTANCE} \\ & + d_6\mathrm{LEGAL\ BONDING} * \mathrm{DISTANCE} + \mathrm{Controls} + v_{\mathrm{it}} \end{aligned} \tag{9.4c}$$

In summary, the present study argues that exposure of firms to additional markets is associated with less financial reporting discretion. The influence of this exposure is attributed to both legal and reputational bonding. Legal bonding is investigated by means of the exposure to at least one market characterized by a stronger institutional environment.

On the other hand, reputational bonding is expected to manifest itself in terms of less financial reporting discretion among firms that are exposed across multiple capital markets in the absence of legal bonding. We further seek to corroborate the presence of reputational bonding by investigating mechanisms and circumstances specific to European markets, and which are likely to enhance awareness and facilitate the assessment of the firm by market participants across different jurisdictions (exchange consolidation, use of internationally understood accounting standards, and geographical proximity).

9.7 Sample Collection and Descriptive Statistics

The data are collected from Worldscope and Datastream for the years between 1995[28] and 2004, for firms originating in 16 European economies. The initial

[27] This information is taken from Sarkissian and Schill (2004).

[28] Since lagged accounting data are necessary for the calculation and estimation of the net accrual, we also employ accounting data from 1994 in order to carry out the estimation for 1995.

sample comprises 39,370 firm-year observations for which the estimation of the discretionary net current accrual (DACC) is feasible. However, given the missing observations for variables that are employed here as controls in the models discussed earlier as well the truncation of the continuous variables at 1 % in order to eliminate the influence of outliers, this reduces the sample to 12,968 firm-year observations.[29]

Information regarding the market exposure of the firm through European listings is collected manually, initially by using Worldscope,[30] and then by identifying in Datastream the date on which the firm has started trading. In the present study, the quotation of a firm's shares in additional markets is established based on the exchange information attached to the Datastream mnemonic for locations other than the firm's primary listing in its home market.

Therefore, the concept of exposure encompasses both formal cross-listing and other cases where a firm's equity may be traded in other markets, even without the issuer's involvement (as in the case, for example, of the Open Market at the Frankfurt Stock Exchange, discussed by Brüggemann et al. 2012) or SEAQ-I at the London Stock Exchange (Bris et al. 2012). Hence, the data collection does not focus strictly on the event of cross-listing, but also on other evidence of trading of a firm's shares in additional markets.[31]

The composition of the sample employed here is presented in Table 9.1, with firms categorized in each year as either 'exposed' or 'non-exposed' with respect to regulatory environments in additional European jurisdictions (in the latter case, it should be recalled that nonexposed firms in a European context may still be traded in the US or elsewhere). Reviewing Panel A, it is possible that firm-year observations in the Public Utilities sector might be over-represented at 8.9 % of the sub-sample for which there is exposure to additional European markets, by comparison to 2.4 % of the nonexposed sub-sample.

This occurrence can probably be attributed to a wave of privatizations with multiple listings across Europe during the period of the study (Pagano et al. 2002).

---

[29] For instance, in the initial sample of firm-year observations for which an estimate of the discretionary net accrual is feasible, there are 14,220 missing observations for analyst following, 14,298 for the item Percentage of Foreign Sales, 10,928 for the item Percentage of Closely Held Shares and 4,420 for the item Accounting Standards Followed. An alternative approach might arbitrarily add zeros where this item is missing (e.g., analyst following, foreign sales). However, by avoiding this approach, we may bias the sample toward including firms whose information environment is more homogeneous.

[30] A similar source of information for identifying exposure to foreign capital markets has been employed in studies that assess earnings quality in an international setting (e.g., the NUMEX variable in Barth et al., 2008) without much further justification or analysis.

[31] Sarkissian and Schill (2009) find that valuation gains related to cross-listing tend to be transitory and concentrated mostly before the cross-listing event. The database compiled for this study contains exposures whose initiation took place before 1995, and the impact of these early cross-listings may be outdated. It is an open question how and whether this might affect the inferences drawn here regarding financial reporting, and whether it is likely to bias against finding a significant relation between foreign capital market exposure and discretion in financial reporting.

Table 9.1 Sample composition

Industry	Exposed			Nonexposed		
	Discretionary accrual DACC (Median)	Number of observations	% in sample	Discretionary accrual DACC (Median)	Number of observations	% in sample
Panel A. Industry						
Basic industries	0.0234	166	14.90	0.0302	1304	11.00
Capital goods	0.0251	230	20.65	0.0353	3410	28.77
Consumer durable	0.0352	12	1.08	0.0377	393	3.32
Consumer nondurable	0.0205	169	15.17	0.0327	1606	13.55
Consumer service	0.0265	136	12.21	0.0318	2541	21.44
Energy	0.0218	52	4.67	0.0374	261	2.20
Health care	0.0244	79	7.09	0.0333	616	5.20
Public utilities	0.0203	99	8.89	0.0240	288	2.43
Technology	0.0458	120	10.77	0.0522	1176	9.92
Transportation	0.0157	51	4.58	0.0266	259	2.18
Total	0.0244	1,114	100 %	0.0343	11,854	100 %
Panel B. Country						
Austria	0.0257	46	4.13	0.0308	138	1.16
Belgium	0.0293	21	1.89	0.0285	261	2.20
Switzerland	0.0232	237	21.27	0.0283	494	4.17
Germany	0.0241	46	4.13	0.0445	1519	12.81
Denmark	0.0251	12	1.08	0.0334	385	3.25
Spain	0.0353	40	3.59	0.0277	365	3.08
Finland	0.0247	44	3.95	0.0344	432	3.64
France	0.0219	134	12.03	0.0310	1655	13.96
UK	0.0246	194	17.41	0.0348	4458	37.61
Greece	0.0095	8	0.72	0.0562	143	1.21
Ireland	0.0239	139	12.48	0.0182	120	1.01
Italy	0.0256	61	5.48	0.0323	424	3.58
Netherlands	0.0312	90	8.08	0.0414	638	5.38
Norway	0.0717	5	0.45	0.0392	120	1.01
Portugal	0.0137	13	1.17	0.0383	122	1.03
Sweden	0.0255	24	2.15	0.0293	580	4.89
Total	0.0244	1,114	100 %	0.0343	1,1854	100 %

Note Table 9.1 reports the median discretionary net current accrual (*DACC*) per sector and country across firm-year observations, where firms are either (1) exposed elsewhere in Europe to one or more capital markets beyond their own jurisdiction, or (2) not exposed elsewhere in Europe, i.e., they have no listing on European stock exchanges other than in the home market

Similarly, in Panel B, a pronounced (net) outward mobility can be observed for Swiss and Irish firms.

In Table 9.2, the most striking differences with respect to exposed and non-exposed firms can be observed in the descriptive statistics for analyst following and ownership structure. Commonly, internationally exposed firms attract the attention of more analysts and are characterized by less closely held ownership, consistent with the motivations of European firms to improve visibility through cross-listing, as described in prior research (Bancel and Mittoo 2001, 2009; Pagano et al. 2002).

The descriptive statistics reported in Table 9.2 also suggest that internationally exposed firms are larger, they tend to engage a reputable auditor and generate a greater percentage of their revenues abroad, and during the period examined made less use of leverage and tended more to report under IAS. While all of the above are consistent with the profile of a typical firm that is exposed to international capital markets, it is also shown that those firms tend to exhibit less financial reporting discretion, by way of a lower absolute discretionary net accrual (DACC).

The correlations reported in Table 9.3 suggest that exercising less financial reporting discretion may be influenced by each of the characteristics mentioned here, which reinforces their inclusion as control variables in the tests discussed below.

9.8 Discussion of Findings

The results reported in Table 9.4 present two different forms of testing the basic model as described in (9.2). Those forms are: a random firm effects estimation with all firm-year observations in the sample (ALL); a similar specification in a sub-sample comprising all observations from firms that are exposed to an additional capital market during the period 1995–2004, i.e., both before and after the first cross-listing (PRE/POST); and again, a similar specification in a sub-sample comprising observations from firms that are never exposed during the period of the study, and which are matched with the firm-year observations in the first sub-sample based on a propensity score (MATCH). All specifications contain year, industry and country effects, and are estimated with firm-level clustered errors.[32]

The first regression includes the main variables of interest, i.e., exposure to additional European capital markets (EXPOSURE) and the number of additional European jurisdictions within which a firm's shares are found to be traded (NUMEX), controlling only for further destinations of European firms on regulated exchanges in the USA, the OTC market in the USA, and other overseas markets.

The evidence in this test corroborates prior research that points to a strong effect of exposure in financial reporting associated with listing in the regulated US market, being statistically significant across all three specifications of model (9.2) (ALL: −0.0087, p-value < 0.01; PRE/POST: −0.0097, p-value < 0.05; MATCH: −0.0117, p-value < 0.01). On the contrary, the exposure elsewhere in Europe

[32] While here we apply a random firm effects model using a GLS approach, we also add year dummies in order to capture cross-sectional dependence in the regressions' residuals.

Table 9.2 Descriptive statistics

	DACC	Analyst following	Ownership	Leverage	Big(n) auditor	Size	Operating assets %	Foreign sales
ALL								
Median	0.0333	5.917	36.786	0.5519	1.0000	5.719	0.5376	41.254
Mean	0.0518	8.352	38.470	0.8289	0.7801	5.815	0.5129	41.344
Standard deviation	0.0591	6.999	25.214	1.0773	0.4142	1.650	0.1962	30.952
EXPOSED (1,114)								
Median	0.0244	12.167	27.756	0.6881	1.0000	7.715	0.5548	61.354
Mean	0.0379	13.273	30.762	0.9492	0.9039	7.440	0.5211	58.505
Standard deviation	0.0447	8.434	23.704	1.1204	0.2948	1.697	0.1853	27.146
NONEXPOSED (11,854)								
Median	0.0343	5.583	38.070	0.5364	1.0000	5.595	0.5356	38.890
Mean	0.0531	7.889	39.195	0.8176	0.7684	5.663	0.5121	39.731
Standard deviation	0.0601	6.665	25.231	1.0725	0.4219	1.561	0.1972	30.799
	Loss	**Tobin's Q**	**Change in equity**	**Change in debt**	**Statutory tax rate**	**IAS**	**US gaap**	**Distance (Km)**
ALL								
Median	0.0000	1.3057	0.0690	0.0211	33	0.0000	0.0000	N/A
Mean	0.1695	1.6181	0.1519	0.4526	34.410	0.1319	0.0304	N/A
Standard deviation	0.3752	1.0278	0.6641	2.1384	7.340	0.3384	0.1716	N/A
EXPOSED (1,114)								
Median	0.0000	1.3332	0.0581	-0.0111	30	0.0000	0.0000	511
Mean	0.1706	1.6901	0.1219	0.3242	30.726	0.3160	0.0817	663.29
Standard deviation	0.3763	1.1513	0.5964	1.6898	6.641	0.4651	0.2740	403.62

(continued)

Table 9.2 (continued)

	DACC	Analyst following	Ownership	Leverage	Big(n) auditor	Size	Operating assets %	Foreign sales
NONEXPOSED (11,854)								
Median	0.0000	1.3037	0.0698	0.0239	33	0.0000	0.0000	N/A
Mean	0.1694	1.6113	0.1547	0.4647	34.756	0.1146	0.0256	N/A
Standard deviation	0.3751	1.0152	0.6701	2.1755	7.308	0.3186	0.1578	N/A

Notes Table 9.2 reports the median, mean, and standard deviation of the discretionary net current accrual and the control variables employed here across firm-year observations, where firms are exposed through trading their equity to European jurisdictions beyond their domicile ('exposed') and firm-year observations where the firms are not exposed to other European jurisdictions ('non-exposed'). DACC is the discretionary net current accrual, estimated as the residual arising from running regression (1) across portfolios of firms sorted by sector and year; ANALYST FOLLOWING is the average number of analysts following the firm during the year; OWNERSHIP is the percentage of closely held shares; LEVERAGE is the ratio of long and short-term debt to equity; BIG(N) AUDITOR is a dummy variable taking the value of 1 if the firm's accounts are audited by one of the large international audit firm and 0 otherwise; SIZE is the natural logarithm of the firm's market capitalization at the year end, denominated in US$; OPERATING ASSETS % is the beginning of the year net operating assets scaled by beginning of the year total assets; FOREIGN SALES is the percentage of foreign sales to total sales; LOSS is a dummy variable taking the value of 1 if the firm reports a loss and 0 otherwise; TOBINS' Q is the ratio of total assets minus the book value of equity plus the market value of equity to total assets; CHANGE IN EQUITY is the percentage change in the book value of equity; CHANGE IN DEBT is the percentage change in total debt; STATUTORY TAX RATE is the statutory tax rate at the firm's jurisdiction of origin for the specific year; AS is a dummy variables taking the value of 1 if the firm reports under IAS according to Worldscope in the year involved and 0 otherwise; US GAAP is a dummy variables taking the value of 1 if the firm reports under US GAAP according to Worldscope and 0 otherwise. DISTANCE is estimated by taking the logarithm of (1 + distance in kilometers) where distance is measured between the capital cities of the jurisdictions where a firm is trading its shares

Table 9.3 Pearson and Spearman correlations

	DACC	Analyst following	Ownership	Leverage	Size	Operating assets %	Foreign sales	Tobin's Q	Change in equity	Change in debt	Statutory tax rate
DACC		−0.1230	0.0558	−0.0623	−0.1749	−0.1065	−0.0633	0.1119	0.1176	0.0667	0.0632
		0.00	*0.00*	*0.00*	*0.00*	*0.00*	*0.00*	*0.00*	*0.00*	*0.00*	*0.00*
Analyst following	−0.1101		−0.1489	0.0941	0.67	−0.0449	0.2193	0.0970	0.0347	0.0648	0.1308
	0.00		*0.00*	*0.00*	*0.00*	*0.00*	*0.00*	*0.00*	*0.00*	*0.00*	*0.00*
Ownership	0.0654	−0.1266		0.0257	−0.1893	−0.0479	−0.0128	−0.1064	0.0088	−0.0256	0.3712
	0.00	*0.00*		*0.00*	*0.00*	*0.00*	*0.14*	*0.00*	*0.32*	*0.00*	*0.00*
leverage	0.0014	0.0224	0.0442		0.0596	0.2011	0.1508	−0.1975	−0.1371	0.2422	0.0538
	0.88	*0.01*	*0.00*		*0.00*	*0.00*	*0.00*	*0.00*	*0.00*	*0.00*	*0.00*
Size	−0.1463	0.6439	−0.1810	0.0040		−0.0641	0.2160	0.3202	0.1450	0.0440	−0.0531
	0.00	*0.00*	*0.00*	*0.65*		*0.00*	*0.00*	*0.00*	*0.00*	*0.00*	*0.00*
Operating assets %	−0.1087	−0.0538	−0.0554	0.0830	−0.0578		−0.0106	−0.2005	−0.0932	0.0008	−0.1462
	0.00	*0.00*	*0.00*	*0.00*	*0.00*		*0.23*	*0.00*	*0.00*	*0.93*	*0.00*
Foreign sales	−0.0501	0.2023	−0.0174	0.0813	0.2062	0.0072		−0.0204	−0.0479	−0.0460	−0.0125
	0.00	*0.00*	*0.05*	*0.00*	*0.00*	*0.41*		*0.02*	*0.00*	*0.00*	*0.16*
Tobin's Q	0.1283	0.0352	−0.0686	−0.1187	0.2289	−0.2059	−0.0084		0.3052	0.0694	−0.0687
	0.00	*0.00*	*0.00*	*0.00*	*0.00*	*0.00*	*0.34*		*0.00*	*0.00*	*0.00*
Change in equity	0.208	−0.0398	0.0016	−0.1074	0.0707	−0.0640	−0.0170	0.1788		0.0303	−0.0202
	0.00	*0.00*	*0.86*	*0.00*	*0.00*	*0.00*	*0.05*	*0.00*		*0.00*	*0.02*
Change in debt	0.1322	−0.0154	−0.0209	0.0038	−0.0098	−0.0840	−0.0586	0.0822	0.0576		0.0435
	0.00	*0.08*	*0.02*	*0.67*	*0.26*	*0.00*	*0.00*	*0.00*	*0.00*		*0.00*
Statutory tax rate	0.0875	0.1666	0.3581	0.0707	−0.0474	−0.1446	−0.0123	−0.0628	0.0067	−0.0055	
	0.00	*0.00*	*0.00*	*0.00*	*0.00*	*0.00*	*0.16*	*0.00*	*0.45*	*0.53*	

Notes Table 9.3 reports the Pearson (left side) and Spearman (right side) correlations between the continuous variables employed here. *DACC* is the discretionary net current accrual, estimated as the residual arising from running regression (9.1) across portfolios of firms sorted by sector and year; *ANALYST FOLLOWING* is the average number of analysts following the firm during the year; *OWNERSHIP* is the percentage of closely held shares; *LEVERAGE* is the ratio of long and short-term debt to equity; *SIZE* is the natural logarithm of the firm's market capitalization at the year end, denominated in US$; *NET OPERATING ASSETS* are at the beginning of the year, scaled by total assets at the beginning of the year; *FOREIGN SALES* is the percentage of foreign sales to total sales; TOBIN'S Q is the ratio of total assets minus the book value of equity plus the market value of equity to total assets; *CHANGE IN EQUITY* is the percentage change in the book value of equity; *CHANGE IN DEBT* is the percentage change in total debt; *STATUTORY TAX RATE* is the statutory tax rate at the firm's jurisdiction of origin for the specific year

Table 9.4 Financial reporting discretion (DACC) and international exposure

	All	Pre/post	Match	All	Pre/post	Match
EXPOSURE	**−0.0101****	**−0.0142****	−0.0004	**−0.0111*****	**−0.0184*****	**−0.0077***
	[−2.228]	[−2.419]	[−0.090]	[−2.584]	[−3.200]	[−1.877]
Numex	0.0035	0.0035	0.0026	**0.0073*****	**0.0115*****	**0.0075*****
	[1.319]	[1.218]	[0.975]	[2.948]	[3.830]	[2.888]
Regulated US	**−0.0087*****	**−0.0097****	**−0.0117*****	−0.0004	−0.0017	−0.0044
	[−2.816]	[−2.397]	[−3.348]	[−0.123]	[−0.426]	[−1.360]
Otc US	−0.0011	−0.0019	−0.0056	0.0051	0.0031	−0.0011
	[−0.235]	[−0.382]	[−1.231]	[1.114]	[0.606]	[−0.248]
Overseas	−0.0154	−0.0159	0.0017	−0.0083	−0.0115	0.0051
	[−1.200]	[−1.048]	[0.255]	[−0.637]	[−0.719]	[0.706]
Analyst following				**−0.0006*****	−0.0004	−0.0004
				[−4.087]	[−1.437]	[−1.584]
Ownership				**0.0001***	0.0000	0.0001
				[1.872]	[0.272]	[1.059]
Leverage				**0.0023*****	0.0009	−0.0003
				[3.461]	[0.741]	[−0.393]
Big(N) auditor				0.0007	−0.0119	0.0030
				[0.422]	[−1.591]	[0.786]
Size				**−0.0032*****	**−0.0058*****	**−0.0041*****
				[−4.760]	[−3.172]	[−3.000]
Operating assets %				**−0.0178*****	**−0.0197****	**−0.0127***
				[−4.185]	[−2.264]	[−1.664]
Foreign sales				−0.0000	−0.0001	−0.0000
				[−1.482]	[−1.109]	[−0.472]

(continued)

Table 9.4 (continued)

	All	Pre/post	Match	All	Pre/post	Match
Loss				**0.0049*****	0.0019	**0.0072****
				[2.918]	[0.359]	[1.961]
Tobin's Q				**0.0058*****	0.0016	**0.0050*****
				[6.183]	[0.675]	[3.061]
Change in equity				**0.0149*****	**0.0096*****	**0.0075*****
				[9.356]	[3.307]	[2.731]
Change in debt				**0.0025*****	**0.0032****	**0.0030****
				[8.095]	[2.197]	[2.465]
Statutory tax rate				−0.0001	0.0005	−0.0001
				[−0.501]	[1.245]	[−0.367]
Euronext				0.0044	**−0.0122***	−0.0051
				[1.527]	[−1.772]	[−1.002]
Norex				0.0021	0.0030	−0.0095
				[0.653]	[0.502]	[−1.232]
IAS				0.0035	0.0028	−0.0019
				[1.476]	[0.630]	[−0.630]
US Gaap				0.0024	0.0114	0.0042
				[0.529]	[1.442]	[0.671]
Constant	**0.0363*****	**0.0600*****	**0.0327*****	**0.0580*****	**0.0954*****	**0.0665*****
	[5.660]	[3.482]	[4.994]	[5.601]	[3.851]	[4.299]

(continued)

Table 9.4 (continued)

	All	Pre/post	Match	All	Pre/post	Match
Industry, year, country controls	Yes	Yes	Yes	Yes	Yes	Yes
Number of observations	12,968	1,659	2,218	12,968	1,659	2,218
Number of firms	3,000	300	659	3,000	300	659
Chi^2	543.9***	93.56***	138.7***	845***	228.9***	209.7***
R^2	0.0549	0.0750	0.0723	0.131	0.153	0.140
VIF (Mean)				3.13	2.77	2.62

Notes The results reported in Table 9.4 present three different specifications of testing the basic model as described in Model (9.2) $DACC_{it} = b_0 + b_1 EXPOSURE_{it} + b_2 NUMEX_{it} + Controls + u_{it}$

Those specifications are: a random firm effects with clustered error at the firm level including all firms year observations in the sample (ALL); a similar specification in a sub-sample comprising observations from firms that will be exposed to an additional capital market at a point in time during the period covered in the sample and exposed firms (PRE/POST); and again, a similar specification in a sub-sample comprising observations from firms that are never exposed during the period of the study but are matched with the exposed firm-year observations based on a propensity score (MATCH). All specifications contain year, industry and country effects, and are estimated with firm-level clustered errors. DACC is the discretionary net current accrual; EXPOSURE is a dummy variable taking the value of 1 if the firm's shares are traded in European capital markets additional to the firm's local market and 0 otherwise; NUMEX is the number of additional European jurisdictions in which a firm's shares are traded; REGULATED US is a dummy variable taking the value of 1 if the firm's shares are traded on NYSE, NASDAQ, or AMEX and 0 otherwise; OTC US is a dummy variable taking the value of 1 if the firm's shares are traded on the US OTC market and 0 otherwise; OVERSEAS is a dummy variable taking the value of 1 if the firm's shares are traded elsewhere in the world (i.e., not in Europe or USA) and 0 otherwise. EURONEXT is a dummy variable that takes the value of 1 if the corresponding observation is either for a firm that originates in France, Netherlands, or Belgium or originates elsewhere and its shares are traded on these exchanges after 2001, and similarly for Portugal after 2003; NOREX is a dummy variable which takes the value of 1 if the corresponding observation is for a firm that originates in Sweden and Denmark or originates elsewhere and its shares are traded on these exchanges after 1998, and similarly for Norway from 2000 and Finland from 2003; IAS is a dummy variable taking the value of 1 if the firm reports under International Accounting Standards according to Worldscope and 0 otherwise; US GAAP is a dummy variable taking the value of 1 if the firm reports under US GAAP according to Worldscope and 0 otherwise. Further controls are as defined in Table 9.2

* refer to significance levels at 10 %

** refer to significance levels at 5 %

*** refer to significance levels at 1 %

appears to be weaker even when evident (ALL: −0.0101, p-value < 0.05; PRE/POST: −0.0142, p-value < 0.05; MATCH: −0.0004, p-value > 0.1).

The right hand side of Table 9.4 introduces a set of possible determinants of financial reporting discretion at the firm level.[33]

Taking into consideration these controls, the effect of listing in the regulated US markets is now found not to be statistically significant, whereas both the magnitude and the significance level of the European exposure are now increased (ALL: −0.0111, p-value < 0.01; PRE/POST: −0.0184, p-value < 0.01; MATCH: −0.0077, p-value < 0.1).

Based on prior evidence which associates the benefits from US cross-listing with increased monitoring by investors (e.g., Lang et al. 2003b), it is possible that the inclusion of variables in the regression which capture visibility and investors' monitoring (analyst following, ownership structure and size) may reflect the market forces that mainly drive the significant effect of the US listing in the first part of Table 9.4.

Nevertheless, those forces are not sufficient to explain the European exposure effect, which now becomes far more obvious. Notably, the number of exchanges where the firm is exposed becomes a very significant determinant of financial reporting discretion, albeit with a positive sign (ALL: 0.0073, p-value < 0.01; PRE/POST: 0.0115, p-value < 0.01; MATCH: 0.0075, p-value < 0.01). Such a result implies that multiple capital market exposure might dilute the initial effect on financial reporting discretion; the omission of multiple exposure or cross-listing in similar studies may also explain the overall weak evidence presented in prior research with respect to European cross-listing.

Although we do not explicitly address the sequence of capital market exposures by individual firms, a possible conjecture based on Sarkissian and Schill (2009) is that those exposures may be motivated by factors that dilute the incentives of managers to exercise less financial reporting discretion, such as being exposed to weaker regulatory environments or to circumstances which do not favor reputational bonding.

The legal bonding hypothesis is represented by model (9.3), which is examined in Table 9.5, and tested here by means of the exposure to a market characterized by a stronger institutional environment than in the home market. Legal bonding here is examined in three contexts: public enforcement, private enforcement, and that aspect of private enforcement that specifically addresses disclosure regulation.

Consistent with the emphasis in prior research on disclosure regulation, the results in Table 9.5 show a persistently significant legal bonding effect with respect to the aspects of regulation that refer to disclosure (ALL: −0.0181, p-value < 0.01; PRE/POST: −0.0233, p-value < 0.01; MATCH: −0.0090, p-value < 0.1), and, although to a lesser extent, to public enforcement (ALL: −0.0075, p-value < 0.1; PRE/POST: −0.0086, p-value < 0.1; MATCH: −0.0012, p-value > 0.1) and to

[33] Given that most of these variables exhibit significant correlation between them, here we also check for possible multicollinearity effects by means of estimating a Variance Inflation Factor.

Table 9.5 Legal bonding—Exposure to another European market with stronger regulation

	Disclosure			Public enforcement			Private enforcement		
	ALL	PRE/POST	MATCH	ALL	PRE/POST	MATCH	ALL	PRE/POST	MATCH
EXPOSURE	**−0.0150*** **	**−0.0191*** **	**−0.0085** **	**−0.0150*** **	**−0.0191*** **	**−0.0087** **	**−0.0167*** **	**−0.0217*** **	**−0.0098** **
	[−3.695]	[−3.478]	[−2.059]	[−3.559]	[−3.336]	[−2.074]	[−3.790]	[−3.650]	[−2.241]
NUMEX	**0.0107*** **	**0.0138*** **	**0.0078*** **	**0.0103*** **	**0.0134*** **	**0.0068** **	**0.0127*** **	**0.0164*** **	**0.0089*** **
	[4.399]	[4.403]	[3.012]	[3.763]	[3.830]	[2.356]	[3.928]	[4.194]	[2.588]
LEGAL BONDING	**−0.0181*** **	**−0.0233*** **	**-0.0090***	**-0.0075***	**−0.0086***	−0.0012	**−0.0103** **	**−0.0125** **	−0.0051
	[−3.576]	[−2.870]	[−1.952]	[−1.857]	[−1.732]	[−0.299]	[−2.236]	[−2.286]	[−1.150]
HOME REGULATION	**−0.0300*** **	−0.0372	**−0.0230** **	**−0.0168*** **	−0.0043	−0.0079	**−0.0132** **	−0.0100	−0.0126
	[−5.392]	[−1.570]	[−2.224]	[−4.003]	[−0.269]	[−0.894]	[−2.068]	[−0.476]	[−1.222]
Constant	0.0689***	0.1034***	0.0561***	0.0546***	0.0881***	0.0449***	0.0544***	0.0943***	0.0516***
	[8.361]	[4.735]	[4.410]	[7.582]	[5.152]	[3.883]	[5.783]	[4.886]	[4.133]
Controls	Yes	Yes	Yes	Yes	Yes	Yes	Yes	Yes	Yes
Number of observations	12,968	1,659	2,218	12,968	1,659	2,218	12,968	1,659	2,218
Number of firms	3,000	300	659	3,000	300	659	3,000	300	659
Chi^2	790.3***	130.7***	163.0***	774.4***	128.9***	163.7***	779.8***	140.2***	166.3***
R^2	0.124	0.141	0.124	0.123	0.142	0.124	0.122	0.145	0.125

Notes The results reported in Table 9.5 present three different specifications of testing the basic model as described in Model (9.3) $DACC_{it} = c_0 + c_1 EXPOSURE_{it} + c_2 NUMEX_{it} + c_3 LEGAL\ BONDING_{it} + c_4 HOME\ REGULATION + Controls + v_{it}$

The three specifications are: a random firm effects with clustered error at the firm level including all firms year observations in the sample (ALL); a similar specification in a sub-sample comprising observations from firms that will be exposed to an additional capital market at a point in time during the period covered in the sample and exposed firms (PRE/POST); and again, a similar specification in a sub-sample comprising observations from firms that are never exposed during the period of the study but are matched with the exposed firm-year observations based on a propensity score (MATCH). All specifications contain year and industry effects, and are estimated with firm-level clustered errors. DACC is the discretionary net current accrual, estimated as the residual arising from running regression (1) across portfolios of firms sorted by sector and year; EXPOSURE is a dummy variable taking the value of 1 if the firm's shares are traded in European capital markets additional to the firm's local market and 0 otherwise; NUMEX is the number of additional European jurisdictions in which a firm's shares are traded; LEGAL BONDING is a dummy variable that takes the value of one when the firm is exposed to at least one market characterized by a stronger institutional environment than in the home market and zero otherwise; and HOME REGULATION is an indicator of the institutional environment in the firm's home market, based on La Porta et al. (2006) securities regulation indices with respect to disclosure, public and private enforcement. The control variables are as in Table 9.4

* refer to significance levels at 10 %

** refer to significance levels at 5 %

*** refer to significance levels at 1 %

private enforcement (ALL: −0.0103, p-value < 0.05; PRE/POST: −0.0125, p-value < 0.05; MATCH: −0.0051, p-value > 0.1).

Note that, in the examination of legal bonding across the three legal contexts, the empirical implementation of model (9.3) accommodates the variation in the corresponding aspects of regulation across the jurisdictions where the firms originate, substituting for the country effects employed in model (9.2) in order to control for the influence of the respective regulation in the home jurisdiction.

The coefficient estimates reported in Table 9.5 (and later in Table 9.6, where a similar approach is taken) are consistently negative and significant across the regression specification that includes all available observations, albeit significant to a lesser extent, when specifically defined sub-samples are employed.

The research design in the present study also enables investigation of another interesting feature of the European setting, i.e., the effect of being exposed to weaker regulatory environments.[34]

As long as exposure to additional markets is associated with significant restraint in financial reporting discretion, even when the firm is exposed to new jurisdictions whose regulation is weaker, such an influence is argued here to stem from the firm's reputational bonding. This effect is now captured by the coefficient on the EXPOSURE variable to which LEGAL BONDING is, in fact, an incremental effect. The findings presented in Table 9.5 support the notion of a pervasive reputational bonding effect, which is denoted by the negative and significant coefficients across both aspects of legal bonding, and in all regression specifications.

The reputational bonding source examined in Panel A of Table 9.6 is the extended visibility brought by stock exchange consolidation. In the period examined, the most prominent development in this respect is Euronext, which enabled a common trading platform across France, Netherlands, and Belgium from 2001, and later Portugal from 2003. A less well-documented development is Norex, which enabled a joint trading platform for the Nordic and Baltic countries, established in 1998 by the Swedish and Danish stock exchanges and extended to Norway in 2000 and Finland in 2003 (Nielsson 2007).

While little is published about the influence of Norex, Pownall et al. (2012) shows that trading through Euronext is associated with higher financial reporting quality for firms listed in high visibility segments. Based on the model presented in (9.4a), which treats stock exchange consolidation as a source of reputational bonding, we examine the separate effects of both legal and reputational bonding mechanisms as well as their possible interactions.

The coefficients of interest here refer to the interaction between EURONEXT and EXPOSURE, and between NOREX and EXPOSURE, referring to the situation where a firm is listed at origin on Euronext or Norex and at the same time has an exposure to other European capital markets whose regulatory environment is

[34] Such an effect cannot be observed in the context of the mainstream cross-listing in the US research, since US regulation is always deemed to be of the highest standard to-date.

Table 9.6 Legal bonding—Exchange consolidation, accounting standards and geographic proximity

	Disclosure			Public enforcement			Private enforcement		
	ALL	PRE/POST	MATCH	ALL	PRE/POST	MATCH	ALL	PRE/POST	MATCH
Panel A. Exchange consolidation									
EXPOSURE	**-0.0169*****	**−0.0193*****	**−0.0093****	**−0.0183*****	**−0.0207*****	**−0.0098****	**−0.0183*****	**−0.0215*****	**−0.0104****
LEGAL BONDING	**−0.0188*****	**−0.0255****	−0.0086	**−0.0092****	**−0.0093***	−0.0024	**−0.0102****	**−0.0124****	−0.0052
NUMEX	**0.0131*****	**0.0133*****	**0.0094*****	**0.0143*****	**0.0140*****	**0.0092*****	**0.0150*****	**0.0154*****	**0.0105*****
EURONEXT	**0.0046***	−0.0088	−0.0009	**0.0052***	−0.0100	−0.0004	0.0037	−0.0108	−0.0010
EURONEXT*EXPOSURE	**−0.0164*****	−0.0088	**−0.0125***	**−0.0186*****	−0.0090	**−0.0144****	**−0.0157****	−0.0066	**−0.0122***
EURONEXT*LEGAL BONDING	0.0076	0.0113	0.0040	0.0088	0.0098	0.0075	0.0035	0.0058	0.0016
NOREX	−0.0022	**−0.0163***	0.0043	−0.0013	**−0.0147***	0.0056	−0.0007	**−0.0154***	0.0057
NOREX*EXPOSURE	**0.0225***	**0.0344****	0.0094	**0.0271****	**0.0372****	0.0112	0.0144	**0.0279***	0.0029
NOREX*LEGAL BONDING	−0.0214	−0.0172	**−0.0195****	**−0.0327****	**−0.0273****	**−0.0227****	−0.0148	−0.0136	−0.0092
HOME REGULATION	**−0.0304*****	−0.0398	**−0.0228****	**−0.0171*****	−0.0030	−0.0083	**−0.0127****	−0.0101	−0.0120
Constant	0.0691***	0.1054***	0.0561***	0.0547***	0.0877***	0.0453***	0.0537***	0.0953***	0.0514***
Panel B. Accounting standards									
EXPOSURE	**−0.0127*****	**−0.0160*****	−0.0063	**−0.0117*****	**−0.0155*****	−0.0049	**−0.0141*****	**−0.0191*****	−0.0072
LEGAL BONDING	**−0.0190*****	**−0.0198*****	**−0.0148****	**−0.0083***	−0.0063	−0.0061	**−0.0096***	−0.0093	−0.0074
NUMEX	**0.0107*****	**0.0134*****	**0.0082*****	**0.0102*****	**0.0130*****	**0.0070****	**0.0128*****	**0.0164*****	**0.0089*****
IAS	0.0026	0.0032	−0.0002	0.0023	0.0040	−0.0001	0.0024	0.0031	−0.0007
IAS*EXPOSURE	−0.0066	−0.0069	**−0.0104****	−0.0087	−0.0085	**−0.0127****	−0.0078	−0.0073	**−0.0108****
IAS*LEGAL BONDING	0.0028	−0.0027	**0.0163***	0.0038	−0.0009	**0.0147****	0.0018	−0.0036	0.0115
US GAAP	0.0047	0.0159	−0.0054	0.0057	0.0212	−0.0037	0.0064	0.0195	−0.0034
US GAAP* EXPOSURE	−0.0020	−0.0079	0.0122	−0.0027	−0.0094	0.0113	−0.0000	−0.0068	0.0139
US GAAP*LEGAL BONDING	0.0030	−0.0078	0.0002	−0.0039	−0.0144	−0.0040	−0.0115	−0.0209	−0.0121
HOME REGULATION	**−0.0299*****	−0.0359	**−0.0225****	**−0.0167*****	−0.0031	−0.0084	**−0.0128****	−0.0127	−0.0120
Constant	0.0689***	0.1022***	0.0556***	0.0546***	0.0869***	0.0457***	0.0541***	0.0961***	0.0522***

(continued)

Table 9.6 (continued)

	Disclosure			Public enforcement			Private enforcement		
	ALL	PRE/POST	MATCH	ALL	PRE/POST	MATCH	ALL	PRE/POST	MATCH
Panel C. Geographic proximity									
EXPOSURE	**−0.0725*****	**−0.0539***	**−0.0462***	**−0.0788*****	**−0.0591***	**−0.0538***	**−0.0720*****	**−0.0565****	**−0.0477****
LEGAL BONDING	−0.0027	0.0025	0.0431	0.0412	0.0425	0.0563	0.0314	0.0394	0.0524
NUMEX	**0.0090*****	**0.0128*****	**0.0072*****	**0.0099*****	**0.0139*****	**0.0074****	**0.0119*****	**0.0163*****	**0.0089*****
DISTANCE	**0.0095****	0.0057	0.0061	**0.0102****	0.0063	0.0071	**0.0090****	0.0056	0.0060
DISTANCE*LEGAL BONDING	−0.0027	−0.0041	−0.0082	−0.0078	−0.0081	−0.0091	−0.0066	−0.0081	−0.0090
HOME REGULATION	**−0.0298*****	−0.0359	**−0.0228****	**−0.0166*****	−0.0020	−0.0067	**−0.0127****	−0.0074	−0.0111
Constant	0.0685***	0.1020***	0.0564***	0.0544***	0.0868***	0.0450***	0.0539***	0.0928***	0.0510***

Notes The results reported in summary form in Table 9.6 are for Models (9.4a–c). The number of firms and observations are the same as in Table 9.5, and the R^2 statistics do not differ substantially from Model (9.3). The response variable DACC is the discretionary net current accrual, estimated as the residual arising from running regression (9.1) across portfolios of firms sorted by sector and year; EXPOSURE is a dummy variable taking the value of 1 if the firm's shares are traded in European capital markets additional to the firm's local market and 0 otherwise; NUMEX is the number of additional European jurisdictions in which a firm's shares are traded; LEGAL BONDING is a dummy variable that takes the value of one when the firm is exposed to at least one market characterized by a stronger institutional environment than in the home market and zero otherwise; and HOME REGULATION is an indicator of the institutional environment in the firm's home market, based on La Porta et al. (2006) securities regulation indices with respect to disclosure, public and private enforcement; EURONEXT is a dummy variable that takes the value of 1 if the corresponding observation is either for a firm that originates in France, Netherlands or Belgium, or a firm that originates elsewhere and its shares are traded on these exchanges after 2001, and similarly for Portugal after 2003; NOREX is a dummy variable that takes the value of 1 if the corresponding observation is either for a firm that originates in Sweden or Denmark, or whose shares are traded on these exchanges after 1998, and similarly for Norway from 2000 and Finland from 2003; IAS is a dummy variable taking the value of 1 if the firm reports under International Accounting Standards according to Worldscope and 0 otherwise; US GAAP is a dummy variable taking the value of 1 if the firm reports under US GAAP according to Worldscope and 0 otherwise; DISTANCE is estimated by taking the logarithm of (1+ distance in kilometers) where distance is measured between the capital cities of the jurisdictions where a firm is trading its shares

* refer to significance levels at 10 %

** refer to significance levels at 5 %

*** refer to significance levels at 1 %

weaker than in the home jurisdiction, providing the ground for establishing reputational bonding.

Indeed, the coefficients for the EURONEXT*EXPOSURE interaction term are always negative, and in most specifications significant, suggesting that extended visibility introduced by exchange consolidation can constrain financial reporting discretion even in the absence of legal bonding. However, this effect appears to be more a reinforcement of the existing reputational bonding that takes place, irrespective of any stock exchange consolidation, denoted by the negative and significant coefficients for EXPOSURE.

Notably, there is no evidence that stock exchange consolidation may have a similar impact on firms that are part of Euronext but do not trade beyond their own jurisdiction, pointing to the asymmetric consequences of capital market integration and harmonization between local and internationalized firms. Surprisingly, we cannot observe similar dynamics for Norex, where we have no evidence of any reputational bonding at all; instead, we observe the effect of legal bonding mechanisms only, in terms of public enforcement.

Given Nielsson's (2007) evidence of limited consolidation in the case of Norex, whose participating markets are relatively small in size, and with thin trading, it is assumed here that the impact of stock exchange consolidation depends on the strength and the integration of the underlying exchanges involved.

The second mechanism examined here is the use of internationally understood accounting standards with a particular focus on the application pre-IFRS of International Accounting Standards, based on the model presented in (9.4b). Motivated by Karamanou and Nishiotis (2009), we seek evidence on whether the use of International Accounting Standards consists of a reputational bonding mechanism in terms of the coefficient on IAS*EXPOSURE.

The results reported in Panel B of Table 9.6 show that this coefficient is negative, but also that it becomes significant only in the specification that employs a sub-sample of matched firms. Interestingly, it is only in those cases where the coefficient on EXPOSURE becomes insignificant, denoting the lack of any reputational bonding *in the absence* of internationally accepted accounting standards.

Furthermore, a positive and significant coefficient for IAS*LEGAL BONDING may be interpreted as International Accounting Standards having a more pronounced role in constraining financial reporting discretion in the absence rather than in the presence of exposure to a stronger regulatory environment, consistent with the arguments in Karamanou and Nishiotis (2009). Moreover, such effects pertain to the application of International Accounting Standards but not US GAAP, which similarly imposes extended disclosure on the preparers. These results may be attributed to International Accounting Standards being more frequently used and hence more familiar among European market participants.

Finally, circumstances that favor the development of reputational bonding pertain not only to stock exchange consolidation and the use of internationally understood accounting standards such as IAS, but also to geographic proximity. Motivated by prior research which investigates a similar question within one jurisdiction (the USA), the model presented in (9.4c) aims to investigate the extent to which exposure to markets that are located closer to the origin of the firm might enable a better monitoring by market participants.

By introducing a variable that is based on a measure of geographical distance between home and destination markets (or, in the case of multiple exposures, the distance between the jurisdiction of origin and the farthest destination), the coefficient of *EXPOSURE* captures the impact of home and destination markets being as close as possible (a 'neighborhood' effect), in the absence of a legal bonding mechanism.

According to the empirical tests reported in Panel C of Table 9.6, proximity has a very pronounced effect towards constraining financial reporting discretion. This effect is now captured by the coefficients on *EXPOSURE* whose magnitude is dramatically different from that of similar coefficients obtained in the previous tests.

Such an effect could be attributed to the intensive information flows across geographically proximate jurisdictions that enable market participants' monitoring activities to an extent that legal bonding mechanisms become irrelevant, as suggested by the consistently insignificant coefficients on *LEGAL BONDING*. On the other hand, there is only very weak evidence that distance has an adverse effect in constraining financial reporting discretion. It is possible that our *DISTANCE* variable is not well specified, in that, while prior research has identified a limit upon which market participants are considered to be 'close' to the firm (in the US context, 100 km), to the best of our knowledge, similar cut-off points have not been reported with regard to the European setting.

Therefore, instead of introducing arbitrary cut-off points, we employ a direct measure of distance (or proximity). However, despite reservations with respect to the appropriateness of the distance measure, the findings do point to a potential substitution effect between information flows and legal bonding. In other words, to the extent that geographical proximity enables information flows, legal bonding may not be as relevant to investors for cross-border investing.

Conversely, legal bonding mechanisms may still be relevant for firms whose information environment is relatively poor due to their distance from the main capital markets. While the coefficient on the interaction term *LEGAL BONDING*DISTANCE* exhibits a negative sign consistent with this conjecture, those coefficients are not statistically significant. Future research that would calibrate the measure of distance in the European setting could revisit this issue.

9.9 Conclusion

In this study, we show that the exposure of European firms across additional European capital markets is associated with significant constraints in financial reporting discretion. By exploiting the variation in the regulatory environment in this setting, we are able to show that incentives for reducing financial reporting discretion stem from a form of legal bonding, in the sense of exposure to at least one capital market with better regulation than the firm's home jurisdiction.

Furthermore, we provide evidence for the presence of reputational bonding in cases where the firm is exposed to capital markets with weaker regulation than at home, in the spirit of Licht et al. (2013).

Moreover, we corroborate the evidence on reputational bonding by extending this investigation to circumstances which are likely to trigger greater financial reporting transparency even in the absence of strong legal regulations, such as exchange consolidation and geographical proximity.

Interestingly, there is consistent and strong evidence to suggest that any legal or reputational bonding influence is diluted by the firm's exposure to multiple capital markets. As little is known about multiple listings (e.g., Sarkissian and Schill 2009), this finding should go some way to help to re-interpret prior reports of a weak or nonexistent effect of European listings, and inform future research accordingly.

This study's findings are subject to a number of caveats.

First, the concept of exposure to additional European capital markets not only encompasses the notion of a formal cross-listing but also includes cases where trading in other markets has been initiated without the issuer's involvement.

Second, the notion of legal bonding employed here is not necessarily fully synonymous with the concept that refers to cross-listing in the regulated US markets, given the SEC supervision and enforcement powers.

Third, our classification of firms reporting under IAS and US GAAP relies on a database that may be subject to errors, according to others (Daske et al. 2013).

Fourth, the geographical distance measure could be further calibrated by establishing specific cut-off points to represent proximity.

However, it is worth noting that each of the points above would have worked against establishing the statistically significant evidence that is reported.

Perhaps, the most important finding in the present study is the presence of reputational bonding. Although we attempt to shed some light on the sources of this type of bonding here by looking at circumstances that facilitate the firm's monitoring by market participants, this quite pervasive influence on financial reporting remains elusive.

Given the points above, and taking into account recent developments that enable cross-border equity investment in the European setting (associated with IFRS implementation, further exchange consolidation, and the enablement of equity trading without the issuer's involvement), it might be fruitful to investigate further how this type of bonding has developed alongside recent initiatives for enhancing the strength of securities regulation, such as the Market Abuse and the Transparency Directives.

References

Abdallah, A. (2008). Do regulations matter? The effects of cross-listing on analysts' coverage and forecast errors: A comparative analysis. *Review of Accounting and Finance, 7*(3), 285–307.

Abdallah, W., & Goergen, M. (2008). Does corporate control determine the cross-listing location? *Journal of Corporate Finance, 14*(3), 183–199.

Aggarwal, R., Klapper, L., & Wysocki, P. (2005). Portfolio preferences of foreign institutional investors. *Journal of Banking & Finance, 29*(12), 2919–2946.

Ayers, B., Ramalingegowda, S., & Yeung, P. (2011). Hometown advantage: The effects of monitoring institution location on financial reporting discretion. *Journal of Accounting and Economics, 52*(1), 41–61.

Bae, K., Tan, H., & Welker, M. (2008). International GAAP differences: The impact on foreign analysts. *The Accounting Review, 83*(3), 593–628.

Baker, H., Nofsinger, J., & Weaver, D. (2002). International cross listing and visibility. *Journal of Financial and Quantitative Analysis, 37*(3), 495–521.

Ball, R., & Shivakumar, L. (2005). Earnings quality in UK private firms: comparative loss recognition timeliness. *Journal of Accounting and Economics, 39*(1), 83–128.

Bancel, F., & Mittoo, C. (2001). European managerial perceptions of the net benefits of foreign stock listings. *European Financial Management, 7*(2), 213–236.

Bancel, F., & Mittoo, U. (2009). Why do European firms go public? *European Financial Management, 15*(4), 844–884.

Barth, M., Landsman, W., & Lang, M. (2008). International accounting standards and accounting quality. *Journal of Accounting Research, 46*(3), 467–498.

Barton, J., & Simko, P. (2002). The balance sheet as an earnings management constraint. *The Accounting Review, 77*(Supplement), 1–27.

Becker, C., DeFond, M., Jiambalvo, J., & Subramanyam, K. (1998). The effect of audit quality on earnings management. *Contemporary Accounting Research, 15*(1), 1–24.

Bradshaw, M., Bushee, B., & Miller, G. (2004). Accounting choice, home bias, and US investment in non-US firms. *Journal of Accounting Research, 42*(5), 795–841.

Bris, A., Cantale, S., Hrnjić, E., & Nishiotis, G. (2012). The value of information in cross-listing. *Journal of Corporate Finance, 18*(2), 207–220.

Brüggemann, U., Daske, H., Homburg, C. & Pope P. (2012). How do individual investors react to global IFRS adoption? Working paper, available at http://ssrn.com/abstract=1458944.

Burgstahler, D., & Dichev, I. (1997). Earnings management to avoid earnings decreases and losses. *Journal of Accounting and Economics, 24*(1), 99–126.

Burgstahler, D., Hail, L., & Leuz, C. (2006). The importance of reporting incentives: earnings management in European private and public firms. *The Accounting Review, 81*(5), 983–1016.

Bushman, R., & Piotroski, J. (2006). Financial reporting incentives for conservative accounting: The influence of legal and political institutions. *Journal of Accounting and Economics, 42*(1–2), 107–148.

Cabán-Garcia, M. (2009). The impact of securities regulation on the earnings properties of European cross-listed firms. *The International Journal of Accounting, 44*(3), 279–304.

Chaney, P., & Lewis, C. (1998). Income smoothing and underperformance in initial public offerings. *Journal of Corporate Finance, 4*(1), 1–29.

Cheng, C., Liu, Z., & Thomas, W. (2012). Abnormal accrual estimates and evidence of mispricing. *Journal of Business Finance and Accounting, 39*(1–2), 1–34.

Christensen, J., & Demski, J. (2003). *Accounting theory: An information content perspective*. NY: McGraw Hill.

Claessens, S., & Schmukler, S. (2007). International financial integration through equity markets: Which firms from which countries go global? *Journal of International Money and Finance, 26*(5), 788–813.

Coffee, J. (2002). Racing towards the top? The impact of cross-listings and stock market competition on international corporate governance. *Columbia Law Review, 102*(7), 1757–1831.

Cohen, D., Dey, A., & Lys, T. (2008). Real and accrual-based earnings management in the pre- and post-Sarbanes Oxley periods. *The Accounting Review, 83*(3), 757–788.

Covrig, V., Defond, M., & Hung, M. (2007). Home bias, foreign mutual fund holdings, and the voluntary adoption of international accounting standards. *Journal of Accounting Research, 45*(1), 41–70.

Dargenidou, C., McLeay, S., & Raonic, I. (2011). Accruals, disclosure and the pricing of future earnings in the European market. *Journal of Business Finance and Accounting, 38*(5–6), 473–504.

Daske, H., Hail, L., Leuz, C. & Verdi, R. (2013). Adopting a label: Heterogeneity in the economic consequences around IAS/IFRS adoptions. *Journal of Accounting Research, 51*(3), 495–547.

Dechow, P., Sloan, R., & Sweeny, A. (1995). Detecting earnings management. *The Accounting Review, 70*(2), 193–225.

Dechow, P., Ge, W., & Schrand, C. (2010). Understanding earnings quality: A review of the proxies, their determinants and their consequences. *Journal of Accounting and Economics, 50*(2–3), 344–401.

DeFond, M., & Park, C. (1997). Smoothing income in anticipation of future earnings. *Journal of Accounting and Economics, 23*(2), 115–139.

Dichev, I., Graham, J., Harvey, C. & Rajgopal, S. (2013). Earnings quality: Evidence from the field. *Journal of Accoundting and Economic, forthcoming*

Doidge, C., Karolyi, G., & Stulz, R. (2004). Why are foreign firms listed in the US worth more? *Journal of Financial Economics, 71*(2), 205–238.

Enriques, L. (2006). EC company law directives and regulations: How trivial are they? *University of Pennsylvania Journal of International Economic Law, 27*(1), 1–78.

Ettredge, M., Scholz, S., Smith, K., & Sun, L. (2010). How do restatements begin? Evidence of earnings management preceding restated financial reports. *Journal of Business Finance and Accounting, 37*(3–4), 332–355.

Florou, A., & Pope, P. (2012). Mandatory IFRS adoption and institution investment decisions. *The Accounting Review, 87*(6), 1993–2025.

Francis, J., & Wang, D. (2008). The joint effect of investor protection and Big 4 audits on earnings quality around the world. *Contemporary Accounting Research, 25*(1), 157–191.

Frésard, L., & Salva, C. (2010). The value of excess cash and corporate governance: Evidence from US cross-listings. *Journal of Financial Economics, 98*(2), 359–384.

Hail, L., & Leuz, C. (2009). Cost of capital effects and changes in growth expectations around US cross-listings. *Journal of Financial Economics, 93*(3), 428–454.

Huijgen, C., & Lubberink, M. (2005). Earnings conservatism, litigation and contracting: The case of cross-listed firms. *Journal of Business Finance and Accounting, 32*(7–8), 1275–1309.

Jaafar, A., & McLeay, S. (2007). Country effects and sector effects on the harmonization of accounting policy choice. *Abacus, 43*(2), 156–189.

Karamanou, I., & Nishiotis, G. (2009). Disclosure and the cost of capital: Evidence from the market's reaction to firm voluntary adoption of IAS. *Journal of Business Finance and Accounting, 36*(7–8), 793–821.

Kothari, S., Leone, A., & Wasley, C. (2005). Performance matched discretionary accrual measures. *Journal of Accounting and Economics, 39*(1), 163–197.

La Porta, R., Lopez-De-Silanes, F., & Shleifer, A. (2006). What works in securities laws? *Journal of Finance, 61*(1), 1–32.

LaFond, R. (2005). Is the accrual anomaly a global anomaly? Working paper, MIT Sloan School of Management.

Lang, M., Smith Raedy, J., & Yetman, M. (2003a). How representative are firms that are cross-listed in the United States? An analysis of accounting quality. *Journal of Accounting Research, 41*(2), 363–386.

Lang, M., Lins, K., & Miller, D. (2003b). ADRs, analysts, and accuracy: does cross listing in the US improve a firm's information environment and increase market value? *Journal of Accounting Research, 41*(2), 317–345.
Lang, M., Raedy, J., & Wilson, W. (2006). Earnings management and cross listing: Are reconciled earnings comparable to US earnings? *Journal of Accounting and Economics, 42*(1–2), 255–283.
Leuz, C., Nanda, D., & Wysocki, P. (2003). Earnings management and institutional factors: An international comparison. *Journal of Financial Economics, 69*(3), 505–527.
Leuz, C. (2006). Cross listing, bonding and firm's reporting incentives: A discussion of Lang, Raedy and Wilson (2006). *Journal of Accounting and Economics, 42*(3), 285–299.
Leuz, C., Lins, K., & Warnock, F. (2010). Do foreigners invest less in poorly governed firms? *The Review of Financial Studies, 23*(3), 3245–3285.
Licht, A., Poliquin, C., Siegel, J. & Li, X. (2013). What makes the bonding stick? A natural experiment involving the US supreme court and cross-listed firms. Working paper, Harvard Business School.
Malloy, C. (2005). The geography of equity analysis. *The Journal of Finance, 60*(2), 719–755.
Nielsson, U. (2007). Interdependence of Nordic and Baltic stock markets. *Baltic Journal of Economics, 6*(2), 9–28.
Peasnell, K., Pope, P., & Young, S. (2005). Board monitoring and earnings management: Do outside directors influence abnormal accruals? *Journal of Business Finance and Accounting, 32*(7–8), 1311–1346.
Pagano, M., Röell, A., & Zechner, J. (2002). the geography of equity listing: Why do companies list abroad? *The Journal of Finance, 57*(6), 2651–2694.
Pownall, G., Vulcheva, M. & Wang, X. (2012). Increasing liquidity on global stock exchanges: The structure of Euronext. Working paper, available at http://ssrn.com/abstract=1800384
Raonic, I., McLeay, S., & Asimakopoulos, I. (2004). The timeliness of income recognition by European companies: An analysis of institutional and market complexity. *Journal of Business Finance and Accounting, 31*(1–2), 115–148.
Roosenboom, P., & Van Dijk, M. (2009). The market reaction to cross-listings: does the destination market matter? *Journal of Banking and Finance, 33*(10), 1898–1908.
Roychowdhury, S. (2006). Earnings management through real activities manipulation. *Journal of Accounting and Economics, 42*(3), 335–370.
Siegel, J. (2005). Can foreign firms bond themselves effectively by renting US securities laws? *Journal of Financial Economics, 75*(2), 319–359.
Sarkissian, S., & Schill, M. (2004). The overseas listing decision: New evidence of proximity preference. *Review of Financial Studies, 17*(3), 769–809.
Sarkissian, S., & Schill, M. (2009). Are there permanent valuation gains to overseas listing? *Review of Financial Studies, 22*(1), 371–412.
Soderstrom, N., & Sun, K. (2007). IFRS adoption and accounting quality: A review. *European Accounting Review, 16*(4), 675–702.
Stolowy, H., & Jeny-Cazavan, A. (2001). International accounting disharmony: The case of intangibles. *Accounting, Auditing and Accountability Journal, 14*(4), 477–497.
Wang, Q. & Pirinsky, C. (2010). Geographic location and corporate finance: a review. Handbook of emerging issues in corporate governance. Available at http://ssrn.com/abstract=1619541
Watts, R., & Zimmerman, J. (1986). *Positive accounting theory*. London: Prentice-Hall.
Wysocki, P. (2004). Discussion of 'ultimate ownership, income management, and legal and extra-legal institutions'. *Journal of Accounting Research, 42*(2), 463–474.
Yu, F. (2008). Analyst coverage and earnings management. *Journal of Financial Economics, 88*(2), 245–271.

Chapter 10
Fair Value and the IASB/FASB Conceptual Framework Project: An Alternative View

Geoffrey Whittington

Abstract This chapter analyses issues arising from the project of the IASB and FASB to develop a joint conceptual framework for financial reporting standards. It discusses, in particular, the possible use of fair value as the preferred measurement basis. Two competing world views are identified: a Fair Value View, implicit in the IASB's public pronouncements, and an Alternative View implicit in publicly expressed criticisms of the IASB's pronouncements. The Fair Value View assumes that markets are perfect and complete and that financial reports should meet the needs of investors and creditors by reporting fair values derived from current market prices. The Alternative View assumes that markets are imperfect and incomplete and that, in such a market setting, financial reports should also meet the monitoring requirements of current shareholders by reporting transactions and events using measurements that reflect the opportunities available to the reporting entity. The different implications of the two views are illustrated by reference to specific issues in recent accounting standards.

This chapter includes a reprinted article first published under the title "Fair Value and the IASB/FASB conceptual Framework Project: An Alternative View" in Abacus in 2008, which is followed by the author's comments by way of a postscript on further developments on the IASB conceptual framework project. It is based on the original paper presented at the Fourth International Workshop on Accounting and Regulation in 2007. The author is grateful for comments on an earlier draft by Richard Barker, Michael Bradbury, Graeme Dean, Andrew Lennard, Stuart McLeay, Geoff Meeks, Steve Zeff and participants in the Fourth International Workshop on Accounting and Regulation, Siena, September 2007, and the ASB Academic Forum, but is solely responsible for any remaining errors or omissions.

G. Whittington (✉)
Centre for Financial Analysis and Policy, University of Cambridge, Cambridge, UK
e-mail: gw12@cam.ac.uk

R. Di Pietra et al. (eds.), *Accounting and Regulation*,
DOI: 10.1007/978-1-4614-8097-6_10,

10.1 Introduction

The project by the IASB and FASB to develop a joint conceptual framework, derived from their existing frameworks, is likely to influence the development of accounting standards for many years to come. It is therefore not surprising that the first discussion papers resulting from the project have attracted much fiercer criticism than the standard setters seem to have anticipated, or that much of this criticism has come from within the European Union, which is committed to adopting the International Financial Reporting Standards (IFRS) of the IASB.

The issue that seems likely to attract most controversy is that of measurement, which has not yet reached discussion paper stage within the conceptual framework project.

In particular, the IASB's perceived preference for fair value as a measurement objective is likely, if expressed in the conceptual framework discussions, to be strongly contested. This issue has already been raised by an earlier discussion paper issued (but not endorsed) by the IASB, and authored by staff of the Canadian Accounting Standards Board (2005), which praised the positive properties of fair value.[1]

Controversy has been stirred further by the IASB's publication, as a discussion paper (November 2006), of the FASB's SFAS 157 (2006), which attempts to prescribe the interpretation of fair value within FASB standards as being a current market sale price, ignoring transaction costs, and free of entity specific assumptions. Many critics feel that the adoption of this within IASB standards would change present practice significantly and adversely, because IFRS apply fair value more widely to nonfinancial assets than do FASB standards. Sale prices are seen as less relevant and less reliable in the case of nonfinancial rather than financial assets.

Although fair value is a focus for much of the recent criticism of the IASB's standards and is also likely to be so for its conceptual framework project, the reasons for the criticism lie in other elements of the framework. Critics of fair value are, in fact, offering an alternative world view of financial reporting, although this view is usually not well articulated. Nor, for that matter, is the fair value world view well articulated: the argument is usually conducted on the basis of accepting a few simple assumptions that make fair value seems to be an obvious choice, whereas the assumptions themselves should be under discussion.

The objective of this chapter is to make some progress toward identifying these alternative world views, and therefore to clarify the nature of the dispute about the conceptual framework in general and fair value in particular.

The perspective is that of the IASB, of which the author was a member from 2001 to 2006, rather than the FASB, which is its partner in the project. The

[1] The paper discusses specifically measurement on initial recognition, but the discussion has wider application.

author's own experiences in writing a number of alternative views to IASB drafts and standards inform the discussion.[2]

These were written piecemeal, but gradually a more coherent pattern began to be apparent, which expressed a different set of assumptions, or world view, described here as the Alternative View. This is in contrast with the view that is implicit in many of the IASB's pronouncements, described here as the Fair Value View. This account is likely to be subjective and incomplete, and there are likely to be many other world views.

However, when there is such a fierce debate between supporters and opponents of a view, it must surely help understanding to identify the main sources of disagreement. It must also be acknowledged that some of the contentious issues arise within the existing conceptual frameworks, but, as the frameworks are being revised, it is appropriate to question them.

The chapter proceeds as follows. First, a description is given of the current project to develop a joint conceptual framework for the IASB and FASB, including its motivation and objectives. Next, there is a discussion of the controversial aspects of the first two draft chapters of the new framework, on the purpose of financial reporting and the desirable properties of accounting information, which have already been issued in discussion paper form. This is followed by a discussion of the issues raised by the subsequent chapters of the new framework that are currently in various stages of development, including definition of the elements of accounts, recognition, and measurement.

An attempt is then made to identify the two competing world views represented by opposing sides of the arguments on specific issues. We then consider how these competing views have been reflected in past IASB pronouncements, and in alternative views expressed on them. We conclude by considering the theoretical support for the Alternative View.

10.2 The IASB/FASB Conceptual Framework Project

Both the FASB and the IASB already have conceptual frameworks. The FASB's was the first, dating mainly from the 1970s, and consists of seven substantial concepts statements, each published separately.[3]

---

[2] An Alternative View is a note explaining the view of a Board member who did not vote in favour of issuing a particular exposure draft or standard (in the latter case, it is described as a 'dissenting view'). The alternative view developed in this chapter is consistent with a number of such views but also draws on the views of external critics of the IASB: it, therefore, has no claim to be an expression of the views of particular members of the IASB, and it is a 'world view' rather than a comment on a particular draft or standard.

[3] A valuable 'insider' account of the development of the FASB Conceptual Framework is given by Storey and Storey (1998). An authoritative account of the development of the IASC Framework is in Camfferman and Zeff (2007, Chap. 9).

The IASB's *Framework for the Preparation and Presentation of Financial Statements* (1989) is a much briefer single document of 110 paragraphs, dating from 1989. Its content shows a strong affinity with the FASB's earlier work, although there are important differences of detail.

One important similarity is that, like the FASB framework, it lacks a treatment of measurement and is therefore incomplete. This is a legacy of the fierce and unresolved debates that took place particularly in the 1970s, when standard setters struggled unsuccessfully to achieve a solution to the inflation accounting problem that would be accepted by both users and preparers of accounts.

Another legacy of the pressures and controversies of that period is that both frameworks emphasize decision usefulness, particularly to investors in capital markets, as the primary focus of general purpose financial statements. This was a bold step at the time, sweeping away the traditionalist view that accounting is primarily for legal and stewardship purposes, with decision usefulness as a useful possible additional benefit. It is argued later that this change of focus may be carried too far by the current revision of the frameworks.

A primary motivation for the joint project is to *converge* the frameworks of the two boards in order to provide a consistent intellectual foundation for the convergence of the two sets of standards, to which both boards committed themselves in the Norwalk Agreement of 2002. Convergence is not, however, the only motivation: *improvement* is equally important.[4]

There are two aspects to improvement: filling gaps to achieve *completeness*, and removing internal contradictions to improve *consistency*. The most obvious gap that needs to be filled is to develop guidance on measurement. There are many aspects of the coherence of the IASB's framework that needs improvement.

An area that has given particular difficulty recently is the definition of a liability and especially the distinction between a liability and equity.

The joint project started in 2005. Its planned sequence of topics and current achievements is listed in Table 10.1.

The working papers for the project are developed by a joint IASB/FASB staff team, there being a different staff team for each stage. FASB's greater staff resources mean that they are usually in the majority, although staffs from the Canadian standard-setting body are currently developing the proposals on elements and recognition.

Each paper is discussed by both boards, usually separately but sometimes in joint meetings. Thus, the project is truly a joint one, although the greater bulk of the FASB's existing framework and its strong staff input mean that the starting point tends to be the FASB's existing document rather than the IASB's. In most aspects, there is little difference between the current IASB and FASB frameworks, so that the FASB's distinct influence is seen mainly in the bulk and style of exposition and argument (which may be politely described as 'thorough') in the two draft chapters and working papers that have appeared to date.

---

[4] Bullen and Crook (2005) provide a staff overview of the objectives.

Table 10.1 Conceptual framework revision timetable, 30 September 2007

Phase	Already published	Publication planned in		
		2007	2008	Undecided
A: Objectives and qualitative characteristics	DP	ED		
B: Elements and recognition			DP	
C: Measurement				DP
D: Reporting entity		DP		
E: Presentation and disclosure				DP
F: Purpose and status				DP
G: Application to not-for-profit entities				DP
H: Remaining issues				TBD

DP Discussion Paper, *ED* Exposure Draft, *TBD* Yet to be determined
Source Abstracted from the IASB Work Plan—Projected Timetable, published on the IASB web site: iasb.org.uk. The full IASB Work Plan is available at http://www.iasb.org/Current+Projects/IASB+Projects/IASB+Work+Plan.htm (accessed, 20 February 2008)

The present chapter is, however, written from the IASB perspective, and this means that some matters which look like changes from that perspective are the result of converging with the FASB's existing position.

10.3 Objectives and Qualitative Characteristics

The first stage of the revision project (Phase A in Table 10.1) was initially considered to be so uncontroversial that it was intended that the first publication would be an exposure draft, which would be the only public consultation.

However, wiser counsel prevailed and it was decided that the first stage would be (as with all subsequent stages of the revision) a discussion paper, which would be followed later by an exposure draft.

This Preliminary Views paper, entitled *The Objective of Financial Reporting and Qualitative Characteristics of Decision-useful Financial Reporting Information*, was published in July 2006, with the comment period ending on 3 November.

The comments received have demonstrated that the proposals are controversial and have justified the decision to issue a discussion paper, allowing further consultation on the subsequent exposure draft. They were originally conceived as being uncontroversial because they substantially reiterate much of the material that is in the existing frameworks. However, they do contain some significant reconstruction of the form and argument, certainly relative to the IASB's currently slender document, and these contain the seeds of controversy.[5]

[5] The first two chapters of the Discussion Paper (including the Basis for Conclusions), covering objectives and qualitative characteristics, are more than twice as long as the entire existing IASB Framework.

Moreover, the retention of some of the concepts in the existing framework is also controversial, particularly in those countries that are recent adopters of IFRS and that were not involved in the original development of the framework.

10.3.1 The Objective of Financial Reporting

Chapter 1 of the discussion paper, on the objective of financial reporting, is fundamental to the remainder of the Framework. It reiterates the existing concern to produce *general purpose financial statements*, that is, ones that meet the needs of all external users who do not have privileged access to the entity's internal information. It also continues the present policy of selecting *investors and creditors* as the focus group for establishing needs.

This includes potential as well as present investors and lenders as well as equity investors. The needs of investors are assumed to be to make *resource allocation decisions*, which will be served by providing 'information to help present and potential investors and creditors and others to assess the amounts, timing, and uncertainty of the entity's future cash inflows and outflows' (para. OB3).

This is consistent with the previous Framework, but to newcomers to IFRS it may seem to understate the special role of present shareholders as the existing proprietors of the entity.

There is certainly a wide range of users of 'general purpose' financial statements, and they have many needs in common, but some might feel that additionally fulfilling the legitimate needs of present shareholders in their special role as proprietors is a *necessary* requirement, whereas other users have a less compelling claim.

This view is expressly rejected, in the Basis for Conclusions (BC1.8–1.13), on the ground that a broad *entity perspective* is more inclusive than a narrow *proprietary perspective*.

This stylization of the proprietary perspective as being narrow and exclusive is contentious: as the discussion paper admits, all investors have substantial common interests, so the proprietary approach does not inevitably entail excluding assets and transactions of a group that may be seen as belonging to outsiders, for example, in the manner of proportional consolidation, but rather might entail more detailed information to existing shareholders on how their share of the total had changed.

The problem of accommodating the specific needs of present shareholders was brought into sharp focus by the issue of *stewardship*, which attracted an Alternative View from two IASB members (AV1.1–1.7) and a substantial volume of adverse comment subsequently, from the respondents to the public consultation.

The discussion paper (OB27–28) acknowledged management's stewardship obligation to present owners but claimed that its reporting requirements could be subsumed within the general objective of decision usefulness, served by providing information relevant to future cash flows (OB3, quoted above). Thus, it was not deemed necessary to specify stewardship as a distinct objective of financial reports.

The reasoning behind this decision is elaborated in BC1.32–1.41. This does not mark a significant change from the current IASB Framework, which places the assessment of stewardship second in a list of uses of financial reports [(b) in the Preface], but asserts that all of the uses are 'economic decisions' which will be aided by similar information.

However, the extensive examination of the issue in the discussion paper drew attention to it, and this sidelining of the stewardship objective was clearly unacceptable to many from countries that were recent adopters of IFRS and inherited a loftier view of stewardship's role.

The Statement of Principles of the UK ASB, for example, although adopting a broad 'decision usefulness for investors' objective, explicitly states that the objective includes 'assessing the stewardship of management' (1.6). It is notable that both of the authors of the Alternative View were former members of the ASB.

The objection to the subsuming of stewardship into the decision usefulness objective is, as expressed in the Alternative View put forward by IASB members, that accountability entails more than the prediction of future cash flows. Its stewardship dimension is concerned with monitoring the past as well as predicting the future and is sometimes as much concerned with the integrity of management as with its economic performance (e.g., with respect to management remuneration and related party transactions).

It is therefore concerned more with the past than is decision usefulness, although the needs of the two typically overlap: information about the past conduct of management may be relevant to predicting future cash flows and the proper assessment of stewardship will entail estimating future prospects in order to evaluate the consequences of management's past policies.

The difference between the two objectives is therefore typically one of emphasis rather than mutual exclusiveness, but both objectives need to be recognized if a proper balance is to be attained.[6]

One issue that was not thoroughly aired in their Alternative View is that of agency theory. The relationship between management and existing shareholders is a classic example of a principal/agent problem. Management, the agent, has scope for free action, and the shareholder needs to monitor that freedom, using the information in the financial reports. This is why, in many jurisdictions, the financial accounts are presented by management to the annual general meeting of shareholders, and it is the context in which the term 'stewardship' has developed.

[6] Some examples of this balancing process in standards are given later under the heading Reliability and Prudence.

The object of this process is to enhance the performance of management from the shareholders' perspective, so financial reporting is involved in *determining* future cash flows, not merely *predicting* them.[7]

The popular term for the process of monitoring management, of which the stewardship process is a part, is *corporate governance* and it may, to some, seem extraordinary that the discussion paper, after acknowledging the agency relationship (BC1.40), attempts (not entirely convincingly) to reject the relevance of financial reporting to corporate governance (BC1.41).

A possible explanation for this lies in the interesting work of Bush (2005), who analyses the different origins and forms of the UK and US regulatory systems for financial reporting and concludes that the former is based on company law, whereas the latter is based on market regulation (the Securities Acts).

The latter basis leads to an emphasis on markets and market prices, and therefore to information relevant to future cash flows, whereas the former leads to greater emphasis on corporate governance and stewardship. The FASB's conceptual framework reflects US institutional arrangements, and therefore favors the market basis. It is therefore not surprising that the EU member states which typically have a strong legal tradition of accounting regulation have favored the company law approach with its emphasis on corporate governance mechanisms, including stewardship.

10.3.2 Qualitative Characteristics of Decision-Useful Financial Information

The title of chapter 2 of the discussion paper, on the qualitative characteristics of decision-useful financial information, indicates the importance of the assumptions made in chapter 1, and particularly the subsuming of stewardship under the general objective of decision usefulness.

This chapter, like chapter 1, claims to retain substantially the principles adopted in the predecessor frameworks. However, it does make substantial changes in both form and language, and these are likely to affect the interpretation of the underlying principles.

The main change in form is the sequential approach to applying the qualitative characteristics, replacing the previous simultaneous approach in which explicit trade-offs were made. The main change of language is the replacement of *reliability* by *faithful representation.*

These changes combine to eliminate the possibility of a *trade-off* between *relevance* and *reliability*, which man regarded as an important aspect of the present

[7] This point is elaborated in the ASB's response to the Discussion Paper, which is available on the ASB's website (http://www.frc.org.uk/asb/press/pub1343.html, accessed, 8 March 2008).

Framework. This trade-off is frequently invoked as a reason for not using fair value measurements, which are perceived as often being relevant but unreliable.[8]

The sequential approach to applying the characteristics is described in paragraphs QC42–7 and discussed in BC2.59–2.65. It is explained that relevance should be considered first because it is essential, and that faithful representation should be considered next, but that both characteristics are necessary for decision usefulness, so that 'they work in concert with one another' (QC45).

What is absent from this explanation is an acknowledgment that neither relevance nor representational faithfulness is an *absolute* property of accounting information; rather, there are different *levels* of relevance and faithful representation, which opens the possibility of a *trade-off* between them. If this is ignored, as it appears to be, the proposed sequence will involve selecting an accounting method first on the basis of highest relevance and then subjecting this selection to a filter based on some absolute minimum level of representational faithfulness.

Above this threshold there will be no question of saying that greater representational faithfulness might compensate for less relevance, even if the latter loss is very small.

The substitution of *faithful representation* for *reliability* has already weakened the possibility of such a trade-off. The IASB's existing definition of reliability is:

> Information has the quality of reliability when it is free from material error and bias and can be depended on by users to represent faithfully that which it either purports to represent or could reasonably be expected to represent (IASB Framework, para 31).

The proposed definition of faithful representation in QC16 is:

> To be useful in making investment, credit and similar resource allocation decisions, information must be a *faithful representation* of the real-world economic phenomena that it purports to represent. The phenomena represented in financial reports are economic resources and obligations and the transactions and other events and circumstances that change them. To be a faithful representation of those economic phenomena, information must be *verifiable*, *neutral*, and *complete* (QC16).

There are significant differences between the two definitions, despite the discussion paper's argument that the new definition is consistent with the intentions of the existing Framework. Not only is faithful representation elevated to be the over-riding concept, but now it refers specifically to 'the real-world economic phenomena' rather than simply 'that [which] it purports to represent'. Moreover, the discussion paper goes on to assert that: 'Information cannot be a faithful representation of an economic phenomenon unless it depicts the economic substance of the underlying transaction or other event' (QC17).

Thus, the essence of the new qualitative characteristic is that it requires judgments about economic substance and real-world economic phenomena, rather than merely the accuracy with which information represents 'that [which] it purports to

[8] Walton (2006), a close observer of IASB meetings, notes the possible implications of this change for the future extension of fair value measurement.

represent'. Thus, if fair value were deemed to better capture 'economic substance', historical cost might be deemed to be an inappropriate measure, despite the latter possibly being a more accurate representation of what it purports to represent (historical cost).

In QC18, the discussion paper attempts, rather clumsily, to explain what it means by a 'real-world economic phenomenon'. It asserts that 'deferred charges and deferred credits do not exist in the real world outside financial reporting'. This is, of course, highly controversial: does, for example, purchased goodwill exist outside financial reporting?

It goes on to use the easy example of a machine as something that is a real-world economic phenomenon and asserts that original cost is also such an economic phenomenon, but would not be a faithful representation of a 3-year-old machine.

In this case, depreciated cost would 'better represent the machine as it now exists' and current replacement cost would be 'even better'. Fair value is offered as another alternative but not evaluated.

This example illustrates why those who are opposed to the IASB's alleged intention to extend the use of fair value see the proposals of the discussion paper as leaning in that direction.

The other important change that is proposed can also be regarded as tilting the criteria in favor of fair value. This is the removal of the phrase 'free from material error and bias', which is in the definition of reliability in the current Framework but absent from the new definition of faithful representation. Many critics of fair value believe that it often involves more estimation and subjectivity (leading to error and bias) than some alternative measures, and the proposed changes reduce the force, within the framework criteria, of this objection.

These measurement error issues are not entirely ignored in the discussion paper. It is argued (QC20–2) that absolute certainty and precision are unattainable in financial reporting, but it is not clearly acknowledged that, nevertheless, greater certainty and precision are preferable to less. What is left of 'free from material error' is subsumed in *verifiability*, a component of faithful representation, and 'free from bias' is included in *another* component, *neutrality*.

> *Verifiability* implies that different knowledgeable and independent observers would reach general consensus, although not necessarily complete agreement, either:
>
> (a) that the information represents the economic phenomena that it purports to represent without material error or bias (by direct verification); or
> (b) that the chosen recognition or measurement method has been applied without material error or bias (by indirect verification) (QC23).

This concept covers part of what is sometimes termed *objectivity*, requiring that independent observers would reach the same (or a very similar) conclusion. However, it does not require accuracy of the estimate in terms of its correspondence with 'that which it... purports to represent' which is required by a stricter view of objectivity and is a critical element in the idea of reliability.[9]

A brief Alternative View to the discussion paper (AV2.1–2.2) pointed out that this is unsatisfactory because there is no requirement that the consensus is based on reliable evidence. Furthermore, in the case of (b), indirect verification, there is no requirement that the method used should be one that would yield an estimate that is free from material error or bias.

Neutrality is another component of faithful representation and is defined as the absence of bias intended to attain a predetermined result or to induce a particular behaviour. Neutrality is an essential aspect of faithful representation because biased financial reporting information cannot faithfully represent economic phenomena (QC27).

This definition is curiously restricted because it requires *intent* to influence consequences. Other forms of bias in measures or estimates, such as that resulting from the natural optimism of managers when they make acquisitions, would presumably be allowed. This reflects the discussion paper's rejection of the concepts of reliability used in econometrics and statistics (BC2.25).

10.3.3 Neutrality and Prudence

The present IASB Framework refers favorably to *prudence* but the discussion paper explicitly rejects the use of the term because of its inconsistency 'with the desirable quality of neutrality, which encompasses freedom from bias' (BC2.22).

The present Framework (37) attempts to reconcile prudence with neutrality by saying that it is 'the inclusion of caution in the exercise of the judgements needed in making the estimates required under conditions of uncertainty, such that assets or income are not overstated and liabilities or expenses are not understated'. It explicitly disallows deliberate under- or over-statement in the cause of prudence.

The UK ASB's Statement of Principles (1999), which adopts a similar approach to the Framework, attempts a reconciliation of prudence with neutrality as follows:

> Prudence is the inclusion of a degree of caution in the exercise of the judgements needed in making estimates required under conditions of uncertainty, such that gains and assets are not overstated and losses and liabilities are not understated. In particular, under such conditions it requires more confirmatory evidence about the existence of, and a greater reliability of measurement for, assets and gains than is required for liabilities and losses (3.19).

By introducing explicitly the role of *confirmatory evidence* to relieve *uncertainty*, the ASB goes some way toward clarifying the relationship between 'two aspects of reliability—neutrality and prudence', but it admits that a 'tension' can exist between the two which requires 'finding a balance that ensures that deliberate

[9] Paton and Littleton (1940, pp. 19–20).

and systematic understatement of gains and assets and overstatement of losses and liabilities do not occur' (3.36).

The discussion paper's position (no prudence) avoids this trade-off, but in doing so it ignores an important aspect of financial reporting, arising from its stewardship role. Much of agency theory is concerned with the problem that the agent has an incentive to exaggerate performance in order to enhance rewards, a problem that is particularly acute when senior executives are rewarded by stock options and stock prices are driven by reported financial performance. There have been a number of recent accounting 'scandals' arising from this scenario. In this context, a 'degree of caution' associated with a requirement for 'more confirmatory evidence' may lead to improved reliability (expressed as confidence by the user in the information) which will adequately compensate for any possible bias.

A specific example of the exercise of prudence which is an important component of the standards of both the IASB and the FASB is the *impairment test* (IAS 36). This *reduces* the carrying amount of an asset to its current recoverable amount, when that is less than the carrying amount. It does not *increase* the carrying amount if the recoverable amount is higher. Hence, it is fundamentally a biased approach to measurement; it is, however, a prudent one.[10]

A similar (biased) measure of liabilities results from the *liability adequacy test* used in the IASB's current standard on Insurance (IFRS 4); this test can result in the carrying value of a liability being increased but not reduced. In the case of both of these tests, strict adherence to neutrality would suggest that the adjustment should be symmetrical, that is, in the case of the impairment test, the asset would always be carried at current recoverable amount (which could, in some cases, be Fair Value).

The consequences of this for accounting for purchased goodwill, which has only recently (IFRS 3, 2004) adopted the impairment test in place of amortization, would be particularly significant and controversial. It was therefore to be expected that there would be many adverse comments on the proposed removal of prudence from the Framework.

The objectors are not simply clinging to past practices; they are concerned with inconsistencies with current practice, some of which has been imposed only recently by the IASB.

10.4 Elements and Recognition

Phase B, Elements and Recognition, has hitherto concentrated on the definition of two basic elements, assets, and liabilities. The other elements defined in the current IASB Framework, equity, income and expenses, have not yet been addressed, and

[10] Bromwich (2004) suggests that impairment tests should not be one-sided.

neither has been the important and potentially contentious issue of recognition, although developments in the IAS 37 (liabilities) revision relate to it.

By starting with the definition of assets and liabilities, the IASB is reaffirming the so-called 'balance sheet' approach that is embedded in its existing Framework and in that of the FASB.

This gives what is sometimes called 'conceptual primacy' (Johnson 2004) to assets and liabilities over flow measures such as income and expense. This approach argues that the accruals resulting from the recognition of flows must meet the definitions of assets and liabilities in order to be recognized in the financial statements, that is, the elements of the income statement, such as income and expense, must give rise to accrued amounts that are consistent with the elements of the balance sheet.

This approach is a means of imposing discipline on the assessment of accruals, avoiding the recognition of what Sprouse (1978) described as 'What-You-May-Call-Its'. This approach does not require the elevation of comprehensive income (total gains measured consistently with changes in the balance sheet) as a central measure of performance, although it might facilitate it.

10.4.1 The Definition of an Asset

The current IASB Framework definition of an asset is:

> A resource controlled by an entity as a result of past events and from which future benefits are expected to flow to the entity [IASB Framework, 49(a)].

The current proposed definition is:

> An asset is a present economic resource to which the entity has a present right or other privileged access.

The new definition deletes two significant phrases in the original: 'as a result of past events' and 'from which future benefits may be expected to flow'. Both of these are likely to affect the recognition criteria, which have not yet been discussed in the conceptual framework revision.

The deletion of 'as a result of past events' was justified on the ground that it was superfluous: anything that exists must have come into existence at some time in the past.

However, the deletion does reduce the emphasis on the importance of past transactions and events, and supporters of the stewardship perspective may regret this. If the recognition criterion were merely to say that anything which *currently* meets the new definition should be recognized as an asset, this would seem to erode the grounding of recognition in past transactions and events, reducing the *reliability* of financial statements. It is less obvious that it would reduce *representational faithfulness*, with its emphasis on the representation of 'real-world economic phenomena'.

Future prospects that have no origin in past transactions might be regarded as real-world economic phenomena, thus allowing the recognition, at fair value, of elements of internally generated goodwill that have not hitherto been regarded as suitable for recognition in financial reports.

The deletion of the reference to *expected* future benefits suggests that there will be a future proposal to remove one of the current recognition criteria from the Framework:

> An item that meets the definition of an element should be recognized if:
>
> (a) it is probable that any future economic benefit associated with the item will flow to or from the entity; and
> (b) the item has a cost or value that can be measured with reliability (IASB Framework, 83).

Clearly, 83(a) will have little relevance if expected future benefits no longer form part of the definition of an asset. The IASB's reason for the deletion is that the phrase has given rise to some confusion, and it must be admitted that this arises, in part, from the explanation of it in the current Framework (85), which confuses *measurement* with *recognition*.

Most elements of financial statements will have uncertain outcomes and, if the *existence* of an asset (or liability) is certain, the fact that its associated cash flows are uncertain can be dealt with by measurement.

For example, it is usual to impair debtors for *expected* losses due to bad debts, and stocks may be impaired for expected wastage. Impairment tests are a common way of reflecting expected future cash flows in the measurement of assets.

The type of uncertainty that is unique to recognition, rather than measurement, is what the UK ASB's Statement of Principles calls *element uncertainty* (ASB 1999, 5.13–5.15).

This is uncertainty as to whether the element exists and meets the definition of an element, and the IASB's criterion of 'probable that any future economic benefit... will flow to the entity' can be interpreted as referring to this type of uncertainty.

An asset is not an asset of the entity, and therefore not recognized in its accounts, if its benefits do not flow to the entity.

Such 'non-assets' of the entity would include assets whose existence cannot be established with an acceptable level of probability, such as internally generated goodwill. This clearly is an existence (recognition) issue rather than a measurement issue, and the proposed amendment to the asset definition appears to ignore it.

The IASB is currently wrestling with that same issue in its revision of IAS 37 (liabilities), where it is attempting to define when a constructive obligation should be recognized as a liability.

Measurement also is part of the recognition process [83(b)], but this is in relation to *reliability* of measurement rather than *uncertainty* of outcome. It is in this context that the IASB Framework (85) is potentially confusing, because the example chosen (credit risk on a receivable) appears to relate to measurement of an uncertain outcome with known parameters (an outcome with known risk, which can be priced and therefore dealt with by measurement) rather than to uncertainty as to what those parameters are (unreliability of measurement itself, which prevents the reliable pricing of the outcome).

In summary, the IASB's (and FASB's) tentative proposals on asset definition involve two changes that potentially erode the recognition criteria in the current Framework. The recognition criteria have not yet been addressed as part of Phase B, and a staff proposal to do so was rejected in July 2007 in favor of continuing work on the definition of an asset.

Critics of fair value may fear that the removal of 'past transactions and events' from the asset definition, the transfer of uncertainty from recognition to measurement (where fair value might be thought to capture it effectively), and the possible modification or even removal of the present reliability of measurement criterion for recognition will open the way for an extension of the application of fair value measurement.

10.4.2 Liabilities

The asset definition has hitherto received most attention in Phase B, for the reason that this will provide the foundation for the other elements in the 'balance sheet' approach.

The other element that has received considerable attention is liabilities, where a parallel definition to that of assets has been proposed. The IASB's current Framework definition is:

> A liability is a present obligation of the entity arising from past events, the settlement of which is expected to result in an outflow from the entity of resources embodying economic benefits [IASB Framework, 49(c)].

The current proposed definition is:

> A liability is a present economic burden for which the entity has a present economic obligation.

Just as the liability definition mirrors that of assets, so do the changes in the definition. As in the case of assets, the reference to past events is deleted, as also is the reference to expectation of future flows. Thus, the same implications arise for assets as for liabilities, particularly with regard to recognition criteria.

As already indicated, the IASB is already confronting recognition criteria in its revision of IAS 37 (1998). It proposes to abolish the concept of *provisions*, classifying all former provisions as liabilities (Proposed Amendments to IAS 37, 2005).

Provisions were liabilities 'of uncertain timing or amount' (IAS 37, para 10) and the IASB's current thinking is that many liabilities are subject to a degree of uncertainty that is reflected in their measurement, so that a sub-category of provisions is unhelpful, despite the fact that it may convey information about the relative predictability of the respective categories.

With regard to the recognition of liabilities, the IASB has focused on the question of whether an obligation exists. It has identified a *stand-ready* obligation, as in a guarantee or insurance contract, as giving rise to a liability, the uncertainty of future outflows being reflected in measurement. It is currently exploring the difficult problem of establishing the circumstances in which a constructive liability should be recognized when there is no contractual obligation.

This is an element uncertainty issue, but the IASB's current preference (*IASB Update*, July 2007) is to draw up a list of indicators rather than confronting directly the probabilistic nature of the decision by defining a probability threshold for recognition, such as 'more likely than not'.

These developments are likely to reinforce the possibility that the IASB, by removing uncertainty criteria from recognition and requiring that uncertainty should, instead, be reflected in measurement, is moving toward a position of requiring that the recognition criterion be the existence of a fair value. Essentially, any expected future cash flow to the entity, however speculative, could be reflected in a fair value that might be said to meet the new element definition and therefore be recognized.

10.4.3 Equity

The definition of *equity* and the difficult problem of defining the distinction between liabilities and equity is another elements issue that will have to be dealt with in Phase B, but which has not yet been addressed directly, although the FASB does have a project on the liability/equity distinction, which is being 'shadowed' by the IASB. This difficulty arises partly because equity is a residual category in the current Framework:

> Equity is the residual interest in the assets of the entity after deducting all liabilities [IASB Framework, 49(c)].

This leads to a wide variety of financial instruments, such as options on equity, being classified as equity, thus confusing the simple picture that would be given if there were only one category of equity instruments, issued shares in the holding company.

It also has led to considerable ambiguity at the margin with liabilities: essentially anything that is not a present obligation to part with economic resources is equity. This has led the IASB to breach the Framework in one instance (a promise to settle in shares to the value of a fixed monetary amount is classified as a liability) and it has issued an exposure draft that proposes to create another breach (*Financial Instruments Puttable at Fair Value*, October 2006) by treating as equity some instruments that have a right to cash settlement and seem, therefore, to meet the current definition of a liability.

One of the possible solutions recently explored in this project is the *claims* approach, which regards all credits in the balance sheet as 'claims', making no debt/equity distinction. This solves the problem by abolishing it, and is unlikely to be adopted.

However, little enthusiasm has been expressed for moving in the alternative direction of having *two-tier equity*, the lowest tier being the claims of existing shareholders, and the other tier including other equity instruments such as warrants, options on equity, and (in group accounts) minority interests.

Such an approach would accommodate the needs of those who regard present shareholders as having a special role as the proprietors to whom the directors owe a special duty of accountability and who are the ultimate controllers of the entity. The 'entity' perspective currently favored by both FASB and IASB makes no concessions to this group and can lead to accounting that makes it quite difficult for them to establish the gain or loss on their interest in a period.

10.4.4 Other Elements of Financial Statements

Other elements have not yet been discussed in Phase B, and it is not yet clear whether all of the elements in the current Framework will be retained. The two elements defined in the existing framework that have not yet been mentioned in Phase B are *Income* (which includes both *revenue* and *gains*) and *Expenses* (which includes *losses*).

In view of the 'balance sheet' approach, it seems likely that these will not be discussed as elements but will instead be discussed as part of the performance statement in Phase E of the Framework revision, Presentation, and Disclosure.

The IASB and FASB already have a joint project on performance reporting, which originally arose from the problem of income statement presentation. This has attracted a large amount of critical comment. Opponents of the IASB's preferred single comprehensive income statement, many of whom are preparers of accounts, are afraid that comprehensive income, possibly based substantially on fair value measurement, will become the central figure for performance evaluation.[11]

They regard fair values and comprehensive income as volatile measures that mask operating profit, which they would regard as a better indicator of the entity's underlying potential for generating future cash flows.

The IASB is still exploring the obvious solution, which is to allow sub-totals such as operating profit (roughly, revenue less expenses, in the current Framework's terms). The difficulty is to define such sub-totals in a way which is based on

[11] For a further discussion of comprehensive income in this journal, see Cauwenberge and De Beedle (2007, pp. 1–26).

sound principles, practical in application, and acceptable to users and preparers of financial statements.

10.5 The Reporting Entity

Phase D of the conceptual framework deals with the reporting entity and has made more progress than the measurement phase (C), possibly, because it is less controversial. A discussion paper on reporting entity issues is expected to be published in 2008. This is not to say that the subject is not important or that it is without controversy (Walker 2007).

One source of criticism is likely to stem from the rather rigid view currently favored by the IASB that only one set of general purpose financial statements is appropriate for a group entity.

The rejection of the importance of separate holding company accounts is a symptom of the rejection of a proprietary perspective in favor of an entity perspective, leading to the view that the interests of those financing the holding company, and particularly the equity shareholders, should not be given special consideration in financial reporting.

The group accounts would be important under either perspective, but a proprietary view would regard the holding company accounts as adding useful information from the perspective of the holding company, for example, showing the extent of its direct control of assets and legal obligation for liabilities.

10.6 Measurement

Work on Phase C, Measurement, has already started, and it is likely to be a lengthy process, because of the importance of the subject and its contentious nature, which caused the predecessor conceptual frameworks to avoid addressing the issue directly, discussing desirable properties of measurements rather than recommending a single preferred measurement objective.

The controversial nature of the subject was partly a result of the inflation accounting debate that raged in the 1960s and 1970s, when the FASB was also developing its conceptual framework which provided a model for successor frameworks such as that of the IASB.

The debate at that time was about whether price changes should be reflected in accounts. In other words, it was about historical cost versus some form of current value. It was then easy to stylize the debate as being between 'old-fashioned' advocates of historical cost, justified by a narrow view of stewardship, and 'modern' advocates of current value who believed in decision-useful information.

However, at the time, it was accepted by many, and acknowledged in the frameworks of the FASB and the IASB, that decision usefulness and stewardship are not necessarily competing objectives and that the needs of stewardship require timely information about performance which would, ideally, be captured by current values.

Since that time, the debate has moved on. Although comprehensive price change accounting did not prove to be successful, recent years have seen an increasing adoption of current values in accounting standards, particularly in accounting for financial instruments (IAS 39), but also in areas such as agriculture (IAS 41 2001).[12]

In these new applications, discussion has been concerned with the question of *which current value* should be used. The failed attempts to introduce price change accounting were based on *current cost* which is supported by *deprival value* reasoning. More recently, standard setters have preferred to use the term *fair value*, meaning a *current market value*:

> Fair value is the amount for which an asset could be exchanged between knowledgeable, willing parties in an arm's length transaction (IAS 16, 6).

This definition is consistent with either an entry value (such as current cost) or an exit value (such as selling price), and it does not define a treatment of transaction costs, so that, for example, it is consistent with net realizable value (selling price less selling costs being the *amount* that the seller would receive). These ambiguities are removed by the recent IASB discussion paper based on SFAS 157 (FASB, 2006):

> Fair value is the price that would be received to sell an asset or paid to transfer a liability in an orderly transaction between market participants at the measurement date (SFAS 157, 5).

Thus, fair value is an *exit* value (the price received to sell an asset) and *transaction costs* are *not* included (hence the substitution of 'price' for 'amount').

Moreover, the reference to a *market* rather than a transaction between parties emphasizes the requirement that the measure be *non entity specific*, that is, it should be based on a hypothetical best market price rather than the price actually paid or that would be actually obtained by the reporting entity.

The discussion paper based on SFAS157 is supposed to be merely a 'how to do it' proposal for existing uses of fair value, rather than extending that use, but the result of its new definition is to draw the lines clearly between different views of the appropriate measurement basis. The difference is not now between historical cost and current value but between *entry* (cost-based) values and *exit* (sale) values, and between those who wish to measure the opportunities available to the *specific entity* and those who prefer to use hypothetical *market prices*.

The discussion paper is not strictly part of Phase C of the Framework revision, although its progress to date is likely to have more impact than that of the Phase C work. The latter has taken the form of drawing up an inventory of valuation bases

[12] Tweedie and Whittington (1984) provide an account of the development of price change accounting standards, and Tweedie and Whittington (1997) describes their rejection (mainly by preparers of accounts) and subsequent withdrawal.

and developing a conceptual approach to measurement that will enable those methods to be evaluated.

The nine candidate valuation bases selected for analysis in Phase C do not include deprival value, once the favorite of standard setters, on the ground that it is a hybrid measure, derived from a comparison of other measures (current entry value, current exit value and value in use). This ignores the fact that deprival value is a coherent valuation *objective*.

Concentrating on the intrinsic properties of specific measures at the expense of considering how objectives might be achieved seems to miss the point of accounting, which is to inform users in an imperfect and uncertain world.[13] It seems possible that this type of analysis will lead to a long and ultimately fruitless debate.

This impression is borne out by the papers on measurement submitted to the IASB's July 2007 meeting. After a careful analysis of measurement theory, a revision of the IASB's definition of measurement is proposed. The current definition is:

> Measurement is the process of determining the monetary amounts at which the elements of financial statements are to be recognized and carried in the balance sheet and income statement (IASB Framework, 99).

The proposed new definition is:

> Financial statement measurement is the numerical ordering or comparison of an asset or liability (or a change in an asset or liability) to other assets or liabilities (or changes in other assets or liabilities) with respect to a preconceived and defined basis in terms of a monetary unit that relates to that same basis, with the result that the asset or liability is properly placed in a monetary ratio scale (*IASB Information for Observers*, Board Paper 2B, July 2007, 69).

This may be rigorously grounded in measurement theory, but it seems unlikely to have as good an intuitive appeal as the present definition, from the perspective of preparers and users of financial statements.

Ultimately, the IASB and FASB will have to stop analyzing the internal consistency of definitions and turn to the *utility* of accounting measures. In evaluating that, it will be necessary to have agreement on the *purpose* of financial statements and the *environment* in which they are used. This is a much wider issue than measurement, or, specifically, whether fair value is judged to be a good measure by certain criteria. It is concerned with what was earlier described as a world view.

---

[13] This is not to say that specific measures cannot be associated with a particular objective. An obvious example is Chambers (1966), who justified the need for exit value measures in terms of an objective of measuring financial adaptability. However, it is notable that Chambers' 'current cash equivalent' measure was not the same as fair value: notably, he came to the view that non-vendible durable assets should be measured at zero value (because there was no cash equivalent available) rather than a hypothetical exit value (Chambers 1970). If there exists a fungible arm's length price for a comparable asset he would use it to report the item. Chambers also advocated valuing bonds at face values rather than current market prices. For a summary see Chambers (1974).

More precisely, this is a model of the purpose of financial accounting and the context in which it operates.

10.7 Competing World Views

In the earlier discussion of the framework review, it is possible to discern two broad schools of thought or world views. They are not well articulated because the argument usually focuses on a particular aspect of the framework rather than the whole system. There is also a variety of individual views within each broad school of thought, so that a degree of stylization is necessary. However, it may clarify the debate if the views of the parties are articulated in a holistic manner, identifying the common ground within each world view and the difference between that and the competing view.

The two competing models identified here are the Fair Value View and the Alternative View.[14] The latter title is justified because many of its ideas are supported by *alternative views* attached to IASB pronouncements.

Another reason for using this rather bland description is that many of the attributes of that view are too easily associated with consequences that do not necessarily follow from them. For example, if it were described as 'a stewardship view' there could be an inappropriate belief that this necessarily implied a preference for historical cost measurement.

10.7.1 The Fair Value View

This is a view that is apparent in many of the proposed revisions of the Framework. Some of its features are also in the existing Framework. This broad view would be supported by a significant number (but not necessarily a majority) of members of the FASB and the IASB, and possibly by a majority of the staff who have worked or are working on the frameworks of the two boards.[15]

Because of its articulation by professional standard setters (albeit with individual differences of view on some aspects) this has been more clearly expressed in a 'joined up' systematic way than has the Alternative View.

[14] A similar (but not identical) identification of two schools of thought is made at the end of Andrew Lennard's very interesting and insightful paper on 'Liabilities and How to Account for Them' (2002).

[15] Staff opinions are not expressed in public, but staff recommendations are expressed to the boards, although only on issues that are referred to them. However, staff do author published papers and their views are sometimes expressed quite forcefully there (e.g., Johnson 2005).

The main features of the Fair Value View are:

- *Usefulness for economic decisions* is the sole objective of financial reporting.
- *Current and prospective investors and creditors* are the reference users for general purpose financial statements.
- *Forecasting future cash flows*, preferably as directly as possible, is the principal need of those users.[16]
- *Relevance* is the primary characteristic required in financial statements.
- *Reliability* is less important and is better replaced by *representational faithfulness*, which implies a greater concern for capturing economic substance, and less with statistical accuracy.
- Accounting information needs ideally to reflect the *future*,[17] not the past, so past transactions and events are only peripherally relevant.
- Market prices should give an informed, *non entity specific* estimate of cash flow potential, and *markets* are generally sufficiently complete and efficient to provide evidence for representationally faithful measurement on this basis.

The implications of the Fair Value View are:

- *Stewardship is not a distinct objective* of financial statements, although its needs may be met incidentally to others.
- *Present shareholders have no special status* among investors as users of financial statements.
- *Past transactions and events* are relevant only insofar as they can assist in predicting future cash flows.
- *Prudence* is a distortion of accounting measurement, violating *faithful representation.*
- *Cost* (entry value) is an inappropriate measurement basis because it relates to a *past* event (acquisition) whereas future cash flow will result from future exit, measured by *fair value.*
- *Fair value*, defined as market selling (exit) price, as in SFAS 157 (FASB 2006), should be the measurement objective.
- *The balance sheet* is the fundamental financial statement, especially if it is fair valued.
- *Comprehensive income* is an essential element of the income statement: it is consistent with changes in net assets reported in the balance sheet.

---

[16] Directly' means that the measure summarizes expected future cash flows, as in a discounted present value.

[17] Barth (2006), an IASB Board member, provides a useful discussion of the orientation of accounting information towards the future, making clear the distinction between recognition (only present rights and obligations should be recognized) and measurement (expected cash flows from those rights and obligations may affect their measurement). She views measurement from a fair value perspective. Bromwich (2004) provides a discussion of future-oriented information from an alternative, deprival value perspective. See also Rosenfield's discussion in this journal of the way to report 'prospects' data within a fair value reporting system (2008, pp. 48–60).

10.7.2 The Alternative View

As indicated above, the Alternative View is more difficult to articulate than the Fair Value View because it is drawn from a diverse range of constituents of the standard-setting process who are typically commenting on particular issues from a practical perspective, rather than attempting to develop a coherent model of financial statement presentation in the manner of the authors of the Framework.

However, this does not mean that an alternative systematic view of the world does not exist and would not attract wide support as an alternative to the Framework, although it does mean that there are probably a number of variations that would be favored by different constituencies.

Below is an attempt to articulate what might be termed an 'enlightened' Alternative View. This would be supported by somebody who did acknowledge the merit of setting accounting standards based on a systematic set of principles and who did recognize the necessity for accounting practice to change in order to meet the needs of users of accounts.

It therefore precludes the totally reactionary views (not uncommon among busy people who are preoccupied with the daily problems of running their business) that nothing in current practice needs to be changed, that financial reporting standards are an unnecessary interference in business, and that thinking conceptually about accounting is an academic, ivory-tower activity of no relevance to the real world.[18]

The main features of the Alternative View are:

- *Stewardship*, defined as accountability to present shareholders, is a distinct objective, ranking equally with decision usefulness.
- *Present shareholders* of the holding company have a special status as users of financial statements.
- *Future cash flows* may be *endogenous*: feedback from shareholders (and markets) in response to accounting reports may influence management decisions.
- Financial reporting relieves *information asymmetry* in an uncertain world, so *reliability* is an essential characteristic.
- *Past transactions and events* are important both for stewardship and as *inputs* to the prediction of future cash flows (as indirect rather than direct measurement).
- The economic environment is one of *imperfect and incomplete markets* in which market opportunities will be *entity-specific*.

---

[18] A feature of standard-setting has been the constructive engagement of the academic and business communities. Standard-setting bodies have always been well stocked with experienced practitioners, but there have also been notable academic inputs. For example, David Solomons was a member of the Wheat Committee that devised the FASB and Robert Sprouse was one of FASB's first members. Robert Sterling and Paul Rosenfield were also early members on the FASB. In the UK, both the Chairman (David Tweedie) and Vice-Chairman (Brian Carsberg) of the ASB, at its inception, started their careers as full-time academics.

The implications of the Alternative View are:

- The information needs of *present shareholders*, including *stewardship* requirements must be met.
- *Past transactions and events* are *relevant* information and, together with *reliability of measurement* and *probability of existence,* are critical requirements for the *recognition* of elements of accounts, in order to achieve *reliability*.
- *Prudence*, as explained in the current IASB Framework and in the ASB's Statement of Principles, can enhance *reliability*.
- *Cost* (historic or current) can be a *relevant* measurement basis, for example as an input to the prediction of future cash flows, as well as for stewardship purposes.
- The financial statements should reflect the financial performance and position of a specific entity, and *entity specific* assumptions should be made when these reflect the real opportunities available to the entity.
- *Performance* statements and *earnings* measures can be more important than balance sheets in some circumstances (but there should be arithmetic consistency—articulation—between flow statements and balance sheets).

10.7.3 A Summary of the Two Perspectives

The Fair Value View emphasizes the role of financial reporting in serving investors in capital markets. It seeks accounting information that has a forward-looking content, impounding future cash flows from a non entity specific market perspective. It is most likely to achieve this when the reference markets are complete and competitive; ideally, perfect markets would be accessible.

The Alternative View also seeks to serve investors, broadly defined, but it gives priority to existing shareholders and regards stewardship as an important and distinct function of financial reporting. It too seeks accounting information that is relevant to forecasting future cash flows, but it assumes that this will often be achieved by providing information that is useful input to investors' valuation models, rather than direct valuation of future cash flows. Such information may be entity specific. This approach assumes that information asymmetry and imperfect and incomplete markets are common.

Possible conflicts between these two competing world views have been apparent in a number of recent IASB pronouncements, and are discussed below.

10.8 Some IASB Proposals Where the Alternative View Supports Criticisms

A number of the IASB's proposals (in discussion papers, exposure drafts and standards) have been subject to strong criticism from constituents and, in some cases, alternative views from within the Board. The following list is by no means complete, but it illustrates instances in which criticisms reflect the Alternative View.

The view expressed by the IASB and its partner, the FASB, usually is consistent with the Fair Value View. This is not surprising because the conceptual frameworks of the two boards, which guide their work, are also consistent with that Views.

10.8.1 The 'Present Shareholder' Focus

IFRS 2, *Share-Based Payment*, adopts the *grant date* approach to measuring stock options. As soon as the grant is made, the option is an equity instrument and subsequent gains or losses in value are treated as transfers within equity rather than gains or losses.

From the perspective of present shareholders, these gains and losses are real and should be reported transparently as such until the exercise date, when they are realized. A significant number of critics of this standard advocated *exercise date* measurement, reflecting a 'present shareholder' perspective.

The IASB Exposure Draft, *Proposed Amendments to IFRS 3* (2005), proposes to amend the existing treatment (under IAS 27) of gains and losses on non-controlling equity investments in subsidiary companies (minority interests). This new treatment is based on the economic entity view, which regards non-controlling (minority) interests as equity of the group.

Gains and losses on trading in minority shares are therefore treated merely as transfers between equity holders and reported in the statement of changes in equity rather than the income statement. However, such transactions are gains and losses from the perspective of the shareholders of the holding company. An Alternative View by three Board members (AV8–10) amplifies this argument. A similar alternative view is attached to the Proposed Amendment to IAS 27, *Consolidated and Separate Financial Statements* (June 2005, paras AV1–3).

The current version of IAS 27 was revised in 2004, when minority interests (now described as non-controlling interests) were classified as equity for presentation purposes. The standard contains a dissenting opinion (DO1–3) by one member who foresaw the consequences of extending this approach to the recognition and measurement of changes in minority interests.

10.8.2 Entity Specific Assumptions

The IASB's current standards do allow entity specific assumptions in some instances. Most notably, IAS 36, *Impairment of Assets*, bases recoverable amount on projected cash flows (when fair value is not an appropriate measure), and these will inevitably be based on entity specific management forecasts. As indicated earlier, impairment testing can be viewed as an application of *prudence*, so that IAS 36 defies the Fair Value View in two respects.

IAS 37, *Provisions*, also allows entity specific assumptions in the estimation of 'the best estimate of the amount to settle an obligation at balance sheet date' (IAS 37, 36). However, the proposed amendment (in the June 2005 IASB Exposure Draft) would narrow, but not eliminate, the scope for entity specific judgement, by moving closer to the FASB's fair value measure (Exposure Draft, IAS 37, Amendments to IAS 37, June 2005, BC77–8).

The proposed measure is: 'the amount that it would rationally pay to settle the present obligation or to transfer it to a third party on the balance sheet date'. Transfer to a third party implies a market transaction, which is a step toward fair value.

The entity specific issue has also arisen in the *revenue recognition* project, where one proposed model advocates that obligations to customers should be measured at fair value, that is, to reflect the costs that a neutral 'market participant' would bear, whereas an alternative would be to reflect the expected costs of the entity holding the obligation.

A specific application of this problem arises in the IASB's recent discussion paper on *Insurance Contracts* (2007). The preferred 'exit value' model can be interpreted as a fair value measurement, but fair value would exclude entity specific assumptions, whereas in practice entities are likely to rely substantially on evidence derived from their own business models, so the IASB has reserved its judgment as to whether the approach should be described as fair value.

10.8.3 The Relevance of Cost

The use of cost measures is widespread in the standards of the IASB and the ASB, particularly for *initial recognition* of assets and liabilities, but also many assets and liabilities are subsequently carried at historical cost or amortized cost.

When items are revalued, this is usually at fair value. We have seen that the SFAS 157 proposals would preclude fair value from being interpreted as replacement cost ('entry' values), although replacement cost might be used as a proxy for fair value in the absence of other measures, at the bottom of the measurement hierarchy.

This would change current practice in areas such as IAS 16, *Property, Plant and Equipment*, and IAS 17, *Leases*, where replacement cost may seem to be a more relevant measure of future cash flows for assets that are to be used in the business, and which therefore represent future costs saved rather than future revenues earned.

The rejection of cost in favor of fair value selling price at initial recognition is particularly controversial. This gives rise to 'day 1' profits on financial instruments (IAS 39). Such profits rely on the entity being able to realize the asset at fair value in the future.

Therefore, some would argue that the profits are not yet 'earned' at day 1, which is why retailers are usually required to record their stock at cost rather than a higher retail price.[19]

In the exposure draft to revise IFRS 3 on business combinations, the proposal to change from a cost allocation model to one based on the fair value of the whole acquired entity has been very controversial, with extensive alternative views by board members (AV1–20).

One of the criticisms made (AV18) is that purchase consideration including acquisition costs (which would be written off under a fair value measurement basis) best captures the economic substance of the acquisition transaction, reflecting the outlay which the acquirer must expect to recover.

10.8.4 Reliability and Prudence

The controversy on the proposed IFRS 3 revision raises a number of issues of reliability, particularly with respect to the measurement of 'full goodwill' (including goodwill in the acquired entity that is attributable to minority interests).

This depends on there being a reliable measure of the fair value of the acquired entity, rather than merely the portion that was acquired. Five board members proposed an Alternative View to this proposal (AV1–7), on grounds of unreliability of measurement.

The existing version of IFRS 3 also attracted a great deal of criticism from constituents, again with particular regard to its treatment of goodwill. Amortization of goodwill, the previous treatment, was abandoned in favor of impairment testing.

Critics of IFRS 3 acknowledged that amortization is arbitrary (as is depreciation of tangible assets) but argued that it guaranteed the *accountability* of management for their expenditure on the acquisition, because over its lifetime the full cost of goodwill would be charged to profit. Under the impairment test, there is no guarantee of this, because of the difficulty of separating acquired from internally generated goodwill (IFRS 3, Dissenting opinions, DO16).

A related issue is that the impairment test is weaker than it need be because it does not include a subsequent cash flow test like that in the UK ASB's original standard (IAS 36, Dissenting Opinions, DO6–10). Such a test might be regarded as an application of prudence, but so is the whole asymmetric principle of impairment testing.

[19] This type of criticism has a long history—see the discussion of the 1930s ideas of George Husband described in this journal (Reinstein et al. 2008, pp. 82–108).

10.8.5 Recognition Criteria

The two recognition criteria in the existing IASB Framework are probability that the entity will receive future cash benefits (in the case of an asset) and reliability of measurement. The probability criterion has been eroded by some recent decisions of the IASB.

IFRS 3, *Business Combinations*, and the consequential amendments to IAS 38, *Intangible Assets*, result in the withdrawal of the probability recognition criterion for intangible assets acquired in a business combination, on the ground that their measurement is at fair value, which incorporates assessments of probability.

As explained earlier, this ignores element uncertainty, and it is inconsistent with the treatment of other intangible assets. A dissenting view to IFRS 3 (DO7) addresses this issue, as does a dissenting opinion on the revised IAS 38 (DO1–3).

Using the same reasoning, IFRS 3 also removes the probability requirement for contingent liabilities acquired in a business combination because they are measured at fair value, and this too is addressed in DO7.

10.8.6 Performance and Earnings

The IASB has a long-running project on reporting financial performance. This has proved to be very controversial, and the project is now part of a joint FASB project, Presentation of Financial Statements.

The main original aim of the project was to improve the presentation of the income statement to include a comprehensive income measure, sometimes referred to as 'clean-surplus' income. This might be achieved by having two statements (as in the UK ASB's FRS 3 format, (Accounting Standards Board, 1992) and one of the options in the FASB's current standard) or one. Some IASB board members had a strong, publicly expressed preference for a single statement and also an aversion to prescribing sub-totals such as operating income.

This was the main source of opposition, particularly from preparers of accounts, but also from some users, who saw a measure of operating income as an important indicator of management performance and an important input to valuing the entity. It is easy to stylize this attitude as resistance to change or management wanting something below operating profit in which to hide bad news, but there is a more worthy rationale.

In many businesses, the operations and margins on operations are drivers of cash flow and, in such cases, it may well be very informative to separate these 'core' activities from other activities such as financing or non- core investments such as property ownership.

A vivid illustration of this approach is given in a recent paper by Penman (2007), which uses the example of valuing the Coca-Cola Company to show how cost-based earnings numbers can be used effectively in valuation.[20]

10.9 Concluding Thoughts: Who is Right in Theory?

The advocates of fair value, and more broadly the Fair Value View, have a consistent view of the world that appears to have attractive attributes of coherence and simplicity from a theoretical standpoint. It is therefore tempting to dismiss it as 'alright in theory but not in practice'.

However, it should be noted that the theoretical underpinnings of the Fair Value View are fairly intuitive and simplistic. Previous advocates of exit value, notably Chambers (1966) and Sterling (1970), developed much more comprehensive theories of business reporting and measurement and would not have been unqualified supporters of the Fair Value View, as outlined above.[21]

The Alternative View, on the other hand, arises from a variety of people with diverse views, commenting on specific issues, often from a practical standpoint. Thus, on the surface at least, it is possible to regard it as somewhat incoherent, pragmatic and lacking in theoretical foundations.

Such an approach might be dismissed as 'practical but not alright in theory'. Neither of these conclusions would be correct. As we have seen, the two views are based on different assumptions about the nature of the economic environment, and it is the accuracy of these assumptions that determines the relevance of the respective views to accounting standards.

If we accept that the world is not characterized by perfect and complete markets, the Fair Value View loses much of its attraction, because it does not relate to the real world in which standard setters operate. In this sense, it is not 'alright in theory' because good theory, from the standard setter's perspective, should be relevant, as well as logically coherent.

The Alternative View, on the other hand, does relate to the real world of market imperfection, but it does not offer simple, coherent solutions. The solutions that come out of the Alternative View will have a much greater entity or industry

[20] The Penman paper uses historical cost earnings for illustrative purposes. This does not preclude current replacement cost, if it were available, from providing an even more useful measure. This is compatible with the Alternative View expressed in this paper. That view does not deny the potential usefulness of current values (entry or exit) when they can be reliably measured and are relevant to the circumstances of the entity.

[21] Chambers' reservations have been noted earlier (note 13). Sterling was extremely careful to point out that his 'conclusions are restricted to trading assets in a trading firm' (Sterling 1970, p. 36) and he acknowledged the difficulties caused by market imperfections. Moreover, unlike the advocates of fair value, he advocated the deduction of transaction costs from exit prices in order to establish exit *values* (p. 327). For a summary of Sterling's later ideas, see Lee and Wolnizer (1997).

specificity, perhaps even allowing more judgement, which tends to offend the orderly instincts of standard setters.

However, the Alternative View does not lack theoretical support. Hicks (1946) is a standard reference for writers on income measurement, and careful readers of his work (of whom there seem to be fewer than those who refer to it) will recall that Hicks confined his analysis of income to static theory (not a realistic view of the business world) and rejected its use in dynamic analysis. In that context, he wrote of Income, Saving and Depreciation:

> In spite of their familiarity, I do not believe that they are suitable tools for any analysis which aims at logical precision. There is far too much equivocation in their meaning, equivocation which cannot be removed by the most painstaking effort. At bottom, they are not logical categories at all: they are rough approximations, used by the business man to steer himself through the bewildering changes of situation which confront him.

The Alternative View is compatible with Hicks' 'rough approximations used by the business man' and, although standard setters may hope to smooth out the roughness as much as possible, some will remain.

Theoretical support for the Alternative View can also be found in the classic work of Edwards and Bell (1961), who were also economists by training. Their analysis emphasized income, rather than the balance sheet (although their system did incorporate 'clean surplus' articulation of total gains with the balance sheet), and considered how *ex post* accounting income, based on past transactions and events, could be used to evaluate performance, using current cost measures rather than fair values (which would be included in what they described as 'opportunity costs').

A great deal of subsequent theoretical work by others during the so-called 'golden age' of accounting theory in the 1960s and during the subsequent debate on inflation accounting was in the Edwards and Bell mould and compatible with the Alternative View.

On the level of pure theory, an important paper by Beaver and Demski (1979) demonstrated that income is an ill-defined concept in a world of imperfect and incomplete markets and that, in such a world, accounting has the role of providing useful information rather than definitive measures: a conclusion consistent with that of Hicks.

Ironically, in the perfect market conditions in which income *is* a well-defined concept, it is not needed, and neither are financial statements: all of the relevant information is impounded in the present value of the entity, which is its market price in a fully informed market.[22]

---

[22] A recent paper by Hitz (2007) evaluates the decision usefulness of fair value accounting both from the measurement perspective and from the informational perspective that Beaver and Demski identify as being the appropriate role for financial reporting in a realistic setting of imperfect and incomplete markets. The conclusion of this evaluation is that the case for fair value measurement is supported only when reliable market values are available.

In the same spirit, when Fischer Black (1993), the pioneer of option pricing theory, came to express his views on how to improve financial reporting, these were very pragmatic and based upon providing information that would help to identify sustainable earnings, rather than offering a Fair Value View.

One reaction to the problem that it is not possible to deduce a general, theoretically 'correct' accounting measure in a world of imperfect and incomplete markets has been for many academics to retreat from theoretical or normative work into empirical studies of how markets react to accounting information, as a test of usefulness. This is unfortunate because such tests can only study what is observable, so that they cannot develop or test new reporting methods: that duty has thus been thrust on the standard setters and on practitioners.

A more constructive approach might be to recognize that theories are not likely to offer panaceas such as a universally valid single measurement method and instead to work in a more limited way to solve specific problems.

Certainly, this approach has worked well in the related discipline of Economics. Keynes (1930), many years ago, hoped for economists to develop in this way and they have largely achieved this, by developing tools of analysis, such as game theory or agency theory which can be applied to specific problems without claiming to provide universal solutions.

Such models are already applied in areas of accounting, such as accounting disclosure.[23] It is suggested that the Alternative View is consistent with this type of theorizing and that it offers more fruitful practical application than the Fair Value View.

One approach to accounting measurement which contains the elements of this approach and is already well-established in the academic literature is *deprival value*,[24] which provides an algorithm for choosing a measurement method (rather than prescribing one universal method) that is grounded in the economics of the firm.

It is unfortunate, and perhaps indicative of standard setters' current preferences, that this approach to defining a measurement objective rather than a single technique has been omitted from the current list of measurement candidates being evaluated in the conceptual framework revision, on the ground that it is a hybrid approach, allowing for the use of more than one 'pure' measurement method.

Therefore, the economists' experience might be relevant to standard setters in their search for a conceptual framework. Perhaps the time has come for them to stop trying to work financial miracles (such as deriving a universal 'best' measurement method from a complex definition grounded in abstract measurement

[23] Verrecchia (2004) gives a concise survey of the application of theoretical models to accounting disclosure. Wagenhofer (2004) provides a broader survey of the application of analytical economic models to financial reporting.

[24] The history of the concept and its role in the inflation accounting debate is surveyed in Tweedie and Whittington (1984). Recent examples of work relating deprival value to fair value are Bromwich (2004) and Van Zijl and Whittington (2006). A good example of economic analysis supporting the use of deprival value is Edwards et al. (1987).

theory) but instead to follow Keynes' advice and 'manage to get themselves thought of as humble, competent people, on a level with dentists'.

10.10 Postscript: Further Developments at the IASB, 2006–2012[25]

The previous paper was a review of the author's own experience as a member of the IASB from its foundation, in 2001, until the end of June, 2006. Since then until the writing of this postscript (May 2012) almost six further years have elapsed, during which the author, as an external observer, has noted a number of decisions which appear to support the Alternative View rather than the Fair Value View, perhaps indicating a change of direction.

However, this change of direction is not consistent, and the lack of progress on revising the conceptual framework means that the future direction of the IASB is unclear.

10.10.1 The Conceptual Framework: 2006–2012

In 2006, the IASB had plans to finish most of the conceptual framework revision by 2012. This has not occurred.

Moreover, the indications in 2006 were that the chapter on Measurement would be completed and would favor Fair Value as the preferred measure, as in the discussion paper, Measurement on Initial Recognition, issued in 2005. This too has not happened: no further discussion papers or exposure drafts on measurement have been issued as part of the conceptual framework project, and work on the project is currently suspended, pending the agenda review.

Moreover, the discussions of measurement at the IASB board prior to the suspension were more concerned with defining the objectives and desirable properties of measurement rather than with attempting to identify and prescribe a single ideal method of measurement, such as Fair Value. Thus, developments in the measurement section of the conceptual framework project have tended to be more consistent with the Alternative View than with the Fair Value View.

However, developments in the conceptual framework project have not entirely favored the Alternative View. In particular, chapter 1 (Objectives) and chapter 3 (Properties of Accounting Information) which were in draft in 2006 have been published in their final form (2010) and this retains the 'Fair Value View'

---

[25] The author is grateful for helpful comments on an earlier draft of this Postscript from Andrew Lennard and David Tweedie, although neither is responsible for the opinions expressed or for any errors that remain.

properties of the original draft. In particular, chapter 1 still advocates decision usefulness as the primary objective, relegating stewardship to a subsidiary role, and chapter 3 still prefers representational faithfulness to reliability as one of the primary properties of good accounting information.

Thus, while the conceptual framework revision has not favored Fair Value measurement as much as might have been expected in 2006, it still retains important features of the broader Fair Value View.

10.10.2 Standards Development: 2006–2012

Work on the development of standards in the period 2006–2012 has shown significant movement toward the Alternative View, although, as in the case of the conceptual framework, the Fair Value View has not been eliminated.

The most notable shift from the Fair Value View has been in the measurement of obligations, which has occurred in three projects, the revision of IAS 37 (Provisions, now retitled Liabilities), insurance contracts, and revenue recognition. In each of these cases, as indicated in the original paper, the prevailing view on the IASB board in 2006 appeared to be that obligations should be measured at Fair Value, i.e., the amount that an independent, arm's length contractor would charge to relieve the entity of the obligation.

Clearly, if the cheapest method of fulfilling the obligation were for the entity to do the work, rather than an outside contractor (an entity-specific approach), the fair value approach would tend to over-state the amount of the obligation. On the other hand, if the fair value of the obligation (as represented by the independent contractor's estimated charge) were less than the consideration receivable from the customer, the fair value approach could lead to the recording of an immediate profit (Day1 profit) when a contract was signed, on the ground that the obligation could be discharged for less than the consideration due on the contract, despite no work having yet been done to fulfill the contract and no specific outside contractor having been identified or employed.

The fair value approach has been modified since 2006 in each of these projects. In the case of *provisions* (and other liabilities not covered by another standard), the 2010 Exposure Draft, *Measurement of Liabilities*, retained measurement as 'the amount that the entity would rationally pay' to be relieved of the obligation. This amount could be the resources that the entity would require to fulfill the obligation, if that were the only costeffective option, but the preferred basis for assessment was a market-based estimate of what an independent contractor would charge to assume the obligation, consistent with the Fair Value View.

The same exposure draft retained the abolition of the 'probable outflow' test for recognition of a liability, which was attributed in the previous paper as a consequence of the Fair Value View, although it substituted a concept of 'judgement', which sounds like an informal probability test.

The Exposure Draft was opposed by a significant minority of Board members and by many constituents. In view of the small likelihood of immediate resolution and the pressure of work on other projects, the IAS 37 revision was suspended in 2010, and remains so. Hence, fair value made no advance in this area after 2006. This project is currently suspended, pending the agenda review.

The *Insurance* project appeared in 2006 to be moving toward measuring obligations on insurance contracts at fair value, which would be based on the price that a reinsurer would charge to assume the obligation. This could have given rise to 'Day 1 profits' where the premium received was greater than the estimated reinsurance cost. This was confirmed by a discussion paper in 2007.

Since then, the IASB has changed its position and its 2010 Exposure Draft favors measuring the obligation initially at *entry* value, the premium charged to the customer, rather than an exit value (the price charged by a notional reinsurer). Subsequently, the initial amount would be amortised on the basis of the entity's estimates of what each stage of performance would cost: an entity-specific measure.

The 2010 Exposure Draft rules out specifically the reporting of 'Day 1 profits' on insurance contracts. These changes move toward the Alternative View and away from the Fair Value View. They will result in the profit on an insurance contract being recognized as the obligations under the contract are fulfilled.

The project on *Revenue Recognition* has followed a similar pattern to that on insurance. In 2006, the IASB's preferred approach was to recognize the performance obligation under a contract at Fair Value: the amount that an independent market participant would charge to assume the obligation.

More recent Exposure Drafts (2010 and 2012) have moved away from fair value to base the initial measurement on the contract price, an *entry* value. The initial measurement is subsequently reduced when specific obligations are discharged by performance.

The identification of specific obligations and attribution of revenue to them is to be based, where possible, on market prices, but in practice it is likely to be entity specific in many cases. Initial ('Day 1') profits will not be recognized (because the obligation is measured at the contract price) but initial losses will be recognized if the contract is onerous. This is an application of *prudence*, and therefore another concession to the Alternative View.

Another project in which the IASB has moved towards the Alternative View is *performance reporting*, and more specifically the presentation of the income statement.

Early IASB discussions were dominated by a concern to report *comprehensive income* as the key performance measure and to discourage, or even prevent, the reporting of component measures such as operating profit.

This reflects the Fair Value View that the aggregate change in wealth, as reflected in a fair value balance sheet, is the ultimate measure of performance and that sub categories such as operating income are potentially misleading and subject to manipulation, because the 'bad news' will be pushed 'below the line' as other comprehensive income. Recent IASB deliberations have shown a retreat from this Fair Value view.

The revision of IAS 1 (2011) acknowledges that profit is a key component of comprehensive income and that reporting components of other comprehensive income is also important.

In other words, it is not just the aggregate change in net assets that is important (as in the Fair Value View) but also the components, which are useful inputs into the valuation models employed by users of accounts (consistent with the Alternative View).

Another area which has seen important developments in recent years is *financial instruments.* The case for fair value measurement and for the broader Fair Value View that markets are deep, liquid and well-informed may be strongest in the case of financial assets and liabilities that are traded on markets, although the recent financial crisis has challenged this view.

The IASB has long been concerned to improve its accounting for financial instruments (IAS 39) and the associated disclosures (IFRS 7) and this was given additional impetus by the Financial Crisis Advisory Group, which was established in 2008 to advise the IASB the FASB on its response to the crisis (which started in 2007).

The first significant change in response to the financial crisis was forced upon the IASB, which reluctantly gave way to political pressure in 2008 (Andre et. al. 2009) by relaxing the restrictions on the reclassification of fair valued financial instruments to the amortised cost category (amendment to IAS 39 2008).

This was undoubtedly a move away from a strict fair value approach to one of mixed measurement, but it did not represent a change of heart by the IASB, because it was made under political duress.

However, the IASB has embarked upon a longer term project, the development of IFRS 9, which is intended ultimately to improve and replace current requirements of IAS 39 for the reporting and disclosure of financial instruments.

This project appears to be confirming the mixed measurement approach, allowing measurement methods appropriate to the circumstances, as in the Alternative View, rather than insisting upon fair value as the universal measurement objective, as in the Fair Value View.

The simplification of financial asset categories, first introduced in an Exposure Draft in 2009, and subsequently adopted in the first stage of IFRS 9,*Financial Instruments* (2009) abolishes the former 'available for sale' category, which required fair value measurement (but with gains and losses by-passing profit and loss) and retains the category that is measured at amortised cost (but with different conditions and no longer called 'held to maturity') in addition to the category that is measured at fair value with gains and losses passing through profit and loss (the latter now having different conditions and no longer called 'held for trading').

Another issue arising from the financial crisis has been the measurement of *loan loss provisions*.

The IASB's current approach is to measure such impairments on the basis of incurred loss, i.e., losses that will result from events that have already occurred. It has been suggested that this led to under-provision for losses during the financial crisis.

As a consequence of this, the IASB has recently issued an Exposure Draft (2011) that proposes a change to the expected loss method. This measures losses in terms of what reasonably could be expected to occur in the future, on the basis of present knowledge. This resembles closely the basis on which a market value would be calculated if there was a market, and it could therefore be characterized as a move toward the Fair Value View. However, this interpretation would not be appropriate because impairment is applied to an historical cost measurement base: essentially it is an application of prudence (certainly not an aspect of the Fair Value View) leading to a mixed measurement approach, the choice of measurement being based on the traditional rule 'cost or market value, whichever is the lower'. The incurred loss method is a strict application of historical cost to the impairment (the loss event must already have occurred) as well as to the original measurement and perhaps arises from a rigid view that adherence to a single measurement method is essential. Adherence to a single measurement method for all circumstances is, of course, one aspect of the Fair Value View.

Another aspect of the development of IFRS 9 on financial instruments has been the treatment of *own credit risk.* When liabilities are measured at fair value, a decline in the issuer's credit rating can cause a lower fair value of its loans and therefore a gain. If this gain is reported as part of profit, advocates of stewardship (part of the Alternative View) would regard the resulting profit figure as misleading: a 'gain' arising from the prospect that the entity will not meet its financial obligations is of a different type and significance to other gains with which it might be aggregated (such as a gain on a fixed interest loan arising from a rise in interest rates). The IASB has recently (in its October 2010 amendments to FRS 9) introduced a requirement to separate gains or losses resulting from changes in own credit risk, reporting them in Other Comprehensive Income, rather than as part of profit and loss. This is consistent with the Alternative View rather than the Fair Value View, which focuses on total comprehensive income, rather than its components, as the central performance measure.

An important new standard that has certainly consolidated and clarified, although arguably not extended, the presence of the Fair Value View in the IASB's literature is IFRS 13, Fair Value Measurement, 2011. This defined fair value and provided guidance on its measurement. It was based on the FASB's earlier SFAS 157 and was therefore an important step in the convergence process between international and US standards. It changed the previous IASB definition of fair value by explicitly stating that it was a *selling price*, i.e., it was a disposal price (exit) rather than an acquisition price (entry) and it was a price rather than a value, so that transaction costs were ignored. This is precisely the definition that was identified with the Fair Value View. The IASB stated that this standard did not *extend* the use of fair value, because it applied only where existing standards required the use of fair value.

However, the IASB did acknowledge that it changed the definition (by excluding entry values and transaction costs), and it conducted a study of existing standards to establish whether the new definition conflicted with the requirements of the standard. It decided that there was a problem in only one case (share-based payments).

10.10.3 Conclusion

It is clear from the above that the dominance of the Fair Value View in IASB decisions, which was anticipated in the 2007 paper, has not occurred. Instead, the IASB has continued to use fair value where it seems to be relevant and reliable, but in other cases it has adopted different measurement methods, including some that are entity specific.

Mixed measurement methods and conservative implementation consistent with stewardship seem to be accepted, in the pragmatic spirit of the Alternative View.

In the absence of an up-to-date conceptual framework that commands respect, this pragmatic approach brings the danger that standards will possibly lose consistency, coherence, and relevance to their central objectives, so it is to be hoped that the revision of the conceptual framework will be resumed promptly when the current agenda consultation is complete.

An obvious question is why the IASB has apparently changed direction. An immediate explanation is the change of Board membership.

The final members of the original Board (2001) retired in June 2011 and their replacements are more diverse in background and geographical origin, with a greater number from outside North America.

Underlying the change of balance on the Board is the continuing process of reforming the IASB Foundation, whose trustees oversee the Board. The thrust of these reforms has been to make the IASB more accountable to its constituency, particularly the users and preparers of accounts in those countries that use IFRS.

The criteria for Board membership have been widened to reduce the emphasis on technical expertise relative to understanding of business and to promote greater geographical diversity of background.

These changes reflect the increasing number of countries that has adopted IFRS and the increasing engagement by constituents as they implement the standards.

The resulting political tensions affecting the IASB have led to a number of crises and confrontations, most notably (but by no means confined to) those involving regulators within the European Union regarding accounting for financial instruments.

These crises have made the IASB aware of its need to persuade and adapt rather than to dictate, and its due process has been refined as a means of achieving this.

With regard specifically to the Fair Value View, the financial crisis, from 2007 onwards, has shaken confidence in the extent to which markets are efficient, deep, and liquid, as assumed by that view, and some commentators have alleged that fair value accounting contributed to the crisis (Plantin et al. 2008, provides a rigorous analysis of the potential destabilising effects of fair value). This created the political pressure that led to the foundation of the Advisory Group.

Hence, the change of direction by the IASB is really an indication of the growth of its worldwide constituency and the consequent need to cater for the needs of a diversity of views.

However, for standards to be effective, they must not simply be the outcome of political compromise. Possibly, the Alternative View requires a conceptual framework more urgently than the Fair Value View, because it is predicated upon a more complex market setting.

Unfortunately, that framework would ideally be different from that assumed by the two chapters of the revised IASB Framework that have been issued to date (chapters 1 and 3).

Therefore, a priority for the IASB should be for it to clarify its conceptual framework in a way that is consistent with the thinking that underlies its recent decisions. It may be the case that starting afresh may be a better approach than attempting to revise and reconcile the two existing frameworks that are derived from FASB's work of the 1970s and 1980s, when the economic environment was very different and a specific institutional setting (that of the USA) was assumed.

References

Accounting Standards Board (1992). FRS, *Reporting Financial Performance*, ASB, (revised 1993 and 1999).

Accounting Standards Board (1999). *Statement of Principles for Financial Reporting*, ASB.

Andre, P., Cazavan-Jeny, A., Dick, W., Richard, C., & Walton, P. (2009). Fair value accounting and the banking crisis in 2008: Shooting the messenger. *Accounting in Europe, 6*, 3–24.

Barth, M. E. (2006). Including estimates of the future in today's financial statements. *Accounting Horizons.*

Beaver, W. H., & Demski J. S. (1979). The nature of income measurement. *The Accounting Review.*

Black, F. (1993). Choosing Accounting Rules. *Accounting Horizons.*

Bromwich, M. (2004). Aspects of the future in accounting: The use of market prices and "fair values" in financial reports. In C. Leuz, D. Pfaff and A. Hopwood (Eds.) *The Economics and Politics of Accounting*, Oxford University Press.

Bullen, H. G., & Crook, K. (2005). *Revisiting the Concepts.* FASB and IASB.

Bush, T. (2005). *Divided by a common language: Where economics meets the law—US versus non-US financial reporting models.* Institute of Chartered Accountants in England and Wales.

Camfferman, K., & Zeff, S. (2007). *Financial reporting and global capital markets: A history of the inter-national accounting standards committee, 1973–2000*, Oxford University Press.

Canadian Accounting Standards Board (2005). Measurement bases for financial accounting-measurement on initial recognition, *IASB.*

Cauwenberge, P. I., & De Beedle, I. (2007). On the IASB comprehensive income: An analysis of the case for dual income display. *Abacus.*

Chambers, R. J. (1966). *Accounting, evaluation and economic behavior.* New York: Prentice-Hall.

Chambers, R. J. (1970). Second thoughts on continuously contemporary accounting. *Abacus.*

Chambers, R. J. (1974). Third thoughts. *Abacus.*

Edwards, E. O., & Bell, P. W. (1961). *The theory and measurement of business income*, University of California Press.

Edwards, J., Kay J., & Mayer, C. (1987) *The economic analysis of accounting profitability.* Clarendon Press, UK.

Financial Accounting Standards Board (2006). SFAS 157, fair value measurements. *FASB.*

Hicks, J. R. (1946) *Value and Capital* (2nd ed.) Clarendon Press, UK.

Hitz, J.-M. (2007). The decision usefulness of fair value accounting—a theoretical perspective. *European Accounting Review 16*(2).

International Accounting Standards Board: Standards

IAS 16 (2004). *Property, Plant and Equipment*, amended.
IAS 17 (2004). *Leases*, revised.
IAS 27 (2004). *Consolidated and Separate Financial Statements*, revised 2004.
IAS 36 (2004). *Impairment of Assets*, revised 2004.
IAS 37 (1998). *Provisions, Contingent Liabilities and Contingent Assets.*
IAS 38 (2004). *Intangible Assets*, amended 2004.
IAS 39 (2005). *Financial Instruments: Recognition and Measurement*, amended 2005.
IAS 41 (2001). *Agriculture.*
IFRS 2 (2004). *Share-Based Payment.*
IFRS 3 (2004). *Business Combinations.*
IFRS 4 (2004). *Insurance Contracts.*

Exposure Drafts

Proposed Amendments to IFRS 3 (2005). *Business Combinations.*
Proposed Amendments to IAS 27 (2005). *Consolidated and Separate Financial Statements.*
Proposed Amendments to IAS 37 (2005). *Provisions, Contingent Liabilities and Contingent Assets*, and IAS 19, *Employee Benefits.*

Discussion Papers

Preliminary Views on an Improved Conceptual Framework for Financial Reporting (2006). *The objective of financial reporting and qualitative characteristics of decision-useful financial reporting information.*
Fair Value Measurements, Parts 1 and 2, November 2006. *Preliminary Views on Insurance Contracts*, Parts 1 and 2, May 2007.

Other Publications

Framework for the Preparation and Presentation of Financial Statements, April 1989.
IASB Update, monthly minutes of Board meetings.
IASB Information for Observers, edited versions of Board papers, on the IASB web site: www.iasb.org.
Johnson, L. T. (2004). The Project to Revisit the Conceptual Framework. *FASB Report*, 28.
Johnson, L. T. (2005). Relevance and Reliability. *FASB Report*, 28.
Keynes, J. M. (1931). Possibilities for our Grandchildren. *Nation and Athenaeum*, 18 October 1930. Reprinted in *Essays in Persuasion*, London: Macmillan.
Lee, T., & Wolnizer, P. (eds) (1997). the quest for a science of accounting: An anthology of the research of Robert R. Sterling, *New Works in Accounting History*, Garland.
Lennard, A. (2002). *Liabilities, and How to Account for Them: An Explanatory Essay*, Accounting Standards Board.

Paton, W. A., & Littleton, A. C. (1940). *An Introduction to Corporate Accounting Standards*. American Accounting Association.
Penman, S. (2007). Financial reporting quality: Is fair value a plus or a minus? *Accounting and Business Research*, Special Issue: International Accounting Policy Forum.
Plantin, G., Sapra, H., & Shin, H. S. (2008). Marking to market: Panacea or Pandora's box? *Journal of Accounting Research, 46*, 435–460.
Reinstein, A., Alvin, G., & Vangermeesch, R. (2008). George R. Husband: Contributions to the development of accounting thought. *Abacus.*
Rosenfield, P. (2008). Prospects: A missing piece of current selling price reporting. *Abacus.*
Sprouse, R. T. (1978). The importance of earnings in the conceptual framework. *Journal of Accountancy.*
Sterling, R. R. (1970). *Theory of the Measurement of Enterprise Income*, University Press of Kansas.
Storey, R. K., & Storey, S. (1998) *Special report: The framework of financial accounting concepts and standards.* Financial Accounting Standards Board.
Tweedie, D. P., & Whittington, G. (1984). *The debate on inflation accounting.* Cambridge University Press.
Tweedie, D. P., & Whittington, G. (1997). The end of the current cost revolution. In C. W. Nobes and T. Cooke (Eds.), The Development of Accounting in an International Context, Routledge.
Van Zijl, A., & Whittington, G. (2006). Deprival value and fair value: A reconciliation. *Accounting and Business Research.*
Verrecchia, R. E. (2004). Policy implications from the theory-based literature on disclosure. In C. Leuz D. Pfaff and A. Hopwood (Eds.), The economics and politics of accounting. Oxford: Oxford University Press.
Wagenhofer, A. (2004) Accounting and economics: What we learn from analytical models in financial accounting and reporting. In C. Leuz, D. Pfaff and A. Hopwood (Eds.), *The Economics and Politics of Accounting.* Oxford: Oxford University Press.
Walker, R. G. (2007). Reporting entity concept: A case-study of the failure of principles-based regulation. *Abacus.*
Walton, P. (2006). Fair value and executory contracts: moving the boundaries in international financial reporting. *Accounting and Business Research.*

Chapter 11
A Comparison of Historical Cost and Fair Value Accounting Systems: General and Some Regulatory Concerns

Michael Bromwich

Abstract A simple and parsimonious example compares the accounting results of two accounting systems in terms purely of aiding investor decision making (buying/holding and selling securities). This article summarises the ideas in Bromwich et al. (2011) though with a slight regulatory emphasis using a different example. A major aim of this chapter is to show that practical accounting models can help the understanding of their utility in predicting the future. A variety of regulators often have recourse to modelling the possible future outcomes of organisations involving accounting simulations and simulated comparisons of the results of different accounting systems. Reconciling the reported results with those derived from benchmark models reveals the deficiencies of accounting systems in supplying information for decision making. Historical cost (HC) accounting is found to perform poorly. Fair value (FV) systems without estimated FVs may perform even worse and may mislead investors but allowing FV estimates increases the subjectivity of financial reports.

11.1 Introduction

This article summarises the ideas in Bromwich et al. (2011) though with a slight regulatory emphasis using a different example. The latter article suggests that empirical comparisons of accounting systems are difficult and therefore suggests

Parts of this article use similar words and phrases to those used in Bromwich et al. (2011) without direct quotation to simplify the presentation. I am very grateful to my co-authors: Frank Clarke and Graeme Dean.

M. Bromwich (✉)
Department of Accounting, London School of Economics, London, UK
e-mail: m.bromwich@lse.ac.uk

R. Di Pietra et al. (eds.), *Accounting and Regulation*,
DOI: 10.1007/978-1-4614-8097-6_11,

drawing upon simulation. A simple and parsimonious example compares the accounting results of two accounting systems in terms purely of aiding investor decision making and also with a benchmark accounting system based on the well-known economic income and wealth concepts which provide the "first best" accounting information system for investment decision making in our setting. The setting assumes certainty and looks at only at the utility of the information provided by the two accounting systems in determining future equity value and income. Reconciling the reported results with those derived from benchmark models reveals the deficiencies of accounting systems in supplying information for decision making both relatively to one another and absolutely with regard to the benchmark model. Here, the major emphasis is primarily on the model building and the utility of simple simulation in comparing accounting systems.

A variety of regulators especially those regulating competition and utilities often have recourse to modelling the possible future outcomes of organisations and this can involve simulations using accounting information and simulated comparisons of the results of different accounting systems. To help in these tasks, a concern of this chapter is to show that practical accounting models can be presented in a way that is useful to help understanding of their utility in predicting the future and that benchmarks can be found that allow the economics of the setting to be understood as is done in Bromwich et al. (2011). It is shown that the integration of economic bench marks needs to be carefully crafted if the results of the modelling are to be meaningful. The results of the economic accounting benchmark systems employed are often quite different to the outcomes of the accounting system(s) being considered. The elements of variances between the systems are often quite nuanced and need to be interpreted carefully, especially in complex simulations.

The results in Bromwich et al. (2011) both endorse and refute some of the statements frequently made about accounting systems. This debate is a topic of current interest as many claims have been made in the literature for fair value (FV) accounting often associated with severe criticism of historical cost (HC) accounting. Similarly, defenders of HC accounting have strongly attacked FV accounting. Although some of this literature is analytical or uses empirical evidence, much is based on assertions.

Some of these results in Bromwich et al. (2011) will be discussed in this chapter as illustrations of what even simple simulations can achieve. These conclusions include that the ability of an accounting system to aid decision making is a function of how and when it reports realised and expected abnormal profits (above normal returns). Some accounting systems perform well on this basis, but require very strong assumptions. As is well known, the usual HC accounting system performs poorly but, perhaps, surprisingly operational (FV) systems also do not perform well. For operational FV systems to be helpful, it is *essential* to employ estimates of the prices that would reign in missing or incomplete markets but such estimates must have economic significance if they are to have validity related to the benchmark model. The possible differential effects of asset price changes on future cash flows which have almost gone unrecognised in the literature are found to be of crucial importance when analysing accounting systems but are not discussed here.

Another aim of this chapter is to illustrate the above results by considering briefly a numerical comparison (a simple simulation) of the relative aid to investment decision making furnished by two accounting systems, the HC and FV accounting systems, using a parsimonious model reflecting elements of practical accounting. Here the aim is to ascertain which, if either of the accounting systems best allows an investor to decide whether to buy equity securities, hold or to retain them using only accounting information. That published financial statements should help in decision making is the avowed primary object of the Financial Accounting Standards Board (FASB) and the International Accounting Standards Board (IASB) (see FASB 1978, SFAC No. 1 and IASB 2010, paragraphs OB5–OB11).

The example focuses on non-financial assets first because there is a view that the standard setters, FASB and the IASB, may extend FV requirements in this area which has not been significantly analysed in the literature (see the discussion in Whittington 2008 and Ronen 2008). Currently, the expansion of FV beyond financial instruments mainly builds upon its use in earlier financial standards and amounts to a gradual exercise. Second, non-financial assets raise some different problems to those generated by financial items. The most important of these latter is that it is believed generally that it is non-financial assets that generate net present values (NPVs) (yield abnormal earnings in the nomenclature of the residual income (RI) literature, that is, periodic earnings greater than the cost of capital on net assets at the beginning of the period) (Felthman and Ohlson 1995). However, the financial reporting of these profits under both accounting systems is limited by the standard setters and in some commentators' views this denies the market timely information and FV accounting is suggested to perform better than HC accounting. The assumed setting is chosen to allow the focus to be on the differences in information provision between the two systems.

Lack of agreement on an ideal accounting information system and limited practical applications of such systems renders impossible empirical comparisons between any proposed ideal accounting system and existing accounting regimes. However, simulations of the accounting results of a chosen "ideal" regime and those of other accounting systems are useful as different accounting systems have diverse strengths and weaknesses and exhibit dissimilar variances with the chosen ideal system.

The evaluation of the two systems uses a number of benchmarks. The first two reflect the economic measures of the value of the firm as obtained by discounting its future cash flows using the opportunity cost of capital and economic income measured as the change in that value over time (Hicks 1946, especially 171–181; see also the recent discussion on Hicksian income, Bromwich et al. 2010 and Clarke 2010). In the example, dividends are based on the economic incomes of the project in the example but these dividends are used only as a benchmark and not as an aid to decision making.

The RI generated in each period of the project is used as a further benchmark. Periodic RI is the accounting profit with the accounting system being used generated in a period less the opportunity cost of capital times the opening book value of net assets at the beginning of the period. The discounted sum of the project's RIs at the opening point of the project is consistent with the project's NPV at this time (Preinreich 1938; Peasnell 1982). The important characteristic of the RI of a period, which is variable across periods and accounting systems, is that it indicates the amount of abnormal earnings deemed realised in the period by the accounting regime in use.

It is not being suggested that these benchmarks generally form an 'ideal' accounting system. However, they do represent an 'ideal' for our example as they incorporate all the information required for investment decision making. More technically, they provide the *first best* accounting system (providing complete information to all) for our problem. The differences between the bench marks and the results of the two accounting systems indicate the limitations of these systems as generators of information (see Hitz 2007). Thus, a measurement approach to income and to valuation is being adopted.

In order to focus only on the strengths and weaknesses of the two accounting systems to be considered, a setting of certainty is assumed to allow the benchmarks to be easily determined.[1] Other assumptions will be introduced below. The objective is to see how far an investor constrained to use only the financial statements of the first period of the two-period example can predict the second period profit and the project's terminal value at the end of the second period. A further aim of this chapter is to urge the use of more complex simulation in comparing accounting systems, given that empirical comparisons of accounting systems are difficult (Leuz et al. 2003; Ball et al. 2000). Moreover, most of the focus of empirical work has been on the informational impact of the outputs of accounting systems on share prices (Barth and Clinch 1998).

Clearly, some of the conclusions generated by very simple models cannot necessarily be generalised (those relating to the utilisation of specific numerical figures and assumptions) but some can and sensitivity analysis is easily done. More complex simulations will need to be employed if this approach proves fruitful (see Choy 2006, for an early example).

Comparisons between the results of different accounting systems have been used infrequently in accounting. Recently, Nissim and Penman (2008) compared what they called the 'ideal' HC accounting system with the 'ideal' FV system but without recourse to numerical examples (see also Plantin et al. 2008). Here such systems will be labelled 'perfect' because they represent applications of the essential elements of the accounting system being used. Perfect HC measures all accounting items at HC based on transactions with the market place,[2] adopts the

---

[1] This simplifies the analysis by avoiding the use of utility functions and the determination of market equilibrium (See Wagenhofer and Ewart 2011). It is not suggested that such refinements are unnecessary for a complete analysis, only that assuming certainty allows sharp focus on the results of the two systems.

[2] Historical cost accounting records can only be based on market transactions because of the use of accruals.

traditional conventions of HC accounting, especially the matching of costs to revenues and maintains HC (monetary) capital. A perfect FV accounting system measures all accounting items including abnormal profits at their exit market prices, it 'marks to market' taking any gains and losses to income, maintains the FV capital of net assets and employs the FV assumptions entertained by standard setters.[3] A perfect accounting system uses only one measurement attribute, excludes mixed attribute accounting, and can therefore also be characterised as a "pure" accounting system. Bell and Johnson (1979) provides a comparative numerical example of a variety of accounting systems, as does the Sandilands Report (1975), a major report to the British government on current cost accounting (entry price accounting).[4] Some papers in Sterling and Thomas (1979) also take this approach and Sterling's introduction provides the justification for using a simplified example as employed here in the simulation. None employ a benchmark or economic comparator.

The accounting systems reviewed are:

1. A perfect historical cost (PHC) system and
2. A Fair Value system with incomplete (missing) markets (FVIM) but otherwise sharing the characteristics of the perfect FV accounting system.

Generally, gaps in the prescribed treatments of accounting items under most accounting systems allow by default the use of elements of current accounting practice as will be assumed in the example.

11.1.1 The Model

A simple of a freestanding, two-period project is used. The focus is on the utility of the accounting information contained in income statements and balance sheets for investment decision making and on accounting for non-financial assets.

As indicated above, the assumed setting is one of perfect knowledge so that only the differential performances of the two entertained accounting systems are being considered. The example is therefore purely representational as the accounting systems reviewed merely rearrange already known information. As an exception to perfect knowledge, the question is asked whether the income statements and balance sheets generated by the two accounting system at the end of the first period *on their own* aid predictions of the equity value of the project at the end of the second period and its second period income. Of course, in the assumed setting of certainty, such information is of no incremental value to investors—they

[3] Such markets are complete—all items are traded and perfect—prices are the same for all. Accounting entries are based on changes in market prices and on market transactions.

[4] Similar examples appear in the Richardson [(NZ) Report issued in 1977] and the similar government sponsored Canadian Report shortly after.

Table 11.1 Details of the example

	T_0	T_1	T_2
Revenues		1,500	1,500
Costs			
Material		100	100
Labour		250	250
Investments			
Conventional asset	1,000		
Development asset	600		

would not pay for it. However, the gaps between perfect information and the different signals given by the accounting systems as shown by variances with the benchmarks utilised helps understanding of the deficiencies of these systems for aiding investment decision making in uncertain and imperfect markets in so far as these variances persist or worsen. The only obvious priors in this exercise are the expectations of earning normal returns on assets.

The opening balance sheet uses the HC accounting system and the final balance sheet consists entirely of cash. Of course, the declared total project profit at the end of the project is identical for all accounting systems. It is the intermediate period's (period one) accounting results that are of interest, that is, which indicate the consequences of the ill-matching of accounting results with cash flows under the different systems. The assumptions of the model allow the foundations of each accounting system to be the focus instead of alleged controversial features of the different systems.

The details of the model used are given in Table 11.1.

T_0 is the beginning of period one when all investments are made financed by equity, T_1 is the end of period one/beginning of period two and T_2 is the end of period 2. Revenue is received in two equal instalments of 1,500 being payments for sales and deliveries in the period. The cash is used to pay operating expenses of 350 in each period producing cash flow retentions of 1,150 in each period prior to dividend payments. The project employs two assets: an operational asset and a development asset. The operational asset costing 1,000 is a specialised asset only used in the industry but trades freely on a well organised market. The development asset is unique to the project [it is a specialised asset in the FV terms of FAS157 (FASB 2008)]. The figure of 600 shown for the development asset represents the costs of the relevant assets which form its inputs. These assets are used widely and also trade on well organised markets. All abnormal earnings (excess profits over the cost of capital) accrue to development asset used in conjunction with the operational asset.[5] Thus, the

[5] Abnormal profits and their discounted sum, often called internal or subjective goodwill, can be generated by a large number of factors including positive net present value opportunities, synergy between activities, special skills and locational advantages, product differentiation and monopoly power (Edwards and Bell 1961, 36–37).

Table 11.2 Price changes with the operational asset

Prices in period 1	Two-period asset	One-period asset
Entry price	2,000	1,000
Exit price	1,500	750
Original price	1,000	500

development asset has an "in use value" in the FAS 157 FV nomenclature (FASB 2008).[6]

The project equity and all assets other than the self-constructed asset are priced by markets at time T_0. Straight line depreciation reflects the fall in market prices with use as seen at the beginning of the project or embeds price changes where appropriate. The assets have no value at the end of the project. The opportunity cost discount rate (r) is 10 % for both borrowing and lending. Any retained cash can be invested at this rate. Dividends equal to periodic economic income (interest on the opening present value (PV) of the project in each period, see below) are paid. However, dividends will be used only as a comparator and not as information used for forming expectations. This assumption is made to sterilise the information which might otherwise be conveyed by dividends. For simplicity, it is assumed only the operational asset is subject to price change during the life of the project which occurs just after time T_0. The prices of the operational asset are given in Table 11.2. These price changes occur because of demand changes for the asset in another sector of the industry. The general price level is assumed to be unchanged. The changed prices shown are those to be paid for an asset having a two-period life and for an asset with a one-period life remaining at the time of the price change just after the beginning of period one.

It is assumed that changes in the prices of this asset do not affect the project's cash flows (see Bromwich et al. 2011). Price increases therefore represent the realisation of expected abnormal earnings rather than increased cash flows (see later sections).

11.2 The Assumed "Ideal" Accounting System

It is generally accepted that the market value of a company on a well-organised securities market is the PV of its expected future dividends to a decision horizon or to infinity. This valuation applies to a separable quoted entity (in our case the stand-alone project) conditioned on the public information available at the time of valuation. In a perfect and complete market, all information is impounded into equity values as soon as known, in our case at the beginning of the project. Thus, we will use the market value of the project as the ideal valuation of the project for

[6] This term has been dropped in the latest FV statement from the standard setters, IASB 2011.

the example. Such valuations cannot generally used in financial reports as they have been proscribed by standard setters because they capitalise unrealised profits and are based on management estimates which standards setters have ruled cannot be used in financial reports other than where necessary to be utilised in the estimates for market values required to estimate FVs where markets are incomplete (FASB 2008).

The PVs of the project at the beginning of the project T_0, at the end of the end of the first period T_1 and at the end of the second period T_2, are the value of the cash flows in the period plus PVs of the future cash flows at these times using an opportunity discount rate of 10 %. The project NPV at time T_0 deducts the cost of investment from the PV of the project's net cash flows at this time. These figures (rounded where necessary) are given in Table 11.3.

The components of the PV calculations for T_0 are the cash flows of the two periods discounted to T_0 using a 10 % discount rate yielding a PV of 1996. (underlined in the Table). Those for T_1 are the cash flows at T_1 of 1,150 plus the discounted value the future cash flows (1,150) received at end of period two having a PV of 1,045.45 giving a value of 2,195. The value of the project at time T_2 is the net cash flows of the period, 1,150, plus the cash flows retained in period one plus interest at 10 % equalling, 1,265 (net cash flows in period one, 1,150 × 1.10 = 1,265) giving a total of 2,415. The increase of the PVs over the project's lifetime reflects the unwinding of the discount rate over time or unpaid dividends at 10 %.

The economic income for each period is calculated (again rounded where necessary) using the well-known No.1 concept of income suggested by Hicks (1946, especially 171–181). This states that income is the maximum that can be spent in each period whilst maintaining the opening economic value of the project, assuming no other transactions with shareholders. The *ex-ante* version of this concept can be used here, as no new information is revealed as the project proceeds. The economic income for the first period (EI_1) is calculated by determining the PV of the project at end of the period comprised of the net cash flows received in the period (1,150) plus the remaining cash flows to be received in period two discounted to the end of the first period (1,045.45) and deducting the value of the

Table 11.3 The periodic cash flows, the PVs of the project in each period and its NPV at T_0

	T_0	T_1	T_2
Revenues		1,500	1,500
Costs		350	350
Net cash flows		1,150	1,150
PV@10 % at T_0	1,996 =	1,150/1.10 +	1,150/1.21
PV@10 % at T_1		2,195 = 1,150 +	1,150/1.10
PV@10 % at T_2			2,415 = 1,150 + 1,265
NPV@10 % at T_1			
PV@10 % at T_0	1,996		
Less investment@ T_0	1,600		
NPV	396		

project at the beginning of the period (1,996). This gives period one's economic income as:

$$EI_1 = 1,150 + 1,045.45 - 1.996 = 199.6$$

The economic income of the project at the end of period two is the value of the net cash flow at end of the period (1,150) minus the value of these cash flows at the end of the previous period (1,045.45 plus the interest received in period two on the retained cash flows of the previous period after paying dividends in that period of 95 [10 % on 950 (1,150-199.6)]. Two-period economic income is:

$EI_2 = 1{,}150 - 1{,}045.45 + 95 = 199.6$ (see Bromwich 1992).

Again this income concept cannot be used in financial reports because it is based on unrealised profits and managerial estimates.

In a well-organised market in equilibrium the aggregate value of a company's individual separable assets (including abnormal profits) and liabilities when measured at their unique market prices will equal the company's equity market value (Revsine 1973; Beaver and Demski 1979). In this type of market with uncertainty all items earn their risk adjusted normal return (Holthausen and Watts 2001). Generally, accounting information is only useful where markets are not well organised and/or are in disequilibrium. Excess or abnormal profits arise both in non-equilibrium markets and in imperfect markets. Abnormal profits are generally recorded by conventional accounting systems only when realised and are not shown separately in the financial reports. Thus, as is generally understood, all practical accounting systems are "second best" from an 'investor perspective'—they neither generate the equity value of the firm nor yield all the information required for investment decisions.

Therefore, it is necessary to build or estimate a 'bridge' between the periodic net assets shown by the accounting systems and economic net worth as shown by the ideal system (Holthausen and Watts 2001).[7] Generally this bridge will be a subjective estimate of items not recognised by the accounting system: the discounted value of future abnormal profits, the value of assets and liabilities not otherwise recognised by the systems and changes in the market prices of assets and liabilities (Feltham and Ohlson 1995).

The reconciliation of income figures with the ideal system utilises the proposition mentioned earlier that the total of the discounted values of the periodic RIs of an entity equal the PV of the entity's abnormal profits at the time of the decision (the project's NPV) (Peasnell 1982). This finding applies to all accounting systems. A further general finding is that for all accounting systems the net assets of a project at the end of any period plus the discounted value of future RIs from the project at that time will equal economic worth (PV) of the project at that time.

[7] Generally, this relation will be equal to the equity value of the firm on the securities market where all markets are well organised and participants share common beliefs and objectives and have the same information and creative (neither aggressive nor conservative) accounting is not being practiced. This is the general case in our example.

The relation between the NPV and the PV of a project's RI does not apply to the individual RI of a period and the RIs under different accounting systems will differ. These differences in the accrual of abnormal profits under the various accounting and benchmark systems allow comparisons between the information provided by the various accounting systems. Periodic RI serves as a measure of how well the realised abnormal profits reported in accounting income in each period capture the total abnormal profits to be realised from the project. Realised abnormal profits can be compared with the total abnormal profits for the project implied by deducting accounting net worth from the value of equity.[8]

The above discussion indicates that setting up useful examples and simulations that portray accounting problems and are economically meaningful needs considerable crafting and the careful choice of benchmarks. Even in this simple example the adjustments required for these reconciliations are quite complex. This is especially the case where regulators are seeking to model regulated firms in a way that aids regulatory decision making.

We now look at the two accounting systems being considered.

11.3 Perfect Historical Cost

Tables 11.4 and 11.5 show the income amounts and the net assets generated using PHC, respectively. Recall that the ascription 'perfect' refers here not to the achievement of accounting objectives but rather to the full and exclusive application to the example of the HC accounting system and its conventions. Accounting for transactions measured at transaction prices is the objective as it reflects the empirics of the market. All accruals are ultimately based on original transactions but are not themselves necessarily based on empirical evidence from the market. Internal goodwill, the value of abnormal profits, is not capitalised. Prudence (sometimes described as conservatism) is central to traditional HC accounting. Thus, for example, traditionally, losses were actioned when known but gains were delayed until deemed 'realised'.

Sales revenue in the first period is 1,500 and the total costs for the period are 1,150 giving an operating profit of 350. This figure can be compared with the economic income for the period of 199.6 being interest at 10 % on the market value of the project of 1,996 at the project's initiation. Economic income includes interest on the project's NPV. The periodic economic income is here also assumed to be the amount paid out as dividends in the period which are deducted from profits to give retained profits.

[8] See Bromwich et al. (2011). Thus, periodic residual incomes can be seen as measuring the distortions generated by the accounting system being utilised relative to the outcomes of the economic income approach.

Table 11.4 Profits, RIs and net asset values with PHC

	T_1	T_2
Revenues		
Sales revenue	1,500	1,500
Interest on net cash at T_1		95
		1,595
Costs		
Material	100	100
Labour	250	250
Depreciation		
Operational asset	500	500
Development asset	300	300
Total costs	−1,150	−1,150
Profit	350	445
Less dividends	199.6	199.6
Retained profits	150.4	245.4
Reconciliation		
Profit	350	445
Interest on assets	−160	−175
RI	190	270
PV of RI	173	+223
		= 396

Table 11.5 Net assets under the PHC

Net assets	T_0	T_1	T_2	
Operational asset	1,000	500		
Development asset	600	300		
Cash		950	1,996	[950 + 951 + 95[a] (interest on retentions)]
Net assets	1.600	1,750	1,996	
Reconciliation				
Abnormal profits	396 (NPV)	246		
Total: stock market value	1,996	1,996	1,996	

[a] Rounded: periods one and two cash 1,150−199.6 = 950.4, Interest on period one's retained earnings 95.04.

Comparing dividends figures with the HC profits in each period indicates the distortion to income caused by not using the benchmark system. The economic income in period one is 199.6; deducting this from the HC profit of 350 in period one gives a variance of +150.4 for this period. Similarly, the variance between economic income and HC profit in period two is +245.4. These variances total to the project's NPV of 396. Thus, these variances quantify the distortion in the provision of information by the HC accounting system.

HC accounting provides all the information concerning the project's income but declares it with a lag over the two-time periods.

The rows below retained profits are not part of financial statements but are benchmarks allowing the reconciliation of accounting profits with the benchmark ideal system described above. The reconciliation section calculates the project's RI in the two periods. The RI in a period is declared accounting profits, less interest or the normal returns on the opening period book value of net assets for the period. The aggregate of the discounted value of the project's RIs reconcile HC profits with the project's NPV at the time of decision. The RI for the first period is profit of 350 less the normal return of 10 % on value of opening net assets of 1,600 (see Table 11.4), an interest charge of 160, which gives a RI for the period of +190. Similarly, the second period RI of +270 is given by deducting from the net profit of 445 the normal return on opening net assets of 175 (on net assets of 1,750, see Table 11.4). The PVs at T_0 of RIs in the first and second periods are 136 and 270, respectively and the last row of Table 11.3 shows that they sum to the project's NPV of 396 at time T_0. Again the total profits declared under HC accounting system do convey all the income information available, though not in the most timely manner.[9] The different individual periodic RIs reflect the periodic distortions caused by using the HC accounting system relative to our benchmark system.[10]

The first period's RI is positive indicating that HC accounting earns a normal return and captures some the abnormal profits from the project. This RI can be compared with the total abnormal profits for the project implied by deducting accounting net worth from the value of equity giving an indication under uncertainty of the risk involved in the project as measured by the abnormal profits not yet obtained and of whether the firm is on track to achieve the abnormal profits implied by the project's equity value. More generally, these RIs help validate the project's market value and aiding in estimating the abnormal profits contained therein. It is impossible to predict future RI without assumptions of its persistence (see Nissim and Penman 2008; Penman 2011 for arguments for using estimates of permanent income in estimating income persistence). The project's HC income statements of themselves do not help formulate such assumptions. Rather such assumptions need to be based on the history of past accounting results.

It would, however, be reasonable for the investor using only the financial statements for investment decision making to assume that the project will at least continue to earn a normal return. This seems all the information contained in the HC income statement for period one unless some type of persistence of the results

---

[9] This is, of course, true of all other accounting for 'cash for cash' projects but we are exploring the different timing of the release of this information by the accounting systems examined.

Total profit—accumulated interest on opening value of assets in each period equals $NPV_0 = (795-199.6-199.6) = 396$.

[10] The declared RI figures are more complex than it might seem. The RI figures for periods 1 and 2 of 190 and 270 respectively, each comprise of two elements. An interest amount equal to the undercharging of interest by the HC accounting system relative to economic income caused by interest on the project's NPV of 39.6 not being charged in the RI calculations in period one; (199.6-160) and 24.5 in period 2 (199.5-175). The second element is the RI net of this interest. Theses RIs net of interest add to the project's NPV (150.4 + 245.4 = 396).

can be assumed. The aid that can be provided by HC income statements in estimating cash flows, their timing and uncertainty as required by standard setters (FASB 1978, SFAC No. 1) is limited especially as accruals which play a substantial part in determining the amounts of declared RI are significantly a matter of managerial discretion. Similarly, regulators seeking to forecast future earnings will obtain little help from HC income statements without making assumptions and using additional information.

Perhaps, surprisingly to the critics of HC, some more timely information is provided by the balance sheet (net assets) at the end of the first period.

11.3.1 The Balance Sheet

The net assets statement (balance sheet) shows the assets recognised by the accounting system and measured at HC, net of depreciation. The net assets at time T_0 and at the end of the two periods are measured at their HCs. The cash at the end of period two is the retained earnings of that period. The assets at the end of period one are in cash made up of the retained cash in both periods plus interest earned on period's 1 retained cash in period two.

The adjustments shown below net assets in Table 11.5 are necessary to reconcile the book value generated by conventional accounting systems for any period with the net worth (market value) of equity generated by our ideal system. They represent 'bridges' necessary to reconcile periodic accounting net assets and the project's market value.[11] With uncertainty the necessary bridge for any period gives an indication of the future risk inherent in judgements regarding a project. This allows investors to use their individual judgements and private information to assess whether these estimates seem reasonable. The relative size of the bridges for different accounting systems are one indicator of how helpful the different accounting systems are to those seeking to make predictions.

To reconcile the net assets at time T_0 of 1,600 with project market value at that time a bridge of equal to the full NPV of the project of 396 is needed as no abnormal profits have yet been realised. Net assets at time T_1 are 1,750 and a bridge of only 246 is required as abnormal profits of 150 (net assets at end of the

[11] In the case of our example, the only adjustment required to net asset values is for omitted abnormal profits as the change in the price of the operational asset is assumed not to affect cash flows. We do not wish to correct for the distortion caused by the use of accrual accounting as this is what we wish to appraise.

The "bridge" required between equity and accounting values may be negative where net asset book value exceeds equity value where companies have not taken the abandonment option. Asset impairments represent one way of reducing the size of a negative bridge.

In the practical world with uncertainty, the existence of bridges may serve to remind investors that equity market prices are estimates and depend for their validity upon the efficiency of the stock market. These estimates could be checked against the investor's private information set, especially where bubbles are likely.

period 1,750—net assets at beginning of the period of 1,600) have appeared during the first period.[12] The necessary bridge at the end of the first period of 246 equals the PV at the end of period one of the abnormal profits accruing in the second period (270/1.1). At the end of the second period no bridge is needed as all abnormal profits have been realised.

Balance sheets do have some information value, as under the traditional HC accounting, managers are seen as committing themselves to achieving, at least, these declared asset values (Edey 1970, 1974). In the example, the value of net assets at T_1 indicates that given our assumptions and the going concern assumption, the project will be valued at the end of the second period at, at least, 1,725 (1,750 plus the normal returns on the assets at T_2, of 175−199.6 dividends at T_3) relative the market value at that time of 1,996. The investor without knowledge of the second period does not obtain information about future abnormal profits using HC accounting balance sheet information or, indeed, any HC information on its own. Only future normal returns can be estimated from accounting information.

Overall, HC balance sheets (contrary to what many commentators say) may provide some information useful to investors by valuing accruals (Mosso 2009). Of course, where price changes affect assets, this information effect will be attenuated over time. For regulators the message is that when using financial statements to help in make predictions, it is necessary to supplement accounting information with relevant economic information.

We now consider the results for our example of using the FV accounting system in a setting of incomplete (missing) markets.

11.4 Fair Value with Incomplete (Missing) Markets

The first innovation of PFV accounting relative to HC accounting systems is that all measurement is based on the current exit market prices of inputs and all assets and liabilities are 'marked to market' with gains and losses being part of profit. This implies fully liquid markets. Here there is a missing market for the development asset. The lack of a market for this asset is assumed to become known immediately after T_0. Following PFV accounting this asset therefore has no FV and therefore no value in the FV accounting system. The costs of the development asset are therefore written off in the first period FV income statement as the PFV system does not recognise assets and liabilities without markets. The standards setters' requirement to use estimates for FV values in these circumstances will be considered later.

[12] The difference between the RI of the first period of 190 and the abnormal profits impounded in that period's net assets of 150 arises as residual income calculations do not incorporate the interest on abnormal profits which are included in dividends.

The second innovation with FV accounting generally is that gains and losses on held assets and liabilities are recognised immediately they are known. Price alterations are therefore reflected in profits, both in terms of gains and losses and in adjusting depreciation and the carrying values of assets and liabilities in the balance sheet. The third innovation is that such gains and losses are taken to income. This implies that the entity gains (losses) from holding assets that have risen (fallen) in price since purchase and gains (losses) from the prices of its liabilities falling (rising). We, in contrast, are assuming that assets gains and losses do not affect the project's future cash flows. Asset price alterations provide only signals about realised abnormal profits and expected abnormal profits from the project.[13]

11.4.1 The Income Statement

This shows the HC profits in both periods at the top of Table 11.6 and by adding/subtracting (shown in brackets) the variances between HC income and FV income determines the FV profits for the periods in columns 2 and 3. Utilising this variance based approach illuminates the differences in the accountings for the two systems. The first variance in both periods adds additional depreciation of 250 to the HC depreciation charge for the operational asset in each period to reflect in periodic costs the price change of 500 for the operational asset. This increases depreciation by 250 in each period (total FV depreciation 1,500).

The second variance applies only to period one. This comprises of an extra 300 write off in addition to the HC depreciation of 300 for the development asset thereby reducing the value of this asset to zero in the FV financial statements of period one as it has no market price. Deducting these variances for period one from HC profit yields the FVIM operational loss of 200 due to the larger write off of the development asset. This figure provides poor signals to the investor by suggesting that the project is not worthwhile and FVIM profit would seem to have less utility than the HC profit. It is for this reason that standard setters require FV estimates for items where markets for which are missing or non-active. If such estimates are correct in the sense of being consistent with the benchmark model and applied to all missing markets, this would yield accurate forecasts of future profits and of equity but requires very strong assumptions.

The gain made from holding the operational asset in the first period (500) is also recognised in the income statement below operational profits yielding FVIM profits of 300. Deducting dividends (199.6) from this profit gives retained earnings of 100.4 With the above figures, the first period RI for the FVIM system is 140 (300—10 % on the opening net asset value of 1,600). In the example and in

[13] Decreased asset prices of this type indicate that the bridge to equate net asset carrying value and equity worth needs to be increased assuming that these changes do not indicate diminished cash flows.

general, this gain serves to disguise the omission of the value of any non-recognised asset. This netting off of the two FV effects means that the FV RI yields less information than the HC accounting system. Without the knowledge of the values of the non-marketable assets at the end of the first period, it is impossible to interpret this RI, though a comparison of the FV of net assets with the stock market value of the project would suggest that the market expects substantial abnormal profits having a PV of 269 at T_1 to accrue in the future.

The standard setters' solution to the problem of missing markets is to require the use of estimates of what FVs would be if markets were not missing. They do not seek to justify this use of estimates as for them all FVs are estimates, differing only in the quality of the information used. The definition of FV requires estimation to determine any FV measurement as this definition of FV is: 'The price that would be received to sell an asset or paid to transfer a liability in an orderly transaction between market participants at the measurement date' IFRS 13, Appendix A, IASB 2011). Why managers should be skilled in making such estimates is not clear nor is why they would avoid the possible temptations to manage earnings via the choice of estimates?[14] The utility of estimates is an empirical matter, though to make economic sense they have to consistent with our benchmark model. Many commentators think that some allowed estimation methods are likely to be too subjective for use in financial reports.

The seductive properties of estimates can be illustrated by estimating the value of the development asset at its HC amount. This changes the first period FVIM financial statements increasing the first period profit to 600 from 300 originally, the RI to 440 from 140 and net asset value to 2,000 instead of 1,700. These changes are reversed in the second period, profit decreases to 195 from 495 and RI becomes −5 instead of 325. Thus, the whole of the abnormal profits appear in the first period because the effect of the gain on the operation can now come through in full. This result appears because the benchmark measures the development asset at only its HC carrying value. In fact, the first period RI on its own overstates the project's abnormal returns. The temptation to over-estimate the FV of assets with no market prices is obvious. Different results would appear with any other estimates with different bases. With a long lived project with asset replacement, HC estimates will measure FV with a lag, which may be substantial for assets with long lives.

The only adjustment to HC profits to obtain FVIM profit required in the second period reflects the increase in the depreciation on the operational asset under the FV accounting system. This updating of depreciation and the value of the associated assets for price changes is generally thought to be an advantage of using FV accounting relative to HC accounting. Here, depreciation has economic meaning

---

[14] It is unlikely in the contemporary environment that the gain accruing from the price increase in the operational asset will be taken to profit as it is with PFV accounting, rather it will be treated as an element of comprehensive income, that is, as capital reserves. This does not affect the value of information provided by capital gains providing that these gains are regarded as of equal quality to gains flowing from marking to market.

being based on the market prices of assets. Adjusting for the increase in depreciation yields a FVIM profit of 495 in the second period and deducting dividends yields retained profits of 295.4. The RI for the second period is 325 after deducting interest on opening FVIM assets of 1,700 (see column 5 of Table 11.5). Again, this is difficult to interpret without knowledge of the value of non-priced asset.

The variances between periodic FV profits and periodic economic income is approximately 100 in period one (300−199.6) and 296 in period two (495−199.6). These variances indicate the realised abnormal profits in the two periods relative to the benchmark model.

As indicated above, a reconciliation with the ideal system and with any forecast of the stock price generally requires a bridge between FV net assets and the project's market value reflecting future abnormal profits. Even minor market failures therefore impair prediction. Thus, at least in the context of the example, FV accounting based only on market prices (without the addition of estimated prices) in the presence of non-marketable items performs poorly in terms of aiding investors but recall that PHC also performs poorly.

The T_1 balance sheet in column 5 commences with HC net assets of 1,750 and the FVIM net assets are then derived. The first variance adds to HC net assets the portion of the gain on the operational asset carried forward to the second period of 250. The second reverses the HC value of the development asset carried forward into the second period of 300 in the HC balance sheet as the total value of this asset is written off in period one under the PFV accounting regime. These adjustments yield FVIM net assets of 1,700. The reconciliation of this with the market value of the project requires the adding to FVIM net assets the PV at time T_1 of the abnormal profit not yet realised in operations. The expected abnormal profits of 325 at T_3, as measured by the RI for period two, have a PV of 296 at the end of period one.[15] Generally, the net assets under FVIM will differ from those reported by HC accounting and therefore the future normal return that can be expected on FV net assets will differ from that determined using HC accounting.

11.5 Comparison of HC and FVIM Accountings and Brief Conclusions

Finally, we will briefly compare the results of the two accounting systems. Table 11.7 shows summary information for HC and FVIM profits, RIs for periods 1 and 2, net asset values at the end of periods 1 and 2 and future abnormal profits at the end of period one.

[15] This is found by deducting from the project's PV of 396 the net gain from the operational asset of 250 (500-250 extra depreciation in period one) which gives the value of the bridge required to give the PV of the project at time T_1 of 1,996.

Table 11.6 Fair value with imperfect markets (FVIM)

Profits and RIs	T_1	T_2	Net assets	T_1
HC profit	350	445	HC net assets	1,750
Variances with HC accounting			Variances with HC accounting	
Less (loss) additional depreciation			Additional value of operational	250
Operational asset	(250)	(250)	Asset (realised gain)	
Less additional write off on development asset (impairment)	(300)	–	Additional write down of development asset	(300)
			FVIM Net assets	1,700
FVIM operational profit (loss)	(200)	495	Reconciliation	
Gain on operational asset	500		PV of unrealised abnormal profits at end of period 1	296
FVIM profit/(loss)	300			
Dividends	(199.6)	(199.6)		
Retained profits	100.4	295.4		
Reconciliation			Total = stock	1,996
FVIM Profit	300	495	Market value	
Less interest on opening assets	(160)	(170)		
RI	140	325		
PV of RI	127+	269 = 396		

Table 11.7 Comparison of HC and FVIM accounting: profits, RIs, net asset values and future abnormal profits

	HC		FVIM	
	Period 1	Period 2	Period 1	Period 2
Profits	350	445	300	495
RI	190	270	140	325
RI less interest on abnormal profits	150	246	100	296
Net asset value	1,750	1,996	1,700	1,996
Future abnormal profits	246	–	296	–

Looking first at income, the first period results of both accounting systems yield imperfect information for investment decision making. This provides an example of the general conclusion in the literature that no practical accounting system can perfectly measure the economic income of organisations, or their economic wealth because of, among other things, not reporting future abnormal returns (Benson et al. 2006). The first period HC income figure cannot be used to predict exactly the second period results without an ability to make completely accurate assumptions about income persistence. This is a strong requirement. HC income statements do report a profit for the period but without any indication whether such results are likely to persist. More helpfully, the periodic RI gives an indication of abnormal profits realised during the period which can be compared with those implicit in the project's market price. RI net of interest indicates that the usual RI calculations over-state realised abnormal profits.

Similarly, the FV accounting system will only fully predict future income and wealth when all assets are priced by the market including the price of expected abnormal profits—again, a strong requirement. FV accounting does have advantages over HC accounting. First, that asset price changes give an earlier indication of abnormal profits or reductions in them than the HC accounting system. Thus, the gains obtained generated by the price change for the operational asset of 500 are recognised in the FV financial statements for the first period whereas the HC accounting recognises only the abnormal profits generated by trading in period one of 190 (HC profit 350-interest on opening assets 160). Both of the accounting systems recognise this element of realised abnormal profits. Second, these price change effects are traced through to costs give more up to date cost figures.

However, both the elements of declared abnormal profits (those from trading and from price gains) in FVIM financial statements are camouflaged by our strict application of PFV which means that the development asset has to be written off in period one.[16] The non-recognition of the development asset and the complete write off of this asset in the FV financial statements adds to the difficulty of interpreting the figures provided by the FV financial statements and can swamp the other effects of using FV when there are missing markets. As an illustration of these effects, focus on only the lack of recognition of the development asset by ignoring the price rise in the operational asset. This amounts to returning to the HC financial statements but without the development asset. The non-recognition of this asset in the example would reduce HC profits in period one to 50, the HC RI to a loss of 110 and net assets to 1,450. Thus, the effect of the non-valuation of assets with missing markets where material could be seen as a fatal flaw in the system, unless estimates of items in missing markets are available under FV accounting. Moreover, it is usually argued that it is the balance sheet with the FV accounting system that provides all necessary information for valuation. In the example the off-setting effects of the gain on one asset and the writing off of the other mean that the FVIM balance sheet is less informative than the HC Balance sheet.

In the example, the offsetting effects of the gain on the operational asset and the omission of the other asset means that the HC accounting system dominates in information provision in period. HC profits and RI are larger than their FV comparators and the size of the required bridge for HC net assets is smaller than that for the FVIM net assets. The use of estimates is essential to avoid these problems but introduces additional subjectivity into financial reports.

As illustrated above, different assumed figures may change the possible conclusions. However, this article has identified general tendencies that affect the choice of accounting systems for decision making irrespective of the actual figures utilised.

---

[16] Period one's FV RI can be written as: HC abnormal profits realised in trading plus the gain on the operational asset unrecognised by HC accounting less the additional depreciation relative to HC depreciation on the operational asset less the additional write off above HC accounting on the development asset. This gives $190 + 250 - 300 = 140$, the FV RI.

Whether regulators seeking to use FV financial information would be willing to allow the use the estimates necessary to restore missing markets, especially give the permitted subjectivity of some of the allowed methods of estimation is not clear. Indeed, whether regulators would wish to use FV accounting systems has not yet arisen as a question. Here, matters of principle arise that can be dealt with only briefly here. Many regulators use long run incremental cost to measure costs and measure assets at their current cost (replacement cost). This amounts to using an entry price system for measuring assets rather than exit prices with the FV accounting system. The former system has a clear theoretical base for regulators. It broadly represents the entry cost of a new equally efficient entrant or of an alternative supplier. The corresponding theoretical base with FV accounting represents either the lowest takeover cost of an incumbent excluding future abnormal returns because FV asset measurements do not include expected abnormal returns or the lowest estimate of the opportunity cost of an incumbent staying in business again excluding future abnormal returns. Information of utility to regulators but, which is, perhaps, not central to their tasks.

Moreover, it is not clear why regulators would wish to impose on regulated organisations a financial capital maintenance base that maintains the exit values of their assets. Generally, most regulators would use, at least, in the first instance, a physical capital maintenance base. Regulated organisations are expected to maintain their physical assets using a given (assumed) technology. This implies using an entry price accounting system.

Finally, we compare the requirements of our ideal or benchmark accounting system with the results of the above two systems. Our ideal system indicates that a complete assessment of future net cash flows requires either full information concerning project abnormal profits and normal returns at the end of period one of the example or the ability to calculate them from information then available. Standard setters who wish to aid investors in fully estimating the amounts, timing and risk of possible future cash flows must consider incorporating information concerning expected abnormal profits into financial reports or into supplementary reports subject to avoiding possibilities for managerial manipulation (IASB 2009, OB 3). It is these profits that drive economic growth. One possible partial approach would be to require that financial reports present the RI of the period. Another would be to show realized abnormal profits as a separate income item. Without incorporating expected abnormal profits, it would seem difficult for the FASB and the IASB to sustain their sole objective for financial reports of aiding decision making as anything other than second best. The declaration of abnormal profits is also of concern to regulators.

To conclude, the two accounting systems that are likely to be used in the practical world for non-financial assets—HC and FV with subjective estimated prices—have major deficiencies for helping investment decision making. Any extension of the application of FV accounting to non-financial assets at the current stage of its development would require consideration of the problems raised here and other concerns that have also been raised.

References

Ball, R., Kothari, S., & Robin, A. (2000). The effect of international institutional factors on the properties of accounting earnings. *Journal of Accounting and Economics, 29*, 1–52.

Barth, M. E., & Clinch, G. (1998). Revalued financial, tangible, and intangible assets: Associations with share prices and non-market-based value estimates. *Journal of Accounting Research, 36*, 199–233. (Studies on Enhancing the Financial Reporting Model).

Beaver, W. T., & Demski, J. (1979). The nature of income measurement. *The Accounting Review, 54*(1), 38–46.

Bell, P. W., & Johnson, L. T. (1979). Current value accounting and the simple production case: Edbejo and other companies in the taxi business. In R. R. Sterling & A. L. Thomas (Eds.), *Accounting for a simplified firm owning depreciable assets* (pp. 95–130). Houston: Scholars Book Co.

Benston, G. J., Bromwich, M., Litan, R. E., & Wagenhofer, A. (2006). *Worldwide financial reporting: The development and future of accounting standards*. New York: Oxford University Press.

Bromwich, M. (1992). *Financial reporting, information and capital markets*. London: Pitmans.

Bromwich, M., Macve, R., & Sunder, S. (2010). Hicksian income in the conceptual framework. *Abacus, 46*(3), 348–376.

Bromwich, M., Clarke, F., & Dean, G. (2011). Fair value accounting: A comparative example of different accounting systems. *Working paper*, London School of Economics and Political Science.

Choy, A. K. (2006). Fair value as a relevant metric: A theoretical investigation. *Working paper*, University of Alberta .H

Clarke, F. L. (2010). 'Alas poor hicks', indeed! sixty years of use and abuse—commentary on Bromwich et al. *Abacus, 46*(3), 377–386.

Edey, H. C. (1970). The nature of profit, *Accounting Business Research*, No. 1 (Winter), pp. 50–55, reprinted in Edey, H. C. (1982). *Accounting queries*, New York: Garland.

Edey, H. C. (1974). Deprival value and financial accounting. In H. Edey & B. S. Yamey (Eds.), *Debits, credits, finance and profits*. Sweet and Maxwell: London.

Edwards, E. O., & Bell, P. W. (1961). *The theory and measurement of business income*. Berkeley and Los Angeles: University of California Press.

Ewert, R., & Wagenhofer, A. (2011). *Earnings quality metrics and what they measure* (August 16). Available at SSRN http://ssrn.com/abstract=1697042 or http://dx.doi.org/10.2139/ssrn.1697042

FASB. (1978). *Objectives of financial reporting by business enterprises*. Statement of financial concepts No. 1, Norwalk: Financial Accounting Standards Board (superseded).

FASB. (2008). *Statement of financial accounting standards 157, 'Fair Value Measurements'*. Norwalk: Financial Accounting Standards Board.

Feltham, G. A., & Ohlson, J. A. (1995). Valuation and clean surplus accounting for operating and financial activities. *Contemporary Accounting Research, 11*(2), 689–731.

Hicks, J. R. (1946). *Value and capital*. Oxford: Clarendon Press.

Hitz, J.-M. (2007). The decision usefulness of fair value accounting- a theoretical perspective. *European Accounting Review, 16*(2), 323–362.

Holthausen, R. W., & Watts, R. L. (2001). The relevance of the value relevance literature for financial accounting standard setting. *Journal of Accounting and Economics, 31*, 3–75.

IASB. (2009). *Fair value measurement*. London: International Accounting Standards Board. (Exposure Draft).

IASB. (2010). *Conceptual framework for financial reporting 2010*. London: International Accounting Standards Board.

IASB. (2011). *IFRS 13, fair value measurement*. London: International Accounting Standards Board.

Leuz, C., Nanda, D., & Wysocki, P. (2003). Earnings management and investor protection: an international comparison. *Journal of Financial Economics, 69*(3), 505–527.
Mosso, D. (2009). *Early warning and quick response: Accounting in the twenty-first century*. Emerald: Bingley.
Nissim, D., & Penman, S. (2008). *Principles for application of fair value accounting*. Centre for Excellence in Accounting and Security Analysis (CEASA), Columbia Business School.
Peasnell, K. V. (1982). Some formal connections between economic values and yields and accounting numbers. *Journal of Business Finance and Accounting, 9*(3), 361–381.
Penman, S. H. (2011). *Accounting for value*. New York: Columbia Business School Publishing.
Peterson, R. (1977). *Waikato inflation accounting project*. Hamilton: University of Waikato. (administrator).
Plantin, G., Sapra, H., & Shin, H. (2008). Marking to market: Panacea or Pandora's box? *Journal of Accounting Research, 46*, 435–460.
Preinreich, G. (1938). Annual survey of economic theory: The Theory of Depreciation. *Econometrica 6*, 219–241.
Revsine, L. (1973). *Replacement cost accounting*. Inglewood Cliffs, NJ: Prentice Hall.
Ronen, J. (2008). *To fair value or not to fair value: A broader perspective* (pp. 181–208). June: Abacus. *44*(2), 181–208.
Sandilands Committee. (1975). *Inflation accounting: report of the inflation accounting committee under the chairmanship of F.E.P. Sandilands*, Cmnd, 6225, HMSO.
Sterling, R. R., & Thomas, A. L. (Eds.). (1979). *Accounting for a simplified firm owning depreciable assets*. Houston: Scholars Book Co.
Whittington, G. (2008). Fair value and the IASB/FASB conceptual framework project: An alternative view. *Abacus, 44*(2), 139–168.

Chapter 12
IASB ED Management Commentary Versus European Regulation: The Impact on Management's Reports of Companies Listed on Italian Stock Exchange

Daniela Argento and Roberto Di Pietra

Abstract This chapter aims to investigate how regulatory change affects corporate disclosure. The explanations are based on institutional theory which provides an understanding of how organizations may react to a change in the regulatory framework. By conducting a content analysis, the chapter focuses on the information disclosed in the Management's Reports prepared by the major Italian listed companies after the enactment of the 2007 law. This law extended companies' disclosure obligations since management has to disclose information pertaining to risks and uncertainties, performance indicators, environment, and personnel. The new requirements not only lead to an increase in the information to be disclosed, but also to a change in the nature of the disclosed information. In addition to the more traditional financial information, also social, environmental, and strategic information should be provided. The main results of the content analysis allow to formulate some tentative reflections on companies' receptivity to the 2007 regulatory change.

This chapter includes an edited version of the paper titled "IASB ED Management Commentary versus European Regulation: The Impact on Management's Reports of Companies Listed on Italian Stock Exchange" and discussed at the Fifth International Workshop on Accounting and Regu lation in 2010. Although this chapter is the result of shared research, Daniela Argento's contribution is 60% and Roberto Di Pietra 's contribution is 40 %. This paper was also presented at the 7th Workshop on European Financial Reporting, University of Bamberg (Germany, 8–9 September 2011), and the 34th EAA Annual Congress, Rome, 20–22 April 2011.

D. Argento (✉)
Centre for Business Studies, Kristianstad University, Kristianstad, Sweden
e-mail: daniela.argento@hkr.se

R. Di Pietra
Department of Business and Law, University of Siena, Siena, Italy
e-mail: dipietra@unisi.it

R. Di Pietra et al. (eds.), *Accounting and Regulation*,
DOI: 10.1007/978-1-4614-8097-6_12,

12.1 Introduction

Corporate disclosure is debated in professional and academic arenas as the right of stakeholders to be informed has highlighted the limitations of traditional financial information provided by annual reports (Beattie 2000). Management should disclose additional information which enables the users of annual reports to better understand and interpret companies' performance (Beattie et al. 2004). Consequently, the supplementing information published in the Management's Report—also called Management's Discussion and Analysis (MD&A) or Operating and Financial Review (OFR)—plays an important role in the overall disclosure package (Clarkson et al. 1999). This report should present management's view on a company's situation with three perspectives: present, past, and future developments. Therefore, the information provided is important as it is the result of managers' willingness (or obligation) to disclose information, which may be sensitive to the company itself and to the users.

This chapter is aimed at contributing to the aforementioned topics by studying the impact of the 2007 regulatory change on Management's Reports compiled by the major companies listed on the Italian Stock Exchange (Borsa Italiana SpA). The explanations are based on institutional theory which provides an understanding of how organizations may react to a change in the regulatory framework.

The research is relevant for two reasons. First of all, the Italian and EU legislators intervened on several occasions to determine the contents of the Management's Report. Thus, it is interesting to investigate the change introduced by the 2007 Italian law that, by adopting the European Directive 51/2003/CE, has expanded the contents to be included in Management's Reports. For instance, managers are now explicitly required to disclose information on company's risks, financial and non-financial performance indicators, and environmental and personnel information (Sottoriva 2007). Second, interest in Management's Report was also demonstrated by the International Accounting Standards Board (IASB), the international standards setter that in June 2009 published the Exposure Draft (ED) Management Commentary ED/2009/6 (IASB 2009). This ED is not a binding international accounting standard, but includes a general framework that can be used by managers as guidance for the preparation and presentation of decision-useful Management's Reports.

In trying to better understand the "disclosure pressures" perceived by companies, the chapter presents a comparison between the contents of the Management's Report required by the Italian regulatory framework, as changed in 2007, and those included in the IASB's ED, identifying similarities and differences.

The chapter also presents the first results of an empirical research on the disclosures of the major companies listed on the Italian Stock Exchange whose stocks are included in the FTSE MIB 40 Index. The empirical research is conducted through a content analysis of the 2008 Management's Reports because it is the first financial year in which the new requirements had to be implemented. The content analysis is aimed at assessing the general level of completeness of the selected

Management's Reports and understanding whether, and how, management disclosed information in compliance with the new requirements. All in all, the research results allow for formulating some tentative reflections on the impact of the 2007 regulatory change on Management's Reports and if managers have been receptive to it.

The remainder of this chapter is structured as follows. First, the theoretical background of the study is presented (Sect. 12.2). Then, a comparison between the contents of the Management's Report required by Italian regulatory framework, as modified in 2007, and those included in the IASB's ED is provided (Sect. 12.3). Thereafter, the research methodology followed for conducting the empirical research is explained (Sect. 12.4) and the main findings of the content analysis are depicted (Sect. 12.5). The final section discusses the main results of this study and highlights the limitations and future developments of this chapter (Sect. 12.6).

12.2 Theoretical Background

The relevance and role of accounting and corporate disclosure are widely debated in the academic and professional literature. Through the compiling and publication of annual reports, the company should be able to disclose the information that meets all stakeholders' information needs (Catturi 1997; Di Pietra 2005; Leuz et al. 2004; Burchell et al. 1980; Hopwood 1983; Roberts and Scapens 1985). In this sense, traditional financial information should be complemented and supplemented with the additional disclosures included in the Management's Report (Clarkson et al. 1999).

Because of the informative power of corporate disclosures, reporting activities need to be governed by rules. Accounting rules are necessary to avoid market failures provoked by the publication of false and misleading information, to guarantee the credibility of annual reports and to facilitate comparability of information disclosed by different companies (Flower 1999). Accounting rules are created and change over time in order to consider the evolution of the outer and inner contexts of a company (March et al. 2003). The outer context refers to the social, economic, political, and competitive environment in which a company operates, while the inner context refers to the structure, corporate culture, and political context within the company (Pettigrew 1987).

The internationalization of economic activities and the integration of capital markets have impacted on companies' reporting activities. On the one hand, companies need to prepare reliable and comparable annual reports, not only within a given country but also in the international sphere. On the other hand, companies also need to meet the expectations of different categories of stakeholders by disclosing both financial and non-financial information (Di Pietra 2002; Flower and Lefebvre 1997; Flower and Ebbers 2002; McLeay 1999; McLeay and Riccaboni 2000; West 2003). The "globalized" social-economic context has limited the effects of national regulation, strengthening and legitimizing the role of international accounting standards. Consequently, when compiling its annual report, each company can not only comply with national accounting rules, but has to take into account also the international accounting standards.

The topic of changes in corporate disclosure is especially relevant in the European context. Over the years, the European Commission has issued Directives and Regulations aimed at stimulating an accounting harmonization process. With Regulation n. 1606 of 2002, the European Commission recognized the IASB as the reference standard setter, obliging the companies listed within the European Union markets to apply the IAS/IFRS for the preparation of their consolidated annual reports (Camfferman and Zeff 2007; Tamm Hallström 2004).

In essence, European companies have to comply with national and European Union accounting rules. A change of accounting rules currently in use affects companies behaviors as the convergence toward the adoption of new rules asks for a (more or less radical) change in their reporting practices and routines.

Applying the theoretical approach proposed by Greenwood and Hinings (1996), a radical change occurs when a company moves to the use of accounting rules that are completely different from those in use. On the contrary, convergent changes consist of slight transformation of the accounting rules adopted by a company.

In general, a radical change occurs when an interaction between exogenous and endogenous factors takes place. The exogenous factors are the market and the institutional contexts, while the endogenous factors are the dissatisfaction of internal stakeholders, their commitment to change, power dependencies, and capacity for action (Greenwood and Hinings 1996). Without an appropriate interplay of those factors, which allows for a certain degree of receptivity and permeability to change, a desired or imposed radical change may ultimately result in a convergent change (Lapsley and Pettigrew 1994; Pettigrew 1987). In other words, the transition toward the use of new rules and, consequently, a change in disclosure behaviors are not only dictated by a regulatory framework change; they also depend on the decisions made by each company.

That is, European Union and national government's ability and power (institutional pressures) to impose the adoption of new accounting rules is not sufficient to ensure an immediate and total convergence. Conformity to accounting regulation change also depends on the reactions of the companies (Phillips et al. 2000). According to DiMaggio and Powell (1983), institutional pressures toward convergence lead, over time, the companies to follow isomorphic behaviors as each company tends to resemble the others. This attitude might not be due to reasons of economic rationality, but could be driven by the need to gain operational and social legitimacy.

Kondra and Hinings (1998), disagreeing with the focus on isomorphic processes leading to conformity, argue that there may be organizations that do not conform and deviate from the behaviors of other companies. Each company can enact a range of strategic and tactical reactions as response to institutional pressures toward conformity. These may vary from total conformity to (more or less active forms of) resistance to change (Oliver 1991). The most hostile reaction to change may depend on the difficulty that companies face in converging toward the adoption of new accounting rules. Accounting practices may in fact be difficult to change especially if the change requires a substantial transformation of the routines currently in use (Burns and Scapens 2000). In this sense, the diffusion and adoption of new rules must be preceded by their theorization, the process by which innovations achieve legitimacy and are considered more appropriate than existing practices (Greenwood et al. 2002).

To conclude, a transformation of the regulatory framework, such as an extension of the contents to be disclosed in the Management's Report, impacts on the companies that have to comply with the new rules. However, the results of such transformation are not certain because of companies' possible deviating reactions.

After having highlighted how a change in the regulatory framework might impact on the preparation of Management's Reports, the next section identifies similarities and differences between the main issues of the IASB's ED the contents of the Management's Report in the Italian regulatory framework, as modified in 2007.

12.3 IASB's Exposure Draft Management Commentary Versus Italian's Regulatory Framework

As highlighted in the previous section, the internationalization and globalization of economic activities have influenced the level and extent of corporate disclosures. The Management's Report, the document which integrates the information disclosed in financial statements, should present management's view on a company's present and past situation as well as future developments. Therefore, the information provided is the result of managers' disclosure behaviors, whose quantity and quality may be sensitive and depending on the mandatory or optional requirements of the regulatory framework (Barron et al. 1999; Beretta and Bozzolan 2004; Pava and Epstein 1993; Penno 1997).

A proof of the value attributed to the Management's Report is that the Italian and European legislators intervened, on several occasions, to establish its contents. Interest in this document was also shown by the IASB, which in June of 2009 published the "Exposure Draft Management Commentary ED/2009/6" proposing a general framework for the preparation and presentation of the Management's Report (IASB 2009).

According to IASB's ED, Management's Report can be an important element of companies' communication with the capital markets, supplementing as well as complementing the financial statements. It provides a context within which to interpret the financial position, financial performance, and cash flows of an entity. It also provides an opportunity to understand management's objectives and its strategies for achieving those objectives. Users of financial reports in their capacity as capital providers use the information provided in Management's Report as a tool for evaluating an entity's prospects and its general risks, as well as the success of management's strategies for achieving its stated objectives (IASB 2009, p. 4).

The IASB's ED is not a binding accounting standard; it proposes a framework for the preparation and presentation of Management Commentary to accompany financial statements prepared in compliance with IAS/IFRS. This framework is intended to assist management in preparing decision-useful Management's Reports. According to the IASB, Management's Reports prepared in accordance with this framework can provide users of the financial statements with historical and prospective commentary on the entity's financial position, financial performance, and cash flows, as it explains management's view on not only what has happened, but also why management believes it has happened and what management believes the implications are for the entity's future (IASB 2009, pp. 7, 9).

According to IASB's ED, when compiling Management's Report, management should include information which is useful for the needs of existing and potential capital providers, as the primary "users" of financial statements. As for the "time frame," the framework explicitly states that Management's Report should communicate information explaining not only the present, but also the past and future performance, position, and development of an entity (IASB 2009, p. 8).

Moreover, management should consider the following "principles" that underpin decision-useful Management's Report, which:

a. provides management's view of the entity's performance, position, and development;
b. supplements and complements information presented in the financial statements; and
c. has an orientation to the future (IASB 2009, pp. 9–11).

On the one hand, the framework does not indicate a specific form for the "presentation" of Management's Report. It will vary between entities, reflecting the nature of their business, the strategies adopted by management and the regulatory environment in which they operate. On the other hand, the framework indicates the "content elements" of decision-useful Management's Report, which are stated below:

1. the nature of the business, discussing (a) the industries in which the entity operates, (b) the entity's main markets and competitive position within those markets, (c) significant features of the legal, regulatory and macro-economic environment that influence the entity and the markets in which the entity operates, (d) the entity's main products and services, business processes and distribution methods, and (e) the entity's structure and its economic model;
2. management's objectives and strategies for meeting those objectives, in order to enable users to understand the priorities for action and the resources that must be managed to deliver results;
3. the entity's most significant (financial and non-financial) resources, (strategic, commercial, operational, and financial) risks and relationships with

stakeholders; how those resources, risks, and relationships affect the entity's long-term value and are managed;

4. the results of operations and prospects, describing (a) the entity's financial and non-financial performance, (b) the extent to which that performance may be indicative of future performance, and (c) management's assessment of the entity's prospects; and
5. the critical performance measures and indicators (both financial and non-financial) that management uses to evaluate the entity's performance against stated objectives (IASB 2009, pp. 12–16).

Table 12.1 summarizes the main contents of Management's Report according to IASB's ED.

In Italy, the contents of the Management's Report are disciplined by Article 2428 of the Civil Code: "Management's Report (in Italian: *Relazione sulla gestione*)," which was amended over time in order to comply with the requirements of EU Directives (for example, the Accounting Modernization Directive 51/2003/CE).

In revising Article 2428 of the Civil Code with the 2007 law, the Italian legislator expanded the contents of the Management's Report by introducing substantial innovations with respect to the past (Sottoriva 2007). The Article's text is presented below, showing *in italics the parts added by the 2007 law*.

The financial statement must be accompanied by a Management's Report *containing an exhaustive, balanced and trustworthy analysis of the company situation, and management trend and results*, in its whole and in the various sectors in which it operates, with particular attention to the costs, revenues and investments, *as well as a description of the key risks and uncertainties to which the company is exposed.*

The analysis above is consistent with the dimension and the complexity of the company's business and contains the financial and non-financial performance indicators pertinent to the specific company activity, including information pertaining to the environment and personnel. The analysis contains, where timely, references to the amounts reported in the financial statement and supplementary explanations on them.

In every case, the report should contain:

1. research and development activities;
2. transactions with controlled (subsidiary), affiliated and controlling (parent) companies;

Table 12.1 Contents of management's report according to IASB's ED

The nature of the business
Management objectives and strategies
The most significant company resources
Strategic, commercial, operational, and financial risks
The most significant business relationships
Management activity results
Future prospects
Performance measures and indicators

3. the number and nominal value of both its own shares and the stock or shares of controlling companies possessed by the company, also through a trustee company or nominee, with an indication of corresponding capital share;
4. the number and nominal value of its own shares, as well as the stock or shares of controlling companies bought or transferred by the company, in the course of the financial year, also through a trustee company or nominee, with an indication of the corresponding capital share, of the amounts and motives for the purchases and transfers;
5. the significant events occurring after the year-end close;
6. the likely evolution of management;

6-bis. with regard to the use by the company of financial instruments, if they are significant for the evaluation of the financial situation of the company and of its income (loss) for the year:

a. the objectives and policies of the company for managing financial risks, including the hedging policy for each main category of operations;
b. the exposure of the company to price, credit, liquidity and variation in cash flow risks.

Finally, the Management's Report has to contain a list of the sub-offices of the company.

A detailed interpretation on the compilation procedures of the "new Management's Report" was supplied by the National Board of Professional and Chartered Accountants (CNDCEC 2009a). The National Board of Professional and Chartered Accountants (CNDCEC) also addressed the information on the environment and personnel that should be disclosed (CNDCEC 2009b).

In summary, in the pursuit of full transparency of information (disclosure), the Management's Report of joint-stock companies—besides the traditional information regarding costs, revenues and investments—should include, starting with the financial year ending December 31, 2008, risks and uncertainties, as well as financial and non-financial performance indicators and information relating to the environment and personnel (Sottoriva 2007). The new requirements do not only deal with a broadening of the quantity of the information to supply. There is also a variation in the nature of the information to be disclosed: besides financial information, Management's Reports should include information of a social, environmental, and strategic nature. This is an enhancement with respect to the past, in which—as stated by Bagnoli (2003)—regulation was too generic and the academic and professional interpretations did not solve doubts regarding the contents of Management's Reports and their degree of depth (Bagnoli 2003, pp. 37–38, 91–93).

Table 12.2 highlights the key contents of the Management's Report according to the Italian regulations, as modified in 2007.

On the one hand, by comparing the innovations introduced by the Italian legislator with the main issues of the IASB's ED, it is possible to affirm that the Italian regulatory framework is—to some extent—ahead of the IASB project because of the explicit inclusion of environment and personnel matters (which are lacking in the ED/2009/6). In this sense, the Italian Accounting Setter (in Italian: *Organismo Italiano di Contabilità*—OIC), in the comment letter to the ED, declared that the IASB should deal with more significant and urgent projects

Table 12.2 Contents of Management's Report according to Article 2428 of the civil code

An analysis of the company situation and of management trend and results, in its whole and in the various sectors in which it operates, with particular attention to costs, revenues, and investments
A description of the risks and uncertainties
Financial and non-financial performance indicators
Information relating to the environment
Information relating to personnel
The Management's Report must contain:
1. Research and Development activities
2. Transactions with controlled, affiliated, and controlling companies
3. The number and nominal value of both its own shares and the stock or shares of controlling companies possessed by the company, also through a trustee company or nominee, with an indication of corresponding capital share
4. The number and nominal value of its own shares, as well as the stock or shares of controlling companies bought or transferred by the company, in the course of the financial year, also through a trustee company or nominee, with an indication of the corresponding capital share, of the amounts and motives for the purchases and transfers
5. Significant events occurring after the year-end close
6. Likely evolution of management
6-bis. With regard to the use by the company of financial instruments:
a. The objectives and policies for managing financial risk
b. Company exposure to price, credit, liquidity, and variation in cash flow risks
The list of company's sub-offices

instead of preparing a guidance on Management's Reports, since this document has a precise discipline in the European Union and also in Italy (OIC 2010).

On the other hand, IASB's ED explicitly asks the companies to disclose the management objectives and the strategies for reaching these objectives, in order to enable the users of Management's Reports to understand company's priorities. Such requirement is not explicitly mentioned in Article 2428 of the Italian Civil Code.

After having highlighted similarities and differences between the contents of Management's Report according to the IASB's ED and the Italian regulatory framework, as modified in 2007, the following section describes the research methodology adopted for conducting this research.

12.4 Research Methodology

The methodology employed in conducting the study presented in this chapter is based on a literature review and an empirical research. After carrying out a review of the national and international literature on changes in accounting regulation and the Management's Report, a content analysis of the Management's Reports compiled by the major companies—in terms of market capitalization—listed on the Italian Stock Exchange (Borsa Italiana SpA) was executed.

In particular, the sample is composed of Management's Reports prepared by the joint-stock companies whose stocks are included in the FTSE MIB 40 Index. From 40 companies identified, the 13 companies afferent to the finance sector (banks, insurance, financial services) were excluded as they are subject to another specific disclosure discipline. The 27 remaining companies work in the following sectors: Consumer Goods (7 companies), Industrials (8 companies), Basic Materials (1 company), Consumer Services (3 companies), Utilities (4 companies), Oil and Gas (2 companies), Technology (1 company), and Telecommunications (1 company).

The Management's Report of each company was found online on the Borsa Italiana SpA web site, using the link to the document archive of each company. Tenaris' Management's Report was not available on the Borsa Italiana SpA web site; it was directly downloaded from the company's Internet site. Instead, STMicroelectronics was excluded because its Management's Report was not available on the Borsa Italiana SpA web site or on the company's Internet site. Finally, Geox (Consumer Goods sector) was not included in the sample because the 2008 consolidated annual report did not include the diction of the Management's Report (even if the consolidated annual report comprises many paragraphs containing information attributable to a Management's Report). In this respect, the researchers have been neutral, focusing only the text explicitly included in the Management's Report.

All in all, the sample is composed of 25 Management's Reports.

Table 12.3 illustrates the sampling process described above, reporting the name of each of the 40 companies included in the FTSE MIB 40 Index (Borsa Italiana SpA), the sector in which it operates and if it was included in the sample.

The content analysis was conducted on the 2008 financial year Management's Reports because it is the first year of application of the new discipline. Specifically, for each company of the sample, a short note was written containing two types of information. The first type of information consists of general information on the company: the dimension (capitalization, sales, capital invested, number employees), the composition of shareholding (to evaluate if there are foreign members in the ownership), the geographic location of company's offices, the sector in which it operates, listed markets, the language used to compile the Management's Report (and financial statement). Instead, the second type relates to specific information which was searched in the Management's Reports. The content analysis was performed in two steps. The first step consisted of a check list aimed at investigating if:

- the Management's Report is a separate document or internal to the annual report for the year ending 31/12/2008;
- all the issues required by Article 2428 of the Civil Code are dealt with. This type of investigation provides an understanding of the general level of completeness of the selected documents;

Table 12.3 Sampling process

Company	Sector	Sample
A2A	Utilities	X
Ansaldo STS	Industrials (industrial goods and services)	X
Atlantia	Industrials (industrial goods and services)	X
Autogrill	Consumer Services (travel and leisure)	X
Azimut	Financials (financial services)	
Banco Popolare	Financials (banks)	
Banca MPS	Financials (banks)	
Banca Popolare di Milano	Financials (banks)	
Bulgari	Consumer goods (personal and household goods)	X
Buzzi Unicem	Industrials (construction and materials)	X
Campari	Consumer goods (food and beverage)	X
CIR	Industrials (industrial goods and services)	X
Enel	Utilities	X
Eni	Oil and gas	X
Exor	Financials (financial services)	
Fiat Group	Consumer goods (automobiles and parts)	X
Finmeccanica	Industrials (industrial goods and services)	X
Fondiaria Sai	Financials (insurance)	
Generali Assicurazioni	Financials (insurance)	
Geox	Consumer goods (personal and household goods)	
Impregilo	Industrials (construction and materials)	X
Intesa SanPaolo	Financials (banks)	
Italcementi	Industrials (construction and materials)	X
Lottomatica	Consumer services (travel and leisure)	X
Luxottica	Consumer goods (personal and household goods)	X
Mediaset	Consumer services (media)	X
Mediobanca	Financials (banks)	
Mediolanum	Financials (insurance)	
Parmalat	Consumer goods (food and beverage)	X
Pirelli and C.	Consumer goods (automobiles and parts)	X
Prysmian	Industrials (industrial goods and services)	X
Saipem	Oil and gas	X
Snam rete gas	Utilities	X
Stmicrolectronics	Technology	
Telecom Italia	Telecommunications	X
Tenaris	Basic materials (basic resources)	X
Terna	Utilities	X
Ubi Banca	Financials (banks)	
Unicredit	Financials (banks)	
Unipol	Financials (insurance)	

- the order established by Article 2428 of the Civil Code is respected. This type of investigation might highlight what choices have been made by managers when compiling the Management's Report.

The second step of the content analysis was dedicated to counting the space dedicated to the innovative issues (introduced in 2007) in terms of number of paragraphs, number of words, and density (the number of words devoted to each innovative issue divided by the total number of words in the entire Management's Report). Similar calculations were carried out as the space devoted to an issue may indicate which issues have received greater importance when compiling the Management's Report (Bagnoli 2009; Unerman 2000). In order to make these calculations, the PDF text was extracted with A-PDF text extractor program and transformed in a word document, enabling to select text parts and to count the number of words dedicated to specific issues.

The following section discusses the key findings that emerged from the content analysis of the Management's Reports included in the sample.

12.5 Findings

From the content analysis of the 25 Management's Reports of the companies listed on the FTSE MIB 40 Index (Borsa Italian SpA), the following considerations can be expressed. In 24 out of 25 cases the Management's Report was included in the consolidated annual report. Only one company, operating in the Utilities sector, prepared its Management's Report as a separate document.

The length of the documents examined (the total number of words) varied from a minimum of 4.272 words to a maximum of 57.432 words, while the average length is 27.912 words. Table 12.4 shows how many companies (and their respective sector) fall in different classes of Management's Reports' length (number of words).

Table 12.4 shows that about one-third of the companies has compiled a Management's Report consisting of a number of words between 10.001 and 20.000 words, and about one-third between 30.001 and 40.000 words. The other companies have other classes of length.

Regarding the general level of completeness of the Management's Reports, the issues required by Article 2428 (as identified in Table 12.2) are not always totally dealt with. In the majority of the cases, the issues excluded are:

- The list of the sub-offices: in 22 out of 25 cases, there is no cross-reference made to other documents, and the reason for such a gap is not included; in substance, isn't there any sub-office or are sub-offices individualized somewhere else?
- The details related to own shares possessed and bought/transferred are lacking in 15 out of 25 cases; in fact, in more than half of the documents examined, only its own shares possessed is indicated, without specification of the number of shares acquired and/or sold and the related nominal value.
- The relationships with related parties (11 out of 25 cases): in some cases, the Management's Report has an explicit cross-reference to the notes to financial statements; in other cases, it was possible to understand that the missing issue is

Table 12.4 Length of Management's Report

Number of words	No. of companies	Sector
Less than 10,000	1	Consumer goods (personal and household goods)
	1	Oil and gas
Between 10,001 and 20,000	1	Basic materials (basic resources)
	1	Consumer goods (food and beverage)
	1	Consumer goods (personal and household goods)
	1	Consumer services (travel and leisure)
	2	Industrials (construction and materials)
	2	Industrials (industrial goods and services)
Between 20,001 and 30,000	1	Consumer goods (automobiles and parts)
	1	Consumer services (travel and leisure)
Between 30,001 and 40,000	1	Consumer goods (food and beverage)
	1	Consumer services (media)
	1	Industrials (construction and materials)
	2	Industrials (industrial goods and services)
	2	Utilities
Between 40,001 and 50,000	1	Consumer goods (automobiles and parts)
	1	Oil and gas
	1	Telecommunications
More than 50,001	1	Industrials (industrial goods and services)
	2	Utilities

dealt with in the consolidated annual report as it is listed in its index. Sometimes, there is no reference at all to the missing issue.

- In 11 of 25 cases, the management of and exposure to financial risks are completely absent or treated in a partial manner with a cross-reference to the notes to financial statements.
- Environmental information is absent in 8 of 25 cases.

The following issues are excluded in a less systematic manner: risks and uncertainties to which a company is exposed, information regarding personnel, research and development activities, likely evolution of management, and the significant events occurring after the year-end close.

- Finally, 14 of the 25 Management's Reports have up to a maximum of three issues excluded, while the remaining documents have greater gaps of information.

In some cases, the issues excluded in the Management's Report are dealt with in the consolidated annual report. It was possible to understand it from reading the Management's Report, because it makes a specific cross-reference to the consolidated annual report or to another document, or from reading the index of contents of the consolidated annual report. In other cases, it was not possible to determine if the issues excluded were dealt with in other documents.

Regarding the order in which the issues are presented in the selected Management's Reports, is it possible to state that the order indicated in Article 2428 (as identified in Table 12.2) is not ever totally respected. In the majority of the Management's Reports, the company's situation, and management trend and results, are the initial issues dealt with. However, there is no substantial uniformity in the order of the issues dealt with in the 25 documents analyzed, showing diverging presentation patterns.

Moreover, in different Management's Reports, multiple issues are dealt with in the same paragraph. The most popular format is to discuss some of the issues required by the regulation in a paragraph entitled "Other Information." The issues most frequently disclosed in such a paragraph are: the number and nominal value of company's own shares (possessed and bought/transferred), relationships with related parties, and the list of sub-offices. In some cases, research and development activities, as well as financial risks, are also discussed.

As regards the innovative issues introduced in 2007, the following picture can be portrayed.

Article 2428 of the Civil Code requires companies to describe the *risks and uncertainties* to which they are exposed. In the majority of the documents analyzed, the risks and uncertainties are treated in a generic manner, without really clarifying the degree of exposure to the risks and the policies for managing them. In some cases, only a general definition of the risks is supplied. The density of words dedicated to the risks and uncertainties fluctuates between a minimum percentage of 0.8 % and a high of 20.8 %, with an average value of the whole sample of 6 %. In almost all of the Management's Reports in which the risks and uncertainties are discussed, there exists a specific paragraph on the issue; however, in one case the risks and uncertainties are introduced in a sub-paragraph inside the "Other Information" paragraph. In the other two cases, the risks and uncertainties are dealt with in a paragraph that also deals with the likely evolution of management.

In the majority of the Management's Reports analyzed, the issues of exposure to and management of *financial risks* are both dealt with in the paragraph on risks and uncertainties, but the risks are not always clarified and the researchers had to identify them in order to determine the number of words devoted to those issues. The density of words dedicated to the financial risks varies between a minimum percentage of 0.6 % and a high of 6.8 %, with an average value of the whole sample of 1.4 %. In general, cross-reference is made to the notes to financial statements for a detailed discussion of these issues.

Another innovation is the insertion of *financial and non-financial indicators* in order to better understand the company situation, and management trend and results. In this regard, the analysis has highlighted that not many indicators are adopted and are not present in all of the selected Management's Reports. Indicators are mainly located in the paragraphs discussing the management trend and results. Thus, in almost all the cases, it is not possible to determine the exact number of the words relating to performance indicators. On the one hand, some items and margins (like cost and revenues, Ebitda, Ebit, capital invested, and net financial position) are presented and discussed, but the only other financial indicators found (not in every Management's Report) are ROI, ROE, ROS, and gearing and leverage. Only in the Management's Reports of two companies is EVA indicated. On the other hand, non-financial indicators are not clearly identified and discussed, meaning that users have to eventually identify and interpret them. Finally, in the Management's Reports examined, there is hardly ever a specific paragraph that listed and explained the performance indicators. In 7 of the 25 cases, there is a paragraph or table related to performance indicators. This implies that the density of words is biased downwards, with values between 0.4 and 2.4 %. The average value of the whole sample is only 0.3 %.

Regarding *environmental information*, the empirical analysis has highlighted that in one-third of the selected Management's Reports no reference is made to environmental information either in a cross-reference to the consolidated annual report, or any other document. The Management's Report of one company, even though it does not supply deep environmental information, refers readers to the Sustainability Report. When the Management's Report discloses environmental information, in the majority of the cases, a specific paragraph on the issue is included. However, in some cases, the environmental matters are incorporated in the paragraphs on "Corporate Social Responsibility (CSR)," "Health, Safety, Environment" or "Sustainable Development." The density of words dedicated to the environment varies between 0.3 and 6.6 %, with an average value of the whole sample of 1.8 %.

Regarding the *information on personnel*, the empirical analysis shows that in almost all the Management's Reports, there is at least one paragraph (or sub-paragraph) dedicated to this issue. Only in 3 of the 25 documents analyzed, there is no reference to that issue. In some Management's Reports, the information on personnel is spread in different paragraphs, such as—for instance—"Health, Safety and Environment." The density of words dedicated to personnel varies between a minimum percentage of 0.5 % and a maximum of 14.6 %, with an average of the whole sample of 4.7 %. Not all the documents analyzed supply complete information on personnel and only indicate the total number of employees and training activities, without specifying the number of those dying in job-related activities, serious accidents, etc.

Table 12.5 summarizes the main research findings pertaining to the new requirements introduced by the 2007 regulatory change.

From the empirical investigation, it emerged that there is no precise correspondence between completeness (quantity of issues dealt with) and the density of words dedicated to the issues dealt with. For example, one of the most complete Management's Reports (omitting just one issue) presents percentages of information on risk and uncertainties and on personnel that are, respectively, below the average and next to the minimum.

Moreover, there is no precise correspondence between the total length of the Management's Reports and the density of words dedicated to the issues dealt with. For example, the Management's Report that is among the briefest has the highest density of words dedicated to risks and uncertainties. Also, the longest

Table 12.5 Findings: average density of innovative issues

Innovative issue	Average density (%)
Risks and uncertainties	6.0
Financial risks	1.4
Financial and non-financial performance indicators	0.3
Environment	1.8
Personnel	4.7

Management's Reports have a density of words relative to risks and uncertainties which is quite lower than the maximum.

From the aforementioned considerations, it is evident that the issues prescribed by Article 2428 of the Civil Code are not always present, or dealt with in a complete manner, in the Management's Reports compiled by the major companies listed on the Italian Stock Exchange (Borsa Italiana SpA). Moreover, the order in which they are presented does not perfectly correspond with that indicated by the Civil Code. It is not possible to state that the order followed is always an indication of the importance attributed to an issue in terms of the space it occupied in the Management's Report. For example, in one Management's Report the information on personnel is the second issue discussed, but the density of words is well below the average. Two other documents discuss the risks and uncertainties before the management trend and results, but have a percentage of words which is below the sample average. On the contrary, the Management's Report that discusses the risks and uncertainties at the end of the document has a density of words well above the average. This evidence highlights that companies have different presentation behaviors.

The following section discusses the findings that emerged from the content analysis. It also highlights the limitations and the future developments of this.

12.6 Discussion and Conclusions

The findings concerning the general level of completeness of the selected 25 Management's Reports seem to be quite in line with the results found by Bagnoli in 2003. The author claims that many Italian companies do not pursue full transparency and avoid disclosing some information. Specifically, many companies do not disclose present and future-oriented information, but only disclose superficial information on their personnel, research, and development activities (without telling the outcomes of such activities), no or partial information on the number and nominal value of own shares, as well as the stock or shares of controlling companies, bought, or sold during the year (Bagnoli 2003, pp. 250–271).

The results from the content analysis also reveal that the innovative issues introduced by the 2007 Italian law, which reflects the requirements of the

European Community Accounting Directives, are not always suitably dealt with in the selected Management's Reports.

Risks and uncertainties have received, on average, a density of words of 6 %. In most cases, their treatment is not fully in line with what was wished for by the CNDCEC. In some Management's Reports, risks and uncertainties are not discussed at all. Additionally, the financial risks are not always treated in a complete manner. Regarding the employment of performance indicators, in order to integrate the information on the company situation and the management trend and results, in many cases only Ebitda and Ebit, capital invested, net financial position, and few other indicators are properly discussed. Further indicators like ROE, ROI, and ROS—when disclosed—are mostly calculated but do not ever receive specific comments. Regarding the information relating to personnel and environment, the picture is not totally satisfactory as well. In many of the Management's Reports these issues are not dealt with or are treated in a partial manner, disregarding what is expected by the CNDCEC.

The Management's Reports analyzed in this chapter are also not in line with the contents of IASB's ED. It becomes interesting to follow IASB's progress with the ED and to understand which role it may play on the preparation of Management's Reports (given that it is not a binding accounting standard). If the IASB approves a final version, it might be challenging when it comes to disclosing management objectives and the strategies for reaching these objectives. The communication of these issues requires that the managers, besides supplying information on past and present events, also communicate specific information on the company's future. This requirement is a considerable challenge, considering that the Italian context was, and still is, characterized by management discretion and avoidance of full transparency (Bagnoli 2003).

The findings suggest that the companies included in the sample were not very receptive to the changes set by the 2007 law. There are very few Management's Reports that respect the normative requirements and present almost all the expected contents. This also means, in accordance with the theoretical section, that companies have not shown an immediate convergence toward the new disclosure rules. This room for deviating behaviors can be explained by the Italian long lasting reluctance to disclose sensitive information, but might also be related to type of pressures exerted by legislators and standard setters. To what extent are companies' disclosure behaviors compelled by the regulatory framework?

All in all, to be able to make a reliable judgment on companies' receptivity to regulatory change, it is desirable to conduct a broader space-temporal analysis. A limitation of this is that the Management's Reports from only one financial year were examined. The documents analyzed are from the financial year ending December, 31st, 2008, as it is the first year in which the new requirements had to be implemented. It would be interesting to also examine the Management's Reports from financial year 2007, the year that precedes the implementation of the new requirements, as well as financial year 2009, so as to formulate more complete considerations.

Another limitation of the current is that the sample is composed of companies operating in different sectors (with the exclusion of those operating in the Finance sector). An option could be to create specific subsamples, with the aim of better understanding the disclosure behaviors of companies operating in the same sector.

In conclusion, the topic discussed in the present chapter offers a starting point for reflection and stimulates further research to contribute to the scientific debate on the Management's Report and on corporate disclosure in general.

References

Bagnoli, C. (2003). *La relazione sulla gestione tra normativa e prassi*. Milano: Giuffrè.

Bagnoli, C. (2009). L'evoluzione delle strategie di disclosure volontaria delle imprese quotate italiane in un contesto di accresciuta incertezza ambientale. *Finanza, Marketing e Produzione, 3*, 104–132.

Barron, O. E., Kile, C. O., & O'Keefe, T. B. (1999). MDandA quality as measured by the SEC and analysts' earning forecasts. *Contemporary Accounting Research, 16*(1), 75–109.

Beattie, V. (2000). The future of corporate reporting: a review article. *Irish Accounting Review, 7*(1), 1–36.

Beattie, V., McInnes, B., & Fearney, S. (2004). A methodology for analysing and evaluating narratives in annual reports: a comprehensive descriptive profile and metrics for disclosure quality attributes. *Accounting Forum, 28*(3), 205–236.

Beretta, S., & Bozzolan, S. (2004). A framework for the analysis of firm risk communication. *The International Journal of Accounting, 39*(3), 265–288.

Burchell, S., Clubb, C., Hopwood, A., & Hughes, J. (1980). The roles of accounting in organizations and society. *Accounting, Organizations and Society, 5*(1), 5–27.

Burns, J., & Scapens, R. W. (2000). Conceptualizing management accounting change: an institutional framework. *Management Accounting Research, 11*(1), 3–25.

Camfferman, K., & Zeff, S. A. (2007). *Financial reporting and global capital markets. A history of the international accounting standards committee, 1973–2000*. Oxford: University Press.

Catturi, G. (1997). *Teorie contabili e scenari economico-aziendali*. Cedam, Padova: Seconda edizione.

Clarkson, P. M., Kao, J. L., & Richardson, G. D. (1999). Evidence that management discussion and analysis (MD&A) is a part of a firm's overall disclosure package. *Contemporary Accounting Research, 16*(1), 111–134.

CNDCEC. (2009a). *La relazione sulla gestione dei bilanci d'esercizio alla luce delle novità introdotte dal d.lgs. 32/2007*. Roma, 14 Gennaio.

CNDCEC. (2009b). *La relazione sulla gestione dei bilanci d'esercizio alla luce delle novità introdotte dal d.lgs. 32/2007—Informativa sull'ambiente e sul personale*. Roma, 11 Marzo.

DiMaggio, P. J., & Powell, W. W. (1983). The iron cage revisited: institutional isomorphism and collective rationality in organizational fields. *American Sociological Review, 48*(2), 147–160.

Di Pietra, R. (2002). *La cultura contabile nello scenario internazionale. Istituzioni, principi ed esperienze*, Cedam, Padova.

Di Pietra, R. (2005). *La comunicazione dei comportamenti aziendali mediante i dati contabili*. Cedam, Padova: Il ruolo della Ragioneria Internazionale.

Flower, J. (1999). Introduction. In S. McLeay (Ed.), *Accounting regulation in europe*. London: Macmillan Press LTD.

Flower, J., & Lefebvre, C. (Eds.). (1997). *Comparative studies in accounting regulation in Europe*. Leuven: Acco.

Flower, J., & Ebbers, G. (2002). *Global financial reporting*. New York: Palgrave.

Greenwood, R., & Hinings, C. R. (1996). Understanding radical organizational change: Bringing together the old and new institutionalism. *Academy of Management Review, 21*(4), 1022–1054.

Greenwood, R., Suddaby, R., & Hinings, C. R. (2002). Theorizing change: the role of professional associations in the transformation of institutionalized fields. *Academy of Management Journal, 45*(1), 58–80.

Hopwood, A. G. (1983). On trying to study accounting in the contexts in which it works. *Accounting, Organizations and Society, 8*(2/3), 287–305.

IASB. (2009). *Exposure draft management commentary, ED/2009/6*. London: IASC Foundation Publications Department.

Kondra, A. Z., & Hinings, C. R. (1998). Organizational diversity and change in institutional theory. *Organization Studies, 19*(5), 743–767.

Lapsley, I., & Pettigrew, A. (1994). Meeting the challenge: Accounting for change. *Financial Accountability and Management, 10*(2), 79–92.

Leuz, C., Pfaff, D., & Hopwood, A. (Eds.). (2004). *The economics and politics of accounting. International perspectives on research trends, policy, and practice*. Oxford: Oxford University Press.

March, G. J., Schulz, M., & Zhou, X. (2003). *Per una teoria delle regole. Nascita, cambiamento e strutturazione delle regole*, Università Bocconi Editore, Milano (edizione italiana di *The Dynamics of Rules. Change in Written Organizational Codes*, Stanford University Press, 2000).

McLeay, S. (Ed.). (1999). *Accounting regulation in Europe*. London: Macmillan Press LTD.

McLeay, S., & Riccaboni, A. (Eds.). (2000). *Contemporary issues in accounting regulation*. Boston: Kluwer Academic Publishers.

OIC. (2010). *Comment on IASB exposure draft management commentary*. Rome, 9 February.

Oliver, C. (1991). Strategic responses to institutional processes. *Academy of Management Review, 16*(1), 145–179.

Pava, M., & Epstein, M. (1993). How good is MD&A as an investment tool? *Journal of Accountancy, 175*(3), 51–53.

Penno, M. C. (1997). Information quality and voluntary disclosure. *The Accounting Review, 72*(2), 275–284.

Pettigrew, A. M. (1987). Context and action in the transformation of the firm. *Journal of Management Studies, 24*(6), 650–670.

Phillips, N., Lawrence, T. B., & Hardy, C. (2000). Inter-organizational collaboration and the dynamics of institutional fields. *Journal of Management Studies, 37*(1), 23–43.

Roberts, J., & Scapens, R. (1985). Accounting systems and systems of accountability—understanding accounting practices in their organisational contexts. *Accounting, Organizations and Society, 10*(4), 443–456.

Sottoriva, C. (2007). L'attuazione della Direttiva 2003/51/CE con il D.Lgs. n. 32/2007. *Le Società, N., 6*, 657–694.

Tamm, H. K. (2004). *Organizing international standardization*. Edward Elgar, Cheltenham: ISO and the IASC in Quest of Authority.

Unerman, J. (2000). Methodological Issues: Reflections on quantification in corporate social reporting content analysis. *Accounting, Auditing and Accountability Journal, 13*(5), 667–680.

West, B. P. (2003). *Professionalism and accounting rules*. New York: Routledge.

Chapter 13
Do Attributes of Management's Explanations of Financial Performance Matter for Analysts? An International Perspective

Walter Aerts and Ann Tarca

Abstract Aerts and Tarca (2010) study attributes of performance explanations in management commentary reports provided by 172 companies from five industries in the USA, Canada, the UK and Australia. They report that, compared to their counterparts in the UK and Australia, companies from the USA and Canada are generally less assertive and less defensive in explicit causal framing of accounting outcomes. They are also more extensive and formal in their explanations, relying more heavily on accounting-technical language in explaining performance outcomes. We investigate whether these differential attributional properties have economic relevance by considering their relationship with analyst forecast dispersion. Using a factor analysis based on firm-level characteristics of explanatory statements for 158 companies included in the above study, we find that defensiveness and extensiveness of performance explanations are negatively associated with analyst forecast dispersion, while assertiveness and formality are not. Our results suggest that analysts benefit from more detailed explanations and that they

This chapter includes the paper originally titled "The effect of Institutional Setting on Attributional Content in Management Commentary Reports" and discussed at the Fourth International Workshop on Accounting and Regulation in 2007. We thank seminar participants at the European Accounting Association Conference Lisbon 2007, the EIASM Accounting Regulation Con ference Siena 2007, the AAA International Accounting Section and IAAER Joint 2008 Midyear Conference, the University of Glasgow and the University of Queensland for their helpful com ments on the material in this article and the related study Aerts and Tarca (2010). We acknowledge the financial support of the UWA Business School and of the National Bank of Belgium. We thank the following research associates for their assistance: Serene Seah, Morris Eggleston, Pirya Altraide, Jamille Payne, Hui Li Siow, Eric Vermuyten and Christophe Nauts.

W. Aerts (✉)
Department of Accounting and Finance, Antwerp University, Faculty of Applied Economics, Antwerpen, Belgium
e-mail: walter.aerts@ua.ac.be

A. Tarca
UWA Business School, University of Western Australia, Crawley, WA, Australia
e-mail: Ann.Tarca@uwa.edu.au

R. Di Pietra et al. (eds.), *Accounting and Regulation*,
DOI: 10.1007/978-1-4614-8097-6_13,

pick up defensive explanations while possibly disregarding more assertive explanations. Not surprisingly, the use of more technical-accounting explanations does not serve to reduce dispersion in forecasts. Our study brings together two strands of literature, being studies of explanatory patterns in narrative reports and studies investigating usefulness of narrative reports for analysts.

13.1 Introduction

The aim of this study is to investigate whether attributes of performance explanations included in companies' management commentary (MC) reports impact on the extent of analyst forecast disagreement. We focus on attributes of performance explanations that tend to differ by institutional context. MC reports[1] are commonly provided by listed companies to give analysts and investors a view of a company's position and performance 'through the eyes of management' (SEC 1987; ASB 2003). Explanations of performance potentially provide insights into events and give a context for greater understanding of the accompanying financial data. However, the content of MC reports is largely discretionary and will reflect management's incentives to portray themselves and the company in a positive light, as highlighted by studies investigating narrative reporting using attribution theory (Aerts 1994, 2001, 2005; Bettman and Weitz 1983; Baginski et al. 2004, 2008; Clatworthy and Jones 2003, 2006; Merkl-Davies and Brennan 2007; Salancik and Meindl 1984; Staw et al. 1983).

Another stream of literature concludes that MC information is an important and useful part of a company's total disclosure package (Jones and Cole 2005; PwC 2007). Research indicates that high-quality information contained in narrative reports can have economic importance for analysts and is associated with lower analyst forecast dispersion (Clarkson et al. 1999; Barron et al. 1999). However, prior studies have not investigated whether attributes of performance explanations affect analyst forecasts. Our study adds to the literature by using a detailed textual analysis of performance explanations and investigating the relevance of various attributes of these explanations for the level of disagreement among analyst when forecasting earnings. Thus our study brings together these two streams of literature and adds to our understanding of the importance of particular characteristics of performance explanations.

Prior studies suggest that the institutional setting for financial reporting affects companies' disclosure practices in MC reports (Frost and Pownell 1994; Beattie and McInnes 2006). Aerts and Tarca (2010) find that expected regulatory and

[1] Management commentary reports include Management Discussion and Analysis (MD&A), Operating and Financial Review (OFR) and similar.

litigation costs embedded in a country's institutional environment influence the nature of attributional statements included by management to explain financial performance in management commentary reports. They report that companies from the USA and Canada are generally less assertive and less defensive in explicit causal framing of performance outcomes compared to their counterparts in the UK and Australia. The North American companies are also more extensive and formal in their explanations, relying more heavily on accounting-technical language. These tendencies are more pronounced in the USA, where the aggregate of private and public enforcement is greatest (La Porta et al. 2006).

We extend the prior studies by investigating whether the differences in attributional framing of performance explanations have economic relevance by considering the relationship between attributional content profiles and analyst forecast dispersion. Specifically, we investigate the data set examined by Aerts and Tarca (2010). Based on their sample of listed companies from five industries and four countries (USA, Canada, United Kingdom and Australia) in 2003, we investigate whether specific profiles in attributional behaviour with regard to performance outcomes can be identified, whether these attributional content profiles differ between countries and whether these differences have economic significance. We carry out a factor analysis on the attributional characteristics investigated by Aerts and Tarca (2010) in order to identify patterns of characteristics which go together (attributional content profiles). We are interested in the extent to which such attributional profiles in performance explanation affect the usefulness of information for analysts.

We propose that when companies' explanatory statements are more informative about performance, there will be less diversity in the opinions of analysts about the entity's position and prospects and therefore less dispersion in their forecasts. Thus we explore the extent to which the characteristics of the performance explanations we observe in companies' MC reports are associated with forecast dispersion. The factor analysis identifies three factors (or attributional profiles) which we label 'assertiveness', 'defensiveness' and 'formality-extensiveness'. The first profile, assertiveness, is dominated by the tendency to ascribe positive outcomes to management actions rather than external events and by avoiding accounting-technical explanations for positive outcomes. Defensiveness (the second profile) mainly captures the tendency to explain negative events as arising more from external causes than management action. The third factor, formality-extensiveness, captures a tendency to use relatively more formal (accounting-technical) explanations to more cognitive effort (relative amount and complexity of explanations).

We find that formality-extensiveness and defensiveness are negatively associated with analyst forecast dispersion, suggesting that cognitive effort invested in explanation (captured in formality-extensiveness) reduces disagreement among analysts. When disaggregating the latter factor into its major components, we find that especially the depth and density elements of explanations are important, while the use of more accounting-technical explanations is not beneficial in reducing disagreement. We find that defensiveness, although potentially self-serving, is useful in reducing disagreement among analysts. Assertiveness, however, is not associated with dispersion in forecasts.

Our study extends the findings of the previous research by showing that the differential empirical framing patterns, likely associated with differences in expected regulatory and litigations costs in the USA, Canada, UK and Australia, are not inconsequential in that they affect dispersion in analysts' forecasts. Our results add to prior studies that have explored the usefulness for analysts of disclosure in management commentary reports (Barron et al. 1999; Lys and Soo 1995; Lang and Lundholm 1993, 1996; Hope 2003a, b) by identifying specific explanatory characteristics that are associated with forecast dispersion.

The importance of high-quality information in MC has been emphasised by regulators and various initiatives have been undertaken to improve narrative content (SEC 2003, 2004; ASB 2003). Our evidence is relevant to regulators' debates about how to promote useful disclosure in MC reports (IASCF 2005). Not surprisingly, we find greater consensus among analysts when more and more detailed explanations are provided by companies so regulators' initiatives should continue to focus on encouraging more comprehensive explanatory reasoning via whichever mechanisms are considered appropriate. Our findings in relation to specific characteristics of attributional framing, particularly defensiveness, suggest that a country's institutional environment should not be too threatening to inhibit an explicit causal stance by corporate management. Causal explanations, even when explicitly self-serving, may reveal useful information and market participants may not be assisted by discouraging such disclosures.

13.2 Background and Research Predictions

The reporting framework for MC varies between countries, with differences in the level of regulation and oversight applied to management commentary reports (IASCF 2005). For example, in the USA a mandatory MD&A has been required since 1968. The SEC provides detailed regulations about content and it also reviews reports and takes action on those reports considered not in compliance with the law (SEC 2003, 2004). In contrast, in the UK the London Stock Exchange has recommended a voluntary report, based on detailed guidance provided by the national standard setter (ASB 2003).

The IASB discussion paper on management commentary raises the question as to whether these differences matter (IASCF 2005). To date, there is little cross-country comparative research to answer this question. Prior international studies have compared various aspects of the content of narrative reports (Collins et al. 1993; Beattie et al. 2002, 2004). Another strand of research investigates the way in which narrative information is presented using an attribution theory approach. Studies identify a self-serving bias in attributional patterns in explanatory cause and effect statements, where managers define situations and events to the firm's own advantage (Baginski et al. 2000; Bettman and Weitz 1983; Clapham and

Schwenk 1991; Clatworthy and Jones 2003; Salancik and Meindl 1984; Wagner and Gooding 1997).

Cross-country studies comparing disclosure practices in the USA and UK suggest that regulatory setting affects firms' disclosure practices (Frost and Pownell 1994; Beattie and McInnes 2006). In this vein, an extensive literature suggests litigation risk varies between countries, being greatest in the USA (Ball et al. 2000; Baginski et al. 2002; Seetharamana et al. 2002; Hughes and Sankar 2006; Khurana and Raman 2004). Aerts and Tarca (2010) find that expected regulatory and litigation costs embedded in a country's institutional environment influence the nature of the statements used to explain financial performance in MC reports. They report that companies from the USA and Canada are generally less assertive and less defensive in explicit causal framing compared to their counterparts in the UK and Australia. The North American companies are also more extensive and formal in their explanations, relying more heavily on accounting-technical language. These tendencies are more pronounced in the USA, where the aggregate of private and public enforcement is greatest (La Porta et al. 2006).

We extend the prior studies by investigating whether the differences in attributional framing of performance explanations have economic relevance by considering the relationship between attributional content profiles and analyst forecast dispersion. Attribution theory relates to how people explain events by ascribing explanations to causes and empirical antecedents. It focuses on perceived causality: people's ideas about what causes things to happen and why things happen as they do. Attributional statements are narrative statements reflecting a cause-effect or antecedent-consequence relationship.[2]

The MC report typically contains performance explanations of two kinds: 'technical-accounting' explanations and causality-based explanations. Technical-accounting explanations use formal accounting language, with its interrelated concepts and inherent calculative relationships, to frame discussion of accounting outcomes. For example, management may explain a rise in the company's profit margin by relating it to an increase in revenue or a decrease of particular categories of operating expenses. These explanations are based on the internal logic of the financial accounting model. Causality-based explanations on the other hand, refer to statements in which causal connections between performance outcomes and internal or external events, actions or decisions are identified as underlying sources for performance. These underlying sources or facilitating factors may be both intentional (i.e. reflecting management purpose) and unintentional. Causality-based explanations include, for example, performance explanations in terms of the company's strategy and underlying business model and explanations of how industry and general economic forces affect business outcomes. Whereas the latter embody interpretative propositional elements (in terms of reasons and causes) that are not transparent from the financial statements, the former typically reflect

[2] In this article we apply an extensive concept of attributional events and we use the terms 'attributional statements' and 'explanatory statements' interchangeably.

accounting logic relationships as embedded in the financial statements and tend to provide an intermediary type of explanation.

Prior studies show a strong link between greater amounts of disclosure and more accuracy in analyst forecasts (Lang and Lundholm 1996; Hope 2003a). Studies also indicate the importance of narrative explanations in MC in the information set used by analysts. Lang and Lundholm (1996) report that analyst forecasts are less disperse for companies with more informative MD&A disclosures (measured by Financial Analysts ratings). Barron et al. (1999) find that better quality MD&A information (based on SEC rankings) is associated with less forecast dispersion. Extending the research question to an international sample, Ang and Ciccone (2001) conclude that more MC disclosure is linked to lower dispersion in forecasts. Similarly, Hope (2003b) finds that disclosures about companies' accounting policies reduce uncertainty, leading to lower disagreement amongst analysts. More public information increases the precision of common and idiosyncratic information generated by analysts (Byard and Shaw 2006). Nichols and Weiland (2009) argue that narrative information improves the quality of publicly available information. They find lower error and dispersion for forecasts for firms providing more non-financial disclosure in information in press releases. Vanstraelen et al. (2003) focus specifically on non-financial information in annual reports identified as important to analysts (based on the Jenkins Committee report) and find lower dispersion in analyst forecasts for companies providing more disclosure. Bozzolan et al. (2010) extend this study by investigating the effect of attributes of forward-looking non-financial information. They show that verifiable information is more likely to be associated with more accuracy and less disagreement in forecasts.

The importance of high-quality information in MC has been emphasised by regulators. A SEC review in 2001 of Fortune 500 companies' reports observed that companies would often choose to present 'boilerplate' analyses that failed to provide insight into the companies' past performance or business prospects. Nelson and Pritchard (2007) note a tendency to 'cut and paste' disclosures from prior years, thus raising the question of the extent to which insights about company performance are provided by formal, ritualised re-statements of self-evident relationships of revenue and expense items. Brown and Tucker (2011) report declining usefulness of MD&A information for US firms, based on reducing amounts of year-on-year change in MD&A content. Lehavey et al. (2011) point to increasing length and complexity of MD&A reports and conclude that higher forecast dispersion among analysts is associated with companies whose reports are less readable (based on the FOG index). Taken together, these studies suggest that the quality of management commentary matters. In this study, we continue the work of Aerts and Tarca (2010) and investigate whether the characteristics of performance explanations that they identified as being sensitive to institutional context affect analyst forecast behaviour.

13.3 Data and Method

13.3.1 Sample Selection: Aerts and Tarca (2010)

The study by Aerts and Tarca (2010) includes five industry groups (building materials, food processing, pharmaceuticals, biotechnology and retail), chosen to include a variety of industries as prior studies suggest that industry membership influences disclosure (Hooks and Moon 1993; Jones and Cole 2005). Aerts and Tarca (2010) study 173 companies, with 53 (30 %) from the USA, 35 (21 %) from Canada, 47 (27 %) from the UK and 38 (22 %) from Australia. Representation from industry groups is as follows: building materials 26 companies (15 %), food processing 36 (21 %); pharmaceuticals 34 (20 %); biotechnology 40 (23 %) and retail 37 (21 %).

Aerts and Tarca (2010) state that 2003 was selected to capture existing differences in the institutional environment for management commentary reports. At that time, regulators in the USA and Canada required mandatory reports while MC reports in the UK and Australia reflected primarily voluntary recommendations. By 2004 the UK had announced the introduction of mandatory reports (an initiative later withdrawn) (Beattie and McInnes 2006) and Australia introduced requirements for management discussion and analysis as part of reform of company law (CLERP 9). The year 2003 was selected so that reports predated the changes in the institutional environment in the UK and Australia, allowing the authors to explore the impact of differences in the institutional setting for MC reports on performance explanations in the reports, which was the major focus of that paper.

13.3.2 Coding of Attributional Statements

In Aerts and Tarca (2010)'s study, the explanatory statements are coded by identifying attributional statements on performance in the management commentary section of the annual report and then coding the statements according to characteristics of explained effects and explanatory factors. The explained effects are coded according to five characteristics: nature, valence, time orientation, qualification and analytical level of explained content. For each characteristic, different elements are discriminated. The explanatory factors (causes and antecedents) are coded according to six characteristics: explicitness of the antecedent—consequence relationship, direction of influence of the antecedent–consequence relationship, time orientation and qualification of the explanatory factor, nature of the antecedent—consequence relationship and locus of causality. As for explained effects, the characteristics are classified according to different elements. Appendix 1 provides definitions of the attributional content characteristics and Appendix 2 shows the coding dimensions. Examples of coding of attribution statements are provided in Appendix 3.

As the company and not the specific instance of attribution is treated as the unit of analysis, the coding results are aggregated at company level, after meaningful selections on relevant attributional dimensions at the individual attributional statement level. The company-level attributional variables are primarily expressed as frequency measures, although some, if relevant, are additionally transformed into proportional measures, reflecting the relative frequencies of specific attributional characteristics. The proportional measures control for variations in the number of attributional statements per company. They add perspective in the analyses by complementing the frequency measures with intensity measures (Gardner and Martinko 1988; D'Aveni and MacMillan 1990).

Table 13.1 presents the explanatory content descriptive statistics in total and by country for Aerts and Tarca (2010)'s sample of 172 companies. The authors state: "the average number of attributional statements is 33.46, relative to an average of 16.19 explained effects, that is, on average each attributed effect is accompanied by 2.04 explanations. There are more positively evaluated effects than negatively evaluated ones (9.50 positives versus 6.52 negatives). Future events represent, on average, 12.31 % of the explained effects, an average of 1.73 prospective attributions per management commentary. Nearly 61 % of the explained effects relate to company level figures (60.90 %) with the balance relating to outcomes on a lower operational level (business or geographical segments, divisions, legal entities, product lines). The majority of the explained effects are quantitatively expressed (68.11 %) and 31.48 % of the effects relate to revenue outcomes. More than one-third of the explanatory statements can be qualified as intermediary accounts (accounting- and consolidation-technical explanations) (38.37 %) and these are biased towards the framing of negative accounting effects, a tendency referred to as 'informality bias on positives' versus 'formality bias on negatives' (Appendix 1)".

Self-serving tendencies become especially apparent in the causal assertiveness bias (i.e. number of positive outcomes explained with reference to internal causes minus number of positive outcomes explained with reference to external causes). The average value of 4.95 indicates a strong acclaiming bias, while a comparable causal defensiveness bias (i.e. number of negative outcomes explained with reference to external causes minus number of negative outcomes explained with reference to internal causes) does not hold for the full sample.

In this study, we add to the results reported in Aerts and Tarca (2010) by employing principal components factor analysis with varimax orthogonal rotation in order to empirically reduce the number of attributional content variables and identify dominant attributional profiles. The factor analysis inputs include attributional properties which have been theorised as impression management sensitive (Bettman and Weitz 1983; Salancik and Meindl 1984; Aerts 1994, 2001, 2005; Clatworthy and Jones 2003; Fiol 1995; Sutton and Galunic 1996) and which could be related to the usefulness of explanations for analysts. Zero values for some of the denominators of proportional measures used as input for the factor analysis

Table 13.1 Explanatory content descriptives

Explanatory content characteristics	Total $N = 173$	US $N = 53$	CAN $N = 35$	UK $N = 47$	AUS $N = 38$
Amount of explanations	Mean (SD)				
Number of explained effects	16.19 (11.48)	16.64 (7.99)	13.74 (9.12)	22.60 (14.95)	9.89 (8.36)
Number of positive effects	9.50 (7.93)	9.42 (5.86)	6.37 (5.29)	14.02 (10.35)	6.92 (6.55)
Number of negative effects	6.52 (5.22)	7.21 (3.67)	7.14 (5.71)	8.36 (6.46)	2.71 (2.40)
Number of neutral effects	0.17 (0.56)	0.02 (0.50)	0.23 (0.49)	0.21 (0.66)	0.26 (0.55)
Number of prospective effects	1.73 (2.04)	1.72 (2.04)	1.17 (2.43)	1.94 (1.86)	1.50 (1.90)
Number of attributional statements	33.46 (24.23)	39.08 (21.08)	28.14 (21.50)	42.11 (28.128)	19.84 (18.39)
Relative content characteristics (%)					
Company level effects	60.90 (31.41)	67.86 (26.24)	73.99 (26.16)	48.53 (31.86)	54.44 (35.50)
Quantitative effects	68.11 (24.96)	78.90 (16.67)	69.07 (27.64)	66.55 (17.68)	54.09 (32.30)
Positivity of effects	55.95 (22.29)	55.45 (18.15)	48.43 (24.40)	60.14 (17.73)	58.39 (28.72)
Prospectively of effects	12.31 (14.36)	10.94 (13.17)	12.28 (14.76)	11.23 (11.21)	15.60 (18.51)
Revenue effects	31.48 (22.40)	28.38 (16.96)	27.13 (20.97)	33.99 (20.22)	36.73 (30.78)
Causal explanations	61.63 (23.81)	52.72 (19.67)	57.44 (20.76)	66.89 (20.61)	71.42 (30.06)
Explanatory effort					
Number of explanations per effect	2.04 (0.60)	2.33 (0.52)	2.01 (0.67)	1.88 (0.38)	1.88 (0.73)
Number of explanations per positive effect ($N = 167$)	2.13 (0.79)	2.33 (0.60)	1.98 (0.84)	2.01 (0.73)	2.13 (1.01)
Number of explanations per negative effect ($N = 161$)	1.96 (0.67)	2.33 (0.67)	2.01 (0.73)	1.73 (0.50)	1.64 (0.53)
Density of explanations	1.25 (0.73)	1.55 (0.71)	1.10 (0.61)	1.38 (0.75)	0.83 (0.62)
Formal language use					
Use of accounting explanations (%)	38.37 (23.81)	47.28 (19.67)	42.56 (20.76)	33.11 (20.61)	28.58 (30.06)
Informality bias on positives	6.38 (11.19)	2.87 (10.46)	2.00 (6.44)	11.28 (13.06)	9.24 (10.17)
Formality bias on negatives	−1.32 (6.40)	−0.15 (6.73)	−0.69 (6.96)	−3.17 (7.36)	−1.24 (2.90)

(continued)

Table 13.1 (continued)

Explanatory content characteristics	Total $N = 173$	US $N = 53$	CAN $N = 35$	UK $N = 47$	AUS $N = 38$
Self-serving content of causal explanations					
Use of enhancements and entitlements (% on total attributions)	24.09 (17.53)	18.81 (13.46)	19.67 (19.78)	27.43 (14.94)	31.40 (20.22)
Use of excuses, justifications and causality denials (% on total attributions)	6.95 (8.57)	6.08 (6.87)	6.67 (7.05)	8.96 (9.35)	5.90 (10.66)
Causal assertiveness bias on positives	4.95 (6.24)	3.92 (5.35)	3.34 (4.10)	8.17 (7.29)	3.89 (6.41)
Causal defensiveness bias on negatives	−0.94 (4.23)	−2.26 (3.72)	−1.43 (4.40)	0.51 (5.31)	−0.42 (2.25)
Inconsistency of explanations					
Formality inconsistency on valence of effects ($N = 158$)	13.15 (11.77)	11.39 (9.46)	9.29 (8.36)	17.64 (14.40)	13.10 (12.07)
Depth inconsistency on valence of effects ($N = 158$)	0.58 (0.66)	0.54 (0.48)	0.61 (0.56)	0.50 (0.72)	0.78 (0.88)

This table provides the mean (standard deviation) for characteristics of performance explanations, in total and for the four countries in the study. The variables are defined in Appendix 1

Table 13.2 Principal components factor analysis—Attributional content profiles

	Factor 1 Assertiveness	Factor 2 Defensiveness	Factor 3 Formality/ Extensiveness	Factor 4 overall Positiveness
Panel A Firm-specific attributional content factors (correlations > 0.35)				
Attributional statement characteristics				
Causal assertiveness bias on positives	0.66		0.38	
Use of enhancements and entitlements	0.76			0.41
Causal defensiveness bias on negatives		0.82		
Use of excuses, justifications and causality denials		0.69		−0.62
Positivity of effects				0.86
Prospectively of effects		−0.37	−0.44	
Revenue effects (%)		0.38		
Divisional effects (%)	0.38	0.62		
Attributional depth			0.64	
Density of explanations			0.82	
Use of accounting explanations	−0.84		0.36	
Informality bias on positives	0.85			
Formality inconsistency on valence of effect	0.61			
Initial eigenvalue	3.86	1.98	1.73	1.03
% of variance explained	29.71 %	15.22 %	13.27 %	7.91 %
Cumulative variance explained	29.71 %	44.93 %	58.20 %	66.11 %
	Mean (Std Dev)			
Panel B Descriptives of attributional content factor scores by country				
AUS ($N = 29$)	0.63 (0.91)	0.03 (1.04)	−0.68 (0.99)	0.31 (1.12)
CAN ($N = 31$)	−0.44 (0.72)	−0.16 (1.01)	−0.15 (0.84)	−0.39 (0.95)
UK ($N = 47$)	0.29 (0.97)	0.38 (1.04)	−0.03 (0.97)	0.15 (1.03)
US ($N = 51$)	−0.36 (0.97)	−0.28 (0.83)	0.50 (0.86)	−0.08 (0.86)

Panel A shows the results of a factor analysis (using Varimax rotated component analysis) based on attributional statements with characteristics sensitive to impression management. The factor analysis provides factors which capture attributional content profiles. Factors are named to reflect the characteristics of attributional statements which dominate in each case. Panel B shows factor scores by country. Data availability for factor analysis reduces the sample size from 172 to 158 companies (consistency/inconsistency variables need at least one positive and one negative explained effect per firm) reduce the number of observations in the factor analysis and in the analyses using the resulting factors to 158.[3]

Table 13.2 (Panel A) shows the variables resulting from the factor analysis model with the highest cumulative explained variance. The variables 'depth inconsistency on valence of effect' and 'formality bias on negatives', initially selected as input for factor analysis, were rejected as disturbing variables in the factor analysis.[4] As shown in Table 13.2 (Panel A), we identify four factors with eigenvalues greater than 1.0 which cumulatively explain 66 per cent of the overall variance. Using a cut-off of 0.38 for factor identification purposes, we label these factors as follows: Assertiveness (factor one), Defensiveness (factor two), Formality/extensiveness (factor three) and Overall positivity (factor four).

The assertiveness factor (factor one) reflects a content pattern based on the self-serving causal tendency to acclaim and enhance positive outcomes, the intensity of causal search in the framing activity, and the tendency to selectively avoid accounting explanations for the framing of positive accounting outcomes. Factor two represents basic defensive tendencies in attributional commentary, with defensive bolstering of negative outcomes through the use of excuses and justifications and a search for compensatory effects at segmental information levels. The distinction between factors one and two indicates that the assertive and defensive components of the basic self-presentational bias in causal analysis are different empirical phenomena with probably different drivers and consequences.

Factor three loads positively on cognitive effort including attributional depth (number of explanations for each effect explained), overall density of explanations (number of attributions/total disclosure items) and the relative use of formal accounting explanations, and negatively on the relative amount of prospective attributions. Factor four reflects content with primarily positive attributional content, accompanied by high causal assertiveness and low causal defensiveness. Interestingly, neither the main opportunistic assertiveness factor (factor one) nor the main defensiveness factor (factor two) loads significantly on overall positivity of attributional content, indicating the presence of significant impression management efforts in attributional content patterns.[5]

---

[3] In addition, in order to study specific properties of attributional content and related attributional profiles, at least one positive and one negative attributional statement had to be present in an MC report.

[4] Interestingly, both the depth inconsistency variable and the formality bias variable did not show up as country-sensitive in the multivariate analysis of individual attributional variables.

[5] The moderate character of the overall positiveness factor has to be interpreted based on the specifics of the content of the coded annual report sections. The coded attributional statements were confined to explanations of effects linked to income statement items (formally stated and audited accounting effects). By purposefully ignoring explanations of company actions and decisions not expressed in profit and loss terminology, managerial discretion in selecting and commenting on facts with positive ramifications is only partially captured in the data set. Given the potential significance of a compensatory leverage effect of explanations of non-accounting positive outcomes (Aerts 2001), it can be expected that overall positivity will be higher if all

Panel B of Table 13.2 shows the mean scores on these attributional content factors by country. On average, Australian companies score high on opportunistic assertiveness and low on formality and cognitive effort. Canadian firms, on average, score low on opportunistic assertiveness, but this seems to be associated with on average higher negativity of attributional content. The UK companies exhibit, on average, both assertive and defensive attributional content, whereas these behaviours are typically avoided by US companies which score high on the properties formality and cognitive effort. Overall, these factor-based international differences are consistent with the country-level analyses of individual attributional content variables as reported in Aerts and Tarca (2010).

13.3.3 Data Analysis

As a company's voluntary disclosure strategy may affect MC disclosure, analyst following and analyst forecasts simultaneously, we considered whether endogeneity exists in these relationships using the Hausman test (the positive outcomes of these tests are reported in the results section of this paper). To control for endogeneity in our analyses, we use two- and three-stage least squares regression models to investigate the relationships of attributional profile factors, analyst following and analyst forecast dispersion.

First, we estimate the relation between attributional profile factors and their determinants with the following model:

Attributional profile factor score = f (20 F filing, Change in leverage, Change in profitability, Negative earnings per share, Foreign revenue %, Number of segments, Market-to-Book ratio, Capital intensity, Corporate governance composite, Analyst following, Size, Industry dummies, Country dummies)$_{it}$ (13.1)

The model includes variables identified in prior research as affecting disclosure in annual reports. Thus, company size, change in profitability, change in leverage, growth, diversification, capital intensity, analyst following, filing status, corporate governance, industry sector and country can affect the demand and supply of attributional statements on accounting outcomes. Larger size is commonly associated with more disclosure, possibly because bigger companies have lower information production costs and lower costs of competitive disadvantage associated with their disclosures (Lang and Lundholm 1993). More disclosure is associated with more equity investors, more foreign revenue and more foreign stock exchange listings (Archambault and Archambault 2003). More disclosure in

(Footnote 5 continued)
company-level attributional statements (accounting and non-accounting effects) are selected as the unit of analysis.

MD&A reports is associated with greater analyst following (Clarkson et al. 1999). Other variables drive the need for explanations, such as level and change in profitability and leverage, growth and diversification (Aerts 2001; Clatworthy and Jones 2006). We include proxies to control for level and change in profitability (change in return on equity and a negative EPS dummy), growth (market-to-book ratio), company diversification (number of segments), capital intensity (fixed assets/total assets) and return variability (variation coefficient of ROE over the previous five years).

Corporate governance structure also tends to affect voluntary disclosure, as better governed companies provide higher quality disclosures to distinguish themselves from other firms. Studies show a relationship between disclosure and some corporate governance mechanisms (Forker 1992; Eng and Mak 2003; Cheng and Courtnay 2006). Beekes and Brown (2006) demonstrate that governance quality is related to informativeness of disclosure. We proxy for corporate governance structure using a composite measure (score out of three, where one is added if board chair is a non-executive director, the majority of the board are independent directors and the company uses a committee structure, i.e. audit, nomination and remuneration committees). Finally, industry membership has been shown to influence disclosure (McKinnon and Dalimunthe 1993; Malone et al. 1993; Meek et al. 1995) reflecting specific features of particular industries which lead to distinctive disclosure patterns.[6]

In a second step we control for endogeneity between attributional reporting and analyst following. We use a 2SLS approach for the above regression with analyst following estimated according to the following model. (We exclude variables for company size in the attributional factor regression due to multicollinearity):

$$\text{Analyst following}_{it} = f\,(\text{20 F filing, Market-to-book ratio, Return variability, Company size, Industry, Country})_{it} \tag{13.2}$$

We expect that a 20 F filing by non-US companies will influence the demand for analysts' services. Lang et al. (2003) find that companies cross-listed on US exchanges have greater analyst following. A US listing is likely to stimulate

[6] The impact of industry membership on attributional content was explored further by rotating the country dummy variables within OLS models (untabulated). Considering significant differences of 5 % or more, we find that there is generally a lack of difference between industries, although some specific differences are observed. For assertiveness (factor one), Pharmaceuticals are more assertive than other industry groups, which are not different from each other. For defensiveness (factor two) Food producers are more defensive than Retail. For formality/defensiveness (factor three) Pharmaceuticals and Biotech companies score significantly lower than Food producers. For overall positiveness (factor four), Retail companies score significantly higher than Pharmaceuticals and Food producers. Considering the few differences by industry, the main conclusions to be drawn are that industry membership does not seem to have a large impact on attributional framing. However, we do observe that Pharmaceutical companies are more assertive in attributional framing, possibly reflecting the nature of their assets (a relatively high proportion of intangible assets).

activity by analysts in the foreign country, adding to the domestic supply of analysts' services. In addition, since foreign investors are likely to experience greater information asymmetry than domestic investors, they create greater demand for analysts' research. From the supply side, analysts may be more inclined to follow cross-listed companies because they are more likely to attract a larger investor base. Prior research on analyst following in the US shows that company size is positively related to analyst following. Bhushan (1989) argues that company size affects both the aggregate demand and the aggregate supply for analysts' services. Moreover, analyst coverage is reported as related to Tobin's Q (Lang et al. 2003). The demand for analyst services may be greater for firms with relatively more intangible assets because the informativeness of their financial reports is lower (Amir et al. 2003; Barth et al. 2001). Since the market-to-book ratio is often used as a proxy for the level of intangibles, we expect a positive relation between this ratio and analyst following. Prior research documents a relation between earnings volatility and analyst coverage (Bhushan 1989; Lang et al. 2003), suggesting that demand for analysts' services is greater for companies with higher financial risk. Therefore, we expect a positive relationship between return variability and analyst coverage. Industries are not likely to equally attract financial analysts. Hence, dummy variables are used to control for industry effects. Additionally, Chang et al. (2000) provide evidence that country-level institutional variables affect the availability of analyst forecasts so we introduce country dummies to control for the country effect.

In the third step, we look at the association of attributional reporting profiles and analyst forecast dispersion. We extend the second model into 3SLS regression mode, as previous research suggests that the properties of analyst forecasts, the level of analyst following of a company and the extent and quality of a company's disclosure practices are to a significant extent simultaneously determined (Alford and Berger 1999; Hope 2003a). These simultaneous relationships imply considerable information dynamics at the company level whereby the level and quality of the analyst services and the disclosure position of a company influence each other.

We define analyst forecast dispersion as the standard deviation in analyst forecasts divided by the absolute mean forecast. To control for endogeneity, the three-stage least squares model shown below is used. In the 3SLS regressions, data constraints (at least two analysts need to follow a company and forecasts are available) restrict the number of observations to 116 firms.

$$\text{Analyst forecast dispersion}_{it} = f\,(\text{Analyst following, Earnings surprise, Return variability, Negative earnings per share, Use of US GAAP accounting standards, Attributional reporting score})_{it} \tag{13.3}$$

$$\text{Attributional profile factor score}_{it} = f\,(\text{20 F filing, Corporate governance composite, Change in leverage, Change in profitability, Foreign revenue, Number of segments, Capital investment intensity, Company size, Market-to-book ratio, Industry, Country})_{it} \tag{13.4}$$

$$\text{Analyst following}_{it} = f\,(\text{20 F filing, Market-to-book, Return variability, Company size, Industry, Country})_{it} \tag{13.5}$$

In addition to the attributional profile measures, several other variables are introduced as possible determinants of analyst forecast dispersion.

Analyst following. Prior studies (Imhoff and Lobo 1992; Marquardt and Wiedman 1998) argue that analyst following functions as a proxy for a company's information that is publicly available. More specifically, Roulstone (2003) provides results that are consistent with analysts reducing information asymmetry by providing public information to market participants, while no support is found for analyst following functioning as a proxy for privately held information. If analyst information is quickly disseminated to large numbers of market participants, then high analyst following represents a 'good' information environment for uninformed and partially informed market participants.

This argument would imply that analyst reports are indeed substitutes and not just complements of corporate disclosures. The substitutory role of analyst following is also consistent with empirical results showing that the impact of corporate disclosures on the cost of capital and on the properties of analyst forecasts decreases with the number of analysts following the company (Botosan 1997; Richardson and Welker 2001; Hope 2003a). Given the evidence of analyst following as a proxy for public information instead of privately held information, we use analyst following as the most efficient proxy for overall company disclosure quality. Moreover, controlling for other disclosure outlets would inflate the number of endogenous variables within our system which would be difficult to control efficiently. Hence, a firm's analyst following is used as a proxy for overall company disclosure quality and the extent of a firm's communication with financial analysts (Leuz 2003). Analyst forecast performance is likely to improve, as more information about a company is processed and disclosed by analysts (Alford and Berger 1999). A negative association between analyst following and forecast dispersion is expected.

Earnings surprise and *Return variability*. Variability in earnings and in historical accounting returns increases the difficulty of forecasting. So, a positive association is expected between the level of earnings change and forecast dispersion. The same reasoning applies for return variability that measures the inherent uncertainty in predicting earnings. A negative relationship is expected between return variability and analyst forecast dispersion.

Negative earnings. We expect that forecasting earnings is more difficult for companies that experience losses. We use an indicative variable for negative earnings and anticipate a positive relationship between this binary variable and forecast dispersion (Hope 2003a, b).

Use of US GAAP. As high-quality standards, the use of US GAAP should be negatively associated with analyst forecast dispersion.

13.4 Results

13.4.1 Regression Results

Table 13.3 reports results for the 2SLS regression models showing the relationship of a company's score on the four attributional profile factors and their determinants. Results from the assertiveness model indicate that attributional assertiveness is significantly higher in Australia and in the UK than in the USA (the omitted country dummy). There is no significant difference in attributional assertiveness between US and Canadian firms. Consistent with the country impact, a Form 20-F filing decreases self-promotional tendencies. A higher quality corporate governance structure also tempers assertive tendencies. The number of segments is positively associated with attributional assertiveness, possibly because more segments create more room for opportunistic attributional framing. Finally, attributional assertiveness is higher in the pharmaceutical industry (with retail as the omitted industry category).

The defensiveness model highlights significantly higher defensiveness in Australia, Canada and the UK relative to the USA. Greater analyst following is associated with more defensiveness while a Form 20-F filing is associated with non-US firms explaining accounting outcomes less defensively. Consistent with previous research (Aerts 2001, 2005), defensiveness is responsive to level and change of profitability, while assertive attributional tendencies are not. Moreover, the effect of number of segments on attributional defensiveness suggests that the existence of more segments promotes opportunistic attributional search.

The formality/extensiveness model evidences more depth and density of explanations in the USA compared to the other three countries. Growth firms (as proxied by the market-to-book ratio) exhibit less formality of explanations and attributional extensiveness, suggesting that such firms prefer a more descriptive approach in their management commentary or probably more explanations with regard to non-accounting outcomes. Increased analyst following has the opposite effect, bringing firms to adopt a more formal and extensive attributional attitude. The fourth attributional profile factor (overall positiveness) appears to capture mainly industry differences, which we discuss further in robustness tests.

Table 13.3 2SLS regressions—Explanatory factors for attributional content profiles

$N = 158$	Assertiveness	Defensiveness	Formality/ extensiveness	Overall positiveness
Constant	−0.427	***−1.711	0.220	0.656
Listing 20F	**−0.592	***−0.755	0.104	−0.068
Change in leverage	−0.028	0.013	−0.030	**0.059
Change in profitability	0.093	***−0.193	*0.136	−0.010
Negative EPS	0.018	***−0.720	−0.092	***−0.717
Industry building materials	−0.007	**0.490	0.124	*−0.468
Industry pharmaceuticals	***0.695	0.260	*−0.433	***−0.795
Industry biotechnology	0.264	*0.539	−0.254	−0.329
Industry food producers	0.250	***0.581	0.299	***−0.627
Foreign revenue %	0.196	0.333	0.008	−0.023
Number of segments	**0.125	**0.137	0.056	−0.001
Market to book	−0.014	−0.001	***−0.059	0.032
Capital intensity	−0.032	*0.104	−0.044	−0.088
Corporate governance composite	**−0.260	0.161	−0.002	−0.082
Analyst following	0.014	***0.047	***0.050	−0.004
Australia	***1.361	*0.415	***−1.019	0.314
United Kingdom	***0.881	***0.538	***−0.816	0.315
Canada	0.095	**0.526	**−0.468	0.036
Adj. R-Square	0.229	0.318	0.266	0.156

Results for 2SLS regression equations examining the association between attributional content profiles and company attributes. The USA is omitted country dummy variable and retail is the omitted industry dummy variable. Listing 20F = 1 if the company has a US listing requiring a Form 20-F reconciliation, 0 otherwise. Change in leverage = (total debt/total equity 2003—2002)/total debt/total equity 2002. Change in profitability = (net profit after tax 2003—2002)/net profit after tax 2002. Negative EPS = 1 if company reports a negative EPS. Foreign revenue = proportion of foreign revenue to total revenue. Market to book = market value of equity at financial year end/book value of equity. Capital intensity = non-current assets/total assets. Corporate governance composite = score out of three, where 1 is added if board chair is a non-executive director, the majority of the board are independent directors and the company uses a committee structure (audit, nomination and remuneration committee). Analyst = number of analysts following a firm

$*p < 0.10$, $**\ p < 0.05$, $***p < 0.01$ (two-tailed tests)

13.4.2 Attributional Content Profiles and Analyst Forecast Dispersion

Since we posit that a firm's voluntary disclosure strategy may affect MC disclosure, analyst following and analyst forecasts simultaneously, we consider whether endogeneity exists between these relations using the Hausman test. Consequently, we reject the null hypothesis of no endogeneity with respect to attributional content profiles reflecting defensiveness and formality/extensiveness and analyst forecast dispersion. Furthermore, the Hausman test confirms endogeneity between analyst

Table 13.4 3SLS regressions—Relationship of attributional content profiles/characteristics and analyst forecast dispersion

	Sign	Assertiveness	Defensiveness[a]	Formality/ extensiveness
Panel A Attributional content profile				
Constant		**0.163	***0.228	**0.130
Analyst following	−	−0.001	−0.001	0.002
Change in earnings per share	+	**0.001	**0.001	**0.001
Return variability	+	*0.011	**0.015	*0.010
Negative earnings per share	+	***0.173		*0.098
US GAAP	−	*−0.069	*−0.085	0.024
Attributional content profile	−	−0.018	**−0.067	***−0.138
R-square		0.168	0.166	0.070
R-square of attributional profile regression[b]		0.375	0.560	0.382
R-square of analyst following regression[b]		0.475	0.475	0.475
N		116	116	116
	Sign	Attributional Depth	Attributional Density	Use of accounting explanations
Panel B Attributional content characteristics of formality/extensiveness				
Constant		**0.554	***0.595	**0.353
Analyst following	−	−0.006	0.004	−0.002
Change in earnings per share	+	*0.001	0.001	0.001
Return variability	+	*0.009	*0.011	*0.009
Negative earnings per share	+	***0.229	*0.121	***0.282
US GAAP	−	−0.031	−0.009	*−0.123
Attributional content characteristic	−	*−0.178	***−0.349	−0.231
R-square		0.102	0.085	0.182
R-square of attributional profile regression[b]		0.341	0.264	0.305
R-square of analyst following regression[b]		0.475	0.482	0.482
N		116	116	116

Results for 3SLS regression equations examining the association between attributional content profiles (Panel A) and individual attributional content characteristics (Panel B) and company attributes. Assertiveness, defensiveness and formality/extensiveness are attributional content profiles, derived from the factor analysis presented in Table 13.3. Attributional depth, attributional density and use of accounting explanations are individual attributional content characteristics which are the key elements of the factor formality/extensiveness (Table 13.3). Attributional depth is the number of explanations per effect statement, attributional density is the number of attribution statements relative to total disclosure, and use of accounting explanations refers to the proportion of explanations based on technical-accounting language (rather than causal explanations). Analyst following = number of analysts following a firm. Change in EPS = ABS(EPS 2003—2002)/EPS 2002). Return variability is the variation coefficient of ROE over the five years preceding 2003. Negative EPS = 1 if company reports a negative EPS

*$p < 0.10$, ** $p < 0.05$, ***$p < 0.01$ (one-tailed if sign predicted, otherwise two-tailed tests)

[a] Negative EPS is not integrated in the Defensiveness regression due to multicollinearity

[b] Attributional profile regression and analyst following regressions are not presented

following and analyst forecast dispersion ($p < 0.059$).[7] Hence, it is important to control for firms' incentives to use specific attributional reporting profiles in order to assess the value relevance of attributional reporting on analyst forecast dispersion, which is done using 3SLS regressions shown in the previous section.

Results of 3SLS models (Table 13.4 Panel A) show a significant association between attributional defensiveness ($p < 0.05$) and attributional formality/extensiveness ($p < 0.01$) and dispersion of analyst forecasts, thus providing support for the economic relevance of the attributional content profiles. The attributional assertiveness factor, however, does not significantly affect analyst dispersion. The results for formality/extensiveness show that there is less disagreement among analysts for companies providing greater density of explanations (i.e. more explanations of performance relative to total narrative content) and more depth of explanations (i.e. more explanations for each effect). The results are consistent with studies that suggest more MC content and higher quality content is associated with lower dispersion in analyst forecasts (Lang and Lundholm 1996; Barron et al. 1999). Control variables in the models in Panel A are largely as expected. Analyst forecast dispersion is positively associated with a company making a loss (not tested in the defensiveness model), larger changes in earnings per share (earnings surprise) and higher variability of returns. As noted previously, companies using US GAAP exhibit less dispersion in analyst forecasts.

We provide further analysis of the major components of the formality/extensiveness factor in Table 13.4, Panel B. Results suggest that it is essentially the extensiveness of attributional reasoning (attributional depth and attributional density) that drives the relevance of the Formality/Extensiveness factor in relation to analyst forecast dispersion. The practice of providing relatively more explanations and more detailed explanations is associated with less forecast dispersion but using relatively more accounting explanations is not. We do not find that analysts prefer one type of explanation over the other. In this sense our results contrast with that of Bozzolan et al. (2009). In our setting, the more verifiable explanations (accounting-technical) are not associated with lower dispersion.

13.4.3 Robustness Tests

We investigate the possible impact of country differences in the models. We control for country in the analyst forecast dispersion regression by introducing country dummies instead of the control for US GAAP (results not tabulated). We

[7] In 3SLS regressions, all dependent variables are explicitly endogenous to the system and as such are treated as correlated with the disturbances in the system's equations. All exogenous variables are used as instruments. In the case that regressions and error terms are not related, i.e. absence of endogeneity, 3SLS will produce the same estimates as OLS. Therefore, if any of the endogeneously specified variables are in fact exogeneous, the 3SLS is still appropriate (Judge et al. 1988, p. 655).

find that both attributional defensiveness and attributional formality/extensiveness are significant at the 1 % level, whereas attributional assertiveness remains not significant. The finding is consistent with our earlier results that attributional optimism seems to be discounted by analysts, while defensiveness and depth and density of explanations are useful in reducing disagreement among analysts.

13.5 Conclusion

Following Aerts and Tarca (2010)'s finding that specific characteristics of explanations of performance outcomes in management commentary reports differ significantly between countries, we investigate whether specific profiles in attributional behaviour with regard to performance outcomes can be identified, whether these attributional content profiles differ between countries and whether these differences have economic significance. We find that more extensiveness in attributional framing of performance outcomes (which means providing relatively more performance explanations and more in-depth explanation of specific outcomes) is associated with less analyst forecast dispersion. More defensiveness in performance explanations is also associated with less dispersion. Interestingly, we find that forecast dispersion is unaffected by more assertiveness in attributional framing, a trait more likely to be observed in UK and Australian reports. Nor is dispersion affected by more intense use of technical-accounting explanations, favoured by US and, to a lesser extent, Canadian firms.

Our study brings together and extends two streams of literature. Our findings about the importance for analysts of the depth and density of both causal and accounting-technical explanations are consistent with prior studies highlighting the role of quality narrative information (Barron et al. 1999; Lys and Soo 1995; Lang and Lundholm 1993, 1996; Hope 2003a, b). The different associative effect of causal defensiveness versus causal assertiveness is consistent with previous organizational research findings, indicating that specific occurrences of defensive impression management are more effective than assertive verbal behaviours in shaping evaluative perceptions of an external audience (Suchman 1995; Kim et al. 2006; Wood and Mitchell 1981; Barton and Mercer 2005; Elsbach 2003), while such direct evidence is absent for acclaiming verbal tactics. Future research could usefully explore the attributes of a broader category of explanations, as we have only considered performance explanations. This approach could also lead to further investigation of analysts' responses to management's compensatory and reputational incentives underlying the explanations in MC reports.

Appendix 1

Aerts and Tarca (2010) Explanation of Terms: Attributional Content Characteristics

Attributional statement	Antecedent—consequence statement. One or more sentences (or part thereof) in which an outcome or effect (relating to firm's financial performance, i.e. revenue, expense or net income/earnings/profits item) is linked to one or more antecedents for that outcome, e.g. Sales increased due to strong consumer demand and an increase in retail outlets
Explained effects	
Company/division	The statement relates to the companies as a whole and/or to a division within the company, e.g. Sales for the company decreased in the current year (company). However, there was strong performance of the Orange division, following restructuring carried out last year (division)
Valence of effect/Positivity	A positive effect is favourable for the company (e.g. revenue increasing, expense decreasing). A negative effect is not favourable (e.g. expenses have increased, without a commensurate increase in revenue)
Prospectivity	The statement relates to a future event or period, e.g. Sales are expected to increase in the following year due to improved economic conditions including lower interest rates
Explanatory effort	
Depth of explanations	Number of explanations for each statement of effect (may be one or more), e.g. Sales increased due to strong consumer demand and an increase in retail outlets (one effect, two antecedents)
Density of explanations	Number of a firm's attribution statements relative to number of items of disclosure about results of operations in MD&A, OFR or equivalent
Formal language use	
Technical-accounting versus causal explanation	Technical-accounting explanations are based on technical-accounting language and are of an intermediary nature (e.g. Profit increased because margins improved). Causal explanations refer to other types of explanation (e.g. Sales revenue increased due to stronger demand and a more buoyant economy)
Formality (informality) bias	Greater (lesser) use of technical-accounting explanations relative to causal explanations
Informality bias on positives	(Relative) tendency to explain positive effects more in explicitly causal terms than in accounting-technical language
Formality bias on negatives	(Relative) tendency to explain negative effects more in accounting-technical language than in explicitly causal terms
Self-serving content	
Causal assertive self-serving bias	(Relative) tendency to explain positive effects more from internal than external antecedents
Causal defensive self-serving bias	(Relative) tendency to explain negative effects more from external than internal antecedents
Enhancement	The framing of a positive outcome relative to negative external factors, e.g. The company achieved strong revenue growth in the Orange division, despite an industry-wide decline in demand for goods produced
Entitlement	Positive effects causally attributed to internal factors (e.g. management decision) rather than external factors (e.g. industry or economy wide factors)

(continued)

(continued)

Excuse	Negative effects causally attributed to external factors (e.g. industry or economy wide factors) rather than internal factors (e.g. management decision), e.g. Sales declined in the period, largely due to poor demand reflecting an unexpected downturn in the economic cycle
Justification	Teleological explanations of negative effects, e.g. R&D expenses increased in order to accelerate the introduction of new high-quality products
Causality denial	Implicit denial of responsibility for a negative effect by referring to internal proactive or remedial factors, e.g. Despite increased efforts of sales staff, sales declined in the period
Inconsistency of explanations	
Formality inconsistency on valence of effects	Relative use of accounting-technical explanations for positive versus negative effects
Depth inconsistency on valence of effects	Number of explanations per effect for positive versus negative effects

Appendix 2

Aerts and Tarca (2010) Coding dimensions of attribution statements

An attribution statement: One or more sentences (or part thereof) in which an outcome or effect (relating to a firm's financial performance, i.e. revenue, expense or net income/earnings/profit item) is linked to one or more antecedents for that outcome. Each attribution statement was coded on dimensions A01–A05 for the outcome/effect phrase and B10–B15 for each antecedent phrase.

A. Outcome/effect	B. Antecedent
A01 Nature of the effect	B10 Explicitness of the antecedent-consequence relationship
Revenue	1. Explicit
1. Expenses	2. Implicit
2. Income/earnings/profit	3. Decomposition (effect = sales, cause = sales)
A02 Valence of the effect	B11 Direction of antecedent-consequence relationship
1. Positive (e.g. increase sales, decrease expenses)	1. Same direction
2. Negative (e.g. decrease sales, increase expenses)	2. Opposite direction
3. Unchanged/flat	B12 Time orientation of antecedent
A03 Time orientation of the effect	1. Past (effect concerns event of preceding fiscal year)
1. Past (effect concerns event of preceding fiscal year)	2. Present (year under review)
2. Present (year under review)	3. Future
3. Future	B13 Antecedent is expressed in quantitative or qualitative terms

(continued)

(continued)

A. Outcome/effect	B. Antecedent
A04 Effect is expressed in quantitative or qualitative terms	1. Quantitative
1. Quantitative	2. Qualitative
2. Qualitative	B14 Nature of explanation
A05 Level of the explained effect	1. Causal explanation
1. Division/product/geographic segment	2. Accounting-technical explanation
2. Company as a whole	B15 Locus of causality of antecedent
	1. Internal cause, explicit reference to management board
	2. Internal cause, explicit reference to segment division in the company
	3. Internal cause with explicit reference to personnel
	4. Other internal causes
	5. External cause; cause is on sector or industry level
	6. External cause; cause is on general economic level
	7. Other external causes

Appendix 3

Aerts and Tarca (2010) Examples of attribution statements

1. Antecedent-consequence relationship: an expense outcome is linked to two explanations, one coded as technical-accounting and the other as causal:

The cost of merchandise sold decreased in 2003 compared to 2002 [*effect*] reflecting lower spending on goods and services due to lower sales [*antecedent* (*a*) *technical-accounting*] as well as favourable procurement conditions [*antecedent* (*b*) *causal*].

Sears Canada Inc. 2003 Annual Report p. 28 (*Canada Retail*)

2. Explicit explanations: characterised by a causal conjunction or connecting phrase (e.g. because of, as a result of) and the verb in the sentence can refer to an explicit explanation (e.g. lead to, result in). For example, consider the following positive outcome with an internal cause which uses 'through' as the causal conjunction:

Foreign exchange losses decreased in the year [*effect*] through better management of the consolidated entity affairs [*antecedent—causal*].

Peptech 2003 Annual Report p. 18 (*Australia Biotech*)

3. Implicit explanation: when cause and effect are not explicitly related. These implicit explanations are only taken into account when cause and effect can be reasonably linked to each other. In the following causal explanations (an excuse and an entitlement) cause and effect are linked by the words 'as a result of':

The company's hog production operations were negatively impacted in 2003 as a result of the sharp rise in the Canadian dollar [antecedent—causal] which immediately reduced producer revenues [effect].

Maple Leaf Foods, 2003 p. 29 (Canadian Food producer).

We are continuing to realise gains in our primary margin [effect] as a result of actions to increase overseas production and consolidate our supply base [antecedent—causal].

Marks and Spencer, 2003 p. 3 (UK Retail)

4. Time orientation: as shown below in a prospective causal statement:

The outsourcing of the liquid sorbitol production at Atlas Point was completed this year [antecedent—causal]. These changes are expected to yield a profit improvement next year [effect].

Associated British Foods, 2003, p. 20 (UK Food producer).

5. Technical-accounting attributions: explanations of accounting effects in financial accounting language:

During fiscal 2003 … lower depreciation expense [antecedent: internal—technical-accounting] contributed to improvement in gross profit and margin [effect].

Other income increased to $3,350,000 in 2003 from $2,285,000 in 2002 [effect] primarily as a result of $932,000 improvement in equity in net earning of affiliates [antecedent: internal—technical-accounting].

Florida Rock Industries Inc., 2003 pp. 8–9 (US Building Materials)

References

Accounting Standards Board (ASB). (2003). Operating and financial review. http://www.asb.org.uk/publications/publication124.html

Aerts, W. (1994). On the use of accounting logic as an explanatory category in narrative accounting disclosures. *Accounting, Organizations and Society, 19*(4/5), 337–353.

Aerts, W. (2001). Inertia in the attributional content of annual accounting narratives. *European Accounting Review, 10*(1), 3–32.

Aerts, W. (2005). Picking up the pieces: Impression management in the retrospective attributional framing of accounting outcomes. *Accounting, Organizations and Society, 30*(6), 493–571.

Aerts, W., & Tarca, A. (2010). Financial performance explanations and institutional setting. *Accounting and Business Research, 40*(5), 421–450.

Alford, A. W., & Berger, P. G. (1999). A simultaneous equations analysis of forecast accuracy, analyst following, and trading volume. *Journal of Accounting, Auditing and Finance, 14*(3), 219–240.

Amir, E., Lev, B., & Sougiannis, T. (2003). Do financial analysts get intangibles? *European Accounting Review, 12*(4), 635–659.

Ang, J.& Ciccone, S.(2001). International differences in analyst forecast properties. Available at SSRN: http://ssrn.com/abstract=275091

Archambault, J. J., & Archambault, M. E. (2003). A multinational test of determinants of corporate disclosure. *The International Journal of Accounting, 38*, 173–194.

Baginski, S., Hassell, J., & Kimbrough, M. (2002). The effect of legal environment on preemptive disclosure: Evidence from management earnings forecasts issued in U.S. and Canadian markets. *The Accounting Review, 77*, 25–50.

Baginski, S., Hassell, J., & Kimbrough, M. (2004). Why do managers explain their earnings forecast? *Journal of Accounting Research, 72*(1): 1–29.

Baginski, S., Hassell, J., & Kimbrough, M. (2008). Macro information environment change and the quality of management earnings forecast'. *Review of Quantitative Finance and Accounting, 31*: 311–330

Ball, R., Kothari, S., & Robin, A. (2000). The effect of international institutional factors on properties. *Journal of Accounting and Economics, 29*, 1–51.

Barron, O. E., Kile, C. O., & O'Keefe, T. B. (1999). MD & A quality as measured by the SEC and analysts' earnings forecasts. *Contemporary Accounting Research, 16*(1), 75–109.

Barth, M., Beaver, W., & Landsman, W. (2001). The relevance of the value relevance literature for financial accounting standard setting: Another view. *Journal of Accounting and Economics, 31*(1–3), 77–104.

Barton, J., & Mercer, M. (2005). To blame or not to blame: analysts' reactions to external explanations for poor financial performance. *Journal of Accounting and Economics, 39*(3), 509–533.

Beattie, V., & McInnes, B. (2006). *Narrative reporting in the UK and US—Which system works best?*. London: Institute of Chartered Accountants in England & Wales.

Beattie, V., McInnes, B., & Fearnley, S. (2002). *Through the eyes of management: A study of narrative disclosures*. London: Institute of Chartered Accountants in England & Wales.

Beattie, V., McInnes, B., & Fearnley, S. (2004). *Through the eyes of management: Narrative reporting across three sectors*. London: Institute of Chartered Accountants in England & Wales.

Beekes, W., & Brown, P. (2006). Do better-governed Australian companies make more informative disclosures? *Journal of Business Finance and Accounting, 33*(3/4), 422–450.

Bettman, J. R., & Weitz, B. A. (1983). Attributions in the boardroom: Causal reasoning in corporate annual reports. *Administrative Science Quarterly, 28*, 165–183.

Bhushan, R. (1989). Firm characteristics and analyst following. *Journal of Accounting and Economics, 11*(2–3), 255–275.

Botosan, C. (1997). Disclosure level and the cost of equity capital. *The Accounting Review, 72*(3), 323–349.

Bozzolan, S., Trombetta, M., & Beretta, S. (2009). Forward-looking disclosures, financial verifiability and analysts' forecasts: A study of cross-listed European firms. *European Accounting Review, 18*(3), 435.

Brown, S., & Tucker, J. (2011). Large-sample evidence on firms' year-over-year MD&A modifications. *Journal of Accounting Research, 49*(2), 309–346.

Byard, D. & Shaw, K. (2006). Corporate disclosure quality and properties of analysts' information environment. SSRN eLibrary.

Chang, J.J., Khanna, T., & Palepu, K. (2000). Analyst activity around the world. HSB Strategy Unit Working Paper No. 01-61. Available at SSRN: http://ssrn.com/abstracts=204570

Cheng, E., & Courtenay, S., (2006). Board Composition, regulatory regime and voluntary disclosure. *The International Journal of Accounting, 41*(3): 262–289.

Clapham, S. E., & Schwenk, C. R. (1991). Self-serving attributions, managerial cognition, and company performance. *Strategic Management Journal, 12*, 219–229.

Clarkson, P. M., Kao, J. L., & Richardson, G. D. (1999). Evidence that management discussion and analysis (MD&A) is a part of a firm's overall disclosure package. *Contemporary Accounting Research, 16*(1), 111–134.

Clatworthy, M., & Jones, M. J. (2003). Financial reporting of good news and bad news: Evidence from accounting narratives. *Accounting and Business Research, 33*(3), 171–185.

Clatworthy, M. A., & Jones, M. J. (2006). Differential pattern of textual characteristics and company performance in the chairman's statement. *Accounting, Auditing and Accountability Journal, 19*(4), 493–511.

Collins, W., Davie, E. S., & Weetman, P. (1993). Management discussion and analysis: An evaluation of practice in UK and US companies. *Accounting and Business Research, 23*(9), 123–137.

D'Aveni, R. A., & MacMillan, I. C. (1990). Crisis and the content of managerial communications: A study of the focus of attention of top managers in surviving and failing firms. *Administrative Science Quarterly, 35*, 634–657.

Elsbach, K. D. (2003). Organizational perception management. In L. L. Cummings, B. M. Staw (Eds.), *Research in organizational behavior* (Vol. 25, pp 297-332).

Eng, L. L., & Mak, Y. T. (2003). Corporate governance and voluntary disclosure. *Journal of Accounting and Public Policy, 22*(4), 325–345.

Fiol, C. M. (1995). Corporate communications: Comparing executives' private and public statements. *Academy of Management Journal, 28*(2), 522–536.

Forker, J. (1992). Corporate governance and disclosure quality. *Accounting and Business Research, 22*(86), 111–124.

Frost, C., & Pownall, G. (1994). Accounting disclosure practices in the United States and the United Kingdom. *Journal of Accounting Research, 32*(1), 75–102.

Gardner, W. L., & Martinko, M. J. (1988). Impression management: An observational study linking audience characteristics with verbal self-presentations. *Academy of Management Journal, 31*(1), 42–65.

Hooks, K., & Moon, J. (1993). A classification scheme to examine management discussion and analysis compliance. *Accounting Horizons, 7*, 41–59.

Hope, O. K. (2003a). Disclosure practices, enforcement of accounting standards and analysts' forecasts accuracy: An international study. *Journal of Accounting Research, 41*(2), 272–273.

Hope, O.-K. (2003b). Accounting policy disclosure and analysts' forecasts. *Contemporary Accounting Research, 20*(2), 295–321.

Hughes, P., & Sankar, R. (2006). The quality of discretionary disclosure under litigation risk. *Journal of Accounting Auditing and Finance, 21*(1), 55–81.

International Accounting Standards Committee Foundation (IASCF). (2005). Discussion paper management commentary. Available on the internet from http://www.iasb.org/NR/rdonlyres/0FE78C14-8AF9-4CFB-A764-40B1A08E0DF5/0/DPManagementCommentary.pdf

Jones, C. L., & Cole, C. J. (2005). Management discussion and analysis: A review and implications for future research. *Journal of Accounting Literature, 24*, 135–174.

Judge, G. G., Hill, R. C., Griffiths, W. E., Lütkepohl, H., & Lee, T. (1988). *Introduction to the Theory and Practice of Econometrics*. New York: Wiley.

Khurana, I., & Raman, K. (2004). Litigation risk and the financial reporting credibility of Big 4 versus Non-B audits: Evidence from Anglo-American countries. *The Accounting Review, 79*(2), 473–495.

Kim, P. H., Dirks, K. T., Cooper, C. D., & Ferrin, D. L. (2006). When more blame is better than less: The implications of internal vs. external attributions for the repair of trust after a competence- vs. integrity-based trust violation. *Organizational Behavior and Human Decision Processes, 99*, 49–65.

La Porta, R., Lopez-De-Silanes, F., & Shleifer, A. (2006). What works in securities laws? *Journal of Finance, 61*(1), 1–32.

Lang, M., & Lundholm, R. (1993). Cross-sectional determinants of analyst ratings of corporate disclosures. *Journal of Accounting Research, 31*, 246–271.

Lang, M., & Lundholm, R. (1996). Corporate disclosure policy and analyst behavior. *The Accounting Review, 71*, 467–492.

Lang, M. H., Lins, K. V., & Miller, D. P. (2003). ADRs, analysts, and accuracy: Does cross listing in the United States improve a firm's information environment and increase market value? *Journal of Accounting Research, 41*(2), 317–345.

Lehavey, R., Li, F., & Merkley, K. (2011). Effect of firms' communication complexity on analyst following and the properties of their earnings forecasts. *The Accounting Review, 86*(3), 1087–1115.

Leuz, C. (2003). IAS versus U.S. GAAP: Information asymmetry-based evidence from Germany's New Market. *Journal of Accounting Research, 41*(3), 445–472.

Imhoff, E. A. Jr. & Lobo, G.J. (1992). The effect of ex ante earnings uncertainty on earnings response coefficients, *The Accounting Review* (*April*), pp. 427–439.

Lys, T., & Soo, L. (1995). Analysts' forecast precision as a response to competition. *Journal of Accounting, Auditing and Finance, 10*, 751–765.

Malone, D., Fries, C., & Jones, M. (1993). An empirical investigation of the extent of corporate financial disclosure in the oil and gas industry. *Journal of Accounting, Auditing and Finance, 8*(3), 249–273.

Marquardt, C. A., & Wiedman, C. I. (1998). Voluntary disclosure, information asymmetry, and insider selling through secondary equity offerings. *Contemporary Accounting Research, 15*(4), 505–537.

McKinnon, J. L., & Dalimunthe, L. (1993). Voluntary disclosure of segment information by Australian diversified companies. *Accounting and Finance, 33*(1), 33–50.

Meek, G. K., Roberts, C. B., & Gray, S. (1995). Factors influencing voluntary annual report disclosures by US., UK and continental European multinational corporations. *Journal of International Business Studies, 26*(3), 555–572.

Merkl-Davies, D.M., & Brennan, N.M. (2007). Discretionary disclosure strategies in corporate narratives: Incremental information or impression management? *Journal of Accounting Literature, 26*: 116–196.

Nelson, K. & Pritchard, A. (2007). Litigation risk and voluntary disclosure: The use of meaningful cautionary language. SSRN eLibrary.

Nichols, D. & Weiland, M. (2009). Do firms' nonfinancial disclosures enhance the value of analyst services? Working paper, Cornell University.

PricewaterhouseCoopers (2007). Corporate reporting—a time for reflection. A survey of the Fortune Global 500 companies' narrative reporting, April 26.

Richardson, A., & Welker, M. (2001). Social disclosure, financial disclosure and the cost of equity capital. *Accounting, Organizations and Society, 26*(7/8), 597–616.

Roulstone, D. T. (2003). The relation between insider-trading restrictions and executive compensation. *Journal of Accounting Research, 41*, 525–551.

Salancik, G. R., & Meindl, J. R. (1984). Corporate attributions as strategic illusions of management control. *Administrative Science Quarterly, 29*(2), 238–254.

SEC. (1987). Securities Act Release No. 6231. Available at http://www.sec.gov

Securities and Exchange Commission (SEC). (2003). Review of the periodic reports of the fortune 500 Companies. February 27. Available at www.sec.gov/divisions/corpfin/fortune500rep.htm

Securities and Exchange Commission (SEC). (2004). Summary by the division of corporation finance of significant issues addressed in the review of the periodic reports of the fortune 500 companies. Available at http://www.sec.gov/divisions/corpfin/fortune500rep.htm.

Seetharamana, A., Gul, F., & Lynn, S. (2002). Litigation risk and audit fees: Evidence from UK companies cross-listed on US markets. *Journal of Accounting and Economics, 33*, 91–115.

Staw, B.M., McKechnie, P.I., & Puffer, S.M., (1983). The justification of organizational performance. *Administrative Science Quarterly, 28*(4): 582–600.

Suchman, M. C. (1995). Managing legitimacy: strategic and institutional approaches. *Academy of Management Review, 20*, 571–610.

Sutton, R., & Galunic, D. C. (1996). Consequences of public scrutiny for leaders and their organizations. In B. M. Staw & L. L. Cummings (Eds.), *Research in organizational behavior* (Vol. 18, pp. 201–250). Greenwich: JAI Press.

Vanstraelen, A., Zarzeski, M., & Robb, S. (2003). Corporate nonfinancial disclosure practices and financial analyst forecast ability across three European countries. *Journal of International Financial Management & Accounting, 14*(3), 249–278.

Wagner, J. A., & Gooding, R. Z. (1997). Equivocal information and attribution: An investigation of patterns of managerial sense making. *Strategic Management Journal, 18*(4), 275–286.

Wood, R. E., & Mitchell, T. R. (1981). Manager behavior in a social context: The impact of impression management on attributions and disciplinary actions. *Organizational Behavior and Human Decision Processes, 28*, 356–378.

Chapter 14
The Consequences to Managers for Financial Misrepresentation

Jonathan M. Karpoff, D. Scott Lee and Gerald S. Martin

Abstract We track the fortunes of all 2,206 individuals identified as responsible parties for all 788 Securities and Exchange Commission (SEC) and Department of Justice (DOJ) enforcement actions for financial misrepresentation from January 1, 1978 through September 30, 2006. A total of 93 % lose their jobs by the end of the regulatory enforcement period. Most are explicitly fired. The likelihood of ouster increases with the cost of the misconduct to shareholders and the quality of the firm's governance. Culpable managers also bear substantial financial losses through restrictions on their future employment, their shareholdings in the firm,

This chapter includes a reprinted article first published under the title "The Consequences to Manager for Financial Misrepresentation" in Journal of Financial Economics in 2008, which is followed by the author's comments by way of a post script on further developments on the Financial Misrepresentation based on the original paper presented at the Fourth International Work shop on Accounting and Regulation in 2007. We thank Jennifer Arlen, John Armour, Chris Ander son, Jennifer Bethel, Sam Buell, Laurie Krigman, Geoffrey Miller, an anonymous referee, and participants at the Harvard Law School Conference on "The Enforcement of Corporate Governance Rules" the Duke Law School/ILEP Roundtable Discussion on "Recent Reform Proposals for Securities Litigation, Corporate Governance, and Reporting Practices" and at seminars at Arizona State University, Babson College, the University of Arizona, the University of Kansas, and the University of Nevada at Las Vegas for helpful comments. We thank Texas A&M University's Private Enterprise Research Center and the University of Washington's CFO Forum and Foster School of Business for support.

J. M. Karpoff (✉)
University of Washington, Foster School of Business, Seattle, WA, USA
e-mail: karpoff@u.washington.edu

D. S. Lee
University of Nevada, Lee Business School, Las Vegas, USA
e-mail: scott.lee@unlv.edu

G. S. Martin
American University, Kogod School of Business, Washington, DC, USA
e-mail: gmartin@american.edu

R. Di Pietra et al. (eds.), *Accounting and Regulation*,
DOI: 10.1007/978-1-4614-8097-6_14,

and SEC fines. A sizeable minority (28 %) face criminal charges and penalties, including jail sentences that average 4.3 years. These results indicate that the individual perpetrators of financial misconduct face significant disciplinary action.

14.1 Introduction

Do managers suffer personal consequences for cooking the books? Much popular sentiment holds that they do not. "They lie, they cheat, they steal and they've been getting away with it for too long," claims a Fortune magazine cover article about financial misrepresentation.[1] This perception helps explain several features of the Sarbanes–Oxley Act of 2002 (SOX), which increased criminal penalties for financial fraud, created new classes of financial fraud, and increased CEOs' and CFOs' personal exposure to liability for financial misrepresentation.

Prior research shows that firm shareholders endure large losses when their firms are accused of misconduct.[2]

But there is little evidence on whether the individual perpetrators bear direct costs. Whether they do has important implications for public policy and corporate governance. Evidence that perpetrators suffer personal consequences would support the view that the current mix of firm governance, managerial labor markets, and regulatory oversight does, in fact, discipline illegal behavior. Evidence to the contrary would suggest that most firms' governance is ineffective in deterring managerial misconduct, and would support arguments for additional regulatory intervention.[3]

We examine a range of consequences to individuals who are caught cooking the firm's financial records. Our data consist of a unique, hand-collected sample of all 788 SEC and DOJ enforcement actions for financial misrepresentation from January 1, 1978 through September 30, 2006. Through public releases and court filings, the SEC and DOJ identify the individuals responsible for the misrepresentation, the interval over which the violation occurred, and (usually) the date the

---

[1] Fortune magazine, March 18, 2002 cover and accompanying story headline.

[2] See Karpoff and Lott (1993), Alexander (1999), the US General Accounting Office (GAO) (2002), and Karpoff et al. (2008a).

[3] Summaries of such arguments are found in Arlen (2007) and Jackson and Roe (2007). See Atkins (2005) for an SEC Commissioner's argument for a greater reliance on individual penalties rather than firm-level penalties, and La Porta et al. (2006) for evidence on enforcement regimes around the world. For an overview of the debate over the optimal mix of individual and firm-level penalties, see Arlen and Carney (1992), Polinsky and Shavell (1993), and Arlen and Kraakman (1997). This literature implies that firm- level penalties, i.e., those paid by shareholders, can be efficient if internal mechanisms work to discipline culpable managers, because firm-level monitoring and control can be less costly than direct monitoring by regulators.

misconduct was revealed to the public. This information allows us to identify the perpetrators with a high degree of precision and to determine whether they: (1) lose their jobs, (2) are barred from similar employment with other companies, (3) lose wealth through their stockholdings, (4) are assessed fines by the SEC, and (5) are subject to criminal charges filed by the DOJ.

Several previous papers examine one aspect of the potential costs borne by managers—whether they lose their jobs. But the evidence is mixed, with some papers inferring that perpetrators frequently lose their jobs and others concluding that they do not.[4] We show that all of these papers use an empirical method that is not well suited for the task. As a result, they omit the ousters of many culpable managers (Type I error) and incorrectly attribute the turnover of innocent managers to the firm's misconduct (Type II error). In Sect. 14.2 we show that the procedure used by Desai et al. (2006), for example, generates a Type I error of 47.2 % and a Type II error of 66.1 % when applied to our data. That is, it misses 47.2 % of all managers who cooked the books and lost their jobs, while 66.1 % of the turnovers it tallies involve managers who are not identified by the SEC as culpable parties. We hasten to add that our criticism of these previous papers is not of their logic or execution. Such efforts used the best available approach and lacked the data we now have on hand.

Our analysis shows that most culpable managers do, in fact, lose their jobs. Of 2,206 individuals identified by regulators as culpable parties, 93.4 % lose their jobs during the violation or enforcement periods. Most are fired, indicating that they do not leave their jobs voluntarily. We also find that the likelihood of removal is positively related to the size of the misconduct's harm to shareholders and the quality of the firm's governance. In particular, the likelihood of removal is positively related to the board's independence and the holdings of outside blockholders.

Culpable individuals suffer consequences beyond losing their jobs. The SEC has barred or is in the process of barring 693 individuals (31 %) from future employment as an officer or director in a public firm. The average culpable manager owns 6.5 % of the firm's equity and experiences a loss in stock value of $15.3 million when the misconduct is revealed. SEC fines average an additional $5.7 million. In addition, 617 (28 %) of these individuals have been charged with criminal violations. To date, 469 of these individuals have pleaded guilty or been convicted and sentenced to an average of 4.3 years in jail and 3 years of probation. In total, the evidence indicates that the large majority of managers who are caught cooking the books lose their jobs. Many also face diminished employment prospects, monetary and non-monetary sanctions, and criminal penalties. Overall, the consequences to these individuals are very significant.

This chapter proceeds as follows. In Sect. 14.2 we review related research and describe the problems that arise in previous attempts to examine whether managers

[4] See Feroz et al. (1991), Agrawal, Jaffe and Karpoff (1999), Alexander (1999), Beneish (1999), Arthaud-Day (2006), and Desai et al. (2006). These papers are discussed in more detail in Sect. 14.2.

lose their jobs when they engage in corporate misconduct. Section 14.3 describes our data and the protracted process of most regulatory enforcement actions for financial misrepresentation. In Sect. 14.4 we describe the job termination and attrition rates of individuals named as culpable parties by the SEC and DOJ in their enforcement proceedings. Section 14.5 presents the results of multivariate tests that examine the factors that contribute to whether a manager loses his or her job for cooking the books. Section 14.6 documents other consequences to the culpable managers, including penalties imposed by the SEC and DOJ, non-monetary sanctions, jail sentences, and losses through their shareholdings in the affected company. Section 14.7 provides concluding remarks.

14.2 Previous Research

Several papers examine whether managers lose their jobs when their firms engage in misconduct and are discovered. Feroz et al. (1991) report that 72 % of the firms that were subjects of SEC Accounting and Auditing Enforcement Releases (AAERs) between 1982 and 1989 fired at least one manager. Similarly, Desai et al. (2006) and Arthaud-Day et al. (2006) conclude that managers tend to lose their jobs following the earnings restatements in the database assembled by the US General Accounting Office (now the Government Accountability Office (GAO) 2003).

In contrast, Beneish (1999) concludes that, following earnings overstatements, "managers' employment losses … are similar in firms that overstate earnings and in firms that do not." Similarly, Agrawal et al. (1999) examine top executive turnover among firms identified in the "Fraud" and "Crime" listings in the General Section of the Wall Street Journal Index. In multivariate tests that control for other influences on managerial turnover, they conclude that top executive turnover does not increase significantly following the discovery of fraud.[5]

Although they reach different conclusions, these studies use a similar empirical approach. Each identifies a specific event (e.g., an earnings restatement or news of a legal violation) and measures turnover among a fixed set of executive titles (e.g., CEO, President, and Board Chair) during a fixed window around the event. Any unusual turnover, controlling for contemporaneous turnover in matched control firms and other firm-specific characteristics, is attributed to the misconduct.

Consider, for example, USA Detergents, Inc., one of the events in the GAO (2003) database that is examined by Desai et al. (2006) and Arthaud-Day et al. (2006). Eight senior managers at USA Detergents, Inc. conspired to inflate income in the last

---

[5] Alexander (1999, Table 4) also reports evidence of employee or managerial turnover in a large fraction of firms accused of a federal crime (see also Alexander 2007). In a new working paper, Agrawal and Cooper (2007) examine turnover among top executives in firms that announce earnings-decreasing restatements. The empirical method in this paper is similar to those of the papers discussed in this section. Helland (2006), Fich and Shivdasani (2007) examine turnover among directors and officers of firms targeted by securities class actions for fraudulent activities.

two quarters of 1996, and the company corrected these misrepresentations by restating its earnings on August 11, 1997. Desai et al. (2006) count turnovers among the CEO, President, and Board Chair during the 2-year period after the restatement date. For this firm there is one such turnover, involving President Giulio Perillo.

One problem with this approach is that Perillo was not a party to the misrepresentation and his turnover should not have been counted. Rather, he was appointed interim President and Chief Operating Officer 11 days before the restatement date and resigned 6 months later. We label this a Type II error in Desai, Hogan, and Wilkins's approach because it counts a turnover that it should not. This approach also incurs a Type I error whenever it misses the turnover of a culpable manager. In the USA Detergents, Inc. case, all eight of the culpable managers left the firm. The Desai et al. (2006) approach misses six of these individuals because they do not hold the titles of CEO, President, or Board Chair. It also misses the departure of President Frank Valdez, named by the SEC as a culpable party, because he left the firm before the date in the GAO database. And it misses the departure of CEO and Chairman Uri Evan, also identified by the SEC as a culpable party, because he did not leave the firm until the SEC served him a "Wells Notice" over 4 years after the GAO date.[6]

The USA Detergents, Inc. example illustrates a systematic tendency in prior studies to misclassify managerial turnover. To measure the magnitude of these errors, we replicated the Desai et al. (2006) empirical method for the 41 firms in the GAO database that also are in our sample of firms targeted by SEC enforcement actions. There are 66 CEO, President, or Board Chair turnovers over a two-year event window starting from the GAO-identified restatement date. Applying the screening process used by Desai et al., we eliminate ten of these turnovers due to the executive's age or because the firm was acquired. Of the remaining 56 executive turnovers, regulators identified 19 as perpetrators and 37 not as perpetrators. This yields a 66.1 % Type II error rate (=37/56). Our data also indicate that 36 perpetrators were associated with these firms (and lost their jobs), so the event method fails to detect 17 (=36–19) of these perpetrators, resulting in a 47.2 % Type I error rate (=17/36).

Applying the Desai, Hogan, and Wilkins procedure to our full sample reveals an even larger Type I error of 67 %. The Agrawal et al. (1999) and Beneish (1999) procedures use longer event windows and therefore have smaller Type I error rates of 36 and 52 %, respectively. But because of their longer event windows, these latter studies undoubtedly have larger Type II errors. (We do not calculate the exact Type II errors for these studies because we would have to replicate their data sets to do so.)

An additional problem results if researchers do not control for the number of executives that occupy the pre-set positions. Put succinctly, the probability of

[6] To repeat, our criticism is of the data available to prior researchers, not of their research design or execution. We highlight the approach taken by Desai et al. (2006) because it is the most recent of these papers. Desai et al. (page 90) explicitly recognize that their approach will miss some relevant turnovers, i.e., have a positive Type I error.

observing a turnover in any given year is greater at firms with three individuals occupying the chairman, president, and CEO posts than at firms with one individual occupying all three posts. Desai et al. (2006), for example, find that at least one turnover occurs among the executives occupying the positions of chairman, president, and CEO in 87 of 146 firms (59.6 %) in the 2 years following a restatement, compared to 51 (34.9 %) in a control sample matched on industry, firm size, and firm age. This difference may be influenced by the fact that the total number of executives in the top three positions is 340 in the restatement sample, but only 181 in the control firms. Consistent with this critique, the variable that Agrawal et al. (1999) use in their analysis to control for the number of executives per firm produces the most significant coefficient in their regression.[7]

In summary, previous studies of misconduct-related turnover use data that have extremely large classification errors. This may explain why these otherwise meticulous studies reach conflicting conclusions. In the following sections we address these problems by tracking the employment of the individuals identified by the SEC and DOJ as the perpetrators of the misconduct. We also document these individuals' wealth losses from their equity positions in the firm, as well as the explicit monetary and non-monetary penalties imposed by regulators, and criminal charges.

14.3 Data on Culpable Manager Turnover

14.3.1 The Enforcement Process

Our sample consists of all enforcement actions initiated by the SEC and DOJ from January 1, 1977 through September 30, 2006 for violation of one or more of three provisions of the Securities Exchange Act of 1934, as amended by the Foreign Corrupt Practices Act of 1977: (1) 15 USC §§ 78 m(b)(2)(A), which requires firms to keep and maintain books and records that accurately reflect all transactions; (2) 15 USC §§ 78 m(b)(2)(B), which requires firms to devise and maintain a system

[7] Even tests that focus exclusively on the CEO position have this problem, because some firms have more than one CEO over the observation period. Yet another problem arises when researchers erroneously assume that all AAERs represent actions taken against perpetrators of misconduct. Some AAERs are issued to forewarn firms of practices that may lead to disciplinary actions. For example, the SEC initiated an administrative proceeding relating to a material overstatement by a Japanese subsidiary of Boston Scientific. (See Securities Exchange Act Release 34-43183, also assigned AAER-1295.) Upon discovery, the firm promptly undertook remedial actions, made appropriate public disclosures, and cooperated with the SEC investigation. The SEC undertook no disciplinary action against the firm or any individual, but issued the AAER to put firms on notice to adjust their internal controls to avert similar problems. A post-event method using AAERs erroneously would count the turnover of Peter M. Nicholas (founder, CEO, Chairman, and President), who relinquished the titles of CEO and President to James Tobin approximately 4 months after the GAO date. We can find no evidence that Nicholas' departure was related to the SEC's administrative proceeding.

of internal accounting controls; and (3) 15 USC yy 78 m(b)(5), which establishes that no person shall knowingly circumvent or knowingly fail to implement a system of internal accounting controls or knowingly falsify any book, record, or account. All enforcement actions initiated by the SEC for financial misrepresentation include charges brought under at least one of these three provisions. These enforcement actions typically include other charges, on which we report in Table 14.1.

Figure 14.1 depicts the typical sequence of events surrounding a federal securities enforcement action.[8]

We use the term "action" to signify the full chain of public releases that relate to a specific company where the books are suspect. Enforcement actions commonly include a mixture of administrative, civil, and criminal proceedings that may implicate the firm itself, other affiliated firms, or individuals employed by or otherwise associated with the firm. Most of these proceedings are publicly disclosed when the SEC files Administrative Releases or Litigation Releases. Some civil and criminal proceedings initiated by the DOJ are disclosed via press releases. Enforcement actions often follow a conspicuous announcement related to the firm that draws the SEC's scrutiny. These trigger events generally are firm-initiated disclosures of potential problems. Common trigger events include self-disclosures of malfeasance, restatements, auditor departures, and unusual trading. Investigations by other federal agencies such as the Department of Defense and Environmental Protection Agency are another source of trigger events, along with delayed SEC filings, management departures, whistleblower charges, and routine reviews by the SEC. Our collection process back-fills the trigger events based on references found in subsequent federal filings. Such filings identify specific trigger events and dates in 575, or 73.0 %, of the enforcement actions.

We find a much higher incidence of firm-initiated trigger announcements than do Dyck et al. (2007), who attribute more discovery of "frauds" to people who are outside the firm. This may represent differences in our samples. The Dyck et al. sample is based on the Stanford Securities Class Action Clearinghouse. As reported in Karpoff et al. (2008b), fewer than 50 % of the enforcement actions in our sample are accompanied by securities class action or derivative lawsuits. Likewise, many class action lawsuits have no accompanying SEC enforcement action.

Following a trigger event the SEC gathers information through an informal inquiry that, if warranted, grows to a formal investigation. During the investigation period the targeted firm may issue a press release indicating that it is the target of an SEC informal inquiry or formal investigation. These press releases occur an average of 7 months after the violation period ends.

After an investigation, the SEC decides to drop the case, proceed with an administrative or civil action, and/or refer it to the DOJ for parallel criminal prosecution. If civil action is warranted, the SEC will send the target(s) a Wells Notice, indicating its intent to initiate civil proceedings against the firm and/or

8 For more information, see the Securities and Exchange Commission (1973), Lucas (1997), Cox et al. (2003), or Karpoff et al. (2008a).

Table 14.1 Regulatory enforcement actions for financial misrepresentation

Panel A: Enforcement actions	N
Total number of enforcement actions	788
SEC involved	782
DOJ involved	240
Number with books and records violations [15 USC §§ 78 m(b)(2) (A)]	747
Number with internal controls violations [15 USC §§ 78 m(b)(2)(B)]	675
Number with circumvention violations [15 U.S.C. §§ 78 m(b)(5)]	334
Number that include fraud violations	622
Number that include insider trading violations	159
Number that include Sarbanes–Oxley violations	40
Panel B: SEC and DOJ proceedings	
Administrative	1,157
Civil	1,130
Criminal	457
Panel C: Respondents	
Total number of firms named as respondents	916
Number of actions in which the subject firm is named as a respondent	607
Number of subsidiary/parent firms named as respondents	42
Number of related agent firms named as respondents	267
Numbers of individuals named as respondents	3,164
Employees	2,206
CEOs	515
Top 3 Executives (CEO, President, or Board Chair)	723
All executive employees	1,433
Non-executive employees	773
Non-employees (agents)	958
Panel D: SEC enforcement releases (total = 3,130)	
Administrative Releases	1,526
Securities Act Releases	189
Exchange Act Releases	1,285
Investment Advisers Act Releases	13
Investment Company Act Releases	8
Public Utility Holding Company Act Releases	2
Administrative Law Judge Releases	29
Litigation Releases	1,604
Number receiving a secondary designation as an Accounting and Auditing Enforcement Release (AAER)	1,959

This table summarizes the number of firms, individuals, cases, and SEC releases related to a comprehensive sample of all 788 enforcement actions for financial misrepresentation from January 1, 1978 through September 30, 2006. All violations include actions under the books and records, internal controls, or circumvention provisions of the Securities and Exchange Commission Act of 1934, as amended by the Foreign Corrupt Practices Act of 1977. The enforcement actions center around 788 target firms at which the misrepresentation occurred. Most enforcement actions involve charges brought under multiple cases, and Panel B reports the number of unique administrative proceedings, civil litigation, and criminal case numbers. As presented in Panel C, each case has one or more named respondents (firms or individuals). Panel D presents the number of unique SEC release numbers assigned to public releases concerning the enforcement actions

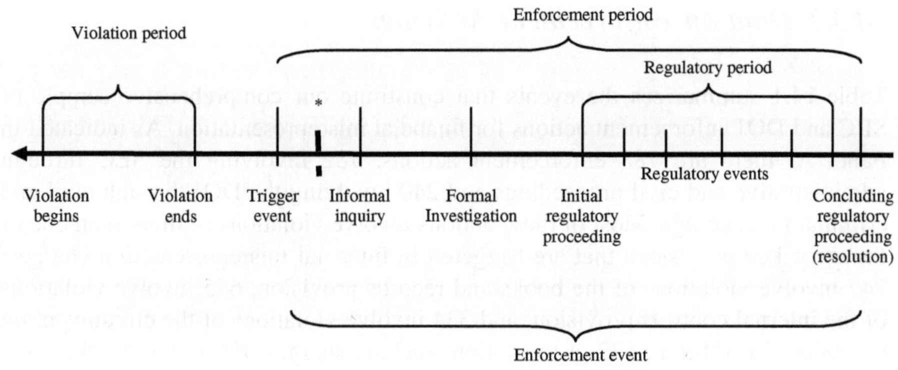

Fig. 14.1 Timeline of an enforcement action. *The Initial filing of a private lawsuit frequently occurs soon after the trigger event

selected individuals. Dropped cases are not reported and do not appear in the sample. Some enforcement actions are settled quickly and resolved simultaneously upon the SEC's initial release of information about the case. But most actions unfold over multiple regulatory proceedings. The SEC makes all of the administrative and most of the civil charges against firms and individuals, while the DOJ pursues the remaining civil charges and all of the criminal charges.

Our information regarding enforcement activities is collected from several sources. We use Lexis–Nexis' FEDSEC:SECREL library for information on SEC securities enforcement actions, the FEDSEC:CASES library for information on litigated enforcement actions, and the Academic Business News, General News, and Legal Cases libraries for news releases (frequently issued by defendant firms) about each enforcement action. Our second source of information is the SEC's Web site at http://www.sec.gov, which contains all SEC public releases relating to enforcement actions since September 19, 1995. Our third source is the DOJ itself, which provided us with further data on enforcement outcomes. Our fourth source, for information on several high-profile cases, is the DOJ's Corporate Fraud Task Force Web site at http://www.usdoj.gov.

For each enforcement action we collect the following information from the proceedings' filings: the date and type of proceeding, the period over which the violation occurred, each law or rule violated, job titles, names, ages, and dates of employment of all individual respondents, and all penalties and sanctions against each respondent. We also record the event that triggered the action if it is provided in the filings. These data are supplemented by searching the firms' public filings and Lexis–Nexis for the first public revelation of an informal inquiry or formal investigation by the SEC or DOJ and the date a Wells Notice was received. If the firms do not appear in the Center for Research in Security Prices or Compustat databases, trading and financial information is gathered manually from the companies' SEC filings, Compact Disclosure/SEC, regulatory proceedings, and Lexis–Nexis. Board data, insider holdings, and blockholder ownership are gathered from regulatory proceedings, proxy statements, or 10-K SEC filings.

14.3.2 Data on Enforcement Activities

Table 14.1 summarizes the events that constitute our comprehensive sample of SEC and DOJ enforcement actions for financial misrepresentation. As indicated in Panel A, there are 788 enforcement actions, 782 involving the SEC through administrative and civil proceedings and 240 involving the DOJ through civil and criminal proceedings. Most of these actions involve violations of more than one of the three key provisions that are triggered in financial misrepresentation charges; 747 involve violations of the books and records provision, 675 involve violations of the internal controls provision, and 334 involve violations of the circumvention provision. In addition, 622 of the actions include charges of fraud under the 1933 Securities Act or 1934 Securities Exchange Act. Fraud charges indicate that regulators believe at least one person acted with intent to misrepresent the firm's financials. A total of 159 of the 788 actions include charges of insider trading. Although 320 of the 788 actions (40.6 %) have violation periods that include the post-SOX period, only 40 of these actions (12.5 %) invoke SOX provisions.

Most of the 788 enforcement actions involve a complicated mix of charges brought under the SEC's and DOJ's different types of authority. Panel B of Table 14.1 tallies the different administrative, civil, and criminal proceedings among the 788 enforcement actions. On average, the SEC and DOJ together bring action under 1.5 different administrative proceedings, 1.4 civil proceedings, and 0.6 criminal proceedings per enforcement action.

Each of the 788 enforcement actions can involve more than one culpable firm or individual. As reported in Panel C, there are a total of 916 firms named, including the target firms, subsidiaries or parent firms, and firms that aided in the violation such as auditors, brokers, bankers, consultants, attorneys, vendors, suppliers, and customers. Target firms are named in only 607 of the 788 actions. Thus, 181 of the target firms were not named either because they were not deemed culpable, or they ceased operations as a result of bankruptcy or acquisition. Of the 309 nontarget firms named, 42 were either a subsidiary or parent of the target firm and 267 were non-related agent firms.

A total of 3,164 individuals were named as respondents, including 2,206 employees of the target firms and 958 nonemployee agents. In the following analyses we focus on the consequences to the 2,206 culpable employees. Of these, 515 were CEOs and 723 held one or more of the Top 3 titles of CEO, President, or Board Chair. A total of 1,433 were executives of any type (including the Top 3), and 773 were nonexecutive employees.

Panel D tallies by classification the 3,130 regulatory enforcement releases issued as part of the 788 enforcement actions. A total of 1,604 Litigation Releases, designated with an LR-prefix, were issued for proceedings involving civil lawsuits brought by the SEC in federal court. A total of 1,526 Administrative Proceedings were issued under the auspices of the various acts that empower the SEC. The Administrative Proceedings fall in six categories: 189 violations of the 1933 Securities Act (designated by a 33-prefix); 1,285 violations of the 1934 Securities

Exchange Act (designated by a 34-prefix); 13 violations of the 1940 Investment Advisers Act (designated by an IA-prefix); eight violations of the 1940 Investment Company Act (designated by an IC-prefix); and two violations of the 1935 Public Utility Holding Act (designated by a 35-prefix). Releases that invoke more than one act have separate release numbers assigned to the same release with the primary release number determined by the earliest act's passage date. Twenty-nine additional releases involve opinions and orders issued by Administrative Law Judges in contested administrative proceedings.[9]

In 1982 the SEC began to assign a secondary designation, an AAER, to some–but not all–public enforcement releases if the proceeding involves accountants or auditors.[10] AAERs frequently are used to construct samples of firms that misrepresent their financial statements (e.g., Feroz et al. 1991; Bonner et al. 1998). AAER designations, however, are not limited to financial misrepresentation actions. They also do not cover all such actions. As indicated in Panel D of Table 14.1, an AAER number is assigned for only 1,959 (63 %) of the 3,130 releases in our sample. A total of 107 (14 %) of the 788 enforcement actions in the sample had no releases with an AAER designation. The DOJ follows no formal release protocol, so information concerning criminal actions comes from DOJ press releases, actual district court filings, Lexis–Nexis searches, or information provided directly by the DOJ.

14.4 Turnover Among Culpable Individuals

14.4.1 Descriptive Data on the Perpetrators

Table 14.2 presents summary information on the age, tenure, and time in position for four groups of culpable individuals at the beginning of their involvement in the misrepresentation. The beginning date is defined as the beginning of the violation period (as defined by the SEC and DOJ) or the individual's first day of employment at the firm, whichever is later. On average, the 515 CEOs identified as perpetrators are 52 years old at the start of the violation, have been with their firms 6.7 years, and have been CEOs for 4.5 years.

Moving to the next column, we add Presidents and Board Chairs to the CEOs to produce the Top 3 cohort examined by other researchers (e.g., Agrawal et al. 1999; Desai et al. 2006). This group includes 723 CEOs, Presidents, and Board Chairs; the mean age is 52 years, the mean tenure at the firm is 6.0 years, and the mean

[9] These include, but are not limited to, such actions as an Initial Decision, Supplemental Initial Decision, Administrative Proceedings Ruling, Opinions, Order Denying Motions for Reconsideration, Order for Summary Affirmance and Filing Opposing Petition for Review, Order Remanding Proceeding, Order Denying Disqualification of Commission, Modifying Order, and Finality Order.

[10] See Accounting and Auditing Enforcement Release No. AAER-1, 1982 SEC LEXIS 2565, May 17, 1982.

Table 14.2 Age and job tenure of respondents for SEC and DOJ enforcement actions

	CEO only		Top 3 executives		All executives		Non-executive employees		All employees	
	Mean	Median	Mean	Median	Mean	Median	Mean	Median	Median	Mean
N	515		723		1,433		773		2,206	
Age	51.9	51.0	52.0	51.0	49.6	49.0	44.9	44.0	48.3	48.0
Tenure at firm	6.7	4.5	6.0	4.0	4.5	2.3	1.5	0.0	3.4	0.9
Tenure in position	4.5	2.6	4.2	1.8	3.0	0.8	0.9	0.0	2.3	0.0

This table presents summary information on the age and job tenure of individual respondents related to all 788 SEC and DOJ enforcement actions for financial misrepresentation from January 1, 1978 through September 30, 2006. Age, tenure at firm, and tenure at position are measured in years as of the beginning of the violation period

tenure in the current position is 4.2 years. Among all 1,433 executive respondents, the mean age is 49.6, the mean tenure at the firm is 4.5 years, and the mean tenure in the current position is 3.0 years.

Our data on the employment histories of the additional 773 non-executive perpetrators are imperfect because firms are not required to provide employment information on non-executives in such regulatory filings as the firm's proxy or 10 K reports. Some of this information is provided in the legal filings and releases associated with the enforcement proceedings. When it is not, we determine an individual's age, tenure at the firm, tenure at his or her position, and (in Table 14.3) turnover from other news reports and company filings. For these 773 non-executive employees, the mean age is 44.9, the mean tenure at the firm is 1.5 years, and the mean tenure in their position is 0.9 years. The median tenures of zero for the non-executive perpetrators reflect the fact that most joined the firm after the misrepresentation was underway.

14.4.2 Turnover Rates

Panel A of Table 14.3 presents the job termination rates for each of these four groups of culpable employees. Consider the top row labeled "End of violation period." The "CEO only" column indicates that 104 of the 515 culpable CEOs (20.2 %) lost their jobs before the end of this period. An additional 56 (10.9 %) culpable CEOs lost their jobs by the trigger date, 138 more lost their jobs by the SEC's investigation date, and 98 more lost their jobs by the date of the SEC's or DOJ's initial proceeding. Cumulatively, 76.9 % of all 515 culpable CEOs were replaced before the initial public release of formal action by the SEC or DOJ. By the time of the last regulatory proceeding, 88.4 % had been dismissed. Because we rely on quarterly filings for these turnover data, we include a "Final proceeding + 90 days" row to account for any turnover that occurs shortly after the regulatory intervention. Our results are insensitive to this distinction.

Table 14.3 Termination rates of employee respondents named in enforcement actions for financial misrepresentation

		CEO only	Top 3 executives	All executives	Non-executive employees	All employees
Panel A: termination rates average months						
Number of respondents		515	723	1,433	773	2,206
Terminated by:						
End of violation period	27.4	104	158	320	196	516
		20.2	21.9	22.3	25.4	23.4
		20.2	21.9	22.3	25.4	23.4
Trigger event	28.6	56	79	164	84	248
		10.9	10.9	11.4	10.9	11.2
		31.1	32.8	33.8	36.2	34.6
SEC investigation date	34.6	138	192	369	199	568
		26.8	26.6	25.8	25.7	25.8
		57.9	59.3	59.5	62.0	60.4
Initial SEC or DOJ proceeding	54.7	98	139	310	188	498
		19.03	19.23	21.63	24.32	22.6
		76.9	78.6	81.2	86.3	83.0
Final proceeding	85.5	59	82	156	74	230
		11.5	11.3	10.9	9.6	10.4
		88.4	89.9	92.0	95.9	93.4
Final proceeding + 90 days	88.5	3	5	5	0	5
		0.6	0.7	0.4	0.0	0.2
		88.9	90.6	92.4	95.9	93.6
Not terminated	–	57	68	109	27	136
		10.7	9.4	7.6	3.5	6.2

(continued)

Table 14.3 (continued)

		CEO only	Top 3 executives	All executives	Non-executive employees	All employees
		100.0	100.0	100.0	99.4	99.8
Unknown	–	0	0	0	5	5
		0.0	0.0	0.0	0.6	0.2
		100.0	100.0	100.0	100.0	100.0
Total	–	515	723	1,433	773	2,206

Group	Failures observed	Failures expected	Failures observed	Failures expected
Panel B: lang-rank test of the equality of the survivor function				
CEO only	458	498.4	458	486.5
Top 3 executives	655	683.8	655	667.8
All executives	1,324	1,316.2	1,324	1,282.7
Non-executive employees	741	714.2		
All employees	2,065	2,030.4		
Total	5,243	5,243.0	2,437	2,437.0
	$\chi^2(3) =$	8.14	χ^2 (2) =	4.19
	Pr > $\chi 2$ =	0.043	Pr > $\chi 2$ =	0.123

Termination rates of 2,206 employee respondents named in enforcement actions for financial misrepresentation from January 1, 1978 through September 30, 2006. Each cell in Panel A presents the number of individuals whose employment was terminated by the given event date, the percentage of the column total, and the cumulative percentage for the column. The column titled "Average months" presents the average number of months until the event date, counting from the beginning of the violation period or the employee's initial date of employment, whichever is later. Panel B presents a log-rank test of the equality of the survivor functions

Culpable employees with less prestigious job titles experience even higher rates of attrition. For example, by the end of the violation period 21.9 % of the culpable Top 3 executives, 22.3 % of all culpable executives, and 25.4 % of all culpable non-executive employees were dismissed. By the time of the final proceeding, 89.9 % of the culpable Top 3 executives, 92.0 % of all culpable executives, and 95.9 % of all culpable nonexecutive employees were dismissed.

In Panel A, the cumulative termination percentage at each event is higher for non-executive employees than for executives. To examine whether this difference is statistically significant, we compute survivor functions for each group. Panel B of Table 14.3 presents the results of a log-rank test for equality of the survivor functions (see Cleves et al. 2004). Considering all four groups, we reject the hypothesis of equality of the survivor functions (p-value =0.043). We cannot, however, reject the hypothesis of equality of the survivor function between the three groupings of executives (p-value =0.12). This indicates that the survival rate is lower for non-executives than for executives, but the differences in survival rates among executives is not statistically significant at normal levels.

Figure 14.2 illustrates the attrition rate of culpable executives. It plots in time the fraction of all 1,433 executives who remain at their posts following their initial exposure to the risk of turnover (Date 0). Exposure begins at the date the violation began, as identified in the regulatory proceedings, or the date the executive began employment with the firm, whichever is later.[11] Exactly 1,283 (89.5 %) culpable executives remain with their firms 12 months after Date 0, and 376 (26.2 %) remain 48 months after Date 0.

As Fig. 14.2 illustrates, a large fraction of culpable managers leave their jobs before the trigger date. Many more leave before regulators take any formal action. As discussed earlier, this explains why previous studies miss the turnover of many perpetrators.

14.4.3 Comparisons to Turnover Rates Among Non-culpable Executives

Table 14.3 and Fig. 14.2 demonstrate that most culpable managers leave their jobs during the violation and enforcement periods. But these periods are quite lengthy. As indicated in the "Average months" column of Table 14.3, the violation period persists for an average of 27.4 months, ending an average of 1.2 months before the trigger date. The enforcement period—from the Trigger event until the Final proceeding—averages an additional 57.0 months. These long periods raise the

---

[11] A total of 402 (28 %) of the 1,433 executive respondents joined the firm after the financial misrepresentation was underway. For these executives, the risk of turnover begins from the date the individual joined the firm.

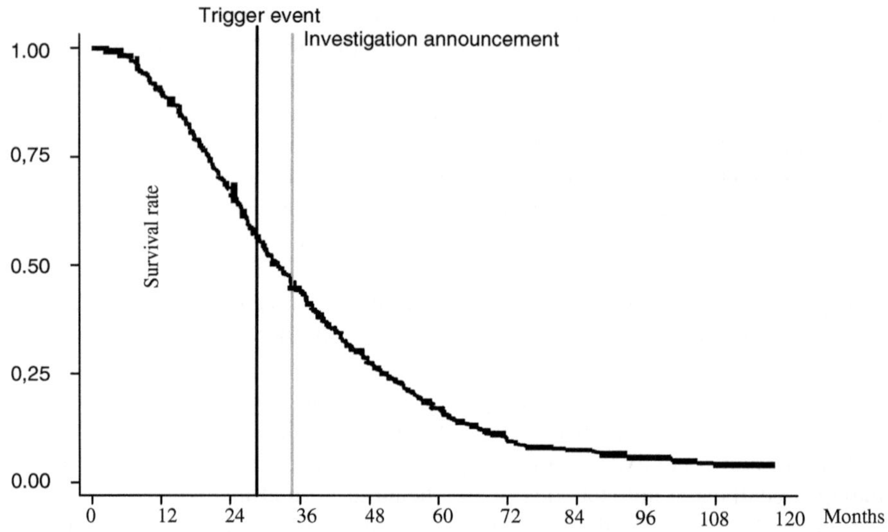

Fig. 14.2 Job Survival Function for Culpable Executives. This figure presents the job survival rates for 1,433 executives named as respondents in SEC enforcement actions for financial misrepresentation from January 1, 1978 through September 30, 2006. Date 0 is the later of the date the violation began or the date the executive began employment with the firm, and represents the beginning of the period in which the executive could lose his or her job for participating in the violation. Two common events in most enforcement actions are also portrayed: the trigger event, which is the first public revelation that a possible regulatory violation has occurred, and which occurs on average 28.6 months after Date 0; and the investigation announcement, which is the first public announcement that the firm is target of an informal inquiry or formal investigation by the SEC, and which occurs on average 34.6 months after Date 0

possibility that turnover among culpable managers, while high, is not much different than among managers who are not charged with financial misrepresentation.

To investigate this possibility, we use the ExecuComp database to create two benchmarks of normal managerial turnover, and compare them to the subset of our culpable executives who also are tracked by ExecuComp. ExecuComp data cover only 144 of the enforcement actions and 145 of the culpable executives in our sample. This subset of culpable executives has a termination rate that is similar to that for our overall sample, as 134 (92.4 %) have termination dates in the ExecuComp data. The first benchmark of normal turnover is based on turnover among all unaccused executives from these same 144 targeted firms. The second benchmark is based on turnover among all executives at non-targeted firms covered by ExecuComp.

To compare the termination rates of culpable executives with our two benchmarks, we measure the time to termination from the executive's date of initial employment at the firm. Figure 14.3 depicts the survivor functions for the 145 culpable executives in the ExecuComp database and for each of the two comparison groups.

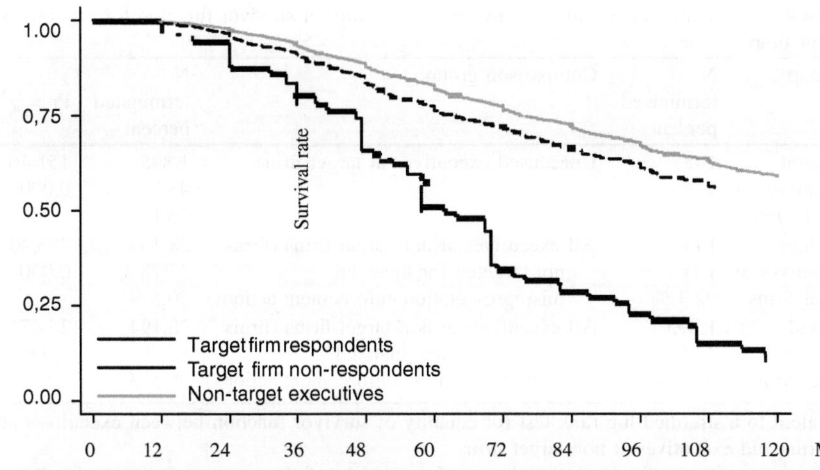

Fig. 14.3 Survivor Functions of Culpable Executives and two Comparison Groups Included in ExecuComp. Survivor functions for three groups using data from the ExecuComp database. Target firm respondents include 145 executives included in the ExecuComp data and also identified as a culpable party by the SEC and/or DOJ. Target firm non-respondents (Unaccused executives) include all 1,895 executives in the ExecuComp data from the same firms as the culpable individuals, but who are not named as culpable parties. Non-target executives include all 28,194 executives included in the ExecuComp data from firms not targeted by SEC and DOJ enforcement activities for financial misrepresentation

The first comparison group consists of the 1,895 unaccused executives from the 144 targeted firms. Of these, 437 (23.1 %) have termination dates reported in ExecuComp. As illustrated in Fig. 14.3, the culpable executives leave their firms at significantly higher rates than the unaccused executives at the same firms. Table 14.4 reports a non-parametric log-rank test for differences in these survival functions. The χ^2 of 151.5 (p-value < 0.0001) indicates that culpable executives have significantly higher termination rates than unaccused executives at the same firms. The top line in Fig. 14.3 represents the survival function of all 28,194 executives at all 2,560 non-target firms covered by ExecuComp. A total of 5,778 (21 %) of these non-target executives have termination dates recorded in ExecuComp. As reported in Table 14.4, the non-parametric log-rank test yields a χ^2 of 296.4 (p-value < 0.0001), indicating that culpable executives have significantly higher termination rates than executives in firms that are not targeted by SEC or DOJ enforcement actions for financial misrepresentation. These results indicate that culpable managers leave their jobs at significantly higher and faster rates than other managers at their same firms, and than other managers in general.

The final row in Table 14.4 reveals that non-respondent executives at target firms leave their jobs at a significantly higher rate than their counterparts at non-targeted firms ($\chi^2 = 25.5$, p-value < 0.0001). This evidence indicates that even non-respondent managers at targeted firms face higher-than-normal turnover rates. This could reflect the ouster of guilty individuals who are not named as

Table 14.4 Termination rates and log-rank test for equality of survivor function for executives in ExecuComp

Test group	N terminated percent	Comparison group	N terminated percent	χ^2 $Pr > \chi^2$
Respondent executives at target firms	145 134 92.4 %	Unaccused executives at target firms	1,895 437 23.1 %	151.46 0.000
Respondent executives at target firms	145 134 92.4 %	All executives at non-target firms (firms not targeted for financial misrepresentation enforcement actions)	28,194 5,778 20.5 %	296.43 0.000
Unaccused executives at target firms	1,895 437 23.1 %	All executives at non-target firms (firms not targeted for financial misrepresentation enforcement actions)	28,194 5,778 20.5 %	25.47[a] 0.000

[a] Equivalent to a stratified log-rank test for equality of survivor function between executives at target firms and executives at non-target firms

Termination rates and pairwise log-rank tests for equality of the survivor functions for three groups of executives in the ExecuComp database. The first group, "Respondent executives in target firms," consists of executives named as respondents in SEC or DOJ enforcement actions for financial misrepresentation (the culpable managers in our dataset who are also listed in the ExecuComp data). The second group consists of unaccused executives from the same firms as the culpable managers. The third group consists of all executives at firms not targeted for financial misrepresentation. Each cell in the second and fourth columns presents the number of executives in the group, the number terminated, and percent terminated. The last column provides the results of a log-rank test for the equality of survivor function between the two groups

respondents by the SEC and DOJ. It could also reflect a high degree of internal turmoil and change at targeted firms, or the effects of stigma from proximity to the misconduct. Cannella et al. (1995), Semadeni et al. (2008) analyze such stigma.

14.4.4 Stated Reasons for Job Termination

Not only are culpable managers removed at unusually high rates; the reasons for their removal indicate that most do not leave their jobs voluntarily. We are able to determine this because the SEC's releases typically summarize the respondents' employment history and the reasons for their removal. Additional information on the reasons for dismissal are reported in EDGAR filings and in articles carried by Lexis–Nexis.

Table 14.5 contains a summary of the stated reasons for removal. Of the 515 culpable CEOs, 300 (58.3 %) were forcibly removed from their positions, i.e., fired. An additional 113 (21.9 %) CEOs resigned or retired, but under circumstances that we cannot assert were involuntary (e.g., these include retirements "to spend more time with my family," and other likely euphemisms for ouster). Thirteen more were removed in a change of control, 29 were removed because the company was in financial distress, and three committed suicide or died. The

Table 14.5 Reasons given for employment termination of respondents named in enforcement actions for financial misrepresentation

N (column %)	CEO only	Top 3 executives	All executives	Non-executive employees	All employees
Number of respondents					
Not terminated	57	68	109	32	141
	(11.1 %)	(9.4 %)	(7.6 %)	(4.1 %)	(6.4 %)
Forced termination	300	434	856	512	1,368
	(58.3 %)	(60.0 %)	(59.7 %)	(66.2 %)	(62.0 %)
Resigned or retired	113	159	343	146	489
	(21.9 %)	(22.0 %)	(23.9 %)	(18.9 %)	(22.2 %)
Death	3	4	6	2	8
	(0.6 %)	(0.6 %)	(0.4 %)	(0.3 %)	(0.4 %)
Change in control	13	15	22	14	36
	(2.5 %)	(2.1 %)	(1.5 %)	(1.8 %)	(1.6 %)
Financial distress	29	43	93	51	144
	(5.6 %)	(6.0 %)	(6.5 %)	(6.6 %)	(6.5 %)
Unknown	0	0	4	16	20
	–	–	(0.3 %)	(2.1 %)	(0.9 %)

Stated reasons for job termination for 2,206 employee respondents named in enforcement actions for financial misrepresentation from January 1, 1978 through September 30, 2006. Each cell presents the reason given for the number of individuals whose employment was terminated and the percentage of the column total. The observation time period is the number of days from the beginning of the violation to 90 days following the final proceeding date. Termination is measured from the beginning of the violation (not the beginning of employment). Forced Termination includes dismissals, forced resignations or retirements, and (in a small number of cases) demotions or reassignments. Change in Control includes terminations due to mergers, proxy fights, and change in majority ownership. Financial Distress includes terminations due to bankruptcy, liquidation, seizure, receivership, dissolution, cessation, and registration revocation

proportions are similar for the other cohorts. Among all employee respondents, 62 % were fired and 22 % resigned or retired, eight died, 36 were removed in control transactions, and 144 lost their jobs because of their companies' financial distress. For comparisons, consider the reasons for removal reported by other researchers. Investigating turnover among CEOs, Chairs, and Presidents following large stock price changes, Warner et al. (1988) find that only one out of 230 executives who left their positions was fired. Ten more left because of "poor performance," and five left because of a "policy difference." None of the other categories listed by Warner, Watts, and Wruck indicate that the executives left involuntarily. Thus, a total of only 16 of 230 (7 %) appear to have left their positions involuntarily. Weisbach (1988) examines CEO resignations and reports similar numbers. Only 21 out of 286 (7 %) turnovers in his sample left for reasons that reflect negatively on the CEO's performance (including four who left because of "Scandal").

In contrast, the data in Table 14.5 indicate that most of the executives caught cooking the books leave their jobs for reasons that are directly related to their misconduct. Most do not leave their jobs voluntarily.

In summary, 92.4 % of all executives who are identified as culpable parties by the SEC and DOJ, and 95.9 % of all non-executive respondents, have their employment terminated before 90 days following the final regulatory proceeding date. These percentages are much larger than those reported in previous studies. This is because we track the job status of all individuals identified by regulators as perpetrators of the financial misrepresentation, and avoid the very large classification (Type I and Type II) errors that accompany prior research designs. Turnover rates of culpable executives are significantly higher than among other managers at their same firms, or among executives in general. Furthermore, a majority of the culpable managers were fired. This evidence indicates that managers who are caught cooking the books do, indeed, tend to lose their jobs, and that their dismissals are directly linked to their misconduct.

14.5 Cross-sectional Differences in Job Survival and Termination

14.5.1 Univariate Comparisons of Retained Versus Terminated Culpable Managers

As reported in Tables 14.3 and 14.5, not all culpable managers lose their jobs. A total of 109 culpable executives, including 57 culpable CEOs, remained with the firm 90 days beyond the final regulatory proceeding. Why are these executives not terminated?

We hypothesize that several forces affect whether a culpable executive loses his or her job, including: (1) the size of the harm imposed by the financial misrepresentation, (2) the firm's governance, (3) other firm characteristics, and (4) characteristics of the violation. Table 14.6 reports on univariate comparisons of these characteristics for the 109 surviving and 1,324 terminated executives. Table 14.7 reports on multivariate logistic regressions for job survival using these same variables.

(1) Size of the harm: We hypothesize that managers' likelihood of job loss increases with the cost imposed on outside shareholders. To measure this cost we use an estimate of "provable loss," a term used to establish damage awards in many class action lawsuits (see Karpoff et al. 2008b). In our tests, provable loss equals −1 times the percentage change in the firms' market capitalization from its highest point during the violation period to the first day news of a possible violation is revealed. (We multiply by −1 to express provable loss as a positive number).

Provable loss is only one of several measures that can be used to measure the cost to outside shareholders. In results that are available upon request, we find that

Table 14.6 Univariate comparisons for retained and terminated executives

	Statistic	Retained (N = 109)	Terminated (N = 1,324)	Test statistic	p-Value
Panel A: Size of harm measure					
Provable loss %	Mean	57.3	66.4	−5.05	<0.001
	Median	57.2	72.2	−4.73	<0.001
Panel B: Governance characteristics					
Board size	Mean	7.0	7.1	−0.10	0.921
	Median	6.0	6.0	−0.34	0.733
Board independence %	Mean	34.4	40.3	−2.30	0.022
	Median	33.3	42.9	−2.62	0.009
CHM/CEO duality	N	83	916		
	% of total	76.2	69.2	1.52	0.128
Unaccused CHM/CEO duality	N	10	196		
	% of total	9.2	14.8	−1.61	0.107
Respondent ownership %	Mean	17.1	9.1	4.81	<0.001
	Median	7.8	1.0	5.05	0.001
Other respondent ownership %	Mean	14.5	14.2	0.16	0.874
	Median	4.1	4.7	−0.36	0.719
Non-respondent blockholder ownership %	Mean	20.4	33.7	−5.19	<0.001
	Median	11.8	29.0	−5.61	<0.001
Non-respondent insider ownership %	Mean	7.5	15.9	−4.25	<0.001
	Median	3.6	8.1	−4.68	<0.001
Panel C: Firm characteristics					
Market capitalization ($mm)	Mean	2,197.0	1,803.1	0.40	0.690
	Median	29.0	50.6	−1.73	0.089
Development stage/reverse merger firm	N	10	189		
	% of total	9.2	14.3	−1.48	0.139
Firm declared bankruptcy during violation or	N	17	613		
Enforcement period	% of total	15.6	46.3	−6.21	<0.001

(continued)

Table 14.6 (continued)

	Statistic	Retained (N = 109)	Terminated (N = 1,324)	Test statistic	p-Value
Panel D: Characteristics of the violation					
Fraud charges included	N	87	1,199		
	% of total	79.8	90.6	−3.55	<0.001
Insider trading charges included	N	16	430		
	% of total	14.7	32.5	−3.86	<0.001
Only administrative action taken	N	26	168		
	% of total	23.9	12.7	3.27	0.001
Charges dismissed	N	5	6		
	% of total	4.6	0.5	4.75	<0.001

Univariate comparisons of the 109 executives who were not terminated by the firm and the 1,324 terminated executives. The column titled "Test statistic", reports the parametric t test for equality of proportions and means and, where medians are presented, the non-parametric Wilcoxon rank-sum test statistic. Provable loss % is the percentage decline in market capitalization from its high point during the violation period to the date the misconduct is publicly revealed. CHM/CEO duality indicates that the CEO also is board chair. Unaccused CHM/CEO duality indicates that the CEO also is board chair and is not named as a culpable party

Table 14.7 Logistic regression of the turnover of executives cooking the books

		CEO only	Top 3 executives	All executives
Size of harm measure	Provable loss %	2.5081	3.3177	3.8039
		0.091*	0.020**	0.005***
Governance characteristics	Board size	0.9593	0.9636	0.9396
		0.518	0.531	0.193
	Board independence %	6.9359	8.2199	8.2850
	CHM/CEO duality	0.025**	0.012**	0.002***
		0.9987	0.9549	1.2026
		0.998	0.925	0.646
	Unaccused CHM/CEO duality		1.6577	2.2871
			0.479	0.087*
	Respondent ownership %	0.7265	0.4269	0.3595
		0.699	0.254	0.132
	Other respondent ownership %	0.5040	1.1231	1.4311
		0.560	0.916	0.652
	Non-respondent	5.5626	7.5321	3.5476
	Blockholder ownership % Non-respondent	0.078*	0.032**	0.088*
		11.4435	17.7341	50.7394
	Insider ownership %	0.083*	0.062*	0.011**
Firm characteristics	Ln(Market capitalization)	0.9673	0.9738	1.0286
		0.694	0.760	0.712
	Development stage/reverse merger firm	2.6824	3.6823	2.1476
		0.084*	0.029**	0.137
	Firm declared bankruptcy	5.8581	5.6632	4.9351
		0.000***	0.000***	0.000***
Characteristics of the violation	Fraud charges included	2.2597	1.5604	1.5485
		0.070*	0.323	0.277

(continued)

Table 14.7 (continued)

		CEO only	Top 3 executives	All executives
	Insider trading charges included	1.7360	1.9212	2.3240
		0.190	0.129	0.025**
	Only administrative action taken	0.7273	0.6569	0.4673
		0.536	0.341	0.022**
	Charges dismissed	0.1673	0.0996	0.1095
	Constant	0.039**	0.008***	0.002***
		0.5010	0.5782	0.5347
		0.494	0.546	0.422
Statistics	*N*	515	723	1,433
	N failed	458	655	1,324
	N clusters	485	550	648
	Log likelihood	−144.06	−175.73	−304.98
	Pseudo r-square	0.1960	0.2205	0.2090
	χ^2	61.93	65.44	86.76
	p-Value	0.000***	0.000***	0.000***

Logistic regressions of the turnover of executives accused of misconduct in all 788 SEC and DOJ enforcement actions for financial misrepresentation between January 1, 1978 and September 30, 2006. The (untransformed) dependent variable equals one if the executive named as a respondent was terminated between the beginning of the violation period and 90 days after the final resolution proceeding filing date. Each cell presents the odds ratio (exponentiated coefficient) and its corresponding p-value using robust standard errors. Observations are clustered at the firm level to adjust standard errors for intra-firm correlation. See Table 14.6 and the text for variable definitions. Superscripts ***, **, and * indicate significance at the 0.10, 0.05, and 0.01 levels provable loss more closely tracks regulators' estimates of damages from 10-b class action lawsuits than do alternate measures discussed by Carleton et al. (1996) and Dyl (1999). Regardless, the empirical results we present are not sensitive to our choice among these alternate measures of shareholder loss.[12] Panel A of Table 14.6 shows that, consistent with expectations, provable loss is higher, on average, for terminated executives (66 %) than for retained executives (57 %). The difference is statistically significant at the 0.001 level using either a parametric t-test or a nonparametric Wilcoxon rank-sum test.

(2) Firm governance: Most commentators argue that the quality of a board's oversight decreases with board size, increases with its independence, and is lower when the CEO also chairs the board (e.g., see Jensen 1993; Yermack 1996; or Boone et al. 2007). This implies that the likelihood of a culpable manager's ouster will be positively related to board independence, and negatively related to board size and the CEO/Board Chair duality indicator variable. The univariate comparisons in Panel B of Table 14.6, however, indicate that only board independence is associated with a higher likelihood of dismissal for culpable managers. Among culpable CEOs, a larger fraction of those who are not terminated also hold the title of board chair (76 %) compared to those who were terminated (69 %). This relation is reversed among unaccused CEOs who chair the board; however, these differences are not significant at normal levels, so we postpone further discussion of these variables until the multivariate tests. We also examine the impact of four measures of ownership. As reported in Panel B of Table 14.6, the shareholdings of retained executives are higher, on average, than for terminated executives (17 % vs. 9 %). Non-respondent block ownership is lower (20 % vs. 34 %) and nonrespondent insider ownership is lower (8 % vs. 16 %) at firms with retained executives. These results suggest that culpable executives are more likely to hold onto their jobs when they have significant stockholdings and when outside blockholders and other insiders own less stock. The fraction of shares held by other respondents (i.e., other culpable managers), however, is not different among the groups of terminated and retained culpable managers.

(3) Firm characteristics: Panel C of Table 14.6 reports on firm size for the groups of retained and terminated executives. Firm size is measured as the natural logarithm of market capitalization on the day before the beginning of the violation period. The mean size is insignificantly larger for the retained group, but the median is smaller. A much higher fraction of the firms at which culpable managers are terminated declare bankruptcy between the beginning of the violation and the final proceeding (46 % vs. 16 %). This is consistent with Gilson's (1989) finding of a positive relation between financial distress and executive turnover. Regulators claim that they scrutinize micro-cap firms particularly closely for evidence of financial manipulation, implying closer monitoring of the managers of such firms.

---

[12] Alternate measures also are discussed by Hall and Lazear (2000) and Barclay and Torchio (2001). We thank the referee for the suggestion to explore different measures of shareholders' loss.

We find that firms in development stage or that went public through a reverse merger are relatively frequent among the group of terminated managers (14 % vs. 9 %), but this difference is not significant.

(4) Characteristics of the violation: Panel D of Table 14.6 indicates that the characteristics of the violation significantly influence the likelihood of termination for culpable managers. Fraud charges are less common among the retained group than among the terminated group of managers (80 % vs. 91 %), as are charges of insider trading (15 % vs. 32 %). A higher fraction of the retained managers faced only administrative actions as opposed to more serious civil or criminal charges—than the managers who lost their jobs (24 % vs. 13 %). And, although few charges are dismissed, the fraction of retained managers against whom all charges were dismissed is higher than for the terminated managers (4.6 % vs. 0.5 %).

14.5.2 Multivariate Tests for the Determinants of Culpable Executive Turnover

Table 14.7 reports on multivariate logistic regressions to examine the factors affecting the likelihood that a culpable manager will be ousted from the firm. The (untransformed) dependent variable equals one if the culpable executive leaves the firm before 90 days after the final regulatory proceeding.[13] The regressors are the variables presented in Table 14.6 and discussed in Sect. 14.5.1.

The first column in Table 14.7 reports on the 515 CEOs named as respondents in SEC enforcement actions. The second column is based on the 723 respondents with any of the titles of CEO, President, or Board Chair. The third column is based on the 1,433 respondents with any executive position in the firm. Rather than reporting the raw coefficients, for each regressor we report the odds ratio (i.e., the exponentiated coefficient) and its corresponding p-value using robust standard errors. Odds ratios greater than 1 indicate that the regressor is positively related to turnover likelihood, whereas odds ratios less then 1 indicate that the regressor is negatively related to turnover likelihood. To account for possible intra-firm correlation of turnover among executives, observations are clustered by enforcement action.

The results generally are consistent with the univariate comparisons, as the size of the harm and the quality of the firm's governance both help explain the likelihood of turnover. The coefficient for provable loss is greater than 1 and statistically significant, indicating that turnover is more likely when shareholders' losses are high. Among the governance variables, turnover is positively related to board independence and, for non-CEO executives, the presence of a strong CEO who is also the board chair. The likelihood of turnover is also positively related to the

[13] We adopt a cutoff 90 days after the final regulatory proceeding because quarterly reports reveal an executive's absence up to 90 days after the actual departure. Using the calendar date of the final regulatory date has no noticeable effect on the results, as only five executives move to the ousted category during this interval.

ownership of outside blockholders and of insiders who are not party to the misconduct. These results indicate that culpable managers are more likely to lose their jobs when they impose high costs on their shareholders and when they face strong accountability from directors, top managers, blockholders, and other insiders who are not parties to the financial misrepresentation.

The likelihood of turnover is relatively high when the firm declares bankruptcy and when the firm is a development-stage firm. This indicates that turnover is more likely when the firm is in financial trouble or consists primarily of growth opportunities. Characteristics of the violation are less important, although CEO turnover is more likely when the violation involves fraud, and for all executives as a group, the likelihood of turnover is greater when insider trading charges are included and lower when the violation leads to administrative actions only (i.e., include no civil or criminal charges). In all three regressions, turnover is less likely when the charges against the manager are dismissed.

14.5.3 Robustness Checks

We conducted a number of sensitivity tests to probe the robustness of these results. King and Zeng (1999) point out that coefficient estimates and standard errors can be biased in logistic regressions that use data with rare events. More than 90 % of the culpable managers leave their jobs, so retention (coded zero in our tests) is a rare event. To examine the potential for bias, we re-estimated the regressions in Table 14.7 using the "RELOGIT" command available in Stata (see Tomz et al. 1999). The results are virtually identical to those in Table 14.7.

We also examined alternate measures of the size of the harm and additional firm characteristics, such as leverage, and whether the firm's audits contained going-concern language. We examined additional characteristics of the violation, including the number of code violations and the length of the violation and enforcement periods. These characteristics, however, are not significantly related to the likelihood of termination, and their presence in the regressions does not qualitatively alter the results in Table 14.7.

Overall, these results indicate that managers who are caught cooking the books are more likely to lose their jobs when their activities are particularly harmful and when strong parties who are not involved in the misconduct (e.g., independent boards, strong CEOs, large blockholders, and other insiders) are present to hold the perpetrators accountable. Culpable managers tend to face discipline through the firm's internal governance, and particularly when such governance is strong.

14.6 Legal Penalties Imposed on Culpable Managers

14.6.1 Non-monetary Sanctions and Debarments

In addition to the prospect of losing their jobs, culpable managers face a variety of potential penalties imposed by the SEC, DOJ, and private lawsuits. This section reports on the non-monetary penalties imposed by the SEC and DOJ. These range from relatively minor slaps on the wrist (e.g., orders to cease-and-desist from the activity) to jail time.

Panel A of Table 14.8 summarizes the non-monetary penalties imposed on individual respondents via civil sanctions initiated by the SEC. Of the 723 Top 3 executive respondents, 134 (18.5 %) received administrative sanctions. Civil sanctions vary from minor cease-and-desist orders to career-threatening prohibitions from appearing before the SEC as an accountant, attorney, broker, or banker, or from being involved with the issuance or promotion of public securities. A total of 627 (86.7 %) Top 3 executives were respondents in civil litigation initiated by the SEC, which tends to result in larger penalties.

One substantive civil penalty is debarment, because it restricts the individual's employment opportunities in the field where he or she has established substantial human capital. A total of 243 (34 %) of the Top 3 executives are barred from serving as officers or directors of public companies or companies that register with the SEC, and 61 (8.4 %) more have bars pending. Thirty-one (4.3 %) are CPAs barred from appearing before the SEC as accountants, and 39 (5.4 %) more are barred (or have bars pending) from appearing before the SEC as an attorney, broker, banker, or other securities related profession. The debarment rates for the CEO, all executives, and all employee cohorts are similar to those of the Top 3 executives.

These data shed light on an important follow-up question to the data in our previous sections; namely, do dismissed executives simply find similar employment at other companies? The high rates of debarments indicate that, for a substantial fraction of culpable executives—over 40 %—the answer is clearly no. These individuals are prohibited from serving as officers or directors of public companies. Anecdotes from our sample indicate that many of these former executives find employment in less lucrative careers, such as real estate or automobile sales.

14.6.2 Criminal Penalties

As summarized in Panels B and C of Table 14.8, a substantial fraction of culpable managers are subject to criminal penalties. A total of 190 (26.3 %) of the 723 Top 3 executives and 617 (28.0 %) of the 2,206 total culpable employees were indicted for their activities. Acquittal occurs rarely for individuals indicted for criminal violations. Four of the 190 (2.1 %) Top 3 executives were acquitted, while 28 of the 617 (4.5 %) of the All Employees cohort were acquitted. Four of the indicted

Table 14.8 Monetary, civil, and criminal sanctions against respondents

	CEO only	Top 3 executives	All executives	Nonexecutive employees	All employees
Total individual respondents	515	723	1,433	773	2,206
Panel A: Civil non-monetary sanctions					
Type of sanction:					
Administrative	83	134	368	242	610
Civil	457	627	1,175	554	1,729
Officer & director bar	175	243	427	105	532
Pending	46	61	135	26	161
Accountant bar	12	31	161	80	241
Pending			11	5	16
Other professional bar	22	32	53	32	85
Pending	7	7	11	2	13
Panel B: Criminal non-monetary sanctions					
Indictments	139	190	394	223	617
Acquitted	1	4	16	12	28
Died	3	4	7	3	10
Awaiting trial	18	24	66	39	105
Convicted/pled guilty	117	157	302	167	469
Sentence pending	19	25	66	53	119
Unknown sentences	11	16	25	15	40
Known sentences	87	116	211	99	310
Panel C: Sentences					
Prison	83	102	168	66	234
Total years	479.9	579.8	849.1	154.5	1,003.6
Average	5.8	5.7	5.1	2.3	4.3
Probation	20	30	62	39	101
Total years	68.7	97.7	189.8	130.0	319.8
Average	23.4	3.3	3.1	3.3	3.2
Halfway house	2	3	7	–	7
Total years	7	10	41	–	41
Average	3.5	3.3	5.9	–	5.9
Home detention	4	7	23	13	36
Total months	26	47	138	72	210
Average	6.5	6.7	6.0	5.5	5.8
Supervised release	10	14	29	13	42
Total months	312	420	840	408	1,248
Average	31.2	30.0	29.0	31.4	29.7
Community service	5	10	16	8	24
Total hours	3,500	5,100	8,500	7,300	15,800
Average	700.0	510.0	531.3	912.5	658.3

(continued)

Table 14.8 (continued)

	CEO only	Top 3 executives	All executives	Nonexecutive employees	All employees
Panel D: Monetary sanctions ($mm)					
Total fines	214.0	1,798.9	2,049.1	15.8	2,064.9
Total disgorgement	3,208.6	8,643.2	9,807.8	585.8	10,393.6
Total monetary sanctions imposed	3,422.6	10,442.1	11,856.9	601.6	12,458.5
Average per individual	6.7	14.4	8.3	0.8	5.7

Panel A presents the monetary sanctions imposed on individuals charged in all 788 SEC and DOJ enforcement actions for financial misrepresentation between January 1, 1978 and September 30, 2006. The civil nonmonetary sanctions against individual respondents are shown in Panel B. The criminal non-monetary sanctions are in Panel C, with the corresponding sentencing information in Panel D

Top 3 executives and ten of the All Employees died before sentencing (including Kenneth Lay, the former Chairman and CEO of Enron, following his July 2006 criminal conviction). Respondents awaiting trial include 24 Top 3 executives and 105 total employees. The DOJ obtained convictions or guilty pleas from 157 of the 190 (83 %) indicted Top 3 executives. Sentences are pending for 25 Top 3 executives, and we are unable to find criminal sentencing information on 16 others.

Panel C summarizes the known sentencing information. A total of 1,003.6 years of prison have been imposed on perpetrators, with 102 Top 3 executives receiving an average sentence of 5.7 years. The average sentence for All Employees is 4.3 years. Top 3 executives that receive probation receive an average of 3.3 years, while the average probation among the All Employees group is 3.2 years. Other methods of incarceration include confinement to a halfway house, home detention, supervised release, and mandated community service.

14.6.3 Monetary Sanctions

Panel D of Table 14.8 summarizes the monetary fines imposed by regulators, including the SEC, DOJ, and state attorneys general. It is important to note that, as of October 1, 2006, 182 (23.1 %) of the enforcement actions have ongoing proceedings, indicating that additional penalties may be imposed in these actions.

A total of 334 of the 723 culpable Top 3 executives received fines from regulators. These executives were fined a total of $1.80 billion and ordered to disgorge another $8.64 billion in ill-gotten gains. On a per-person basis, the average unconditional monetary penalty for the 723 Top 3 executives is $14.4 million. The fines imposed on non-executive employees tend to be smaller, averaging only $0.8 million. Among all culpable employees, the unconditional mean fine is $5.7 million.

14.6.4 Wealth Effects via Stockholdings

In addition to the penalties meted out by regulatory authorities and courts, perpetrators typically lose from their shareholdings in the target firm when their financial misrepresentation is discovered. To estimate the magnitude of such losses, we gather ownership information from regulatory filings (10-Ks and proxy statements) and the proceedings filings. As reported in Table 14.9, mean ownership per respondent among Top 3 executives is 17.5 % of the firm (the median is 10.0 %) measured as close as possible to the trigger event. Mean ownership per respondent among all employees is 6.5 % (the median is 0.02 %).

We provide upper and lower bound estimates of the wealth loss experienced by managers. The "upper bound wealth loss" is related to "provable loss" (used in the tests reported in Table 14.7) and is consistent with Federal guidelines for estimating economic loss in securities suits (see Hall and Lazear 2000). The upper bound wealth loss is the product of the manager's ownership times the firm's largest decline in market capitalization as measured from the violation period's peak value to its value on the day news of a possible violation is revealed. We label this upper bound wealth loss because it values the manager's shares as though they were acquired at the highest possible price induced by the misrepresentation. The market-adjusted upper bound wealth loss subtracts the dollar return on an equivalent investment using the value-weighted index of all stocks in CRSP. Using this measure, the mean (median) wealth loss is $46.1 ($5.6) million for CEOs, $36.9 ($3.9) million for top executives, $22.1 ($1.0) million for all executives, and $14.5 ($0.03) million for all employees. While assuming the respondent purchased all shares when the firm's market capitalization is at its peak may seem unreasonable, it does, however, reveal the loss in the respondent's shareholdings from their highest value.

"Lower bound wealth loss" is calculated similarly to "upper bound wealth loss" except the change in market capitalization is measured from the last trading day preceding the violation period. The mean (median) market-adjusted wealth loss using this more conservative estimate is $13.1 ($1.7) million for CEOs, $12.2 ($1.0) million for top executives, $5.4 ($0.1) million for all executives, and $3.6 ($0.01) million for all employees.

Overall, the data in Tables 14.8 and 14.9 indicate that regulators and lawsuits impose explicit costs on a substantial fraction of culpable managers. Among the group of 1,433 culpable executives, 39 % are debarred from serving as officers or directors of public companies and 27.5 % face criminal indictments.

The mean regulatory penalty for these executives is $8.3 million, and our estimate of the average loss from their personal holdings of their firms' stock ranges from $5.4 million to $22.1 million. Similarly, large pecuniary and non-pecuniary penalties are imposed on the cohorts of culpable CEOs, Top 3 executives, and non-executive employees. Finally, it must be noted these results are understated because the proceedings have not concluded in 180 of the 788 (23 %) enforcement actions.

Table 14.9 Ownership and wealth losses

	CEO only		Top 3 executives		All executives		Non-executive employees		All employees	
	Mean	Median	Mean	Median	Mean	Median	Mean	Median	Mean	Median
N	515		723		1,433		773		2,206	
Ownership %	20.1	12.9	17.5	10.0	9.7	1.1	0.5	0.0	6.5	0.0
Regulatory penalties:										
N	243		334		615		294		909	
Total ($mn)	3,422.6		10,442.1		11,856.9		601.6		12,458.5	
Per respondent fined ($mn)	14.1	0.2	31.3	0.2	19.3	0.1	2.1	0.0	13.7	0.1
Per all respondent ($mn)	6.7	0.0	14.4	0.0	8.3	0.0	0.8	0.0	5.7	0.0
Wealth loss ($mn)										
Upper bound	48.4	4.8	38.7	3.5	23.4	0.8	0.4	0.0	15.3	0.0
Lower bound	5.8	0.6	5.7	0.4	1.8	0.0	0.1	0.0	1.2	0.0
Market-adjusted wealth loss ($mn)										
Upped bound	46.1	5.6	36.9	3.9	22.1	1.0	0.4	0.0	14.5	0.0
Lower bound	13.1	1.7	12.2	1.0	5.4	0.1	0.3	0.0	3.6	0.0

This table presents the ownership and share value losses of employee respondents to charges of financial misrepresentation. Ownership is measured as close as possible to the market revelation of the transgression or the last reported ownership prior to bankruptcy, whichever is earlier. Wealth loss is determined by multiplying the percentage ownership by the change in market capitalization measured on the revelation date. The market-adjusted wealth loss is the wealth loss minus the change in value from a hypothetical investment of the same number of dollars in the CRSP value-weighted portfolio. The revelation date is the earlier of the date that problems were first disclosed to the public or the date of bankruptcy. For firms that filed bankruptcy, the settlement, if any, for the equity class was used to determine market capitalization. The maximum wealth loss is measured using the day—the firm had the highest closing market capitalization over the period from the beginning of the violation to the market revelation date. The minimum wealth loss is measured using the market capitalization at the beginning of the violation period. Market-adjusted wealth loss is computed using the value-weighted return of all stocks in CRSP. The average period of time over which the maximum wealth loss is measured is 13.6 months, and 31.9 months for the minimum wealth loss

14.7 Conclusions

Previous research establishes that shareholders lose substantial value when their firms are charged with misconduct. This paper provides evidence that managers who are responsible for the misconduct also suffer meaningful personal consequences. We track the fortunes of all 2,206 employees named as culpable parties in SEC and DOJ releases for all 788 regulatory enforcement actions brought from January 1, 1978 through September 30, 2006 for financial misrepresentation. Our main findings are as follows:

(1) Most (93.6 %) of all employees cited by the SEC or DOJ as responsible parties for financial reporting violations lose their jobs. Among culpable executive employees, the fraction is 92.4 %. Culpable managers lose their jobs at significantly higher rates than unaccused managers at the same firms, and than managers at non-targeted firms. A majority of culpable managers are explicitly fired—a dramatic result compared to the very low incidence of explicit firings in most studies of managerial turnover.

(2) Culpable managers are more likely to lose their jobs when their activities are particularly harmful to shareholders and when they face strong governance controls. The likelihood of dismissal is positively related to board independence, the ownership of large blockholders and other insiders, and for nonCEOs, the presence of a strong CEO who is not party to the misconduct. Culpable managers are more likely to keep their jobs when the SEC drops its charges against them.

(3) In addition to the prospect of ouster, culpable managers face legal penalties and direct losses in the values of their shares. The average culpable executive (n = 1,433) owns 9.7 % of the firm's equity and experiences a loss in stock value ranging between $1.8 million and $23.4 million when the misconduct is revealed. SEC fines average an additional $8.3 million, and 562 (39.2 %) of the executives have been barred or are in the process of being barred from serving as an officer or director in a public firm. In addition, 394 (27.5 %) culpable executives have been charged with criminal violations. To date, 168 of these individuals have pleaded or been found guilty and sentenced to an average of 5.05 years in jail and 3.06 years of probation. Similar fractions of culpable nonexecutive employees (n = 773) have faced such regulatory and criminal penalties.

We begin this article by quoting from Fortune magazine: "They lie, they cheat, they steal and they've been getting away with it for too long."[14] The evidence, however, belies such popular sentiment. Managers who are caught misrepresenting their companies' financial statements typically lose their jobs and substantial personal wealth through their ownership stakes in the firm. Regulators impose additional penalties on many of these managers, including fines, non-monetary sanctions, and criminal penalties. It is noteworthy that only 40 (5.1 %) of the 778 enforcement actions in our sample invoke Sarbanes–Oxley provisions. Thus, firms' internal governance and the SEC's and DOJ's oversight worked to penalize

[14] Fortune magazine, March 18, 2002 cover and accompanying story headline.

much financial misrepresentation even before the 2002 Sarbanes–Oxley Act. In short, a more accurate version of the sentiment in the Fortune article would be: "Some managers may lie, cheat, and steal, but most face serious consequences when they are caught."

14.8 What has Changed Since the Consequences to Managers for Financial Misrepresentation was Published?

The sample for our study began in 1978 and ended in September 2006. Shortly thereafter, the world economy abruptly fell from irrational exuberance to near depression.

In the eternal wisdom of Warren Buffett, "when the tide goes out … you learn who was swimming naked." The credit crisis of 2008 exposed plenty of flesh (i.e., financial misrepresentation) and enforcement actions per year against corporations roughly doubled in the years following our study. The number of actions taken against individuals experienced a similar jump, peaking with 42 actions initiated against individuals in 2009.

In recent years, regulators and Congress have adopted measures intended to more efficiently deploy their scarce resources. Through the Dodd-Frank Act, Congress has enhanced whistleblowers incentives. The Securities Exchange Commission (SEC) and Department of Justice (DOJ) have attempted to reward corporate self-reporting and cooperation through promises of leniency. Files et al. (2012) find that being credited for cooperation by regulators reduces the monetary penalties firms pay by 35 % (conversely, non-cooperation increases monetary penalties by 53 %). Even greater benefits result for cooperative firms that conducted independent investigations and made the results available to regulators.

Deferred Prosecution Agreements (DPAs) and Non-Prosecution Agreements (NPAs) came into their own in the years following our study to encourage reforms and enhance better internal controls, compliance programs, and training. The theory behind these measures was that the firms (specifically their shareholders) should not be further punished for the transgressions of the firm's managers. Our evidence clearly demonstrates that the perpetrators of the crime paid large penalties in the form of monetary penalties, job losses, censures, incarceration, and lost wealth in the form of disgorgements and losses on their shareholdings in the firm. The DOJ and SEC continue to dispense staggering penalties, with one 2011 defendant receiving a 15 year sentence, the largest FCPA-related sentence to this date.

Politics and resource constraints lead to uneven enforcement of the many laws that the SEC is charged with enforcing. Following the Credit Crisis, an underfunded SEC has been overwhelmed with naked swimmers. Choi et al. (2012) examine the short-lived media furor surrounding option backdating to document how the SEC was compelled to temporarily shift resources to these backdating investigations from more egregious accounting cases. Infamous scandals involving Bernie Madoff, the Galleon Group hedge fund, and others also have drawn the SEC's attention in recent years to the arenas of Ponzi schemes, affinity fraud, and insider trading.

Our study relied on violations of the Foreign Corrupt Practices Act (FCPA) of 1977. As its title implies, the FCPA banned bribery of foreign officials, but it also has three provisions that are commonly invoked to combat financial reporting abuses. Through the end of 2011, FCPA charges for financial misrepresentation have been leveled against 1,099 publicly traded firms. Until recently, the FCPA's namesake, bribery provision was rarely invoked. Recently, the SEC dramatically increased enforcement of the FCPA's anti-bribery provision. Over half (66) of the 115 FCPA bribery allegations made between 1977 and 2011 occurred during the last five years (Karpoff et al. 2012). This anti-bribery enforcement surge coincides with the adoption of similar anti-bribery resolutions by European and Latin American countries. The SEC has worked in concert with other country's regulators to deal with multinational giants like Siemens. Inevitably, the SEC's resource constraints mean that an increasing emphasis in bribery leads to diminished vigilance in other areas such as financial misrepresentation. In fact, financial misrepresentation enforcement has declined steeply with the SEC's increased efforts in other areas.

References

Agrawal, A., & Cooper, T. (2007). Corporate governance consequences of accounting scandals: Evidence from top management, CFO and Auditor Turnover. Unpublished Working Paper. University of Alabama.

Agrawal, A., Jaffe, J. F., & Karpoff, J. M. (1999). Management turnover and governance changes following the revelation of fraud. *Journal of Law and Economics, 42*(1), 309–342.

Alexander, C. R. (2007). The market consequences of financial reporting frauds: toward a reputation-rebuilding hypothesis. Unpublished working paper. Securities and Exchange Commission.

Alexander, C. R. (1999). On the nature of the reputational penalty for corporate crime: evidence. *Journal of Law and Economics, 42*(1), 489–526.

Arlen, J. H. (2007). Public versus private enforcement of securities fraud. Unpublished working paper. New York University.

Arlen, J. H., & Carney, W. J. (1992). Vicarious liability for fraud on securities markets: theory and evidence. University of Illinois Law Review, pp. 691–740.

Arlen, J., & Kraakman, R. (1997). Controlling corporate misconduct: An analysis of corporate liability regimes. *NYU Law Review, 72*, 687–779.

Arthaud-Day, M. L., Certo, S. T., Dalton, C. M., & Dalton, D. R. (2006). A changing of the guard: executive and director turnover following corporate financial restatements. *Academy of Management Journal, 49*, 1119–1136.

Atkins, P. S. (2005). Speech by SEC Commissioner: Remarks before the Atlanta Chapter of the National Association of Corporate Directors. www.sec.gov/news/speech/spch022305psa.htm

Barclay, M., & Torchio, F. C. (2001). A comparison of trading models used for calculating aggregate damages in securities litigation. *Law and Contemporary Problems, 64*, 105–136.

Beneish, M. D. (1999). Incentives and penalties related to earnings overstatements that violate GAAP. *Accounting Review, 74*(4), 425–457.

Bonner, S. E., Palmrose, Z.-V., & Young, S. M. (1998). Fraud type and auditor litigation: an analysis of SEC accounting and auditing enforcement releases. *Accounting Review, 73*(4), 503–532.

Boone, A. L., Field, L. C., Karpoff, J. M., & Raheja, C. G. (2007). The determinants of corporate board size and composition: an empirical analysis. *Journal of Financial Economics, 85*, 66–101.

Cannella, A. A, Jr, Fraser, D. R., & Lee, D. S. (1995). Firm failure and managerial labor markets: evidence from Texas banking. *Journal of Financial Economics, 38*, 185–210.

Carleton, W. T., Weisbach, M. S., & Weiss, E. J. (1996). Securities class action lawsuits: a descriptive study. *Arizona Law Review, 38*, 491.

Choi, S. J., Pritchard, A. C., & Wiechman, A. C. (2012). Scandal enforcement at the SEC: salience and the arc of the option backdating investigations (March 6, 2012). ssrn.com/abstract=1974976.

Cleves, M. A., Gould, W. M., & Gutierrez, R. G. (2004). An Introduction to Survival Analysis Using Stata. Stata Press, College Station, TX.

Cox, J.D., Thomas, R.S., Kiku, D., 2003. SEC enforcement heuristics: An empirical inquiry. *Duke Law Journal, 53*, 737–779.

Desai, H., Hogan, C. E., & Wilkins, M. S. (2006). The reputational penalty for aggressive accounting: earnings restatements and management turnover. *Accounting Review, 81*(1), 83–112.

Dyck, I., Morse, J. A., & Zingales, A. L. (2007). Who blows the whistle on corporate fraud? Unpublished working paper, University of Toronto, University of Michigan, and University of Chicago.

Dyl, E. A. (1999). Estimating economic damages in class action securities fraud litigation. *Journal of Forensic Economics, 12*, 1–11.

Feroz, E. H., Park, K., & Pastena, V. S. (1991). The financial and market effects of the SEC's accounting and auditing enforcement releases. *Journal of Accounting Research, 29*, 107–142.

Fich, E. M., & Shivdasani, A. (2007). Financial fraud, director reputation, and shareholder wealth. *Journal of Financial Economics Forthcoming, 86*, 306–336.

Files, R., Martin, G. S., & Rasmussen, S. J. (2012). The monetary benefit of cooperation in regulatory enforcement actions for financial misrepresentation (March 19, 2012). http://ssrn.com/abstract=2026282

Gilson, S. C. (1989). Management turnover and financial distress. *Journal of Financial Economics, 25*, 241–262.

Hall, R. E., & Lazear, V. A. (2000). Reference guide on estimation of economic losses in damage awards. Reference Manual on Scientific Evidence, second ed. Federal Judicial Center, Washington www.niatec.net/Publications/wyndrose/CASMAT/EVID/SCIEV/10DAM.pdf, pp. 471–523.

Helland, E. (2006). Reputational penalties and the merits of class action securities litigation. *Journal of Law and Economics, 49*(2006), 365–396.

Jackson, H. E., & Roe, M. J. (2007). Public enforcement of securities laws: preliminary evidence. Unpublished working paper. Harvard Law School.

Jensen, M. C. (1993). The modern industrial revolution, exit, and the failure of internal control systems. *Journal of Finance, 48*, 831–880.

Karpoff, J. M., & Lott, J. R, Jr. (1993). The reputational penalty firms bear from committing criminal fraud. *Journal of Law and Economics, 36*, 757–802.

Karpoff, J. M., Lee, D. S. & Martin, G. S. (2008a). The cost to firms of cooking the books. *Journal of Financial and Quantitative Analysis ssrn.com/abstract, 43*, 581–612.

Karpoff, J. M., Lee, D. S., & Martin, G. S. (2008b). The legal penalties for financial misrepresentation (May 2, 2007). papers.ssrn.com/sol3/papers.cfm?abstract_id=933333.

Karpoff, J. M., Lee, D. S., & Martin, G. S. (2012). The economics of bribery: Evidence from FCPA enforcement actions (July 29, 2013). http://ssrn.com/abstract=1573222.

King, G., & Zeng, L. (1999). Logistic regression in rare events data. Unpublished working paper. Department of Government, Harvard University. http://gking.harvard.edu.
LaPorta, R., Lopez-de-Silanes, F., & Shleifer, A. (2006). What works in securities laws? *Journal of Finance, 61*, 1–32.
Lucas, W. R. (1997). A practitioners guide to the SEC's investigative and enforcement process. *Temple Law Review, 53*, 53–70.
Polinsky, A. M., & Shavell, S. (1993). Should employees be subject to fines and imprisonment given the existence of corporate liability? *International Review of Law and Economics, 13*, 239–257.
Semadeni, M. B., Cannella, A. A, Jr, Fraser, D. R., & Lee, D. S. (2008). Fight or flight: Managing stigma in executive careers. *Strategic Management Journal, 29*, 557–567.
Tomz, M., King, G., & Zeng, L. (1999). ReLogit: Rare Events Logistic Regression, Version 1.1. Harvard University, Cambridge, MA http://gking.harvard.edu/ (Oct. 1).
US General Accounting Office (GAO), (2002). Financial Statement Restatements: Trends, Market Impacts, Regulatory Responses, and Remaining Challenges. GAO-03-138. US Government Accountability Office, Washington, DC. www.gao.gov/new.items/d03138.pdf.
US General Accounting Office (GAO), (2003). Financial Statement Restatement Database. GAO-03-395R. US Government Accountability Office, Washington, DC. www.gao.gov/new.items/d03395r.pdf.
US Securities and Exchange Commission, (1973). Commencement of Enforcement Proceedings and Termination of Staff Investigations Release No. 5310 (Feb. 28).
Warner, J. B., Watts, R. L., & Wruck, K. H. (1988). Stock prices and top management changes. *Journal of Financial Economics, 20*, 461–492.
Weisbach, M. S. (1988). Outside directors and CEO turnover. *Journal of Financial Economics, 20*, 431–460.
Yermack, D. (1996). Higher market valuation of companies with a smaller board of directors. *Journal of Financial Economics, 40*, 185–211.

Chapter 15
National Standard-Setters' Lobbying: An Analysis of its Role in the IFRS 2 Due Process

Begoña Giner and Miguel Arce

Abstract As the IASB's due process sustains, the national standard-setters play a key role in the development of IFRS. There is still much to learn, however, about their lobbying practices, which arguments they use and when they do it. This chapter focuses on the accounting of share-based payments that were under-regulated before IFRS 2. To analyze lobbying behavior of this relevant group of stakeholders, we conduct a content analysis of the 27 comment letters addressing the documents issued by the G4+1 and the IASB that preceded IFRS 2. Consistent with institutional theory, our analysis of lobbying activity by national standard-setters shows that participation increased at the end of the process, and they supported the IASB's final proposals although they were not as much supportive at the beginning.

15.1 Introduction[1]

This research addresses the lobbying activity toward the international accounting standards board (IASB) in the development of international financial reporting standard (IFRS) 2—*Share-based Payments*—by a group of relevant stakeholders: the national standard-setters (NSS). Following Sutton (1984, p. 81), lobbying

---

[1] Earlier versions of the paper benefited from presentations at the 3rd Workshop on Accounting and Regulation held in Siena and 30th European Accounting Association Congress held in Lisbon.

B. Giner (✉) · M. Arce
Universitat de València. Facultat d'Economia. Dpt. de Comptabilitat,
Valencia, Spain
e-mail: begona.giner@uv.es

M. Arce
e-mail: miguel.arce@uv.es

R. Di Pietra et al. (eds.), *Accounting and Regulation*,
DOI: 10.1007/978-1-4614-8097-6_15,

activity includes 'All the actions which the interested parties take to influence the rule-making body'.

In the new international context where the IASB is the *de facto* accounting standard-setter worldwide, the complexity of this procedure has increased considerably. Besides the traditional interested groups, corporate managers, investors, and auditors, one should consider the NSS,[2] who play a different and very important role. Although they are not responsible for the production of the standards, their active participation in the IASB standard-setting process is necessary to achieve high quality global accounting standards. To the extent they have a good knowledge about the local institutions they are in a good position to find out how the standards may be understood and applied locally; they can undertake research, encourage stakeholders input from their jurisdictions, and identify emerging issues, in summary they can act as a channel between the IASB and the other stakeholders. An obvious recognition of this important role is the recent proposal of the IFRS Foundation[3] to create an accounting standards advisory forum (ASAF). In addition as the changes in the IFRS may put pressure on the NSS to modify country-specific standards they become a potentially affected group. Moreover within the EU, the European Commission (EC) and other relevant groups, mainly the European financial reporting advisory group (EFRAG), are very much involved in the process as the standards must be endorsed to be applied throughout Europe; they are also considered in this research.

The IASB's due process relies on wide consultation, including a formal process of inviting public comment letters on discussion chapters (DPs) and exposure drafts (EDs) (IASCF 2006). As Leuz et al. (2004) argue, the legitimacy of the standards depends on the participation of those affected, thus lack of participation suggests failure in the process. This chapter is based on the assumption that participation results in the submission of comment letters. In this respect, our investigation provides knowledge about the lobbying activities of the NSS, when their lobbying practices occur, and the arguments employed by them.

Some prior lobbying literature examines the motivations and characteristics of the groups that participate in the process (Tandy and Wilburn 1992; Kenny and Larson 1993, 1995; Tutticci et al. 1994; Jupe 2000; Larson and Brown 2001; Stenka and Taylor 2010), while other chapters focus on one particular group, such as academics (Tandy and Wilburn 1996), auditors (Puro 1984; Meier et al. 1993), or preparers (Watts and Zimmerman 1978; McArthur 1988, 1996; Guenther and Hussein 1995; Schalow 1995; Larson 1997; Ang et al. 2000; Georgiou 2002, 2004), and in particular on preparers that lobbied against SFAS 123 (Dechow et al.

[2] In Giner and Arce (2012) we make an analysis of the lobbying procedure by all interested groups. This paper could be considered an extension of this analysis focused on the NSS.

[3] See the Invitation to Comment 'Proposal to Establish and Accounting Standards Advisory Forum' (IFRS Foundation 2012). As stated in the document the two main reasons behind the proposal are the end of the convergence program with the FASB and the widely spread use of IFRS around the world what make necessary to rationalize the relationships of the Board with NSS and regional bodies.

1996; Hill et al. 2002). We are not aware about any chapter that focuses on lobbying by the standard-setters, which is understandable due to the relatively new regulatory structure that makes them a potential lobbying group. Some of the prior chapters look at the content of submissions, as we also do in this research (McArthur 1988; Kenny and Larson 1993; Tutticci et al. 1994; Ang et al. 2000; Jupe 2000; Stenka and Taylor 2010).

Although most of the previous literature deals with the standard-setting process at the country level, some chapters focus on lobbying an international accounting body. Thus Guenther and Hussein (1995), Larson (1997), MacArthur (1996) ,and Kwok and Sharp (2005) deal with the international accounting standards committee (IASC). More recent chapters deal with the IASB, such as Georgiou (2010) who examines the users' attitudes and Orens et al. (2011) that focus on preparers, while Jorissen et al. (2012) and Giner and Arce (2012) analyze the participation of all stakeholders. Finally, Larson (2007) considers lobbying the IASB's international financial reporting interpretations committee (IFRIC).

We adopt a single-case approach that highlights some neglected aspects of the lobbying behavior. Although this type of analysis does not allow generalization of the lobbying activity, it enables to explore the sense of comments issued by the interested parties. Consequently we avoid some of the limitations noted by Walker and Robinson (1993), such as submissions are interpreted as "votes", there is failure to consider arguments provided, and shifts in preferences.

The accounting regulation of share-based payments—transactions whereby an entity obtains goods and services from other parties with payment taking the form of shares or share options—generated an unprecedented debate in the United States in the 1980s and 1990s, and the financial accounting standards board (FASB) maintained a non-expense-recognition policy. Moreover, expense recognition of share-based payments was not required in other countries. In 2001, the IASB included this project in its agenda, and 3 years later approved IFRS 2, forcing recognition of share-based payments as an expense.

In this study we analyze the lobbying activity of the NSS prior to the adoption of IFRS 2 in February 2004. To this end we analyze the 27 comment letters submitted by this interested group to the previous documents, going as far back as 2000. The IFRS 2 requires an entity to record all share-based payments as expenses, regardless of the form of settlement (shares or cash) and the counterpart involved (employees or others). We have chosen IFRS 2 as the subject of this study for several reasons. First, it deals with fundamental accounting notions—assets versus expenses, liabilities versus equity—in an area in which, as already stated, there was no previous standard. Second, it has a big impact on the two key accounting figures: net income and equity. Third, the discussion held in the United States on this topic ended with a compromise solution that allowed companies not to recognize the expense, what suggests a difficult decision faced the IASB, and provides an ideal setting to examine lobbying strategies. Fourth, the project had three consultation periods, as the DP was initially published by the G4+1[4] in 2000, then the IASB adopted it and reissued it in 2001, and later the IASB published the ED 2 in 2002. In particular, the second publication of the DP enables us to examine the lobbyists' attitudes as a function of the differential status of the issuer. We argue that the lobbyists' concerns might increase as a consequence of the eventual impact of the new standard which was particularly evident when IFRS become mandatory. In addition, the relevance of IFRS 2 is evidenced by the participation of interested parties.[5]

Our examination of the comment letters consists of a content analysis focusing on three key issues: recognition, valuation criteria, and reference date. Our analysis is further aimed at identifying the underlying conceptual and economic arguments that used to justify the position on each of these issues. As most of the prior literature, this study relies on the rational-choice model of lobbying developed by Sutton (1984), which explains participation by the lobbyists if their expected benefits exceed the cost of lobbying. However, the institutional theory is particularly relevant as well. Indeed as Kenny and Larson (1995, p. 288) note: 'In an institutional context, lobbying may be evidentiary of the perceived importance or viability of the organization being lobbied'; the considerable participation of NSS after the ED 2 is consistent with the insights of this theory. This theory also predicts the standard-setter 'will try to accommodate the strongest wishes of its constituency when doing so enhances the organization's acceptability without seriously impairing its integrity' (Kenny and Larson 1993, p. 214). Consequently, our investigation draws on a combination of the institutional theory and rational-choice literatures.

In order to understand the IASB's attitude it is useful to consider the IASB Constitution and the Framework. As stated in the paragraph 2 of the Constitution (IFRSF 2010), the aim of the IFRS is to achieve high quality, transparent, and comparable information to help investors, other participants in the world's capital markets (as well as other users) make economic decisions. It cannot be denied that accounting information has economic effects, but if it is accepted that information should be neutral these should be ignored when making decisions on how economic transactions should be recorded. In other words, although it is recognized that different accounting treatments will have a different impact between competing constituencies, only conceptual and technical considerations should be considered when developing the standards. In Whittington's (2005, p. 152) words: 'Ultimately, markets need full, transparent information, untainted by concessions to vested interests. The IASB is attempting to meet this need by following the ultimate objective "tell it the way it is". In this line of argument, in 1993, James J.

[4] The G4+1 was an association of the accounting standards-setting bodies of Australia, Canada, New Zealand, United Kingdom and United States. The IASC participated as an observer. The G4+1 was disbanded in 2001 when the IASC was transformed into the IASB.

[5] Between 2002 and 2006 the IASB received 103 comment letters per document on average; IFRS 6 received the lowest number (24), and the DP on share–based payments received the most (281).

Leisering, Vice-Chairman of the FASB at that time (and member of the IASB when IFRS 2 was adopted), declared in a hearing of the Subcommittee on Securities of the Senate Committee on Banking, Housing and Urban Affairs when debating the FASB's proposal on accounting for stock options: 'We believe that economic goals are best achieved directly, by subsidies, tax policy, and the like. Capital markets, on the other hand, are best served by unbiased financial statements designed to inform policy makers rather than to promote policies. Decision-makers need financial statements that tell it like it is, in short' (quoted in Zeff 2002, p. 181).

This research adds to the literature on the politics of standard setting. It focuses on the IASB's due process, and given the role of the IASB as a global standard setter, it is relevant to gain insights about the standard-setting process for both the IASB and the NSS. This is particularly the case in the current context in which the producer of the standards, the IASB, has a supranational dimension, and the NSS act as interested parties. Moreover, as stated in the Due Process Handbook (IFRSF 2012) and the current developments are evidencing, the interaction of this group with the IASB is key in the development of IFRS.

The structure of the chapter is as follows. In Sect. 15.2, we provide a brief summary of the institutional developments. Section 15.3 deals with the development of IFRS 2. Section 15.4 focuses on the research questions, the data and the results. Finally, Sect. 15.5 provides the main conclusions.

15.2 Institutional Developments

Although the main purpose of this research is to analyze the lobbying behavior prior to the publication of IFRS 2, we consider it helpful to provide some background to understand the new institutional arrangements that have given wide acceptability and authority to the IASB, in other words that provide power, both competent authority and legitimacy (Hope and Gray 1982). Our analysis is consistent with the institutional theory which considers that organizations, such as the IASB, have to be acceptable to their constituency to survive; Kenny and Larson (1993) applied this framework to its predecessor the IASC, while Fogarty (1992) made an application to the FASB. The former study explains the changes that took place in 1989, when the IASC started an open due process, using the mimetic institutional influence explanation (DiMaggio and Powell 1983). Kenny and Larson (1993) argue that the IASC tried to imitate the FASB's format as it was perceived the most successful and legitimate. Although the replacement of the IASC by the IASB in 2001 was subject to a strong debate between those that preferred a bicameral solution and proponents of the independent model, the latter solution won out, and the IASB structure is very similar to that of FASB (Stevenson 2007).

The IASB members have the sole responsibility for setting the standards, so in contrast to the previous IASC in this case individuals cast votes. As for the composition of the Board, the Constitution establishes some geographical criteria to ensure a broad international basis, and the Trustees have to ensure that the group provides an appropriate mix of recent practical experience among auditors, preparers, users, and academics. The IASB is assisted by regular meetings with the IFRS Advisory Council, also appointed by the Trustees from a wide range of nationalities and backgrounds. The Advisory Council provides advice before adding an item to the Board's agenda, and offers comments on its on-going work. In addition the IASB keeps regular contacts with NSS and with international organizations, such as the international organization of securities commissions (IOSCO) and the EFRAG. An annual meeting has also been instituted with all NSS, in order to widen the IASB's world-wide contacts. In short, these different consultation levels help to provide legitimacy of action to the IASB. A Monitoring Board created in 2007 provides a formal link between the Trustees and public authorities.

The open due process that follows the IASB before issuing an IFRS is also consistent with the institutional theory framework. This is the process by which the Board deliberates and decides on the content of its standards; it allows all interested groups to give their opinions when the standard is under deliberation. 'A proper due process ensures that the issue has been properly understood, that all sides of the argument have been identified and properly considered, and that the rationale underlying the conclusion eventually reached has been tested. It is therefore very important for the credibility and authority of the conclusion reached' (EFRAG 2005, paragraph 3.19). Indeed it is a way of receiving input from the stakeholders in order to better understand the possible divergent views, and so make more effective decisions, but it can also be seen as an attempt to capture the interest of all participants in the standard-setting process, as a strategy that helps to legitimate the organization. Another important aspect of the due process, comes from its open nature; as Richardson and Eberlein (2011, p. 219) argue, 'is a (potential) means for disciplining the exercise of power by the IASB and perhaps more importantly, for forcing influence attempts by networked entities on the IASB into a public forum'.

The IASB due process allows several opportunities to participate: developing views as a member of the Advisory Council, taking part in advisory groups, submissions of issues to IFRIC,[6] submissions of comment letters to DPs and EDs, participation in public round-tables, as well as field visits and field tests. Those who participate in the process want to be listened and to exercise influence over the final standard, in so doing they normally provide arguments to support their positions. Comment letters is probably the most visible mechanism of lobbying to the researchers as they are available on the IASB website. As Walker and Robinson (1993, p. 15) argue this tries to 'ensure that rule-making bodies can be held accountable for the way they go about making their decisions'. Moreover, the public availability of these letters and the open nature of the Board meetings provide transparency in the formulation of the standards.

[6] The IASB also issues interpretations that are prepared by the IFRIC. IFRIC members are appointed by the Trustees.

Once an item is on the Agenda and considered a major project, the IASB due process may start with the publication of a DP. After a normal period of about 120 days for responses, the technical staff prepare an ED, which requires the votes of nine Board members to be approved if there are fewer than 16 members or 10 members if there are 16 members.[7] After its publication a similar consultation period starts and in the light of the responses received, a final draft standard is submitted to the Board (public hearings and field tests are conducted if desired), which requires the same number of votes to be adopted. Consequently, throughout the process the lobbyists have to decide whether to take action, when to take it, and what to argue. It is assumed that in deciding to take action constituents consider both the benefit and the associated costs. Referring to the FASB's structure, Fogarty (1992) sustains the *due process*, a *balanced background of members*, and the *public relations efforts* are three elements that provide legitimacy to the FASB. It is indeed no coincidence that these three aspects are also well-covered in the IASB structure.

Although prior research has explored the extent of political influence in the development of accounting standards through the study of the constituents lobbying activity, Walker and Robinson (1993) point out that to explain the political process undertaken attention should be paid to the manner in which responsibility has been assumed by the standard-setter, or delegated to it; thus before concluding our analysis of the current standard-setting context, we think it is useful to comment on the arrangements that give power to the IASB. The IASB has no direct powers of its own; consequently it has to persuade those with regulatory and enforcement powers to approve the use of international standards. The acceptance of IFRS in a number of jurisdictions has given the IASB a leading position in the international accounting standard-setting (and by 2002 it was clear that they were going to be used in the EU, Australia, and New Zealand), although certain organizations keep the right to endorse the standards. For instance, Europe has moved away from the previous policy of harmonizing the national standards through the Directives to apply IFRS when endorsed by the Commission (this measure had a direct impact on about 8,000 entities[8]). The endorsement mechanism is a two-tier structure that involves the technical advice given by the EFRAG, an independent private body created in 2001, and a political consultation to the accounting regulatory committee (ARC), which is a committee established under the "comitology" procedure commonly followed by the EC to make decisions. Consequently, the EC and the EFRAG have become relevant interested parties as their view on the standards is crucial to their being made compulsory in the EU. It is important

[7] The supermajority rule was introduced in the reform on the IASB Constitution that took place in 2005. It aims to get more unity among the Board members in order to increase the perception of acceptance of the standards.

[8] This is the estimated number of listed companies that prepare consolidated accounts. There is also an indirect and very important impact if Member States of the EU use the option included in the Regulation 1606/2002 and allow or oblige to use endorsed IFRS for individual accounts and for consolidated purposes to non-listed companies.

to remark that in order to endorse any standard it should be conducive to the "European public good"—that there should be no competitive disadvantages for European companies.

15.3 Accounting for Share Options: The Evolution Towards IFRS 2

The early inclusion of share-based payments in the IASB agenda may be seen as a clear sign to the objective of the IASB to lead the development of high quality standards especially in those areas where there is no national standard that adequately addresses the problem; Whittington (2005), at that time an IASB Board member, refers to the share-based payment project as one obvious example of this commitment. We find rather symbolic that the first 'new' standard produced by the Board deals with this controversial accounting issue.

The history of the SFAS 123 (FASB 1995) shows that the accounting for share-options is a very cumbersome topic. The strong opposition especially from the technology industry refrained the FASB from producing an advanced standard on this issue; accordingly it finally took a step back and did not require the expensing of these payments, but adopted a compromise solution that allowed companies not to recognize the expense (Dechow et al. 1996). The decision about expensing stock options does imply economic consequences, not only on the companies directly affected, but also on wider issues such as human resources management. It has been suggested that the recognition of an expense corresponding to promised option plans could discourage companies from introducing retributive schemes based on shares or options compensations or even encourage them to be completely abandoned. But this 'is inconsistent with the view that current granting practices are optimal, because, if they were, imposing an accounting change should not affect option grants' (Murphy 2003, p. 144).

Nevertheless, it is thought that the IASB might have faced lesser difficulties than NSS. As Crouzet and Veron (2004, p. 12) sustain 'the IASB's principal advantage over the FASB is its greater immunity to corporate lobbying, which, in principle should result in superior standards quality'. It can be argued that it is easier to be immune to the adverse consequences argument when dealing with standards to be used worldwide than when dealing with a particular country. In the words of Whittington (2005, p. 134): 'The IASB, as an international standard setter, has the advantage of being less susceptible to the 'level playing field' argument, that stringent national standards may disadvantage domestic companies relative to those overseas, which have less stringent regimes. However, because international standards are not followed in the largest economy in the world, the US, this advantage is not as strong as it will be if international standards are converged with the US standards. European companies listed in the US are particularly sensitive to this issue'.

As already explained, the screening mechanism established in the EU for the legal endorsement of the IFRS requires the standards to be conducive to the "European public good", and no doubt share-based payments is a very sensitive topic. Nevertheless in January 2005, 1 year after the promulgation of IFRS 2, the EC, with the support of the EFRAG, endorsed the standard. As explained later, the EFRAG's position changed over the period under analysis from rejection to acceptance of recognizing the expense. To understand these positions, it has to be considered that there were parallel changes in the United States, so that the competitive disadvantages argument frequently used to justify the European constituents' opposition to recognition lost its relevance (Giner and Arce 2012). Thus, in March 2003, the FASB added the project to its agenda,[9] and 1 year later issued an ED showing a substantial amount of convergence with IFRS 2, and SFAS 123 (revised) was published at the end of 2004. This was an important step to avoid or reduce strong criticisms based on competitive disadvantages.

The importance of share-based payments derives from the huge development of such transactions. At the time when the DP was issued Towers Perrin (2000) reported that, in reference to companies with sales of over $500 million , share options represented between 20 % of annual salaries in Germany, and 40 % in both Sweden and the UK (other figures included 25 % in Belgium, 32 % in France, and 35 % in Spain and the Netherlands). These percentages represent less than half of those in the US. In 2000, 99 % of the S&P 500 companies, gave share options to their employees, but only two of them registered an expense, and as such profits were overvalued by 12 %. The importance of these compensation schemes differs between industries. Murphy (2003) provides some data on the new and old economy firms. Using 1999 pretax income figures, he suggests that 45 % of the new economy firms and 16 % of the old economy firms would have had negative figures (compared with 23 and 13 % as reported ignoring compensations).[10]

A somewhat generalized opinion even among academic researchers (Aboody 1996; Garvey and Milbourn 2001) is that the spread of option plans for employees was at a certain extent favored by the lack of an adequate accounting treatment. Indeed companies prefer to avoid recognition and disclose the *pro forma* net income that results when the fair value of options is included as a cost. If the market were able to efficiently price the options disclosed in the notes, the discussion between recognition and disclosure could be considered irrelevant;

[9] The comprehensive Basis for Conclusions that accompanies IFRS 2 explains that the IASB worked with the FASB after the latter added to its agenda in March 2003 a project to review US accounting requirements on share-based payment.

[10] As a consequence of the accounting changes US firms reduced the use of stock options. The Towers Perrin's (2004) report indicates that many US companies redesigned their executive incentive plans: they estimate a reduction of 16 % in the value of long-term incentives and an increase of cash compensation in 2004. According to Bear, Stearns & Co (2004) the impact of stock options on the 2004 earnings figure of S&P 500 and NASDAQ 100 is about 5 and 22 %, respectively.

however, the conclusions resulting from empirical research do not uphold this position. A number of studies carried out in the US after SFAS 123 on 'Accounting for stock-based compensations' evidences that prices negatively reflect the information disclosed on option costs (Aboody et al. 2001), which leads us to question the quality of the accounting earnings figure without considering this expense. Other studies show that investors have only a partial understanding of the whole reality (Garvey and Milbourn 2001); it seems the market undervalues the cost of the options given out until vesting date, meaning that those companies which agree to hand over large numbers of options tend to be overvalued. Definitively, Garvey and Milbourn (2001, p. 14) claim: 'The aggressive use of employee stock options may thus represent a transfer of wealth from long-term to short-term shareholders'. Consequently, it could be argued that the extensive use of unrecognized performance-based schemes linked to share prices has favored the boom of the stock market during 1990s and this situation also favored the expansion of these schemes. In contrast, the great stock market crisis at the beginning of this century probably facilitated the adoption of IFRS 2. This is consistent with a causal relation between a crisis and the entrance of an issue in the political process (Watts 1977; Nobes 1991). At the time the IASB started the share-based payments project there was a major crisis of confidence in the market and in the accounting system as a whole.

In 2004 IFRS 2 was issued; the project had started 4 years earlier with the publication of the DP by the G4+1, which received 29 comment letters, 4 of them came from the NSS. In September 2001, the recently created IASB backed and reissued that chapter. Following its due process, a period for comments was established and a considerable larger number of responses were received 281 letters (83 % from the preparers), only 4 of them came from the NSS. An Advisory Group, including individuals from different countries and backgrounds (investment, corporate, audit, academic, compensation consultancy, valuation, and regulatory communities) helped the Board in the development of the ED, ED 2. It also received the assistance from experts at a panel discussion held in New York in July 2002. Thus on November 2003, the IASB published ED 2 and received 229 letters (53 % from the preparers), 19 of them from the NSS. The final step was taken in February 2004 when the standard was published, with the full backing of the 14 Board members.

Figure 15.1 is a timeline of the development of this standard in connection with some relevant events that happened at that time, such as the EC announcement after the Lisbon Council in June 2000 about the adoption of IAS, and the Norwalk Agreement in 2002.

Table 15.1 gives some details on the documents under study about the three issues of interest in this study: recognition, valuation, and reference date, and compares them with SFAS 123. It is remarkable that the three selected items were subject to different accounting treatments in the DP and the original SFAS 123.

The basic idea of the share-based project is that the transaction whereby an entity obtains goods and services from other parties, with payment taking the form of shares or share options should be recognized as equity in the balance sheet with

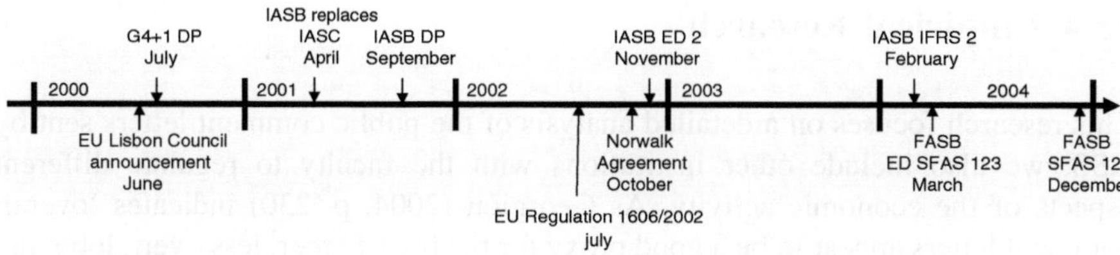

Fig. 15.1 Timeline of the standard development and other relevant events

Table 15.1 Comparison of SFAS 123, DP, ED 2, and IFRS 2

	SFAS 123 (1995)	DP	ED 2	IFRS 2
Recognition of the expense	Yes	Yes	Yes	Yes
Exceptions from recognition	Fixed plans[a]	No	No	No
Fair value of goods and services received	Yes	No	Yes, not to employees	Yes, not to employees
Fair value of share-based instruments issued	Yes	Yes	Yes	Yes
Reference date for valuation	Grant date	Vesting date	Grant date, exceptions	Grant date, exceptions

[a] This option was eliminated by the revised SFAS 123 (2004)
Source Giner and Arce (2012, p. 660)

a corresponding charge in the income statement. This fundamental principle has remained in the three documents. In the SFAS 123 there was an exception to recognition for fixed-option plans (common in the USA) that did not exist in the DP; the revised SFAS 123 eliminated the exception. As for valuation, the DP established that the fair value of equity instruments issued should be used and admitted that, in most cases, an option pricing model should be applied. Nevertheless SFAS 123 allowed using this criterion or the fair value of the goods and services received the one that is more reliably valued. This was later allowed in ED 2 but not for employees. Thus ED 2 differentiated between payments to employees and those made to the providers of goods and other services, it kept the same criteria for the former, but established a refutable presumption about using the fair value of goods and services for the latter. IFRS 2 keeps this distinction. Regarding the measurement date, according to the DP vesting date[11] should be used to measure the fair value of the shares or options issued, while SFAS 123 required gran date.[12] ED 2 changed the criteria and established that grant date should be used when determining fair value by reference to an equity instrument, while when fair value considers the value of the goods and services, the date when the entity obtains them should be considered; IFRS 2 did not introduce any change on that.

[11] The date at which the other party, having performed all of the services or provided all of the goods, becomes unconditionally entitled to the options or shares.
[12] The date at which the contract between the entity and the other party is entered into.

15.4 Empirical Research

This research focuses on a detailed analysis of the public comment letters sent by NSS, we also include other institutions with the faculty to regulate different aspects of the economic activity. As Georgiou (2004, p. 230) indicates 'overall comment letters appear to be a good proxy for the use of other, less overt, lobbying methods'. Indeed they have been often used in previous lobbying research (Tutticci et al. 1994; Kwok and Sharp 2005; Jorissen et al. 2012; Giner and Arce 2012). Lobbying research based on written submissions has attracted criticism, however, because it has frequently interpreted the submissions as "votes", without consideration for the arguments provided (Walker and Robinson 1993). Nevertheless Brown (1982), a former member of the FASB, asserts that the standard setters are influenced by both the nature and strength of the arguments provided by respondents. Consequently, in this research we look at the arguments in detail.

15.4.1 Research Questions and Methods

The research questions address the NSS lobbying strategies. Our first question deals with the decision about *whether or not* to participate in each of the three comment periods associated with the development of IFRS 2. The rational-choice model of lobbying developed by Sutton (1984) contends that parties will take action in the lobbying process if their benefits, adjusted by the probability that lobbying will change the outcome of the standard-setting process, exceeds the cost of lobbying.

The position of the NSS can be also explained by the self-interest argument that is associated with the constituent's position (Puro 1984). As Giner and Arce (2012) note political, economic, and perhaps social factors could explain the position of the national standard setters as they need to be considered respectful and influential to maintain their respective roles. Their special status is recognized in paragraph 28 of the IASB's Constitution (IFRSF 2010); it is expected to establish and maintain liaison with them in order to assist in the development of IFRSs and promote the convergence of NSS and IFRSs. Moreover, as stated in the introduction, the IASB aims to establish a new group, ASAF, to strength the links with them.

There were three comment periods in the development of the share-based payments project, which allows us to focus on the two stages in the production of IFRS 2—the DP and ED—enabling us to consider the lobbyists' decisions about *when* to participate. Sutton's (1984) model suggests that it is easier to influence the decision maker when general views and ideas are required (e.g., when a DP is under discussion) than after the publication of an ED. Following this reasoning, respondents would be prone to providing comments in the first stage of the process, as they may think there is a greater probability of influencing the final result. As for the nature of the issuer, the DP was published twice—first by the G4+1 and then by the IASB—implying a change in the mandatory status of the outcome of the project. In this context, non-compliance with the accounting proposal is not a feasible alternative for preparers and NSS are in good position to know the attitudes in their jurisdictions; on the contrary, it becomes costly not to follow the IASB's requirements. The model also suggests that raising the cost of non-compliance increases the lobbying efforts, as the benefits of this activity are higher. Consequently there could be an increase in lobbying activity after the second publication of the DP—once the EU and other jurisdictions announced that they were to adopt the IFRSs.

Overall, this reasoning leads to our first research question, RQ1: Was the NSS lobbying activity related to IFRS 2 equally distributed across comment periods? To address RQ1, we classify the comment letters by periods of response and use χ^2 test to compare responses among periods.

The second question refers to the decision about *what* to argue. The use of arguments to justify the opinions stated in the letters is perceived as a strategy of persuasion. In this respect, prior research distinguishes between conceptual arguments and those based on economic consequences (Tutticci et al. 1994; Jupe 2000). Conceptual arguments refer primarily to the accounting notions linked to the Conceptual Framework and to technical issues related to the topic under consideration. Arguments based on economic consequences refer to economic changes associated with the proposed standard and the implications of those changes. As economic-based arguments would conflict with the image of professionalism and objectivity (Stenka and Taylor 2010), NSS might hesitate to use them and prefer to provide erudite and conceptually based responses.

Prior research has not examined the behavior of interested parties in agreement or disagreement with the proposals on accounting standards (see Tutticci et al. 1994; Giner and Arce 2012 as significant exceptions). We assume that respondents who agreed with the proposed standard had fewer incentives to present a supporting argument than did their counterparts that disagreed with such proposals. Thus, we raise the following question, RQ2: Did the NSS provide different arguments in their comment letters to support their positions in favor of or against the proposals?

As in Jupe (2000) and Stenka and Taylor (2010), our examination related to the lobbying strategies requires us to analyze the content of comment letters. As mentioned above, we identify the issues considered (recognition, valuation, and reference date), the position (agree, disagree, or no opinion) and the arguments used (conceptual, economic consequences, both arguments, or neither argument) in each comment letter (Giner and Arce 2012).

The detailed reading of the comment letters implies a certain degree of subjectivity, which we have tried to reduce by focusing on three issues and double-checking the content of the letters. The Kappa statistic for inter-annotator agreement suggested by Cohen (1960) shows non-significant differences between the two annotators in the three issues analysed. Nevertheless, we admit some subjectivity exists in the selection of the three key issues, but we have considered the *Invitation to comments* included in the DP, the responses, as well as those aspects that in our view are fundamental for the accounting of these transactions. It is also important to remark that the three selected items were subject to different accounting treatments in the DP and the original SFAS 123.

15.4.2 Data

As Table 15.2 shows fourteen NSS participated in the lobbying, they come from Australia, Canada, France, Germany, Japan, Malaysia, the Netherlands, Norway, Poland, Singapore, South Korea, Spain, Sweden, and Thailand. In this group we also include the EC and EFRAG that as explained above play a relevant role in the endorsement of IFRS in the EU. We also consider the responses of other institutions with the faculty to regulate different aspects of the economic activity, such as the Basel Committee and the IOSCO, one answer from a US Congress members group, other from the Securities Commission of New Zealand, and another from the Ministry of Economy, Trade, and Industry of Japan. In total there are 21 different respondents considered as NSS.

We collected the comment letters from the IASB website. As some respondents replied more than once, there are more letters (27) than respondents (21). Table 15.2 indicates the six respondents (EC, EFRAG, and the standard-setters of France, Germany, the Netherlands, and Spain) that participated in two stages (no one did it three times). They represent 28.5 % of respondents. This percentage is lower than in other groups, 45 % in the profession, but larger than in others, such users, 21 %, and preparers, only 9 % (Giner and Arce 2012).

More than half of the comment letters (17) came from the EU and Australia/New Zealand jurisdictions where IFRSs would be compulsory. It is also remarkable the high number of letters coming from Asia. These figures should be interpreted with caution however, as the small number of comments from the NSS represents a high proportion of the potential respondents in this group.

15.4.3 Results

Table 15.2 provides a detailed overview and a geographical breakdown of the sample. In the last row we include for comparative purposes the number of letters coming from all respondents. It provides evidence on RQ1 regarding the decisions of when they do the lobbying. The IASC received 4 responses when issued the DP (DP1), and then the IASB received another 4 when issued it again (DP2) and 19 when issued the ED 2. The χ^2 tests confirm that there is a significant difference (at 0.001 level) in the participation of the NSS in the three comment periods. As Giner and Arce (2012) indicate this occurs with the other groups of respondents as well, and the χ^2 tests confirm that the participation of the groups differs statistically from the first publication of the DP to its second publication and from the second DP to

Table 15.2 Respondents

Geographical zone	Name		DP1	DP2	ED2
International	Basel committee on banking supervision				x
	International organization of securities commissions				x
ASIA					
Japan	Accounting standards board of Japan	NSS[a]			x
Japan	Ministry of economy, trade and industry		x		
Malaysia	Malaysian accounting standards board	NSS			x
Singapore	Council on corporate disclosure and governance	NSS			x
South Korea	Korean accounting standards board	NSS			x
Thailand	Accounting standards committee of Thailand	NSS			x
AUSTRALIA-NZ					
Australia	Australian accounting standards board	NSS			x
New Zealand	Securities commission				x
EUROPE					
	European commission		x	x	
	European financial reporting advisory group			x	x
France	Conseil National de la Comptabilité	NSS		x	x
Germany	German accounting standards board	NSS	x		x
Netherlands	The Netherlands council for annual reporting	NSS	x		x
Norway	Norsk RegnskapsStiftelse	NSS			x
Poland	Accounting standards committee in Poland	NSS			x
Spain	Instituto de Contabilidad y Auditoría de Cuentas	NSS		x	x
Sweden	Swedish financial accounting standards council	NSS			x
US-CANADA					
Canada	Accounting standards board	NSS			x
USA	Members of the United States Congress				x
	Total NSS responses		4	4	19
	Total responses		29	281	229

[a] *NSS* National accounting standard setters

ED 2. Nevertheless our examination of the individual periods reveals a different pattern of the NSS with the other of respondents.

The standard setters sent 5 times more letters to the ED 2 than to the DP in each of the two comment periods (19 vs. 4 letters). This finding departs from Sutton's (1984) contention that there should be a stronger reaction in the earlier stages of the process, due to the greater effectiveness of lobbying. On the contrary, this result is consistent with Walker and Robinson (1993) who point out that those who lobby could merely be showing support for the overall activities of the regulatory agencies. As explained later, this appears to have happened in this case, as most of the responses to the ED 2 were in support of the IASB's proposals. This interpretation is consistent with the institutional theory, as it may be seen as 'a visibility-enhancing maneuver and as a maneuver to increase another organization's (the IASC's) viability' (Kenny and Larson 1995, p. 298); the same could be argued of the IASB.

We then examine the three issues under discussion on the accounting for stock options to employees (recognition, valuation, and reference date). Most of the letters (21) dealt with the key issues under consideration, as shown in Table 15.3 panel A. This strategy is common to other groups such as the profession and users, whereas preparers and consultants usually addressed only the recognition issue (Giner and Arce 2012). Notwithstanding, the European Commission in response to the DP and the accounting standards board (ASB) of Japan in its letter to the ED 2 did not address directly any of the identified issues. Instead they made general comments on accounting policy. The ASB of Japan stated: ‘We have concern about consistency between the way of applying the asset/liability approach in several major projects of IASB (…) and the explanation for the consistency with the Framework shown in the Basis for Conclusions of the ED. We do not express arguments for or against the proposals in the ED (…). However, we would like to take this opportunity to state our views on how the Framework should be applied, because we believe it is a very critical issue in conjunction with other projects’ (ED2 comment letter n. 75).

As for the supporting arguments of the opinions we identify two types: conceptual and based on economic consequences. Table 15.3 panel B summarizes them. Although most of the respondents did not justify their opinions, when they did it, they employed mainly conceptual arguments, particularly when agreed with the proposals. According to Giner and Arce (2012) NSS behaved as the profession and users, but differently to the preparers and consultants, that frequently employed arguments related to economic consequences. We found that NSS commonly provided no argument when in favor of a position, which is the strategy followed by other groups (Tutticci et al. 1994; Giner and Arce 2012).

Although the self-interest theory suggests that lobbyists could be prone to arguments rooted in economic consequences that account for unintended effects of the standards, they may be reluctant to provide these arguments, in case they are seen as self-serving, and consequently less likely to be considered by a regulator

Table 15.3 Panel A: number of comment letters that address 0, 1, 2, or all 3 of the of key issues. Panel B: Use of arguments about the three issues in the comment letters according to positions

Panel A					
Key issues	0	1	2	3	Total
Comment letters	2	3	1	21	27

Panel B			
	Agree	Disagree	Total
Conceptual	8	3	11
Economic consequences	1	2	3
Both	2	1	3
No arguments	47	4	51
Total	58	10	68[a]

[a] If one letter dealt with all three issues, we counted it three times. Thus the maximum count would have been 81

(Jupe 2000). Given the IASB's mission 'to serve the information needs of participants in capital markets' (IASB 2010: paragraph BC 1.23), respondents might have realized that the IASB would be reluctant to consider vested arguments per se—especially arguments in favor of a solution contrary to the interests of users—as they could seriously damage their credibility.[13] In addition, we suggest that the economic-consequences argument might have lost ground as a consequence of the convergence policy of the IASB and the FASB that followed the 2002 Norwalk agreement. As expected, we find no economic consequences-based arguments after the ED 2 was issued among the responses of the NSS. Next we provide a more detailed analysis of the responses about the three identified issues, as well as the arguments provided by the respondents.

15.4.3.1 Recognition

Regarding the opinions on recognition to the DP (that received 8 letters in total), 4 were in favor, 3 against and 1 with no clear opinion. Thus, the DP received full support from the Deutsches Rechnungslegungs Standards Committee of Germany, the Raad voor de Jaarverslaggeving (Council for Annual Reporting—RJ) of the Netherlands, and the Instituto de Contabilidad y Auditoría de Cuentas (ICAC) of Spain. The Ministry of Economy, Trade and Industry of Japan was also in favor, but stated that it would not be applicable to venture capital companies, unlisted companies and those recently listed on the stock exchange (DP1 comment letter n. 29). The need to encourage the growth of these types of companies—and the possible detrimental effects of the proposal—as well as the difficulties involved in measuring the fair value of equity instruments were the two reasons claimed to justify its position. Even the RJ expressed its concern over the economic effects of a regulation that negatively affects earnings especially if the new treatment was not going to be adopted worldwide (DP1 comment letter n. 20).

The Conseil National de la Comptabilité (CNC) of France rejected the DP when published by the IASB using conceptual arguments mainly due to problems with the definition of expense in the IASB Conceptual Framework (DP2 comment letter n. 113). Giner and Arce (2012) also identify respondents other than NSS that rejected the expensing of stock options arguing problems with the reliability requirement, the competitive disadvantages of companies treating stock options as expenses and the convenience of maintaining a level playing field.

The EC replied twice to the DP; in the first answer did not take a clear position, but in the second was opposed and recommended to 'convert this to a two-track project with one track focusing on the conceptual, recognition, measurement and practical aspects, and the other dealing with disclosure' (DP2 comment letter n.

[13] The experience surrounding the changes in IAS 39 and IFRS 7 that occurred in 2008 questions this assumption, however. See the Minutes of Evidence by Sir David Tweedie, Chairman of IASB, taken before the Treasury Committee of the House of Commons of the UK Parliament (Tuesday 11 November 2008).

279). EFRAG admitted that share-based payments are an expense in its response to the second publication to the DP, although suggested that due to problems with the Framework it would be better to adopt a disclosure standard as an interim measure. EFRAG also placed special emphasis on the need for worldwide convergence of accounting practices (DP2 comment letter n. 146).

However, the respondents to ED2 accepted recognition with the sole exception of the ASB of Japan that did not address directly this issue. It is interesting to note the change in EFRAG's view, which in its letter refers to the support of the Norwalk agreement on convergence and the changes in the FASB agenda (ED2 comment letter n.136). Nevertheless, EFRAG was critical about the reliability of the measurement and highlighted the strong desire from several EFRAG commentators[14] to achieve global convergence on recognition and measurement; the CNC also supported recognition, but mentioned inconsistencies with the IASB Framework and competitive disadvantages.

15.4.3.2 Valuation

Regarding the valuation criterion, NSS accepted the accounting treatment as included in the DP and ED2, and only the CNC was against it not only in its response to the DP but also to ED2 because 'its valuation causes major difficulties, one of them dealing with reliability of measurement' (ED2 comment letter n. 147). Giner and Arce (2012) identify other arguments used by other groups to criticize the use of option valuation models to measure these transactions, such as the special characteristics of employees' options, the impact on taxes; they also find that many respondents proposed the use of the intrinsic value as in SFAS 123.

15.4.3.3 Reference Date

In relation to the reference date, all the NSS preferred grant date, except the Spanish ICAC that supported vesting date, not only in its letter to the DP but in the one to ED2. The Spanish ICAC stated in its letter 'as the performance occurs between the grant date and the vesting date, the entity should account for an accrual of the best estimation of the transaction amount during the performance period' (ED2 comment letter n. 31). But the use of the vesting date was rejected for the following conceptual reasons: (1) the obligations beginning and the equity instruments being issued at the grant date, (2) the contracts being established in terms of the value at that date, and (3) there are inconsistencies between the Framework and the use of this criteria, as it would require remeasurement of equity until that date. Giner and Arce (2012) also identify respondents that argued

[14] When EFRAG produces the comment letters, it follows a due process as well, and requires comments to its constituency before considering them final.

about income volatility when discussing the use of vesting date as a possible reference date.

In summary there were shifts in the opinion of most of the respondents that replied more than once, and the support of ED 2 was due not only to these changes, but to the 13 respondents that participated for the first time at the end of the process to show agreement with the IASB's proposal. According to institutional theory, this may be seen as a sign of support for the IASB's role as a global standard-setter.

15.5 Conclusions

Taking the development of IFRS 2 as the case under study, this chapter considers the IASB's due process, and also discusses the institutional arrangements that have given wide acceptability and authority to the IASB. The latter provides the framework to understand the current position of the IASB as the global standard-setter. As Fogarty (1992) sustains the due process, a balanced background of members, and the public relations efforts are three elements that provide legitimacy to a standard-setter; our analysis of the IASB structure and *modus operandi* suggest that they are well covered in the current framework.

The IASB's due process relies on wide consultation, including a formal process of inviting public comment letters on DPs and EDs. This chapter is based on the assumption that participation results in the submission of comment letters. In this respect, our investigation provides knowledge about the lobbying activities of the NSS, when their lobbying practices occur, and the arguments employed by them.

We focus on the NSS, as they are a very special and relevant lobbying group. They have a good knowledge about the local institutions and consequently they are in a good position to find out how the standards may be understood and applied locally; they also undertake research, encourage stakeholder input from their jurisdictions, and identify emerging issues, in summary they act as a channel between the IASB and the other stakeholders. An obvious recognition of this important role is the proposal to create an ASAF that the IFRS Foundation has been recently announced.

In this study, we analyze the lobbying activity prior to the adoption of the IFRS 2 in February 2004. To this end we analyze the 27 comment letters submitted to the previous documents, the DP and ED2. It is important to highlight that the DP was issued twice, first by the IASC and later by the IASB, thus the project had three consultation periods. The standard requires an entity to record all share-based payments as expenses, regardless of the form of settlement (shares or cash) and the counterpart involved (employees or others). By the time it was adopted, these transactions were not recognized as expenses anywhere; in fact due to the strong pressure the FASB could not impose recognition in the 1990s.

Our examination of the comment letters consists of a content analysis focusing on three key issues: recognition, valuation criteria, and reference date, and confirms that most of the respondents dealt with the three issues. Our analysis is further aimed at identifying the underlying conceptual and economic arguments used to justify the position on each of these issues. We find that respondents did not employ normally arguments to show support of the proposals, but mainly used conceptual arguments when disagree. No economic consequences-based arguments were used after the ED 2 was issued, and we argue it could be due to the fact that the economic consequences argument might have lost ground as a consequence of the convergence policy of the IASB and the FASB after the 2002 Norwalk agreement.

As most of the prior literature, this study relies on the rational-choice model of lobbying which explains participation if their expected benefits of the lobbyists exceed the cost of lobbying (Sutton 1984). However, the institutional theory is particularly relevant as well, as lobbying may evidence the perceived importance or viability of the organization being lobbied (Kenny and Larson 1995); the considerable participation of NSS after the ED 2 is consistent with the insights of this theory. Moreover the majority of the respondents only participate at the end to show agreement with the proposal.

In summary, this analysis is consistent with the institutional theory which considers that organizations, such as the IASB, have to be acceptable to their constituency to survive. In our view, the attitudes of NSS in the IFRS 2 due process may be seen as a sign of support for the IASB's role as a global standard-setter.

References

Aboody, D. (1996). Market valuation of employee stock options. *Journal of Accounting and Economics, 22*, 357–392.

Aboody, D., Barth, M., & Kasznik, R. (2001). *SFAS 123 stock-based compensation expense and equity market values*. Working paper, University of California, Los Angeles.

Ang, N., Gallery, N., & Sidhu, B. K. (2000). The incentives of Australian public companies lobbying against proposed superannuation accounting standards. *Abacus, 36*(1), 40–70.

Brown, P. R. (1982). FASB Responsiveness to corporate input. *Journal of Accounting Auditing and Finance*, 282–90. (Summer).

Cohen, J. (1960). A coefficient of agreement for nominal scales. *Educational and Psychological Measurement, 20*, 37–46.

Crouzet, P., & Veron, N. (2004). *Accounting for globalisation—The Accounting Standards Battle*, En Temps Réel—Cahier 3 bis, Sept 2004 (English version of *La mondialisation en partie double—la bataille des normes comptables*, Trans.). En Temps Réel—Cahier in April, 2002.

Dechow, P. M., Hutton, A. P., & Sloan, R. G. (1996). Economic consequences of accounting for stock–based compensation. *Journal of Accounting Research, 34*(3), 1–20.

DiMaggio, P. J., & Powell, W. W. (1983). The Iron Cage revisited: institutional isomorphism and collective rationality in organizational fields. *American Sociological Review, 48*, 147–160.

EFRAG (European Financial Reporting Advisory Group). (2005). Achieving consistent application of IFRS in the EU: A discussion paper, EFRAG, Available at: www.efrag.org.

FASB (Financial Accounting Standards Board). (1995). *Statement of financial accounting standard no. 123: Accounting for stock–based compensation*. Stamford, Connecticut: FASB.

FASB (Financial Accounting Standards Board). (2004). *Statement of financial accounting standard no. 123: Accounting for stock–based compensation* (revised). Stamford, CT: FASB.

Fogarty, T. J. (1992). Financial accounting standard setting as an institutionalized action field: constraints, opportunities and dilemmas. *Journal of Accounting and Public Policy, 11*, 331–355.

Garvey, G. T., & Milbourn, T. T. (2001). *Do stock prices incorporate the potential dilution of employee stock options?* Working paper, Claremont Graduate University, Claremont.

Georgiou, G. (2002). Corporate non–participation in the ASB standard–setting process. *European Accounting Review, 11*(4), 699–722.

Georgiou, G. (2004). Corporate lobbying on accounting standards: methods, timing and perceived effectiveness. *Abacus, 40*(2), 219–237.

Georgiou, G. (2010). The IASB standard–setting process: Participation and perceptions of financial statement users. *The British Accounting Review, 42*(2), 103–118.

Giner, B., & Arce, M. (2012). Lobbying on accounting standards: Evidence from IFRS 2 on share-based payments. *European Accounting Review, 21*(4), 655–691.

Guenther, D., & Hussein, M. E. A. (1995). Accounting standards and national tax laws: The IASC and the ban on LIFO. *Journal of Accounting and Public Policy, 14*(2), 115–141.

Hill, N. T., Shelton, S. W., & Stevens, K. T. (2002). Corporate lobbying behaviour on accounting for stock–based compensation: Venue and format choices. *Abacus, 38*(1), 78–90.

Hope, A., & Gray, R. (1982). Power and policy making: the development of an R&D standard. *Journal of Business Finance and Accounting, 9*(4), 531–558.

IASB (International Accounting Standards Board). (2002). *ED 2: Share-based payments*. London: IASCF.

IASB (International Accounting Standards Board). (2004). *IFRS 2: Share-based payments*. London: IASCF.

IASB (International Accounting Standards Board). (2010). *The conceptual framework for financial reporting 2010*. London: IFRSF.

IASC (International Accounting Standards Committee). (2000). *G4+1 position paper: Accounting for share–based payment*. London: IASC.

IASCF (International Accounting Standards Committee Foundation). (2006). *Due process handbook for the international accounting standards board*. London: IASCF.

IFRS Foundation. (2012). *IASB and IRFS interpretations committee due process handbook*. IFRS Foundation.

IFRSF (International Financial Reporting Standards Foundation). (2010). *Constitution*. London: IFRSF.

Jorissen, A., Lybaert, N., Orens, R., & Van der Tas, L. (2012). Formal participation in the IASB's due process of standard setting: a multi–issue/multi–period analysis. *European Accounting Review, 21*(4), 693–729.

Jupe, R. (2000). Self–referential lobbing of accounting standards board: The case of financial reporting standard no. 1. *Critical Perspectives on Accounting, 11*(3), 337–359.

Kenny, S., & Larson, R. K. (1993). Lobbying behaviour and the development of international accounting standards: The case of the IASC's joint venture project. *European Accounting Review, 2*(3), 531–534.

Kenny, S., & Larson, R. K. (1995). The development of international accounting standards: An analysis of constituent participation in standard setting. *The International Journal of Accounting, 30*(4), 283–301.

Kwok, W. C. C., & Sharp, D. (2005). Power and international accounting standard setting. Evidence from segment reporting and intangible assets projects. *Accounting, Auditing and Accountability Journal, 18*(1), 74–99.

Larson, R. K. (1997). Corporate lobbying of the international standards committee. *Journal of International Financial Management and Accounting, 8*(3), 175–203.

Larson, R. K. (2007). Constituent participation and the IASB's international financial reporting interpretations committee. *Accounting in Europe, 4*(2), 207–254.

Larson, R. K., & Brown, K. L. (2001). Lobbying of the international accounting standards committee: The case of construction contracts. *Advances in International Accounting, 14*, 47–73.

Leuz, C., Pfaff, D., & Hopwood, A. (2004). *The economics and politics of accounting*. Oxford: Oxford University Press.

MacArthur, J. B. (1988). An analysis of the content of corporate submissions on proposed accounting standards in the UK. *Accounting and Business Research, 18*(71), 213–226.

MacArthur, J. B. (1996). An investigation into the influence of cultural factors in the international lobbying of the international accounting standards committee: The case of E32, comparability of financial statements. *The International Journal of Accounting, 31*(2), 213–237.

Meier, H. H., Alam, P., & Pearson, M. A. (1993). Auditor lobbying for accounting standards: the case of banks and savings and loan associations. *Accounting and Business Research, 23*(92), 477–487.

Murphy, K. J. (2003). Stock–based pay in new economy firms. *Journal of Accounting and Economics, 34*(1–3), 129–147.

Nobes, C. (1991). Cycles in UK standard setting. *Accounting and Business Research, 21*(83), 265–274.

Orens, R., Jorissen, A., Lybaert, N., & Van Der Tas, L. (2011). Corporate lobbying in private accounting standard setting: does the IASB have to reckon with national differences? *Accounting in Europe, 8*(2), 211–232.

Puro, M. (1984). Audit firm lobbying before the financial accounting standards board: An empirical study. *Journal of Accounting Research, 22*(2), 624–646.

Richardson, A. J., & Eberlein, B. (2011). Legitimating transnational standard-setting: The case of the international accounting standards board. *Journal of Business Ethics, 98*, 217–245.

Schalow, C. M. (1995). Participation choice: The exposure draft for postretirement benefits other than pensions. *Accounting Horizons, 9*(1), 27–41.

Stenka, R., & Taylor, P. (2010). Setting UK standards on the concept of control: An analysis of lobbying behaviour. *Accounting and Business Research, 40*(2), 109–130.

Stevenson, K. M. (2007). The IASB: Some personal reflections. In J. M. Godfrey & K. Chalmers (Eds.), *Globalisation of accounting standards*, Edward Elgar, London.

Sutton, T. G. (1984). Lobbying of accounting standard setting bodies in the UK and the USA: A dowsian analysis. *Accounting, Organizations and Society, 9*(1), 81–95.

Tandy, P. R., & Wilburn, N. L. (1992). Constituent participation in standard setting: The FASB's first 100 statements. *Accounting Horizons, 6*(2), 47–58.

Tandy, P. R., & Wilburn, N. L. (1996). The academic community's participation in standards–setting: Submission of comment letters on SFAS Nos. 1–117. *Accounting Horizons, 10*(3), 92–111.

Perrin, T. (2000). *Worldwide total remuneration.*

Perrin, T. (2004). Companies pursuing major changes in executive pay strategies http://www.towersperrin.com/hrservices/global/default.htm.

Tutticci, I., Dunstan, K., & Holmes, S. (1994). Respondent lobbying in the Australian accounting standard setting process: ED49. *Accounting, Auditing and Accountability Journal, 7*(2), 86–104.

Walker, R. G., & Robinson, P. (1993). A critical assessment of the literature on political activity and accounting regulation. *Research in Accounting Regulation, 7*, 3–40.

Watts, R. L. (1977). Corporate financial statements, a product of the market and political processes. *Australian Journal of Management, 2*, 0.

Watts, R. L., & Zimmerman, J. L. (1978). Towards a positive theory of the determination of accounting standards. *Accounting Review, 53*(1), 112–134.

Whittington, G. (2005). The adoption of international accounting standards in the European union. *European Accounting Review, 14*(1), 127–153.

Zeff, S. (2002). Political lobbying on proposed standards: A challenge to the IASB. *Accounting Horizons, 16*(1), 43–54.

Chapter 16
Commentary. Current State and Future Challenges of the IFRS: Some Thoughts

Begoña Giner

16.1 Introduction

My first words are to congratulate and thank Roberto, Stuart, and Joshua for bringing this most interesting and timely book on Accounting Regulation into the public domain. Indeed accounting regulation is a major issue, not only for us, the accountants, but also for society as a whole. Despite this, I often have the impression that there is a real lack of understanding about its implications and links with other institutions that shape the real economy. Moreover, the present economic crisis has highlighted the varied opinions on the role accounting standards and financial accounting in the economy. Should they be oriented to the financial market? Or should they act as another instrument to ensure economic and financial stability?

I also very much appreciate the chance I have been given to write a short piece for the forum. Of course, this should be related to the general topic of the book, an area I enjoy immensely as, after all, it makes the core of my own research and teaching activities. Therefore, I intend to share some of these more personal thoughts on the current state of affairs as well as the future challenges facing accounting regulation, and in particular the International Financial Reporting Standards (IFRS).

The main objective of the IFRS Foundation as stated in its constitution is to provide high quality standards, which help to prepare information that meets the user's needs (IFRSF 2010); it focuses on the needs of a particular group of users, investors, and mainly on capital providers. However, it would seem that this is frequently ignored or at least forgotten in the discussions about the role and success of the IFRS. With this idea in mind, principle-based standards are developed, and some jurisdictions have adopted the standards voluntarily. As frequently mentioned principle-based standards are a double-edged sword. While

---

B. Giner (✉)
Universitat de València. Facultat d'Economia. Dpt. de Comptabilitat, Valencia, Spain
e-mail: begona.giner@uv.es

R. Di Pietra et al. (eds.), *Accounting and Regulation*,
DOI: 10.1007/978-1-4614-8097-6_16,

some discretion is given to managers which allows them to convey private information, other incentives may also come into play.

Bearing this in mind, next I wish to explore both sides of the previous statements: the development of standards and the decision to adopt them. After that I will insist on two-related aspects that drive the final success of the aforementioned objective: implementation and enforcement. I will conclude with some final remarks.

16.2 The Development of the IFRS

The production of the standards lies with the International Accounting Standards Board (IASB) itself, as this is its main task. To achieve this, the Board is composed by a team of excellent independent experts, selected by the Trustees of the IFRS Foundation. This team is publicly accountable to a monitoring board of capital market authorities and other regulators; a strong due process has been established to guarantee the standard-setting procedure, and make it transparent for both the standard-setter and the participants who provide both input and feedback. Although preparers have traditionally been very active in the standard-due process due to their incentives to lobby, other stakeholders have been less interested (Dechow et al. 1996; Ang et al. 2000; Hill et al. 2002; Jorissen et al. 2012; Giner and Arce 2012).

In particular I want to highlight the scarce participation of academics, though this is not altogether surprising, as tends to happen with other standard-setters. In this case incentives fail to encourage academics to participate, on the contrary we are more often than not most concerned with getting published in highly ranked journals, and so spending time on other activities is frequently perceived as mere time wasting … Despite this, or more probably because of this, the Trustees of the IFRS Foundation in its Strategic Review have recommended establishing or facilitating the establishment of a research capacity that could be based on a combination of internal and external intellectual resources, including a more active engagement of the academic community. This will allow the IASB to rely on evidence to support its decisions and to persuade those who use IFRS that the IASB has made the right choices between competing solutions when developing standards.

Indeed given that academics are the main experts in research activity, it would only seem quite natural to rely on us to perform this task. Larson et al. (2011) provide details about the role of academic research in the development of standards and encourage us to participate in the development of IFRS. Although it is up to individuals to react and participate in the standard-setting process, either by responding to the call for responses to discussion papers and exposure drafts, or by showing an interest in the calls of the IFRS Foundation to occupy a temporary position (such as academic or research fellow), there is also the possibility to act in a more organized way, and this is what the European Accounting Association

Financial Reporting Standards Committee (EAA FRSC) is doing. This committee has been providing input to IASB, as well as European Financial Reporting Advisory Group (EFRAG), in the form of comment letters, but has also liaised with IASB and EFRAG, and now includes two liaison members who help us remain in permanent contact with them.

Another interested group that deserves special attention is the standard-setters' group; in Chap. 13 we pay attention to their role (Giner and Arce 2013), but here I want to highlight some aspects of the new group just promoted by the IASB, namely the Accounting Standard Advisory Forum (ASAF). ASAF mainly aims to provide support to the IASB on technical issues. Indeed national standard-setters and regional bodies are experts on accounting issues, but in my view there is another important aspect that could leverage their input in the process. Based on their good knowledge of the institutional arrangements in their own jurisdictions and on how the proposed standards could affect them, they are in a unique position to evaluate the impact of the changes, So, sharing this information could only help the IASB to make better-informed decisions.

Despite the previous comments, it is important to keep in mind that the IASB is the standard-setter and the purpose of the IFRS is to have good information for the capital markets, so that the unintended consequences of the standards should not drive the discussions, leaving aside the actual decisions. As I see the role of the Forum, it could make local bodies engage more easily with their own stakeholders in order to accept and use the IFRS following the IASB's objectives. In this way I believe it could give them a real sense of ownership of the standards, To the extent those bodies have endorsement powers; ASAF could also be useful to facilitate the adoption of IFRS without any carve out or delay, I will insist later on these problems.

16.3 The Decision to Use the IFRS

The decision to adopt IFRS is made at the national or jurisdiction-level as the IASB has neither the power to impose its standards nor to enforce its proper application. As some authors have pointed it is a "leap of faith" that the adoption of IFRS will bring the desired output of improved decision-making, and indeed this was the case when the first followers, the EU, Australia, and New Zealand, made that decision. More importantly, and with reference to the EU, Pope and McLeay (2011, p. 211) posit "the Commission has placed considerable trust in the ability of the primary system of devolved enforcement to deliver uniformly consistent high quality financial reporting." This brings me to the role of enforcement and each country's institutions in shaping the final content of financial information. However, before that I would like to make a brief comment on the politics of the accounting standard-setter process.

As Bushman and Landsman (2010) argue, the economic recession has brought into sharp focus the reality that the regulation of corporate reporting is just one piece of a larger regulatory configuration. The pressure of prudential regulators, financial institutions, and some national standard-setters, who put the emphasis on the unintended consequences of the standards, might endanger the ability of the IASB to maintain its role as producer of standards that promote corporate transparency to support market discipline and capital allocation. Indeed there is strong pressure on the IASB to accommodate the requirements of the prudential regulators, but this strategy contradicts its own constitution. Moreover, this discussion questions the extent to which those authorities who adopted IFRS were aware of the real impact of their decision. As mentioned in the introduction, this suggests there is a real lack of understanding about the implications and links of accounting regulation with other institutions that shape the real economy; and it is not clear whether both objectives, capital market transparency and prudence, cannot be achieved simultaneously.

16.4 The Implementation and Enforcement of IFRS

Implementation and enforcement are the key aspects to the achievement of high quality global accounting information as Leuz (2010) and Brown (2011), among others, sustain. It can be argued that to some extent the main difficulty nowadays is not to produce highly technical accounting standards but to guarantee they are used and enforced properly. Although none of these aspects are under the control of the IASB, in a way they are key to judging the success of the IASB. Having said that, it would not be acceptable to discard the idea that in order to achieve high quality information, one must first start with high quality standards.

Nowadays IFRS are used in many jurisdictions. Philip Danjou (2013), a current Board member, has recently confirmed that more than 100 jurisdictions require or permit the application of IFRS for financial reporting, and two thirds of G20 countries have adopted IFRS. However, the approaches followed to adopt them substantially vary from one country to another. In some countries the standards are directly applied, such in as South Africa, while in others there is an endorsement process, as in the European Union. This allows some not to accept a given standard or even some paragraphs of the standards (as the *carve out* made in IAS 39), as well as delay in the endorsement decision (as happened with IFRS 9), or even the delay in the application of a standard (such as with IFRS 10, 11, and 12, as well IAS 27 and 28). In some countries IFRS have been imposed for certain types of companies and accounts, consolidated accounts of listed companies in the EU, while in others, such as Australia individual accounts, as well as nonlisted companies are also affected. In addition there are some countries that allow IFRS for foreign companies, such as in Japan and the US. Finally other countries have convergence programs, but they are far from real adopters as what they finally decide could be rather different to the full IFRS package. I am not implying that these programs are useless, as according to the constitution, the convergence of national accounting standards and IFRS is a strategy to promote and facilitate adoption of IFRS, which is another objective of the IFRS Foundation. This scenario introduces serious doubts about the use of full IFRSs in the world. Indeed that IFRS have been accepted so widely is an impressive achievement of the IASB, and its predecessor the IASC, but it is necessary to keep the mind clear and think about the real use of IFRS.

Although there is an array of studies that confirm the advantages of using IFRS in terms of improved efficiency of capital market operations and promotion of cross-border investment, there is the perception that the IFRS benefits go together with a framework that encompasses legal protections, competent professionals, and adequate monitoring and enforcement (see Tarca 2012 for a good summary of recent research). Thus, there is a growing stream of literature that questions the possibility of obtaining the desired achievements unless there are further changes in the institutions (Hail et al. 2010; Leuz 2010; Walker 2010; Isidro and Raonic 2012). In their view, due to the role of the country's institutional infrastructure, unilateral changes in accounting standards (such as IFRS adoption) may not yield the desired outcomes. In fact Landsman et al. (2012) found that IFRS firms' accounting amounts have greater comparability with those of US firms when IFRS firms apply IFRS than when they apply non-US domestic standards. However, comparability is generally greater for firms that adopt IFRS mandatorily, common law firms, and firms in countries with high enforcement. Even within the most harmonized context, the European Union, Pope and McLeay (2011) confirm that although some of the benefits from increased transparency appear to have been realized, the results are far from uniform due to heterogeneous preparer incentives and differing enforcement mechanisms in member states.

Following this line of argument Wysocki (2011) states that the advantages of IFRS compared with local standards are not evident in countries that have evolved different institutions and thus lack the necessary infrastructures to support the effective application and enforcement of the uniform global standards. Moreover, Ball (2006) argues that as long the incentives of preparers and enforcers remain primarily local, there are fundamental reasons for being skeptical about uniformity of implementation of the standards. Having said that, it is important to keep in mind that this is a real challenge for the IASB as the constitution also includes the following objective: "to promote the use and rigorous application of those standards." The challenge is how to achieve it given the lack of enforcement power in the different jurisdictions. Perhaps as previously mentioned, the strategy to launch the new ASAF could help to advance this objective.

16.5 Final Remarks

To conclude I want to insist on a couple of ideas mentioned above. First of all IFRS are developed to improve the transparency of financial information in order to help investors, so other alternative objectives, as well as the unintended consequences of the information should be left aside in the discussions. Second the IFRS's adoption will not bring the desired impact if there are no further changes in other institutions, and thinking of the EU, the obvious one must be enforcement. At times one has the impression that too much time and effort is being wasted unless a more unified enforcement takes place within the EU.

References

Ang, N., Gallery, N., & Sidhu, B. K. (2000). The incentives of Australian public companies lobbying against proposed superannuation accounting standards. *Abacus, 36*(1), 40–70.

Brown, P. (2011). International financial reporting standards: What are the benefits? *Accounting and Business Research, 41*(3), 269–285.

Bushman, R., & Landsman, W. R. (2010). The pros and cons of regulating corporate reporting: A critical review of the arguments. *Accounting and Business Research, 40*(3), 259–273.

Danjou, P. (2013). An update on international financial reporting standards (IFRS). 1 Feb, Available at: http://www.ifrs.org/Features/Pages/An-Update-on-IFRSs-by-Philippe-Danjou.aspx

Dechow, P. M., Hutton, A. P., & Sloan, R. G. (1996). Economic consequences of accounting for stock–based compensation. *Journal of Accounting Research, 34*(3), 1–20.

Giner, B., & Arce, M. (2012). Lobbying on accounting standards: Evidence from IFRS 2 on share-based payments. *European Accounting Review, 21*(4), 655–691.

Giner, B., & Arce, M. (2013). National standard-setters' lobbying: An analysis of its role in the IFRS 2 due process. In: R. Di Pietra, S. McLeay, J. Ronen (Eds.), *Accounting regulation* (pp. 311–332).

Hail, L., Leuz, C., & Wysocki, P. (2010). Global accounting convergence and the potential adoption of IFRS by the U.S. (Part I): conceptual underpinnings and economic analysis. *Accounting Horizons, 24*(3), 355–394.

Hill, N. T., Shelton, S. W., & Stevens, K. T. (2002). Corporate lobbying behaviour on accounting for stock–based compensation: Venue and format choices'. *Abacus, 38*(1), 78–90.

IFRSF (International Financial Reporting Standards Foundation). (2010). *Constitution*. London: IFRSF.

Isidro, H., & Raonic, I. (2012). Firm incentives, institutional complexity and the quality of "harmonized" accounting numberss. *The International Journal of Accounting, 47*, 407–436.

Jorissen, A., Lybaert, N., Orens, R., & Van der Tas, L. (2012). Formal participation in the IASB's due process of standard setting: a multi–issue/multi–period analysis. *European Accounting Review, 21*(4), 693–729.

Landsman, W. R., Maydew, E. L., & Thornock, J. R. (2012). The information content of annual earnings announcements and mandatory adoption of IFRS. *Journal of Accounting and Economics, 53*, 34–54.

Larson, R. K., Herz, P. J., & York Kenny, S. (2011). Academics and the development of IFRS: An invitation to participate. *Journal of International Accounting Research, 10*(2), 97–103.

Leuz, C. (2010). Different approaches to corporate reporting regulation: How jurisdictions differ and why. *Accounting and Business Research, 40*(3), 229–256.

Pope, P., & McLeay, S. (2011). The European IFRS experiment: Objectives, research challenges and some early evidence. *Accounting and Business Research, 41*(3), 233–266.

Tarca, A. (2012). The case for global accounting standards: Arguments and evidence. Available at: http://www.ifrs.org/search/Pages/Results.aspx?k=tarca

Walker, M. (2010). Accounting for varieties of capitalism: The case against a single set of global accounting standards. *The British Accounting Review, 42*, 137–152.

Wysocki, P. (2011). New institutional accounting and IFRS. *Accounting and Business Research, 41*(3), 309–328.

Index

R. Di Pietra et al. (eds.), *Accounting and Regulation*,
DOI: 10.1007/978-1-4614-8097-6,

MIX
Papier aus verantwortungsvollen Quellen
Paper from responsible sources
FSC® C105338

If you have any concerns about our products,
you can contact us on
ProductSafety@springernature.com

In case Publisher is established outside the EU,
the EU authorized representative is:
Springer Nature Customer Service Center GmbH
Europaplatz 3, 69115 Heidelberg, Germany

Printed by Libri Plureos GmbH
in Hamburg, Germany